Theo-Politics?

Theo-Politics?

Conversing with Barth in Western and Asian Contexts

Edited by
Markus Höfner

LEXINGTON BOOKS/FORTRESS ACADEMIC

Lanham • Boulder • New York • London

Published by Lexington Books/Fortress Academic
Lexington Books is an imprint of The Rowman & Littlefield Publishing Group, Inc.
4501 Forbes Boulevard, Suite 200, Lanham, Maryland 20706
www.rowman.com

6 Tinworth Street, London SE11 5AL, United Kingdom

British Library Cataloguing in Publication Information Available

Library of Congress Cataloging-in-Publication Data

Names: Höfner, Markus, 1972– editor.
Title: Theo-politics? : conversing with Barth in Western and Asian contexts / Markus Höfner.
Description: Lanham : Lexington Books/Fortress Academic, [2021] | Includes index. | Summary: "Using the theological work of Karl Barth as a resource for present-day inquiry, the contributors discuss the complex interconnections between the religious and the political and address the contemporary challenges these interconnections pose for Western and Asian societies"—Provided by publisher.
Identifiers: LCCN 2021028600 (print) | LCCN 2021028601 (ebook) | ISBN 9781978710054 (cloth) | ISBN 9781978710061 (epub)
Subjects: LCSH: Barth, Karl, 1886-1968. | Christianity and politics.
Classification: LCC BX4827.B3 T435 2021 (print) | LCC BX4827.B3 (ebook) | DDC 230/.044—dc23
LC record available at https://lccn.loc.gov/2021028600
LC ebook record available at https://lccn.loc.gov/2021028601

Contents

List of Figures and Tables

FIGURES

TABLES

Acknowledgments

The contributions in this volume grew out of the multiyear international research project, entitled *Theo-Politics: Conversing with Barth in Western and Asian Contexts (2013–2015)*, composed of three symposia held at Bochum University, Germany. The rectorate of Bochum University provided support for the preparation of the research application. The research project itself was made possible by a generous grant from the Volkswagen Foundation, which supported the three symposia and the publication of the resulting papers in this volume. I wish to express my gratitude to both institutions. A special thanks goes to Robert Lahmert, who not only brilliantly managed the logistics of the symposia, but was also a most reliable help in the editing process.

Introduction

Theo-Politics? Conversing with Barth in Western and Asian Contexts

Markus Höfner

THEO-POLITICS?

Theo-Politics? This term may be taken as a shorthand reference to the complex of interconnections between the religious and the political. It can also refer to the challenges and questions concerning the arrangement of both spheres that can be judged appropriate, functional and desirable by religious and/or political criteria.[1] In that respect, traditional binaries such as religion and politics or church and state, which have dominated many theo-political discussions in the past, continue to have relevance for current debates, but are misleading if they are intended to capture the whole field of theo-politics. For the religious sphere is wider than the Christian church or even the ensemble of faith-based communities and organizations representing different religious traditions. In order to capture the rich diversity of the theo-political, one must also consider the everyday lives of individual believers, as well as the religious motives and motivations that are present in seemingly secular contexts, to name just a few examples. Moreover, in order not to reduce the political sphere to state institutions and procedures, one will have to take into account the distinction between politics (*la politique*) and the political (*le politique*), which is prominent in recent discussions of political ontology and democratic theory.[2]

CONVERSING WITH BARTH IN WESTERN AND ASIAN CONTEXTS

This volume discusses Theo-Politics *in conversation with* Swiss theologian *Karl Barth* (1868–1968).[3] The contributions collected here use the breadth

1

of Barth's rich theological work (not only his explicit theo-political theses) as a resource to address theo-political questions in and for the present. This conversation with Barth takes multiple forms; in-depth analyses of Barthian texts and comparisons of Barth with other approaches to theo-politics sit alongside essays that take inspiration from Barth in order to discuss theo-political questions that are not present in Barth nor classical Barth studies. Some scholars writing in this volume follow Barth's basic theological decisions while others are more critical of his theological project. Taken together, these essays make clear that Barth's theology is a fertile resource for present theo-political discussions. Indeed, Barth's thought has been discussed and critically appropriated in theological discussions all over the world, more than any other German-speaking theologian of the twentieth century. Such global reach renders a comparative theo-political discussion in and between different cultural and political contexts possible, by making their differences visible *and* communicable by a common reference to Barth's theology. While knowledge that the complex relations of the religious and the political are increasingly affected by processes of globalization[4] may lead one to ask for a truly global perspective, or at least a conversation comprising all cultural and political contexts, the more modest and focused aim of this volume is to present a theo-political conversation with Barth *in Western and Asian contexts*. The scholars contributing to this conversation come from Germany, the United Kingdom, and the United States and from Hong Kong, Taiwan, and the People's Republic of China, yet they aim to speak from their contexts in a manner that can be useful for those from other contexts.[5] Most contributions in this volume speak from the perspective of Christian theology in the Protestant tradition.[6] Theological reflection, however, has much to learn from non-theological perspectives,[7] not only, but especially, when it comes to questions of theo-politics. In order to highlight this insight and to build on it for the theo-political conversation with Barth, this volume includes contributions by sociologists and political scientists, from different Western and Asian contexts.

SECULAR POLITICS OR THE POLITICAL IN THEOLOGICAL FRAME? BEYOND AN APPARENT OPPOSITION

Some may assume that answers to the various questions concerning theo-politics today can be sorted according to a basic alternative: *Either* one opts for a strict and clear separation of the religious and the political, thus assuring the proper functioning of secular politics, a religiously neutral state, and a rule law unaffected by religious preferences. *Or* one considers this supposed religious neutrality of politics, state, and law as an oppressive ideology and opts for a religious politics without reserve, centered on the Christian church—and not the modern state or civil society—as the one example of true politics. And if one follows the first option, the most desirable arrangement of the religious and the political would be a restriction of religion to a nonpolitical, private realm over against a religiously neutral public realm of the political, while the second option will lead one to wish for the establishment—or re-establishment—of a Christian society dominated by faith-based convictions and goals.

This imagined alternative is a consensus shared by thinkers as diverse as the liberal philosopher Mark Lilla and the Radical Orthodoxy theologian John Milbank. Lilla follows Hobbes' rejection of all political theology as the attempt to ground the legitimacy of basic political institutions in divine revelation. It is this "great separation" of the political and the religious, in Lilla's view, that marks the fragile project of modern liberal Western politics which has to be defended against the constant temptation to conflate spiritual and political redemption and to translate religious eschatology into a messianic politics with anti-modern and anti-humanistic goals.[8] For Milbank, on the contrary, the very idea of a religiously neutral modern reason, as well as religiously neutral state and civil society, must be refuted by Christian theology. The "Radical Orthodoxy" he proposes aims to develop a Christian vision of the communion of God and man that leaves no room for the supposed autonomy of the secular, but re-interprets the world exclusively within a theological framework—a framework which finds its visible correlate in the practices of the Christian church as *the* exemplary political community.[9] Lilla and Milbank thus stand on opposite sides of the supposed alternative, but they agree that these are the only options available. In Lilla's words: "Theorists like John and theorists like me are standing on opposite shores looking at each other with a mutual disdain for those who think that they can somehow negotiate the middle."[10]

And this consensus shapes how Lilla and Milbank view the theo-political thought of *Karl Barth*. Lilla pictures Barth as a prominent example of the (dangerous) messianic politics he aims to overcome. This is because even though Barth, as Lilla reads him, advises Christians to "keep their eyes fixed on eternity rather than on the 'game' of contemporary politics," he could not avoid his "talk of spiritual redemption [. . .] transforming itself into a talk of political redemption." He thus offers only "two models of Christian action in politics: the prophetic scold and the citizen without qualities"—and both models, in Lilla's view, violate Hobbes' "great separation."[11] Milbank, likewise, positions Barth on his own shore of the supposed alternative, counting him with Augustine and Aquinas among those who do not apologetically appeal to a supposedly neutral reason, but develop a genuinely theological perspective "in terms of the imaginative explication of texts, practices and beliefs."[12] Still, in Milbank's view, Barth "remain[s] captive to a modern—even liberal—duality of reason and revelation, and [runs] the risk of allowing worldly knowledge an unquestioned validity within its own sphere."[13] And this is why "Barthian neo-orthodoxy," for Milbank, must be surpassed by "radical orthodoxy" in "refusing all 'mediations' by other [i.e. non-theological] spheres of knowledge and culture."[14]

Contrary to these descriptions of Karl Barth by Lilla and Milbank, this volume aims to show that Barth's theology and his reflections on the politics can hardly be grasped within the limits of the supposed alternative just sketched. Barth does not advocate for the retreat of religion to a private, nonpolitical realm, nor is he engaged in a radical orthodox fight against modern secular reason or the secular state, covertly wishing for the (re-)establishment of a Christian society. And he is certainly not representing liberal theology, the only impossible possibility Lilla and Milbank see between their respective shores. Barth's position, rather, is more nuanced than what is allowed by the supposed alternative of "secular vs. theological politics"—and is thus a more interesting resource for theo-political discussion. This is what the contributions to this volume show with a great variety of approaches to and interpretations of Barth's theology in addressing theo-political questions for today.

THEO-POLITICS—TODAY AND TOMORROW

Theo-Politics has attracted much attention and analyses in the past twenty years, both within theology and other academic disciplines, as well as beyond, in the media and other publics. The reasons for this new attentiveness are multiple. The fall of communism and the subsequent reconstruction of Christian churches in Eastern Europe, the experience of horrendous violence justified by religious motives on 9/11 and beyond, and the effects of processes of globalization and digitalization have contributed to the awareness that modern societies and their politics (still) have to deal with the ambivalent phenomenon of religion.[15] There is probably some truth in traditional secularization theories, but the hope or fear that religion will eventually disappear amid processes of societal modernization has certainly been proven wrong.[16] The term post-secular, often applied to the current theo-political situation (at least in the West), may point not so much to a global trend toward religious affiliations and convictions, but to a changed attitude toward religion by politics and academia alike.[17] But it is clear that religion is back on the agenda and theo-political discussions are needed in order to cope with these challenges, and to use the opportunities arising from the continuing presence of religion in Western and Non-Western contexts.

In order to orient oneself, one can heuristically map the complex field of present theo-political discussions with a matrix comprised of three differences:

A *first* difference concerns the *perspective* from which the theo-political complex is approached: Is it from a religious perspective aiming to orient religious communities or organizations by applying criteria and imaginaries derived from religious traditions? Or are the analysis and the evaluation of religion and politics conducted from a decidedly non-religious point of view?

A *second* difference concerns the *diagnosis* of the main challenges arising in the field of theo-politics. While such diagnoses, of course, can take many forms, they will tend to see a given arrangement of the political, the religious, and their relatedness as inappropriate or as endangered by current political or religious dynamics. The problem a theo-political approach responds to, in other words, can be seen in a given status quo *or* in a dynamics that challenge it.

A *third* difference can be seen in the *therapy* recommended, that is, the specific approach suggested and supported by the author. Amid all nuances, the proposed therapy may aim at the stabilization or the dynamization and transformation of a given theo-political status quo, corresponding to the respective diagnosis of what is problematic within the field of theo-politics.

In sum:

	Dynamics as problematic: *Stabilization*	*Status quo as problematic:* *Transformation*
Religious Perspective		
Non-Religious Perspective		

Now while these differences are, of course, only heuristic tools and one will see much overlap when applying them to specific theo-political approaches, they offer a glimpse of the deep grammar governing theo-political discussions. And it is noteworthy that, from religious and non-religious perspectives alike, religion can be promoted both as a means of stabilization and as a force of dynamization of given theo-political constellations.

The factors that were named earlier as contributing to renewed interest in theo-politics in recent years certainly mark the historical difference between current discussions of theo-politics and the theo-political thought of Karl Barth. As the contributions in this volume show, however, this historical difference points to some limits of Barth's theology, but does not diminish the value of his thought as a resource for current theo-political discussions in Western and Asian contexts.

NOTES

1. The term "theo-politics" thus is used here in a capacious sense, comprising what can also be called political theology in the many senses of the later term. For a narrower use of "theopolitics," signifying *God's* kingship and thus naming an alternative to (especially Carl Schmitt's concept of) political theology cf. Martin Buber, *Kingship of God (1936)*, trans. Richard Scheimann (New York: Harper & Row, 1967).

2. Cf. e.g. Claude Lefort, "The Permanence of the Theologico-Political?" in *Political Theologies: Public Religions in a Post-Secular World*, ed. Hent de Vries and Lawrence E. Sullivan (New York: Fordham University Press, 2006), 148–187. 150–155 and the comprehensive study Oliver Marchart, *Post-foundational Political Thought: Political Difference in Nancy, Lefort, Badiou and Laclau* (Edinburgh: Edinburgh University Press, 2007).

3. For an overview of Karl Barth's life and work, see Eberhard Busch, *Karl Barth: His Life from Letters and Autobiographical Texts*, trans. John Bowden (Eugene, OR: Wipf & Stock, 2005) and the excellent recent study Christiane Tietz, *Karl Barth: A Life in Conflict* (Oxford: Oxford University Press, 2021). A good overview of Barth's political thought and political engagement is provided by Frank Jehle, *Ever against the Stream: The Politics of Karl Barth, 1906–1968* (Grand Rapids: W.B. Eerdmans, 2002).

4. Cf. e.g. the contributions in *The Routledge Companion of Religion and Politics*, ed. Jeffrey Haynes (London: Routledge, 2009, 2016).

5. These are, to be sure, only *some* Western and Asian contexts. There is a unique and interesting reception of Barth's theology, worthy of engagement, in theo-political discussion in most other Western contexts as well, and in order to cover Asian contexts more comprehensively, additional scholars, certainly from Korea and Japan, would have to be included.

6. There is a significant and highly insightful reception of Barth's theological thought in the Roman-Catholic tradition of Christian theology worldwide. Adding specific confessional differences to the various contexts, however, would have created an overly difficult complexity within the limits of this volume. For an overview of the Roman-Catholic discussion of Barth's theology, cf. Benjamin Dahlke, *Karl Barth, Catholic Renewal, and Vatican II* (London: T&T Clark, 2012).

7. And hopefully sometimes the other way round.

8. Cf. Mark Lilla, *The Stillborn God: Religion, Politics, and the Modern West* (New York: Vintage Books, 2007), esp. 55–103. 251–295. Cf. for a critical discussion of Lilla's approach Mark R. Schwehn et al., "Critical Dialogue," *Politics and Religion* 1 (2008): 300–316.

9. Cf. John Milbank, *Theology & Social Theory: Beyond Secular Reason* (Malden, MA: Blackwell Publishing, 1990, 2006), esp. 7–47. 382–442 and John Milbank, Graham Ward, and Catherine Pickstock, "Introduction: Suspending the Material: The Turn of Radical Orthodoxy," in *Radical Orthodoxy: A New Theology*, ed. John Milbank, Graham Ward, and Catherine Pickstock (London: Routledge,

1999), 1–20. For a lucid criticism of Milbank's thought, see Jeffrey Stout, *Democracy & Tradition* (Princeton: Princeton University Press, 2004), 92–117.

10. José Casanova, Michael Jon Kessel, John Milbank, and Mark Lilla, "A Conversation," in *Political Theology for a Plural Age*, ed. Michael Jon Kessler (Oxford: Oxford University Press, 2013), 13–40. 17.

11. Lilla, *Stillborn God*, 279, 259, 271.

12. Milbank, *Theology & Social Theory*, 329. This is the only, but highly significant, instant in which Barth is mentioned in that book.

13. Milbank et al., "Introduction," 2.

14. Ibid.

15. Cf. e.g. José Casanova, *Public Religions in the Modern World* (Chicago: Chicago University Press, 1996), Hent de Vries, *Religion and Violence: Philosophical Perspectives from Kant to Derrida* (Baltimore: Johns Hopkins University Press, 2002), *Political Theologies: Public Religions in a Post-Secular World*, ed. Hent de Vries and Lawrence E. Sullivan (New York: Fordham University Press, 2006), and Charles Taylor, *A Secular Age* (Cambridge, MA: Harvard University Press, 2007).

16. Cf. e.g. Detlef Pollack, Gergely Rosta, *Religion and Modernity: An International Comparison*, trans. David West (Oxford: Oxford University Press, 2017) and David Martin, *On Secularization: Towards a Revised General Theory* (Aldershot: Ashgate, 2005).

17. Cf. Jürgen Habermas, *Zwischen Naturalismus und Religion* (Frankfurt: Suhrkamp, 2005) and Habermas, "Notes on Post-Secular Society," *NPQ: New Perspectives Quarterly* 25, no. 4 (2008): 17–29, and Hans Joas, *Braucht der Mensch Religion? Über Erfahrungen der Selbsttranszendenz* (Freiburg: Herder, 2004), 122–128. For a critical discussion in theological perspective, see Michael Welker, "The Future Tasks of Political Theology: On Religion and Politics Beyond Habermas and Ratzinger," in *Political Theology: Contemporary Challenges and Future Directions*, ed. Michael Welker, Francis Schüssler Fiorenza, and Klaus Tanner (Louisville: Westminster John Knox Press, 2013), 75–86.

Part I

CHRISTIANITY, POLITICS, AND CULTURE

A COMPLEX RELATION IN WESTERN AND ASIAN CONTEXTS

Chapter 1

Religion, Politics, and Sino-Christian Theology

Chloë Starr

Karl Barth's life (1886–1968) parallels that of the first cohort of Chinese Protestant theologians, active in the 1920s through the 1950s, and his theology maps in remarkable ways onto the questions and decisions of the incipient Chinese church. An examination of these parallels, and especially three "moments" of correspondence which form the focus of this chapter, shows, inter alia, just how integrated the Chinese church was into currents of world thought for much of the twentieth century—and how concentration on the high communist period of church inactivity and on church-state relations can distort the fuller picture of theological dialogue. A reading of Barthian discourse alongside the writings of contemporary Chinese theologians allows us to see how prominent voices inside the church have positioned themselves firmly within international theological debates on society and politics, even as commentators have been keen to define the Chinese (Protestant) church by its difference, focusing attention on contextualization and Buddhist/Confucian dialogues. The three "moments" of this chapter relate to particular texts and debates in China from the 1930s, 1950s, and 1990s, and all address the central question of how the people of God are to live in the world. The chapter explores evolving thinking on the topic in both Barth and Chinese theologians as political circumstances change, whereas the juxtaposition asks how parallel moves might inter-illumine experiences. A reading between Barth and Chinese thinkers of pivotal debates on church and state provides a theological biography of the twentieth century in snap shot, and prompts further thought on wartime debates and assumptions in Europe, as well as China.

THE KINGDOM OF GOD

A first moment of correspondence between Barth's theology and the Chinese church concerns the foundation of the Kingdom of God. If the impact of Karl Barth's early, Safenwil phase on the remainder of his theological thinking is a matter of continued debate, the ongoing presence of a socialist vision within mainstream Chinese theology in the decades after the 1911 revolution, the year Barth published his germinal "Jesus Christ and the Movement for Social Justice," has never been in doubt. Commentators might separate out Barth's thinking into a number of phases or periods and argue over the degree to which he eschewed aspects of his own thought, but later reverberations of his texts are important in a discussion of dialogue. If for Barth, the kingdom is very much an issue for the state, and the state a parable of the kingdom in its reflection of Christian beliefs, the kingdom has an autonomous aspect too, foregrounded in Chinese writings, and a comparison of the two architectures is revealing.

Kingdom theology, and its relation to contemporary social issues, permeated the thinking of a cross-section of more liberal Christianity in China in the 1920s and 1930s, from YMCA and YWCA personnel to members of the many denominations represented in the National Council of Churches. Zong Weicong (W. T. Zung), who traveled to the International Federation of Working Women's meeting in Geneva in 1921 as a representative of the Chinese YWCA, wrote:

> The Church has for her object the establishment of the Kingdom of God on this earth, so she directs her activities toward the uplift of humanity. Here comes the new industrial system, which involved legions of evils. Under this system human lives are of less value than soulless machinery. Because of the evils of the system we see social injustice spreading more and more each day. Is the Church concerned with this social injustice? Will the Church make attempts to help solve the problems resulting from the evils of the industrial system?[1]

The kingdom of God is, in Zong's estimation, antithetical to industrial working patterns. It is brought about by Christian efforts for social justice, and offers something to a humanity "yearning for a new order of life."

> If we wish to see the Kingdom of God on earth, China included, we cannot allow the continuance of the miserable state of labor. It is true that the Church is ever ready to do any kind of charitable work but the cry of these exploited poor is, "We want no charity—we want justice." . . . The church is *the* place from where the public opinion may emanate. Will the Chinese Church again lay the foundation stone of standing for social justice and humanity as she did nobly for other causes in her earlier days?[2]

Roman Catholic theologians of the era likewise grappled with the foundation stone of social justice and the role of the church in social issues, including alleviating the pain of workers across the world. Xu Zongze's exposition of Pius IX's 1931 encyclical and discussion of labor conditions in his articles "Labor Contracts" and "How Catholicism Resolves Social Questions" is a notable example.[3]

The theologian who articulated perhaps most extensively a vision of the kingdom of God in China, Wu Leichuan (1870–1944), understood religion as a force for progress in society, directing individuals from the material to the spiritual, the individual to the communal.[4] From adjacent starting points, Barth and Wu converge on the kingdom of Heaven. Barth, who had argued a few years earlier that Jesus *was* the movement for social justice, and who coined the phrase "Jesus was a worker, not a pastor,"[5] to express Jesus' alignment with the laboring poor, focuses through the lens of socialism; Wu through that of culture, and specifically, the compatibility of Chinese culture with Christian. Their kingdom shares many attributes: a preference for the poor; a strongly material aspect and disdain for a spirit/material dualism; an impetus to change attitudes, especially toward social misery, that which "*ought not to be.*"[6] The visions have different focal lengths: Barth explores the inherent connections between Jesus and socialism, where Wu mostly takes these for granted, turning his attention to explain the economic implications of the gospel parables. The Kingdom in Wu Leichuan stems less from a theological vision of community than from an analysis of Jesus' actions, within the framework of building a Christian China. In an era where the rallying cry was "save the nation," this vision of the kingdom represented a highly practical, Christian solution to the building of a strong China. If for Barth in his early "religious-socialist phase," the movement for social justice, "the greatest and most urgent word of God to the present," was paramount; for Wu, the pressing imperative was to work out how to reconstruct the nation and revivify China. The kingdom functioned, in both cases, to guide the individual to transform society, if the emphasis on means and end differed.[7]

In both sets of writings, we hear the voices of detractors at work: for Barth, these are a disparate group of religious conservatives and critics of party politics or of aligning Jesus with any political faction, together with a minority of "atheists and Darwinists" who might embrace his political vision but not his religious one; for Wu, the sounding board is the voice of nationalists, of the Anti-Christian movement, including pro-science skeptics and an anti-imperial clamor. There are parallels between Barth and Wu in the criticisms each received and defences offered. As Clifford Green points out in questioning the attention Marquardt draws to Barth's socialism, theology grounds Barth's socialism, rather than vice versa, "socialism is a *consequence* of community, which is theologically grounded, rather than the hermeneutical key to the theology."[8] Wu was similarly read and criticized as a nationalist, yet this underplays the theological vision of the Kingdom that is central to his state-building project.[9]

While "Jesus Christ and the Movement for Social Justice" is a relatively short essay in Barth's oeuvre, it is of a piece with the "Socialist Speeches" written between 1911 and 1917, and with Barth's ministry at that time, split between worker education meetings, union work with the SDP and Gruetli Association, and church pastoring, demonstrating the conviction that the kingdom would be built in the real world, where there was "in the essential endeavor of socialism, a revelation of God."[10] In his concurrent work in fledgling state institutes and education throughout the early decades of the twentieth century, Wu's life echoes the activist streak in Barth. Wu's early career spanned imperial and revolutionary governments, and he combined the roles of educator and civil servant, putting his scholarship to the use of the state in the manner of traditional gentry. He later worked in the Jiangsu governor's office, and was briefly a magistrate in the Hangzhou military government when the city declared independence from the Qing in 1911.[11]

Wu Leichuan's thinking on the Kingdom was strongly influenced by his reading (in translation) of the writings of various Social Gospel proponents of the 1910s and 1920s.[12] He draws on Charles Gore's 1927 lectures, which argue for a social element to "salvation" in scripture and remind of the voluntary system of communal ownership in the early church,[13] and quotes Sherwood Eddy's *Religion and Social Justice* (1927), where Eddy explores how the social gospel embraces social justice in the commercial world and the economic sphere.[14] Wu draws on thinkers like Gore, Eddy, and Rauschenbusch in his understanding of the relationship between stewardship and property ownership; of the need for a small vanguard whose ideas would transform wider society; of the construct of the early church; and of the relationship of the Kingdom with society and with the eschaton. In these writers, Wu found an echo of his own unease with contemporary society, and a shared interest in teasing out what a Christian life expended in Kingdom-building would look like. While Barth's thinking may have drawn on a "more sophisticated" Continental version of the Social Gospel via Kutter and Ragaz, there were points of contact.[15] Eddy's "growing dissatisfaction with 'things as they are'" and desire to find a way to "things as they ought to be,"[16] and Gore decrying contemporary society as "a parody of the divine intention,"[17] were anticipated by Barth in his damning charge that the church's recourse to piety when faced with social misery was "the great, momentous apostasy of the Christian church, her apostasy from Christ."[18]

The core to building the kingdom for Wu, as in Barth's socialist vision, is economic reform. Since the greatest inequalities cause the most division, the first task was to remove private property, a point Barth underlined in asserting that there was "no doubt" Jesus rejected the concept of private property.[19] Wu held that the notion Jesus looked down on material goods was a later misunderstanding, and believed that the rejection of private ownership was a prerequisite to getting rid of class distinctions. For Wu, the economics of the kingdom permeate Jesus' parables: those who refuse to attend the wedding banquet do so to pursue their own private mercantile interests; the parable of the lost coins exposes ideas on property; the prodigal son's enlightenment comes after he has squandered private property and becomes a hired laborer.[20] Wu follows Gore in believing that a new ideal of property, regulated by society and predicated on "use" not "power," was needed to accompany the realization that the self is always brought to being in community.[21] The wording is almost a paraphrase of Barth, and the sentiment akin to Barth's dictum that salvation is effected by a "collective, solidary, communal, social God." A social understanding of capital precludes individual greed or gain: as Wu explains to his readers, everything humans have is received from others, "you received without payment, give without payment." Property is important to the functioning of society, but as Wu points out, intelligence too is nurtured by society, and it is only natural and proper that its use should be returned to society. "It's a pity most people don't get this," he notes laconically.[22] Barth is less sanguine: Lazarus is held up as someone excluded from the kingdom not because of any evil committed, but as one who belatedly realizes the effect of class contradiction in his earthly life, and Barth attacks strenuously the complicity of church and state in Europe in valorizing wealth.[23]

The differences between Barth and Wu in their respective constructions of the kingdom presage different faith outcomes when the building is delayed, or the edifice does not emerge as anticipated. While Barth elides the humanity/person of Christ with the social justice movement, for Wu and many of his Republican-era counterparts, it was the character of Christ which enabled the advent of the kingdom: this is not a debate about divinity but about (a more Confucian) perfectibility.[24] If the Kingdom of Heaven is pre-eminently a matter of economic justice, its realization is brought about through Jesus' perfected, Messianic nature. "The center of Christianity," argues Wu, "is Jesus' character, and Jesus-as-Messiah is the center of Jesus' character."[25] If there is to be a revolution, it is an upturning of the old ways, and a pruning of regressive traditions. The Jesus who "taught us that to be human was to take on the task of improving society" modeled salvation in the act, and in his confrontation with evil, enabled his spirit of courage to be replicated.

If there is base agreement between Wu and Barth on the negative social side to the capitalist mode of production and on Jesus' alignment with the poor, the way that the Kingdom is brought about in each reflects crucial differences in perspectives. Wu's verdict that without change in the economic system there will never be any progress in morality is a natural outcome of rooting the kingdom in personal moral transformation. For Wu, sin is structural. It has economic and postcolonial properties, and it is overcome by Christ and in Christ-like lives. For Barth, and not just a late Barth, "God's kingdom comes to us," rather than by a human ascent toward heaven. From the divine point of view, the movement is downward.[26] As Herberg notes, Barth's insistence on God's otherness attacks a world "that had lived by a confidence in the essential divineness of its own aspirations and achievements," while his "word of divine transcendence, relativizing everything, absolutely everything, that was not God" is already present in the "movement from above" of his 1911 address.[27] Human effort is important for Barth—since social action has value in God's eyes, and judgment will be based on whether one clothed the poor and fed the hungry—but humans do not, themselves, bring about the kingdom. Wu's replication of Christ-actions will never, of itself, found the kingdom. Socialism creates the conditions that maximize the possibility of the kingdom flourishing—especially for the proletariat—but does not actualize it. (Later Chinese advocates of the TSPM such as Wu Yaozong or Ding Guangxun would take a similar line on the positive intermediary function of socialism.) Where Social Gospel writers had warned against utopia-building, or the anticipation that a change in human conditions could eliminate selfishness, Wu remains deliberately naïve, promulgating the (Confucian) notion that the right conditions would produce moral goodness, which itself would ensure good governance.

While Wu Leichuan spent 1936 envisioning the kingdom of God in China, other Chinese thinkers were beginning to be disillusioned with the failure of Christianity to establish a peaceful or secure nation, a failure to which Wu's human-horizon Christianity could not easily respond. Stalwarts of the church like Gu Ziren (T. Z. Koo) spoke of "how deeply troubled he was at the ineffectiveness of Christianity in the world," and of the deleterious effects on his faith of the failure of the League of Nations to prevent the annexation of Manchuria.[28] The aggression of Christian imperialism, and China's failure to repel Japanese imperialism problematized, to say the least, the project of cultural transformation and salvation. Barth's evolving construct of the kingdom, "which is not capable of realization in this age"[29] may have spoken to this gap between ideal and reality, but a stronger point of connection with Chinese Christians in the 1930s was the transformation in Barth's thinking in the face of state oppression. If the experience of living under an increasingly totalitarian state had a decisive effect on Barth, the experience of life under Japanese occupation had a polarizing effect on Chinese theologians. Six months imprisonment under the Japanese, for example, caused the theologian and author of the first Chinese language study of Barth, Zhao Zichen, to revert to an orthodox evangelical faith.[30]

If the Kingdom of God formed an early point of connection between Barth and Chinese thinkers, a second "moment" where the Chinese situation and Barth's writings speak insightfully to each other occurs in the mid-1950s, when the church was beset by bitter debates over how to respond to the state's demands. Between these two stood the war. The threat to the nation under Japanese occupation and the perceived failure of international capitalism help explain why the liberal wing took such an accommodating stance toward the state. The War of Resistance against Japan and its effects on Chinese society have been well documented by historians,[31] but the effects of anti-Japanese sentiment in strengthening anti-imperialism in the church have rarely been discussed. The war united people in resistance and was heralded by some Christians as the cornerstone of a broader liberatory movement. It was instrumental in eliding "Divine Service" and "political service" in many minds.[32] In an example of the closing distance between church and state, St. Peter's Parish board in Shanghai called on members to purchase government bonds in 1937, arguing that "because these bonds are part of the plan to save our country, our church cannot simply stand by."[33] Wu Yaozong (Y. T. Wu), who was to emerge as a key figure mobilizing Protestants to work with the fledgling PRC government, argued in his long pamphlet "Abiding Faith for a Nation in Crisis," that Chinese victory against Japan would bring stability and discourage other aggressors.[34] For Wu as for others, the turning point toward supporting the (communist) state was a growing belief that the root problem was not just links between mission and imperialism, but also between imperialism and capitalism.

THE KINGDOM IN THE WORLD,
OR: CHURCH AND STATE

If the young Barth and the incipient Chinese-run Protestant church focused on the invocation "thy kingdom come," just how this might be done on earth in the face of opposition from worldly kingdoms occupied much thought in the middle decades of the century. Barth's combination of biblical exegesis and attempts to rethink Reformation theologians' understanding of the relation between the kingdoms of heaven and earth, and between the church and the state, proves to be a surprisingly vital source for parsing and balancing the bitter debates within the Chinese church in the mid-twentieth century, providing insight into why passions ran so high, and how this legacy might potentially be mediated. Barth's thinking relates to the Chinese situation in two ways: in the careful crafting of theological thought in his essays "Gospel and Law," "Church and State," and "Christian Community and Civil Community," and in his pastoral response to the East German question, as espoused in "How to Serve God in a Marxist Land."

The question of the relation of church to state drove deep theological and ecclesiological divides through the Christian denominations of China in the 1950s, as is well known. Republican-era debates on Chinese Christian identity and allegiance in the face of (Christian) imperialist aggression, re-emerged in questions of whether taking part in building the new China was a Christian project, or how the church might enter into dialogue with the atheist party-state. As the demands of the state on religious leaders gradually intensified throughout the early 1950s, the threat of internal division in the churches grew accordingly. Protestants and Roman Catholics who rejected the new regime and its claims continued to worship outside the authorized bounds of the newly co-opted Three-Self Patriotic Movement (1951/54) and Chinese Catholic Patriotic Association (1957), setting up alternative structures and networks (which culminated in the Roman Catholic Church in the ordinations of "underground" bishops and total severance from the CCPA). The vehemence of debate and of personal attacks by different factions within Christian groups show how deeply the relationship with the state touched central claims of faith (and for Roman Catholics, of authority). The divisions of the 1950s over this question have proved, so far, impossible to reconcile.

It is not coincidental that the two representative figures in the Protestant debates of the early 1950s each became revered leaders within their respective spheres.[35] Ding Guangxun (K. H. Ting) was a spokesperson for that sector of the church which chose to work with the government, and spent much of the next six decades of his leadership of the TSPM and China Christian Council justifying this project theologically. Wang Mingdao, preacher, publisher and independent church leader, spent most of the first twenty years of communist rule in prison for his stance. Although certain precepts of Barth seem strongly to support the principled stance of a Wang Mingdao against Ding, a close reading across Barth's essays show how both figures adhered to core principles that Barth articulated in his dissection of the role of the church on earth, and points to why the two positions led to such protracted and entrenched antagonism. What Barth helps show, is the different emphases of each, rather than absolute contradictions.

Karl Barth held an exceedingly high view of the state. As he points out, while the ultimate State for Christians is not on earth but in heaven, the church's hope in the age to come is precisely in a *state* (polis), and not a church body; the church which "stands over against the earthly State as a sojourning," will ultimately be absorbed into a heavenly state.[36] Barth follows Calvin in the distinction between a *regnum spirituale* governing eternal life and a *regnum politicum* for the present, with the church and the state "each being competent in its own sphere," while holding that the Reformers did not articulate adequately the relationship between the two.[37] Adamant that the state is involved in the order of Redemption, Barth demonstrates its legitimacy (and neutrality in Christian terms) through the misuse of state power by Pilate. The state, Barth claims, may be constrained to do good even when aiming for evil, but in any case, must always be honored, as God-instituted. The state belongs "originally and ultimately to Christ" and cannot be understood apart from Christ, yet can become demonic, "by a renunciation of its true substance, dignity, function and purpose."[38] The baseline for the church is that the state should supply it with its one central freedom to preach and exercise its function of proclaiming divine justification, while the church should act in a priestly capacity toward the state, reminding it of the limits and truths of its own sphere.

The principles of active involvement in the church and the world derive from these tenets. The difficulty in terms of the Chinese church and the debates between Ding and Wang, is their respective weighting. While the core duty of a Christian citizen vis-à-vis the state, according to Barth, is to support it in its godly functions of administering justice and protecting the law, the church also has a duty to withstand any state that is not acting as a state should under God; it renders its unique service to the state precisely by dissenting, even when this "will consist in becoming its victims."[39] While the Maoist state in the 1960s represents one of the most egregious forms of Caesar-worship and state-mythology the world has known, fulfilling Barth's criteria for the demonic, its nature was far less obvious in the early years of the People's Republic. The tension in Barth between the duty to withstand a warped state and the need to live out the core function of the church, its proclamation of the Gospel, is one of the critical pivot points between Ding and Wang; part of this is the question of timing and discernment, and part is the question of *how* one dissents, whether by challenging from within state structures, or by principled disengagement. Ding favored the Sadducees' route; Wang the Pharisaical (or even the Essenes; in Yoder's terms[40]).

Barth understood that determining the nature of the state was "a question of continual decision, and therefore of distinction between one state and another, between the State of yesterday and the State of today."[41] For Wang Mingdao, how the church should proceed under the PRC was clear, and he maintained a sure sense of what was, and was not, of God. In a sermon of the early 1950s, Wang explores how incremental concessions or accommodation negate faith. "Spiritual victory is obtained by being faithful in small matters. . . . Maybe someone will say, 'If I should say that a white sheet of paper is black, at most I myself only speak a lie. This will not hurt anyone nor disgrace the name of God.'"[42] For Wang, any small unfaithfulness was serious sin. He refused to sign the Manifesto drawn up in May 1950 condemning the church as a tool of imperialist powers, and denounced all forms of compromise, including the establishment of the Three-Self Patriotic Movement. In 1955, shortly after his public debates with Ding, Wang received a fifteen-year prison sentence for "anti-revolutionary" activities. He was coerced into signing a public "self-examination" or confession, which he subsequently recanted—a text which, like those of many intellectuals, is remarkable for its potential counter-reading, in its restatement of "crimes" and erroneous beliefs intertwined with the self-criticism.[43] Wang remained in the prison system until 1980.

Wang's actions are consonant with Barth's vision of the church's relation with a distorted or demonic state. Subjection to the state's authority, Barth writes, "can in no case mean that the Church and its members will approve, and wish of their own free will to further, the claims and undertakings of the State, if once the State power is turned not to the protection but to the suppression of the preaching of justification." They cannot, moreover, accept responsibility for any undertakings of the state aimed against the mission of the church, its preaching of justification.[44] For Wang, the structure of the TSPM amounted to such an undertaking. Barth held that the freedom to preach and exercise the function of church was foundational, to be defended to death, if necessary, while Wang wrote "Nothing should prevent us from preaching the gospel, not does anyone have the authority to interfere with out witness to the resurrected Lord."[45] While his ordering of priorities for the church differs from Barth, Wang's plea for freedom closely echoes Barth:

> Christians should obey all the rules and regulations of man and those in authority. But Christians should also obey God's will, which is to fellowship with believers, serve God with others in the church, keep the church holy, witness for the Lord and spread the gospel of salvation. All these should absolutely not be interfered with by anyone. For the cause of *freedom to do these things*, we should count no sacrifice too costly.[46]

For Wang, moreover, persecution was inevitable; the only alternative to being hated by the world was to become a collaborator like Judas.[47] "Arm yourself with the spirit of suffering," he exhorts, and elsewhere castigates those who preach "safe sermons" and do not rebuke sin, who "have totally lost their function before God."[48]

Wang's theology foregrounds holiness and repentance, where holiness meant separation from the world and a steadfast persistence in doing what one believed to be right, no matter how strong the opposition. His sermons are rich in exhortations to a life lived to please God not humans, he lauds, for example, the prophet Micaiah, "who did not care that others slandered him, because he was determined simply to be faithful to God," noting that "The situation in the nation of Israel in those days is parallel to that in the church of God today."[49] While Wang's arguments are often naïve appeals to scripture, his principled stand fulfills a prophetic role to both church and state, an embodiment of Barth's claim that "Even though the Church prefers to suffer persecution at the hands of the state . . . rather than take part in the deification of Caesar, yet it still knows that it is responsible for the State and for Caesar." It is possible to argue that Ding Guangxun was equally aware of his responsibilities of the state, and exercised them differently to enable the church to continue functioning, but once the state started demanding thought-reform and self-criticism on the part of believers, it is difficult to get round Barth's "unhesitating 'No'!" to such internal demands, and almost impossible to square a theology of *aiguo aijiao* (爱国爱教 "love the country (and) love the church") with Barth's claim that such a demand denotes an unjust state, since "love is not one of the duties which we owe to the State."[50] Where Wang differs markedly from Barth, is in his ascription of the world to Satan; the world does not become, but *is* demonic, under the control of Satan.[51]

On the question of working alongside atheists and communists, Ding Guangxun consistently took an opposite view to Wang. "Can the church only glorify God by placing itself in opposition to the nation and its people?"[52] he asked incredulously in 1954. Consecrated an Anglican Bishop in China in 1955, Ding reiterated on different occasions:

> It is the conviction of many of my colleagues that, as long as there is space for Christian witness to be borne and for dialogue on issues to be carried on, we must for the good of the church refrain from adopting confrontation and mar-tyrdom as church policy.[53]

Barth had argued that the "essential service" of the church to the state "consists in maintaining and occupying its own realm as church," which lay in "true scriptural *preaching*, and *teaching*, and in the true and scriptural administration of the *sacraments*," and that the performance of these actions is the "force which founds and maintains the state."[54] This was Ding's justification and aim. In an article of 1954, "Why Must We Still Be Preachers?" Ding combines a conviction of commission to preach the truth and belief that "people of all times and places need the gospel," with the beginnings of a systematic response to the moral and theological niceties of whether to work with the government.[55] Barth notes, too, the church has a role which only it can fulfill in conveying to the state an understanding of its true function, something one could argue Ding undertook faithfully during his decades of service on the national Chinese People's Political Consultative Conference. Yet Barth, as we have seen, also lays out the circumstances under which not resisting would make it an enemy of the state.

In different times and places, Ding expressed a mixture of philosophical and personal reasons for working within state structures. Where Barth argues from first principles of the State and the Kingdom, Ding opts for a cultural, contextual argument. (One of the difficulties in reading Ding is the dearth of contemporary writings, and the preponderance of later recollection.) The historical context for Ding and other intellectual leaders of the period is clear: the overriding issue for the Chinese church was the resolution of its colonial legacy, and the institution of an independent, non-denominational "Chinese" church and Chinese theology. Part of that Chinese identity was its identification with the fate of the nation. Among Protestants, there was genuine admiration for what the Communists had achieved in the areas under their occupation, and hope for what Liberation and the "new China" might achieve. Love for one's nation, especially in times of suffering, argued Ding repeatedly, using texts from Isaiah, Jeremiah or the psalms, is a thoroughly biblical standpoint.

Ding was as scathing in his remarks on those who could not work with the (state) church or hold a positive theological vision for China as Wang was in his condemnation of the "so-called servants of God." Ding's rhetoric grew stronger over time: in a speech in Tokyo in 1984 he belittled the "theological but highly political" arguments used to negate the new China, and especially those who claimed that the Christian should love the world or anything in it. "To them, God has lost the world he created to Satan" Ding wrote, demonstrating why this could not be a theologically acceptable argument.[56] Ding's textual base was wider than Barth, and he drew on the Chinese classics, the Bible and theology to argue to Christians that humanity is not utterly depraved, and that the created world is God's sphere. Central theological tenets for Ding were a concentration on the incarnation and "divine yes to creation," and a Christology that proclaimed the "Christlikeness of God."[57] The universal nature of Christ's care and Christ's ongoing role in creation is fundamental to Ding, and the experiences of the second half of the twentieth century did not change his fundamental allegiance to a God of Love, or to socialism as the path forward for China.[58]

Two of Barth's best known and most courageous acts thus speak incisively to the situation in China: the declarations against Hitler and the role of the German church, and his later refusal to condemn Communism, or, as his son Markus Barth wrote, his refusal to "give religious sanctification to the superficial or hysterical condemnations of communism."[59] In "How to Serve God in a Marxist Land," the most striking note is the pastoral wisdom of reticence. In speaking about the pressure Christians in the DDR were facing, Barth cuts into the debates between Ding Guangxun and Wang Mingdao with his understanding that a situation is impossible to assess from outside. There is no simple answer: "One would need to have spent all these years with you, to have experienced in one's life the growing pressure under which you stand," he begins. This rare empathy extends to moral exigencies, since "one would need to have tried out personally the various possibilities of withstanding it in order to avoid coming up with some kind of wisdom which because of a deficient knowledge of the facts, situations and persons, might be totally irrelevant to your questions."[60] Given the overwhelming tendency in the debates surrounding the divisions of the Chinese church—divisive precisely because of the power of the belief invested and the huge impact on life of implementing faith decisions—Barth's honest ignorance is profoundly helpful. Faced with Wang's unwillingness to call black white, but also Ding's perceived calling to keep the church going and save others through continued preaching, who is fitted to impute right or wrong? In a move which is affirmative of Christians in the Communist East, but also prescient regarding the West, Barth condemns not only the "spirit, and the words, the methods and the practices" of East Germany, but also the distortions and "creeping totalitarianism" of the West, with its tyrannous press, systems of private enterprise, and "snobbish presumption."

All regimes, Barth implies, are potential "prowling adversaries" and demand resistance; identifying Communism as the "lion" of I Peter might prove to be "the trap of a dangerous optical illusion." Chiming with Ding, Barth affirms that God is sovereign over atheism, and that much atheism has arisen "from misunderstandings caused by the prevailing teaching, attitudes and practices of the Christian Church,"[61] while he suggests, contra Wang, that loyalty does not signify approval of a particular government ideology, and opens a way up to a conditional recognition, where acknowledging the authority of the state does not preclude retaining the "right of freedom of thought, right of opposition, even resistance" in particular instances. Barth's anti-state movements in Germany place him alongside Wang Mingdao in his resistance and denunciation, yet his theology of community and the affirmation of possibility in the Communist state draw Barth alongside Ding, and Ding's iteration of the Cosmic Christ finds much support in Barth's view of the church community's scope and service.[62] Barth is adamant, moreover, that the existence of the Christian community is itself political, and that a Christian decision to be "indifferent" or "non-political" is "quite impossible."[63] If Barth's wisdom leads to the acceptance that only those present can discern right and wrong before God, then the onus on the contemporary church in China must be to understand, and not judge, those who survived the persecutions of the Maoist years. Re-evaluating these debates of the 1950s is a starting point.

CHURCH, COMMUNITY, AND THE SINO-CHRISTIAN THEOLOGIANS: A FOOTNOTE

Debates over church-state relations in China have been complicated more recently by the growth of a sector of Christianity outside of the church. If

Barth's anti-capitalism and worker-activism was tempered in middle age, one thing that remained constant from his formative, socialist, years was an insistence on community. *CD* 4/2 emphasizes the provisional nature of the church, between Christ and the end time. The task of the community of Christ is to fulfill this provisional representation, and for Barth, individual contributions to this representation are only possible when "surrounded and supported and nourished" by the community.[64] A saint cannot function "in and for himself," but only as part of the communion of saints; "extra ecclesia, nulla salus." On the face of it, Barth would seem to have little sympathy for the burgeoning Sino-Christian theology movement, the third "moment" of this chapter.

Sino-Christian Theology, a term coined in the 1990s, refers to a specific movement in Chinese academic theology, circling initially around scholars such as Liu Xiaofeng and He Guanghu, and more broadly to all Chinese-language theology. The movement raises sharp questions over the relationships between church, community, and theology.[65] Two stand out: the faith of individuals, and the relation of theology to church. The "extra ecclesia" debate surfaced in the 1990s in China and Hong Kong over the issue of "Cultural Christians," proving eventually to be as much a question of terminology as authority. A related debate on whether one has to be a theologian to do theology, continues to the present. In the mid-1990s, use of the term "Cultural Christians" as a label for academics studying Christianity with no church affiliation or necessary personal belief led to arguments over whether academics from "outside the church" could *be* theologians, setting mainland philosophers of religion against Hong Kong theologians, and subsiding when the phrase "Scholars in Mainland China Studying Christianity" (SMSC) was more widely adopted.[66] As Jason Lam writes, "the special feature of the emergence of scholars studying Christianity in mainland China is that they have no relationship with existing ecclesiastical institutions and are all located in the cultural and educational system run by the communist government."[67] As Lam argues, the fact that scholars have learnt their Christianity not from institutional churches but through their academic studies and translation experiences has profound effects on the theology produced.

Sino-Christian theology never set itself up as a theology of the church, for the church, as in orthodox Western theology, but aimed to be "from Chinese academia, for Chinese academia, facing the Church and society." Chin Kenpa, in this volume, considers the notion of Sino-Christian theology as "a non-Christian public theology."[68] While some Sino-Christian theologians are believers, some are not, at ease operating outside the paradigm where theology, the reflexive thinking of the church, must come from within the body of believers. Liu Xiaofeng has argued that the church is secondary, a historico-social product formed to stave off the effects of persecution. Liu finds historical precedent for a dispensable church in German and Russian examples.[69] He is not the first to argue the case: when Wu Leichuan asked in the 1930s whether the relation of culture to religion is fundamentally differ- ent in a convert nation, he noted that if the Kingdom of God were to be built in a minority Christian country like China, it would necessarily be through the wider apparatus of the state, in a broad coalition. If there was no need for miracles for liberals in Republican and Nationalist China, the church was no more necessary for building the kingdom either (and here Wu concurs with an early Barth).[70]

Barth, who in "The Church and the Community" argued that 'The Word and Spirit of God are no more automatically available in the church than they are in the State,'[71] also held that 'the community exists only in the common being and life and action, in the faith and love and hope, of its members, and therefore of individual Christians.'"[72] If (if!) academics have found this sustaining community and commonality of service in their universities and scholarly networks, a question still remains over the locus of theology in China today. Seminaries run by the mainstream (TSPM) Protestant church have been seen by academics as low-level "Bible Schools," and regional seminaries indeed do accept students directly from high school, or even mid- dle school. Even Nanjing Union Seminary degrees do not allow their holders to access MA courses within the state university system. From the former leader of the church, Bishop Ding, commenting that much good theology was coming from the university sector, to Liu Xiaofeng arguing that until the church raised the level of its thinking it could never compete with Buddhism or Confucianism, to the Director of World Religions at CASS, Zhuo Xinping, claiming that ecclesiastical theologies are peripheral "and receive little atten- tion from either society or Chinese intellectuals," there has been no shortage of detractors of church theology.[73] The reasons for individuals to remain outside the church system are many and complex, including disdain for the level of preaching, and lack of breadth in liturgical or theological offerings, but there are also numerous new communities, both real and virtual, attracting urban intellectual Christians.[74]

For Barth's provisional church to have purchase in China, the definition of "church" may need to be amplified. The parameters of the debates on com- munity and church in China have been set by many factors, some practical and local—laws on religious services taking place only at registered loca- tions, the division between registered and unregistered churches in any given area—and some more structural: the legacy of Christianity as a "foreign" religion, and the broader framework of China's quest for its own (socialist, modernized) identity; the history of church-state interactions and residual fear and mistrust on the part of many Christians; the post-denominational stance as a rejoinder to the imperialist mission era; the separation of seminary and university training and therefore the possibilities for Christian education. The growth in academic studies of Christianity over the last three decades has had an effect on these boundary lines too, because of their impact on the public understanding of religion and in creating communities of Christian scholars. In renegotiating the relationship of Christianity to Chinese culture and in promoting the value of the methods of theological study in the search for truth for the wider humanities, academic scholars of Christianity have created an important new, legitimizing, space for Christianity in society. Outside the strictures of the church, they have also had more leeway to develop their own thinking on aspects of Christianity, from church-state relations to philosophical theology and beyond, insisting on China's right to set its own theological agenda, to rethink certain (Western) norms and expectations, including that of "who speaks?"

AFTERWORD

As the "moments" of debate discussed here show, the intensity with which Barth's thought speaks to the situation of the Chinese church and vice versa is at times striking. Using Barth as a foil for Chinese thinkers can serve to clarify what is particular both in experience and in theological thought, and what fits with longer historical or global currents. Barth's longevity, the breadth of his writings, and his experience of socialist fervor, wartime desolation, and Communist divisions make him a perceptive and shrewd dialogue partner for Chinese theology of the twentieth century and its questions of state power, national identity, and ecclesial development. The iteration of "moments" shows how these questions are both historically discrete and timeless; they can be framed in one context and transposed to another, and it is the transposition that makes the particular contextual frame stand out. This is, if anything, more evident for Barth, whose scriptural reading of, say, the relation of earthly church to the heavenly State looks a shade less assured or more parochial in the light of very different Chinese concerns and methodologies.

The "moments" also remind us that these are ongoing debates that intersect and recur. In August 2015, for example, the leaders of a Chengdu-based new urban Protestant house church published online a document entitled *Reaffirming our stance on the House churches—95 theses*.[75] In it, Pastor Wang Yi and the other leaders of his church set out their core beliefs under four broad categories: opposing the "Sinicization" of Christianity; the church as Christ's body and kingdom; the division of church and state, and opposing the TSPM and supporting the Gospel mission. As the section headings indicate, the church leaders present a fairly prescriptive view on the nature of the church in the world. The language of the church as a spiritual kingdom in the world, pledging its loyalty only to Christ (#44), of a China under the sovereign power of Christ (#43), of God handing the power of the sword to secular rulers while the church holds the keys to Heaven (#62), and of the church's mission to the world which no country can limit, reprises the debates of the 1950s for a new generation. These twenty-first century representatives of the evangelical house churches, who scarcely favor Barth, have produced a credal document suffused with Barthian precepts, a rejoinder to state church adherents and to the Sino-Christian movement—a text which cries out for a new dialogic reading of the type modeled here.

NOTES

1. Zung Wei Tsung, "The Chinese Church and the New Industrial System," *Chinese Recorder* LIII (1922): 186–190.

2. Zung, "The Chinese Church and the New Industrial System," 190.

3. Xu Zongze (P. Joseph Zi, SJ), "Laodong qiyue," 勞動契約 *Shengjiao Zazhi* 10 (1932): 576–581, and "Tianzhujiao zenyang jiejue shehui wenti 天主教怎樣解決社會問題," *Shengjiao Zazhi* 9 (1933): 514–519. For discussion of Xu, see Starr, *Chinese Theology: Text and Context* (New Haven: Yale University Press, 2016), Chapter 4.

4. Wu Leichuan, *Jidujiao yu Zhongguo wenhua* 基督教与中国文化 [Christianity and Chinese Culture] (repr. Shanghai: Shanghai Guji, 2008). Discussion of Wu Leichuan draws on chapter 5 of Starr, *Chinese Theology*.

5. Karl Barth, "Jesus Christ and the Movement for Social Justice," repr. in *Karl Barth: Theologian of Freedom*, ed. Clifford Green (London: Collins, 1989), 99, 101.

6. Barth, "Jesus Christ and the Movement for Social Justice," 104.

7. In his critique of social democracy and argument for the prior need for human transformation to bring about earthly transformation (p. 107), Barth shows how the means to the Kingdom are as important as the outcome; Wu is less explicit on this distinction.

8. Green, *Karl Barth*, 43.

9. C.f. e.g. Chu Sin-jan, *Wu Leichuan, A Confucian-Christian in Republican China* (New York: Peter Lang, 1995); Li Wei, *Wu Leichuan de jidujiao chujinghua sixiang yanjiu* 吴雷川的基督教处境化思想研究 (Beijing: Zongjiao Wenhua, 2010); Frank K. P. Chan, *Liji liren: Wu Leichuan bense shenxue* 立己立人：吴雷川本色神学重构 (Hong Kong: Chinese Mission Seminary, 2008).

10. From Barth's lecture "Religion and Socialism," December 7, 1915, quoted in Marquardt, *Theological Audacities*, 105.

11. Details of Wu's biography can be found in English in Chu, *Wu Leichuan*, 5–15.

12. For a cogent discussion of the Social Gospel movement, its relation to Barth, and its meaning throughout the twentieth century and into the present, see Charles Mathewes' article in this volume, "Whatever Happened to the Social Gospel? Religion and Political Economy in the USA Today, and for the Future."

13. Translated into Chinese by (Rev.) Yu Ensi 俞恩嗣, published by the Anglican Church in China in 1931.

14. Translated into Chinese and published by the Youth Association, in its Books and Newspapers Translation Journal in 1930.

15. Herberg, "The Social Philosophy of Karl Barth," 22.

16. Sherwood Eddy, *Religion and Social Justice* (New York: George H. Doran, 1927), 9.

17. Charles Gore, *Christ and Society – Halley Stewart Lectures, 1927* (London: George Allen and Unwin, 1928), 154.

18. Barth, "Jesus Christ and the Movement for Social Justice," 104.

19. Barth, "Jesus Christ and the Movement for Social Justice,"109.

20. Wu, *Jidujiao yu Zhongguo wenhua*, 43.

21. Charles Gore, Introduction to "Property, its duties and rights, historically, philosophically and religiously regarded," (London: Macmillan, 1915), xv, xi. Both Barth and Wu note Jesus' disinheritance of his family, but Barth is the more radical, arguing that the family question is here an extension of the issue of private property, see "Jesus Christ and the Movement for Social Justice," 109–110.

22. Wu, *Jidujiao yu Zhongguo wenhua*, 45.

23. Barth, "Jesus Christ and the Movement for Social Justice," 108–109.

24. As various scholars have noted. See e.g. John Yueh-Han Yieh, "Chinese Biblical Interpretation," in *Ways of Being, Ways of Reading*, eds. Mary Foskett and Jeffrey Kah-Jin Kuan (St Louis: Chalice, 2006), 23–24.

25. Wu, *Jidujiao yu Zhongguo wenhua*, 55.

26. "Wholly and Completely a Movement from Above to Below," Barth, "Jesus Christ and the Movement for Social Justice," 105.

27. Karl Barth, *Community, State, and Church*, ed. Will Herberg (Gloucester, MA: Peter Smith, 1968), 16.

28. See R. O. Hall, *T. Z. Koo: Chinese Christianity Speaks to the West* (London: SCM Press, 1950), 25.

29. Barth, "Church and State," in *Community, State, and Church*, 126.

30. See e.g. Ying Fuk-tsang, "寻索基督教与中国文化的关系：自由神学以后的赵紫宸," repr. in *Xunsuo Jidujiao de dute xing: Zhao Zichen shenxue lunji* 寻索基督教的独特性：赵紫宸神学论集, ed. Ying Fuk-tsang (Hong Kong: Alliance Bible Seminary, 2003).

31. See e.g. Rana Mitter, *China's War with Japan 1937–45* (London: Allen Lane, 2013), 5, 14.

32. Cf. Barth, "Church and State," 101–102.

33. Duan Qi, trans. Brian O'Keefe, "St Peter's Church in Shanghai during the War against Japan," in *Christian Encounters with Chinese Culture: Essays on Anglican and Episcopal History in China*, ed. Philip L. Wickeri (Hong Kong: Hong Kong University Press, 2015), 126, 119–134.

34. Wu Yaozong, *Da shidai de zongjiao xinyang* 大時代的宗教信仰 (Chengtu, Szechuan: The Association Press of China, 1938; repr. 1941), 4–5.

35. Cf. quotation in Thomas Alan Harvey, *Acquainted with Grief: Wang Mingdao's Stand for the Persecuted Church in China* (Grand Rapids: Brazos Press,

2002), 7: "Understand two men, and you will understand Chinese Christianity. " This section on Ding and Wang draws on chapter 7 of Starr, *Chinese Theology*.

36. Barth, "Church and State," 127, 124.

37. Barth, "Church and State," 102.

38. Barth, "Church and State," 118.

39. Barth, "Church and State," 138.

40. In *The Original Revolution*, John Howard Yoder created a typology of four tried-and-tested ways for a Jewish Jesus to develop the Kingdom of God in the Roman state: revolutionary violence (à la Zealots), realist accommodation (the Saducees' mode), withdrawal (Essenes) or careful segregation (the Pharisees' preference).

41. Barth, "Church and State," 119–120.

42. Wang Ming-dao, "Nitty-Gritty Faithfulness," in *A Call to the Church*, trans. Theodore Choy (Fort Washington, PA: Christian Literature Crusade, 1983), 19.

43. For English text, see Harvey, *Acquainted with Grief*, 167–173.

44. Barth, "Church and State," 138.

45. Wang Ming-dao, *A Call to the Church*, 104.

46. Wang Ming-dao, *A Call to the Church*, 27, from a sermon on Romans 13: 1.

47. Wang Ming-dao, *A Call to the Church*, 72.

48. Wang Ming-dao, *A Call to the Church*, 34, 68.

49. Wang Ming-dao, "The Missing Voice," in *A Call to the Church*, 41.

50. Barth, "Church and State," 143.

51. Wang Ming-dao, *A Call to the Church*, 31.

52. Ding Guangxun (K. H. Ting), *A Chinese Contribution to Ecumenical Theology*, eds. Janice and Philip Wickeri (Geneva: WCC Publications, 2002), 23. From 1954 essay "Why Must We Still be Preachers?"

53. K. H. Ting, "The Cosmic Christ," (1991) in *God is Love*, 14.

54. Barth, "Church and State," 146–147.

55. See Ting, *A Chinese Contribution to Ecumenical Theology*, 14–26.

56. K. H. Ting, "Love and Optimism," (1984) in *God is Love*: *Collected Writings of Bishop K. H. Ting* (Colorado Springs, CO: CCMI, 2004), 62–3, 110.

57. K. H. Ting, "My View of God," (1993) in *God is Love*, 68.

58. K. H. Ting, "My View of God," (1993) in *God is Love*, 38–39.

59. Markus Barth, "Current Discussion on the Political Character of Karl Barth's Theology," in *Footnotes to a Theology: The Karl Barth Colloquium of 1972*, ed. Martin Rumscheidt (Canada: Corporation for the Publication of Academic Studies in Religion in Canada, 1974), 80.

60. Karl Barth, "How to Serve God in a Marxist Land," 47, 48.

61. Karl Barth, "How to Serve God in a Marxist Land," 56, 57, 58.

62. Karl Barth, "The Christian Community and the Civil Community," (1954) in ed. C. Green, *Karl Barth*, 269.

63. Karl Barth, "The Christian Community and the Civil Community," 272.

64. *CD* IV/2, 622.

65. For a practical application of Barth to recent political movements in Hong Kong such as the Occupy Central protests, see Lai Pin-chiu's essay in this volume, "Religious Diversity, Democracy, and Public Theology: Conversing with Barth in

a Hong Kong Context," for more detailed exploration of the relationship of church to state in mainland China as conceptualized by different groups of Christians, see Thomas Xutong Qu, "'Gleichnis Wagen': Karl Barth's Political Theology and its Meaning for the Church-State Relationship in Mainland China Today. "

66. See Hanyu Jidujiao wenhua yanjiusuo (ed.) (1997). *Wenhua Jidutu: xianxiang yu lunzheng* 文化基督徒：現象與論爭 (Hong Kong: Institute of Sino-Christian Studies); also Fredrik Fällman, *Salvation and Modernity: Intellectuals and Faith in Contemporary China* (Stockholm: Stockholm University, 2004), 38–48; and articles by Peter K. H. Lee and Chan Shun-hing in Lai, Pan-chiu and Lam, Jason, eds., *Sino-Christian Theology: A Theological Qua Cultural Movement in Contemporary China* (Frankfurt: Peter Lang), 2010.

67. Jason Tzs-shun Lam, "The Emergence of Scholars Studying Christianity in Mainland China," *Religion State and Society* 32, no. 2 (2004): 177–186, 179.

68. Cf. Chin Ken-Pa, "Sino-Theology as Public Theology: The Reception of Karl Barth's Theology and Its Significance in the Chinese Context," in this volume.

69. Liu cites Richard Rothe, Simone Weil, Kierkegaard, Solovyov as examples of or promoters of an intellectual Christianity outside of the church, see Liu Xiaofeng, "Sino-Christian Theology in the Modern Context," in *Sino-Christian Studies in China*, eds. H. Yang and D. Yeung (Newcastle-upon-Tyne: Cambridge Scholars), 87.

70. Cf. Barth, "Jesus Christ and the Movement for Social Justice," 100.

71. Barth, "The Christian Community and the Civil Community," (ed. Herberg, 1968), 152.

72. *CD* IV/2, 615.

73. Zhuo Xinping, "Introduction," in *Christianity*, ed. Zhuo Xinping, trans. Chi Zhen and Caroline Mason (Leiden: Brill, 2013), 2.

74. See e.g. Gerda Wielander's study of the use of the Internet for creating virtual communities, and the range of online Christian publications and service podcasts, *Christian Values in Communist China* (London: Routledge, 2013).

75. "我们对家庭教会立场的重申," accessed at http://weibo.com/p/1001603881 634431670754.

Chapter 2

Yes! Intercultural Existence Today

Volker Küster

Christianity today is a globalized religion and the expansion of western Christendom a past history for many.[1] Even more, while Christianity in the secularized West—which against all predictions at the same time has in parts become multi-cultural-religious—has to face painful demographic setbacks,[2] it seems to flourish in the Southern hemisphere.[3] Instead of "mission in six continents," occasionally one speaks of the "Re-evangelization of Europe"; migrant churches and "mission in reverse" from South Korea or Nigeria included. Christian faith is at present confessionally and culturally poly-morphic and is lived out in contexts which are not only religiously plural. Intercultural theology explores the unavoidable interconfessional, intercul-tural, and interreligious processes of exchange that result from the develop-ments sketched earlier. I initially go into the matter, what Karl Barth still has to do with all that, dip back into the missiological discussion; and then sketch the irruption of contextual and intercultural Theology.[4]

KARL BARTH—A THEOLOGICAL TRICKSTER

If it comes to contextual and intercultural theology, Karl Barth is a sort of trickster. He seems to neglect everything that is central to them, yet still many of the founding fathers are referring particularly to him. Paradoxically enough, in the course of their lives they come to conclusions that are the opposite of pure Barthian teaching and still claim that Barth would agree with them. James Cone (1938–2018), for instance, describes his departure toward Black Theology:

I will never forget the event of writing that essay.[5] It seemed that both my Christian and black identity was at stake. My first priority was my black identity, and I was not going to sacrifice it for the sake of a white interpretation of the gospel that I had learned at Garrett. If Christ was not to be found in black people's struggle for freedom, if he were not found in the ghettos with rat-bitten black children, if he were in rich white churches and their seminaries, then I wanted no part of him. The issue for me was not whether Black Power could be adjusted to meet the terms of a white Christ, but whether the biblical Christ is to be limited to the prejudiced interpretations of white scholars. I was determined to set down on paper what I felt in my heart.

I decided to write a brief manifesto identifying Black Power with the gospel of Jesus. [. . .] From Barth and others I knew all about the ideological dangers of my procedure. Identifying the gospel with historico-political movements was anathema to anyone who bases his theology on divine revelation. But I purposely intended to be provocative in much the same way that Barth was when he rebelled against liberal theology. As Barth had turned liberal theology upside-down, I wanted to turn him right-side-up with a focus on the black struggle in particular and oppressed people generally.[6]

Cone makes his faith in Jesus Christ explicitly disposable, if it cannot prove its relevance for the black liberation struggle. Nevertheless, he claims Barth for his argument, on whose anthropology he wrote his dissertation[7]: "I was angry not with Barth but only with European and North American Barthians who used him to justify doing nothing about the struggle for justice. I have always thought that Barth was closer to me than to them [the Barthians]."[8] Indeed, on closer inspection, the seemingly so consistent Barth is himself not free of antagonisms.

Barth's first intervention in the mission scene was his lecture "Theology and Mission today" at a mission conference in Brandenburg in 1932.[9] Following his own flow, Barth pointed out the Trinitarian foundation of mission, "that in the ancient church the term *missio* was located in Trinitarian teaching, designating God's self-sending, the sending of the son and the Holy Spirit into the world."[10] The mission of the church takes place as a service in allegiance with this self-revelation and mission of God. This idea would become influential through the term *Missio Dei*, the origin of which is often ascribed wrongly to the World Missionary Conference in Willingen 1952. In the official conference proceedings, however, it does not occur. It virtually became the guiding theme of the whole conference through the later report of the director of the Basel Mission Karl Hartenstein (1894–1952). Hartenstein had been friends with Barth since the years he spent in Basel, and early on pointed out the relevance of Barth's theology for mission thinking.[11] Together with Walter Freytag (1899–1959), Hartenstein was a representative of the salvation history school, which was inspired by the New Testament scholar Oskar Cullmann (1902–1999), who also taught in Basel. Barth himself was rather reserved with regard to this eschatological, sometimes even apocalyptic thinking "with a view to the End."[12]

At the Willingen conference, the American delegation headed by Paul Lehman (1906–1994), which was inspired by the Social Gospel, talked about the "mission of God" referring to God's acting in history. A vanguard for their time, they already anticipated ideas of liberation theology when they proclaimed that "God is carrying out His judgment and redemption in the revolutionary movements of our time."[13] The first draft of the report of Section 1 was consequently declined by the plenary. Yet this interpretation was unfolding in the study process "The missionary structure of congregations,"[14] masterminded by Hans Hoekendijk (1912–1975) and Hans Jochen Margull (1925–1982), and continues to thrive in liberation theologies. Ahn Byung-Mu (1922–1996) and Suh Nam-Dong (1918–1984), for instance, the founding fathers of South Korean Minjung Theology, explicitly refer to *Missio Dei*.[15]

Hoekendijk, innately informed by Pentecostalism and evangelicalism, himself sympathized with Barthian thinking and feared the ghosts that he had conjured up. Banished from the theological faculty of the University of Utrecht because of his allegedly liberal thinking, he got into the vortex of Black Theology at Union Theological Seminary in New York. In addition, Hoekendijk lived in a second marriage with the feminist theologian Letty Russell (1929–2007). Therefore, all his life he was sitting between chairs and became the tragic figure of Dutch missiology.

The other stream of reception of Barth's *Missio Dei* concept leads directly into the salvation history school, which, however, received it according to their own agenda—the executive organ of the mission of God remains the church. The Lutheran missiologist Georg Vicedom (1903–1974), who is unsuspicious of liberation theological thinking, made it the guiding idea of his theology of mission.[16] Before, during, and after Willingen, the meaning of *Missio Dei* always depended on who was using it.

Barth's second interesting intervention in regard to our subject is his categorical "No!" to Brunner's discourse on a "point of contact."[17] His explicit and implicit critique of Schleiermacher, Troeltsch, Tillich, and the whole of cultural Protestantism is legendary. A Protestant theology of culture is not done with Barth. The Taiwanese theologian C.S. Song (born 1929), who studied in Edinburgh under Barth's pupil Thomas F. Torrance (1913–2007), but had also still sat at Barth's feet himself in Basel and later wrote a dissertation about "Revelation und Religion" in the theologies of Barth and Tillich at Union Seminary in New York,[18] writes in retrospect:

I just referred to the two great Western theologians of the 20th century [Barth und Tillich]. They were aware that they were doing theology in Western setting. But I am not sure whether they were aware of the "contextual" nature of their theology, even less so most Western theologians who have come after them. But after the initial stage in which I was held captive by my Western theological mentors such as Karl Barth and Paul Tillich as well as T. F. Torrance. [. . .] I ventured into the quest of the nature and truth of Christian theology on my own and developed my theology informed by stories. Stories, especially stories from Asia and stories from Taiwan, enabled me to develop theological methods and construct Christian faith and theology quite different from Western theologies.[19]

Song speaks in this regard of a "transposition"[20] "From Israel to Asia"[21] which leads to "doing theology with a third eye."

The term "third eye" is derived from Buddhism. [. . .] The theology with which we are familiar and in which most of us are brought up is a first- or a second-eye theology—a two-dimensional theology that is not capable of a third-dimensional insight. Because of its two dimensionality it is a flat theology. It canvasses a long stretch of terrain, which is the two thousand years of church history colored strongly by Western thought forms and lifestyles. [. . .] Those who are not endowed with German eyes should not be prevented from seeing Christ differently. They must train themselves to see Christ through Chinese eyes, Japanese eyes, Asian eyes, African eyes, Latin American eyes.[22]

Phrased in Barth's terminology, Song is searching for those "points of contact," which the master countered with a clear-cut "No!"

He [the missionary] will know that this is about the freedom of service, his service as messenger, whose master is the word, namely the written word and not the freedom to give the gospel an Indian, Chinese, or African form according to his pedagogical discretion, i.e. bringing it into a new system. [. . .] Therefore he will not rivet on a particular historical form of the gospel, neither on a European, nor an Asian or African, but on the one essential and superior form, the reification of which is the revelation, that is attested to him only through the scripture and only the scripture just as to the preacher at home.[23]

The consequences can, for instance, be observed in the case of the missiologist Klauspeter Blaser (1939–2002) from Lausanne, who in the 1980s wrote a booklet about contextual theologies which he originally wanted to give the title *From the Third Reich to the Third World: From Barmen to the Poor (Armen).*[24] The master himself on his part asked his assistant Eberhard Busch (born 1937) to draft a letter that he himself later signed, to respond to an invitation by Kosuke Koyama (1929–2009) to contribute to a special issue of the South East Asia Journal of Theology on Barth's Theology:

> Dear Christians in South East Asia! [. . .] Can the theology, presented by me, be understandable and interesting to you—and how? And can you continue in the direction in which I believed I had to go, and at the place where I had to set a period—and to what extent? [. . .] Now it is your turn. Now it is your task to be Christian theologians in your new, different, and special situation, with heart and head, with mouth and hands. [. . .] I can only encourage you: Yes do that: say that which you have to say as Christians for God's sake, responsibly and concretely with your own words and thoughts, concepts and ways! [. . .] You truly do not need to become "European," "Western" men, not to mention "Barthians," in order to be good Christians and theologians. You may feel free to be South East Asian Christians. Be it! Be it, neither arrogantly nor faint-heartedly with regard to the religions around you and the dominant ideologies and "realities" in your lands! Be it in all openness to the problems which are so burning in your region, and for your own, special and unique fellowmen.[25]

Most far-reaching in a negative sense was Barth's third intervention, namely the declaration that all religions—nota bene including the Christian—are disbelief.[26] Theologically founded in God's immediacy just as the *Missio Dei*, this statement does not leave room for a Christian theology of religions, let alone for interreligious dialogue. Hendrik Kraemer (1988–1965) has enforced this idea with his pamphlet "The Christian Message in a non-Christian World," written in preparation for the World Mission Conference in Tambaram 1938, which was commissioned by the International Missionary Council.[27]

D.T. Niles (1908–1970) from Sri Lanka, one of the pioneers of the modern ecumenical movement, not only in Asia, hawks a conversation with Barth (1935):

> Barth talked to me about our Christian communities in Asia in the midst of other faith. In the course of the conversation he said: "Other religions are just unbelief." I remember replying with the question "How many Hindus, Dr. Barth have you met?" He answered: "None." I said, "How then do you know that Hinduism is unbelief?" He said: "A priori." I simply shook my head and smiled.[28]

A good half century later, C. S. Song writes:

> In his doctrine of the Word of God Karl Barth speaks of "the Revelation of God as the Abolition of Religion" and "Religion as Unbelief" [. . .] Although Barth did not exempt Christianity as a religion from his theological judgement, his negative view of religion did not contribute to understanding of other religions.[29]

Barth himself de facto swiveled with his reflection on the light in other religions (*Lichterlehre*)[30] toward the exclusivism-inclusivism dilemma of a Christian theology of religions. With this argumentation he comes close to the other great Karl, Rahner's teaching regarding "anonymous Christians."[31] A constant thorn in his flesh was for Barth in this respect certainly Katsumi Takizawa (1909–1984), who was sent to him by his Buddhist master Kitaro Nischida (1870–1945).[32]

> He [Nishida] replied to me: "Today it is better to study with theologians than with philosophers, as the former are far more interesting than the latter. For the moment something needed in truth, namely God, is lacking even in Heidegger. So it is best for you to go to Karl Barth, who is also the firmest of theologians."[33]

Takizawa describes his first impression of Barth's teachings in eloquent words:

> In the great lecture hall in which almost 500 students were gathered, I took a place right at the front, in the fifth row and immediately before the desk, so that I did not miss a word of the teacher. Around me there were perhaps 20 students from Switzerland. When Professor Barth entered, around ten SA students got up with a jingling of spurs and shouted out "Heil Hitler!" Karl Barth stood rock-steady like an oak behind the desk, prayed briefly, and sang some verses from the hymn book with the students. Then he began to lecture. The topic this semester was "The Virgin Birth." I listened as though I had become an ear, body and soul. I do not know what happened to me. Nowhere else, in no philosophical lecture room or seminar, did I feel as free as I did here. Despite my ignorance and my linguistic difficulties his explanation of the creed, "conceived by the Holy Spirit, born of the Virgin Mary," was not wholly alien to me, but as clear and familiar as if it were going directly to me and my very soul.[34]

As a consequence, Takizawa committed his further life to develop a synthesis of the teachings of his two masters and to find the common ground of Buddhism and Christianity. Not without being critical in both directions. Nishida did not emphasize enough the irreversibility of the relationship between God and man, and Barth did not know how to differentiate between "Christ, the eternal Son of God" and "Jesus in the flesh." This resulted for Takizawa in a reduction of Christology to Jesus's function as an ideal and a concurrent revaluation of anthropology. God is represented in every human being.

On his death bed, Barth reportedly wanted to do everything again differently and rewrite his *Dogmatics* in view of other religions. Eberhard Busch recalls:

In the further course of our conversation, I tried to distract him from his depression by pitching a task to him. He quickly seized my suggestion and declared that he would indeed very much like to once again write a new book—a really new one—about a topic hardly anyone would put past him—a *symbolics* of religion, that would cover not only Christianity but the current major religions of the world as well. He would, however, proceed in an inverse order from how such a task is usually pursued. He would strictly proceed from the inner to the outer. Thus, he would not rely on a general concept of religion and subsequently treat the different religions according to that concept. Rather, he would start from the perspective and the primary insight of the biblical gospel and ask how all different religions need and are surrounded by God's grace. To begin, the major insights of the Reformed doctrine would have to be discussed, followed by an analysis of their relation to Lutheran doctrine and the doctrines of other Protestant churches. Next, this picture would have to be expanded by reflecting on the relation of Protestant doctrine to Roman-Catholic and Eastern-Orthodox perspectives. The symbolics would thus develop into an ecumenical theology, which in Barth's view, would necessarily need to include Jewish theologies as well. This, however, would not be enough. For, in a last step, the analysis should be expanded to cover the relations of the gospel perspective to non-biblical religions as well. This endeavor would demand flexibility and openness, the decisive point, however, would be to start analysis from the Gospel of Jesus Christ and not from a general concept of religion. "Well then!" I said to Barth, and he replied: "wait and see!" In any case, he thought that this topic was on the agenda for a current theology.[35]

Yet the formulation leaves open whether Busch only suggested that Barth start with a new book project, or with a new theme as well. In any case, Barth's considerations, conveyed here, follow along the lines of his thinking hitherto. Therefore Barth's Meta-universe and the *bricolage* of contextual and intercultural theology remain two parallel worlds. Only the trickster Barth would probably be happy to haunt both worlds and fool the Barthians just as well as "the cultured among his despisers."

MISSION REVISITED

The theological reflection on mission has subtly vanished from the curricula of European theological faculties. Chairs for missiology and comparative religion and/or ecumenics have been discarded, graded down, or simply not reopened, as at Tübingen, Birmingham, and what is left over from the Dutch faculties. When it has come to new appointments on the remaining chairs, the emphasis has usually been put on comparative religion. Ecumenics in its form of classical controversial theology has become part of dogmatics. Certain areas of missiology like church growth and planting have found a new home in practical theology.

What is the outcome of one century of academic-theological reflection on mission, which started from the missionary awakening of the nineteenth century and reached the Protestant theological faculties in Germany with Gustav Warneck? Theo Sundermeier has differentiated between six models of a theology of mission which still can serve as a framework of orientation in a dictionary of missiological terms, of which he was one of the initiators, and that has been one of the first and at the same time last of its kind in Europe.[36]

Sundermeier's models may be grouped according to their historical development and their theological references into three pairs. The two oldest are oriented toward their recipients. The conversion model can be located on the evangelical wing of the missionary movement. Often eschatologically/apocalyptically oriented, it has as its goal the conversion of the individual before the end is coming. The church-planting model, of Catholic origin, on the other hand, aims at the establishment of structures and community building.

As a first answer to the "crisis of mission," which after the end of World War II should never regain its old influence,[37] the conversion model finds in the salvation history school its ideological superstructure and at the same time becomes ecclesiologically embedded. In a progressive reduction, the "chosen ones" are condensed from the whole of creation to the people of Israel, to the "remnant," and finally Jesus Christ; and afterward salvation history widens itself in a "progressive expansion" from the apostles via the churches toward the kingdom of God.[38] The history of promise model, in contrast, changes the order God—Church—World into God—World—Church. The church is "ex-centric" to the world. This does not marginalize the church, but to the contrary puts it in relation with the world. Church is "church for others," to refer to Bonhoeffer. These models, which are oriented toward the theological foundation of mission, both claim the *Missio Dei* idea for themselves.

A second strategy to counteract the "crisis of mission" has been of a methodological nature. Again on the evangelical wing, the communication model was developed. If we learn to understand how communication processes function, the missionary as the sender can optimally transmit the message of the gospel to the receiver, who is supposed to be converted. The risk of a one-way traffic from the sender to the receiver is countered by Sundermeier with the hermeneutical model that presupposes a dynamic interaction and wants to accept the stranger in his strangeness. Quietly, Bonhoeffer's "for" others becomes a "with" others. Insofar one could also speak of a model of being present.

Even though developed consecutively, all these models are still in use. With the conversion and the hermeneutical model, the two possible extreme

Table 2.1   Theological Models of Mission (Theo Sundermeier)

Conversion Model	*Church-Planting Model*
(oriented toward recipients)	
individual	church
evangelicals; Church Growth School;	Louvain School (P. Charles;
J. Schmidlin	J. Masson)

Salvation History Model	*History of the Promise Model*
(oriented toward theological foundation)	
salvation history versus world history	salvation history = world history
God—church—world	God—world—church ("ex-centric")
	("for" others)
	"Missio Dei"
O. Cullmann; B. Sundkler; D. Bosch	J. Hoekendijk; H.J. Margull

Communication Model	*Hermeneutic (being present) Model*
(oriented toward methods)	
risk: one-way street (S⇒E)	dynamic interaction
H. Kraemer; E. Nida; H. Balz	("with" others)
	T. Sundermeier

positions are identified: conversion of the individual beyond existing church structures, or *être présent* among the people, striving for a dialogical living together. Yet the first impression can deceive. My Ghanaian doctoral student, for example, a former Muslim converted by a Korean missionary, has managed the project "Share" in Gushegu in Northern Ghana, financed by free evangelical churches in the Netherlands. He prays for the conversion of his Muslim neighbors, but he does this with an attitude of respect, by living his faith in their midst. In his PhD research, he deals with Muslim–Christian relations among the Dagbon, his own tribe.[39] Therefore, today various combinations even between seemingly contradictory models seem to be possible.

There remains the question of the relation between mission and dialogue. In the circles of a pluralist theology of religions, the decision has already been made. The age of mission and of a Christian claim to absoluteness is over. The religions are equal ways to salvation; interreligious dialogue is the order of the day. While the Lausanne declaration of the evangelical wing of the mission movement of 1974 still explicitly discards dialogue (LE 3), a formulation of the Manila Manifesto of 1989 already indicates a reversal of the trend: "in all aspects of our evangelistic work including inter-faith dialogue" (B.3).[40] Postmodern evangelicals do not have a problem anymore with dialogue, as long as we talk about the adequate form of mission for today in any case. Yet this does justice neither to the spirit of dialogue nor of mission. What is labeled dialogue should contain dialogue, and the same goes for mission. The mainline churches are aware of these tensions between so-called ecumenicals and evangelicals among their members and are therefore anxious to keep mission and dialogue apart if possible. The WCC has a Program for Inter-religious Dialogue and Cooperation and a Commission on World Mission and Evangelism; the Vatican maintains a Pontifical Council for Inter-religious Dialogue and a Congregation for the Evangelization of Peoples.

My own take on this complicated relationship is comparable to the nuanced solution of the Christological debates in the ancient church: mission and dialogue are hence "united with neither confusion nor division." The double commandment of dialogue is: (1) to understand the others in a way that they can recognize themselves in what is said about them and (2) to give witness to the best of one's own tradition. A dialogue without having one's own standpoint is not a dialogue and does not take seriously the other. At the same time, one should retain that whoever wants to get involved in missionary activities today, and this is not only true for Christianity but to the same degree also for the other two missionary religions, Islam and Buddhism, should do this in a dialogical way. An attitude of respect for the other is indispensable.

Dialogue has, in contrast, its purpose within itself. Depending on who is having a dialogue with whom about what, the objective may differ. Today there is usually a differentiation between three types of interreligious dialogue. The *dialogue of life* aims at the peaceful formation of the daily living together. It is pre-conceptual. People can respect the feasts of the religious others and even take part in their rites, without having a deeper understanding of them. In the *dialogue of the mind,* on the other hand, the learned of the different religions meet and embark on a common search for truth. This conceptual dispute reaches sooner or later a point where we have to agree that there are incommensurable differences between religions. Because here loyalties to the particular dogmatic system are at stake, the potential for conflict is the highest. In the post-conceptual *dialogue of the heart,* the mystics of all religions share their spiritual experiences. The conversion of the other is not a goal in any of these different types of dialogue.

Table 2.2 Typology of Interreligious Dialogue

Type	Subjects	Level	Goal
Dialogue of Life	all humans	pre-conceptual	ethical: good living together
Dialogue of the Mind	intellectuals	conceptual	intellectual: common search for truth
Dialogue of the Heart	mystics	post-conceptual	spiritual: sharing of spiritual experiences

In the ecumenical thinking on mission of the postwar era, shaped by the history of promise and hermeneutical models, respectively, liberation, inculturation, and dialogue emerged as generative themes. Barth's three interventions, sketched out at the beginning, cover this spectrum thoroughly. At the same time, the generative themes mirror the theological developments in the Third World, into which we are going to look now.

CONTEXTUAL THEOLOGY—INTERCULTURAL THEOLOGY

While the former sending churches of the West were unsettled by a "crisis of mission," in Africa, Asia, and Latin America it came to an ecclesiological and theological irruption. The repercussions of World War II overseas had often led to deportation or internment of missionaries. The contact between the Western mother churches and the so-called "younger churches" was interrupted, with the consequence that the latter established their own structures and cut the umbilical cord. In the wake of secular emancipation movements and cultural renaissances, soon contextual theologies also developed. Christian intellectuals who wanted to participate in the process of nation building had to justify why they wanted to stick to the religion of the colonizers.[41]

Due to the lack of priests in Latin America, the poor organized themselves in basic Christian communities, which soon became centers of resistance against oppression by the military dictatorships. They became the laboratories of liberation theology. In Asia, with the exception of the Catholic Philippines and South Korea, with a strong Protestant share of the population, Christianity is in an absolute minority position. In Africa, it competes with Islam for the remaining adherents of traditional religion. In the two last mentioned continents, theologically the engagement with the cultural-religious dimension of the particular context is in the foreground. Yet also here, liberation theologies existed early on in the Philippines, South Korea, and South Africa.

Contextual theology was in the beginning a purely male business, making it little different from Western academic theology, from which it tried to emancipate itself in an epistemological break. African theologian Mercy Amba Oduyoye (born 1934), however, proclaimed an "irruption within the irruption" at the general assembly of Ecumenical Association of Third World Theologians (EATWOT) in New Delhi in 1981.[42] Since then a self-contained theology of women from the Third World has developed, among women who are searching their way in dialogue with, but independent from their male colleagues in the Third World as well as Western feminists. Ecology and the ethnic identity of tribal communities emerged as new generative themes.

The thematic plurality is accompanied by a methodological unity, which can be described as hermeneutic circle between text and context. Since the text itself has also been produced in a particular context, a twofold question for the context arises, namely that of the actual reader and that of the author. What is the relevance of the text for the particular reader in his/her context and how can the "nasty ditch" (*garstige Graben*) be bridged? The contextual theology developed in the process has to be checked with the text. Does it follow-through with the identity of the Christian faith? The hermeneutical process is also progressing. The text cannot be exhausted in a single interpretation. At the same time, each interpretation is an addition of meaning to the text. In the dispute of interpretations, they have to prove themselves in the ecumenical forum. This criterion of dialogue presupposes the formulation of an intercultural theology, which operates between the different contextual theologies. The intercultural dialogue within the EATWOT, which was already founded in Dar es Salam in 1976, corresponds with the theoretical reflections among academic theology in Western Europe, which can be characterized as the "discovery of the other." Werner Ustorf talks in this respect about an act of "theological repentance of the North."[43] Today, on the other hand, a strategy of self-immunization can be observed. In Western Europe, theology is done in a way as if the contextual theologies had never existed.

CONTEXTUALITY AND DIALOGICAL IMPERATIVE AS FORMS OF THEOLOGICAL EXISTENCE

"Doing theology" is a contextual business. It has to be responsive to the experiences of the local people in their particular situation. If one does not succeed in deploying the relevance of the "Word of God" for them, the message trails off unheard. This is not only the creed of confessing Barthians among the contextual theologians like James Cone or C. S. Song; Ernst Lange (1927–1974) also knew it and was therefore badly vilified by the Barthian Rudolf Bohren (1920–2010).[44] Such dissonances prick up one's ears. James

Table 2.3   Typology of Contextual Theology

Cultural-Religious Type	Socio-Economic and Political Type
accommodation/indigenization/translation models (kernel-and-husk model)	development theology/new political theology (evolution; reform)
inculturation and dialogue theologies (onion model)	liberation theologies (revolution)

contextual theologies:
cultural religious, socio-economic and political, ecological, gender and ethnic dimension

Cone claims Barth against the Barthians; considering what I said at the beginning about Barth as a trickster, he might have a point.

Already Emil Brunner pointed to Jesus Christ as the hermeneutical key to disclose points of contact in a given culture. Barth condemned this idea with his "No!" driven by his worries about the Nazi specter of the German Christians. In his own captivity to that context he went beyond the target. The criteria of identity and dialogue prevent the "Word of God" from being instrumentalized in the interest of the context. Intertwining the generative themes of the text with those of the context means that the Word comes into its own. Human beings are enmeshed in stories, which are never only their own.[45] We always share these stories with somebody and recognize ourselves in the countenance of the other. This encounter with the other is principally open for the encounter with God.

Nevertheless, dialogue and conflict are two sides of the same coin. The encounter with the other throws us back onto ourselves. It disturbs, and can lead to hate of foreigners. Our image of God is also not free from ambivalences and the "dark sides of God" terrify us.[46]

Interreligious dialogue and inculturation are generative themes that do not have a space in Barth's system. Jesuit Aloysius Pieris (born 1934), one of the most prolific dialogue theologians in Asia, writes concerning this:

> In dismissing the immanentist thesis coming down from Schleiermacher to Otto, a thesis that postulated "a religious a priori" in the human person, Barth initiated an evangelistic theology that reduced the notion of religion to a blasphemous manipulation of God or at least an attempt at it. [. . .] In the militant stream of liberation theology, this Barthian view of religion dovetails neatly with Marx's equally evangelistic and Eurocentric evaluation of religions and cultures.[47]

Yet Protestant liberation theologians in South Korea and South Africa, for example, have repeatedly referred to Barth and Barmen for their cause.[48] Public Christian theologies developed in Hong Kong also make use of Barth's theology in an explicitly multireligious context.[49] While Barth in his manifesto "Theological Existence today" early on hints at the predicament of the Jews,[50] the Barmen Theological Declaration remains silent in this respect. In his anxiety to honor the Word of God, the Gospel—the good news to the poor and oppressed—falls by the wayside. What remains is a critical attitude founded in the *Missio Dei*. Barth's interventions had contextual impact because of their performative character; they were however never contextual theology in a programmatic sense. Or the trickster Barth may have directed the monomania of his project as an alternative draft to the monstrosities of the Third Reich. Anyhow, intercultural existence is today not an option, but a given, and whoever says "No!" to it can only refrain from the world, which is still God's creation. Intercultural theology on its part wants to continuously encounter God in the world.

NOTES

1. This chapter was first published in German as "Ja! Interkulturelle Existenz heute," in *Zeitschrift für Dialektische Theologie* 29 (2013): 82–100, translation Volker Küster.
2. Cf. for a nuanced account of the German context the contribution of Gert Pickel in this volume.
3. Trustworthy statistics about the relation between population growth and the increase in membership of a particular religion are not available. Werner Ustorf, *Robinson Crusoe Tries Again: Missiology and European Construction of "Self" and "Other" "in a Global World 1789–2010* (Göttingen: Vandenhoeck, 2010), 238f. comments that in spite of enormous efforts nothing much has changed over the last one hundred years regarding the percentage of Christians among the world population (ca. 33 percent). Regarding Asia, Aloysius Pieris laconically states: "But Asia, as circumstances clearly indicate, will always remain a non-Christian continent" [Aloysius Pieris, *An Asian Theology of Liberation* (London: T&T Clark, 1988, 74)].
4. Cf. in more detail Volker Küster, *Einführung in die Interkulturelle Theologie* (Göttingen: Vandenhoeck, 2011).
5. It is based on the manuscript of a lecture about "Christianity and Black Power" at Elmhurst College.
6. James H. Cone, *My Soul Looks Back* (Maryknoll, NY: Orbis Books, 1986), 44f.
7. Cf. James Cone, *The Doctrine of Man in the Theology of Karl Barth*, PhD Northwestern University 1965.
8. Cone, *My Soul*, 45.
9. Already in 1926, Barth had talked about "Church and Culture" at a meeting of the Continental Association for Inner Mission and Social Welfare (*Kontinental Verband für Innere Mission und Diakonie*) in Amsterdam. Cf. Karl Barth, *Vorträge und kleinere Arbeiten* 1925–1930 (Zürich: Theologischer Verlag, 1994), 6–40.
10. Karl Barth, "Die Theologie und die Mission in der Gegenwart. Vortrag gehalten an der Brandenburgischen Missionskonferenz in Berlin am 11. April 1932," in *Zwischen den Zeiten* 10, 1932, 189–215 [reprint: *Theologische Fragen und Antworten. Gesammelte Vorträge 3*, 100–126], 204. Cf. *KD* IV/3, §72 bes. 991–1007.
11. Cf. Karl Hartenstein, "Theologische Besinnung," in *Mission zwischen gestern und morgen: Vom Gestaltwandel der Weltmission der Christenheit im Licht der Konferenz des Internationalen Missionsrats in Willingen*, ed. Walter Freytag (Stuttgart: Evangelisches Missionswerk, 1952), 51–72; id., "Was hat die Theologie Karl Barths der Mission zu sagen?" *Zwischen den Zeiten* 6 (1928): 59–83.
12. Walter Freytag, "Mission im Blick aufs Ende," in: id., *Reden und Aufsätze II* (München: Chr. Kaiser, 1961), 186–198. Cf. Oskar Cullmann, *Christus und die Zeit. Die urchristliche Zeit- und Geschichtsauffassung* (Zürich: Theologischer Verlag,

1946); id., *Heil als Geschichte. Heilsgeschichtliche Existenz im Neuen Testament* (Tübingen: Mohr, 1965).

13. Quoted in H. H. Rosin, *Missio Dei: An Examination of the Origin, Contents and Function of the Term in Protestant Missiological Discussion* (Leiden: Interuniversity Institute for Missiological and Ecumenical Research, 1972), 25.

14. Cf. *Mission als Strukturprinzip. Ein Arbeitsbuch zur Frage missionarischer Gemeinden* [The Missionary Structure of the Congregation], ed. Hans Jochen Margull (Genf: Ökumenischer Rat der Kirchen, 1968).

15. Cf. Ahn Byung-Mu, "Was ist die Minjung Theologie? Zur‚Theologie des Volkes' in Südkorea," *Junge Kirche* 43 (1982): 290–296, 290; Suh Nam-Dong, "Zwei Traditionen fließen ineinander," in *Minjung. Theologie des Volkes Gottes in Südkorea*, ed. Jürgen Moltmann (Neukirchen-Vluyn: Neukirchener Verlag, 1984), 173–213, 206, etc.; Volker Küster, *A Protestant Theology of Passion. Korean Minjung Theology Revisited* (Leiden: Brill, 2010).

16. Cf. Georg F. Vicedom, *Missio Dei. Einführung in eine Theologie der Mission* (München: Chr. Kaiser, 1958).

17. Cf. Karl Barth, *Nein! Antwort an Emil Brunner* (München: Chr. Kaiser, 1934). Already in id., Die Theologie und die Mission, 199 und 214 [110 und 125].

18. Choan-Seng Song, *The Relation of Divine Revelation and Man's Religion in the Theologies of Karl Barth and Paul Tillich*, PhD thesis, Union Theological Seminary, New York City, 1964.

19. C.S. Song, "Theological Transpositions," *Theologies and Cultures* 7 (2010): 10–28.

20. Cf. C.S. Song, *The Compassionate God* (Maryknoll, NY: Orbis Books, 1982), 5–12.

21. C.S. Song, "Von Israel nach Asien. Ein theologischer Sprung," in *Europäische Theologie herausgefordert durch die Weltökumene* (Genf: Ökumenischer Rat der Kirchen, 1976), 10–29.

22. Choan-Seng Song, *Third-Eye Theology. Theology in Formation in Asian Settings* (Maryknoll, NY: Orbis Books, 1979, Revised Edition 1990), 26f.

23. Barth, *Die Theologie und die Mission in der Gegenwart*, 214 [124f], translation Volker Küster.

24. Cf. Klauspeter Blaser, *Volksideologie und Volkstheologie. Ökumenische Entwicklungen im Lichte der Barmer Theologischen Erklärung* (München: Chr. Kaiser, 1991).

25. The letter, written originally in German ["Brief Nr. 96: An Christen in Südostasien 1968," in Karl Barth, *Offene Briefe 1945–1968* (Zürich: Theologischer Verlag, 1984), 551–556], has been translated into English by William Rader. Cf. *South East Asia Journal of Theology* 11 (1969): 3–5. This quote from Barth seems to have become a kind of itinerating word (*Wanderlogion*). Barth is supposed to have said, for example, to an Indian student: "My dear friend, to answer your question I would have to be an Indian myself. That is *your* task. [. . .] I have done, what I could do, here in *this* country and in this continent. And it is impossible to me to tell you, what you have to do in India. You may be happy, because you are younger than I am, and because you are an Indian [. . .] and then you will have to explain the same matter

in an *Indian* way: not in the continental, European way, but *the same matter*—please the same matter, not by changing the matter itself through the language. This is *your* task." Karl Barth, *Gespräche 1964–1968*, ed. Eberhard Busch (Zürich: Theologischer Verlag, 1997), 344 (English original). Cf. Alle Hoekema, "Barth and Asia: 'No Boring Theology,'" *Exchange* 33 (2004): 102–131.

26. Cf. *KD* I/2, §17, 304 und 327.

27. Hendrik Kraemer, *The Christian Message in a Non-Christian World* (New York, 1938).

28. D.T. Niles, "Karl Barth—A Personal Memory," *The South East Asia Journal of Theology* 11 (1969): 10–13, 10f.

29. Choan-Seng Song, *Jesus in the Power of the Spirit* (Minneapolis: Fortress Press, 1994), 87 fn. 26.

30. Cf. *KD* §69, 2.

31. Cf. Karl Rahner, "Das Christentum und die nichtchristlichen Religionen," in: id., *Schriften zur Theologie 5* (Einsiedeln: Benzinger Verlag, 1962), 136–158.

32. Cf. Volker Küster, *The Many Faces of Jesus Christ. Intercultural Christology* (Maryknoll, NY: Orbis Books, 2001), 92–117; Susanne Hennecke, "Incarnation as Awakening. Katsumi Takizawa Reading Karl Barth," *Exchange* 36 (2007): 144–155.

33. Katsumi Takizawa, "Zen-Buddhismus und Christentum im gegenwärtigen Japan," in *Gott in Japan. Anstöße zum Gespräch mit japanischen Philosophen, Theologen, Schriftstellern*, ed. Yagi Seiichi and Ulrich Luz (München: Chr. Kaiser, 1973), 139–159, 144.

34. Katsumi Takizawa, "Was ich bei Karl Barth gelernt habe," type written manuscript 21 pp., 6f.

35. Cf. Eberhard Busch, *Meine Zeit mit Karl Barth. Tagebuch 1965–1968* (Göttingen: Vandenhoeck, 2011), 520 (Dienstag 16.1.1968; translation Markus Höfner, Virginia White [English translation forthcoming: Eberhard Busch, *My Time with Karl Barth: Diaries 1965–1968*, trans. D. L. Guder (London etc: Bloomsbury Academic, 2021)].

36. Cf. Theo Sundermeier, "Theologie der Mission," in *Lexikon missionstheologischer Grundbegriffe*, ed. Karl Müller and Theo Sundermeier (Berlin: D. Reimer, 1987), 470–495.

37. See below.

38. Cf. Bengt Sundkler, *The World of Mission* (London: Lutterworth Press, 1965), 12f.

39. Cf. Abdul-Rahman Yakubu, *The Gods are not Jealous. Lived Contextualization of Religious Identity and Dialogue through Dagomba Rites of Passage*, Leipzig: EVA 2022 (forthcoming).

40. Cf. www.lausanne.org.

41. Cf. Küster, *The Many Faces of Jesus Christ*; id., *Einführung in die Interkulturelle Theologie*.

42. Mercy Amba Oduyoye, "Reflections from a Third World Women's Perspective: Women's Experience and Liberation Theology," in *Irruption of the Third World: Challenge to Theology*, ed. Virginia Fabella and Sergio Torres (Maryknoll, NY: Orbis Books, 1983), 246–255, 247.

43. Werner Ustorf, "The Cultural Origins of 'Intercultural Theology,'" *Mission Studies* 25 (2008): 229–251, 229 and 243.

44. Cf. Peter Krusche, "Die Schwierigkeit Ernst Lange zu verstehen. Anmerkungen zu dem Versuch von Rudolf Bohren," *Wissenschaft und Praxis in Kirche und Gesellschaft/Pastoral Theologie* 70 (1981): 430–441.

45. Cf. Wilhelm Schapp, *In Geschichten verstrickt. Zum Sein von Mensch und Ding* (Frankfurt/M.: Klostermann, 1985).

46. Cf. Walter Dietrich and Christian Link, *Die Dunklen Seiten Gottes*, 2 Vols. (Neukirchen-Vluyn: Neukirchener Verlag, 1995, 2002).

47. Pieris, *Asian Theology of Liberation*, 91.

48. Cf. Ahn, Byung-Mu, "Zur dritten These der Barmer Erklärung," in: id., *Draußen vor dem Tor. Kirche und Minjung in Korea: Theologische Beiträge und Reflexionen* (Göttingen: Vandenhoeck, 1986), 146–150; Nico Koopman, "The Reception of the Barmen Declaration in South Africa," *Ecumenical Review* 61 (2009): 60–71.

49. Cf. the contribution of Pan-Chiu Lai in this volume.

50. Karl Barth, *Theologische Existenz heute! (1933)* (München: Chr. Kaiser, 1984).

Chapter 3

Male Circumcision Controversies, Barth, and Infant Baptism[1]

Grace Y. Kao

Long-standing male circumcision customs on minors are being subjected to critical scrutiny. In the United States and Western Europe, several prominent medical associations have recently revised their official statements on male circumcision, while lawmakers, human rights organizations, and other interested parties continue to debate the rights, goods, benefits, and harms allegedly involved or commonly invoked in extant practices. The broader discussion in Western contexts has largely centered on legal and political considerations—on adjudicating between and among competing claims and on considering the practical impact any changes in facially neutral laws pertaining to circumcision will likely have on the religio-cultural practices of Jewish and Muslim minorities.

This essay proceeds in a different manner. After providing several snapshots of recent circumcision controversies in the West and then identifying the quandary of legal and political issues they raise in section I, I consider the matter *theologically* in section II. I suggest therein debates about neonatal circumcision particularly as performed among Jews are evocative of internal Christian discussions from the Reformation onward about the propriety of infant baptism (paedobaptism), given comparable concerns about covenant membership, sacraments, God's commands, and human freedom.[2] I contend a focus on Karl Barth's break with classical views on baptism in general and Reformed baptismal practices in particular could prove illuminating by helping Christians think through contemporary circumcision controversies in the political sphere, given Barth's rejection of the Reformed tradition's defense of infant baptism on analogy with the Abrahamic covenant of circumcision.[3] While acknowledging any interpretation of the meaning of Christian baptism should still underdetermine public policy responses to contemporary challenges concerning male circumcision, I demonstrate how a comparison between both practices could nevertheless serve to inform our understanding of what well-intentioned parents should be able to do—and not do—for their children. I conclude by demonstrating how Barth's more nuanced account of human freedom serves as a helpful contrast to—and even critique of—the more common liberal understanding of freedom as the self-determining ability to do what one wishes to do amid a sea of options in the absence of restraint held by many activists on different sides of the circumcision debates.

So understood, my essay falls thematically under a "Barth and Political Theology" heading, even as I apply what might be described as a "bottom-up" approach to his work.[4] That is, I do not begin with theory—be it a reconstruction of Barth's understanding of the proper relationship between theology and politics or of Barth's views on the posture that a majority-Christian population in a modern liberal democracy should take toward other religious communities—and then move to application in a concrete case. Rather, I begin by attending to contemporary political and cultural debates on a complicated matter and only turn to a portion of Barth's work in systematic theology on the meaning and significance of baptism for its surprising potential to help Christians formulate a response to the concrete issue at hand.

RECENT CONTROVERSIES OVER
MALE CIRCUMCISION

Male circumcision is estimated to be the most common surgical procedure globally: an estimated 30–33 percent of the world's males aged fifteen years or older are circumcised, and two-thirds of these (69 percent) are believed to be Muslim.[5] Despite long-standing traditions of male circumcision for a variety of nontherapeutic reasons across the globe—religious observance, cultural belonging, coming-of-age, aesthetic preference, personal hygiene, preventative care—recent controversies about non-medically indicated circumcision on minors have erupted in several regions in Western Europe and the United States. Consider the following four snapshots:

Case #1: In San Francisco, California, a proposal to ban nontherapeutic male circumcision on children—ostensibly for the sake of human rights, bodily integrity, and children's welfare—had been cleared to appear on the November 2011 ballot, thus setting the stage for the first public vote on the procedure anywhere in the United States.[6] After several Jewish groups filed a lawsuit challenging the ballot initiative, the City Attorney took the unusual step of commenting upon the impending measure in light of the "patently unconstitutional" religious animus behind the proposed ban (i.e., the anti-Semitic literature circulated by some ballot initiative leaders).[7] In the end, the proposed ban was struck down from even appearing on the ballot because California law only grants the state, not individual cities, the authority to regulate medical procedures. Despite losing that round, organizations such as the Bay Area Intactivists continue to fight for "genital autonomy" for all.

Case #2: In Cologne, Germany, an incident of a four-year-old Muslim boy's severe medical complications following circumcision for (non-medically indicated) religious reasons by a Muslim doctor eventually led a regional court in July 2012 to outlaw male circumcision on minors as being against the "best interests" of the child.[8] Following the ripple effects of the regional court's decision even beyond its jurisdiction, the national and international uproar that ensued, and months of debate by lawmakers, German Parliamentarians approved a bill in December 2012 (434 votes to 100) to keep male circumcision legal for boys up to six months old if conducted by a trained practitioner with adequate pain management and with both parents' consent; after six months of age, only a medical doctor could perform it.[9] While Germany's Central Council of Jews and Central Council of Muslims are reportedly satisfied with the new law and the former has begun to develop guidelines to certify *mohalim*,[10] a left-wing opposition group in the *Bundestag* (the lower house of Parliament) had hoped the new law would have required parents to wait until their boys were fourteen to give informed consent to what they said amounted to irreversible foreskin "amputation."[11]

Case #3: In New York City, recent debates have centered on a particular kind of circumcision method practiced within some Hasidic and other Haredi Jewish communities called *metzitzah b'peh* (MBP). In MBP or oral suction, a *mohel* (Jewish ritual circumciser) puts his lips directly on the newborn's newly circumcised penis and sucks away the blood from the wound to clean it.[12] Following a report by the Center for Disease Control (CDC) that circumcision with orogenital suction has been linked to eleven cases of laboratory-confirmed neonatal herpes infections from 2000 to 2011 and that two of these infants suffered permanent brain damage and two died,[13] the New York City Health Department and Commissioner began discouraging the practice in press statements, distributing free "Before the Bris" hospital brochures explaining the health risks of transmitting oral herpes (HSV-1), and requiring the child's parents to sign a consent form provided by the circumciser prior to any circumcision with oral suction as per new health code regulations.[14]

Leaders of several Hasidic and other Haredi Jewish communities have vehemently opposed these measures. Several Orthodox Jewish groups and *mohalim* are still (at the time of this writing) fighting the constitutionality of the consent form requirement on free speech and free exercise grounds, the former because it allegedly compels *mohalim* to disseminate a message (about the increased risk of herpes infection) they do not believe to be true.[15] For a host of political reasons, New York officials have reportedly *not* been enforcing the consent form requirement; New York City Mayor Bill De Blaiso also announced in late February 2015 his administration's intent to scrap existing health code regulations in exchange for cooperation with the ultra-Orthodox community: After any new confirmed case of oral suction-related neonatal herpes, the *mohel* who performed the procedure would be required to submit to DNA testing and would be banned from performing any subsequent circumcision via MBP for life if the DNA of the virus in the *mohel* matches the strain in the infected infant.[16] To be sure, the tentative agreement leaves important matters unresolved, including whether the city would release the names of any banned *mohalim* or what it would do if a *mohel* tested positive for herpes but not for the strain that infected the baby; it also remains unclear whether the Board of Health would even grant the administration's request to repeal the consent form requirement. In the midst of these and other uncertainties, the New York City Department of Health and Mental Hygiene continues to alert the public of additional cases of neonatal herpes following circumcisions with MBP, which stands at the time of this writing at seventeen laboratory-confirmed cases of HSV-infection since 2000.[17]

Case #4: In a manner reminiscent of the Cologne regional court ruling (case #2), the Council of Europe, a leading pan-European intergovernmental human rights organization, passed a Parliamentary Assembly resolution on October 1, 2013 by an overwhelming majority (seventy-eight in favor, thirteen against, fifeen abstentions) that identifies "circumcision on young boys for religious reasons," among other practices, as violating children's "physical integrity." The resolution calls upon member states to initiate a public debate on the rights of children to bodily integrity and to "clearly define the medical, sanitary and other conditions to be ensured for practices which are today widely carried out in certain religious communities, such as the *non-medically justified circumcision of young boys*" (emphasis added).[18] Though nonbinding, critics fear the resolution could eventually serve as the basis for a legal prohibition against nontherapeutic circumcision in any of the Council of Europe's forty-seven member states. Predictably, Jewish and Muslim communities have decried the resolution: several Jewish groups convened a special task force later that month to mount a "proactive defense" of ritual circumcision, while Muslims have responded in their own ways as they simultaneously contend with growing anxieties about Muslim immigrants and the rising tide of anti-Muslim attacks across several European countries.[19]

As might be gleaned from these four snapshots of recent circumcision controversies, the approach most commonly taken as the way out of the morass involves disentangling the rights, duties, and interests belonging to the parents, child, and the state and then advocating for some elements to take moral and legal precedence over others.[20] While any adequate ethical, political, or legal response to these controversies must involve a careful adjudication of completing claims and while Jewish and Muslim minorities have generally been viewed as the primary stakeholders in these debates, I submit that Christians themselves would be well-served to reflect on these controversies by first considering their own real or potential investments in them. These include (1) the not insignificant number of Christian parents (mostly outside of Europe) who also circumcise their sons, though primarily for nonreligious reasons,[21] (2) the ritual commemoration of Christ's own circumcision (Luke 2:21) still observed by the Eastern Orthodox Church and several other Christian groups, (3) the vulnerability Christian ecclesiological practices—not just Jewish or Muslim initiation rites—could also face under increasing demands by children's rights activists today for children to be self-determining in all important matters of religion, and (4) the arguably Christian and civic duties Christians have to nurture good Jewish-Christian-Muslim relations particularly in Western liberal democracies still struggling with the legacies of anti-Semitism and Islamophobia.

Beyond the matter of self-interest lies the important political contribution Christians could make by accessing traditions of theological inquiry. That is, while respecting the distinct activities and authority of the separate realms of politics and theology, Christians could nevertheless bring theology in conversation with other modes of critical thought to bear on contemporary social issues and accordingly serve the common good by empowering the faithful to, in the words of Max Stackhouse, "address the world in its wider structures and dynamics by developing the kind of reasonable moral theology that is able to assess and reform the institutions of civil society."[22] In addition, in ways I will explain below, this resultant "reasonable" theology might be simultaneously distinctive to Christians and illuminating for other people of goodwill, without necessarily needing to constrain or translate its content into any such Rawlsian notion of "public reason," wherein argumentation in the public arena on constitutional essentials would remain purely "political," not "metaphysical" in character.[23]

KARL BARTH ON BAPTISM

In mining resources from Christian theology to think through recent concerns about male circumcision particularly as they implicate Jewish ritual practices, I will largely draw upon Karl Barth's break from tradition both on the theological significance of baptism and widespread church practice of infant baptism. To be sure, other—and more obvious—aspects of Barth's work could be mined for these purposes, including Barth's overall approach to ethics, his broader understanding of Jews, Judaism, and Israel, and his explicit remarks on circumcision, the law, and Jew-Gentile relations in his *Epistle to the Romans*. While my turn to Barth is more indirect, I am guided by the conviction even not immediately relevant portions of Barth's theology could serve as a helpful resource for Christians as they attempt to think through a contemporary cultural and political controversy. Of course, my narrower focus on Barth's mature views on baptism, specifically his rejection of the covenantal analogy between circumcision on the eighth day and infant baptism, will touch upon the more obvious aspects of his work that could also be brought into play for this topic: it will presuppose his general enclosure of ethics within dogmatics (option #1), but without having to sort through his highly nuanced understanding of Jews, Judaism, and Israel (option #2); it will also invoke several of the themes already presented in the second edition of his *Epistle to the Romans* (option #3), though will privilege his remarks in his unfinished *Church Dogmatics* IV/4 in what was to be §75: The Foundation of the Christian Life over *Romans* II given the maturity of thought it represents.[24]

Barth's reflections on baptism in that self-contained fragment are structured around two baptismal theses: one positive, one negative. Put negatively, the mature Barth rejected both of the two major arguments for infant baptism Christian theology has historically provided: (1) the *sacramental* view articulated by Augustine and upheld for the most part in Roman Catholicism, wherein baptism is necessary for salvation as a means to remove sin, and (2) the *covenantal* view advanced by Zwingli, Calvin, and other Reformers, wherein infant baptism serves as a sign of the same covenant with God circumcision had served in the Old Testament.[25] Barth's positive account of baptism as the foundation of the Christian life can best be explained by first unpacking the sharp distinction he draws between baptism with the Holy Spirit and baptism with water. The former is what God accomplishes—it is the "objective" element, the "self-attestation and self-impartation of Jesus Christ . . . which actually reconciles the world to Him,"[26] and thus "makes possible and demands human decision as conversion from unfaithfulness to faithfulness" to God. The latter is the corresponding "subjective" element or the free human response to God's faithfulness, wherein the individual participates in a ritualized "bodily washing of water" and confession of faith in the context of her church body (*CD* IV/4 41, 31–32, 44, 73, 83). Christian (water) baptism is for Barth "the first form of the human decision which in the foundation of Christian life corresponds to the divine change," wherein baptizands respond to God's gift and command in gratitude and obedience (*CD* IV/4, 136).[27]

To be clear, Barth had already interrogated the widespread practice of infant baptism in his 1943 work, *Die Kirchliche Lehre von der Taufe,* on the dual grounds that baptism requires a free, active, and responsible movement toward God of which infants are incapable and that pedobaptism serves the interests of the *Volkskirche,* though it is the very "present day form of the National Church" and "Constantinian system" that needs to be reexamined.[28] Through his son and New Testament scholar Markus Barth's book *Die Taufe ein Sakrament?* (1951), Barth eventually came in his 1959–1960 lectures to "abandon the 'sacramental' understanding" of baptism he still retained in that earlier publication with respect to the "work of the candidates and the community which baptizes them" (*CD* IV/4 41, ix–x).[29]

The crux of Barth's sharp parting of ways with classical Roman Catholic, Lutheran, and Reformed baptismal teaching and practice is neither primarily to be found in his understanding of baptism's biblical basis (i.e., Christ's baptism by John in the Jordan), nor in his account of baptism's transcendent *telos* (*CD* IV/4 41, 67–69, 71, 105). Rather, it lies in his dissenting view that "the praise of baptism is not served but fatefully damaged" when it is improperly characterized as an "immanent divine work," not a human one (*CD* IV/4 41, 101). Barth writes:

> Baptism, as water baptism, takes place in the light of the baptism of the Spirit, and with a view to it. As such, however, it is not itself the baptism of the Spirit; it is always water baptism. Baptism takes place in active recognition of the grace of God which justifies, sanctifies, and calls. *It is not itself, however, the bearer, means, or instrument of grace.* Baptism responds to a mystery, the sacrament of the history of Jesus Christ, of His resurrection, of the outpouring of the Holy Spirit. *It is not itself, however, a mystery or sacrament.* (*CD* IV/4 41, 102; emphasis added)

Barth essentially "demythologizes" the received view of baptism by advising against "docetic" interpretations, wherein the human response is either "overshadowed and obscured" by the divine work and thus "robbed of significance," or "integrated" into the baptism of the Spirit and thus rendered "superfluous" (*CD* IV/4 101–102, 105).

Of chief importance for our present purposes is Barth's rejection of the Reformed tradition's depiction and defense of infant baptism as a sign of the covenant on analogy with Israelite circumcision. As Calvin argues in the *Institutes*, baptism serves not only as a sacrament but also as a "symbol for bearing witness to our religion before men."[30] Indeed, an anagogic relationship for Calvin exists between baptism and circumcision, wherein the "promise" and "inner mystery" of "God's fatherly favor, of forgiveness of

sins, and of eternal life" is purportedly present in both rituals, despite differences in "outward ceremony."[31] Calvin's teaching on the significance of
baptism was not idiosyncratic to the Reformed tradition, as belief in the link
between those two rites predated him in Zwingli and continued thereafter.[32]
Consider, for instance, the Belgic Confession's affirmation "children ought
to be baptized and sealed with the sign of the covenant, as little children
were circumcised in Israel on the basis of the same promises made to our
children" (Art. 34) and the Heidelberg Catechism's understanding infants
are "included in God's covenant and people" and thus "by baptism . . . they
should be incorporated into the Christian church and distinguished from the
children of unbelievers" as was "done in the Old Testament by circumcision" (HC Q&A 74).

In contrast to those who claim to have found in baptism the "New
Testament equivalent to the Old Testament rite called circumcision," Barth
reasons while several biblical passages could be interpreted accordingly, no
passage requires viewing baptism in such a sacramental or covenantal manner
and many others "more or less completely rule [such an interpretation] out"
(*CD* IV/4, 128, 119).[33] Thus in rejecting the "theologoumenon of the identity
between Christian baptism and the circumcision which was administered to
Israelite boys on the eighth day of their lives," Barth opposes treating the
meaning of the two practices as if "interchangeable" (*CD* IV/4, 178–9). In
his own words:

> The people of the covenant of grace in its Old Testament form was the nation of
> the twelve tribes of Israel, elected and called by God to serve Him. The physical
> descendant of this nation was such a member of the covenant. . . . *Newborn male
> members received the sign of circumcision as active bearers of the propagation
> of this nation.* . . . [T]hrough circumcision proselytes also became a 'holy seed'
> in so far as they hereby received the same distinguishing mark as the members
> of this nation. *The people of the new covenant . . . is not a nation. It is a people
> freely and newly called and assembled out of Israel and all nations.* It is not
> made up of succeeding generations. It is not recruited through procreation and
> birth. . . . In this sense they are without father, mother, or descent. (Ibid.)

For Barth then, only those "who are already serious Christians and those who
seek to be such" should be baptized (*CD* IV/4 101, *cf.* 166). Thus Barth contrasts Christian baptism, properly understood, with both Jewish circumcision
on the eighth day and infant baptism as widely practiced across the church for
essentially the same reason: only in the former case is the indispensable first
step of faithfulness taken by each individual herself, not by the individual's
"most believing parents . . . [or] the whole Church" (*CD* IV/4, 186).

DRAWING UPON CHRISTIAN THEOLOGY TO
INFORM CURRENT DEBATES ON CIRCUMCISION

Fortunately for our purposes, we need not determine *whose* view of baptism has the force of the better argument before mining these intra-Christian debates for helpful insights on the recent scrutiny over male circumcision in Western contexts. Given my sympathy for the manner in which these political controversies disproportionately affect already vulnerable religious minorities as well as my desire to move the (majoritarian Christian) public toward a deeper understanding of the significance of the religiously grounded circumcision rites at issue, I submit that Christian theology could be marshaled in service of these controversies in three ways. The first would be in demonstrating how a Christian could provide tradition-specific support for the continuation of Jewish ritual circumcision in particular, regardless of whether she sides with or against Barth on the matter of infant baptism, through a theological model of either sameness or difference between the two practices. This is to say that Christians could well provide "thick" reasons internal to Christianity for supporting the extant religiously grounded circumcision customs of *others*—reasons that may well prove persuasive only to them, since they would be grounded in their particularized (Rawlsian) "comprehensive doctrines"—apart from the public political culture shared by all.[34] The second would be in comparing the permanent alteration to a boy's body *via* circumcision and the irrevocable change to a person's status before God many Christians believe baptism brings about, so as to prompt Christians to appreciate how their own liturgical rites might be implicated in recent male circumcision controversies that place a premium on the child's self-determination. The purpose of doing so would not be to serve self-interest in the first instance, but to query why public controversy has fallen on circumcision and not infant baptism if the two can rightfully be compared in the ways I name. The third point would be in turning to Barth's more nuanced understanding of freedom for an alternative to the more popular liberal account centering on volition or choice. Doing so would not only augment the public's understanding of what is at stake in these male circumcision debates but also remind Christians they may have recourse to deeper—and potentially more satisfying—notions of freedom from which to draw than the popular Enlightenment-inspired notions in wide circulation in society today.

Christians hoping to affirm extant Jewish circumcision rites on specifically theological grounds might be encouraged to turn to the aforementioned historical debates on infant baptism and then reason either analogously or disanalogously in their support. In the first case, followers of the Reformers and their historic creeds on infant baptism might find reason to support the continuance of *brit milah* by creatively reversing the order of their argument on an analogous model of "sameness." Insofar as they or others (already) affirm the historical-conceptual linkage between Abrahamic circumcision and infant baptism and additionally maintain in non-supersessionist fashion that God's covenant with Israel endures even after the advent of Christ, Christians who already support infant baptismal rites (for Christians) might then have vested theological and ecclesiological interests in supporting Jewish ritual circumcision as well. They might accordingly challenge those (in the law, courts, broader society) who would legally or morally oppose nontherapeutic neonatal circumcision on the grounds of the child's autonomous self-determination, for they would regard circumcision on minors in *brit milah*—like baptism for infants—as matters of great importance for pointing children to a reality greater than themselves and for signaling to the world they have been born into a covenant community antecedent to choice.

Paradoxically, Christians more sympathetic to Karl Barth's break with the Reformed tradition on the meaning and practice of baptism might also find tradition-specific support the right of Jews to continue *brit milah* on explicitly theological grounds, but this time on a model of "difference." Recall while Barth affirmed (with Calvin) the "material unity of the old and new covenants," he maintained it would be inappropriate to analogize, as Calvin and others in the Reformed tradition did, from the one to the other: the new covenant is to be comprised of a "people freely and newly called," while the "covenant of grace in its Old Testament form" "recruit[s]" in hereditary fashion through "procreation and birth" (*CD* IV/4, 177–178). While Barth intended to underscore in this disanalogy the non-genealogical character of the people of the new covenant, contemporary proponents of this "difference" model might constructively use it to support Jewish notions of belonging instead as ritualized through the covenant of circumcision.[35] They might accordingly critique any political, legislative, or judicial measures prohibiting nontherapeutic circumcision on minors without the boy's consent (e.g., before age fourteen as per the *Bundestag*'s losing minority faction in case #2)—as if the logic of Jewish ritual circumcision needed to conform to that of Christian baptism from a Barthian perspective (i.e., as "free" and "responsible."). Adherents of this theological "difference" model could then make an important contribution to these political debates in Western liberal democracies by exposing the hidden or unnamed Christian bias of those who would push for the state to tolerate only those religious rituals pertaining to children that conformed to this (Christian) model of free and voluntary consent.

The second way in which intra-Christian debates on baptism could be brought to bear on recent controversies over circumcision neither turns on one's acceptance nor rejection of the covenantal analogy, but on the significance of the common (though not universal) Christian understanding of baptism as a permanent, life-altering event. Roman Catholics, Lutherans, followers of the Reformed tradition, and Barthians may disagree with one another on what exactly baptism signifies, but they are nearly united in their conviction the rite brings about an immutable transformation in a person that need not, should not, and technically could not be repeated.[36] As Barth understood the matter, baptism signifies "the once-for-allness of the event," thus its "actual efficacy" cannot be impugned by any "abuse of baptism" on behalf of the administering church or by the baptizand's own ignorance or "impiety" (*CD* IV/4, 39, 198; 1948, 36, 40, 56–57, 64). The indissoluble change in one's *spiritual* status before God to which baptism purportedly gives witness could thus be compared with the irreversible change in the *bodies* of newly circumcised males who have undergone the procedure for religious reasons. Insofar as parties including the Bay Area Intactivists and the Cologne regional court object to the nonmedical circumcision of boys in the absence of their consent on the grounds that parents should avoid determining the *religious* identity of the children in ways that are irreversible, we might ask whether principles of fairness would require similar public scrutiny over *pedobaptism* as well, given that Christian parents who present their children for baptism might be said to be similarly compelling their children to participate in an irreversible religious ceremony. For as Barth himself warned in his earlier 1943 lecture, we are not to think less of the sign of baptism "because its mark—*unlike that of the circumcision of the Israelites*—cannot afterwards be seen; because the few drops of water . . . dried up long ago," for the newly baptized person may later end his own life or become a "Mohamedan [*sic*], . . . atheist, a Nationalist Socialist . . . a heretic" or something else, but he "cannot divest himself of his baptism" (1948, 60–61, emphasis added).

A possible retort to the hypothetical question posed earlier about the asymmetry in response to the two practices would proceed as follows: it would be unwise for a secular liberal society to wade into contentious theological waters concerning what kind of *spiritual* change, if any, is brought about by infant baptism, but society does have a right—perhaps even an obligation—to concern itself with any painful, permanent, and objectively verifiable changes to the *body* through circumcision when not medically justified. While not without merit, such a retort falsely assumes that deciphering the propriety of infant baptism from a public policy perspective would invariably entail advancing one thick account of the good or Rawlsian "comprehensive doctrine"[37] over another, while doing the same about circumcision would not. And yet, as Richard Amesbury has shown, we cannot settle public policy disputes about circumcision by turning to the "presumed facticity of something called 'the body,' which exists prior to something called 'culture,'" for what even counts as a "whole body and what as a violation of its integrity belongs to what is in dispute."[38] Thus, in comparing the purportedly permanent change baptism brings about in the relationship between the baptizand and God (in the eyes of many Christians) and the irreversible alteration to the anatomy of boys circumcision brings about, we can see more clearly how societies that have enacted public policy regulations concerning the latter but not the former have indeed weighed-in on contestable matters of value (e.g., what constitutes bodily harm or disfigurement, whether the phenomenon of "forced baptism"—a fear not unknown to Jews and Muslims in the history of Christianity[39]—merits legal protection). The point here is less about denigrating those judgments than about underscoring how they favor majoritarian attitudes and practices and thus may have well-contravened ideals of liberal neutrality.

The third point we might draw from Barth's reflections on baptism is a different and more complex understanding of freedom than the Enlightenment notions of autonomy in wide circulation in secular discourse among both liberal critics and defenders of male circumcision alike. Barth's insistence of the "free" response in Christian baptism is not the same kind of freedom that many circumcision opponents have sought for minors, be they the San Francisco intactivists pushing for genital autonomy, the opposition group in the *Bundestag* who lobbied unsuccessfully to set the age of consent for the procedure at fourteen, or the Council of Europe's desire to protect the right to children to decide for or against circumcision for themselves, among other practices. Nor, however, is it to be likened to those who would defend extant circumcision practices from either outright bans or governmental regulation out of the principle of the parental right to direct the upbringing of their children, including in their religion of choice. This is because Barth characterized the free and responsible human response in baptism more in terms of obedience than voluntariness—the "freedom of the children of God" to be baptized because they desire to respond faithfully to the "baptismal command of Jesus" and thus "have no other choice as such" (*CD* IV/4, 153–154). As Jesse Couenhoven has noted, Barth's conception of human freedom was not what Barth himself characterized as the "heathen notion of freedom"—the "freedom of Hercules: choice between two ways at a crossroad," but instead the power that God has provided us to be as we were created.[40] In what Couenhoven reads (with some caution) as a philosophical compatibilist reading, Barth believes we are genuinely free,[41] but true freedom requires us to choose and to act rightly—and grace leaves us with only one genuine option (obedience).[42]

We might apply Barth's reflections on the nature of human freedom obliquely to contemporary circumcision debates in at least two ways. First, we could draw upon it to demonstrate how the ideal of freedom itself has multiple meanings. Indeed, Barth's normative conception of freedom in terms of obedience to the command of God comes much closer to the ancient conception of religion in terms of ties or bonds (*religio*)[43] than the contemporary understanding of the freedom of religion in liberal democracies and international human rights law as the "freedom to have or to adopt a religion or belief of his choice" (ICCPR, Art. 18). Barth's conception also comes closer to the kind of freedom many Jews have been seeking to protect in *brit milah*: not the freedom to do as they please, but the freedom to do what they have long interpreted as what God requires of them: to circumcise on the eighth day in accordance with Jewish law, with or without MBP (depending on differing interpretations of Halakhic requirements).[44] Is it thus no wonder these two notions of freedom—one tied to a notion of binding obligations—the other tied to the self-making power to decide among alternatives, were—and still are—bound to clash. Second and relatedly, Christians might use Barth's deeper conception of freedom not to disparage modern liberal democracies for recognizing a wide range of civil and political liberties, but to remind them that the deepest sense of their freedom arises metaphysically, not politically (to use Rawlsian terms)—not in having choices between alternatives but in being guided by the light of Christ.[45]

CONCLUSION

To submit, as I have, that Christian theological views about the meaning of baptism and circumcision can play a role in one's examination of the recent male circumcision controversies is not to suggest a straight line runs from Christian theology to public policy. For, as I have suggested, any adequate resolution to recent circumcision controversies would have to go beyond these internal discussions in Christian theology about the meaning and significance of baptism and when adjudicating between competing rights and duties claims, weighing real or potential medical benefits against risks, and providing serious attention to the political consequences of altering extant circumcision policies. Nor is to suggest Christians in a modern Western liberal democracy should, from a public policy standpoint, favor traditional *Jewish* practices of circumcision above all other (religious or secular) varieties on the grounds that comparisons (of the type that I have provided above) could be made between Jewish circumcision and Christian pedobaptism in contravention of the principle of fairness. Though one's theological beliefs about baptism and circumcision accordingly underdetermine how one should respond to these male circumcision controversies, I have offered these Barthian reflections on sacraments, covenant, and freedom to inform Christian reflection on what well-intentioned parents should and should not do for their children.

NOTES

1. Work for this essay was completed on July 11, 2015. The debates on circumcision may well have changed since then, but this essay does not capture any such developments due to a lag in publication.

2. While beyond this chapter's scope, my theological examination of recent circumcision controversies through the rite of baptism would be enhanced if contextualized within the lengthier history of Christian ambivalence toward Jewish circumcision and also with reference to Jewish conceptions of the relationship between these two practices. For an exploration of these themes, see Yaacov Deutsch, *Judaism in Christian Ethics: Ethnographic Descriptions of Jews and Judaism in Early Modern Europe* (New York: Oxford University Press, 2012) and Elizabeth Wyner Mark, *The Covenant of Circumcision: New Perspectives on an Ancient Jewish Rite* (Lebanon, NH: Brandeis University Press, 2003).

3. One caveat: my appeal to Barth in Sections II and III is intended more for constructive purposes than as an attempt at Barth scholasticism. In light of this essay's origins in the international research project directed by Markus Höfner entitled "Theo-Politics? Conversing with Barth in Western and Asian Contexts," my use of Barth owes more to our shared commitment to use his theology as common referent for critical discussion than any subject expertise on my part as a nonspecialist. Among my fellow participants who helped me to think through several ideas in this chapter, I owe special thanks to Stephen Lakkis for providing written responses to the earlier drafts I presented at the colloquia and Markus Höfner for inviting me to participate, hosting such wonderful gatherings in Bochum, Germany, and for providing written feedback on an earlier draft.

4. For a comparable "bottom-up" approach, see Martin Wendte's essay in this volume on what he finds to be the troubling matter of the increase in cesarean sections.

5. World Health Organization, "Male Circumcision: Global Trends and Determinants of Prevalence, Safety and Acceptability," World Health Organization and Joint United Nations Programmed on HIV/AIDS 7.29E (2007), 7.

6. See Robin Hindry, "San Francisco Circumcision Ban to Appear on Ballot" *Associated Press*, May 18, 2011, and "Initiative Measure to Be Submitted Directly to the Voters" as prepared by the City Attorney and cleared by the Department of Election on October 13, 2010.

7. The lead organization had "expressly demonize[d] the Jewish faith" by disseminating comic books that were "darkly evocative of Nazi propaganda of the 1930s and 1940s." See Office of City Attorney, "News Release: Circumcision Ban Unconstitutional If Court Exempts Medical Professionals, City Argues," June 30, 2011. Following the dismissal, the California Senate Judiciary Committee unanimously approved a bill to preemptively block local jurisdictions from pursuing similar ballot measures. See "California Circumcision Ban Bill Signed by Gov. Jerry Brown: Circumcision Bans Will Not Make the Ballot," *Associated Press*, October 2, 2011.

8. While the doctor involved, "Dr. K," was ultimately acquitted because of a lack of clarity in the law, the Cologne regional court nonetheless concluded that circumcision on boys too young to give consent would amount to "bodily harm" and "assault"—even if done properly by a doctor at parental request for religious reasons. See "Circumcision Debate has Berlin Searching for Answers," *Speigel Online International*, July 25, 2012.

9. See Kate Connolly, "Circumcision Ruling Condemned by Germany's Muslim and Jewish Leaders," *The Guardian*, June 27, 2012; Gareth Jones, "Circumcision Ban Makes Germany 'Laughing Stock': Merkel," *Reuters*, July 17, 2012; Sylvia Poggioli, "German Lawmakers Move to Quell Uproar Over Circumcision," *National Public Radio*, October 19, 2012.

10. See Kay-Alexander Sholz, "Circumcision Remains Legal in Germany," *Deutsche Welle*, December 12, 2012. A *mohel* (plural: *mohalim*) is someone trained to conduct the covenant of circumcision or *brit milah (bris)* ceremony in accordance with Jewish law, including on the eighth day as per Genesis 17: 1–14. In response to a criminal charge of assault against the chief representative of Chabad in Berlin (Rabbi Yehuda Techtal) for using *metzitzah b'peh* as part of the circumcision of his own son (see case #3, below), the president of the Central Council of Jews in Germany informed Germany's main Jewish newspaper of his organization's opposition to MBP and that *mohalim* who circumcise accordingly would not receive certification. See A. J. Goldman, Donald Snyder, and Nathan Jeffay, "Circumcision Controversy Endangers Fight to Keep Rite Legal in Germany," *The Jewish Daily Forward*, May 6, 2013, and "Wir Befürworten Dies Nicht," *Jüdische Allgemeine*, April 15, 2013.

11. Toby Axelrod, "German Lawmakers Propose Barring Circumcision Before Age 14," *Jewish Telegraphic Agency*, November 14, 2012.

12. As bioethicist Dena Davis explains, *metzitzah b'peh* was "originally done to care for the wound, as a crude form of antisepsis. The Babylonian Talmud declares that, for the sake of the infant, the *mohel* must perform this act, 'so as not to bring on risk'" (456). See her "Ancient Rites and New Laws: How Should We Regulate Religious Circumcision of Minors," *Journal of Medical Ethics* 39 (2013): 456–458.

13. Less severe symptoms included fever and lesions on the infants' abdomen, buttocks, genitals, and perineum. According to the CDC, the risk of HSV-1 in baby boys following circumcision with orogenital suction is 3.4 times greater than in those who are not circumcised accordingly. See Center for Disease Control and Prevention, "Neonatal Herpes Simplex Virus Infection After Ritual Circumcisions that Included Direct Orogenital Suction—New York City, 2000–2011," *Morbidity and Mortality Weekly Report*, June 7, 2012.

14. Thomas Farley, "New York City Statement on Jewish Ritual Circumcision with Direct Oral Suctioning - *Metzitzah B'peh*," June 6, 2012. According to Title 24 of the New York City Health Code, Section 181.21 "Consent For Direct Oral Suction As Part of Circumcision," the parent or legal guardian must sign the following statement: "I understand that direct oral suction will be performed on my child and that the New York City Department of Health and Mental Hygiene advises parents that direct oral suction should not be performed because it exposes an infant to the risk of

transmission of herpes simplex virus infection, which may result in brain damage or death."

15. For reports of resistance, see Liz Robbins, "Baby's Death Renews Debate Over a Circumcision Ritual," *New York Times*, March 7, 2012 and Kate Briquelet, "Despite Baby Dying After Getting Herpes, Orthodox Rabbis Say They'll Defy Law On Ancient Circumcision Ritual," *New York Post*, September 1, 2012. Though a district judged ruled against the preliminary injunction in 2013 holding that the new health code provision does not compel speech and that it is a neutral and generally applicable law, the Second Court of Appeals overturned that ruling in August 2014 when finding that the regulation is neither neutral nor generally applicable, targets a religious practice for special burdens, and thus must be held to "strict scrutiny." See Paul Berger, "U.S. Court Rules NYC Metzitzah B'Peh Regulation Must Go Under 'Strict Scrutiny,'" *The Jewish Daily Forward*, August 15, 2014.

16. Paul Berger, "New York City Changes Policy on Controversial Circumcision Rite," The *Jewish Daily Forward*, February 25, 2015.

17. Paul Berger, "New York Fails to Enforce Consent Forms for Metzitzah B'Peh Circumcision Rite," *The Jewish Daily Forward*, February 5, 2015. See also New York City Department of Health and Mental Hygiene, "2014 Alert #40: Fourth Case of Neonatal Herpes Infection Following Ritual Jewish Circumcision Reported in New York City in 2014," December 23, 2014.

18. Other targeted practices include female genital mutilation, "early childhood medical interventions" in cases of intersexuality, and "the submission to, or coercion of, children into piercings, tattoos or plastic surgery." See Parliamentary Assembly, Council of Europe, Resolution 1952 (2013): Children's Right to Physical Integrity.

19. See "European Groups Set up 'Proactive' Brit Milah Task Force," *Jewish Telegraphic Agency*, October 13, 2013, and Maria Kristiansen & Aziz Sheikh, "The Debate on Male Infant Circumcision in Europe: A Challenge for Islamic Biomedical Ethics," Research Center for Islamic Legislation and Ethics, August 26, 2014. To be sure, these four case-studies do not exhaust debates on male circumcision across Europe and the U.S; for example, a fifth case could have concerned leading Scandinavian medical associations' recent policy recommendations to prohibit circumcision on minors when not medically indicated. See "Ritual Circumcision Ban Recommended in Sweden and Denmark by Medical Associations," *Huffington Post*, January 27, 2014.

20. For example, most contributors to a recent special issue on "The Ethics of Male Circumcision," *Journal of Medical Ethics* 39, no. 7 (2013) pursued this general strategy when teasing out *non*-medical goods and harms before issuing disparate recommendations. Some defended extant religious rites by invoking the right and good of religious freedom and toleration, the parental right to direct the religious education of their children, and the child's best interests. Others who either opposed all nontherapeutic circumcision on minors or who sought more stringent regulations (but not a total ban) emphasized the parent's and state's obligations to preserve and protect the child's rights to bodily integrity, health, self-determination in matters of religion, an open future, and even the principle of nondiscrimination based on sex, the

latter because FGM is widely condemned and outlawed in many jurisdictions where male circumcision is not.

21. The contrast between American attitudes and practices associated with circumcision and those of many Western European countries is stark. In the majority-Christian United States, circumcision prevalence varies across races and geographic regions and is in slight decline, but more than half of all male newborns are still being circumcised—and primarily for *non-religious* reasons (e.g., some out of a belief that, in the words of the American Academy of Pediatrics, the "health benefits of newborn male circumcision outweighs the risks"). In contrast, newborn male circumcision is not the norm in the United Kingdom or the rest of Europe more generally, since circumcision is not generally undertaken as a preventative health measure and thus is "predominantly related to Muslim and Jewish religion, medical indications or immigration from circumcision" (WHO 2007, 12, 17). See also American Academy of Pediatrics, "Circumcision Policy Statement," *Pediatrics* 130, no. 3 (2012): 585–586; Center for Disease Control, "Trends in In-Hospital Newborn Male Circumcision in the United States, 1991–2010," *Morbidity and Mortality Weekly Report* 60, no. 34 (2011): 1167–1168 and Cordelia Hebblethwaite, "Circumcision: The Ultimate Parenting Dilemma, *BBC News*, August 21, 2012.

22. Max Stackhouse has identified this view as "public theology." See his "Civil Religion, Political Theology and Public Theology: What's the Difference," *Political Theology* 5, no. 3 (2004): 275–293, 286.

23. See John Rawls' "Introduction to the Paperback Edition" and Lecture 1 of his *Political Liberalism*, 2nd ed. (New York: Columbia University Press, 2005) for his "political" vs. "metaphysical" distinction. For Rawls' notion of "public reason," see especially §9 and §26 of his *Justice as Fairness: A Restatement*, 2nd ed. (Cambridge, MA: Belknap Press, 2001).

24. Barth was still a young pastor in Safenwil when he published the second edition of *Romans* (1922), but described his reflections on baptism in the unfinished *Church Dogmatics* IV/4 as not only representative of the "late Barth" but also as something that would likely be his "last major publication" (*CD* IV/4, viii, xii). Unless otherwise stated, all references to Barth will be taken from his *Church Dogmatics IV: The Doctrine of Reconciliation, 4: The Christian Life (Fragment): Baptism as the Foundation of the Christian Life*, trans. G. W. Bromiley (Edinburgh: T&T Clark, 1969). To see how another contributor has found Barth's work in *The Christian Life* helpful for thinking through theo-political matters, see Paul Dafydd Jone's "Karl Barth's *The Christian Life* and the Task of Political Theology," in this volume.

25. See W. Travis McMaken, *The Sign of the Gospel: Toward an Evangelical Doctrine of Infant Baptism After Karl Barth* (Minneapolis, MN: Fortress Press, 2013), 21–24 for a good overview of these two traditional arguments for infant baptism. For Catholic teaching, see the Sacred Congregation for the Doctrine of Faith, *Infant Baptism*, October 20, 1980, particularly §13: "The Church has thus shown by her teaching and practice that she knows no other way apart from Baptism for ensuring children's entry into eternal happiness."

26. As McMaken explains, the "supreme objectivity" of Barth's doctrines of election, atonement, and reconciliation in *CD* II/2 and IV/1 undercuts the logic of "traditional sacramental soteriology," such that the personal faith of the individual is not required to insure the validity of what has already taken place in Jesus Christ (McMaken 83). As Barth himself states: a person does not become a Christian "through his human decision or his water baptism"—"Jesus Christ Himself, and He alone, makes man [*sic*] a Christian" (*CD* IV/4 32–33).

27. Though Barth regarded his positive thesis about locating the foundation of the Christian life in baptism as more important than his negative thesis, he foresaw that his objections to the commonplace practice of and rationale for infant baptism would "leave [him] in . . . theological and ecclesiastical isolation"—or at least until some future time when his minority views might be vindicated (*CD* IV/4, xii).

28. Karl Barth, *The Teaching of the Church Regarding Baptism*, trans. E. A. Payne (London: SCM, 1948), 52–54. This is the published lecture he delivered to Swiss theological students on May 7, 1943, at Gwatt am Thunersee.

29. According to Eberhard Busch, the influence also went the other way. Markus Barth was not initially persuaded by his father's critique of infant baptism, but came around by the spring 1950 when he began working on that aforementioned book and stopped having his own children baptized. See Eberhard Busch, *Karl Barth: His Life from Letters and Autobiographical Texts* (Eugene: OR, Wipf & Stock, 2005), 369.

30. In *Institutes* 4.16.2, Calvin describes baptism as "point[ing] to the cleansing of our sins," the "mortification of our flesh," and the "symbol for bearing witness to our religion before men." See *Institutes* 4.15.1 for more on the sacramental function of baptism. Jean Calvin, *Institutes of the Christian Religion II*, *The Library of Christian Classics vol. 21*, ed. John T. McNeill, trans. Ford Lewis Battles (Philadelphia: The Westminster Press, 1960).

31. John Calvin, *Institutes* 4.16.3–4.

32. To be clear, the Swiss Reformer Zwingli did not subscribe to a sacramental view of baptism (out of belief that that "an external thing cannot do an internal work … a material thing cannot accomplish or reveal what is spiritual"), though held with other Reformers the view that infant baptismal rites serve as a "sign of loyalty" for the covenant people of God. See Bryan Spinks, *Reformation and Modern Rituals and Theologies of Baptism: From Luther to Contemporary Practices* (Burlington, VT: Ashgate, 2006), 31–35. In upholding Zwingli's anti-sacramental view of baptism, Barth remarked that his own doctrine of baptism might be characterized by others as "neo-Zwinglian" (*CD* IV/4, 129–130).

33. The biblical passages that are commonly believed to substantiate either a sacramental or covenantal interpretation that Barth reconsiders include 1 John 5: 5–8, John 19: 33–37, Heb. 10: 22, Eph. 5:25, Titus 3:5, Gal. 3:27, John 3:5, Acts 22: 16, 1 Pet. 3: 21, Rom. 6:3f, Col. 2:12, and Mark 16:16 (*CD* IV/4, 107–127).

34. See supra, note #22 for these Ralwsian terms.

35. As Elizabeth Wyner Mark recounts, circumcision is generally understood even by nonreligious Jews as "absolutely essential to male Jewish identity," though there is no Halakhich Jewish "entry ritual" for a person born to a Jewish mother. Additionally, while there is no initiation ceremony for Jewish girls equivalent to *brit milah*, girls

"nevertheless convey Jewish status to the next generation" (xiii). See her "Crossing the Gender Divide: Public Ceremonies, Private Parts, Mixed Feelings," in *The Covenant of Circumcision: New Perspectives on an Ancient Jewish Rite*, xiii–xxvi.

36. See, for example, Canon 845 §1 for Catholic teaching, the *Westminster Confession of Faith* 28:7 for Reformed teaching, and Martin Luther, "Concerning Rebaptism" (1528) in *Martin Luther's Basic Theological Writings*, third edition, eds. Timothy F. Full and William R. Russell (Minneapolis, MN: Fortress Press, 2012) for Lutheran teaching. Barth, too, was neither advocating for rebaptism for those who were baptized as infants, nor for a "supplemental rite" to infant baptism such as (Catholic) "confirmation," for baptism on his account—even if done for the afore-mentioned "questionable" and "doubtful" reasons—nonetheless remained "valid" (*CD* IV/4, 188–189).

37. See John Rawls, *Political Liberalism,* expanded ed. (New York: Columbia University Press, 2005 (1993) for his distinction between "comprehensive doctrines," which address broader questions of value and how to live, and the "political concep-tion of justice" narrowly concerned with the basic structure of society.

38. Richard Amesbury, "Is the Body Natural? Bodily Integrity and Religion," *Bioethics Forum* 7, no. 2 (2014): 51–52. Because the widespread norm in many European countries is not to circumcise, the bodily practices of (mostly) Jewish and Muslim minorities who may seem to many in the mainstream as *other* in comparison. Where the norm differs, such as in the United States where the majority of males undergoes neonatal circumcision for nonreligious reasons, or among Jewish com-munities, wherein Talmudic support can be found for the view that circumcision "is the completion and perfection of the human body," males who have had their fore-skins removed prior to their consent are not widely viewed as having experienced affronts to their bodily integrity. For Jewish oral tradition, see Avraham Steinberg, "Circumcision," in *Encyclopedia of Jewish Medical Ethics*, trans. Fred Rosner (Jerusalem: Feldheim Publishers, 2003), 194–224 at 195.

39. See, for example, Marina Caffiero, *Forced Baptisms: Histories of Jews, Christians, and Converts in Papal Rome*, trans. Lydia G. Cochrane (Berkeley, CA: University of California Press, 2012).

40. Karl Barth, *Table Talk*, ed. John Godsey (Richmond, VA: John Knox Press, 1963), 37 as quoted in Jesse Couenhoven, "Karl Barth's Conception(s) of Human and Divine Freedom(s)," in *Commanding Grace: Studies in Karl Barth's Ethics*, ed. Daniel L. Migliore (Grand Rapids, MI: Eerdmans, 2010), 246.

41. Barth's insistence on human freedom is clear in his mature work on baptism: one's free first act of faithfulness in baptism should neither be understood "mecha-nistically, under any physical or moral compulsion," nor as originating autonomously in one's own "free will and action"; rather, baptism should be understood as an indi-vidual responding in obedience to the "justification and sanctification ... which God has accomplished and revealed in Jesus Christ" (*CD* IV/4, 43, 101, 159).

42. Couenhoven, "Karl Barth's Conception(s) of Human and Divine Freedom(s)," 249.

43. See, for example, Lactantius, *Divine Institutes* IV:28: "For we are created on this condition, that we pay just and due obedience to God who created us, that we

should know and follow Him alone. We are *bound* and *tied* to God by this chain of piety [religati], from which religion itself received its name, not, as Cicero explained it, from carefully gathering [religendo]." Taken from Christian Classics Ethereal Library, http://www.ccel.org/ccel/schaff/anf07.iii.ii.html.

44. So understood, perhaps the most effective way to encourage Jewish groups who circumcise with MBP to cease doing so (for the sake of children's safety and public health) would *not* be through the threat of coercive sanction from the state, but from internal discussions among Jewish groups themselves about what is and is not required for circumcision under Jewish law.

45. Alexander J. McKelway, "Freedom," in *Westminster Handbook to Barth*, ed. Richard Burnett (Louisville, KY: Westminster John Knox Press, 2013), 79; Couenhoven, 246–247.

Chapter 4

Cesarean Section between High-Tech Medicine and a Theology of Birth

Developing an "Ethics of the Middle Range"

Martin Wendte

This chapter sets a stage for four players who do not usually perform together: Karl Barth, Martin Luther, the feminist theologian Hanna Strack, and the contemporary chorus of voices airing theo-politically tinged views upon technical progress in the field of medicine, with particular focus on the issue of the rise in the rate of cesarean sections (C-sections).[1] My basic premise is that in this particular context, Barth and Luther need not be seen any longer as irreconcilable opponents within one play or, indeed, as protagonists in their own separate plays. Rather, both figures can enter a productive dialogue on one and the same stage, even though some important differences do remain. For in tandem with Hanna Strack, they offer one another methodological and material insights that open up theological perspectives upon a development in many Western societies that raises concerns and begs important questions, namely the sharp rise in the rate of C-sections. Fifty percent of births in German cities are already performed with the help of the surgeon's knife, and this upward trend shows no sign of stalling in the near future. Surprisingly, this happens in spite of the facts that (a) at the beginning of a pregnancy, only few women imagine that they may eventually come to opt for a birth via C-section, (b) only the minority of C-sections is medically strictly indicated, and (c) many C-sections carry a greater risk than vaginal births. Although medically indicated C-sections are undoubtedly imperative, the sharp rise in the rate of C-sections leads to the paradoxical situation that this surgical procedure is often chosen out of a desire for safety although in actual fact it is more often than not exactly that option which presents the greater risk. How can we explain this paradoxical situation, and how can theology help to ease its negative aspects?

The guiding thesis of the following consists of two aspects. Human action in all its spheres—in the private as well as the public—is steered by conceptions (or ideas) of the good life characterized by particular religious- and world-views, which in, with, and under a number of technical, economic, cultural and other factors, are central for action. In other words: In truth, seemingly technical questions ("Shall we do a cesareans or not") are cultural and political questions, questions about the way we want to lead our life. Cultural and political questions are partly driven by religious convictions and ideas of the good life, which always appear in plural. Technical questions thus are questions of "theo-politics." What seems to cause the rise in the rate of C-sections, then, is a concert of technical, economical, cultural, and ideological (or theo-political) causes, and it is the very task of theology to analyze these causes and to present alternative theo-political horizons.

Second: Theo-political questions are best treated by an "ethics of the middle-range," that is, by an ethics which takes the plurality of factors into account that shape our acting in the real world. An ethics of the middle range is a "bottom-up approach" to public theology.[2] It starts with the analysis of a concrete situation and displays the many implicit factors shaping this question. It will become obvious that the rise in the rate of C-sections can serve as a particularly apposite example to focus paradigmatic issues relating to technical progress in general and developments within the medical sector in particular. Finally, an ethics of the middle range presents an alternative theo-political horizon (shaped by Luther, Barth, and Strack) and concrete alternatives.

To develop my thesis, I shall stage a conversation between Barth and Luther about methodological and material aspects, expose the framework of an ethics of the middle range, the reasons for the rise in the rate of C-sections, and the risks of this procedure. Thereby, theological perspectives on birth will come to the fore, especially when Barth's and Luther's insights are developed further through exposure to the thinking of the feminist theologian Hanna Strack. In drawing upon Strack, I also hope to dispel the notion that the present chapter may be yet another attempt by a male scholar to tell women how to handle their body and convince the reader that she is instead witnessing a modest theological attempt at the clarification of some pressing issues in a heavily debated field. In the final section, I shall offer some thoughts about possible practical consequences.

METHODICAL REFLECTION 1: KARL BARTH'S BARMEN II, AND THE LUTHERAN "ESTATES": NEW ALLIANCES

As Jesus Christ is God's assurance of the forgiveness of all our sins, so, in the same way and with the same seriousness he is also God's mighty claim upon our whole life. Through him befalls us a joyful deliverance from the godless fetters of this world for a free, grateful service to his creatures. *We reject the false doctrine, as though there were areas of our life in which we would not belong to Jesus Christ, but to other lords—areas in which we would not need justification and sanctification through him.*[3]

Karl Barth wrote these famous words as the second Barmen theses. In the Barmen Theological Declaration Theses I and II were, on the one hand, written against a specific strand of Lutheran theology, namely Emanuel Hirsch and Werner Elert, who among other things represented specific ways of reading the Doctrine of the Two Realms.[4] As a result, Barmen was also criticized over the decades by certain theologians of Lutheran provenance.[5] On the other hand, since the co-address to the Barmen Theological Declaration given by Lutheran Hans Asmussen at Free Synod of Barmen in 1934,[6] there are ways of reading the text of the declaration which emphasize that Barmen takes important impulses from Lutheran theology and translates them for the times. In this chapter, we will follow this second reading and will understand Barmen—borrowing from the words of Ernst Wolf—as a "call forwards."[7] Ernst Wolf continued these consensus-oriented lines in the debate over Christ's lordship in particular. On the basis of new research on Luther, these lines also led to the fact that at the end of the 1970s a consensus was reached in the subject between mostly Lutheran advocates of the doctrine of the two realms on the one hand and mostly Reformed and Barthian advocates of a concept of the lordship of Christ on the other.[8] At present, for many theologians the debate over the two different approaches, and therefore also over the debate going on since 1945 over the second Barmen Thesis, is seen as outdated.[9] Luther and Barth are no longer to be understood as the great opponents—hero or villain—on the stage of European theology. We have reached a point where they need to be reconfigured as mutually helpful agents with a common goal. The task at present seems to me to be, in accepting the consensus reading, to adopt impulses from the second Barmen Thesis for an effective social ethic in a Lutheran tradition; four impulses are of particular import:

First—what is theologically speaking the least disputed—all human striving toward sanctification is grounded in the alien righteousness of Jesus Christ, which precedes all human deeds (in the words of Barmen: "Jesus Christ is God's assurance of the forgiveness of all our sins"—from this follows the description of the human task). Second: in accepting insights from the notion of Christ's lordship there is the emphasis that human striving for sanctification encompasses the entire life. There are no spheres of life, either noetic or ontic, in which Christians can act suitably in abstraction from the Lordship of Jesus Christ. What obtains noetically is that all thinking and action with respect to all spheres of human life is perspectival—that is, it is not worldview neutral. Suitability in thinking and action does not come by disregarding the particular perspective of the agent in question and not by disregarding the conception (or the idea) of the good directing the action that is characterized by a religious perspective and a worldview.[10] On the other hand, corresponding to this ontologically is precisely what recent Luther research holds to be Luther's own theological notion: human action from the Christian perspective is not limited solely to the private sphere, but rather encompasses all areas of life.[11] This is because God acts in all spheres and God orders God's action in specific ways to each: God's action of creation and preservation does not include these spheres in itself in an autotelic manner, but is so ordered in itself that action of creation and preservation serves that of salvation.[12] Thus the *"Andergesetzlichkeit"*[13] of particular societal functional systems will not be denied opposite the way that spiritual manner of God's governance functions. This, however, will contradict all attempts to bracket out segments of societal interaction by means of reference to the respectively reigning set of standards (*Eigengesetzlichkeit*) from all of those ethical discourses that are seen as being shaped by religion and worldview.[14]

Third, the "deliverance from the godless fetters of this world for a free, grateful service to his creatures" (Barmen II) is a procedure that is always to be repeated anew. Theology as a whole, and theological ethics as well, come about as a conflict about reality and thereby always have to attend to a kind of tentative, investigative, exploratory—that is, a genuinely hermeneutical—task. Fourth, in accepting insights from the second and third point, and now accepting insights that are particularly emphasized by advocates of the doctrine of the two realms: the always renewing process of liberation made possible by divine action occurs in all its actuality precisely in that concrete place of human existence and therefore with regard to its own traditions, *Andersgesetzlichkeiten* and institutions together with their formative powers and additional factors, which enable humans to live and live together as bodily entities in the fallen world[15]; that is, at the location of the estates, foundations, institutions, orders of creation or mandates.[16]

In order to conceptualize the kind of mediation envisioned here of the basic impulse from Barmen II with this foundational element of Lutheran social ethics, the underlying understanding of the estates or orders has to be clarified with greater precision: here we should not understand either a place of a too absolutized autonomy (a reading that Barth used against his Lutheran opponents) nor—recognizing all the necessary differences in individual points in a line running from Bonhoeffer through Wolf up to Eilert Herms[17]—the place of a sphere of duties in which human life and action are taking place at all times. On the contrary, in connection with the Ernst Wolf's student Hans G. Ulrich and even Luther himself the estates are described as places for the differentiated interplay of divine action with that of human action. "Through this process of life (in the estates or institutions, to the best of my knowledge) human life is set into God's economy as *creaturely* life. And conversely God's economy is set into the reality of human life, its beginning and its end, as well as the logic of its course."[18]

The doctrine of the estates deals with what is the fundamental theme of the theology of the Reformation, the right ordering of divine and human action. At the same time, this ordering comes into view in its specifically concrete form and with regard to its particular danger within the sphere of action of an individual estate; for our topic, in relation to the economy: "The loss of creaturely life enters into the *Oeconomia*, when what humans had received as God's co-workers fell from view. The nonsensical form of a kind of economy arises that believes itself to be able to design and produce everything, an entire world."[19] Our goal, therefore, is to develop a posture within an estate and under the direction of a specific picture of the good which is suitable for the creaturely life in this estate. The following is thus presented as a nexus of an ethics of the good, the estates, and the virtues.

METHODICAL REFLECTION 2: AN ETHICS OF THE ESTATES AS AN ETHICS OF THE MIDDLE RANGE FOR—AMONG OTHER THINGS—QUESTIONS OF HEALTH CARE

The following will make clear that in the economy (in the widest possible sense) it is not only that the guiding difference between receiving from others and producing on one's own is central, but that this guiding difference is also expressed with regard to ultimate concern and assured action.[20] This guiding difference will be examined in relation to its determinative efficacy, which, on the basis of technical progress, great economic pressure, and the changing mental "state of things" in recent years, has become a significant theme in social ethics: the politics of health care, and indeed with regard to an exemplary contemporary theme in health care, the rapid increase in the number of C-sections being performed in Western industrial nations.

With this I am working on a theme, which in relation to its fit into an ethics of the estates, falls under what I would like to call an "ethics of the middle range." This attempts to be an ethics related to the often not-all-that-dramatic, but still in many ways ethically challenging biographies of many Christian women and men in Western society. It is notable, first, for the fact that the problems it handles are not questions of the ultimate, existentially dramatic kind, which are to be answered with a clear yes or no. They therefore present questions, second, of only relative preferability of one good over another. Phenomena come into view that certainly pose weighty questions, but which would not be labeled either intrinsically good or bad. Third, the presentation of the problem being handled leads back to a myriad of factors, which characterize actions in the respective estates and which therefore deserves to be perceived and assessed with differentiation—even when a factor (the respective image of the good life) is oftentimes the most fundamental and most important. In correspondence to this layer of problems, the solutions proposed aim at relative improvements. What this asks of theology is for it to prepare a set of tools that is differentiated enough in analysis and problem-solving to be capable of providing information for the sought-after middle range. We now need to consider how an ethics of the middle range is affected by the issue of the increase in the rate of C-sections. To this end, we first need to take a look at the causes of that development in the medical sector.

THE "CLASH OF THE SPIRIT OF THE AGE WITH NATURE"—REASONS FOR THE RAPID INCREASE IN THE RATE OF CESAREAN SECTIONS

How are we to explain the fact that at the beginning of a pregnancy only 4 percent of women aim at having a C-section—but in Germany, more than 30 percent of the births are C-sections? How are we to understand the fact that the rate of C-sections in Germany and other industrialized countries increased by 10 percent between 1993 and 2003, and in many bigger cities come close to 50 percent—although no more than 10 to 15 percent of the C-sections are necessary in a strictly medical sense?[21]

We begin with some detailed material observations. Five aspects are of importance. We will present them in turn and then observe the mutual influence of these aspects—the network which becomes so persuasive for many women. Technical Progress forms the basis of the whole story we tell. Until 1950, the C-section was a highly risky operation with very high maternal mortality rate.[22] Since the 1960s, thanks to cardiotocography (CTG), the prenatal condition of the child could be determined, and the cesarean-rate increased. A peculiar dialectic of progress becomes evident: The increase in knowledge "is accompanied by the danger that minor anomalies are declared to be pathological."[23] The result is perplexing: According to the maternal logs [Mutterpass] issued by gynecologists, more than 80 percent of pregnant women belong to a high-risk-group![24]

The second factor is a political one, since displaying hospitals as organizational and economic factors. Many hospitals prefer C-sections, because they are easier to organize. Hospitals also receive three times the amount of money for a C-section than for a vaginal birth, which is especially interesting for private patients. [25]

The third factor is the doctors themselves. Medical training "tends toward action, not towards waiting,"[26] and "gynecologists tend to see pregnancy and birth as a potentially pathological process, which has to be corrected by medical intervention."[27] In addition, doctors lose their knowledge about complicated natural births; a downward spiral takes place. Doctors also fear high recourse claims in the case of mistakes.[28] Due to these factors, many doctors pre-emptively advise C-sections.[29]

The fourth factor is the parents themselves, naturally. For a number of good reasons, more and more women are having their children at higher ages, and they are having increasingly fewer children. Attitudes toward birth and children are changing. A child now often becomes a project that should achieve as much success as possible.[30] This attitude is accompanied by a distinct need for control and security. It is driven by insecurity and anxiety in face of the uncontrollable outcome of a birth. As an experienced midwife pointedly put it: "People were always anxious of what could happen during birth. But in earlier times, people were ready to trust—in destiny, a divine power, in nature, in whatever. Women prayed and hoped—they cherished their hopes [waren guter Hoffnung—this is a play on words as it also means: they were expecting]! Today they face their anxiety with control—with the compulsion to be active."[31] This need for control is enforced by the fathers and their (often) more technical views on birth. The more fathers accompany births, the more their perspective becomes influential—and the rate of cesareans rises.[32]

Fifth: doctors and parents alike are influenced by the extremely influential (but: hard to grasp) phenomenon called the "spirit of the age" or the "mental state of things"—the idea of the good life. For one, help with the birth is now understood as kind of service, fitting to the wishes of the customer, the mother. Two, the attitude toward birth is formed by the need for control so characteristic of Western societies. They want to tame all strong feelings, all pain and everything unforeseeable—or at least they try to. As the philosopher Peter Sloterdijk puts it: "Modern social climate as a whole changes. Our society distrusts all kinds of immigration. Two borders are controlled in a most extreme way: the borders of a country, and the borders of the body."[33] Empirical research displays that these general aspects are of major importance for the rise in the number of cesareans.[34]

In the end, though, the interplay of all five factors provides the full picture. During pregnancy, women with their raised need for control are accompanied by doctors—and less by midwifes. Due to their training and experience and due to the parent's willingness to put forward recourse claims, doctors tend to see pregnancy and birth as a risky occurrence and advise preventive medical checkups, which often display minor deviations from the norms. Women become more and more insecure. The image of the women concerned thus also changes decisively: They come to be seen as weak and endangered, as patients in need of help.[35] Accordingly, the image of pregnancy and birth also shifts: Pregnancy as a state of good hope becomes an accumulation of risks.[36] Also driven by economic reasons and the overall decline of pregnancies, hospitals tend to see themselves as service providers willing to fulfil women's wishes. Due to this network of factors, the quality and quantity of indicators pointing toward a cesarean themselves have changed. In the present, less than 10 percent of the cesareans are done because of absolute indicators—and among the relative indicators, anxiety about the uncontrollable situation and pain during birth are widely accepted.

In summary: Due to the interdependence of the five factors, a mental state of things has come about in which cesareans seem to be the "natural" option. Three steps can be distinguished: One, although there is a great deal of rhetoric about self-determination in play, women are nevertheless both active players and aggrieved parties in a mutually reinforcing network of need for security composed of doctors, the women and their partners, as well as the practice of prenatal diagnosis. The mental state of things has changed: The state of good hope increasingly appears to be an accumulation of risks, and women appear to be weak patients. Two, quite often, cesareans now become an option. Three, before pregnancy only 4 percent of the women aim at a cesarean, and many women appreciate birth as a natural occurrence. According to WHO, a C-section is a medical necessity for no more than 10 to 15 percent of births. Nevertheless, in many bigger cities in Germany, the rate of performance of the procedure has reached 50 percent, with an increasing tendency.

Why is this development so problematic? Why write an article on such a development, which is not perhaps so well known, but which at first sight seems more or less to be harmless? Why deal with this problem in ethics of middle ranges?

ON STILLBIRTHS, RITE DE PASSAGES AND ANXIOUS HEARTS: THE PROBLEMS OF THE INCREASE OF CESAREAN BIRTHS

From well into the past all the way to the present, assessment of the increasing number of C-sections has been a true battlefield. As early as in 1929, the famous doctor Martius emphasized that we should let go of the "Caesarean frenzy."[37] Today, both defenders and opponents of cesareans fight for their position with great zeal—natural births, too, need to be defended with high art.[38] In late modernity, the mental state of things always appears as a pluralistic phenomenon.

The following position does not oppose cesareans as such: I am most grateful for all those cesareans which are medically necessary. Other cesareans, however, do appear to be problematic according to classic insights of academic medicine, according to psychological developments, and according to the wider horizon of mental states.

Although in the last decades, cesareans have become a much safer option, they nevertheless pose a much higher risk for both mother and child than a natural birth.[39] Children suffer from a lack of oxygen much more often, their oxygen supply as such is much lower and they are threatened by damage from the incision. Most of all, their death rate is twice as high as it is with non-cesarean born children.[40] The mothers suffer a higher risk of thrombosis; and, most of all, their death rate is much higher—between two and nine times as high![41]

A closer look at the psychological aspects adds further cracks in the picture of a smooth, unproblematic cesarean. The knowledge of prenatal- and natal-psychologists might be accompanied by some inaccuracies. But experts such as prenatal psychologist Ludwig Janus emphasize that during pregnancy, the depth emotionality of the babies are heavily shaped. While vaginal birth presents a smooth transition from the world without polarity to the world of polarities, in a cesarean birth the world of polarities is reached without preparation and participation of the child and therefore in an often traumatic way. It is more difficult, then, to experience it as true home.[42] Many mothers also have the impression of having lost the privilege to have a successful birth and have to fight the experience of helplessness and failure. This is all the more problematic as the camp of cesarean skeptics propagate the notion of natural birth as a fundamental female experience, thereby putting pressure and a bad conscience on mothers who have had cesarean births.[43]

Two further aspects are of importance: at least in the first days and weeks, cesarean-mothers experience bonding—the mother-child relationship—less strongly, and there are physiological reasons as well. Bonding begins during the first days of pregnancy—but during birth, first the "bonding-hormone" oxytocin, and then the "bonding-and happiness-hormone" endorphin is poured out. Together they tie mother and child in the tightest way.[44] Additionally, a natural birth is a rite de passage not only for mother and child but also for the parents.

As for the third level, we refer back to the main insight of the last subsection, which also forms the background to the second level we just developed. A cesarean is the incarnational point of culmination or at least the visible indicator of an all-encompassing mental state of emphasis on risks—of the anxious heart (as a mirror of a certain idea of the good) as the main reason and the biggest problem. The mental state of emphasizing risks promotes a further hardening of hearts, because women are seen as patients and do not gain the same self-confidence which often comes along with a natural birth. With these aspects, a paradox comes to the fore which is characteristic for the whole debate about cesareans (as well as for other debates in the realm of the politics of health care): In order to avoid risks, people tend to choose the even riskier way.[45] Or, mentally speaking: that which is supposed to alleviate concerns causes even greater ones.

We have thus entered a field of tasks which are themes of a theological ethics, because at its deepest level, technological questions are political questions ("how shall we lead our lives"), and political questions are driven by ideas about the good life, which are theological questions. Questions of cesareans are theo-political questions. The following section thus develops a theology of birth in three steps. Following Barth, I perform a theological re-lecture of the anxious heart and of the paradox, that in order to avoid risks, people tend to choose an even riskier way. Then, following Luther, I present a re-lecture of the main characteristics of pregnancy and birth in a theological perspective: they are God's good gifts, which humans should accept in gratefulness and confidence—a perspective which displays advantages in the classic perspective of academic medicine as well. This perspective is, finally, enriched with insights that stem from the feminist theology of Hanna Strack which helps to grasp the experience of birth as holy, and women as God's co-operators.

Aspects of a Theology of Birth

The Lordless Powers: Barth's Theological
Re-Lecture of the Anxious Heart

"They take away his little anxieties but create new and bigger ones. They seem to promise him courage and a greater zest for life, but increased worry about life is the fulfillment of their promise."[46] Barth's late lectures on ethics, posthumously published under the title "The Christian Life" ("Das Christlichen Leben"), expose the same phenomenon that we diagnosed earlier, with reference to the C-section, as the idiosyncratic paradox of technical progress. Interestingly, Barth relates this phenomenon to the development of technology, too.[47] Barth's analysis of the dialectic of technical progress highlights aspects that we know from the contemporaneous writings of the great philosophers of technology and progress, Adorno and Heidegger.[48] Importantly for us, though, Barth places his analysis and his suggestions for possible solutions to the conundrum of modern technology into an explicitly theological context.

Barth develops his analysis within the framework of his exegesis of the Lord's Prayer, more precisely: as an interpretation of the second petition: "Your kingdom come." When uttering this petition, Christians express that kind of obedience to God that signifies an encompassing, just and righteous relationship between man and God. Within the bounds of this righteous, obedient relationship, the human subject is equipped with the capacities and the liberties to act in a righteous and humane way. Due to the fall, however, the human subject has lost this close relationship to God. At the same time and for the same reason, said capacities and liberties are uncoupled from the human subject. Originally meant to serve the human subject, these capacities and liberties take on a life of their own and become subjugating forces.[49] Man finds himself in the position of the Sorcerer's Apprentice, unable to re-establish control over the forces that he has set free, who now turn to control him in accordance with their own proper law.[50]

In this state of free flotation, man's capacities and liberties become "Lordless Powers" with an ambivalent ontological and epistemic status. Their ontological Lordlessness stems from the fact that they are dissociated from man and no longer controlled by him. God himself, however, does of course retain His mastery over and His ability to utilize or dispel these forces. "This relativity in their relationship to God and man causes the *darkness*, ambivalence and opaque nature of their reality and their workings as well as the ghostly fleetingness of their manifestation."[51] Related to this relativity of their relationship both to God and man is the obscurity, ambivalence, and unintelligibility of their reality and efficacy. Also related to it is the "wraith-like transitoriness with which they manifest themselves."[52] This ontological in-between status has its epistemical parallel in the difficulty one faces when attempting to recognize and describe the Lordless Powers. It therefore makes good sense that the New Testament and many contemporary descriptions, including Barth's, recur to mythological diction in order to account for such phenomena. The language and logic of myth are therefore not archaic remnants that could be dissolved in the rational, scientific concepts of modernity. Quite the contrary: only mythological diction is adequate for the issue at hand. Barth's ontological and epistemological reflections elucidate why the previous section's descriptions of the condition of the "restless heart," which (in)voluntarily affects many peoples' lives, were cast in searching and mythologizing language—the only language apt to capture the essence of the phenomena under scrutiny here.

Barth's closer description of the Lordless Powers is instructive because it is rich in detail and at the same time seemingly pre-emptive of Foucauldian insights. For in Barth, the Lordless Powers take their effects not only in destructive but also and especially in productive ways. They are the driving forces of the constellations that shape our day-to-day lives: "They are the secret guarantee of man's great and small concerns, customs, habits, traditions, and institutions. They are not just the supports but the motors of society. They are the hidden wirepullers in man's great and small enterprises. They are not just the potencies but the real factors and agents of human progress, regress, and stagnation in politics, economics, scholarship, technology, and arts."[53] In order to exemplify the efficacy of the Lordless Powers, Barth explores different dimensions of human agency, among them the realm of the "chthonic"[54] powers, that is the realm of man's domination of nature, first and foremost by means of technology. It is this latter realm where man is, in fact, dominated by the Lordless Powers, uncoupled as they are from the human subject whom they oppose as adversarial forces in ways that were described in our opening quote and, with reference to various empirical studies, in the previous section (IV): "They take away his little anxieties but create new and bigger ones. They seem to promise him courage and a greater zest for life, but increased worry about life is the fulfillment of their promise."[55]

Barth explains in two steps how these powers are banished. First, he emphasizes that it is not the task of the human subject, but of the Lord of the whole world—Jesus Christ—to banish the Lordless Powers in bringing the Kingdom to this world.[56] Barth's second, and very different, point relates to the human subject's role in this process. This consists first and foremost in pleas to God to let His Kingdom come. Moved by such prayers and hopes for the advent of the Kingdom of God, man is also supposed to strive, in accordance with divine justice, toward concrete justice in his own day-to-day life, with the aim of serving his fellow man.[57]

Perhaps driven by the fear that the Kingdom of God may be seen as attainable through human deeds, Barth, holding on to the fundamental premise of his theology as expressed in the *finitum non capax infiniti*, remains remarkably unspecific as to a more precise account of the human subject's role in the taming of the Lordless Powers. These are rendered in thick descriptions while the human deeds to be done in accordance with divine justice are merely sketched (although Barth emphasizes that these deeds should take place in our daily life).[58] My own theology makes stronger claims upon the Lutheran tradition and includes a conviction that God's agency, while categorially different from human agency, materializes in, with and under the conditions of creaturely existence. I shall therefore now draw upon Luther's doctrine of the three estates, which offers a differentiated account of the interplay of divine and human agency, especially as regard birth and family life. Such a Lutheran move will, however, necessitate certain terminological shifts: that which in Barth is cast mostly in terms of the advent of the Kingdom of God, is described by Luther with partial recourse to Aristotelian terminology as participation in an encompassing reality of God's gift.

Luther's Doctrine of the Three Estates in His Exegesis of the Psalms (1533)

In prominent texts from his late theology, Luther explains his Reformation theology in the terminology of gift. Reality as a whole is understood as a circulation of gifts. It is grounded in God's Trinitarian self-giving. God comes close to human beings in creation, reconciliation and sanctification, empowering human beings for grateful handling of these gifts. In his exegesis of Psalm 127 from 1533,[59] entitled "If the Lord does not build the House, those who work on it build it in vain," Luther further develops this theology by connecting his wide theology of gifts and his ethics of goods with his doctrine of the estates, connected with his virtue ethics.

Among the good gifts which mankind receives from God are the "estates," in which human beings are placed. As Luther develops in his lectures on Genesis, in paradise human beings are put both in the estate of the church and in the estate of economy, which includes the setting of the family and economic actions in a broader sense.[60]

Luther's decisive insight emphasizes that, God, at present, is unceasingly active.[61] In order to gain a deeper understanding of the present reign of God, Luther operates with two distinctions. They originate in the Aristotelian tradition, but Luther reshapes their semantics with the basic insights from the theology of the Reformation. Luther operates with a new definition of the scheme of the four causes, and the scheme of primary and secondary causes.

All human beings including the pagans know about the *causa materialis* and the *causa formalis* of worldly things and thus about the material and formal causes of the estate of economy. God empowers human beings to use this estate according to their own responsibility.[62] But pagans do not know about the true *causa finalis* and the true *causa efficiens*: The final cause consists in that everything is God's good gift and that everything exists in order to serve the honor of God, not the peace or wealth of human beings. And the efficient cause of all things is God's reign and action, not the actions of human beings.

In order to gain a closer understanding of God's reign and action as the efficient cause of all things, as a second scheme, Luther applies the scheme of primary and secondary causality. God's reign relates to human deeds as the primary cause relates to the secondary cause. In their estate and as secondary causes, human beings should act actively to reach their aims—at the same time, everything depends on God's action as the primary cause. Luther provides an anthropological insight which solves this apparent paradox: According to the old human being—that is: according to human beings who act in worldly settings as the formal and material cause—human beings ought to act busily. According to faith and heart, however, humans are to rely on God completely.[63] With the help of this terminology, Luther can define divine and human action both as categorically distinct and as related—thus he can follow the basic insights of Reformation theology, which grasps divine and human action as both completely distinct and as completely related. If the Lord does not build the house, those who build it work in vain—but those who build should work as well. God builds his house in, with and under the activity of human beings.

Accordingly, it is adequate to understand everything in the estate of the economy as God's gift.[64] Specified to the realm of pregnancy and birth, Luther writes: "Holy Spirit teaches us to listen to the Word of God which is in the first book of Moses, so that we learn [. . .] that kids are God's gift, not your own work. [. . .] As long as the embryo is in the mother's womb, it is fed without its works and her sorrow, by God alone. For what should the embryo do, which is lying there without all reason? And after being born, the baby has got a well-filled cellar, the breasts of his mother, well prepared as a source of all good. [. . .] Alas, where God preserves his gifts, He also donates plenty of things through which they are preserved."[65]

Luther's theology is realistic and attractive for contemporary discourse, because he relates these theological insights with the experience of human beings in the estates and under the conditions of the fall. We encounter descriptions which work with the guiding difference of anxious hearts versus hopeful hearts, and we thus encounter descriptions which we met in subsection III of this chapter. In their day-to-day life, human beings experience their life in the economic estate and during the dealing with children especially, as dominated by sorrows and risks—and often enough they feel driven by all kinds of Lordless Powers.[66] More precisely, due to the fall, human beings forget that they are not themselves the efficient cause of all things. They thus hold that not only the process of work but also its success depends on their work. This sin in the estate of economy leads to permanent excessive demand, impatience, or dejection. Human beings either try to control everything in an excessive way—they hold pregnancy and birth to be an accumulation of risks which need to be managed with strenuous effort. Or they lose courage altogether[67] since they realize that in spite of all efforts they cannot master the Lordless Powers.

This is to be contrasted by an attitude which Luther calls the attitude of a calm, grateful heart. This attitude accepts God as final cause and as efficient cause of all things. It is thus shaped by—(its idea of the good consists of)—the insight that reality as a whole is a circulation of gifts, not the result of human works. Although sorrows and failures are not ignored, the anxious heart is lightened. It is characterized by an attitude of gratefulness toward God for His rich giving of gifts, of carefulness and equanimity toward worldly activities, and of the consolation that—in success and failure—all things work out the way God wants them to (which, as a human reaction, may include lament as well).[68]

The attitude of the calm heart, too, is a gift of God. The Holy Spirit gives himself and with himself faith, which makes human beings certain that they are loved by God, and that thus (as the idea of the good) reality as a whole is a circulation of gifts, thereby enabling human beings to love themselves. With Barth, we can emphasize: The Holy Spirit is able to instill this certainty in us since, in Jesus Christ, the Lord of the world has developed mastery over the Lordless Powers. This certainty determines the will of human beings, and in the concordance of love and will consists the power of virtue—of grateful equanimity.

Hanna Strack's Phenomenology of the Holiness of Birth, and Women as Co-operators of God's Creative Action

The feminist theologian Hanna Strack provides a successful demonstration of the mutual divine and human agency during birth, while giving heed to the Barthian notion of liberation. For Strack emphasizes that the modern medical view of birth as a risky process turns women into patients, thus subjecting women to a patriarchal, technocratic worldview and robbing them of a key moment of female gender identity. Strack, in contrast, aims to liberate women by enabling them to develop a different perception of birth and their own role. To this end, Strack recurs to accounts of birth by midwives and mothers who are able to offer first-hand experiences of births outside clinical institutions, and reads these accounts as experiences of the holy. As we know from Rudolf Otto's influential phenomenology of the holy, part and parcel of the experience of the holy is a captivating effect, a liminal experience, a moment where space and time feel distinctly different. It is exactly in this way that the midwives and mothers interviewed by Strack describe birth, namely as "a process wherein a transformation occurs in which all partake: mother, infant, father and midwife."[69] Liminal experiences materialize on several levels: on the child's way from twilight to light, in the mother's simultaneous feelings of pain and bliss, but also in the accompanying father's emerging new identity.[70] Space and time take on a new, different quality: Space is filled with a dense atmosphere and time seems to stand still, a state of things that is impossible to capture within the horizon of chronological metrics.[71] It is in these ways that, during birth, the categorially different divine and human agencies described by Luther can interlock in such a way that birth becomes an experience of the holy. God acts in, with, and under the bodily activity of the expecting mother and the child—an experience that can, as we have seen, be cast quite adequately in phenomenological terms.

Our understanding of the role of women is substantially altered by such thinking. Strack as well as other Germanophone and Anglo-American feminist theologians see the expecting mother not as ill or as a patient who, with an anxious heart, undergoes birth as a risky process.[72] Rather, the figure of the mother comes into view as an active co-operator of God. His Spirit liberates her heart from anxiety and lends her the strength, courage, and serenity that enables her to give birth to her child.

Strack's further tenets about the co-operation of God and woman are just as vital as her redefinition of the role of woman in the process of birth. Yet, in spite of her insight that the experience of the holy can comprise negative emotions such as anxiety, pain, and sadness, her separation of surgically assisted birth and experiences of the holy in vaginal births, which often occur outside of clinical institutions, seems to be rather strict. We do need to stress, therefore, that the mother who embraces vaginal birth remains exposed to economical, technical, and mental dimensions of the Lordless Powers, which do in many ways offer a degree of safety that is indeed helpful. And experiences of the holy can be had in clinical institutions and in the process of a pregnancy that ultimately leads to a C-section. The points that I am getting at here are, indeed, Lutheran in kind: Before the eschaton, the dialectic of law and Gospel has to be suffered through continuously. Temptation never ends.

Making Connections and Brief Look at Ethical Concretization

What can we say concretely from all this? Any concretion has to react to the myriad of factors in their interdependence and at the same time address the central issue, the respective conception of the good life. If the churches face the problem of the high rate of C-sections, then they have to promote and foster the position of the peaceful, grateful heart in the frame of their possibilities. This happens above all in worship and in other places where the Gospel is communicated: the secondary cause, with which we humans bring other humans close to the good gifts of God and can introduce them to a corresponding disposition, is first and foremost the Word in its bodily, even liturgical form.[73] In addition, there could be the possibility of a theological thematization of the increasing number of C-sections in the framework of adult Christian formation for those who are to become parents, and for the mothers especially.[74] Furthermore, awareness of the theme could be raised by offering discussions or seminars during the initial and continuing education of doctors, nurses, and midwives or aligned with those persons and their groups (doing public theology in the public). The goal would then not only be to develop an ethic of the estate, but furthermore an ethic of the estate in the style of a duty ethics. At the national level the church should support political movements like the Association of Midwives

(Hebammen-Vereinigung) in order to be active within the sphere of the economic and organizational reasons for the increasing in C-sections. The Association of Midwives is now proposing a compensatory payment for clinics with high rates of C-sections.[75]

In any such activities, two key points ought to be kept in mind. Medically indicated C-sections are a blessing indeed. The culture of the anxious heart, however, causes ever-increasing cesarean rates, thus creating the paradoxical situation that in order to avoid risks, people tend to choose the even riskier option. To counter such developments, Christians do well to characterize birth as a possible experience of the holy wherein God gives the expecting mother a hopeful heart and lets her act as His co-operator.

NOTES

1. A warm thanks to the whole group of scholars who were gathered by Markus Höfner, and to Paul Jones and his insightful and stimulating response to my paper especially: these impulses greatly improved the initial version of my paper.

2. For a comparable "bottom-up" approach see Grace Y. Kao's essay on male circumcision controversies in this volume.

3. Alfred Burgsmüller, Rudolf Weth (ed.), *Die Barmer Theologische Erklärung. Einführung und Dokumentation* (Neukirchener: Neukirchen-Vluyn, 1983), 12.

4. A reconstruction of the powerful political implications of important strands of Barth's doctrine of God which were originally attacking certain Lutheran theologians is presented by Alexander Massmann's essay on Barth's understanding of the righteousness of God in this volume.

5. On the historical placement and the most important theological accents, cf. Carsten Nicolaisen, *Der Weg nach Barmen. Die Entstehungsgeschichte der Theologischen Erklärung von 1934* (Neukirchener: Neukirchen-Vluyn, 1985).

6. On this cf. Hans Asmussen, "Vortrag," in *Die Barmer Theologische Erklärung. Einführung und Dokumentation*, ed. Alfred Burgsmüller, Rudolf Weth (Neukirchener: Neukirchen-Vluyn, 1983), 23–52.

7. Ernst Wolf, "Königsherrschaft Christi und Lutherische Zwei-Reiche-Lehre," in *Peregrinatio. Band II, Studien zur reformatorischen Theologie, zum Kirchenrecht und zur Sozialethik*, ed. Ernst Wolf (Kaiser: München, 1965), 217.

8. For a short overview of the historical development of this debate, cf. Hans Walter Schütte, "Zwei-Reiche-Lehre und Königsherrschaft Christi," in *Handbuch der christlichen Ethik, Bd. 1*, ed. Anselm Hertz (Herder: Freiburg, 1978), 344–353.

9. For a Lutheran perspective on this, cf. Wilfried Härle, *Ethik* (deGruyter: Berlin/New York 2011), 458 and Eilert Herms, Art. "Zwei-Regimenten-Lehre," *RGG* 4, no. 8 (1939).

10. On this, cf. also Karl Barth, "Christengemeinde und Bürgergemeinde," in *Rechtfertigung und Recht*, ed. Karl Barth (Theologischer Verlag Zürich: Zürich, 3. Auflage, 1984), 60–62.

11. A rejection of the Christian life as being exclusively focuses on the private sphere can already be found in a pronounced form in Wolf, "Königsherrschaft," 212–214.

12. On this, cf. also Wilfried Härle, "Luthers Zwei-Regimenten-Lehre als Lehre vom Handeln Gottes," *Marburger Jahrbuch Theologie 1*, ed. Wilfried Härle (Evangelische Verlagsanstalt: Leipzig, 1987), 12–32; Barth, as is well known, also advocated this thesis; for a summary cf. Barth, "Christengemeinde," 62.

13. Härle, *Ethik*, 457.

14. Cf. also Barth, "Christengemeinde," 65.

15. Barth, of course, also recognized this; cf. Karl Barth, Kirchliche Dogmatik III/4 (Theologischer Verlag Zürich: Zürich, 1951), 17f.

16. On the background to Luther's understanding of the three estates, cf. Reinhold Schwarz, "Luthers Lehre von den drei Ständen und die drei Dimensionen der Ethik," *Luther-Jahrbuch* 45 (1978): 15–34.

17. Ernst Wolf, *Sozialethik. Theologische Grundfragen* (Vandenhoeck: Göttingen, 3. Auflage, 1988), 173, Eilert Herms, "Die Lehre von der Schöpfungsordnung," in *Offenbarung und Glaube: zur Bildung des christlichen Lebens*, ed. Eilert Herms (Mohr: Tübingen, 1992), 455.

18. Hans G. Ulrich, *Wie Geschöpfe leben: Konturen evangelischer Ethik* (LIT-Verlag: Münster, 2007), 103.

19. Ulrich, *Wie Geschöpfe leben*, 115.

20. On this, cf. Ulrich, *Wie Geschöpfe leben*, v.a. 104ff., and Brian Brock, "Why the Estates? Hans G. Ulrich's Recovery of an Unpopular Notion," *SCE* 20, no. 2 (2007): 179–202.

21. Cf. for this development the important, representative study Ulrike Lutz, Petra Kolip, *Die GEK-Kaiserschnittstudie* (Asgard: Bremen, 2006), 15ff.

22. Cf. Lutz, *GEK-Kaiserschnittstudie*, 18ff.

23. Lutz, *GEK-Kaiserschnittstudie*, 20.

24. This is emphasized by the former president of the federation of German midwives, Magdalena Weiß, cf. Magdalena Weiß, Peter Sloterdijk, "Wie soll ich dich empfangen? Die Hebamme und der Philosoph über Glück und Schrecken der Geburt im 3. Jahrtausend nach Christus," in: EKD, *Taufe und Freiheit*, 14.

25. Cf. Lutz, *GEK-Kaiserschnittstudie*, 22f.

26. Lutz, *GEK-Kaiserschnittstudie*, 22.

27. Lutz, *GEK-Kaiserschnittstudie*, 129. Most midwives conceive of birth as a natural happening and orient their action on the available resources, cf. Lutz, *GEK-Kaiserschnittstudie*, 130 and V.3.

28. Cf. Lutz, *GEK-Kaiserschnittstudie*, 24f.

29. Lutz, *GEK-Kaiserschnittstudie*, 24.

30. Martin Spiewak, "Wie man in Deutschland geboren wird," *Die ZEIT* 41(2003): 23.

31. Hauke Schütt, "Die Kollision des Zeitgeistes mit der Natur. Ein Interview," *medizin individuell* 37 (2009/2010): 5.

32. This is the guiding idea of Michel Odent, *Es ist nicht egal, wie wir geboren werden—Risiko Kaiserschnitt* (Mabuse: Düsseldorf und Zürich, 2005), cf. also Lutz, *GEK-Kaiserschnittstudie*, 28.

33. Sloterdijk in Weiß, Sloterdijk, "Wie soll ich dich empfangen," 14.

34. Cf. Lutz, *GEK-Kaiserschnittstudie*, 136.

35. Hanna Strack, *Die Frau ist Mit-Schöpferin: Eine Theologie der Geburt* (Christel Göttert Verlag: Rüsselsheim, 2006), 33.

36. This is the conclusion of Weiß and Schütt; cf. also Theresia Maria de Jong, Gabriele Kemmler, *Kaiserschnitt. Wie Narben an Bauch und Seele heilen können* (Kösel Verlag: München, 2003), 106–114.

37. Cf. Volker Lehmann, *Der Kayserliche Schnitt. Die Geschichte einer Operation* (Schattauer: Stuttgart, 2006), 241.

38. Cf. also Lutz, *GEK-Kaiserschnittstudie*, 130, and de Jong, *Kaiserschnitt*, 123–130.

39. For all risks cf. also the following article which includes a vast number of contemporary literature on the theme Beate Schücking, "Selbstbestimmt und risikolos?, Wunschkaiserschnitt,"*Mabuse* Nr. 148, S. 27–30.

40. Cf. Schütt, "Kollision," 7.

41. Cf. Lutz, *GEK-Kaiserschnittstudie*, 39f.

42. Cf. Ludwig Janus, *Der Seelenraum der Ungeborenen. Pränatale Psychologie und Therapie* (patmos Verlag: Stuttgart, 2007).

43. Cf. also Lutz, *GEK-Kaiserschnittstudie*, 47.

44. Cf. also Bund Deutscher Hebammen, *Kaiserschnitt ohne strenge medizinische Indikation*, 5. https://www.hebammenverband.de/index.php?id=788.

45. Cf. Lutz, *GEK-Kaiserschnittstudie*, 135–145.

46. Karl Barth, *The Christian Life: Church Dogmatics Volume IV, Part 4: Lecture Fragments*, trans. Geoffrey W. Bromiley (London: T&T Clark, 2004), 229.

47. Barth, *The Christian Life*, 230.

48. Cf. Martin Wendte, *Die Gabe und das Gestell. Luthers Metaphysik des Abendmahls im technischen Zeitalter* (Mohr: Tübingen, 2013), 21–93.

49. Cf. Barth, *The Christian Life*, 233f. For a further analysis of the Lordless power, see also the essay of Hanna Reichel on the The Political Theology of the Surveillance Society in this volume.

50. Barth, *The Christian Life*, 215.

51. Barth, *The Christian Life*, 367.

52. Barth, *The Christian Life*, 216.

53. Barth, *The Christian Life*, 217.

54. Barth, *The Christian Life*, 228.

55. Karl Barth, *The Christian Life*, 229.

56. Cf. Barth, *The Christian Life*, 240–249.

57. Cf. Barth, *The Christian Life*, 250f., 260–271.

58. I thus present a different reading from this passage in Barth than Paul D. Jones in his outstanding essay on Karl Barth's *The Christian Life* in this volume. I agree with Paul Jones on the importance of this paragraph of the Christian Life and on the fact that it is very helpful for analyzing the technological age from a theological perspective. But I differ in my assessment of how helpful Barth's own alternative material ethics is for an ethics of the middle range (or any realistic ethics at all).

59. During his last, extended lecture on the psalms from 1532 to 1533, Luther also read about Psalm 45 and on the Psalms 120–134. For the historical setting cf. Martin Brecht, Martin Luther, *Band 3: Die Erhaltung der Kirche* (Calwer Verlag: Stuttgart), 137–139.

60. Due to the Fall, God initiated a third institution, politics.

61. Martin Luther, *Sämtliche Schriften. Band 4: Auslegung des Alten Testaments*, ed. Johannes Walch (Harms: Groß Oesingen, 1910), 1940.

62. Cf. Luther, *Sämtliche Schriften. Band 4*, 1914.

63. Luther, *Sämtliche Schriften. Band 4*, 1942.

64. Luther, *Sämtliche Schriften. Band 4*, 1963.

65. Luther, *Sämtliche Schriften. Band 4*, 1963f.

66. Cf. Luther, *Sämtliche Schriften. Band 4*, 1917.

67. Luther, *Sämtliche Schriften. Band 4*, 1922f.

68. Luther, *Sämtliche Schriften. Band 4*, 1922.

69. Strack, *Die Frau ist Mit-Schöpferin*, 184.

70. Strack, *Die Frau ist Mit-Schöpferin*, 186f.

71. Strack, *Die Frau ist Mit-Schöpferin*, 190–192.

72. Strack refers to Ulrich, Johnson and others, cf. Strack, *Die Frau ist Mit-Schöpferin*, 191.

73. For a number of examples of prayers, parts of liturgy, blessings, etc., cf. Strack, *Die Frau ist Mit-Schöpferin*, 309–329.

74. This is the reason why academics and midwives are always asking for better clarification and guidance in cases where anxiety arises about prenatal issues and the birth process, cf. Lutz, *GEK-Kaiserschnittstudie*, 136–138.145f.

75. Bund Deutscher Hebammen, *Kaiserschnitt ohne strenge medizinische Indikation*, 6. https://www.hebammenverband.de/index.php?id=788.

Chapter 5

The Ecclesiological Implications of the Political Attitude of the Chinese Authority toward Christianity

Kim-Kwong Chan

INTRODUCTION

When a Christian community finds itself in a hostile sociopolitical environment, it must reflect upon its relation to this particular environment to achieve ecclesiological self-understanding. It must also do so to ensure its survival. Often hostility has characterized historical encounters between Christianity and "local" cultures, and that has had an impact both on the way that a particular government views a Christian community and on the way that a particular Christian community formulates its political theology. This chapter looks at the situation in contemporary China, whose government typically views Christianity as a Western religion that is hostile toward Chinese culture—and has developed a policy that reflects this view. Christian communities in China, in turn, have developed theological outlooks that are unique to their situation.

Chinese Communist theoreticians have concluded that the collapse of the USSR was merely a *result* of the Cold War, in contrast to the common interpretation that it marked the *end* of the Cold War.[1] This interpretation indicates that China continues to look at the world through the lens of the Cold War and that China formulates foreign policies, as well as its policies that affect Christianity, based upon this political perspective. And if that is indeed the case, the Chinese government's attitude toward Christianity[2] is more historical-political than socio-administrative, and it stands to reason that it will differ in character from other religions. This chapter, then, looks first at the general hostility toward Christianity in China before the Cold War, followed by the Chinese government's policy toward Christianity during the Cold War period (that is, from 1950 to 1980). It next considers the Chinese government's current religious policies, focusing on patriotic education schemes and "anti-infiltration" vigilance. These policies suggest a continuation of a Cold War mentality, despite the rapid liberalization in other Chinese social spheres (such as in urbanization or with respect to the free-market economy). Finally, the chapter highlights the ecclesiological challenges that face Chinese Christians living in this historical-political context—challenges that stem from the fact that the very existence of this community is often perceived, by civil authorities, to be a liability that endangers national security. This situation, I suggest, resonates with Barth's claims about the Confessing Church in relation to National Socialism in Germany during the 1930s.

PRE-COLD WAR PERIOD (1840S TO 1946)

Christianity came to China in the mid-nineteenth century, when Western powers were most intensively pursuing colonialist projects. China was forced to open its ports for trade with the West through a force often described as "Gunboat Diplomacy," and it was in this context that missionaries began to proselytize, beginning with coastal cities and gradually moving into all parts of China. There had also been a series of unequal treaties signed between China and various Western powers that granted foreigners, including missionaries, extraterritoriality and other privileges. In effect, China became a semi-colonial territory under different Western forces.[3] This foreign intrusion, along with the inept Qing dynastic government, triggered strong anti-Western sentiments among the Chinese public and intelligentsia. One result was Chinese nationalism, which played a significant role in the eventual overthrow of the more than three-hundred-year-old Qing Imperial Dynasty in 1911.

During this turbulent period, from the mid-nineteenth century to the fall of the Qing Dynasty, hostility toward Western influence could be seen all over China as a general instance of xenophobic expression (consider, for instance, the resistance to building railways and the Boxer Rebellion). Despite the contributions made by missionaries in the fields of education, medicine and social service, Christianity was often identified with the powers that invaded China, since it came to China under the general protection of the Western forces, be they diplomatic, military, or commercial. Furthermore, some missionary pioneers did not have the most honorable status in the eyes of the Chinese. Consider, for instance Robert Morrison: He was praised in the missionary circles as the first Protestant to translate the Bible into Chinese, yet also served in the East India Company as the interpreter involved in the selling of opium to China. There were also hundreds of local conflicts between Western missionaries and the local Chinese that Western powers exploited, resulting in more and more concessions to Chinese interests and the further expansion of foreign influence. Humiliations of this kind became a trauma haunting the Chinese national psyche, and Christianity was often identified as bound up with Western imperialistic forces that undermined Chinese sovereignty. Indeed, hostility toward the introduction of Christianity into China can still be noted among intellectuals in some influential Chinese publications.[4]

The 1911 Republican revolution ushered in a new political era for China as the Imperial Qing Dynasty was overthrown by revolutionaries, many of whom were Christians—including the father of modern China, Sun Yat-sen. Nonetheless, Christianity and the Republican revolutionary endeavor have hitherto not been linked or highlighted, even granted that a high percentage of these revolutionaries were Christians—a rarity in those days.[5] Although Republican China soon embraced science and democracy as symbols of a new and modern China, Christianity—an icon of modernism for many—was only on the fringe of the building of the nation. Ironically, one of the early national movements, the May Fourth Movement of 1919,[6] gave rise to the Anti-Christian Movement, which challenged Christianity as serving the interests of Western powers and undermining Chinese nationalism. Indeed, whereas Korea's nationalist movement had a disproportionally large number of Christian members, who opposed the Japanese colonization of Korea, and later Korean Churches became the incubator for Korean nationalism, the opposite was the case in China. Perhaps Korea identified Christian missionaries to Korea—westerners and ethnic Koreans and Chinese from China—as liberation forces to empower Korean nationalism, whereas missionaries in China were seen by the Chinese as allies of the Western colonial and imperialistic forces. (This topic has not been sufficiently considered by scholars.)

Chinese Christianity, led by Western missionaries, did not seem to notice this tide of emerging nationalism. At the time, it seemed more preoccupied with self-congratulation regarding the growth of ecclesiastical influence in China than interested in echoing the national aspirations of China. Such attitudes are illustrated by the meticulous records of missionaries' work in China in a monumental volume entitled *Christian Occupation of China*.[7] Either extremely insensitive to the rising nationalism in China, or utterly arrogant, or simply naive, the very title of this missionary publication carried strong colonialist overtones. Fortunately, it was published in English, not being intended to be read by Chinese "heathens," but by those foreigners who undertook such "occupying" endeavors; and, as such, it was not widely known outside the small Christian circle in China. Otherwise, this publication about China could easily have triggered another wave of anti-Christian campaigning.[8]

During the following three decades (from the 1920s to 1949), China entered into a period of protracted conflict, first among the warlords, and later between the Nationalists and the Communists, and also with war against Japanese invasion when Japan annexed Manchuria. There was no effective central government, and the country was ruled at different times, often simultaneously, by various government bodies: the Nationalist government, Communist (Soviet) governments, the Japanese Occupied government, the Japanese-sponsored Manchukuo government, and regional warlords. The overwhelming desire of most Chinese people was therefore to defend China from foreign aggression and to build a united, sovereign nation. This intense patriotic sentiment drove many to search for ideological and political solutions that would "save" China: socialism as modeled by the USSR after the Bolshevik Revolution and democracy as modeled by the Western parliamentary system being the two main options, represented respectively by the Chinese Communist Party and the Nationalist Party. Both camps had their supporters and a quite large segment of the intelligentsia sided with the Communists (who were seen as the underdog), since the Nationalist government was perceived to be corrupt, authoritarian, and riddled with cronyism. However, within missionary circles and among Chinese Christians, leaders generally favored the Western-backed Nationalist Party. Both the Generalissimo Chiang Kai-shek and his wife were baptized Christians, with strong ties with the United States, and few dared to side with Communism as it was regarded as anti-Christian, especially from the 1920s to 1940s.[9] In political terms, then, Christianity in China tended to take the side of the Nationalist government and adopted a hostile stance toward Communism.[10] It was this political position that later led to the church being viewed as an enemy of the state and being targeted for political suppression.

Given this course of events, the Christian missionary endeavor is often thought to have taken advantage of colonialism for missiological purposes, while also denying Chinese Christians the opportunity to support national sovereignty and to take pride in the nation. This has put an obvious strain on church-state relations. Furthermore, the ecclesial self-understanding of Chinese Christians often seems to challenge a core value of the Gospel: liberation from political bondage. The ultimate question, one might say, is whether a Chinese Christian can genuinely identify with the national sentiment of his or her sovereign nation and, at the same time, be truly faithful? Often Chinese Christians have been forced to stand against their own national aspirations in order to do justice to their faith—itself brought by Western missionaries tagging along with political forces hostile to China. Such dilemmas serve as the backdrop to the Chinese political arena in which the Chinese Church would later pay a dear cost.

COLD WAR PERIOD 1 (1946 TO 1966)

The Cold War generally refers to the confrontation between the two super-powers—the United States-NATO bloc and the USSR-Warsaw Pact bloc—that lasted from 1947 to 1991. During this period there was no large-scale direct fighting, but two major regional wars did occur: Korea and Vietnam. Rather than direct confrontation, two camps seeking to achieve global dominance through indirect means: psychological warfare, espionage, and technological competition, for instance. At first, China sided with the USSR, but later rallied with other nonaligned nations to form a third camp, following the reestablishment of diplomatic relations with the United States in the 1970s. China, in some sense, was part of the Cold War formulation for only a decade, from the 1950s to the early 1960s.

On the eve of the founding of the People's Republic of China in 1949, there was an exodus of the Nationalist government and army, rich tycoons, foreign expats, Christian leaders and missionaries, all of whom sought to flee the Chinese Communists—this being, in part, the result of Cold War propaganda by the Nationalists that portrayed communists as anti-religious beasts. Most went to Taiwan; some left for Hong Kong. Once the Korean War began in 1950, China faced the US-led UN forces, and regarded the countries to which these forces belonged as enemy states. The official Chinese title for this con-flict is the "Anti-America Aid-Korea" War, and soon there were nationwide Anti-America Aid-Korea Movement campaigns to rally support for China's military involvement in Korea. This name carries strong political implica-tions for understanding the Sino-US confrontation, by way of the Korean conflict. The *real* enemy seemed to be the United States, which also backed the renegade regime—as seen by the new Chinese regime—of the Nationalist government that had retreated to Taiwan. This new Chinese regime soon confiscated all US assets in China and expelled most of remaining western-ers, of which a significant portion were missionaries, as it was feared that these people would become a "fifth column" serving the interests of China's enemies.[11] Concomitantly, the United States imposed economic sanctions on China, confiscated China's assets (and handed them to the Nationalist gov-ernment), and blocked China's entry into the United Nations. A Cold War was, in effect, fought between China and the United States, with the ultimate prize being dominance in Asia.

Since the majority of the Christian churches in China had long been led, influenced, and supported by Western missionaries, it was natural for the new Chinese regime to entertain suspicions as to the loyalty of Chinese Christians toward the socialist government. In the context of Sino-US hos-tility, Christians were forced to demonstrate their loyalty to the regime by renouncing relations with their Western counterparts, denouncing the West (and especially the US-led aggression in Korea), and pledging allegiance to the new Communist government. Endorsed by the government, in September 1950 some Christian leaders issued a "Three Self Declaration" (self-administer, self-support, and self-propagate) in order to declare the independence of the Chinese Church from Western control, and initiated a Chinese Protestant "Three Self Patriotic Movement." It is particularly noteworthy that patriotism was tied to the "Three Self" ecclesial position—the implication being that if one were to refuse separation from the Western mother church, denomination, or missionary board, one would not be patriotic toward the new China. Ecclesial independence from Western Christian institutions became, in fact, the litmus test for acceptance by the new Chinese government. And by 1951, this movement included the Cold War element—anti-Americanism—and was renamed as the "National Preparatory Committee for the Anti-America Aid-Korea Three-Self Reform Patriotic Movement for the Protestant Church of China." This long title sent a clear message: a Chinese Christian would not be regarded as patriotic if he or she retained ties with the West.

After the cessation of the Korean conflict,[12] this Committee dropped the "Anti-America Aid-Korea" term from its title and became commonly known as the "Three Self Patriotic Movement," or simply the "Three Self Movement." Soon all Christian churches were urged to join the "Three Self Movement," which effectively led to the expectation that all Christians in China would follow the government's political direction, and do so under the banner of patriotism. Those who failed to join were regarded as anti-government or anti-revolutionary—a serious crime in China, subject to harsh punishment and usually long sentences in a labor camp. Congregations that failed to join were disbanded, and some Christians soon disappeared from public. Ironically, these events led to clandestine Christian communities meeting in homes, and thereafter what is now known as the House Church Movement.

During this period of the Cold War, Christianity in China in general bore a negative social, political and historical connotations, and became almost an outcast group associated with anti-government forces. It had to work extremely hard to gain acceptance in the new regime and to prove its patriotism. As such, its official national body—the Chinese Protestant Three Self Patriotic Movement—repeatedly issued statements denouncing the West, especially the United States, and supported the USSR on such matters as the US involvement in the Indo-China Conflict and the Cuban crisis.[13] Its leaders, such as Bishop K. H. Ting of Nanjing, openly endorsed the USSR's suppression of the 1956 Hungarian Uprising.[14] The pulpit in Chinese Churches was frequently used for sermons that praised the new socialist government's achievements: the class struggle was presented in terms of the triumph of the working class, with Jesus depicted as a model carpenter, and the Jerusalem community in Acts was presented as a prototype of the modern commune.

It is interesting to note that during this period only Catholics and Protestants, among all religious groups in China, were asked to denounce the West and to prove their patriotism. There was actually a Slavonic Orthodox Church in China which had, at its height in the mid-1950s, two hundred thousand members and more than one hundred and twenty parishes. Yet because of USSR-China relations, the Orthodox Church was not required to renounce Russia; in fact, some factions that belonged to the Russian Orthodox Church in exile, and that expressed antagonism to Moscow's Patriarchate, were asked to pledge allegiance to Moscow. Later in 1956, the Orthodox Church in China became autonomous, yet retained spiritual ties to Moscow. In contrast, the Buddhist, Daoist, and Muslim communities were simply regarded as parts of Chinese society. No attempt was made to draw them under the banner of Chinese patriotism. These three religious groups have no link with the West nor have they been linked with foreign forces hostile to China; and, unlike the Protestant and Catholic Christian communities, none of these three religious organizations were required to add a "patriotic" prefix to their names. They were simply asked to scale back some of the traditional practices, given that religion in general was regarded as backward and superstitious—a hindrance to the progress of the scientific society that China was supposed to become.

In general, the government's policy was a form of confinement in religious venues and containment at the individual level, the purpose of which was to ensure that religion could be practiced by believers but not have a negative influence on society. Different religions in China were therefore treated differently in this period of Cold War. Those with no Western ties were accepted as part of society subject to general socialist education; those with ties to the West (i.e., the Christian church) were targeted as potential enemies of the state and were required to denounce these ties and to earn their place in society by showing patriotism. Chinese Christians, in other words, were always suspected of being opposed to socialism in China.

During the 1950s and 1960s, then, the Chinese Church had to justify its existence as a Christianized proletarian community that supported the socialist class struggle and opposed capitalist aggression. The theological justification for the "Three Self Movement" during this period was to interpret the Gospel as a liberation force for the peasants and workers against the exploitation of greedy capitalists, with Jesus being presented as the model worker par excellence. This theological justification has been largely overlooked and ignored by Western theologians, who have simply regarded it as nothing more than Communist propaganda. Yet the perspective adopted by Chinese Christians is, ironically, somewhat similar to the liberationist perspective developed by later Latin American theologians. Could this neglect be another example of political discrimination or prejudice against Christians in the developing world, in this case Christians in Communist China? Or does it represent a patronizing attitude of the Western Christian academia against the "younger churches"—those without fluency in Greek and Hebrew, and those who are not well versed in Barth's *Kirchliche Dogmatik*; communities that are thought hardly qualified to undertake serious and credible theological endeavors—and therefore reprises the same colonial mentality that China and the "Three Self Movement" opposed when making Christianity credible and relevant in socialist China? Or was it a form of Christian anti-communism, popular among Christians in the West, yet regarded by Barth to be as "a matter of principle an evil even greater than communism itself,"[15] given that it interprets any theological endeavor from Christians in Communist regions as heretical or merely propaganda by the government?

COLD WAR PERIOD 2 (1966–1990)

China soon fell under the Great Proletarian Cultural Revolution (1966–1976), in which all religion, patriotic or otherwise, was suppressed. In terms of development, this ten-year period of turmoil effectively set China back more than a decade. Although some Western theologians in the early 1970s tried to present the Chinese Cultural Revolution as God's attempt to build a new heaven and earth, and China's "new Communist man" as the new creation of the New Testament epistles,[16] such naive idealizations—propaganda, really— were soon discredited by the horror stories about the reality of the Cultural Revolution, which became public in the late 1970s,

In political terms, during this period the Cold War was at its height, with the United States and the USSR engaged in multiple races for supremacy: space technology, nuclear armament, missiles, sport, culture, manufacture, and so on. China rebelled against the USSR's communist leadership by challenging the USSR's communist ideology in the early 1960s, and later reestablished ties with its former archenemy, the United States in the early 1970s. These developments released China from Cold War dynamics and perhaps accelerated the end of the Vietnam War, freeing up US resources to refocus its attention on Europe. Yet it was not until the late 1970s that China's "Reform and Open" policy put the nation back on a track for progressive development. From the end of the 1970s until the early 1990s, with China temporarily out of the Cold War equation, the United States and the US-led NATO alliance (under Ronald Reagan and Margaret Thatcher's leadership) put many resources and much effort into Europe to challenge the USSR, eventually leading its collapse—and thus ending the Cold War's European front. Meanwhile, China no longer viewed the West as an enemy, but rather as a partner and the object of learning. The international order was a tripartite situation with two superpowers confronting each other and China as the emerging power taking a sideline: embracing socialism, yet experimenting with capitalism.

During the later period of the Cold War, religion was also liberalized in China. However, unlike other social spheres, such as education, economics, and science—where new liberalized policies were in place such that they could develop rather freely—religion still followed the basic policy of containment and confinement that had been used in the 1950s. While all other spheres were encouraged to have contact with their counterparts aboard to learn the latest developments in their respective fields, religion was limited in its contact with the West. A special clause was included in the constitution to make sure that religion would not be under "foreign" domination as it had in the past. Furthermore, strong anti-infiltration measures were put in place to limit foreign influences on the Chinese Church, namely the foreign missionary activities in China, from exposure to Western influence. It seemed that the same paranoid fear of Western influence, along with intense mistrust of the Chinese Christians concerning their intentions, lingered on from the Cold War since the 1950s. The sudden influx of foreign missionary activities from the so-called China ministry especially targeted the House Churches, which had mushroomed since the early 1980s; this fed paranoia about Western influence on Chinese sovereign affairs and re-enforced the Chinese authority's decision to adopt a very cautious attitude toward Christianity, depicted as a Western agent to undermine China.

In this context, the Chinese Church had few options other than to parrot the government's desires and to justify its existence theologically. Because no criticism of the state was permissible, the Chinese Church adopted a seemingly apolitical stance.[17] One of the early attempts by Chinese theologians in the 1980s was the advocacy of a Theology of Reconciliation by Chen Zeming, a faculty member of the Nanjing Theological Seminary. Zeming encouraged reconciliation between the church and China,[18] acknowledging that the church had in the past committed sins that sought to rob the country of its pride, dignity, and sovereignty. It is rather refreshing to note theological work that looks at the sins of the church against a nation or a society, and confesses its past misdeeds! However, the "crimes" identified seem politically shaped and not all Christians agree with such a confession. Nevertheless, given the context, what other theological option did the Chinese Church have?

POST-COLD WAR (OR CONTINUATION OF THE NEW COLD WAR): 1991 TO 2013

The fall of the Berlin Wall marked a new era in Europe, and was followed by rapid changes in Eastern Europe and the disintegration of the USSR in 1991.

From this point onward, the US-NATO bloc faced no archenemy, and the new international order became a US-led financial-economic global network. Yet the emergence of China as a global power (second, in economic terms, to the United States after 2015) challenged US dominance. It also gave rise to what Chinese Communist theoreticians construed as the continuation of the Cold War, whereby the United States and its political-economic allies aim to contain China, perceiving it as the major threat to the United States' global interests. Furthermore, the United States is seen to be fighting a non-military proxy war with China through economic warfare, technological competition, and ideological agendas such as democracy, religious freedom, human rights, and so on.

Despite the tension with the United States, China has continually maintained its "Reform and Open" policy. This Policy of the Chinese Government since the early 1990s to the present, has fundamentally changed many spheres of livelihood—market, economics, employment, housing, social service, education, traveling, and foreign interactions, for instance. However, China's basic attitude toward religion remains unchanged. Containment and confinement are still the fundamental policies. Among the various religious groups, the government has given vast resources to Buddhists and Daoists, ushering them into the international arena as part of China's "soft power" initiative,[19] and local governments have often supported local religious practices as a vehicle to bolster communal cultural identity. Since Islam is closely associated with the policy on ethnic minorities—of which many are Muslim—the government's stance toward Islam is in accordance with its National Minority Policy, not Religious Policy, which amounts to a generous approach to win supports from the ethnic minority groups that embraced Islam in China. The government even officially recognizes certain New Religious Movements recently introduced to China, such as the LDS Church (Mormon) and Baha'i. However, the policy toward Christianity remains stiff and hostile, as noted by the recent government campaigns to tear down hundreds of crosses from church buildings in Zhejiang Provinces.[20] The following issues bear the impress of the Cold War, and have appeared in all major government documents associated with Christianity: "Peace Evolution," "Patriotic Education," and "Anti-infiltration."

With the fall of the Berlin Wall and the collapse of the USSR, the Chinese authorities commissioned a team of social scientists to investigate the cause of the collapse, in order to ensure that China would not share USSR's fate—especially as China had just experienced the Tiananmen Square incident on June 4, 1989, contemporaneous with the unrest in Eastern Europe that led to the eventual fall of Communist rule in the Eastern bloc. The team concluded that the collapse of Communism was primarily due to long-term, coordinated efforts of the United States and NATO to undermine the basic structure of socialist countries through cultural, political, and economic means. For example, Radio Free Europe spread propaganda behind the Iron Curtain to promote the supremacy of capitalism; the Vatican worked with the United States (via the Catholic Church in Poland) to organize workers to confront the government through the Solidarity Movement; various cultural foundations—the Ford Foundation, for example—promoted democracy and human rights through academic and cultural exchanges; the Lutheran Church in East Germany provided refuge for dissidents; and various commercial enterprises applied pressure on exports from the Eastern bloc as a form of economic sanctions. All these factors, suggested the researchers, were carefully orchestrated by the United States as part of the grand strategy of the Cold War. The Chinese named this strategy "Peace Evolution" (*He Ping Yan Bian*). Nothing was said about the inefficiency of the Soviet economic system, its near-economic bankruptcy due to the arms race, the steady decline of quality of life in the Eastern bloc, and increasing dissatisfaction with corrupt and autocratic governmental regimes—as in Romania—that deviated from communist ideals. Regardless of the accuracy of the team's report, "Peace Evolution" became an important political concept used by the party leadership to describe the Western strategy to undermine communism via non-military means, from the Cold War, to the "Color Revolutions," to the current containment strategy of the United States and its allies. Christianity, allegedly, played an important part on all fronts.[21]

Since that time, the concept of "Peace Evolution" has often been used when formulating religious policy, and especially as it pertains to Christianity, since Christianity is seen as vulnerable to manipulation by hostile Western forces as a way to undermine the Chinese regime. One representative view is that of Secretary General Wang Zuoan of the State Administration for Religious Affairs. He suggests that in order to protect the security of China, the country must be careful to implement "Peace Evolution" in the area of religion, so as to ensure that China does not follow in the footsteps of the USSR.[22] The government is encouraged, in other words, to make sure that the Christian church is not used by enemy forces to promote Western values that might jeopardize China, since China perceives that the West continues to employ this strategy,[23] for example in the name of Human Rights, as they did with the USSR in the past.[24] Consequently, the government limits the contact of Chinese Christians with their Western counterparts, especially those who may promote ideas such as human rights, freedom, democracy, and so on, through their support of Autonomous Christian Communities in China.[25] As a result, the Christian Church in China cannot autonomously make contact with its overseas counterparts: all contact must be vetted by the civil authority. This measure is undertaken because of the fear that "Peace Evolution" is occurring in China. And it is, indeed, a challenge to ecumenism and inter-ecclesial fellowship, since the church forfeits the right to relate to other Christian groups in exchange for political acceptance by the government.

Since 2005, the State Administration for Religious Affairs (SARA) of the Chinese Central government has initiated a nationwide campaign for patriotic education among religious groups, and particularly for professional religious workers such as pastors and monks. A general textbook has been produced, along with a defined curriculum, to be taught first at all religious schools, such as seminaries or Buddhist schools, and later to all professional religious workers.[26] The general curriculum states that the current development and achievements of China in recent years is the result of the Party's leadership, which means that patriotism and support of this leadership is required. There are also particular textbooks that cater to individual religions, such as books for Muslims, Protestants, and Daoists.[27] Teaching materials for Daoists emphasize the religion's historical support of the regime, as well as its preservation of Chinese traditional culture, and encourage the continuation of this stance.[28] In terms of Islam, the emphasis is on the inclusion of Muslims in the Chinese population for national unity and ethnic harmony, so as to challenge the separatist movement among the Uighurs, who constitute the largest group of Muslims in China. Patriotic education for them means striving for national unity.[29] The Protestant textbook highlights the unpatriotic past of the Christian Church in China, given that it entered China via Imperial forces, and notes Protestantism's links to political forces hostile to China. Patriotism for Christians would, then, mean independence from Western influence and domination, as well as wholehearted support of the current regime. Christianity, on this reckoning, is still associated with anti-Chinese Western forces, and is still stigmatized as potentially unpatriotic—despite the contributions that this community has made to the building of the nation for the last sixty years. This emphasis on the past is either an unhealthy fixation that refuses to face reality or an excuse to maintain vigilance over Christianity in China, interpreted through the lens of the continuing Cold War. Such patriotic education also raises an interesting theological issue: What is the role of Patriotism and nationalism in the context of church-state relation, particularly in the context of China, when Christianity is an extremely small community that carries a political stigma and has virtually no sociopolitical bargaining power? Can a Chinese Christian genuinely love his or her country, even though this country is ideologically anti-Christian? Love thy enemy? Should a Chinese Christian suffer because of the political "crimes" committed by his or her predecessors? And what characterizes the relationship between the Chinese Church and the ecumenical family when so many of its Western counterparts sided with political forces hostile to China, as in the current situation of Sino-US tension?

In all the major documents of the officially sanctioned Christian Church in China (the TSPM/CCC), there is always the term "anti-infiltration," used against non-sanctioned foreign missionary activities in China. In its latest national report, not only did TSPM/CCC stress the significance of anti-infiltration, but it also identified the need for the Christians to build up an "anti-infiltration" capacity as one of its main ecclesial objectives.[30] It seems that the government is concerned about unmonitored foreign relations with the Christian community, as if this community could potentially be a "fifth column" serving anti-government forces. Talk of "anti-infiltration" does not appear in other religions in China, and it applies particularly to Christians—as if this community is not only untrustworthy but also poses a national security threat. Identifying a community as a national security risk normally happens only if a nation is at war or under the threat of war (such as in the case of World War II when the US government interned ethnically Japanese people, regarding them as potential enemies of the state). In this case, the Chinese government again interprets Christianity through the prism of the post-USSR Cold War and classifies Christianity, because of its historical ties and current affinity to the West, as a national security issue. The issue of anti-infiltration also raises some important theological issues. For instance: Should the issue of national security preclude Christians from embracing missionary efforts and evangelism when non-nationals are involved? What kind of the theological reflection ought to be undertaken with respect to the issue of nationality, foreign and local, as it relates to ecclesiastical structures? Finally, could there be theological reflection on the ecclesiology of a national church, situated within a xenophobic state, that can still incorporate the universality of ecclesial community?

CONCLUSION

In principle, the Chinese Constitution grants all citizens the freedom of religious belief and grants all religions equal rights.[31] In practice, however, the Chinese government seems to favor Buddhism and Daoism, supposing that both are well integrated with Chinese culture and society and neither engage in confrontations with the government. Islam is treated more as a minority population than a religious issue. Christians are singled out as threats to the state in the context of "Peace Evolution," and is viewed in terms of specific measures, such as "anti-infiltration" and patriotic education. Motivating this treatment is a very strong anti-Western sentiment, which views all elements of Western culture as a form of infiltration and as part of the "Peace Evolution," which aims to destroy China. This view has been widely circulated by intellectuals and popularized among Party Members.[32]

Despite such hostility, the Christian Church in China strives not only to survive and prosper but, in recent years, has even developed a vibrant community numbering tens of millions of adherents, and it operates the largest Bible printing press in the world. What is the modus operandi of Chinese

Christians to overcome political constraints, both historical and contemporary? Not only the leaders of the TSPM/CCC churches but also most of the leaders of the Autonomous Christian Communities, express support of the current government as law-abiding citizens. Is their submission to the government in conflict with the ecclesial vision of the Confessing Church, supported by Barth through the Barmen Declaration, which urged German Christians not to pledge political allegiance to the Nazi regime—a confrontational stance that led to the eventual suppression of the Confessing Church? Does the lack of a public theology of the mainland Chinese Church, unlike its counterparts in other Chinese-speaking parts of the world—such as those in Hong Kong who have loudly and publicly advocated public values, formed alliances with sectarian forces for sociopolitical actions like the Occupied Central movement in 2014[33]—make the church more or less socio-politically relevant in the long run?

Unlike the Presbyterian Church in Taiwan, which heroically stood up against the regime to witness like a martyr and suffered accordingly, expressing the immanence and the incarnate nature of God, the church in China has taken a silent role, suffering without raising its voice in public and thereby expressing the transcendence of the divine. However, a seemingly powerless ecclesial community in China seems to have become one of the most powerful ecclesial communities in contemporary Christendom, and one that may challenge many theological assumptions about missiology and ecclesiology—the paradoxical power of the powerlessness. It echoes the spiritual power suggested by the Christology of Philippians and the parable about the dough and the yeast, which silently yet powerfully transforms society. Most importantly, what theological paradigm emerges from the living example of the Chinese Church? Does it challenge our view of church-state relations, whereby the church should depend on the state? How can the church live in relation to a state that offers a constant academic and a spiritual challenge?

Theological speculations notwithstanding, the outcome seems to be that the Chinese Christian communities have experienced unprecedented growth without taking a confrontational stance toward the government. This ecclesial paradigm from China, be it within the framework of the Cold War or not, is making its presence felt in Chinese society, and is making its imprint in Christendom.

NOTES

1. In October 2013, the National Defense University of the People's Liberation Army released a movie entitled *Silent Contest*, which represents the thinking of the

Leftist fraction that is currently gaining control in China. At the beginning of the movie, the Chinese Communist Party's view on the Cold War is reprised: the collapse of the USSR is a result, not the end, of the Cold War. The narrator then goes on to suggest that China is the United States's next target. This movie went "viral" in China and had been briefly suspended during the Party's Central Committee meeting in November 2013; however, it has now become the framework for national policy by the new Chinese leadership relating to foreign and domestic affairs. It has also generated numerous discussions among Chinese "netizens," even as it has been almost ignored by Western scholars. The movie is easily obtainable on websites such as Youtube; see, for instance, http://www.youtube.com/watch?v=M_8lSjcoSW8.

2. Christianity in this chapter refers to Protestantism. The Chinese government classifies Protestantism, Roman Catholicism, and Orthodox Christianity as three different religions. This chapter will not discuss the situation of the Catholic Church, which is complicated by Sino-Vatican relations, and is a diplomatic as well as a religious matter. The Orthodox Church has perhaps only 20,000 to 30,000 adherents in China: a tiny and scattered community, currently not significant enough to bear major implication on socio-religious matters in China.

3. Although Japan is not a Western nation, its successful Meiji Restoration made Japan a rather powerful and western*ized* nation—one that was part of the Western forces that occupied China from the late nineteenth century until the end of World War II.

4. See, for instance, Tong Xuan, "The Criminal History of Christianity in China," *American Studies* (Mei Guo Yan Jiu) Volume 3 (2007). Reprinted at Globalview.cn #428, January 2012; see http://www.globalview.cn/ReadNews.asp?NewsID=27541.

5. There seems to be either a subconscious or a deliberate omission of the impact of Christian faith on these Chinese revolutionary leaders by secular historians of contemporary China, perhaps due to ignorant, unsympathetic, or even hostile attitudes to Christianity. It was not until a hundred years after Dr. Sun's revolution that Professor John Y. Wong, an internationally recognized expert on Sun Yat-sen, conducted a landmark study on Sun's Christian faith and its impact on his political thinking. See *Sun Yetsen: Bible and Yijing* (Hong Kong: Chung Hwa Press, 2015).

6. Although China was on the winning side in World War I, at the signing of the Treaty of Versailles, the German-occupied territories in China were not given back to China; instead, they were given to Japan, another occupying force in China. The Chinese were angry and students from Beijing University led a protest on May 4, 1919, which soon became a nationwide movement of nationalism later referred to as the May Fourth Movement.

7. Milton T. Stauffer (ed., assisted by Tsinforn Wong and M. Gardner Tewksbury), *The Christian Occupation of China: A General Survey of the Numerical Strength and Geographical Distribution of the Christian Forces in China, Made by the Special Committee on Survey and Occupation, China Continuation Committee, 1918–1921* (Shanghai: 1922).

8. Somehow the official Chinese title of this publication is "China for Christ (Zhong Hua Gui Zhu)," a much less provocative rendering than the original English.

9. Bishop Ronald Hall of the Anglican Church was one of the very few church leaders who held a sympathetic attitude toward the Chinese Communist Party (CPC)

during the Sino-Japanese War. Several Chinese Anglican priests also went to Yan'an, the CPC revolutionary base, and even joined the Communist Party. See Edgar Snow, *Red Star Over China* (New York: Random House, 1938). Snow mentions a pastor named Wang serving as his interpreter; this man was a Chinese Anglican priest.

10. The political stance of "Christianity versus Communism" had been used by Nazi Germany as a justification for their invasion on the USSR—this being a "holy war" to protect Christian Europe against the Bolshevik atheism. Similar justifications were employed during the Cold War by the West to stress the confrontation between Christianity and Communism, rallying the church to support the ideological position held by the US-led Western world.

11. In 1949, some Catholic missionary priests were arrested and tried as spies for attempting to assassinate Communist leaders in Beijing. Later many US missionaries in China, mainly the Maryknoll Fathers, were arrested and tried as US spies. See Beatrice Leung and William Lau, *The Chinese Catholic Church in Conflict: 1949–2001* (Boca Raton: Universal Publishers, 2004), pp. 64–65.

12. The Korean War has not officially ended. There has simply been a ceasefire, agreed upon in 1953.

13. A cursory reading of the official Christian national publication *Tian Feng* from 1950 to 1966 would grant the reader a glimpse of heavily politicized Christian statements, echoing the political stance of the Chinese government on both domestic and foreign affairs.

14. The Theological Seminary of the Hungarian Reformed Church awarded Bishop Ting an Honorary Doctorate in Divinity at the end of 1956 when Ting visited Budapest, and the *causa honorais* was his support of the USSR's suppression of US-backed, anti-revolutionary action against the peace-loving Warsaw Pact community. In 1956, Ting was newly consecrated as a Bishop yet had no substantial publications—be the theological or otherwise. This writer saw this record at the Seminary in 2000.

15. Karl Barth, "No Angel of Darkness and Light," in *Christian Century*, January 20, 1960, pp. 72ff.

16. For example, see Lutheran World Federation/Pro Mundi Vita, ed., *Christianity and the New China*, 2 Volumes (South Pasadena, CA: William Carey Library, 1967), in which there was an article by an ananymomous writer titled: "Red China and the Self Understanding of the Church: Marxism, Leninism-Mao Tse-tung Thought and the Phillippine Revolution," Also Chu Mei-fen, *The Religious Dimension of Mao Tse-tung's Thought*, unpublished doctoral dissertation, Divinity School, University of Chicago, 1976.

17. Cf. Thomas Xutong Qu, "'Gleichnis wagen' Karl Barth's Political Theology and Its Meaning for the Church-State Relationship in Mainland China today," in this volume.

18. Chen Zemin, "Reconciliation with the People," in *A New Beginning: An International Dialogue with the Chinese Church*, eds. Theresa Chu and Christopher Lind (Toronto: Canada China Program, 1983).

19. Kim-kwong Chan and Alan Hunter, "Religion, Culture and Confucius Institute in China's Foreign Policy," in *China Foreign Policy*, ed. Emilian Kavalski (Surrey, UK: Ashgate, 2012), pp. 135–150.

20. Gao Shan, "Chinese Officials Tears Down Another Cross Ahead of Christmas," December 22, 2014, from Radio Free Asia, see http://www.rfa.org/english/news/china/cross-12222014171202.html.

21. See Jiang Zemin's "Party Secretary Jiang Zemin's talk on Resist Peace Evolution and Strengthen the building of the Party," in *Beijing Youth Daily*, August 23, 2001, see http://www.people.com.cn/GB/guandian/26/20010823/542133.html.

22. See Wang Zuoan, *The Religious Issues and Religious Policy of China* (in Chinese) (Beijing: Religious Cultural Press, 2002), p. 398.

23. Some missionary agencies' use of missionary rally slogans (such as "Christianization of China"), suggest a hope for the radical conversion of China from Communism to Christianity or conversion of large groups of the Chinese population. This fuels fears among the Chinese Communist leadership, leading to further entrenchment into the Cold War mentality of the Party members, with a particular hostility toward Christianity. See Fenggang Yang, *Religion in China: Survival and Revival Under Communist Rule* (Oxford: Oxford University Press, 2012).

24. Wang, *The Religious Issues and Religious policy of China*, p. 335.

25. The term "Underground Church" is often misleading: many of these officially non-sanctioned Christian groups are not clandestine. Rather, most of them are known and monitored by the authorities. The term "Autonomous Christian Communities," in contrast to those who registered with the "Three-Self Movement," is a more accurate description for the non-registered Christian groups. See Alan Hunter and Kim-kwong Chan, *Protestantism in Contemporary China* (Cambridge: Cambridge University Press, 1993).

26. SARA Edited, *Teaching Material for Patriotic Education (Aiguo Zhuyi Jiaocheng)* (Beijing: Religious Cultural Press, 2005).

27. There was no edition for the Catholics because they already had a series of "Patriotic Educational Materials" published by the Catholic Patriotic Association as a political defiance against the Vatican. These materials have been widely circulated. The Buddhist edition has not been published as the Buddhists in China are well known for their overwhelming support of the government, so that the need for such education is doubtful.

28. SARA Edited, *Patriotic Educational Curriculum for Daoism (Daojiao Aiguo Zhuyi Jiaocheng)* (Beijing: Religious Cultural Press, 2011).

29. SARA Edited, *Patriotic Education Curriculum for Muslim (Musilin Aiguo Zhuyi Jiaocheng)* (Beijing: Religious Cultural Press, 2006).

30. See the Work Report (2013), p. 22. From http://www.ccctspm.org/quanguolianghui/gongzuobaogao.html

31. See Kim-kwong Chan, Eric R. Carlson, *Religious Freedom in China: Policy, Administration, and Regulation—A Research Handbook* (Santa Barbara, CA: Institute for the Study of America Religion, 2005).

32. For example: Xi Wuyi, "Be careful of the Cultural Infiltration of the International Christian Right," in *Studies in Marxism* (2013) appeared at www.wyzxwk.com/Article/guofang/2013/07/303743.html, or Huang Cao, "The New Model of American Religious Infiltration to China and the Changes on Its Ideology," in *Forum of Chinese party Cadres* (2012), appears at www.wyzxwk.com/Article/gu

oji/2012/03/293387.html, and Zuo Peng, "Highly Aware the Spread of Christianity through Internet," in *Studies on Chinese Youth* (2012), appears at www.wyzxwk.com/Article/yulun/2012/05/296486.html.

33. Cf. Lai, Pan-chiu, "Religious Diversity, Democracy, and Public Theology: Conversing with Barth in a Hong Kong Context," in this volume.

Chapter 6

The Power of the Religio-Poietic Complex in Politics

Karl Barth's Strategies against the Nation Becoming Religiously Charged

Günter Thomas

INTRODUCTION

When Protestant theologians reason about the relation between politics and religion, they tend to focus on the relation between the church and the state. In doing so they concentrate on legal issues, legal privileges, and the historical trajectory of church-state interaction.[1] The political relationship is then assessed based on legal regulations. This perspective, however, overlooks a crucial element in politics, and hence a critical interface between religion and politics: political psychology. Both, a Habermasian universe of political theory and Protestantism, overlook the management of emotions that occurs in politics and religion.[2] Political psychology, in contrast, shifts attention to the muddy waters of emotional politics, attachment to the nation, and patriotism.[3]

Political psychology concerns everything before or beyond the rational exchange of arguments that characterizes political philosophy, such as rituals, body politics like demonstrations, inflammatory speeches and other forms of political mobilization, as well as seemingly nonrational motivations for political behavior in general and of voting in particular.[4] What matters most, in the field of political psychology, are all forms of special political bonds and loyalties between the individual and humankind.

Last but not least, nationalism is the hotspot for political psychology. As a matter of fact, a large part of the educated liberal disgust for populist politics is the apparent return of more emotional and less rational forms of public politics. At the same time, on the side of liberal Protestantism, the concepts of public theology tend to neglect political psychology as well.[5]

For that reason, a future-oriented debate about religion and politics, or Christianity and the state, must be expanded to a triangle: religion, nation/culture, and the state. In addition, this triangle opens the view to political dynamics which create forms of a political religion (or secular religion) which interact with "positive" or traditional religions such as Christianity. Any religious charge to politics seems to connect to such a religio-poiesis inside politics. In current media-societies, these religio-poietic processes will take place in large part on social-media.[6]

The central theses of this essay are the following:

During his whole intellectual development, Karl Barth's relation to politics was always concerned not only with the principle pattern of political and legal structures of the state but also with the inadequate religious charging of politics. To better understand Karl Barth's theology, I will look at two counter texts: First, I will shortly analyze a speech given by Otto Dibelius in 1918, which spells out religious nationalism. Second, I will turn to the mastermind behind many variants of religious nationalism: Fichte's eighth speech to the German nation, written under the sound of Napoleon's canons. Given key ideas and the reception of this speech by national socialists, this is a text from a "theo-political poison cabinet." In terms of hermeneutics, the following considerations acknowledge that in some cases—not in all cases—the removal of an inadequate answer does not eliminate the underlying question and problem. In such cases, a hermeneutic of moral disgust is not helpful, but only a hermeneutic of curiosity which is willing to look into the cabinet of such poisoned texts. Moreover, Fichte's text needs to be analyzed because its observations concerning political psychology are highly dated today.

This background needs to be highlighted since it is often overlooked in research on Barth's dealing with politics.[7] In a third step, I will have a closer look at two texts by Barth, first the classic Tambach lecture, and then at a more neglected text which is his discourse with the title: "Die Nahen und die Fernen," "The close and the distant ones." The fourth and final step will be a critical evaluation of Barth's responses to the problem posed by political psychology.

THE NATION AND THE FATHERLAND AS MEDIUM OF THE DIVINE, WHERE IMMANENCE AND TRANSCENDENCE MEET: OTTO DIBELIUS IN 1918

By many standards, Otto Dibelius was one of the vital public theologians not only of the first part of the twentieth century but through the 1960s. Born in 1880, he worked during World War I in a parish and later began his career in church administration. Before and during World War II, he was part of what is called national Protestantism and was a fervent proponent of anti-Semitism. In 1926, he published a hugely influential book: *Das Jahrhundert der Kirche* (The Century of the Church) in which he responded to the November Revolution of 1918. Due to conflicts with the National-Socialist Government, he lost his position as a high church official and later joined the Confessing Church. He was, however, a typical representative of those theologians who only resisted the political interventions into the church administration, not the other parts of the National-Socialist's politics. After World War II, he was not only the long-time chairman of the German Churches (1949–1961) but also a founding member of the executive committee of the World Council of Churches, and from 1954 to 1961, he served as its president. His public reputation as a leading public theologian is mirrored by the fact that he delivered the opening sermon to the first meeting of the democratic German parliament in 1949.[8] In Otto Dibelius' work, we can find two contrarian understandings of the state which can be characterized as "divinization of the nation-state" and "demonization of the nation-state."

The text in question was originally a speech Otto Dibelius gave in the first part of 1918 when he was a young pastor in Heilsbronnen. The series has the title: "Gott und die Deutsche Zuversicht"—"God and the German hope." The third speech is titled: "Das Ewige und das Vaterland. Diesseits und Jenseits"—"The Eternal and the Fatherland. Immanence and Transcendence."[9] The 38-year-old pastor declares:

> It is the highest religion, to conquer and die for justice and truth, to love the fatherland more than lords and princes, as fathers and mothers, as wives and children. This is the highest religion, to leave to his grandchildren a free land, a proud sense! (E.M. Arndt). For the sake of eternal life, which I feel within me and in which my hope for a future of my life extends beyond death, I am bound to this world of eternal, patriotic goods. [. . .] When I denied my fatherland, I denied love in its deepest, holiest power. If I denied my fatherland, then I denied humility and duty, sacrifice, and faithfulness. I don't want that. I can not do that. [. . .] But because my love for the Fatherland is a love for sacred, eternal goods, it therefore also rises on the wings of joyfulness above all the misery and anxiety of the present. [. . .] Nations of grocers, whose fatherland is nothing more than an insurance company for personal well-being, can go to ruin forever. [. . .] But a people for whom the fatherland is an eternally holy good can never break completely. The power of the Eternal will be stronger than all the calamities of this earthly time.[10]

What are the critical elements of Dibelius' strategy of divinizing the nation? First, religion is considered to be the force, the medium, and the practice of transcending one's own private and familial life. Religion provides the means of moving beyond "one's own, small and earthly life." This transcendence has a social, a temporal as well as a spatial dimension.

This power for transcending one's own life, however, does not lead into bad infinity or a realm of sheer otherworldliness. In religion we live, Dibelius argues, a higher life and belong to an eternal, invisible world; religion is not questionable escapism that leaves behind this earth.

Dibelius is not arguing for a religion of pure immanence, nor just an immanent transcendence, as some sociologists would do today. Like many theologians of the nineteenth century, Dibelius is convinced that "heaven and earth," the visible and the invisible, are united in what is called the "Gemüt." By focusing one's power of self-perception on this "Gemüt," one inevitably makes a stunning discovery: the fatherland is, as a matter of fact, the entity, in which the invisible is present in the visible—beyond any false immanentism or bad transcendence. According to Dibelius, only faith in some "Eternal" which shines in our life can give us the necessary energy and drive to love our fatherland. Only Christian faith can provide this love with the necessary seriousness. Dibelius vividly argues against pure and mundane immanence or—to use a term coined by Max Weber—a pragmatic "this-worldliness" concerning our understanding of one's fatherland. The functional and technical state apparatus as technical administration and service institution, as well as religion, both serve the fatherland, that is, the nation. In his opinion, the fatherland is God's craft shop, not just a "pile of ants."

"Only the belief in an eternal, which sheds light on our earthly life, gives patriotism the piercing earnestness and devotion to the people, the obligatory power we need when it comes to the ultimate" (4). In Dibelius' view, it is the Christian religion, that can add ultimate weight to the divinization of the nation. Since "eternity is carrying us like in the wings of an eagle," people can transcend everyday concerns, sorrows, and political suffering—because in the presence of the Eternal in the visible there is the power of the spirit. It is the Holy Spirit who carries the people into the sphere of the eternal, which makes them participate in eternal goods: "Love and humility, reverence and faith, truth and confidence, purity and joy of sacrifice" (8). "They set the radiance around the life of earthly things, which also transfigures and sanctifies them" (8). Halfway using tools from ecclesiology and pneumatology, Dibelius claims that the fatherland becomes the presence of the transcendent. The love of the fatherland brings Christians closer to Christ, simply because one of the eternal goods is the fatherland. "That I love my country and am obliged to sacrifice everything to it, I thank my Lord Christ. And the more sacred my country becomes, the closer I feel to Him" (11). Dibelius ends his speech with a final declaration: "In such a spirit, we lay hands on the sword, on the sword of German need, ready for resistance, ready to fight for the last.

And the God who in hard times was with our fathers, he will also be with us! Yes, he will be with us!" (14).

Looking at Dibelius' rhetorical moves, it becomes clear that he fashions the fatherland in analogy to the church. It is one spirit which unites the whole community, mobilizes a willingness to sacrifice. The new spiritual body can transcend all other social divisions and communities of solidarity. It is the presence of the spirit, which makes people endure and maintain hope—despite all counterevidence. As the church is elected in order to witness to the world, the specially elected German nation will testify to the world God's might and glory. As Christian discipleship asks for sacrifices, so the fatherland asks for sacrificial acts up to giving one's life. The symbols of Christianity become interpretive tools for constructing analogies, which in the end are not analogies. They are framing devices which eventually become, in their very function as framing devices, invisible. The resulting theological mix is not very clear.

To use our own distinctions: In Dibelius' speech, it is difficult to perceive where Christianity is meeting and framing, reinforcing and empowering theopoetic processes in the political world. Its function appears to be self-evident: The religious framing of politics serves the emotional mobilization. Religion, in its ability to mobilize and orchestrate deep-seated emotions, becomes part and parcel of political psychology. This is the function it serves. Religion becomes a cultural resource for forming and bonding a political community. It helps to activate a hot collective memory of fight and liberation.[11] The German national state was to a significant extent a "Protestant project."[12]

The interface between politics and religion, however, becomes much clearer by looking at the long tradition in which Dibelius stands. Dibelius' text "Das Ewige und das Vaterland" explicitly positions himself in a tradition dating back to the early nineteenth century. It was the philosopher Johann Gottlieb Fichte who inaugurated a specific kind of German nationalism in his famous "Addresses to the German Nation"—a text to which Dibelius refers at the very outset of his speech.

THE THEOLOGICAL AND CULTURAL DYNAMICS IN FICHTE'S DEIFICATION OF THE NATIONAL STATE: A THEORY OF LIFE

In order to understand the inner logic and the destructive potential of the deification of the nation-state and an utopian political romanticism, it is necessary to reach into the theological poison cabinet and to grant a patiently analytical look at a truly toxic text: Johann Gottlieb Fichte's eighth speech in his "Addresses to the German Nation." It is a text of liberation-theology and of a philosophy of resistance that emerged under the cannon-thunder of Napoleon in 1807 in Berlin. For us, the eighth speech, which is about the religious charge of the nation, is especially important. Without delving into the details of the philosophical reception of Fichte, there are ten basic decisions that contour his position—and, according to the thesis, make it seem extremely relevant, both for contemporary Protestant theology and for an up-to-date analysis of the wider political culture in 2019.

1. The starting point is Fichte's plea for a radically *naturalized religion of eschatology-free and transcendence-free immanence*. It is about "finding heaven on this earth, and to endow his daily work on earth with permanence and eternity, to plant and to cultivate the eternal in the temporal."[13] This life must not only be made to be "a forecourt of true life" (112). Fichte is utterly disinterested in the tropes of traditional Christian eschatology.

2. An *anthropology of self-transcendence and immanent transcendence* allows the individual to transcend himself socially (toward other people) and in time (toward his own future and the futures of others). In this social and temporal self-transcendence, man works on his own finitude. "What man of noble mind is there who does not earnestly wish to relive his own life in a new and better way in his children and his children's children, and to continue to live on this earth, ennobled and perfected in their lives, long after he is dead?" Who does not "want to scatter, by action or thought, a grain of seed for the unending progress in the perfection of his race, to fling something new and unprecedented into time, that it may remain there and become the inexhaustible source of new creations?" (113).

3. In these acts of moral self-transcendence, man transcends his self-referential nature through acts of love. These *acts of love create a "bond*, which unites first his own nation, and then, through his nation, the whole human race, in a most intimate fashion with himself, and brings all their needs within his widened sympathy until the end of time" (116). This band spans all intervening particularities. Any shorter span would indicate selfishness and would document that "the higher view of the human race" (118) has not yet been reached.

4. In an idea of *culture as a gift of life* (receiving and giving), Fichte sums up the insight that individual life owes its existence in many dimensions to previous lives. At the same time, life is passed on to others, not only those temporally and socially co-present but also to those in far distant times and spaces.

5. In the face of a *permanent endangerment life* and the giving of life, this notion of a life's endowment is linked by Fichte to a *theory of sacrifice*.

Those who have received life need to be prepared to use their own lives to pass on their lives. The self-abandonment as a sacrifice is the limit-case and the deep truth in the process of the passing on life. This notion of sacrificial behavior leading to a far-reaching conclusion: What people are willing to do for dying in their exchange of life is sacred to them. Sacrifice is self-sacrifice, which is in essence a sacrifice to the exchange of life. It is at this point where the moral self-transcendence reaches a religious level. Fichte's strong thesis is: Sacrifice for life lies at the core of the religio-poietic process in politics.

6. The *social form* in which the moral self-transcendence takes place, in which life-receiving and life-giving is accomplished and for which people are ready to sacrifice themselves (as a real sacrifice), is now for Fichte, not the family, not the city, not humanity as a whole, but truly *the nation*. It is the nation that evokes for their adherents the "confident expectation that they themselves would eternally continue to live in the eternity in the stream of time" (117).

7. Based on that insight, Fichte draws an important distinction *between the state and the nation or the people (Volk)*. People and fatherland, in this sense, as support and guarantee of eternity on earth and as that which can be eternal here below, far transcend the state in the ordinary sense of the word.

8. State and nation are not only separated but also related. It is undoubtedly clear to Fichte, "that the state, merely as the government of human life in its progress along the ordinary peaceful path, is not something which is primary and which exists for its own sake, but is merely the means to the higher purpose of the eternal, regular, and continuous development of what is purely human," and now Fichte comes to the point of "this nation" (125). This is the place of all transcending humanity. The nation itself is ultimately an imaginary construction that allows participation in the whole. The relation between state and fatherland is radically asymmetrical: "Love of fatherland must govern the state itself" (119).

9. This religious-moral self-transcendence is embedded in the idea of passionate politics, indeed *politics of passions*. What mobilizes people? Fichte poses a rhetorical question that touches the heart of political psychology: "What spirit has an undisputed right to summon and to order everyone concerned whether he himself be willing or not, and to compel anyone who resists, to risk everything including his life?" In hindsight directly formulated against Jürgen Habermas' constitutional patriotism, Fichte claims: "Not the spirit of the peaceful citizen's love for the constitution and the laws, but the devouring flame of higher patriotism, which embraces the nation as the vesture of the eternal, for which the noble-minded man joyfully sacrifices himself, and the ignoble man, who only

exists for the sake of the first one [the constitution] must likewise sacrifice himself. It is not the love of the citizen for the constitution, that love is quite unable to achieve this, so long as it remains on the level reason. [. . .] The promise of life here on earth extending beyond the period of life here on earth—that alone it is which can inspire men even unto death for the fatherland" (120f.).

10. The *particularity of a people* emerges out of history, related to its language and region (not blood and soil!). Also, a people is not just an emerging socio-cultural formation. In a people, and according to Fichte, in particular in the German people, two things come together, something which could be called as the fusion of emergence and election: A people viewed "from the standpoint of the spiritual world" is "the totality of men continuing to live in a society with each other and continually creating themselves naturally and spiritually out of themselves [emergence], a totality that arises together [*sic!*] out of the divine under a certain law of divine development" (115). This law determines the national character and is essentially divine. It is the "law of the development of the original [Ursprünglichen] and the divine" (115). It appears that this law creates a particular character and forms the distinct destiny of these special people and nation. The particularity of a distinct nation and people is perceived as a divine act. One could conclude that every people has its divine election and hence mission.

THE "TIMELESS" RELIGIO-POIETIC DYNAMIC— AN INTERMEDIATE REFLECTION

Looking at our reading of Fichte's theory of life and the dynamics of the religio-poietic complex (in short: RPC) with a more contextualizing and analytical gaze, we can hold on to the following key features and functions:

1. The religio-poietic dynamic in the theory of life sketched above is an integral, self-supporting cultural phenomenon, creating the RPC. It links both anthropology and cultural life and lies at the core of political psychology.

2. In the reading of Fichte proposed in this chapter, RPC can be detached from the sanctification of the nation. As a cultural theory of life, foci of attention, affection, adoration, preservation, development, defense, and worship can be other entities in the web of life. As seen in many regions of the world, an intensely perceived crystallization of life can be the family. As already envisioned by Fichte, humankind is a possible candidate. "Ultimate dependencies" (F. Schleiermacher) or "ultimate concerns" (P.

Tillich) can vary. There are many ways in which people go beyond a mere "immanent frame" (C. Taylor).

3. Can RPC be pluralized and democratized? In order to use a comparison: Is monotheism at the core of RPC, or can it be modeled along the line of polytheism? And: If yes, are the many gods in a battle or peaceful collaboration? Max Weber's famous image of the Gods ascending out of their graves in a disenchanted world points to a battle in a world of competing ideals and values in autonomous realms of reality (spheres of value).[14] Niklas Luhmann is convinced that the inescapable pluralism of value orientations in general and in particular in terms of last and final values are fueling conflicts and not creating unity—even though he considers shared values as a civil religion.[15] In a pluralized form, RPC can be used to decode the splintering of late modern societies in conflicting groups nourishing their own identity, with their own entity of worship and sacrifice.[16]

4. Contrary to Dibelius' use of it, RPC does not need to be clothed in or supported by traditional religion. RPC might borrow elements and transform, even banalize them. Even more, in order to function in real life, RPC does not need to be labeled (or self-labeled) as religion. It does not require a theistic semantic in order to excercise its power.

5. RPC is highly flexible and offers an enormous degree of plasticity so that different elements can move into the center. Over against traditional religions with their "Hinterwelt" (Max Weber and Friedrich Nietzsche) its truly *naturalized character* can be emphasized (1 above).[17] The dimension of *election* and manifest destiny can be stressed (10). Focusing more on *communication*, the creation of *community* bonds (3) or the nation as a unity of real and imaginative communication can come to the forefront.[18] The *intergenerational exchange* can be highlighted in issues of sustainability and preservations of the unity in question (4). If the *endangerment* is becoming prominent, a *battle* motive can be combined with the notion of a necessary *sacrifice* (5).[19] The bonds of love can remind us of the need to generate solidarity and compassion in distinct communities (3).[20] This plasticity is not a disadvantage but certainly an advantage in favor of specific adaptations.

6. Due to the many possible motives, RPC can serve as an attractor of many elements of Christian faith. Ranging from the preservation of nature in creation theology to the sacrifice of Christ, eschatology and the betterment of life, the uniting Holy Spirit or the doctrine of election—all these tropes and themes can be connected to RPC, depending what is placed at its center. Seen the other way around, many Christian tropes can supercharge RPC.

7. As dangerous as RPC might be—especially with a focus on the nation— Fichte's explicit thesis is that the procedures, services, and legal set-ups

of the state need a cultural grounding. There are, admittedly, quite a few ambivalences and even tensions in Fichte's use of the three concepts of the fatherland (Vaterland), nation, and people (Volk). RPC in its connection to language, history, story, and memory is, however, in essence, a thick concept of culture. As a consequence, the relation of Christian theology to the state cannot be detached from the other relation between culture on the one side and the state embedded in legal regulations and social structures on the other side. In reality, religion, state, and culture form a triangle.

Even if one launches all the necessary criticism against Fichte's fierce nationalism, his option for the nation remains at least an open question: to what extent does the state rely for its functioning on something like a united nation, a people with memory, community, and shared visions of the future.[21]

8. If RPC has some empirical traction and if also the connection to the nation has at least some evidence, it is pulling the rug from beneath a thin constitution-based patriotism (Verfassungspatriotismus), so beloved by the many adherents of Jürgen Habermas philosophy and those rightly concerned by the destructive powers of zealous nationalism. So the question is: "What type of national culture is supporting the constitutional democracy?"

9. Given the highly ambivalent history of RPC in Europe and Germany in particular, the issue on the table is the following: Can RPC be avoided or eliminated? If the answer is no, how can it be formed and shaped in favor of humanity? Metaphorically speaking, can it be dosed in a way, that is nontoxic? If it can be formed and shaped, what other cultural force can do that?

10. When Christian theology is facing RPC, a vexing question arises: Is Christian religion looking into the face of a sibling or even into a mirror? Alternatively, is Christian faith eyeball to eyeball with an enemy it has to fight? How should theology behave in this inevitable encounter with what is political culture's own religion—at least in the eyes of a comparative study of religion and in view of Christian faith?

In short: Most of Fichte's observations and ideas are not only powerful but seem to be well-timed. His plea for a religion of transcendence in immanence, his appreciation of the dynamics of life transmission, his view on the policies of the passions, his observation of the readiness of people to sacrifice themselves, his insights into the longing to improve this life and to care for the life of future generations—all this sounds very timely. Such ideas can easily be found on the left and the right. They are present in publications of Greenpeace, Physicians without Borders, or the Green party. Fichte's theory of life and sacrifice is embedded in many current, broadly speaking, left-wing NGOs. His ideas resonate with many ecological initiatives trying to preserve the planet for future generations.[22] The adored and simultaneously endangered objects in which the dynamics of life are manifest, one could say, incarnated, today include the ecosystem, human rights, the world's climate, and so on, while in the globalized world the working class appears to be more outdated. He appears to be contemporary—despite a temporal gap of 200 years. The problems he looks at are "daueraktuell" (N. Luhmann)—always timely.

There should be no doubt: Fichte's argument for the fatherland and nation, his sacrificial cult, his national chauvinism of the higher vocation of the German nation, and last but not least, his anti-Semitism in the approach are to be criticized. They had been fatal and deadly in their consequences. And yet, quite often underneath his questionable solutions are valid problems.

KARL BARTH'S STRATEGIES IN HIS FIGHTS AGAINST THE POWER OF POLITICAL RELIGIONS

If RPC is seen as an ongoing challenge, the responses given in Karl Barth's theology can be seen in a new light. The breadth and scope of his struggle with political religion and political psychology become visible. Given the nature of the religio-poietic dynamic, Barth's struggle is placed "in-between" his dealing with religion and his dealing with the state. For this reason, this struggle tends to be overlooked by both strands of research.[23]

In this chapter, I will only very briefly sketch out two types of responses we can find in Barth's writings. They do not exhaust Barth's dealing with theo-politics but are highly exemplary. Moreover, I will concentrate on two texts which are not the beaten track of Barth research. The extent to which Barth implicitly, at least, and partially explicitly moved beyond the dualism and the shortcut of church and state increasingly attracts scholarly attention.[24]

I will distinguish two models of response: (1) Decoupling of the Shortcut; and (2) Radical Desacralization and Demythologization. Another third strategy is manifest in Barth's classical texts on church and state. It has been interpreted many times (also in this volume).[25] I will, therefore, concentrate on the first and second strategy.

Strategy 1: A Theological Decoupling of the Shortcut—Karl Barth's Tambach Lecture of 1919

Karl Barth's sentences about his disappointment and theological irritations due to his theological teachers' plea in favor of World War I are well known. The ideology of "God with us," materialized on the buckle of the uniform belts, was sharply criticized.[26] However, the most direct and openly explicit critique of a sacralization of politics, that is to say, a version of RPC, can be found as early as Karl Barth's Tambach lecture. The Tambach Conference had been the founding event of a German section of Christian Socialists. Karl Barth was invited as a replacement for Leonard Ragaz, the leading Swiss religious socialist. The topic of the lecture was "Der Christ in der Gesellschaft"/"The Christian in Society."[27]

Barth's overall target in the long and complicated lecture is to decouple Christian faith from the RPC of political movements—without giving up the hope for God's transformative presence in the sphere of society and politics. He is, however, rejecting the religious supercharging of political movements—without reducing Christian hope and the work for justice.

Even though Barth's sincere sympathy with the social democratic party and his moderate closeness to religious socialism had been well known, the Tambach lecture is surprisingly critical of political instrumentalization, not on the nationalistic right, but the side of religious socialism. He targets the religious socialism represented by Leonard Ragaz, something astutely observed by Ragaz himself.[28] Specifically, Barth rejects the way religious socialism combines the presence of God in society with the certainty that God is present in the acts of Christians and this particular political movement.[29] Barth openly criticizes the equation of human political acts and divine acts. In short: Barth objects to the religious-socialist motto: "God with us." "Immediately to hand we have all those combinations—'social-Christian,' 'social-evangelical,' 'social-religious' (christlich-sozial, evangelisch-sozial, religiös-sozial), and the like—but it is highly questionable whether the hyphens we draw with such intellectual courage do not make dangerous shortcuts."[30] In what follows, the Tambach lecture presents not a political or a philosophical, but a genuinely theological critique of a Christian charging of RPC.

Barth does so by raising the bar for his critique. Barth rejects the simple, but theologically popular idea, that God is absent in society and present in the church, so that the sphere of the church needs to be expanded in order to bring God's transforming presence to the society. His bold claim is that both the political right and political left rely on "God with us" as a way of "secularizing Christ."[31] Barth justifies this claim by pointing to the wholeness and independence, that is to say, the living reality of God. "The Divine [. . .] does not permit of being applied, stuck to, and fitted in [. . .] for that it is more than religion." It is a two-sided argument. By religiously charging the socialist RPC with Christian faith and pretending that there is this distinct window of the Word of God and our world, God's power and presence are as actually domesticated and downsized. The sacralization is an act of domestication and hence an act of secularization, theologically speaking: another betrayal of Christ.[32] In reverse, the alternative model of a church expanding into the seemingly godless space of society is "the most dangerous way of betraying society."[33]

In order to dissolve this double-bind, Barth introduces a moderate version of what later will be called anonymous Christian. What both the religious socialists as well as the adherents of clericalism overlook is Christ's presence in the society which precedes any of their actions. For Barth, the title of the lecture given to him "Der Christ in der Gesellschaft" is interpreted as Jesus Christ present and active in this sphere. Christians can witness to this fact because they know the world to be in God's threefold movement and rule from regnum naturae, to regnum gratiae and eventually to the regnum gloriae.[34]

What can Christians do when they are neither directly building the kingdom of God nor waiting for it to come? What place can they occupy vis-à-vis RPC when they are neither "heated up" political Zealots nor "cool" political flaneurs?

Barth's far-reaching suggestion already put forth in 1919 is the building of parables of the kingdom.[35] The sphere of society and politics becomes the sphere of both careful and courageous building of parables which in this world of the regnum naturae and regnum gloriae become anticipations, models, so to speak, of the coming reign of God. Building parables transcends the verbal preaching of the Gospel. The criteria, however, to any criticism of RPC by building parables is Jesus Christ—which has far-reaching consequences not only for politics but also law.[36]

In terms of the religious management of revolutionary emotions, parables occupy a space in between the hot zeal of the revolutionary and the detachment of the flaneur. Although what is done in the fight for peace and justice does not have ultimate value, it is not without some value and significance. To rephrase Barth's theo-political intention, parables of the kingdom of God are faithful to the old and the new world of God. In the eyes of Leonard Ragaz, however, such an emphasis of "only relative significance" and this rejection of the real presence of the kingdom of God in the developments in history are equal to "eschatological pessimism."[37] What Barth is doing by decoupling both Christ himself and the Christian's building of parables from RPC is—seen clearly by his opponent—a betrayal of "the religious meaning of socialism."[38] Even though Barth is not decoupling faith from politics, Ragaz openly declares against Barth's strategy of decoupling: "Socialism [is] certainly something God willed and in this sense something absolute. For what God, the Absolute, wants is absolute."[39] The proponent of moral absolutes in politics is explicitly accusing Barth of "relativizing all ethical."[40]

Strategy 2: Radical Desacralization and Demythologization— Karl Barth's Treatment of Nation in 1951

In the last volume of his four-volume doctrine of creation, Karl Barth turns to the issue of humanity and human creatures' forms of social relations. After unfolding his anthropology and ethics of man and woman as well as parents and children, he turns to the issue of the nation as a form of social life. Shortly after World War II, he has to address the issue of nations and nationalism. Without explicit references, Barth's treatise is a direct address of Paul Althaus' and Walther Künneth's texts of a Christian embrace of the nation which could not resist a sacralization of the nation.[41]

Karl Barth's first implicit, yet decisive, decision is to separate the issue of a nation from the state. The nation-state is not the problem he wants to discuss. By rejecting the idea that a "nation" refers to a one-nation state, he is making a strong statement—both as a Swiss and as a theologian. At the same time, he opens up the possibility of considering nationhood in an ethics of creation—which was also the inroad to the problem for conservative Lutheran theologians. What Barth develops is almost paradoxical: a theological "non-theology" of the nation through deconstruction and a phenomenology of nationhood. Both strands of argumentation lead to a radical desacralization of the "hot topic" of nationhood.[42]

The fundamental doctrinal starting point, which Barth spelled out in length in other sections of his treatment of creation, is a theological anthropology open to social life.[43] According to Barth, the "basic form of humanity" is "fellow-humanity." As a consequence of this social understanding of being human, Barth has to ask what social forms of life embody this fellow-humanity and echo the will and the intention of the creator. The nation is after man/woman and parent/children, the third form of social life in which "freedom in fellowship" is realized.

In order to theologically devalue the nation, he formally uses the orthodox distinction between divine orders as permanent determinations and divine ordinations or dispositions which are not essential but accidental. Based on this distinction, Barth sets apart the community of the nation as mere divine disposition, "which does not contain any imperative" from marriage as permanent determination.[44] In contrast to marriage, which is a fundamental and essential natural form of creaturely life, nationhood is not. A nation is not a "natural creaturely relationship."[45] Nations are in some way created, but are highly contingent, emerge and perish and embody in their very existence no special divine command. Nations are frameworks in which human responsibility unfolds, and Christian obedience needs to be practiced—though they do not determine the content of this obedience. Quite pointedly, Barth affirms: "The fact that he finds himself in this relationship to near and distant neighbours cannot tell him anything new or distinctive concerning what God requires of him."[46] This is Barth's way of saying that they do not carry religious significance. In short: "To maintain and teach that the being of man within his people and its relationship to other peoples is a determination of human nature [. . .], is to give free rein to arbitrary fancy."[47]

This assessment of no particular theological significance opens the door to a phenomenological deconstruction. In a severely antiessentialist move, Barth suggests a particular image: "Die Nahen und die Fernen," the near and the distant inside shared humanity. This spatial distinction is only one of degrees, not of kind. Barth emphasizes that the distant neighbor is still in a relationship—but a distant one. The circle of the near ones has "the character of an allotted framework" in which every person "has to express his distinctive obedience" and finds certain self-evident relationships and obligations.[48] The distinction between the near and the distant is highly fluid and always takes place in a broader context. Over against alternative treatments of nation Barth underlines that one "should take expressly into account from the outset the wider sphere of man and humanity by which the first sphere [of the nation] is bordered and enclosed."[49]

Part of the phenomenological deconstruction is a high sensitivity for the particularities which make up a nation. Barth considers a shared language, even down to the dialect. Similarly, he ponders the impact of the geographic location, even as far as the distinct valley, the climate and the customs and feelings of local attachments. While Barth describes in detail the aspects of local rootedness, he repeatedly emphasizes that no particular form of life is holy. "Economic, social, cultural, political and religious factors are the historical realities which underlie the existence and distinction of peoples."[50] Nations are all the way down historical constructs.[51]

Far beyond having a specific religious significance, a nation with its obligations is a sphere of responsibility in which human beings have to receive God's command.

Both the theological devaluation and the phenomenology of the nation converge in a clear cosmopolitan horizon. Man "is not first and intrinsically in his own people, and then perhaps in humanity as well. In his own people, he is on the way to humanity, and in humanity on the way from his own people."[52]

Barth acknowledges in passing that there are tensions between the obligations in the nation and other nations as well as humanity. "To unite loyalty towards those who are historically near with openness towards those who are historically distant will always involve the enduring of a tension and overcoming of an antithesis within which the individual practical decisions may be very different."[53]

Barth's specific theological strategy of devaluating the nation raises many questions. He certainly needs to be criticized for his blunt natural theology or halfway sanctification of marriage. The theological devaluation of the nation comes at the high cost of a religious supercharging of marriage. The claim of "a special sphere of *natural* fellow-humanity and an *independent* form of the divine command" does not stand even against his own criticism. If one rejects—with Barth against Barth—his natural theology of marriage, however, the qualitative distinction between marriage and nation falls apart. The invalidation of Barth's tool for desanctification does not invalidate his insight into the historical contingency of the nation as a "sphere of responsibility."

By radically setting apart the issue of the nation and the problem of the state Barth avoids a question he puts center stage in "The Civil Community and the Christian Community": What are the cultural resources or even requirements for cultivating the civil community—besides the Christian community? More pointedly: Is the nation as a community of solidarity a prerequisite of a just legal and political community? Is nationhood an implicit yet powerful background assumption? Does not the analogy between the Christian community and the civil community open the door to a robust notion of nationhood, in which the unity and plurality of the church—its celebratory character, its inescapable emotional bonding—are mirrored in the nation-state? Is it both theologically and politically realistic to separate the church's relationship to the state from its relationship to the nation? His treatment of the nation leaves the many conflicts between citizenship and cosmopolitanism untouched. The conflicting spaces of responsibility and conflict are not in sight—also in Barth's earlier and later treatment of church and state. These are the issues where a post-Barthian dealing with nationhood needs to start.

PARADOXES AND TEMPTATIONS— CONCLUDING REMARKS

Our starting point was the sacralization of the nation in Protestant theology during World War I and World War II, following Otto Dibelius' reference to Johann Gottlieb Fichte's speeches to the German nation. Contrary to a reading of Fichte which focuses on his nationalism and especially his reception in later religious nationalisms, we analyzed the steps of his argumentation. As a result, we reconstructed his theory of the nation as a theory of the dynamics of life—which arbitrarily takes the nation as the decisive node in the receiving, giving, defending, and optimizing of life. As a result of this approach, we took Fichte as describing a process in politics we labeled RPC.[54] So the theological critique of religiously charged nationalism has to be expanded into a critique of the RPC present not only in right-wing nationalism but also in other political movements. The willingness for sacrifice is an indicator of what is considered holy and of utmost importance. The emergence of RPC is not necessarily tied to explicit religious practice. Explicit religion can, however, charge or even supercharge RPC. In this constellation, a theological critique of political ideologies becomes a critique of religion.

This widening interpretation of misplaced religious nationalism opens up new conversations with Karl Barth: A theological critique of politics overlaps with a theological critique of religion. As can be seen in Barth's 1919 Tambach lecture, he confronts RPC on two levels. He first rejects the theological charging of political movements with ultimate and absolute claims. He does, however, unfold on a second level a theological, and more specific, a Christological framework which allows him to claim Christ's anonymous presence in society. Already in Barth's Romans and then in the Tambach lecture, the society and the sphere of politics are not without Christ—as co-creator, reconciler, and redeemer. In 1951, Barth rejects the nation as a place of a natural fellow-humanity with a specific divine command. Instead, it is a sphere of responsibility inside the wider humanity.

These two texts represent only two of many strategies which can be found in Barth's wartime lectures, in the Barmen Declaration of 1934 and the widely discussed classics such as "The Christian Community and the Civil Community." So, the two texts do not by any means cover the territory. Moreover, there is already a tension visible between the two. On the one side, Barth can desacralize as in his treatment of the nation. On the other side, he emphasizes—over against large parts of the Lutheran tradition—that the state is in the frame of reconciliation already under Christ's rule. The world is never "gottlos"—godless—because of the theological, that is to say, Christological framework. Any secularization, any critique of RPC, of any political religion and false sovereignty takes place inside this frame. So, any secularization of RPC has a paradoxical character: Religion is denying religion. There is, quite obviously, an inbuilt temptation in Barth's construction: The collapse of the distinction between the frame and what is framed. The Christological perspective on society and politics then divinizes particular aspects of society because they are hotspots of divine presence. When the frame collapses, the worldliness of the world is denied in favor of a robust moral rule of Christ. When the frame collapses, the church wants more than parables of the kingdom. Christians are then tempted to deny that what they pray for, do and say "is not itself the new thing but the reflection of the great new thing of the kingdom of God within and over against the disorder and demonization of human life."[55] In this case, then the humanity of God present in the humanity of Christ serves to over-moralize the society and to refute the distinction between reconciliation and redemption, between the reflection and radical novelty coming from God alone. If this happens, Christians, unknowingly, use Johann Gottlieb Fichte's RPC as a script. They haste without waiting.[56] Withstanding this temptation, Christians practice "faithfulness to the

Spirit of God, faithfulness in the community [. . .] in the world which has been reconciled in J[esus] C[hrist] with God and with [?] itself, and which even though it is not yet redeemed, exists in the light of its coming redemption. They are to be achieved and displayed in deep solidarity with this world's misery and hope, also under severe attack by it, but above all in humble but resolute witness in and to it."[57]

NOTES

1. Gerhard Robbers, ed., *State and Church in the European Union* (Baden-Baden: Nomos, 2005).

2. For a left post-marxist critique of an inadequately non-emotional concept of politics, see Chantal Mouffe, *The Return of the Political* (London: Verso, 1993); Chantal Mouffe, *Über das Politische: Wider die kosmopolitische Illusion* (Frankfurt am Main: Suhrkamp, 2007); and Lasse Thomassen, *Deconstructing Habermas* (New York: Routledge, 2008).

3. Interestingly enough the bare fact that Karl Barth was Swiss does not become a piece in the jig-saw puzzle of Barth research. The same holds true for Bonhoeffer-research. For a widely neglected but nonetheless valuable and exceptional study on Dietrich Bonhoeffer, see K. W. Clements, *A Patriotism for Today: Love of Country in Dialogue with the Witness of Dietrich Bonhoeffer* (London: Collins Liturgical Publications, 1986).

4. On emotions, see Martha L. Cottam, *Introduction to Political Psychology* (Mahwah, NJ: Lawrence Erlbaum Associates, 2004), 191–221; Ted Brader and George E. Marcus, "Emotion and Political Psychology," in *The Oxford Handbook of Political Psychology*, ed. Leonie Huddy (Oxford: Oxford University Press, 2013), 165–204; Nicolas Demertzis, "Political Emotions," in *The Palgrave Handbook of Global Political Psychology*, ed. Paul W. Nesbitt-Larking and Catarina Kinnvall (Basingstoke: Palgrave Macmillan, 2014), 223–241; also, the contributions in Nicolas Demertzis, ed., *Emotions in Politics: The Affect Dimension in Political Tension* (Basingstoke: Palgrave Macmillan, 2013).

5. In place for many others Eberhard Jüngel, *Christ, Justice and Peace: Toward a Theology of the State in Dialogue with the Barmen Declaration* (New York: Bloomsbury, 2014). Evidently, the second essay in Heinrich Bedford-Strohm, *Liberation Theology for a Democratic Society: Essays in Public Theology* (Wien: Lit, 2018), 23–44, carries the title: "Nurturing Reason: The Public Role of Religion in the Liberal State," not "Nurturing Passion."

6. As shown by Benedict Anderson, the newspaper played a major role in the emergence of the nation-state. See Benedict R. Anderson, *Imagined Communities: Reflections on the Origin and Spread of Nationalism* (London: Verso, 1983).

7. A noteworthy exception is Rudy Koshar, "Demythologizing the Secular: Karl Barth and the Politics of the Weimar Republic," in *The Weimar Moment: Liberalism, Political Theology and Law*, ed. Leonard V. Kaplan and Rudy Koshar (Lanham: Lexington Books, 2012), 314–334.

8. For more details of this dazzling personality, see Hartmut Fritz, *Otto Dibelius: Ein Kirchenmann in der Zeit zwischen Monarchie und Diktatur* (Göttingen: Vandenhoeck & Ruprecht, 1998).

9. Otto Dibelius, "3. Das Ewige und das Vaterland: Diesseits und Jenseits," in *Gott und die deutsche Zuversicht: Drei Reden in dunkler Zeit* (Berlin: Vaterländische Verlags- und Kunstanstalt, 1918).

10. Ibid., 10–11. this and the following translations are mine.

11. For a current distinction between cold and hot collective memories, see Jan Assmann and Rodney Livingstone, *Religion and Cultural Memory: Ten Studies* (Stanford, CA: Stanford University Press, 2006).

12. With further references Hartmut Ruddies, "Religion und Nation: Reflexionen zu einem beschädigten Verhältnis," in *Gott im Selbstbewusstsein der Moderne: Zum neuzeitlichen Begriff der Religion*, ed. Ulrich Barth and Wilhelm Gräb (Gütersloh: Gerd Mohn, 1993), 196–221.

13. Johann Gottlieb Fichte, *Addresses to the German Nation*, ed. George Armstrong Kelly (New York: Harper & Row, 1968), 126. The page numbers in the text refer to this edition.

14. "Today the routines of everyday life challenge religion. Many old gods ascend from their graves; they are disenchanted and hence take the form of impersonal forces. They strive to gain power over our lives and again they resume their eternal struggle with one another" (Max Weber, *From Max Weber: Essays in Sociology*, ed. C.W. Mills and H. Gerth [London: Routledge & Kegan Paul, 1970], 149).

15. On the role of basic values in a nation, see Niklas Luhmann, "Grundwerte als Zivilreligion," in *Soziologische Aufklärung Bd. 3: Soziales System, Gesellschaft, Organisation*, ed. Niklas Luhmann (Westdeutscher Verlag, 1981), 293–308.

16. On the fragmentation of a nation by reinforced identity of particular groups, see Mark Lilla, *The Once and Future Liberal: After Identity Politics* (New York: Harper 2017).

17. The issue of the theistic or non-theistic semantics of a civil religion is a constantly debated topic.

18. James Carey, "Das Fernsehen und der Nationalstaat: Glaube, Zugehörigkeit und technischer Wandel," in *Religiöse Funktionen des Fernsehens? Medien-, kultur- und religionswissenschaftliche Perspektiven*, ed. Günter Thomas (Wiesbaden: Westdeutscher Verlag, 2000), 45–75. This relates well to Benedict R. Anderson, *Imagined Communities: Reflections on the Origin and Spread of Nationalism* (London: Verso, 1983), who studied the newspaper as a nation-building medium.

19. This is why the religio-poietic complex is crucial for the support of war. For good reasons, RPC resonates quite well with the political philosophy of Carl Schmitt. For the sacrificial dimension, see, that is, Carolyn Marvin and David W. Ingle, *Blood Sacrifice and the Nation: Totem Rituals and the American Flag* (Cambridge: Cambridge University Press, 1999); Carolyn Marvin, "Was Gruppen wissen müssen: Implikationen der Medienpraxis für Ritualtheorien," in *Religiöse Funktionen des Fernsehens? Medien-, kultur- und religionswissenschaftliche Perspektiven*, ed. Günter Thomas (Wiesbaden: Westdeutscher Verlag, 2000), 179–188.

20. This connection is emphasized in Robert N. Bellah, *The Good Society* (New York: Random House, 1991), and his account of civil religion.

21. This is a case made by Nigel Biggar, *Between Kin and Cosmopolis: An Ethic of the Nation* (Eugene, OR: Cascade Books, 2014); but also David Miller, "Conclusion," chap. 9 in *Strangers in our Midst: The Political Philosophy of Immigration* (Cambridge, MA: Harvard University Press, 2016), 151–164; and Margaret Moore, *The Ethics of Nationalism* (Oxford: Oxford University Press, 2001), 88.

22. For one example among many, see Melanie Johnson-DeBaufre and Catherine Keller, ed., *Common Goods: Economy, Ecology and Political Theology* (New York: Fortham University Press, 2015).

23. The problem of this "in between" position can clearly be seen in Tom Greggs, *Theology against Religion: Constructive Dialogues with Bonhoeffer and Barth* (New York: T&T Clark International, 2011).

24. Carys Moseley, *Nations and Nationalism in the Theology of Karl Barth* (Oxford: Oxford University Press, 2013); Carys Moseley, *Nationhood, Providence and Witness: Israel in Protestant Theology and Social Theory* (Eugene, OR: Cascade Books, 2013). For a recent overview, Rebekka A. Klein, *Depotenzierung der Souveränität: Religion und politische Ideologie bei Claude Lefort, Slavoj Zizek und Karl Barth* (Tübingen: Mohr Siebeck, 2016), 191–246. For a decisively strong political reading of Barth, see Timothy Gorringe, *Karl Barth: Against Hegemony* (Oxford: Oxford University Press, 1999). For a contextualization Günter Thomas, "Karl Barth's Political Theology: Contours, Perspectives, and Lines of Development," in *Dogmatics after Barth: Facing Challenges in Church, Society and the Academy*, ed. Günter Thomas and Rinse Reeling Brouwer (Leipzig: Create Space, 2012), 181–197.

25. The literature on Barth on church and state is legion. See the analyses in David Fergusson, *Church, State and Civil Society* (Cambridge: Cambridge University Press, 2004); for an overview Haddon Willmer, "Karl Barth," in *The Blackwell Companion to Political Theology*, ed. Peter Scott and William T. Cavanaugh (Malden, MA: Blackwell Pub., 2004), 123–135; William Werpehowski, "Karl Barth and Politics," in *Cambridge Companion to Karl Barth*, ed. John Webster (2000), 228–242; Eberhard Jüngel, "Zum Verhältnis von Kirche und Staat nach Karl Barth," in *Zeitschrift für Theologie und Kirche: Beiheft 6; Zur Theologie Karl Barths* 108, no. 4 (1986): 76–135.

26. See Jochen Fähler, *Der Ausbruch des 1. Weltkrieges in Karl Barths Predigten 1913–1915* (Bern: Peter Lang, 1979). For a critical reconstruction of Barth's reaction to the Declaration of the 93 intellectuals, see Wilfried Härle, "Der Aufruf der 93 Intellektuellen und Karl Barths Bruch mit der liberalen Theologie," in *Zeitschrif für Theologie und Kirche* 72, no. 2 (1975): 207–224.

27. Karl Barth, "The Christian's Place in Society (1919)," in *The Word of God and the Word of Man*, ed. Karl Barth (Gloucester, MA: Peter Smith, 1978), 272–327. Barth took advantage of the fact that the German title "Der Christ in der Gesellschaft" could be taken as being ambiguous.

28. See Leonhard Ragaz, "Von der schweizerischen religiös-sozialen Bewegung zur dialektischen Theologie," in *Reich Gottes, Marxismus, Nationalsozialismus: Ein Bekenntnis religiöser Sozialisten*, ed. Georg Wünsch (Tübingen: J. B. C. Mohr, 1931), 1–65. This text, given as a lecture in 1930, offers a harsh and bitter reckoning with the early dialectical Karl Barth. It reads like a late commentary to the Tambach

lecture. At the same time it validates—in hindsight—Barth's critique of religious socialism. Interestingly enough, this important self-positioning text by Leonard Ragaz is neglected in the reconstruction of Friedrich-Wilhelm Marquardt, *Theologie und Sozialismus: Das Beispiel Karl Barths* (München: Kaiser, 1972).

29. This orientation is already present in Karl Barth, *Der Römerbrief (Erste Fassung) 1919* (Zürich: Theologischer Verlag, 1985), 508–9: "ihr werdet euch schwerlich anderswohin stellen können als auf die äußerste Linke [...]. Daß ihr als Christen mit Monarchie, Kapitalismus, Militarismus, Patriotismus und Freisinn nichts zu tun habt, ist so selbstverständlich, daß ich es gar nicht zu sagen brauche. [...] Viel näher liegt euch natürlich die andere Möglichkeit, die im Christus kommende Revolution willkürlich vorauszunehmen und dadurch hintanzuhalten. Und davor warne ich euch! Die Sache der göttlichen Erneuerung darf nicht vermengt werden mit der Sache des menschlichen Fortschritts. Das Göttliche darf nicht politisiert und das Menschliche nicht theologisiert werden, auch nicht zugunsten der Demokratie und Sozialdemokratie."

30. Karl Barth, "The Christian's Place in Society (1919)," in *The Word of God and the Word of Man*, ed. Karl Barth (Gloucester, MA: Peter Smith, 1978), 276.

31. Ibid., 277.

32. The German original is much more pointed than the translation: "Ja, Christus zum soundsovielten Male zu *säkularisieren*, heute z.B. in der Sozialdemokratie, dem Pazifismus, dem Wandervogel zu Liebe, wie ehemals den Vaterländern, dem Schweizertum und Deutschtum, dem Liberalismus der Gebildeten zu Liebe, *das möchte uns allenfalls gelingen. Aber nicht wahr, da graut uns doch davor, wir möchten eben Christus nicht ein neues Mal verraten*" (Karl Barth, "Der Christ in der Gesellschaft (1919)," in *Anfänge der dialektischen Theologie: Teil 1*, ed. Jürgen Moltmann, 6th ed. [München: Kaiser, 1962], 6).

33. Ibid., 8 (trans. G.Th.).

34. In this respect the Tambach, located in between the first and second edition of Barths commentary of Romans, offers a lucid first variant of a model he never gave up but always developed: The events and movements of the world follow the events and movements in God's own life—and Christ is the interface between both. Also with respect to the political theology suggested by Barth a mirror image of the Tambach lecture is the very late Karl Barth, *The Christian Life: Church Dogmatics IV, 4; lecture fragments* (London: T. & T. Clark International, 2004): Christians fight the principalities and powers of their time but always have to take into account that God is not totally unknown in the society. For a location of Barth's later "political theology" within a similar covenantal framework, see Paul Daffyd Jone's contribution in this volume.

35. For an excellent study of both background and emergence of this concept, see Thomas Xutong Qu, *Barth und Goethe: die Goethe-Rezeption Karl Barths; 1906–1921* (Neukirchen-Vluyn: Neukirchener Verl.-Ges., 2014); also, Qu's contribution to this volume.

36. Barth's christological perspective on law is analyzed by Alexander Massmann's contribution in this volume. Massmann is calling this christological orientation a "desecularizing move."

37. Leonhard Ragaz, "Von der schweizerischen religiös-sozialen Bewegung zur dialektischen Theologie," in *Reich Gottes, Marxismus, Nationalsozialismus: Ein Bekenntnis religiöser Sozialisten*, ed. Georg Wünsch (Tübingen: J.B.C. Mohr, 1931), 46–47.

38. Ibid., 54.

39. Ibid., 56.

40. Ibid., 55.

41. See, that is, Paul Althaus, "Kirche, Volk und Staat," in *Kirche, Volk und Staat: Stimmen aus der deutschen evangelischen Kirche zur Oxforder Weltkirchenkonferenz*, ed. Eugen Gerstenmaier (Berlin: Furche, 1937), 17–35; and Walter Künneth, "Die biblische Offenbarung und die Ordnungen Gottes," in *Die Nation vor Gott: Zur Botschaft der Kirche im Dritten Reich*, ed. Walter Künneth and Helmuth Schreiner (Berlin: Wichern, 1933), 1–23; for an overview see Roland Kurz, *Nationalprotestantisches Denken in der Weimarer Republik: Voraussetzungen und Ausprägungen des Protestantismus nach dem Ersten Weltkrieg in seiner Begegnung mit Volk und Nation* (Gütersloh: Gütersloher Verlagshaus, 2007).

42. For a recent creative appropriation of Barth's treatment of nation, see Luke Bretherton, *Christianity and Contemporary Politics: The Conditions and Possibilities of Faithful Witness* (Chichester, UK: Wiley-Blackwell, 2010), 126–174. See also David Haddorff's essay in this volume.

43. Karl Barth, *Church Dogmatics: Vol. III; The Doctrine of Creation; Pt. 2* (Edinburgh: T. & T. Clark, 1961), 222–285.

44. Karl Barth, *Church Dogmatics: Vol. III; The Doctrine of Creation; Pt. 4* (Edinburgh: T. & T. Clark, 1961), 305.

45. Ibid., 285.

46. Ibid., 289.

47. Ibid., 305. The English translation is misleading at this point. Barth is speaking of a free invention, a "freie Erfindung," not of a "free discovery."

48. Ibid., 288.

49. Ibid., 288.

50. Ibid., 294.

51. This judgment resonates strongly with the mindset of Eric Hobsbawm.

52. Karl Barth, *Church Dogmatics: Vol. III; The Doctrine of Creation; Pt. 4* (Edinburgh: T. & T. Clark, 1961), 298.

53. Ibid., 297.

54. We consciously leave open the question whether there can be a vital political life without this religio-poietic process. Whether one rather welcomes it or rejects it, there is quite some evidence that it is almost unavoidable, an essential part of receiving and giving of life. Posttheistic times appear to be most vulnerable to this non-theistic religion.

55. Karl Barth, *The Christian Life: Church Dogmatics IV, 4; lecture fragments* (London: T. & T. Clark International, 2004), 235.

56. I borrow this phrase from Nigel Biggar, *The Hastening that Waits: Karl Barth's Ethics* (Oxford: Oxford University Press, 1993), and change it accordingly.

57. Karl Barth, The *Christian Life: Church Dogmatics IV, 4; lecture fragments* (London: T. & T. Clark International, 2004), 285.

Part II

LEGITIMACY AND SOVEREIGNTY

POLITICAL POWER IN
THEOLOGICAL PERSPECTIVE

Chapter 7

Constitutional Theology

Karl Barth and Carl Schmitt on Legitimacy and the Rule of Law

Clifford B. Anderson

INTRODUCTION

Does Karl Barth's theology support the rule of law? I approach this question by comparing Karl Barth (1886–1968) with a near contemporary, Carl Schmitt (1888–1985). Karl Barth and Carl Schmitt had strongly overlapping interests. Schmitt was a German constitutional scholar who drew on theology for inspiration. Barth was a theologian who wrote about legal and political questions facing Germany. However, Karl Barth and Carl Schmitt did not interact directly. We can speculate about the reasons: Barth was Protestant, Schmitt was Roman Catholic; Barth was a vocal opponent of National Socialism who was forced out of Germany in 1935; Schmitt became a proponent of National Socialism after 1933 and never formally renounced the party. So Karl Barth and Carl Schmitt mostly passed each other by. Scholars, notably German philosopher and Jewish scholar, Jacob Taubes (1923–1987), have subsequently engaged both and drawn comparisons between them.[1]

In what follows, my approach is theological, not biographical or historical. I bracket questions like the relations between Karl Barth and the Confessing Church or Carl Schmitt and National Socialism. Instead, I limit my comparison primarily to two texts: Karl Barth's *Rechtfertigung und Recht* (Justification and Justice, 1938)[2] and Carl Schmitt's *Legalität und Legitimität* (Legality and Legitimacy, 1932).[3] The guiding question of our enquiry is whether Barth offers a sufficient basis for the rule of law in his political theology. By drawing on Schmitt's understanding of the distinction between legality and legitimacy, I hope to provoke greater insight into the distinctiveness of Karl Barth's christological approach to legitimating the legal order. To anticipate, I will defend Barth's reconfiguration of the relation between church and state against two possible charges: on the one hand, that it denudes the secular authority of the ability to act mercifully and, on the other, that it leaves the legitimacy of the state dangerously open to question. In defending him against both charges, I show how Barth's indirect political theology avoided the dangers intrinsic to Schmitt's concept of legitimation.

SOVEREIGNTY AND THE RULE OF LAW

Among the ideals of political liberalism, the rule of law stands as the most cherished.[4] John Adams's adage, "a republic [is] a government of laws, and not of men," guides the American people to this day.[5] The Constitution of the United States of America puts all branches of government—executive, legislative, and judicial—under the purview of the law. Defining the rule of law is not as easy, however. The ideal encapsulates values such as publicity of the law, equality before the law, non-retroactivity of the law, and legal constraints on the exercise of political power, among other things. While defining the rule of law may be a scholarly exercise, it does not take special training to recognize its absence. "The hallmarks of a regime which flouts the rule of law are, alas, all too familiar," writes Tom Bingham in *The Rule of Law*: "The midnight knock on the door, the sudden disappearance, the show trial, the subjection of prisoners to genetic experiment, the confession extracted by torture, the gulag and the concentration camp, the gas chamber, the practice of genocide or ethnic cleansing, the waging of aggressive war."[6] When talking about the rule of law, the stakes are high. The ideal of the "rule of law" protects us against anarchies like the Hobbesian state of nature, on the one hand, and absolutisms like dictatorship, on the other.

Acting against the rule of law normally numbers among the most grievous of political transgressions. The decade following the events of September 11, 2001, saw many exceptions made to the rule of law in the United States, including the use of national security letters without sufficient judicial oversight, clandestine programs of national rendition, and the opening of the prison camp in Guantanamo Bay, Cuba. In a 2013 speech to the National Defense University, President Barak Obama acknowledged, "I believe we compromised our basic values—by using torture to interrogate our enemies, and detaining individuals in a way that ran counter to the rule of law."[7] Violations of the rule of law—such as the infliction of cruel and unusual punishment or the practical suspension of habeas corpus—damage the standing of the United States among the community of nations.

However, these exceptions to domestic and international law were far less controversial in the United States than abroad. The public support in the wake of September 11 for these extraordinary measures may be attributed to another, conflicting ideal—the exceptionalism of the "American way of life." Violating the rule of law to defend the rule of law seems paradoxical until we understand, as Paul W. Kahn explains, the political theology of the American people.

> The exceptional turn to violence against the enemy will always be understood as the defense of sovereign existence. This includes, but is not exhausted by, the defense of the order of law that the sovereign put in place: to defend the state is not just to defend the border, but to defend a way of life. For Americans, the rule of law is not that which eliminates the need for the violent defense of the nation, but that for the sake of which violence is deployed.[8]

The exercise of sovereignty stands in tension with the ideal of the rule of law. Are there times when leaders of a nation ostensibly devoted to the rule of law may legitimately make exceptions to defend the rule of law?

This question transcends any difference between the political right and left. A political theology forms a shared point of reference for a nation, though it may be interpreted and deployed for opposing political causes. Returning to his speech at the National Defense University, President Obama criticized Congress for placing legal barriers in the way of transferring prisoners from Guantanamo Bay. A heckler interrupted him to demand its immediate closure.

THE PRESIDENT: And given my administration's relentless pursuit of Al Qaeda's leadership, there is no justification beyond politics for Congress to prevent us from closing a facility that should have never have been opened. (Applause.)
AUDIENCE MEMBER: Excuse me, President Obama—
THE PRESIDENT: So—let me finish, ma'am. So today, once again—
AUDIENCE MEMBER: There are 102 people on a hunger strike. These are desperate people.
THE PRESIDENT: I'm about to address it, ma'am, but you've got to let me speak. I'm about to address it.
AUDIENCE MEMBER: You're our Commander-In-Chief—
THE PRESIDENT: Let me address it.
AUDIENCE MEMBER: —you [can] close Guantanamo Bay.[9]

What is fascinating about this exchange is the interplay between the rule of law and sovereign authority. The president complained that Congress has passed regulations limiting his ability to close Guantanamo Bay. The heckler urged the president to act—using the military term "Commander in Chief"— rather than allow prisoners to languish.[10] The president and the heckler both recognized an injustice—Guantanamo Bay as an exception to the rule of law.

The president, however, called for a legal resolution whereas the heckler demanded a sovereign action.

Again, the question we need to address is whether a state legitimately can make exceptions to the rule of law, especially for the sake of showing mercy.

THE POLITICAL USE OF THE LAW

The history of Christian interpretation of the law and of political authority is complex and multifaceted. Briefly put, two of the most significant passages in the New Testament are Rom. 13:1–7 ("Let every person be subject to the governing authorities; for there is no authority except from God, and those authorities that exist have been instituted by God" [Rom. 13:1]) and 1 Peter 2:13–17 ("For the Lord's sake accept the authority of every human institution, whether of the emperor as supreme, or of governors, as sent by him to punish those who do wrong and to praise those who do right" [1 Pet. 2:13–14]). The history of the exegesis of these passages literally fills books. Only a few points need to be made here. First, both hold that secular authority derives from divine authority. Christians are admonished to obey the secular authorities as God's agents in the secular realm. The legitimacy of secular authority is theological, not political. Second, since legitimation is theological rather than political, differing political configurations do not affect the legitimacy of the state. Paul does not say, "Let every person be subject to the governing authorities in a constitutional state that upholds the rule of law." As Ernst Käseman argued about Rom. 13:1–7, any attempt to find a constitutional basis for political authority in these texts cannot be sustained. "Every sentence can apply also in a police state and it simply should not be overlooked that the apostle is in fact writing under a dictatorship with largely corrupt and capricious representatives, not to speak of the petty despotism of departments and officials."[11] These passages are difficult to interpret because they seem to legitimate any existing political order without regard to its legality or justice.

The political effects of the interpretation of these passages sharpened during the Reformation. Luther expounded the paradoxical freedom of the Christian, setting the understanding for the Reformation as a whole.[12] The New Testament admonition to obey the secular authorities became enshrined in the so-called "civil" or "political" use of the law. As Luther stated in his Commentary on Galatians, "This civil restraint is extremely necessary and was instituted by God, both for the sake of public service and for the sake of preserving everything, but especially to prevent the course of the Gospel from being hindered by the tumults and seditions of wild men."[13] The rule of law may be a necessity in a sinful world, but it is not an ideal. The law constrains us from sinning against one another, but it does not foster love between us. Rather, the law judges—sometimes harshly and cruelly. Still, it does so with a legitimate purpose: the maintenance of public order, which indirectly serves the freedom of the gospel.

JUSTIFICATION AND JUSTICE

In *Rechtfertigung und Recht*, Karl Barth proposed a conceptual redescription of the relation between church and state. He argued that the Reformation model of church and state had been inadequately grounded in christology. In part, the Reformation's dichotomous model arose from its starting point, namely, opposition between church and state, which mirrored the opposition between law and gospel. While not denying that church and state may clash, Barth argued that we must also understand the connection between church and state—the *"positive* connection between the two realms."[14]

Barth contended that both church and state are christological entities. The difference between them is, basically, that the church knows Christ directly whereas the state knows him indirectly—that is, through the church. As with Luther, the state serves the church by providing the political order required for the freedom of the gospel. But Barth made the point more strongly, arguing the state represents a "secondary Christological sphere" "uniting the church with the cosmos."[15] The state is not incidental but essential to the mission of the church. The order imposed by the state, however imperfect, provides a prolepsis of the divine order. The church does not look forward to the dissolution of the state but to the elevation of the human state into the divine state.[16] The church must thus never stand in simple opposition to the state but rather pray for the state as a *"ministri extraordinarii ecclesiae."*[17]

What about the relation between the state and the church? What value does the church have for the state? In the classical view, this question was not explicitly addressed. Theologians wrestled with the place of the church in the state, presupposing the value of the church and putting the state in question. Barth broke new ground by asserting that the church is also essential to the state because the church provides indirect legitimation of the political order through its proclamation of the gospel. Barth claimed, "it is the preaching of justification of the Kingdom of God, which founds, here and now, the true system of law, the true state."[18] The "true system of law" that the church knows and to some extent models in its own legal structures functions as the norm and source for secular law.[19] Cleverly, Barth also introduced the concept of right (and, by extension, the rule of law) into the relation between the church and state by way of the concept of legitimacy. "The right of the church to liberty," Barth wrote, "means the foundation, the maintenance, the restoration of everything—certainly of all human law."[20] The quality of the relationship between church and state can be judged by the robustness of the right to preach the gospel. The right to preach the gospel is the highest legal norm and the tacit source of the state's legitimacy.

LEGALITY AND LEGITIMATION

The relation between legality and legitimacy was a major subject of debate during the Weimar Republic (1919–1933). What legitimated the Weimar Republic in the face of such hostility from so many divergent parties? This question formed the subject of a long-running debate between Carl Schmitt and another prominent jurist of the period, Hans Kelsen (1881–1973), an Austrian legal philosopher and constitutional scholar. Put starkly, Carl Schmitt argued that the source of legitimacy must be extralegal while Hans Kelsen argued that only legality ensures legitimacy.

Hans Kelsen defended a form of legal positivism.[21] That is, Kelsen aimed to purify the law of metaphysical concepts such as divine right, natural law, and—more controversially—justice itself. He believed that appeal to any extralegal source of legitimation for the legal system introduces metaphysical elements into the system of laws. "Values are fragile standards that constitute a 'metaphysical' source of legitimacy that Kelsen cannot come to terms with," writes Sandrine Baume in *Hans Kelsen and the Case for Democracy*. "So with great consistency, he turns to legality as the ultimate criterion for legitimacy."[22] Kelsen considered the search for extralegal sources of normativity akin to the search for spiritual forces directing the laws of nature. He argued that the legal philosophers need to follow the example of the natural philosophers, who first conflated God and the natural order ("*Deus sive Natura*") and then dispensed with God as an unnecessary hypothesis.

> And if the absorption of the concept of a supernatural God by the concept of nature was the presupposition, first created by pantheism, for a genuine natural science devoid of all metaphysics, so likewise is the reduction of the superlegal concept of the state to the concept of law the indispensible precondition of the development of a genuine science of law, as a *science of positive law* purified of all natural law.[23]

The concept of the sovereignty of the state in particular represents a "pseudo-problem." There is no legitimate sovereign above and beyond the laws. That said, Kelsen did not deny the existence of political theology. He simply ruled it out of scope. Kelsen argued, pace theologians like Emil Brunner and Reinhold Neibuhr, that the state requires no Christian justification.[24] For

Kelsen, the appeal to extralegal norms is always a flight to authority and an escape from secular responsibility.

Carl Schmitt defended a perspective diametrically opposed to Hans Kelsen. In his view, legal positivism's refusal to acknowledge extralegal sources of legitimacy threatened the Weimar Republic. While his two most influential books, *Political Theology* (1922)[25] and *The Concept of the Political* (1927)[26] indirectly addressed the situation of the Weimar Republic, Schmitt explored its sources of normativity directly in *Legality and Legitimacy* (1932).[27] *Legality and Legitimacy* is an exploration of whether a liberal polity like the Weimar Republic can succeed—à la Kelsen—in collapsing legitimacy into legality. Can the constitution avoid making reference to a sovereign authority above the law? Is it possible to reduce legitimacy to adherence to the constitution and to the rule of law alone?

Schmitt considered these questions of signal political significance because the legitimacy of liberal parliamentary polities like the Weimar Republic stood or fell by their outcome. "The parliamentary legislative state, with its ideal, closed, and gapless system of legality of all state action, developed a thoroughly distinctive system of justification," wrote Schmitt. "'Legality' here has the meaning and purpose of making superfluous and negative the legitimacy of either the monarch or the people's plebiscitarian will as well as of every authority and governing power, whether in a form that provides its own foundation or one claiming to be something higher."[28] Schmitt directed his inquiry in *Legality and Legitimacy* at the constitution of the Weimar Republic. To what extent did the constitution succeed in putting extralegal presuppositions out of effect? And could the state survive without those presuppositions?

Schmitt concluded in *Legality and Legitimacy* that a "formal-functional" view of law poses a grave danger to the state. The problem with a functional approach is its identification of legitimacy with legality. So long as parliament passes a statute according to defined constitutional procedures, the law is valid. "The lawmaker creates what he wants in the lawmaking process; that process is always 'law,' and it always creates 'right.'"[29] There is no basis for claiming that a law is unjust because a pure parliamentary system does not allow appeals to extralegal norms. While there is a constitution in a parliamentary system, it is essentially formal, not substantive. The ideal of the parliamentary system was to select representatives from among the people who could articulate the nation's shared commitments. But could it cope with a situation in which "the people" have been fractured into parties, several of which seek to undermine the constitution? The threat is that elections will deliver a sufficient majority for a party to revise the constitution in such a way as to make all other parties illegal. "If legality and illegality can be arbitrarily at the disposal of the majority, then the majority can, above all, declare their domestic competitors illegal, that is *hors-la-loi*, thereby excluding them from the democratic homogeneity of the people."[30] Schmitt intended his analysis of the Weimar Constitution to demonstrate that it was not a purely formal system based on the rule of law alone and thus contained substantial elements that could be invoked against its enemies. As Sandrine Baume remarks, "If one were to summarize the danger that Schmitt tried to avoid, it would be the situation in which the state dies legally."[31]

Tragically, the situation Schmitt warned against in 1932 came to pass in 1933. A democratically elected parliament employed legal measures to repeal the rule of law and to declare its opponents illegal. The collapse of the Weimar Republic in 1933 does not, however, necessarily vindicate Schmitt's proposed solution to the problem of legitimacy. At the time, Schmitt belonged to a circle of conservatives who favored using Presidential authority to uphold "the substantive characteristics and capacities of the German people."[32] What gave this circle the right to decide on these "substantive characteristics"? Who can legitimately speak for the nation against the constitution?

The question of the sovereign exception to the rule of law is among the most contested in political philosophy. In his *Political Theology*, Carl Schmitt held that sovereignty could be equated with the ability to decide on the exception to the rule of law. As he famously wrote, "Sovereign is he who decides on the exception."[33] In *Legality and Legitimacy*, he argued in practical terms that invoking extraordinary sources of authority—most particularly the President's "emergency powers"—was necessary to defend the Weimar Republic against its enemies. But employing emergency powers or declaring a state of exception contravenes the rule of law and promotes authoritarianism. Giorgio Agamben has identified the "state of exception" as an essential trait of totalitarianism. "Modern totalitarianism can be defined as the establishment, by means of the state of exception, of a legal civil war that allows for the physical elimination not only of political adversaries but of entire categories of citizens who for some reason cannot be integrated into the political system."[34] In face of our experiences during the twentieth century, the attempt to preserve the constitution (and, by extension, the rule of law) by suspending constitutional liberties seems too risky, no matter how "legitimate" the authority.

BARTH ON LEGALITY AND LEGITIMACY

Karl Barth's understanding of the relation between legality and legitimation seemingly rules out the possibility of a "legitimate" exception to the rule of law. For, as we have seen, he posited an asymmetric relation between law and gospel in his description of church and state in *Rechtfertigung und Recht*. On the one hand, the church is structured not only by the gospel but also by the law. According to Barth, "There is and must be within the Church itself (and here its close relation to the State asserts itself) *something like . . .* a commonwealth: with its offices and orders, divisions of labour and forms of community."[35] Barth rejected the notion of a pure church founded only on the gospel. The gospel is always an ordered liberty—or, as he made the point in *Gospel and Law* (1935), the law is always the "form" of the gospel and the gospel is always the "content" of the law.[36] The state, in contrast, knows nothing of the gospel. The state only knows the law. "The State as State knows nothing of the Spirit, nothing of love, nothing of forgiveness."[37] The state cannot declare a "legitimate" exception to the law because the state does not have direct access to the source of its own legitimacy.

A consequence is that the state—in contrast to the church—can act justly but not mercifully. For what is mercy in the sphere of the state? As Paul W. Kahn shows, mercy cannot be explained by reference to the rule, only to the exception. He points to several examples, including the executive power of pardon.

> When we assign the pardon power to the chief executive, we worry that we are putting him above the law: where is justice outside of law? Yet when Grant Gilmore writes, "In Hell, there will be nothing but law," we understand his point. The pardon power still has something of the character of the laying on of hands, of the mark of the sacred, indeed of the blessing. It is not quite the same as an act of forgiveness, for there is no need for the beneficiary even to admit guilt. The pardon is always undeserved. It literally takes the bearer outside of law. It is a gift that comes as if from nowhere.[38]

The executive pardon is not the only example of sovereign exception to the rule of law in the political system of the United States. Kahn also points to jury nullification as an example from the judicial branch.[39] In fact, the closer we look at the practice of government the more we find exceptions to the rule of law. As Bonnie Honig notes, the exercise of administrative discretion is, in effect, an exception in miniature that may smooth the way for the rule of law.[40] The point is clear. Without the ability to make these forms of exceptions, the rule of law threatens to become oppressive. Barth himself argued for acknowledging exceptional cases in the ethical sections of the *Church Dogmatics*. But did Barth deny the state's ability to act mercifully in the exceptional case by restricting secular authority to the sphere of law alone? What effect does this restriction have on the popular perception of the state's legitimacy?

A merciless state will not garner the affection of its citizens. Citizens will not love a state that remains impartial to them. While this outcome sounds negative, it may actually represent Barth's intentions. As Carys Moseley argues in *Nations and Nationalism in the Theology of Karl Barth*, Barth's turn from liberal theology also had the effect of "displacing" his Swiss patriotism.[41] She notes that Barth drew on the concept of patriotism in his early theology, even pointing to Calvin as "a model of true patriotism."[42] While not rejecting the historical and cultural distinctiveness of the Swiss nation, Barth's dismay at the virulence of German nationalism in the wake of World War I and his desire to cut off any identification of the spirit of the nation with the Holy Spirit led him to avoid naïve appeals to Swiss patriotism. In a more sophisticated vein, Barth regarded Switzerland (and the Holy Roman Empire before it) as models for what Moseley terms the "containment of nationalism."[43] In modern times, we might think about the European Union as Barth's ideal of a supra-national state. Citizens of the European Union may enjoy its economic benefits and appreciate its fostering of continental peace, but few citizens "love" the European Union. At best, Barth might have regarded the European Union as a parable of the Kingdom.

While rejecting European nationalism, Barth might have allowed for what Jan-Werner Müller has described as "constitutional patriotism"—that is, patriotism "not primarily tied to a state, but to political principles."[44] In other words, he might have permitted a much more sober form of patriotism than the one expressed in the hymns we sing in American churches on Independence Day. While Barth's political theology cannot allow for the concretization of "national values" to the extent required for Schmitt's elevation of legitimacy above legality, this line of thinking nevertheless seems to permit some form of political mercy to be exercised alongside justice. Might we say that his theology permits occasional parabolic acts of political mercy? These parabolic acts would perhaps be few and far between, but it seems to me that Barth leaves the door ajar to a form "constitutional patriotism," whereby a limited range of extralegal acts of mercy may be legitimated.

This raises a second question for Barth's understanding of church and state, namely, whether Barth opened a dangerous legitimation gap. In *Rechtfertigung und Recht*, as we have seen, Barth asserted that the state has no secular legitimacy, but depends on the church's proclamation of the gospel for its legitimacy. This claim is, indeed, central to Barth's view of the relation between church and state.

> After all that we have seen as constituting the relation between the realms, the answer must be given: that apart from the Church, nowhere is there any fundamental knowledge of the reasons which make the State legitimate and necessary. For everywhere else, save in the Church, the State, and every individual state, with its concern for human justice, may be called into question.[45]

Secular law is essentially ungrounded because it cannot address the source of its legitimacy in the gospel. The gospel serves as the (hidden) presupposition of the state's legitimacy. A problem with this solution is that it creates a vacuum within the secular state that other institutions apart from the church may wish to fill. By denying the secular legitimacy of the law, Barth opens the door for others to supply its justification. Certainly, the gospel may provide this justification. But, in our pluralist world, there are other contenders. A political vacuum will inevitably be filled. This brings us back to Hans Kelsen—a legal system dependent on extralegal legitimation easily falls prey to illegitimate metaphysics. Does the church need to rush in to supply legitimations before others do?[46]

I argue that the church's task is not to supply legitimizations but rather to hold open the vacuum by delegitimizing patriotisms and nationalisms of all forms. This represents a form of its indirect service to the state. Theology's delegitimizing function comes to the fore in an occasional piece of writing from 1931: *Fragen an das "Christentum."*[47] In that piece, Barth argued that in face of the three major ideological threats to the church—(Russian) Communism, Fascism, and Americanism—the concept of "worldview" appears dépassé. These states do not simply uphold worldviews, which are after all only human constructions and not binding over life and death, but have become something more insidious, namely, political religions. He cautions that the church cannot tolerate such religions of the state. The church, he writes, "must know that it only has enemies before it in these surrounding foreign religions—in spirit, in principle, in will, in their daemon—and that it expects no tolerance from them because it can also extend them none."[48] Is this a way of saying that whenever a state develops a political theology—either implicitly or explicitly—the church must combat that theology or face its own destruction? So the church may live quietly and peacefully in a state that does not evince much inclination toward self-divination (such as, perhaps, Switzerland or Singapore) but remain vigilant whenever the temptation toward political theology arises.[49]

CONCLUSION

The extralegal basis for constitutionalism and the rule of law continues to elicit debate in modern times. What legitimates the rule of law in our pluralist world? This question is global, spanning any difference between East and West. In *The Rule of Law: The Common Sense of Global Politics*, Christopher May argues for a continuum between "thick" and "thin" conceptions of the rule of law.

> Following many other writers, I refer to these as a 'thick' view of the rule of law encompassing a wider set of legal norms such as equity and justice, and a more process and institution-focused 'thin' rule of law that seeks only to specify method rather than content.[50]

The "thin" view of the rule of law regards its implementation primarily as a matter of increasing administrative efficiency and economic predictability whereas the "thick" view ascribes normative ends—such as justice, fairness, and human flourishing—to the rule of law. In other words, the "thick" view incorporates broad political ends to the enactment of the rule of law. Of course, political debates may arise within polities about these normative ends. These disagreements sharpen in cross-cultural contexts. As May notes, scholars continue to discuss the effects of legal pluralism on the rule of law.[51] Should the rule of law look different in non-Western contexts, for instance? Certainly, a "thin" rule of law would seem to have a better chance of adapting to different national circumstances than a "thick" rule of law program.[52]

By way of conclusion, consider the contemporary conversation in Mainland China over the legitimacy of its constitution. While China does have a constitution, many of its provisions presently remain unenforced—the Chinese Communist Party effectively governs as a sovereign power in a state of (undeclared) exception. But the Chinese Communist Party faces a crisis of legitimacy as it departs from classical Marxism to a capitalist market economy with "Chinese characteristics." Qing Jiang, director of the Yangming Confucian Academy in Guizhou, and Weifang He, professor of law at Peking University in Beijing, both anticipate constitutional revision in China. But they take distinctly different approaches to its legitimation. The first argues for a "thick" conception based on traditional Chinese values, whereas the second argues for a mostly "thin" conception.

Qing Jiang advocates a "Chinese constitutionalism" explicitly based on Confucianism. He is acutely attuned to the problem of political theology. For Jiang, the legitimacy of the Chinese legal system depends on its connection with the Chinese people and their history. In *A Confucian Constitutional Order*, Jiang writes, "China's ancient sages have already established the eternal and unchanging principle of legitimization. Our duty today is to put that eternally valid norm into practice at the level of implementation."[53] If the legitimating norm is Confucian, then legal institutions cannot be directly imported from the West. The differences in political theologies require careful attention to differences in practices, including foregoing such basic beliefs as equality before the law. Jiang winds up posing a stark choice between East and West. "There is no other Chinese constitutionalism outside Confucian constitutionalism, bar Western constitutionalism. For Chinese constitutionalism to be Chinese, it must be Confucian and cannot be called by any other name."[54] While quixotic, Jiang's proposals for a Confucian constitutionalism remind us that political theology generally provides direct legitimation of a state's legal system.

In contrast, Weifang He proposes that China embrace a form of Western constitutionalism to promote the rule of law and to bring an end to authoritarian rule in China. "From a long-term perspective," writes He in *In the Name of Justice: Striving for the Rule of Law in China*, "rule of law is the only way for China's ancient civilization to escape the historical cycle of order and chaos."[55] He openly acknowledges that Christianity has provided the historical background—dare we say, the political theology?—for the rule of law in the West.[56] However, when asked about the role of Christianity in the struggle for the rule of law in China, He demurs. "As for the religious dimension of constitutional government, since we believe in Marxism, there is no place for any religion, and therefore it is impossible for us to worship constitutional government or establish a theology-based jurisprudence."[57] The comment may represent a wry critique of the role of Marxism in the Chinese legal system since, as Barth remarked in *Fragen an das "Christentum,"* Marxism is also a kind of political religion. In any case, He comes closer to Barth's view: the role for Christianity—or any political theology, for that matter—must always be indirect; a religion should not be used to legitimate a legal system directly.

The contemporary conversation in China between He and Jiang and others signal the ongoing significance of the Weimar-era debates about the legitimacy of the liberal legal system.[58] Perhaps surprisingly, the pairing of Kelsen's emphasis on legality (or a "thin" rule of law) with Barth's theological concept of legitimacy seems a more stable and more portable solution than Carl Schmitt's appeal to substantive national values (or a "thick" rule of law) when grounding legality. Seen from another perspective, though, this result should not be surprising. Barth's theology provokes us to reject natural theologies of all kinds, including in the political realm. Barth's writings on justification and justice thus fit hand-in-glove with Hans Kelsen's legal positivism. Advocating for a "thin" rule of law may seem overly modest to many theologians, who naturally gravitate toward substantive concepts of justice and mercy. But it may be the most prudent political path forward for Christian churches in pluralist societies, especially in non-Western contexts. In traditionally non-Christian societies like China, appeals to Schmitt, "patriotism," and "national values" could easily justify the political exclusion of the Christian churches.[59] The combination of a "thin" rule of law with Barth's theology of church and state provides a more flexible solution to the fraught relation of legality and legitimacy in pluralist societies.

NOTES

1. See Jacob Taubes, "Theodicy and Theology: A Philosophical Analysis of Karl Barth's Dialectical Theology," *The Journal of Religion* 34, no. 4 (October 1954): 231–243; see also Jacob Taubes, *To Carl Schmitt: Letters and Reflections* (New York: Columbia University Press, 2013); see further Mathias Eichhorn, *Es Wird Regiert! Der Staat im Denken Karl Barths und Carl Schmitts in den Jahren 1919 bis 1938* (Berlin: Duncker & Humblot, 1994).

2. Karl Barth, *Rechtfertigung und Recht* (Zürich: Theol. Verl., 1998); English translation Karl Barth, *Church and State* (London: Student Christian Movement Press, 1939).

3. Carl Schmitt, *Legalität und Legitimität* (München: Duncker & Humblot, 1932); English translation Carl Schmitt, *Legality and Legitimacy*, ed. Jeffrey Seitzer (Durham: Duke University Press, 2004).

4. The term of "rule of law" arises from the jurisprudence of English-speaking nations. The continental equivalent is the *Rechtsstaat* or "legal state." These concepts are related, though not necessarily identical. Most significantly, it is possible to have "rule of law" without a written constitution, as is the case in Great Britain, but a *Rechtsstaat* presupposes that the power of the sovereign is bounded constitutionally. For the purpose of this study, we use the terms interchangeably. On the differences between "rule of law" and *Rechtsstaat*, see Dietmar von der Pfordten, "On the Foundations of the Rule of Law and the Principle of the Legal State/Rechtsstaat," in *The Legal Doctrines of the Rule of Law and the Legal State (Rechtsstaat)*, ed. James R. Silkenat, James E. Hickey Jr, and Peter D. Barenboim, Ius Gentium: Comparative Perspectives on Law and Justice 38 (Springer International Publishing, 2014), 15–28; Stephan Kirste, "Philosophical Foundations of the Principle of the Legal State (Rechtsstaat) and the Rule of Law," in *The Legal Doctrines of the Rule of Law and the Legal State (Rechtsstaat)*, ed. James R. Silkenat, James E. Hickey Jr, and Peter D. Barenboim, Ius Gentium: Comparative Perspectives on Law and Justice 38 (Springer International Publishing, 2014), 29–43; Martin Krygier, "Rule of Law (and Rechtsstaat)," in *The Legal Doctrines of the Rule of Law and the Legal State (Rechtsstaat)*, ed. James R. Silkenat, James E. Hickey Jr, and Peter D. Barenboim, Ius Gentium: Comparative Perspectives on Law and Justice 38 (Springer International Publishing, 2014), 45–59.

5. John Adams, *The Political Writings of John Adams: Representative Selections* (Indianapolis: Hackett Publishing, 2003), 44.

6. T. H Bingham, *The Rule of Law* (London: Allen Lane, 2010).

7. "Remarks by the President at the National Defense University | The White House," accessed May 27, 2013, http://www.whitehouse.gov/the-press-office/2013/05/23/remarks-president-national-defense-university.

8. Paul W. Kahn, *Political Theology: Four New Chapters on the Concept of Sovereignty* (New York: Columbia University Press, 2011).

9. "Remarks by the President at the National Defense University | The White House."

10. On the interpretive difficulties of the "Commander in Chief" clause of the US Constitution (II.2.2), see Ingrid Brunk Wuerth, "International Law and Constitutional Interpretation: The Commander in Chief Clause Reconsidered," *Michigan Law Review* 106, no. 1 (2007): 67ff.

11. Ernst Käsemann, *Commentary on Romans*, trans. Geoffrey William Bromiley (Grand Rapids: Eerdmans, 1980), 356.

12. See Martin Luther, *The Freedom of a Christian* (Minneapolis: Fortress Press, 2008).

13. Martin Luther, *Lectures on Galatians, 1535*, ed. Helmut T. Lehmann and Jaroslav Jan Pelikan, Luther's Works (Saint Louis, MO: Concordia Publishing House, 1963), 309. Luther is commenting on Gal 3:19.

14. Barth, *Church and State*, 12.

15. Ibid., 33f.

16. Ibid., 41f.

17. Ibid., 61.

18. Ibid., 44.

19. Intriguingly, Devin Singh suggests that analogies or "homologies" also exist between the political economy of the state and the theological economy of the Trinity. See Devin Singh, "Incarnating the Money-Sign: Notes on an Implicit Theopolitics," *Implicit Religion* 14, no. 2 (July 19, 2011): 136.

20. Barth, *Church and State*, 84.

21. The most accessible statement of his legal positivism for English-speakers is probably Hans Kelsen, *Pure Theory of Law* (Berkeley: University of California Press, 1967).

22. Sandrine Baume, *Hans Kelsen and the Case for Democracy*, trans. John Zvesper (Essex: ECPR Press, 2012), 10.

23. Hans Kelsen, *Essays in Legal and Moral Philosophy* (Dordrecht: Reidel, 1974), 82.

24. Baume, *Hans Kelsen and the Case for Democracy*, 15.

25. Carl Schmitt, *Political Theology: Four Chapters on the Concept of Sovereignty*, trans. George Schwab (Chicago: University of Chicago Press, 2005).

26. Carl Schmitt, *The Concept of the Political*, trans. George Schwab, Expanded ed. (Chicago: University of Chicago Press, 2007).

27. Schmitt, *Legality and Legitimacy*.

28. Ibid., 9.

29. Ibid., 23.

30. Ibid., 30.

31. Sandrine Baume, "On Political Theology: A Controversy Between Hans Kelsen and Carl Schmitt," *History of European Ideas* 35, no. 3 (September 2009): 369–381.

32. Schmitt, *Legality and Legitimacy*, 93.

33. Schmitt, *Political Theology*, 5.

34. Giorgio Agamben, *State of Exception*, trans. Kevin Attell (Chicago: University of Chicago Press, 2005), 2.

35. Barth, *Church and State*, 56.

36. Karl Barth, *Evangelium und Gesetz* (Munich: Chr. Kaiser Verlag, 1935).

37. Barth, *Church and State*, 55.

38. Kahn, *Political Theology*, 38.

39. Ibid., 40.

40. Bonnie Honig, *Emergency Politics: Paradox, Law, Democracy* (Princeton: Princeton University Press, 2009), 84ff.

41. Carys Moseley, *Nations and Nationalism in the Theology of Karl Barth* (Oxford: Oxford University Press, 2013), 48–49.

42. Ibid., 39.

43. Ibid., 63.

44. Jan-Werner Müller, *Constitutional Patriotism* (Princeton, NJ: Princeton University Press, 2007), 80.

45. Barth, *Church and State*, 70f.

46. Indeed, as Devin Singh points out in his contribution to this volume, upholding the transcendence of God (and divine justice) over secular forms of political legitimacy can itself supply a backhanded metaphysics of political absolutism—and also, as he cautions about my position, a theology of indifference toward absolutist politics. See Devin Singh, "A Tale of Two Sovereignties: Karl Barth and Carl Schmitt in Dialogue," in this volume.

47. Karl Barth, "Fragen an das 'Christentum,'" in *Theologische Fragen und Antworten*, vol. 3 (Zollikon: Evangelischer Verlag, 1957), 93–99. I thank Devin Singh for calling this article to my attention in his contribution to our seminar.

48. Ibid., 96.

49. Devin Singh suggests that liberalism may also "betray enduring theological assumptions" (See Singh, "A Tale of Two Sovereignties," in this volume). While undoubtedly true as an historical claim, I take Kelsen's position to be that genuine liberalism constantly subjects its lingering metaphysical assumptions to ideological critique.

50. Christopher May, *The Rule of Law: The Common Sense of Global Politics* (Cheltenham, UK: Edward Elgar Pub, 2014), 36.

51. Ibid., 170–183.

52. See ibid., 172.

53. Qing Jiang, *A Confucian Constitutional Order: How China's Ancient Past Can Shape Its Political Future*, ed. Daniel A. Bell and Ruiping Fan, trans. Edmund Ryden (Princeton: Princeton University Press, 2012), 42.

54. Ibid., 48.

55. Weifang He, *In the Name of Justice: Striving for the Rule of Law in China* (Washington, DC Brookings Institution Press, 2012), 143.

56. Ibid., 76ff.

57. Ibid., 98.

58. In his contribution to this volume, Lai Pan-Chiu underscores that Barth's putative position toward contemporary political developments in China necessarily remains underdetermined. He notes, for instance, that "Barthian" rationales can and have been mustered for and against participation in the "Occupy the Central" movement. Any "Barthian" argument advanced in the present must also be constructive. See Lai Pan-chiu, "Religious Diversity, Democracy, and Public Theology: Conversing with Barth in a Hong Kong Context," in this volume.

59. As Kim-kwon Chan recounts in his contribution to this volume, Christianity is regarded as "unpatriotic" in some Chinese political circles. See Kim-Kwon Chan, "The Ecclesiological Implications of the Political Attitude of the Chinese Authority on Christianity," in this volume.

Chapter 8

A Tale of Two Sovereignties

Karl Barth and Carl Schmitt in Dialogue

Devin Singh

This study aims to make an intervention—both historical and theoretical—into contemporary discussions of political theology by bringing the work of Karl Barth and Carl Schmitt into conversation.[1] Doing so is not only useful in shedding light on their respective theoretical systems and agendas. It is also worthwhile in opening up a political-theological analysis of a critical historical juncture in European thought and society signaled, if only in shorthand, by the Weimar period.[2] My aim is not a simple exercise in comparative and contrastive analysis, however. Nor is it merely a historical retrieval of two Weimar era theoretical giants. My interest is in examining and problematizing the category of the theological-political itself.

In bringing Barth and Schmitt into conversation around the topic of sovereignty, in particular, I intend to demonstrate the proximity of their systems, a proximity that in turn is evocative of the zone of indistinction between the theological and political. In other words, in pointing out the connections between one who prioritized the theological over the political (Barth) and a champion of politics as the final word (Schmitt), I mean to speak to the persistent intermeshing of theological and political spheres. Considering the terms and implications of this encounter will be, I hope, useful to the wider conversation about political theology currently taking place.

Highlighting a proximity between Barth and Schmitt may understandably be unsettling to readers who have come to appreciate much of Barth's theological project and legacy. After all, what could a leading theologian of the *bekennende Kirche* have in common with the "crown jurist" of the Third Reich? What can it mean to speak of a proximity between Barth's stalwart resistance to the Führer as ultimate authority and Schmitt's theoretical justification of this very role? Counterintuitive as this may seem, however, I want to explore what appear as significant similarities and structural parallels between their positions on the nature of sovereignty.[3] Given the recent retrieval of and renaissance in studies of Schmitt, particularly as the limits of the liberal paradigm become more evident, those attempting theological interventions in debates about liberalism might find inroads through this interface of Barth and Schmitt. Thus, theologically informed diagnoses of and prescriptions for what ails Western liberal regimes do well to consider the proximity and difference between these two thinkers, influential as they both have been in their respective fields and in modern thought more broadly.

Indeed, there are good reasons to bring Barth and Schmitt into conversation, and considerations of the potential connections should aid inquiries into twentieth-century theopolitical thought. Both Barth and Schmitt are products of the same historical moment and context, writing in the interwar and Weimar years. Yet, each chose radically different political options. Both draw on theology, one aligning Reformed Protestantism and a separation of church and state with his socialist tendencies, the other conservative Catholicism and a proximity of church and state with national socialist advocacy.[4] Both thinkers can be taken as critics of modernity in its epistemological and sociopolitical implications. Both also attack Western liberalism, choosing alternatives on the left and right. For both, the figure of the sovereign remains central and determinative in their projects.

For Schmitt, the political sovereign is the highest authority, for it is he who "decides on the exception."[5] The sovereign creates order, sustains the space of rule, and can suspend the force of law. For Barth, God is the sovereign, calling creation into being and ordering it by divine decree and according to the logic of the covenant. Questions need to be asked as to whether or not their models are structurally identical, with the political sovereign or God as exchangeable referents. Barth radically opposed political exceptionalism and the exalted leader. But, does it matter that in opposing the extreme political sovereign, he apparently reasserts an exalted view of sovereignty in the name of God? Does outdoing Caesar with a more powerful, glorious, and exalted Christ offer adequate challenge to earthly modes of power? How does one take the apparent formal similarities between their two models of sovereignty, given the material differences in content in their ideas of the sovereign?

In this chapter, I review various points of apparent connection between Barth and Schmitt on the attributes of sovereignty, arguing that a baseline formal similarity exists. Material differences remain, to be sure, and the impact of such differences on their respective systems requires consideration as well. The point is not to impugn Barth or declare guilt by association. It is rather to open a conversation about the depths of such affinities and their implications, raise questions about the possibility of such comparisons and the methods employed, and spur further research into what I take to be a perpetually ambiguous overlap or interconnection between theology and politics that calls for ongoing reflection and clarification.

AGAINST THE LIBERAL ORDER

Barth and Schmitt share an antipathy toward Western liberalism. Barth aims his critique at liberalism's theological failures and its corrupting potential on the soul of the Christian church, while Schmitt levels his challenge against liberalism's erosion of the political will and community. Undergirding both are similar methodological and ideological concerns. Resistance to liberalism can take many forms, however, and this in no way immediately places Barth and Schmitt in the same camp. Indeed, Schmitt opted for a far right political conservatism that supported Hitler's rise, while Barth leaned left and favored socialism and social democracy. Yet, this common opposition, despite different political alternatives chosen, indexes similar assumptions about how power and authority might be arranged.

Schmitt's early work in *Political Theology* and *Roman Catholicism and Political Form* offers a skeptical image of human nature, which requires God-ordained rule and dominion if true political community is to be established and preserved.[6] Schmitt does not articulate a robust theological model or justification for such rule. Neither does he seek to retrieve or re-establish an explicitly theological ground for sovereignty. His purposes are political in nature and aimed at what he takes for granted as the secular sphere. Yet, undergirding his theorizing of secular politics is his now famous claim that "*all* significant concepts of the modern theory of the state are secularized theological concepts."[7] Schmitt seeks to recover and signal the theological aura to politics undermined by modernity and under threat in particular by the liberal project. In retrieving the long history of theological justification for monarchy (starting at least as early as Eusebius of Caesarea), Schmitt seeks to mobilize the prestige, esteem, and horizon derived from such a legacy. Signaling the theological roots to modern politics is to invoke the enduring necessity of notions of transcendence, of ontological excess beyond the immanent sphere that grounds the political.[8] The flattening effect of liberal cosmology dismantles authority structures that require hierarchy and unity, catalyzing a process of atomization and individualism that disrupts authentic politics.

For Barth, liberalism could provide no theologically robust resistance to National Socialism, in part because of an insufficient conception of human sinfulness and capacity for moral and spiritual failure. Only God is righteous, holy, and just. Liberalism atomizes humans as individuals and exalts their rational capacity for independent judgment and decision apart from revelation and the authority of the divine Word. Liberalism centers on the human in a way that deemphasizes not only divine alterity but sovereignty as well. Barth's resistance to liberalism thus seeks a recuperation of the sovereignty of God and God's radical priority and uniqueness in all matters. Not only must the radical qualitative distinction between God and creation be maintained in order to prevent a liberal sacralization of culture, but the sovereignty of God is essential such that the human sphere can respond in obedient conformity to the divine plan.

It is noteworthy that Barth has been seen as problematically antagonistic toward the fragile Weimar republic.[9] Some even charge his attack on liberalism as facilitating the republic's ultimate failure. As Christophe Chalamet notes, Barth himself retrospectively admitted that he was insufficiently supportive of the republic.[10] Yet, Chalamet charges such critics, many associated with the so-called "Munich School," with gross misreadings and oversimplifications of Barth's works and the history of their effects. This group of thinkers, including Trutz Rendtorff, Falk Wagner, and Friedrich Graf, read Barth as epitomizing Enlightenment themes of autonomy and self-sovereignty, if projected now upon God. Rather than representing a radical break with modernity or a reclamation of pre-modern "orthodoxy," Barth radicalizes modern themes and comes dangerously close to a fascist authoritarianism in theological guise.[11]

Discussions of the political implications of Barth's theological system can degenerate into debates about his original authorial intentions versus various (mis)interpretations of his position. That seems to be the state of the conversation in response to the Munich School's criticism. While such debate has its place, I am more interested in the legacy of his theological model and the courses it has taken and may take, regardless of "original intent." While tracing these trails is in no way possible here, I want to argue against foreclosing consideration of the provocative proximity between Barth's views on divine sovereignty and authoritarian political models. The critiques associated with the Munich School, raising concerns about Barth's absolutism, should remain part of such consideration.[12]

Chalamet cautions further that Barth's critique of *theological* liberalism should not be taken as a critique of political liberalism or liberalism in general.[13] The two must be kept distinct as separate objects of thought. This would perhaps then disrupt swift comparisons with Schmitt. But the two movements are assuredly related. The conception of the human is similar in both, and liberal theology, at least the lineage linked to Schleiermacher, articulated its theological anthropology in explicit conversation with dominant humanist tropes associated with political liberalism. That theological liberalism was seen (fairly or not) as a theological accommodation to cultural constraints and challenges posed by an emerging liberal paradigm further justifies the association. Furthermore, Barth explicitly links liberal forms of parliamentary democracy with his theological critique, asking "Why does

Christianity engage in parliamentary discussion, when it believes in revealed truth?"[14] Some tension and possible opposition are here implied. From the other angle, Schmitt explicitly sought a critique of political liberalism in transcendent and theological registers, further blurring the lines. The mutual implication of theology and politics within liberalism highlights the need to think the two together. Chalamet's defense of Barth here inserts too stark a divide between the theological and the political.

DECISION AND AUTONOMY

Over against this liberal order, with its endless deliberation and overconfidence in the sanctifying effects of human discourse, both Barth and Schmitt posit a decisive and autonomous sovereign. The centrality of these themes for both thinkers prompted Jacob Taubes to consider the two together as "Zealots of the Absolute and of Decision," and to label Schmitt the "Catholic variant" of Barth.[15] Such an association may ultimately be deemed premature and lacking nuance, but its provocation invites closer scrutiny. For, indeed, both Barth and Schmitt resisted modern, liberal ideals of personal decision and autonomy. Both condemned the hubris of contemporary ideologies of autonomous self-determination, of a liberalism that contributed to the atomization of humanity and the loss of a fundamental sociality. To the contrary, decision and freedom remain, first and foremost, the prerogative of sovereignty.

For Schmitt, decision is essential to the definition of the sovereign, given the decision on the exception.[16] Schmitt resists what he took to be liberalism's emphasis on endless discussion, seen in the erosion of parliamentary democracy, and he calls instead for political will and action. A centralized decision maker is necessary to unite political space and implement the will of the people. The sovereignty of this decision maker is maintained in that the leader as representative of the people ultimately retains independence and is not a mere cipher for their will. In this way, Schmitt also resists what he sees as the economic logic of liberalism (one person-one vote), which reduces humans to numbers and makes politics a matter of statistics, proportions, and measurements. His concern with the parliamentary model is what he saw as a proliferation of interest groups and a majoritarian logic. Such processes were not only open to corruption but ultimately stymied action. Seeing the disintegration of authentic politics, Schmitt asserts a personalist and decisionist sovereign, a clear and authoritative center whose actions and will, while taking into consideration the interests of the governed, originate in the heart of sovereignty itself.

Yet, the sovereign decision is not merely the basis on which to get things done. More fundamentally, it is the will of the sovereign that forges political space. The sovereign decision, for Schmitt, is prior to law and ultimately grounds the order to which law is applied. This is what is revealed in the sovereign decision over the exception, as the capacity to suspend the force of law indexes a more originary capacity to set such law and order into place. Consider the creation-theological resonances in one commentator's observation that, for Schmitt, "the figure of the sovereign, and thus the figure of the legislator, achieves for Schmitt a victory over formless matter."[17] Concerned to retain a personalism over against the leveling, dehumanizing, and disenchanting forces of a market economy, Schmitt invests the figure of the sovereign with a will that does not mechanically apply law or the general will, but rather makes these possible in the first place.

For Barth, divine decision is of ultimate concern.[18] Such a "turning-point or decision has not, however, taken place in time, but in that eternity which is the frontier of time."[19] Rooted in eternity, God's decision before all time to elect humanity in Jesus Christ is the basis of the divine covenant. Such a covenant is itself the internal basis of creation, which is, in turn, the covenant's external basis. The authority of decision resides with God. This is part of the mark of divine sovereignty, that the entirety of decision is God's and that God's decision has ultimate consequence for humanity and all of creation. It is because of God's free and sovereign decision that creation exists, and because this results in human life—a life of election in Jesus Christ—it is interpreted as a gracious decision. Divine decision brings the created order into being and human community into existence, formed around the covenants and united to God in gratitude and obedience. Thus, the right of decision is a divine prerogative and signals sovereign freedom and priority.[20]

The right of decision resides so much with God that Barth will resist notions of "decisionism" when it comes to faith. Humanity in no way chooses to accept what God has done in a way that renders this more real or effective. Instead, humanity agrees with and affirms God's decision, responding in gratitude and praise. Divine sovereignty is such that this modest human response is also construed as an act of divine will, as something that divine revelation accomplishes by its own power. It does not align with any innate human capacity to perceive and respond to the Word (hence Barth's debate with Brunner). This relates to Barth's critique of the liberal agenda, as he undoes the sovereignty of independent human decision-making in the spiritual realm. Divine decision obviates the liberal, deliberative process of rational human actors, since such agents can in no way meaningfully opt for the divine but must respond to a call from above, as it were. Because God's Sovereign Word does not return empty, the promise which is also a command accomplishes its response in elect humanity.

This vision of a God who decides, and whose decisions are definitive for creation and humanity, bringing order and existence, is predicated upon a

God who is supremely free. Thus, autonomy emerges as a central theological principle, indeed, the theological principle that, along with love, defines who God is: the one who loves in freedom. Barth explicitly links divine freedom with sovereignty, and distinguishes it from all other forms of such supreme authority:

> If we enquire how, according to His revelation in Jesus Christ, God's lordship differs in its divinity from other types of rule, then we must answer that it is lordship in freedom. It would be senseless to ascribe this characteristic to other kinds of sovereignty, or to any other living and loving but that of God. There are other sovereignties, but freedom is the prerogative of divine sovereignty.[21]

But, how, we might ask, is divine freedom a mark of distinction, for certainly earthly sovereigns possess a type of autonomy and priority, at least in the Schmittian schema. No apparent constraint exists in the sovereign decision for the state of exception. None dictate the prerogatives of sovereignty in forging the order in the first place. Indeed, in speaking of the norm and so-called "normal situation" under sovereignty, Schmitt suggests that it is simply the arbitrary norm enforced by the power.[22] What marks the divine difference?

> Freedom is, of course, more than the absence of limits, restrictions, or conditions. This is only its negative and to that extent improper aspect— improper to the extent that from this point of view it requires another, at least in so far as its freedom lies in its independence of this other. But freedom in its positive and proper qualities means to be grounded in one's own being, to be determined and moved by oneself. This is the freedom of the divine life and love. In this positive freedom of His, God is also unlimited, unrestricted and unconditioned from without.[23]

Here we see that, according to Barth, nothing is dictated to God from without; all decision comes from within, from the divine nature. Divine freedom is not defined simply negatively as freedom from constraint. Even this is not free enough for God, for the absence of constraint implies another from whom one is independent. But God is one, sole, primary, ultimate. Divine freedom is here not understood relationally but constitutively: God's sovereignty is grounded from within, in God's own being, and the freedom that arises is unconditioned and originary.[24]

In this sense, divine freedom surpasses all earthly modes of sovereignty. Other sovereignties, Barth correctly notes, are still conditioned by a related non-relation, positing freedom negatively as unconstrained by another. This dynamic can be seen in Giorgio Agamben's exploration of Schmittian notions of sovereignty.[25] The sovereign, related to the sphere of rule by virtue of the exception, is fundamentally linked by this exclusion. Sovereignty is inconceivable outside of some association—even a wholly excluded relation—with the sphere of the governed. What Barth postulates here seeks to free divine sovereignty from even these fetters. God is so sovereign, so absolutely free, so as to generate sovereignty and freedom internally, from the ground of the being of the divine person. This divine sovereign exceeds all earthly sovereigns in being the source of sovereign freedom.

It is such sovereign freedom that is primary and that, because of the divine love that is also primary, becomes God's decision to be *for us*.[26] The relation that is expressed between God and creation, seen in the covenant and in the election of humanity, is posited a posteriori to the pure, sovereign, loving freedom of God. The sovereign decision to be for humanity and in relation to creation logically precedes this creation, even as Barth insists on always thinking the two together, given his Christological paradigm. As Barth will go on to elaborate when discussing divine omnipresence, nothing is remote from God, and all depends upon and is subject to God as the Lord.[27] Yet, this proximity results from the primary and originary freedom of God that stems from God's being in itself, not in contradistinction to creation.

Barth's sovereign God is pure freedom. A question that should be explored is whether this exalted notion of freedom functions as a horizon toward which earthly sovereignties strive. If so, it may serve a legitimating role, despite protestations to the contrary. Whether or not it is conceptually consistent to extrapolate from earthly sovereignties to this divine model and back again—given claims, for instance, about radical ontological distinction—such moves may still be made and arguably have been made continually throughout history.

In order to disrupt earthly sovereignties, it would need to be shown that Barth's understanding of originary, non-relational and non-oppositional divine freedom is somehow *antithetical* to the logic of political sovereignty and therefore an illegitimate *telos*. The textures of this sovereign logic as explored by Agamben may prove to be one route toward important distinctions and resistance.[28] If sovereignty persists by way of this relation of exception, a related non-relation, does it find its fulfillment or undoing in this vision of a sovereign God who is pure freedom outside of all—even the most negative—of relations?[29]

EXCEPTIONAL REVELATION

Closely related to the decision and the autonomous priority of the sovereign in Schmitt's thought is the idea of the exception. "Sovereign is he who decides on the state of exception."[30] The sovereign has the power of decision and also the capacity to recognize or determine and to declare the exception. In a sense, the sovereign decision is itself part of the exception, the originary exceptional act. In juridical terms, the exception pertains to the suspension of law in states of emergency, where direct power is assigned to the leader in an extralegal capacity. The leader may decide to suspend the rule of law and initiate martial law and emergency rule. Following Kierkegaard, Schmitt asserts that the exception in fact proves the norm, showing the true logic of the political system.[31] Thus, the emergency situation of the suspension of the law, where all now rests and resides with the decision and will of the sovereign, reveals the backbone of the system that operates on a day-to-day basis through the "regular" employment of law. Elements like due process, deliberation, and delegated acts of judgment in courts are stripped away to reveal the basic power structure where the whole inheres in sovereign will.

For Schmitt, "the exception in jurisprudence is analogous to the miracle in theology."[32] The miracle is that moment of in-breaking or disruption that is ultimately not an aberration but reveals what is most fundamentally true. Just as the miracle reveals an underlying truth that all power and authority reside with the God who irrupts into the immanent sphere of creation, the exception displays the logic that law and order rest upon sovereign will. The miracle and exception preserve the autonomy and authority of the sovereign, while still paradoxically expressing a relation between the sovereign and the governed order. This is why the exception reveals indirectly, by way of negation, and appears as chaos. It is not a didactic moment or simple assertion of authority, but a stripping away and disruption that shows that all hangs upon the will of the sovereign.

The exceptional character of revelation is central to Barth's system. At the heart of this conception is the desire to preserve the sovereign freedom of God, asking "How in God's freedom is it possible for His revelation to encounter man?"[33] Even perception and understanding for Barth imply a kind of authority, such that the human encounter with the divine raises concerns about God's priority. Revelation of the Word is something that irrupts and interrupts, intervening in human existence in a display of total divine sovereignty. Through revelation humans encounter this sovereign God in Jesus Christ, even as this God, paradoxically (or dialectically), remains hidden. Revelation reveals that in Christ alone God is free for humanity and as such "it stamps itself . . . as a mystery and in token thereof as a miracle, i.e., as an exception from the rule of the cosmos of realities that otherwise encounter man, it claims to be attested and known in this exceptional way corresponding to its exceptional character."[34]

As exceptional, the miraculous revelation reveals by way of inversion or negation. Barth is adamant that the incomprehensibility of God and blindness of humanity are at the core of what is revealed. "Revelation itself is needed for knowing that God is hidden and man blind."[35] In other words, revelation does not mark movement from blindness to light and understanding, for human conceptions of divine incomprehensibility and creaturely finitude are themselves deeply flawed. What is revealed shows the frontier between God and humanity:

> If [the message of Revelation] is heard, then and not till then the boundary between God and man becomes really visible, of which the most radical sceptic and atheist cannot even dream, for all his doubts and negations. Since the boundary is visible, revelation, which crosses this boundary, is also visible as a mystery, a miracle, an exception.[36]

Revelation as exception shows this reality of divine otherness, stripping away human pretension to agency and self-definition. Human existence is a derived existence, taking its form and logic from the Word in the person of Jesus Christ. From the apparent chaos and negativity of revelation emerges a deeper truth that God is nevertheless for humanity, and has created the world in concert with this disposition and decree. Revelation, following the logic of exception, reveals the reality that all rests upon God.

Seen in terms of the wholly-other, radically prior, triune God who initiates revelation *and* accomplishes the response of belief in humans, Barth's sovereign also operates in a way that makes deliberative consideration, and more micro acts of faith and practice, secondary to the will, decision, and plan of this figure of authority. Many have critiqued Barth's seeming erosion of human agency and freedom in this image of an overwhelming, sovereign God.[37] Yet, here my interest is in the sociopolitical implications of this model, which lends itself to an understanding of sovereignty focused on obedience to and adoration of the one in authority.

Giorgio Agamben's recent passing critique of Barth in this regard is worth considering. Agamben notes Barth's claim that the very ontological composition and existential foundation of humanity is glorification of and hence obedience to God (as a response to this exceptional revelation). Agamben claims that this is structurally identical to the very politics of utmost adoration of and fealty to the earthly sovereign, which Barth, of course, rejected in wartime Germany. In either the theological or political arena, "the highest dignity and the highest freedom are to be found in the glorification of the sovereign . . . glorification is due to the sovereign not because he needs it but, as his resplendent insignia, his throne, and crown reveal, because he is glorious in himself."[38]

Does Barth's project lend itself to a theology of glory for glory's sake, glorifying God because God is glorious? Agamben thinks so, and takes this as easily transferable from theology to politics. Although Barth of course rejected glorification of the Führer, the question persists of whether or not he sets forth the model of such glorification with even greater tenacity and theological legitimation by ascribing it to God.[39]

TRANSCENDENCE AND COMPETITIVE SOVEREIGNTIES

While both Barth and Schmitt invoke notions of transcendence, they must be understood differently, given the different objects to which the term is applied. Schmitt's project indexes the theological aura to politics and so roots the political order and its center in an implicit understanding of the transcendent God. Again, Schmitt here is drawing on (although rarely in explicit fashion[40]) a long history of theological legitimation of rulers, not to reiterate this legitimation in the same manner, but to express the need for a transcendent ground even in secular modernity. That political values and the (sovereign and collective) will refer to something outside of the human and political sphere is critical for him in resisting the flattening effects of liberalism, which is ultimately self-referential.[41] Transcendence denotes the sovereign's relation to the political order itself. The sovereign stands outside the governed sphere to a significant extent in order to create its conditions of possibility.[42] Theologically, we might compare this to God creating a space that is not-God in order to allow creation to exist in dependent and yet distinct identity. Thus, we can speak of a limited or secular-political transcendence in the relation of the sovereign to the political order that is drawn together and sustained by sovereign will and decision.[43]

Transcendence is, of course, central to Barth's reassertion of divine sovereignty and alterity. God is the wholly and radically other, standing outside of and before creation. Jesus Christ is the bridge and link between God and creation. Creation depends upon this wholly-other God, having been drawn into being from God's sovereign, free, and loving decision to be in relation with an Other. Even in Jesus Christ, however, God remains transcendent and distinct. Indeed, as contemporary interpreters of this Barthian vision have emphasized, it is because of radical and complete transcendence that incarnation is possible, since God can exist in a noncompetitive relation with creation and thus be fully proximate and present with it while being not of it.[44]

It is this extreme transcendence of God that marks one potential Barthian reply to concerns that his model legitimates earthly sovereigns. Because of the infinite qualitative distinction between God and creation, no innate or natural link exists that would allow one to transfer these divine attributes to a monarch or dictator. God is not simply higher on the chain of command or being but of a completely different order such that no legitimate authorization of earthly power is possible.

My concern is that, at best, this undoes the link between theological legitimation and earthly authority in word only, but not in implication. One can protest all one wants that one's image of a glorious, exalted, all-powerful and completely efficacious divine sovereign is ontologically distinct from and therefore not a legitimate ground for earthly rulers. This does not stop (and has not stopped throughout Christian history) the application of that model nevertheless.[45] Ironically, even this exalted and radical view of transcendence may be co-opted and deployed in political theology to undergird a theopolitics of radical distinction between ruler and ruled (seen already in applications of the Persian Great King in Hellenism).[46] Rather than undercutting attempts to provide theological legitimation to rulers, radical transcendence may offer new possibilities for it.

In a thoughtful article exploring the resonances and differences among Barth, Schmitt, and Agamben, Clifford Anderson highlights the implications of divine sovereignty and transcendence for Barth's political sensibilities. Drawing on reflections in the *Römerbrief* and Barth's *Theological Existence Today*, Anderson claims that for Barth, conservative endorsement of and revolutionary reaction to political regimes are both wrongheaded.[47] Neither gives divine sovereignty its full due. The revolutionary, in particular, runs the risk of replacing one illegitimate sovereign with another.

Alignment with and obedience to the one, sovereign, transcendent Lord leads one to recognize the profound insignificance of earthly regimes in light of the eschatological reality of God's kingdom. "The real revolutionary gives witness to the coming divine revolution through his inaction. . . . By calmly rejecting any political theology, the genuine revolutionary drains the state of its religious 'pathos.'"[48] Anderson is quick to note that this need not entail passive quietism, but can fuel prophetic witness against the legitimacy of earthly regimes. But at base it grounds a life and an ecclesial activity lived as if the state and its claims to authority do not matter. This, in my view, is a Barthian politics of the transcendence of God, a conformity to a divine sovereign whose noncompetitive relation with earthly sovereigns leads to a calculated indifference to earthly regimes.

Though not contradictory, a different voice emerges in some of Barth's more strident writings against the Nazis. In *The Church and the Political Problem of Our Day*, Barth explains that the Christian church must reject and oppose the claims to supremacy of the National Socialists. When confronted with this regime, "the Church cannot but answer with Yes or No," for it "cannot persist in an attitude of neutrality."[49] No third way exists. While in other political situations the options may look different, in the concrete situation facing the church in Germany, Christians must either be for or against the state.

The cause of this opposition is the religious aura of Nazism, the claims of a false "Man-God" and "false Messiah." The regime set itself up as an alternative religious option and means of salvation. Here Barth problematically invokes the ancient archenemy of Christendom, Islam, labeling the Nazi state a *"new Islam*, its myth as a new Allah, and Hitler as this new Allah's Prophet."[50] The regime exists in competition with and as a threat to the church and its proclamation, and so must be opposed. Commitment to Jesus Christ and allegiance to the Nazi party are, for Barth, "mutually exclusive."

What is apparently insidious here is the wedding of alternative religious and political agendas. Thus, Barth seems to recognize—if oppositionally—the claims of Schmitt and other Nazi theorists about the theological aura to political sovereignty. The Schmittian exalted sovereign trades on a divine model. In resisting this, Barth appears at first to advocate a politics stripped of religious legitimation. This is what is implied in Anderson's observation that, for Barth, "the Christian theologian retains a political task, namely denying the legitimacy of theological-political concepts by insisting on the secularity of political discourse."[51]

This might lead one to conclude that Barth respects the legitimacy of the secular, political order, which assuredly is not the case. For Barth, the state, like all reality, remains rooted in Jesus Christ, who is its center.[52] While the state may not be aware that Christ is its center, it is nevertheless called to execute justice in the service of God's grace, and the church must remind the state of this task. The state maintains a level of independence, where the church chides and may advise it, but must accept the state's own freedom as rooted in Jesus Christ. Barth will go so far as to assert that functioning state churches are preferable to free church arrangements, given the unity they display in Christ.[53] The decision faced by the church under National Socialism, then, is not between either political theology or affirming secular-political discourse. Rather, it is a matter of choosing between two different political theologies. For Barth's views root the state in divine authority.

In opposing the religiosity of National Socialism, Barth's resistance is not due to its fusion of religion and politics, its use of political theology. Rather, the challenge is its difference. It is not Christianity. The values that this state upholds and the sovereign it exalts are not the Christian sovereign. It is a religious competitor, with an incompatible political theology (again, the comparison with Islam here is significant). The two options are competing and mutually exclusive positions. There are two sovereigns to choose from and one threatens to usurp the other. There is no noncompetitive relation leading to neutrality and indifference.

At least as deployed in Nazi context, the political sphere here draws upon the theological in a way that must be confronted, because its transcendent sources are different.[54] Of course, God's being remains the same for Barth, and so God must not be thought of here as in competitive relation. But the competitive—as opposed to neutral or indifferent—response of the church displays a type of competition between a vision of God and the false sovereigns who would threaten to obscure humanity's response to the divine.

While the sovereignty of God is never in itself under threat, such divine sovereignty is under apparent attack in the hearts of would-be worshippers, inviting vigorous confrontation by the church.

CONCLUSION

What presents itself in this exploration is the persistent ambiguity in attempts at theological self-distinction from the political and vice-versa. Barth can be interpreted in at least two ways with regard to the implications of his views of divine sovereignty for political engagement. On the one hand, he seems to posit a God whose radical sovereign transcendence engenders on the part of the church a profound distanciation from and conscientious indifference to various political regimes. This would support a reading of a noncompetitive relation between his ideal of divine sovereignty and a model of earthly sover-eignty championed by Schmitt. Fundamental formal and material differences persist, ensuring that such sovereigns do not in fact face a head-on collision. Comparisons of Barth and Schmitt on sovereignty thus render dissimilarity as the final word. Of course, the critique often raised at such a position is that it promotes quietism and passivity in the face of radical evil, leading to various sins of omission. The challenge remains of how to conceptualize strategies of resistance on the basis of a divine transcendence that may draw ecclesial vision outside the world.

On the other hand, Barth faces the particularity of National Socialism with critique and opposition, and rightly so, given the horrors and abuses carried out by the regime.[55] In this case, however, the basis of his position reveals a competitive relationship, where the option of either God or Hitler presents itself. In other words, the criterion for resistance stems from an impossibility of co-existence between two focal points of sovereign power. In such a reading, Barth and Schmitt appear to have proximate notions of sovereignty and ultimate authority. That they end up in contrasting political positions is not a function of different understandings of sovereignty so much as it is an exchange of terms—God or Führer—with their attendant material differences.[56] The challenge that Barth poses to the national socialist ideology of ultimate allegiance to the sovereign leader is not a radically different understanding of authority and sovereignty but a more extreme one. God in Barth's view is higher and more exalted than any earthly leader such that ultimate allegiance belongs only to God. One sovereign—an earthly, mortal, and political one—is displaced by another—eternal, divine, and transcendent.

This option presents a quandary: while the formal similarity and resultant competitive relation certainly provide a fulcrum for protest and resistance, questions of ultimate legitimation of such earthly modes of power persist.

In what ways might opposing excessive earthly power with models of more authoritative divine legitimacy double back upon political models and end up sacralizing them?[57] Caveats about radical divine otherness do not sufficiently mitigate transferals of models from theological to secular-political registers, nor can they stave off implicit and indirect influence. Certainly this is a problem that applies far beyond the Barth-Schmitt dialogue here pursued. Yet the tensions, paradoxes, and practical challenges of such a concern present themselves vividly in this exchange. The task of theorizing the theopolitical, whether in critiquing political theology or outlining a theological basis for political engagement, is to tease out the persistent intermeshing of spheres— if only for moments of heuristic clarity. Lines of influence must be mapped and directions of legitimation considered.

Furthermore, champions of a Barthian paradigm might consider what the encounter with Schmitt reveals about the implications of a high view of God's sovereignty. In what ways might a radically different understanding of sovereignty be retrieved from Barth? How, for instance, might an understanding of the cross and a suffering savior—tropes certainly present throughout his works—challenge claims to exalted authority? Why has the Barthian legacy of interpretation done so comparatively little with such images? Perhaps a more efficacious and subversive response to the image of an exalted and glorious leader—mobilized so effectively by Schmitt and the Nazi party—is not a picture of an even more glorious and sovereign God but a broken and humble servant of all.

NOTES

1. In addition to the feedback of my fellow colloquium participants—in particular, Clifford Anderson—I am grateful to Michael Hoelzl, Paul Kim, Justin Stratis and Derek Woodard-Lehman for input and critique.

2. See the excellent collection of essays addressing these themes in Leonard V. Kaplan and Rudy Koshar, *The Weimar Moment: Liberalism, Political Theology, and Law* (Lanham, MD: Lexington Books, 2012).

3. A history of concern for possible links or affinities between Barth and Schmitt exists, with early critiques appearing in Friedrich Wilhelm Graf, "Die Freiheit der Entsprechung zu Gott. Bemerkungen zum theozentrischen Ansatz der Anthropologie Karl Barths," in *Die Realisierung der Freiheit. Beiträge zur Kritik der Theologie Karl Barths*, ed. Trutz Rendtorff (Gütersloh: Gerd Mohn, 1975); Friedrich Wilhelm Graf, "'Der Götze wackelt'? Erste Überlegungen zu Karl Barths Liberalismuskritik," *Evangelische Theologie* 46 (1986): 422–41. See also the comparisons in Mathias Eichhorn, *Es wird regiert!: der Staat im Denken Karl Barths und Carl Schmitts in den Jahren 1919 bis 1938*, Beiträge zur politischen Wissenschaft (Berlin: Duncker & Humblot, 1994); Jacob Taubes, *The Political Theology of Paul*, trans. Aleida Assmann (Stanford: Stanford University Press, 2004), 62–70.

4. Carl Schmitt, *The Concept of the Political*, trans. George Schwab, Expanded ed. (Chicago: University of Chicago Press, 2007). See also, e.g., John P. McCormick, *Carl Schmitt's Critique of Liberalism: Against Politics as Technology* (Cambridge: Cambridge University Press, 1997). Barth's views on church-state relations are articulated most explicitly in Karl Barth, "The Christian Community and the Civil Community," in *Karl Barth: Theologian of Freedom*, ed. Clifford Green (Minneapolis: Fortress Press, 1991). See also Frank Jehle, *Ever Against the Stream: The Politics of Karl Barth, 1906–1968*, trans. Richard and Martha Burnett (Grand Rapids: Eerdmans, 2002); George Hunsinger, ed., *Karl Barth and Radical Politics* (Philadelphia: Westminster Press, 1976); Timothy Gorringe, *Karl Barth: Against Hegemony* (Oxford: Oxford University Press, 1999). See Paul Dafydd Jones's chapter in this volume for an exploration of how we might position Barth vis-à-vis today's political-ideological options.

5. Carl Schmitt, *Political Theology: Four Chapters on the Concept of Sovereignty*, trans. George Schwab (Chicago: University of Chicago Press, 2005), 5.

6. Ibid.; Carl Schmitt, *Roman Catholicism and Political Form*, trans. G. L. Ulmen (Westport, CT: Greenwood Press, 1996). See the discussion in John P. McCormick, "Authority Beyond the Bounds of Mere Reason: A Political-Theological Sketch of the Schmitt-Strauss Exchange," in *The Weimar Moment*, ed. Kaplan and Koshar.

7. Schmitt, *Political Theology*, 36.

8. See the summary and critique in Paulina Ochoa Espejo, "On Political Theology and the Possibility of Superseding It," *Critical Review of International Social and Political Philosophy* 13, no. 4 (2010): 475–94.

9. See the review and assessment in Christophe Chalamet, "Karl Barth and the Weimar Republic," in *The Weimar Moment*, ed. Kaplan and Koshar.

10. Ibid., 242.

11. See, e.g., Trutz Rendtorff, ed., *Die Realisierung der Freiheit. Beiträge zur Kritik der Theologie Karl Barths* (Gütersloh: Gerd Mohn, 1975); for a recent survey see Stefan Holtmann, *Karl Barth als Theologe der Neuzeit: Studien zur kritischen Deutung seiner Theologie* (Göttingen: Vandenhoeck & Ruprecht, 2007).

12. It is interesting that these works have been muted in the English reception of Barth and, indeed, remain untranslated. Ben Myers's observes insightfully that Anglo-American reception of Barth rarely questions the view that Barth's project "overcame the problems of modernity," that in general the success and authority of his dogmatics is "fundamentally beyond question." Criticism restricts itself to pointing out "some relatively benign deficiency." In such context, positing Barth as somehow distinctively modern appears almost incoherent. And yet this has been the claim of some outside such tradition, in Germany and particularly in the Munich School. See Benjamin Myers, review of Holtmann, "Karl Barth als Theologe der Neuzeit,"in *Reviews in Religion and Theology* (2009): 632–635. It has been easy for some to dismiss this School in part because of its efforts to assert Ernst Troeltsch's methodology as the ideal alternative to Barth's and to search for a universalizable theological method. While the optimism of this agenda can and should be questioned, it strikes me as wholly appropriate and necessary to historicize Barth and to under-stand him as a product of his modern environment. While, for Barth, Revelation may

be qualitatively distinct from this world, his own theology is not. One stellar example of situating Barth within a genealogy of modern, Enlightenment theology is Gary J. Dorrien, *Kantian Reason and Hegelian Spirit: The Idealistic Logic of Modern Theology* (Malden, MA: Wiley-Blackwell, 2012), 454–529.

13. Chalamet, "Karl Barth and the Weimar Republic," 256.

14. "Warum parlamentiert das 'Christentum,' wenn es an eine offenbarte Warheit glaubt?" See Karl Barth, "Fragen an das Christentum," in *Theologische Fragen und Antworten*. Gesamelte Vorträge. 3 Band. (Zollikon: Evangelische Verlag, 1957), 98. Cited in Holtmann, *Barth als Theologe der Neuzeit*, 295 n. 204. Holtmann also notes here Graf's critique of Barth's proximity to Schmitt on this issue: Barth's question "wird hier gegenübergestellt: 'Auch Carl Schmitt hat den Parlamentarismus gerade wegen der—vermeintlichen—Unfähigkeit verworfen, der Wahrheitsfrage gerecht zu werden.'" Citing Graf, "'Der Götze wackelt'?" 439.

15. Taubes, *The Political Theology of Paul*, 62, 64.

16. For studies of this theme, see e.g., Christian Krockow, *Die Entscheidung: Eine Untersuchung über Ernst Jünger, Carl Schmitt, Martin Heidegger* (Stuttgart: F. Enke, 1958); George Schwab, *The Challenge of the Exception: An Introduction to the Political Ideas of Carl Schmitt between 1921 and 1936*, 2nd ed. (New York: Greenwood Press, 1989).

17. Astrid Deuber-Mankowsky, "Nothing is Political, Everything Can Be Politicized: On the Concept of the Political in Michel Foucault and Carl Schmitt," *Telos* 142 (Spring 2008): 155.

18. Of many possible sections with this theme, consider, e.g., *CD* II/2 §38 "The Command as the Decision of God," esp. 38.1, "The Sovereignty of the Divine Decision."

19. Karl Barth, *The Epistle to the Romans*, trans. Edwyn Hoskins, 6th ed. (London: Oxford University Press, 1933), 272.

20. Schmitt himself posits a link between "the old Calvinist doctrine of decrees [which] has become transformed into the political terror of the dictator who wields the inscrutable decision in all politics." See Clifford B. Anderson, "The Unexceptional Church: An Exploration of Carl Schmitt, Giorgio Agamben and Karl Barth," *Zeitschrift für Dialektische Theologie* Supplement Series 5 (2010): 16; citing Carl Schmitt, *The Leviathan in the State Theory of Thomas Hobbes: Meaning and Failure of a Political Symbol*, trans. George Schwab and Erna Hilfstein (Chicago: University of Chicago Press, 2008), 32.

21. *CD* II/1, 301.

22. "There exists no norm that is applicable to chaos. For a legal order to make sense, a normal situation must exist, and he is sovereign who definitely decides whether this normal situation actually exists." Schmitt, *Political Theology*, 13.

23. *CD* II/1, 301.

24. It is here that Trutz Rendtorff sees Barth as radicalizing the Enlightenment's autonomy theme, placing it squarely on God. Barth's *Römerbrief* is "der erste Schritt einer neuen Aufklärung, die den Prozeß der Aufklärung noch einmal aufrollt ... Sein Zielpunkt ist nicht die Freiheit und Autonomie des Menschen, sondern die Freiheit und Autonomie Gottes" Trutz Rendtorff, "Radikale Autonomie Gottes.

Zum Verständnis der Theologie Karl Barths und ihrer Folgen," in *Theorie des Christentums: historisch-theologische Studien zu seiner neuzeitlichen Verfassung* (Gütersloh: Gerd Mohn, 1972), 164.

25. Giorgio Agamben, *Homo Sacer: Sovereign Power and Bare Life*, trans. Daniel Heller-Roazen (Stanford: Stanford University Press, 1998). This encounter is further explored in Devin Singh, "Exceptional Economy: Sovereign Exchanges in Carl Schmitt and Giorgio Agamben," *Telos* 191, Summer (2020): 115–36.

26. The Schmittian sovereign is also the one who leads the charge to distinguish between friends and enemies, defining the boundaries of political space. The distinction is necessary, for without it words like "sovereignty, constitutional state, absolutism, dictatorship, [etc] … are incomprehensible if one does not know who is being affected, combatted, refuted or negated by such a term" (Schmitt, *Concept of the Political*, 31). An opposition is necessary, as light is distinguished from darkness, as boundary lines are drawn, as demarcations are made to define the political order. In Barth, we discover a sovereign who has opted to be friends with humanity. If a divine enemy does exist in Barth's system, it is *das Nichtige*. Although God is in no way oppositionally defined in relation to it, it does demarcate creation and human existence as their shadow side and undoing. In this way, it might be viewed in a Schmittian friend-enemy paradigm, for *das Nichtige* helps define the created order negatively and marks the advancing front of God's kingdom. For a different application of Schmitt's friend-enemy distinction in explicit association with Barth's ideas of Christian love for enemies, see Luke Bretherton, "'Love Your Enemies': Usury, Citizenship, and the Friend-Enemy Distinction," *Modern Theology* 27, no. 3 (2011): 386–387.

27. *CD* II/1, 461.

28. See Clifford Anderson's exploration of this relation in his chapter in this volume.

29. As John Macken notes, "In Rendtorff's view, the radical autonomy of God has a radical *function*, that of affirming pure freedom against every claim of a historical structure to be the realisation of freedom. This radicalism may lead to the statement that the self-consciousness of autonomy is not ultimately grounded in the world that it creates." John Macken, *The Autonomy Theme in the Church Dogmatics: Karl Barth and his Critics* (Cambridge: Cambridge University Press, 1990), 132. Such otherworldly autonomy can still be taken either to undermine or ground earthly authority, depending upon the system one constructs. Indeed, Barth's claim about otherworldly autonomy remains itself a historical claim and liable to various historical uses.

30. Schmitt, *Political Theology*, 5.

31. Ibid., 15. The common influence of Kierkegaard on Barth and Schmitt is worth exploring, particularly in notions of radical decision (either/or), as well as ideas of separation (infinite qualitative distinction) between God and creation or the sovereign and the governed space. Barth also makes use of the "exception proving the rule" logic in the *Dogmatics*. For an impressive exploration of the intellectual heritage of Weimar era thinkers see John Stroup, "Political Theology and Secularization Theory in Germany, 1918–1939: Emmanuel Hirsch as Phenomenon of his Time," *Harvard Theological Review* 80, no. 3 (1987): 321–68.

32. Schmitt, *Political Theology*, 36.

33. *CD* I/2, 27.

34. Ibid., 28.

35. Ibid., 29.

36. Ibid.

37. See some critiques and the possible readings of Barth in response that support a divinely grounded yet robust human agency in Macken, *Autonomy Theme*; John Webster, *Barth's Ethics of Reconciliation* (Cambridge: Cambridge University Press, 1995).

38. Giorgio Agamben, *The Kingdom and the Glory: For a Theological Genealogy of Economy and Government*, trans. Lorenzo Chiesa and Matteo Mandarini (Stanford: Stanford University Press, 2011), 215.

39. The respective theories of representation in Schmitt and Barth are also here applicable and must be considered. Schmitt's model expresses a Catholic *analogia entis*, while Barth famously set forth *analogia fidei* in opposition to Catholic positions (cf. the debate with Przywara). Schmitt invoked the incarnation, tied to the Roman Catholic Church as witness, as the ground and legitimation for political form. Incarnation provides the bridge between God and creation (see Schmitt, *Roman Catholicism and Political Form*). Barth's non-sacramental view of incarnation eliminates this link. Indeed the event-like nature of revelation for Barth is calculated to undercut any support of institutions that might claim privilege in matters of God. Yet Barth's understanding of the church as witness and as keeping the political community in check may offer points of connection (see Barth, "Christian Community and Civil Community"). Representation will reveal how divine authority and power are manifest in the world.

40. One of his most direct engagements with theological tradition and the figure of Eusebius is in Carl Schmitt, *Political Theology II: The Myth of the Closure of any Political Theology*, trans. Michael Hoelzl and Graham Ward (Cambridge: Polity, 2008).

41. See McCormick, "Schmitt-Strauss Exchange," 174. This move of reclaiming the transcendent register in the face of immanent, modern politics is also seen in Eric Voegelin, *The New Science of Politics: An Introduction* (Chicago: University of Chicago Press, 1952). Schmitt was a trenchant critic of Hans Kelsen and his positivist legal theories. Voegelin carried on this type of critique, much to the chagrin of Kelsen, his former mentor. See also Clifford Anderson's exploration of Kelsen and Schmitt in this volume.

42. This is most explicitly explored in Giorgio Agamben, *State of Exception*, trans. Kevin Attell (Chicago: University of Chicago Press, 2005).

43. Whether or not such transcendence persists or is necessary in contemporary politics is at the heart of current debates. See, e.g., Claude Lefort, "The Permanence of the Theological-Political?" in *Political Theologies: Public Religions in a Post-Secular World*, ed. Hent de Vries and Lawrence Eugene Sullivan (New York: Fordham University Press, 2006).

44. See Kathryn Tanner, *God and Creation in Christian Theology: Tyranny or Empowerment* (Oxford: Blackwell, 1988); Kathryn Tanner, *Jesus, Humanity*

and the Trinity: A Brief Systematic Theology (Minneapolis, MN: Fortress Press, 2001).

45. This is my critique of Erik Peterson's famous essay "Monotheism as a Political Problem," which makes similar protestations about the impossibility of Christian political theology, claiming that the Trinity cannot be modeled in the earthly realm. This has stopped neither centuries of court theologians from attempting such models nor emperors and kings from trading on the prestige of representing the Triune God. See Erik Peterson, *Theological Tractates*, trans. and ed. Michael J. Hollerich (Stanford: Stanford University Press, 2011). Note that Schmitt and Peterson engaged in extended debate about these themes, a matter that is significant to the present exploration but exceeds its scope. See Devin Singh, "Eusebius as Political Theologian: The Legend Continues," *Harvard Theological Review* 108, no. 1 (2015): 129–54.

46. See, e.g., Lily Ross Taylor, *The Divinity of the Roman Emperor* (Middletown, CT: American Philological Association, 1931), 1–34.

47. Anderson, "Unexceptional Church," 21–26.

48. Ibid., 23. Anderson suggests affinities between Barth here and Agamben's vision of an inactive, indifferent community living outside the gaze of sovereign biopolitics as articulated in, e.g., Giorgio Agamben, *The Coming Community*, trans. Michael Hardt (Minneapolis: University of Minnesota Press, 1993).

49. Karl Barth, *The Church and the Political Problem of our Day* (New York: Scribner, 1939), 38, 40.

50. Ibid., 43. Barth returns to this theme of Islam several times in the text. Interestingly, in his discussion of the friend-enemy distinction, Schmitt also invokes the specter of Islam. In maintaining that the enjoinder to love one's enemies does not apply to the political enemy, he recalls that "Never in the thousand-year struggle between Christians and Moslems did it occur to a Christian to surrender rather than defend Europe out of love toward the Saracens or Turks" (*Concept of the Political*, 29). It would be worthwhile here to explore Barth's Islamophobia in light of Gil Anidjar's Schmittian study of the figures of the Arab and Jew in European theopolitical tradition: see Gil Anidjar, *The Jew, the Arab: A History of the Enemy* (Stanford: Stanford University Press, 2003).

51. Anderson, "Unexceptional Church," 23.

52. Barth, "The Christian Community and the Civil Community." Cf. Robert Hood, *Contemporary Political Orders and Christ: Karl Barth's Christology and Political Praxis* (Allison Park, PA: Pickwick, 1985), 65–67.

53. "A state church that knows and is true to its cause, and to the unity of this cause, is to be preferred to even the freest of churches as a symbol of the ultimate unity of church and state." Karl Barth, "Appendix: Theses on Church and State," in *Ethics* (New York: Seabury, 1981), 521.

54. In explicitly opposing National Socialism in distinction from other political systems, Barth seems to imply that these other systems (liberalism, state monarchies, atheistic socialism, etc.) do not claim theological legitimation or transcendent ground. Nazism comes into competition and confrontation with the church because of the explicitly different sovereign it worships. But the question is whether liberalism

provides merely a better cloak and suppression of its theological legitimation or whether it represents a genuine break with political theology and thus poses no threat. Barth seems to take the latter route (despite his critiques of liberalism), raising questions for those who want to suggest that liberalism too, and indeed all political systems, betray enduring theological assumptions.

55. Although, lamentably, the basis of Barth's condemnation here appears to be less about Nazi abuses or the attempted annihilation of the Jews, but about Nazism's apparent threat to the church and attenuation of the sole worship owed to God.

56. We should note that Schmitt does not explicitly equate the sovereign with Hitler or any other specific leader. The sovereign is a concept and structural necessity. Neither can we define the sovereign simply as God from a Schmittian perspective. As Tracy Strong notes, for Schmitt, "the sovereign is not like God: there *is* no 'Sovereign.' Rather, sovereign acts have the quality of referring only to themselves, as moments of 'existential intervention.'" (Tracy B. Strong, "Foreword," in *Concept of the Political*, ed. Schmitt, xiv).

57. Laurel Schneider sees the radical monotheism invoked by Barth against Hitler as ultimately undermining Christian truths about incarnation and relationality, asserting a divine one-sidedness that has often coincided with imperial strategies: "In such an explicit move against multiplicity and toleration of multiplicity, Barth exposes the logical conclusion of monotheism as the identity of God and takes up the very tools of those he rails against. Faced with the atrocities of tyrants, Barth did not see his position as faulty, even in the decades following the fall of Nazi Germany. Against the likes of governments that will grasp at the image of the ultimate rule, Barth sets the ultimate rule of God. This approach is and has been a comfort to those who suffer under tyrants. But rather than rail against absolute righteousness, radical monotheism claims absolute righteousness for God, and even Barth cannot keep that claim from slipping to the shoulders of God's righteous defenders." Laurel C. Schneider, *Beyond Monotheism: A Theology of Multiplicity* (London and New York: Routledge, 2008), 193–194.

Chapter 9

The Political Theology of the Surveillance Society

Lordless Powers, Drones, and the Eye of God

Hanna Reichel

INTRODUCTION

It was Carl Schmitt who famously pointed out that all political terms are originally theological ones—in a historical as well as a systematic sense.[1] As a complement to this thesis, Jan Assmann has argued that theological terms, in turn, are originally political ones if you consider their longer-term history.[2] Without going into the details of their positions, it would still seem plausible today to say that the hyphen in the term "theo-politics" cuts both ways. Political concepts and theological ideas are intricately linked and inspire each other. Images of the divine and conceptions of state sovereignty, or, more generally speaking, divine and human power have time and again been developed in close analogy and mutually informed one another throughout history.

I will employ such an understanding of political theology as an underlying conceptual framework in order to assess the dynamics of what could be called today's "Surveillance Society."[3] Doing so will allow us to show how much these developments are not only open to interpretation in religious terms, but are already in many instances producing such interpretations which call for their theological assessment. I propose that, particularly, Karl Barth's analysis of "lordless powers" can provide a theological lens for the spread and autonomization of surveillance technologies in our times. His conception describes human creaturely capacities which, disengaged from their original purpose of serving God and men, turn not only against the creator but also the creature and, rather than empowering them, subdue humans to their false—but no less potent—rule. The development of surveillance from instrumental technologies into policy-making and life-shaping realities of frighteningly inescapable and all-encompassing scope can be seen as an instance of such "lordless powers," in the way of *knowledge* gone wild. Karl Barth contributes a hamartiological foundation to the reflection of these processes which goes beyond scandalization or resignation but sees the true extent both of human responsibility as of human suffering under these powers. Furthermore, Barth's conception allows for a theological assessment and critique of the surveillance society and its idols by entailing their confrontation and comparison with the reality and characteristics of the true, "Lordly" power whose distortion they are.[4]

The chapter proceeds along the following lines. I will lay out how our lives to date are thoroughly regulated on multiple levels and by a variety of actors (not least ourselves) by surveillance technologies. After explicating Karl Barth's understanding of "Lordless Powers," I then proceed to examine some of the metaphors and conceptualizations appearing in "surveillance studies" which might easily be reckoned among theo-political concepts as inferred by Schmitt and Assmann. Specifically, the "all-seeing eye," the "Big Other," and the "panopticon" reference images of divine omniscience in whose likeness surveillance technology is perceived and conceptualized.

However, the hyphen cuts both ways. Not only is the political rhetoric of the surveillance society rife with theological images—the surveillance narrative creeps into the religious realm, as well. Outside of institutional religion, we witness phenomena of quasi-religious adherence to practices and politics of surveillance that have prompted talk about emergent forms of "surveillance religion." But also within Christian discourse, we find images of God re-articulated in surveillance terms and structures.

Finally, I sketch venues for a theological assessment and ideological critique of the "political theology" of the surveillance society, in this instance by confronting surveillance interpretations of quasi-divine power with their biblical foundations in Ps 139. The chapter concludes by indicating the need for new, "demonological" models of political ethics in order to better conceptualize the reality of the encountered "lordless powers."[5]

"WELCOME TO SURVEILLANCE SOCIETY!" POLITICS OF VISIBILITY, MARKETS OF VISIBILITY, AND THE VISIBLE SELF

Surveillance as such—understood broadly as "any collection and processing of personal data, whether identifiable or not, for the purpose of influencing or managing those whose data have been garnered"[6]—is, of course, not a new phenomenon. To some degree, there have always been techniques and practices of surveillance in every existing society. In recent years however, we have witnessed unprecedented developments in the technological possibilities and political deployment of surveillance technologies. In the wake of 9/11, a politics of fear and disenfranchisement in the name of security has reigned particularly, but not exclusively, in the Western world. The declaration of the "War on Terror" has led to a rapid spiraling of the use of surveillance technology in domestic and foreign affairs, most prominently on behalf of the United States.[7] The USA PATRIOT Act and its setbacks for citizens' (and non-citizens!) rights has only been the beginning. Reinforced border control, no-fly-lists assembled by profiling algorithms, the monitoring of worldwide communication and—not to be forgotten—the employment of unmanned, but armed drones in wars at a distance mirror external fears. But also internally, CCTV systems survey institutions and public areas, malls, subways, and highways. The activities of secret services have gained momentum, and seem to have surpassed control by national or international law. Today's extent of automatic gathering, storing and analysis of "big data" allows for accumulation of much more information than any human observation has ever been able to provide.[8]

Surveillance changes public hermeneutics. Every citizen is a potential criminal or terrorist and has to be kept under close watch. Transparency, once hailed as an objective of enlightenment and precondition of the free and open, non-corrupt and democratic society, has shown itself in very different colors. The "total transparency" of the digital society threatens to destroy any private sphere, and with it, the very foundations of democracy.[9] The scandals around *wikileaks*, INDECT, PRISM, and NSA data mining reveal deep tensions of power and powerlessness of nation states, secret services and civil societies in the face of technological feasabilities. However, the revelations about the extent of data gathering by the NSA in Germany—unprecedented in amount and at least partially illegal—did not lead to huge public protests. What has been seen as the "Chernobyl moment"[10] of the digital age died away almost quietly. Today, the ever-new headlines about the extent of state surveillance are mostly met with a mix of cultural pessimism, resignation, and, most alarming, cynicism. It seems as though the public has accepted the idea that living under the potentially all-seeing eye of security politics and being monitored, profiled, and analyzed in all areas of life is a necessary condition of human existence in the modern world.[11]

Of course, the "new surveillance"[12] of the digital age has not been an invention of 9/11. It was the tremendous advancements in information and communication technology along with the digital storage and computing capacity that allowed for the technological possibilities of surveillance as well as the political employment of surveillance technologies in all areas of private and public life and by a variety of actors. Also, their use has not been limited to a quasi-totalitarian nation-state of "Big Brother is Watching You"[13] (with Big Brother, in our present world, often posing as "Uncle Sam"). Automatic monitoring and analysis of movement, consumption, and communication profiles permeate private and commercial life, as well. Information has become a new currency in itself. Highly valuable for personalized advertisements as well as for risk assessment of banks, insurance companies, and health-care providers, consumer profiles are bought and sold by international corporations, often without knowledge or explicit (much less informed) consent by consumers. RFID-tags in jeans, intelligent Google online searches and Amazon accounts, social media like Facebook or Twitter and finally, the "Internet of Things"— they all gather massive amounts of personal data often under the banner of convenience and entertainment for the individual, but always for commercial use. "Big data"—whether revealed unknowingly or voluntarily, or even meticulously curated by individuals—can not only predict criminal or purchase behavior. Algorithms based on statistical correlations reveal more about an individual's behavior, feelings, thoughts, past and future development than she knows about herself.[14] These algorithms, however, do not only record and analyze people's lives passively, they also actively shape them. The analysis of past consumer behavior prefigures the world the individual is going to see and interact with in the future. Profiling algorithms are filtering mechanisms for social, commercial, and even political participation and create individualized and exclusive sets of possibilities and constraints of action. Knowledge, prediction, and predetermination seem to go inevitably hand in hand—just as in many a reflection about divine foreknowledge.

It would, however, still be shortsighted to regard surveillance just as an *external* force employed by political systems and big corporations. In the personal and highly voluntary-compulsive communication of social networks, the very individual works actively toward constituting herself as an effect of the annihilation of her privacy. The public exhibitionism displayed in social networks gives the impression that life is only what is seen by others. What constitutes the individual is not enjoying the meal, but posting a picture of it; not living a romantic moment but changing her "relationship status"; not spending time with friends, but "liking" their posts and so on. This "sharing" of activities, preferences, beliefs, and moods—self-expository to a mostly uncontrollable public—can be characterized as a horizontal practice of "participatory surveillance."[15]

Furthermore, quasi-religious movements like the "Quantified Self" advertise the use of surveillance technology for comprehensive self-perfection—from medical monitoring to personal fitness. Self-tracking devices (monitoring individual fluid or calorie intake, steps walked per day, sleep phases, work efficiency and, of course, communication) leave no area of life unsubjected to measurement, statistics, and comparison. The commercial distribution of

"Google glass"—turning the human eye itself into a surveillance camera—is only the next step in the transversal surveillance of private life.

In the face of the technological development and the political, commercial, and private deployment of surveillance technology today, George Orwell almost seems like a "naive optimist."[16] His dystopic visions of a preemptive fight against crime or TVs that monitor our every move have long been surpassed by the reality of automatized surveillance of public and private spaces. With the high degree of permeation of everyday life by surveillance technology, one does not have to be a conspiracy theorist to talk about a global *Surveillance Society*. The major threat today might not be the totalitarian state anymore as much as liquid and intransparent channels of information power, themselves seemingly uncontrollable by national law and governance. The transition from dystopian fantasies to background realities has come to pass by small, sometimes even inconspicuous steps. The fact that there has been no significant public outcry against these developments may well be their most thorough effect and success as this in itself speaks of the deep transformations of our conceptions of public and private space. The emergent surveillance society is structured by notions of omniscience, prediction and the transparency of the individual to higher, intangible and unseen powers which control life in subtle, yet pervasive ways.

THE POLITICAL THEOLOGY OF THE SURVEILLANCE SOCIETY

"Lordless Powers": Knowledge Gone Wild

In posthumous fragments of *CD* IV/4, Karl Barth sketched an analysis of "lordless powers" that can illuminate our reflections on these technological and societal developments.[17] For Barth, politics, economics, and other powers cannot be seen as originally benign divine ordinances or orders of creation. On the other hand, for Barth it is clear that there is no evil power next to or opposed to God. Rather, "man's fall and alienation from God is the root of all evil."[18] Thus, the "disorderly" powers structuring our world are in fact creations of man who, "alienated from God, tries to live a lordless life." In the realm of politics, such an attempt at autonomization might look as follows:

> Now if power breaks loose from law, if the one who should be active in the service of the divine order chooses to value and love as such his sovereignty and dominion, his power and force over others, if he undertakes to establish and exercise these things for their own sake, as the man does who emancipates himself from God, then inasmuch as they too emancipate themselves from him and become his master, the demonism of politics arises. (219f.)

This attempt at human autonomy, however, does not at all succeed and "result in his becoming the lord and master of the possibilities of his own life" (214). Rather,

> in the foolish and hopeless attempt to escape from the sphere of God's lordship, it is not so simple for man to become and be even a little God and Lord with the implied approximation to God's supremacy and controlling power in the fashioning of human existence. Even a partially free control has always been everywhere the myth, but only the myth and illusion, of the person who thinks and claims that he has come of age and is now sovereign and autonomous. In thinking this—and the more self-consciously and emphatically he does so, the more—he is overtaken by the opposite. He ceases to be the free lord and master he could and should have been in the sphere of God's lordship if, instead of fleeing from God, he had oriented himself to him. (214)

The human being is unable to keep the originally creaturely human powers under control. As lordless powers, they now turn against humanity. Goethe's *The Sorcerer's Apprentice* provides an illustration for the particular type of disorder the human being lives in.

> Inevitably, in the form of the forces which he has unleashed and which have become lordless, his own strength turns not only away from him but against him. They rob people of the freedom which they have misused and thus for-feited in advance. (233)

Wild "principalities and powers" gain a life of their own of almost demonic quality. In his analysis, Barth therefore concedes that certain "magical views of the world" actually might have seen more clearly the truth of human existence than many a rationalist point of view (216).[19]

As examples of such powers gone wild, Barth analyzes incidents of political absolutism ("sovereignty" or "Leviathan," the "demonic which is visibly at work in all politics," 219) and economic absolutism ("money" or "Mammon," the "very mobile demon" of human "resources," 222). Additionally, Barth predicts that "corresponding to the fact that there always seem to be unknown as well as known powers and possibilities of human life—we have to reckon not only with some very familiar but also with some new and unfamiliar forms of this kind" (215).

Thus, I propose to consider what we witness in the Surveillance Society as a new form of lordless power: the power of *knowledge* gone wild. In the face of the rampant surveillance technology and its permeation of everyday life, Barth's analysis can help us to navigate between the pitfalls of a simple technophobic view condemning new technology as such as evil (unfortunately, an approach rather common in much of—especially protestant—theology) and a view of technology as simply "neutral," to be judged according to the specific use to which it is put. Ever since McLuhan's "the medium is the message,"[20] at the latest, we know that there is no such thing as a neutral medium. Rather, the medium creates its own contents. This, of course, also holds true for new media including social media. So while it would be erroneous to demonize information and communication technologies as such, it would be just as shortsighted to regard them as fundamentally benign and simply call for care and control in their application. Rather, it is necessary to analyze their potential of self-autonomization and idolization, their tendency of claiming quasi-divine authority and attributes in today's society.

It may be a first step toward a critical engagement with the political theologies of the surveillance society to scrutinize its use of religious metaphors. In the following pages, I will examine the pivotal metaphor of the panopticon, external identifications or labeling of surveillance practices as "religious," and "living under drones" as the epitome of the nexus between surveillance and power over life and death.

"Cave, cave, Dominus videt!" Panoptic Inspection and the "Eye of God"

No metaphor has been used as widely to characterize the Surveillance Society as the panopticon (see figure 9.1). The architectural structure was devised by philosopher Jeremy Bentham, primarily as a model for prisons, but also for schools, hospitals, asylums, factories, and any other area that required systematic surveillance (*"watching over"*), or, as Bentham called it at the time, "inspection" (*"looking into"*).[21] Its design is of circular build with a clear center (watchtower) and periphery (cells open for inspection toward the watchtower). Drawing upon the idea of a watcher who is able to watch everything while remaining himself invisible, the panopticon structures space in such a way that every inmate is potentially being surveyed at any given moment of time, while not being able to see those who watch him from the center. The discipline exerted by such a structure relies not so much on force as on an internalization of morale. As the inmates do not know whether they are *actually* being watched at any given moment but can never be certain of *not* being watched, they themselves will discipline their own behavior *as if* they actually *were* being watched all the time. Thus, discipline is not only internalized but also exerted in voluntary subordination. By enacting total and permanent visibility of the individual, the architecture itself thus spares the controlling institution true round-the-clock watch and in fact makes physical intervention all but obsolete. "Visibility is a trap,"[22] observed

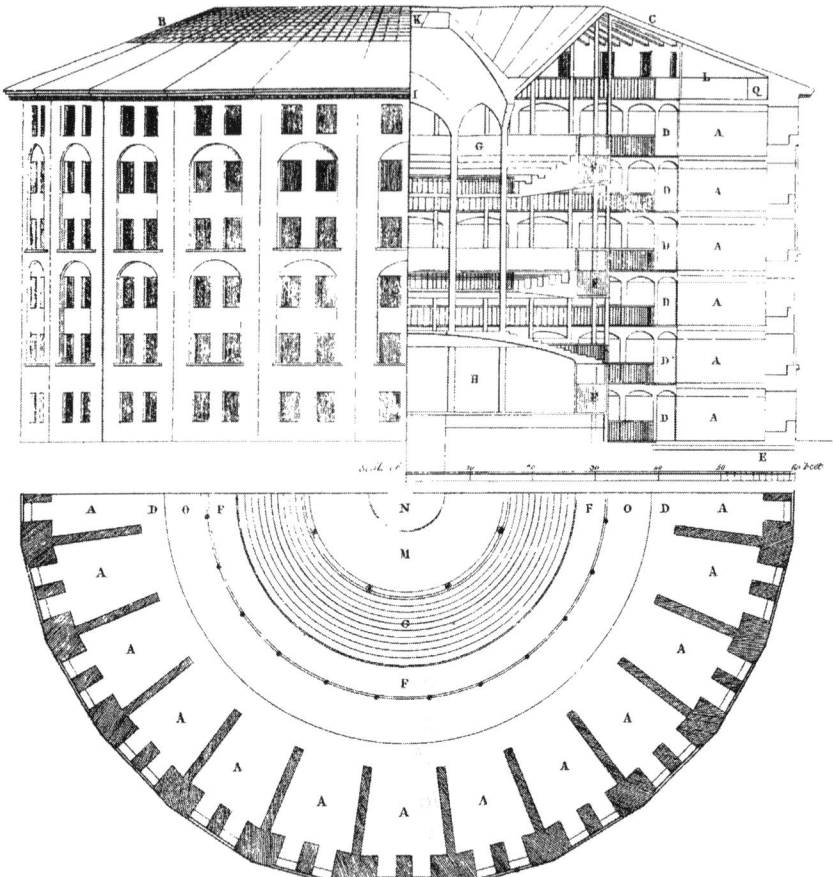

Figure 9.1 A General Idea of a Penitentiary Panopticon in an Improved but as Yet (January 23, 1791) Unfinished State. *Source: Jeremy Bentham, Panopticon, Constitution, Colonies, Codification (The Works of Jeremy Bentham, vol. 4; Edinburgh: Tait, 1843), plate 2 (in the public domain).*

Michel Foucault. Bentham's panopticon is much more efficient as a device of behavioral control than any system relying on punishment alone could ever be. This is why for Foucault the panopticon marked the transition from "societies of sovereignty," relying on physical force, to the much more subtle and internalized, even bureaucratic force of "societies of discipline."

It is no coincidence that Bentham's conception of the panoptic prison structurally resembles pictures of the all-seeing eye of God, such as Hieronymus Bosch's famous depiction of the seven deadly sins (see figure 9.2). In this painting, it is Christ who is the pupil at the center of the all-seeing eye, where a banner reads: "*cave, cave, D[omin]us videt*" ("beware, beware, the Lord sees"). Bentham himself had an emblem sketched for his panoptic prison that portrays an ever open eye with the catchphrase "mercy, justice, vigilance"— a traditional image of divinity complete with classic divine attributes (see figure 9.3). As an epigraph for the description of his panopticon, he chose a Psalm verse: "Thou art about my path and about my bed; and spiest out all my ways" (Ps 139:2).

Images of an all-knowing, all-seeing God thus serve as a model for worldly systems of control and discipline. They intimate to be a prolongation or application of the already ever-existent watch of the eye of God and thus legitimize human justice as a surrogate or even a representative agent of divine justice. Within the raging debates about prison reforms in his times, Bentham's model was actually a "strategic move" of "secularizing prison reform"—although drawing on religious imagery, it "rested on the kind of rational abstract knowledge prized by the Enlightenment thinkers" and "sought to impose its own order, its own rationality."[23] In this sense, it assumes a Godlike position for the punitive system itself and can thus be seen as a first step toward an emancipation or autonomization of powers.

While the panopticon from Bentham to Foucault served as a disciplinary institution at the margins of society, in today's realm of unbridled surveillance technology, the panopticon has expanded its boundaries and shed its walls. Today, we all live within the panopticon, in a global panoptic society.

Figure 9.2   Hieronymus Bosch, *The Seven Deadly Sins and the Four Last Things* (1485). *Source: Museo del Prado.*

Figure 9.3 Willey Reveley, Emblem of the Panopticon. *Source: The Bentham Papers/, UCL, Box 118, Folio 174, p. 1, http://transcribe-bentham.ucl.ac.uk/td/JB/118/174/001.*

However today, there is no clear center anymore. We do not actually know who is watching us, what kind of knowledge is gathered, to what use it is put, and from where control over it (and our lives) will be exerted. While this remains within the panoptic paradigm claiming that the position of power should be able to watch everything without being watched itself, it leaves the clear architectural spacing as well as the visible embodiment of power behind. In addition, the visibility created by the "new surveillance" is not so much a literal reality anymore (although it still is, too) as it is also a metaphor: today's surveillance relies not only on actual *images* from direct observation, CCTV systems, or drone systems, but mostly on the analysis of *data* and especially, communication meta-data. Rather than *confining* problematic elements into the disciplinary panopticon, "ban-optic" mechanisms such as screening and profiling algorithms *exclude* certain elements from participation in society.[24] These significant restructurings have led some scholars to criticize the metaphor of the panopticon or propose alternate versions of it.[25] Beyond the paradigm of the panopticon, it has been suggested that Kafka's *Trial* with its vision of faceless and unfathomable bureaucratic processes comes closer to today's experience of surveillance[26]—and bureaucracy in its relentless extreme might well be described as a lordless power all in itself.

However, while panoptic control is certainly not the only type of control exerted anymore, it does remain one of the predominant patterns of surveillance. It has even been argued that while the architectural structure has obviously mostly vanished, the initial idea of the panopticon—internalized and voluntary discipline—is even stronger than before, thriving in what could be called the "DIY panopticon": "Everything moves from enforcement to temptation and seduction [. . .] and everything shifts the principal role in achieving the intended and welcome results from the [. . .] surveyors to the surveyed."[27] According to Berlin philosopher and media theorist Byung-Chul Han, it is more than ever before not the body, but the mind that is controlled by surveillance mechanisms, turning Foucault's bio-political society of discipline into a "psycho-political transparency society."[28] The main difference between the rising "a-perspectival panopticon"[29] and the traditional panopticon is that now, the inhabitants believe themselves to be free. Rather than being forced into visibility, they are being seduced by convenience and entertainment to cooperate in making themselves transparent, thus contributing to their own self-surveillance. "The inmate of the digital panopticon is victim and culprit at the same time. Thus is the dialectic structure of his freedom."[30] Hence for Han, the classic term Neoliberalism best describes the conditions of the a-perspectival panopticon,[31] where "the fear of ceding ones privacy and intimacy is replaced by the desire to exhibit them shamelessly, this means: freedom and control become indistinguishable."[32] The new wall-less and boundless panopticon is one of seemingly free will surveillance of everyone by everyone.

"Dataism" and the End of Theory: Surveillance as Religion

Not only do politics of surveillance rely on religious imagery and metaphors for their conceptualization and legitimization, surveillance itself is increasingly worshiped like a religious idol in some ways. Very generally speaking, surveillance technologies serve to optimize processes. Thus, they become instruments of dealing with contingency and finitude. Within many a definition, coping with contingency is already what constitutes the religious. Han goes even further by declaring: "The recent data rage does not only have to do with the NSA. It expresses a new faith which might be called dataism. At the moment, dataism almost reaches religious or totalitarian traits. The euphoria for big data is part of the worship of this faith of the digital age."[33]

While traditional churches run out of members, social media requiring ever more self-exhibition in order to take their place. Han attests that the religious techniques of the "Quantified Self" or of the exhibitionism witnessed on Facebook as "a new church" are quite different from Christian practices like confession of sins: They only serve to optimize individual performance and efficiency, but do not contribute to self-awareness or meaning, let alone truth. "We cannot escape death by Facebook. And because we feel this, we communicate ever more and ever faster."[34] Such practices only serve the "ego become self-referential" (which almost seems like a translation of Luther's "*homo incurvatus in seipsum*"), thus ultimately leading to nihilism. Arguing against Villem Flusser's view of digital communication as a new "pentecostal community," Han asserts: "The messianism of networks has not come true. Instead, digital communication erodes the community, the 'we.' It destroys the public realm and reinforces the solitude of man. Not the love of one's neighbor, but narcissism rules digital communication."[35] One might also put it like this: While traditional churches may emphasize community but fall short in fostering strong participation, surveillance-based religious movements tend to boost participation without fostering real community-building.

In the context of the NSA scandals, where "super-human knowledge [is hailed] as a religious-political ideology," Bernhard Taureck anticipates a religious turn on the political scene, as well:

> Whoever possesses significantly more knowledge about human beings than they themselves do is already in a superhuman position. In order to justify this superhuman monopoly of knowledge, there will be no other option in the long run than to invent a religious language to be accepted by the population.[36]

According to Taureck, only two aspects are needed to eventually turn the NSA itself into a religion: first, generate a "feeling of absolute dependence" in the population and, second, supply means of collective socialization. Drawing from the religious roots since the foundation of the United States, the NSA might be able to transform its knowledge into an instrument of domination and government by creating "trust in a religiously colored surveillance democracy."[37]

In a different, but no less ambitious vision, editor-in-chief of technology journal *Wired*, Chris Anderson even announced the end of all belief systems, indeed the "end of theory" as such due to "big data."[38] He argues that theories and scientific models are always abstractions and oversimplifications built on uncertain reasoning and hypotheses about causes and correlations. As such, they are by nature "flawed, no doubt a caricature of a more complex underlying reality." Big data supposedly makes all these shortcuts unnecessary. Once the database is big enough, thus Anderson's belief,

> We can stop looking for models. We can analyze the data without hypotheses about what it might show. We can throw the numbers into the biggest comput-ing clusters the world has ever seen and let statistical algorithms find patterns where science cannot. [. . .] Correlation supersedes causation, and science can advance even without coherent models, unified theories, or really any mecha-nistic explanation at all.

Hermeneutics, interpretation and even theory as such become dispensable, Anderson claims. In the hyper-reality of perfect data, theories and even scientific models become ineffective and obsolete idols. In Anderson's hypertrophic vision, it would seem like it is only a matter of time until data become "all in all."

It is easy to see from these diverse examples how the powers to knowledge linked to the development of surveillance technologies themselves acquire religious attributes and contribute to human aspirations at self-authorization and empowerment with visions of superhuman possibilities.

"Whither Shall I Flee?" Living under Drones

As we have seen, surveillance technologies do not only employ religious imagery as a political theology, providing itself with religious legitimacy and authority, they even in turn arouse religious sentiments. But, as initially stated, the hyphen cuts both ways: Not only do we find religious imagery in the realm of surveillance, surveillance metaphors also migrate into the religious sphere.[39] Consider drone warfare. Drones are, in a way, the epitome of the transparency and visibility produced by the Surveillance Society. Disembodied machinery, they are able to watch everything everywhere without being seen, and, what is more, to strike and intervene without any possibility of escape or defense. Just like divine justice, it would seem. And it does seem like this, to some.

In a promotional video for Fellowship Church, Pastor Ed Young uses drones as an image for the omnipresence and omniscience of God. The opening lines run as follows:

> Who you are when no one is looking is who you are. What would it be like if you knew someone saw everything you do? What would it be like if I knew someone heard every single word uttered from my mouth? Today we hear about drones. Drones supposedly know it all, they see it all. Well, the reality is, our great God sees and knows everything. If we really understood that, would it change our lives? I believe the answer is yes.[40]

Headed by the video caption: "Someone is always watching," Young comments on an encounter with a video drone while on a fishing trip:

> The drone was behind me while I fished, on top of me, it seemed, above me, in front of me [. . .]. Drones are everywhere and they kind of bring up a kind of a voyeuristic type vibe, they kind of bring up "Big Brother is watching," they kind of bring up all sorts of privacy issues . . . —and then immediately, I thought about God. Because God is everywhere. It seems as though a drone can be everywhere when you're involved in filming but in reality, drones can't, yet our great God can. God is above us, he is behind us, he is beyond us, he is our all-everywhere God.

From these provocative starting lines, Young goes into an extensive exegesis of Ps 139 in order to back up his comparison between drones and God. It seems not to disturb Young to translate the talk of drones into a positive and even supposedly favorable image of God while the drone displayed in the background is clearly a military, armed model. The line of argument is not at all ambivalent: God is a better, more efficient drone than any drone could be. These policing, military and livestock monitoring agents of surveillance provide a model image for the divine.

In the United States, the deployment of drones has been greatly advertised during the past years as a way of protecting the nation from terrorist threats while at the same time preserving the security of one's own military personnel. A recent study of US military drone strikes in Pakistan between 2004 and 2012 by Stanford Law School has challenged this narrative thoroughly. They compile data that shows how drone strikes are not only highly questionable in terms of international law as well as ethics of even the most conservative persuasion but also the official narrative of minimal collateral damage is simply false.[41] Even beyond the immediate death toll, "their presence terrorizes men, women, and children, giving rise to anxiety and psychological trauma among civilian communities." This anxiety significantly alters social behavior, especially due to the common US practice to strike one area multiple times, targeting those who come to rescue and assist victims of the initial strikes.[42] Far from making even the United States a safer place while "merely" affecting the population of the "enemy," the experiences of drone strikes have actually spurred international terrorism, replacing "Guantanamo as the recruiting tool of choice for militants."[43]

What does it mean if these concepts—the "all-seeing eye" of the drone, inescapable "justice" executed from the skies—are used as religious resources? What images of the divine do they create? Are they really apt to describe the God of Israel, incarnate in Jesus Christ, or are they merely idolized overglorifications of political and military power symbols into quasi-divine status?

"DEMYTHOLOGIZATION": TOWARD A THEOLOGICAL CRITIQUE OF THE POLITICAL THEOLOGIES OF THE SURVEILLANCE SOCIETY

Reclaiming the "Panoptic Psalm"

Bentham and Young are no isolated examples—Ps 139 is prominently employed in most "religious" accounts of surveillance:

O Lord, thou hast searched me, and known me. Thou knowest my downsitting and mine uprising, thou understandest my thought afar off. Thou compassest my path and my lying down, and art acquainted with all my ways. For there is not a word in my tongue, but, lo, O Lord, thou knowest it altogether. [. . .] Such knowledge is too wonderful for me; it is high, I cannot attain unto it. Whither shall I go from thy spirit? Or whither shall I flee from thy presence? If I ascend up into heaven, thou art there: If I make my bed in hell, behold, thou art there. If I take the wings of the morning, and dwell in the uttermost parts of the sea; even there shall thy hand lead me, and thy right hand shall hold me. (Ps 139:1–10)

In the surveillance rationale, Ps 139 points out that God is always already watching us, knowing every detail of our actions, thoughts, and feelings. Therefore, the implicit conclusion is that surveillance technology following this model cannot be ethically wrong. It can even be justified and legitimized as enforcing God's vision on earth.

At least two objections must be made to this reasoning. First and simply, what is the prerogative of God might not necessarily be what humans should be able to do (or, as the Romans used to say, *"quod licet Iovi non licet bovi"*). Claiming the Godlike position of omniscience is actually *hubris*, a human denial of God's lordship and establishing of lordless powers.

Second, Bentham et al. might not even have read the text well with regard to the image of God conveyed here. Certainly, Ps 139 does speak of God's omniscience at the extreme end of the biblical range of doing so. The psalmist's reaction is one of awe, oscillating between fascination and horror. In no other psalm is this penetrating knowledge ever reached. Rather, the psalmist time and again even has to claim God's attention by calling out: "Look at me!" (see, e.g., Ps 13:4; 31:17; 59:5; 119; 153). Even more fearsome than the prospect of being known through-and-through by God seems to be the prospect of not-being-seen. Being seen thus amounts not so much to being registered within the unfathomable depths of some divine knowledge, but to the pro-vision and attention of a caring relationship, which is never all-encompassing, but rather highly personalized and selective. Even in Ps 139, the important point revealed by a closer reading is not as much that God holds infinite amounts of personal data and uses them for some heavenly social sorting. Rather, the tone is that of a loving engagement with and commitment to the psalmist. God's view on the psalmist is relational rather than abstract and technical, it strives to engage with the reality of the psalmist rather than with his data double or profile, and it is based on a hermeneutic of "retrieval" rather than on a hermeneutic of suspicion.[44]

In support of this point, the story of Hagar comes to mind. Hagar, cast out, pregnant, deserted in the middle of the desert, is utterly vulnerable and

exposed. God finds her in the desert, promising her and her son life and protection. Hagar in turn exclaims: "You are a God who sees me. [. . .] Truly here I
have seen Him who looks after me" (Gen 16:13)—the Hebrew wording very
close to Mary's song: "He has looked on the humble estate of his servant. For
behold, from now on all generations will call me blessed" (Lk 1:48). Womanist
theologians have pointed out that the looking-out and looking-after of this God
is not necessarily unambiguously liberative,[45] is not the "knowledge" of the
sum of "perfect data." Rather, it is a caring-for those God beholds. In addition,
there is a measure of reciprocity or accountability introduced in Hagar's (the
slave woman's!) "naming" of God as "El-Roi", "The One Who Sees Me".

The "lord of drones" (*"Baal-ze-bub"*?) is not the God of the Bible.[46] Thus,
the surveillance imagery used for characterizing God might actually say more
about us and our own claim to lordship, which relies on force and terror and
fosters fear and suspicion, than about God.

Demonology Wanted: New Perspectives in Political Ethics?

Within the panorama of the emergent Surveillance Society, the call for digital
ethics or stricter privacy laws (while much needed!) is a trap if it is the only
call we raise. It is necessary to conceptualize and critically analyze the very
realities we face before we can think of devising coping mechanisms. Thus,
before we can adequately apply an "ethics of care,"[47] we might first need a
theological demonology. Especially in the German context, received models
of political ethics are mainly quasi-institutional ethics relying on stable
and manifest power structures such as "the state" or "the church." Such
conceptions resulting in modelings of "two kingdoms" or "two regiments" are
inherently unable to even describe the fluid and fleeting, faceless, and lawless
powers at work in today's world. We need new theological models that are
able to assess power and control in their more elusive and liquid forms.

Barth's account of "lordless powers" provides a promising starting point for
such a model. He is very reserved about granting evil more than a "quick, sharp
glance," but he is also opposed to ignoring its reality.[48] While the nature of the
demonic lies in nothingness, this does not make it unreal at all. If we simply deny
its existence, this would be evil's first triumph and increase its potency, while
being worshiped as a powerful truth is its even higher triumph (525f.). Thus, Barth
develops a confidently non-alarmist, yet highly realistic conception of powers
which are as potent as they are elusive, which can be theologically analyzed with
the resources of the doctrine of divine sovereignty on the one hand and hamartiological anthropology on the other hand, and which can be unmasked by a rigorous
demythologization based on a biblical account of God's power.

The Christian stance, therefore, considers the demonic as a reality, but a false
reality. Rather than ignoring it, it takes it into account. Rather than granting it

truth, it pronounces it as a lie, an idolous imitation at best of the true God. Barth's response to the lordless powers of his own time is twofold: Most importantly, he points out, they already *have* their limit in God's lordship. While this assertion reflects not optimism about Christians, but rather a trust in God, it does become manifest and visible "in their own sphere in the simple fact that the Christian and the Christian community pray 'Thy kingdom come.'"[49] While Christians do not bring about or inaugurate the Kingdom of God, their steadfast and free prayer within all of human disorder "proves the majesty and might of *another* kingdom."[50] This prayer for the Kingdom of God "is the true and essential thing about the revolt [. . .] against the unrighteousness and disorder in whose sphere they find themselves and indeed whose guilt they share (with a sharper sting than others) and whose consequences they also suffer (again with a livelier awareness than others)."[51]

Second, from the real revolution of the Kingdom of God coming toward them, Christians on their part are called to live toward the coming Kingdom. In the wake of this movement, they, too, strive for human (not divine!) justice in solidarity with the suffering of the earth. In the face of lordless powers, this might mean:

> The demythologization which will really hurt them as required cannot consist in questioning their existence. Theological exorcism must be an act of the unbelief which is grounded in faith. It must consist in a resolute denial that they belong to this exalted company. It must consist in the fact that in the light, not of a world-view but of Christian truth, they are seen to be a myth, the myth which lurks in all myths, the lie which funds all other lies, so that a positive relationship to them, an attitude of respect and reverence and obedience, is quite impossible.[52]

Christians themselves, of course, are not out of reach and control of such powers in this world. Still, their attitude toward lordless powers is to "deprive them of their pathos"[53] and to "pray: Thy kingdom come!"[54] They might embark on this truly theo-political enterprise by assessing the political theologies of the Surveillance Society and subjecting them to theological criticism: How do theological and quasi-religious images and metaphors serve to create political legitimacy and power? Barth's account of "lordless powers" might be a first step in the quest for new, theological *demonologies* to devise models of political ethics for our times.

NOTES

1. Carl Schmitt, *Politische Theologie: Vier Kapitel zur Lehre von der Souveränität* (München and Leipzig: Duncker & Humblot, 1922), 43.

2. Jan Assmann, *Politische Theologie zwischen Ägypten und Israel* (München: Carl Friedrich von Siemens Stiftung, 1992), 35.

3. The term was coined by Gary T. Marx, "Surveillance Society: The Threat of 1984-style Techniques," *The Futurist* (1985): 21–26 in his study of undercover police work as the "all-encompassing use of computer surveillance technology in modern society for total social control." A few years later, the "Surveillance Society" was analyzed by Oscar H. Gandy as a sophisticated development of bureaucracy (Oscar H. Gandy, "The Surveillance Society: Information Technology and Bureaucratic Social Control," *Journal of Communication* 39, no. 3 [1989]: 61–76), and then by the seminal work of David Lyon as an all-encompassing reality (David Lyon, *The Electronic Eye: The Rise of Surveillance Society* [Cambridge, UK: Polity, 1994]). While Foucault had described the transitions of "societies of sovereignty" to "societies of discipline," epitomized in Bentham's panopticon as a model for prisons, Gilles Deleuze pointed out that we now are passing into a new era of "societies of control" (Michel Foucault, *Discipline and Punish: The Birth of the Prison* [New York: Vintage, 1979]; Gilles Deleuze, "Postscript on the Societies of Control," *October* 59 [1992]: 3–7).

4. Cf. in this volume the contribution by David Haddorff who also departs from the assumption that it is the doctrine of God—in contrast and comparison with the political structures in the human realm—which needs to be brought into focus by political theology. Haddorff's main insights and gains from Barth's theological engagement in this course are a trinitarian reformulation of sovereignty as well as several a specification of democratic freedom and practices through the relation to this sovereign, trinitarian creator.

5. I am deeply grateful to the participants of the *Theo-Politics* colloquia for their comments, inputs, and criticism. My special thanks go to Markus Höfner for a very thoughtful and enriching response to my paper. I am also much obliged to Grace Kao for linguistic revisions. In the meantime, some parts of this chapter have been taken up in my article, "All/Macht/Wissen. Politische Theologie als Zwei-Wege-Deutungsmodell in der Überwachungsgesellschaft," in *Macht und Deutungsmacht*, ed. Philipp Stoellger (Tübingen: Mohr Siebeck, 2016).

6. David Lyon, *Surveillance Society: Monitoring Everyday Life* (Buckingham and Philadelphia: Open University Press, 2002), 3.

7. Previous to 2001, the United Kingdom was leading in the use of surveillance technology in public spaces, cf. David Murakami Wood, ed. *A Report on the Surveillance Society* (Cheshire, UK, 2006), 19.

8. See the estimation by Bernhard Taureck, *Überwachungsdemokratie: Die NSA als Religion* (Paderborn: Fink, 2014), 10. There have also been revealing visualizations of comparisons between data gathering by the Eastern German "Stasi" and the NSA (cf. http://apps.opendatacity.de/stasi-vs-nsa/).

9. Hanna Reichel, "Transparenz und Öffentlichkeit in der Überwachungsgesellschaft: Bedingungen von Zivilgesellschaft im 21. Jahrhundert," *ZEE* 59 (2016): 102–116.

10. Marin Majica, "Der Tschernobyl-Moment der Digitalisierung," *ZEIT* (July 25, 2013), www.zeit.de/digital/datenschutz/2013-07/nsa-skandal-tschernobyl-vergleich.

11. Leonhard Dobusch, *Digitale Zivilgesellschaft: Stand und Perspektiven 2014* (Berlin: Bridge, 2014), 2f.

12. Gary T. Marx, "What's New About the 'New Surveillance'? Classifying for Change and Continuity," *Surveillance & Society* 1, no. 1 (2002): 9–29, http://library. queensu.ca/ojs/index.php/surveillance-and-society/article/view/3391.

13. This quote almost as ubiquitous in surveillance studies as the panopticon metaphor is the party slogan in George Orwell, *Nineteen Eighty-Four* (Cutchogue, NY: Buccaneer, 1949).

14. Exemplary at the time was the highly accurate prediction of pregnancies by Target's algorithms on buying data from their customers, cf. Kashmir Hill, "How Target Figured Out a Teen Girl Was Pregnant before Her Father Did," *Forbes* (February 16, 2002), http://www.forbes.com/sites/kashmirhill/2012/02/16/how-target -figured-out-a-teen-girl-was-pregnant-before-her-father-did/.

15. Anders Albrechtslund, "Online Social Networking as Participatory Surveillance," *First Monday* 13, no. 3 (2008), http://www.uic.edu/htbin/cgiwrap/bin/ ojs/index.php/fm/article/view/2142/1949.

16. Kopfkompass, "Indect: War George Orwell ein naiver Optimist?" *der Freitag* (November 8, 2009), https://www.freitag.de/autoren/kopfkompass/indect-war-orwell -ein-naiver-optimist.

17. Cf. in this volume the contribution of Paul Dafydd Jones, who in broader scope explicates how this posthumous piece by Barth could contribute immensely to current trends in the theo-political discussion.

18. Karl Barth, *The Christian Life: Church Dogmatics IV, 4, Lecture Fragments* (Grand Rapids: Eerdmans, 1981), 213. Barth does not employ gender-inclusive language, all following citations are left in the originally exclusively masculine form; however, their theological meaning has to be understood as encompassing all sexes and genders.

19. Ibid., 216. Barth proceeds to ask: "Might it be that our fellow Christians from the younger churches of Asia and Africa, who come with a fresher outlook in this regard, can help us here?" (219). In fact, pentecostal scholars, have been developing theological approaches to demonology over the last twenty years that might be worth considering, see e.g., Amos Yong, *Discerning the Spirit(s): A Pentecostal-Charismatic Contribution to Christian Theology of Religions,* Journal of Pentecostal Theology: Supplement Series Vol. 20 (Sheffield: Sheffield Academic Press, 2000); Carolyn D. Baker and Frank Macchia, "Created Spirit Beings: Satan and Demons," in *Systematic Theology*, ed. Stanley M. Horton (Springfield, MO: Logion, 1994), 179–213; Eldin Villafañe, *The Liberating Spirit: Toward an Hispanic American Pentecostal Social Ethic* (Grand Rapids: Eerdmans, 1993); Anthony N. S. Lane, ed., *The Unseen World: Christian Reflections on Angels, Demons and the Heavenly Realm*, Tyndale House Studies (Carlisle, Cumbria: Paternoster Press, 1996); Samuel Solivan, *The Spirit, Pathos and Liberation: Toward an Hispanic Pentecostal Theology,* Journal of Pentecostal Theology: Supplement Series Vol. 14 (Sheffield: Sheffield Academic Press, 1998).

20. Marshall McLuhan, *The Medium Is the Massage: An Inventory of Effects* (New York: Random House, 1967).

21. Cf. Jeremy Bentham, "Panopticon; or, the Inspection-House," in *The Works of Jeremy Bentham*, vol. 4; Edinburgh: Tait, 1843, 37–172.

22. Michel Foucault, *Discipline and Punish: The Birth of the Prison* (New York: Vintage, 1979), 200.

23. David Lyon, "Surveillance and the Eye of God," *Studies in Christian Ethics* 27, no. 1 (2014): 26.

24. Didier Bigo, "Globalized (In)Security: The Field and the Ban-Opticon," in *Terror, Insecurity and Liberty*, ed. Didier Bigo and Anastassia Tsoukala (Abingdon: Routledge, 2008), 10–48.

25. E.g., the "superpanopticon" (Mark Poster, *The Mode of Information: Post-Structuralism and Social Contexts* [Chicago: University of Chicago Press, 1990]), the "electronic panopticon" (David Lyon, *The Electronic Eye: The Rise of Surveillance Society* [Cambridge, UK: Polity, 1994]), the "synopticon" (Thomas Mathiesen, "The Viewer Society: Michel Foucault's 'Panopticon' Revisited," *Theoretical Criminology* 1, no. 2 [1997]: 215–234), the "post-panopticon" (Richard Boyne, "Post-panopticism," *Economy and Society* 29, no. 2 [2000]: 285–307, see also Gilles Deleuze, "Postscript"). For an overview of the debate and the search of new metaphors beyond the panopticon see Manuela Farinosi, "Deconstructing Bentham's Panopticon: The New Metaphors of Surveillance in the Web 2.0 Environment," *tripleC* 9, no. 1 (2011): 62–76.

26. Franz Kafka, *Der Process: Roman* (Berlin: Die Schmiede, 1925).

27. Zygmunt Bauman and David Lyon, *Liquid Surveillance: A Conversation* (Cambridge, UK; Malden, MA: Polity, 2013), 57.

28. Byung-Chul Han, *Im Schwarm: Ansichten des Digitalen* (Berlin: Matthes & Seitz, 2013), 98, see also idem, *Psychopolitik: Neoliberalismus und die neuen Machttechniken* (Frankfurt/Main: Fischer, 2014). The translations from Han's texts are mine, as are all subsequent translations of originally German quotes, unless otherwise indicated.

29. Idem, *Transparenzgesellschaft* (Berlin: Matthes & Seitz, 2012), 74.

30. Ibid., 82.

31. Idem, "Warum heute keine Revolution möglich ist," *Süddeutsche Zeitung* (September 2, 2014), http://www.sueddeutsche.de/politik/neoliberales-herrschaftssystem-warum-heute-keine-revolution-moeglich-ist-1.2110256.

32. Idem, *Im Schwarm*, 93.

33. Idem, "Dataismus und Nihilismus," *ZEIT ONLINE* (September 27, 2013), http://www.zeit.de/digital/internet/2013-09/big-data-han-dataismus/.

34. Tobias Haberl, "'Wir steuern auf eine Katastrophe zu': Interview mit Byung-Chul Han," *Süddeutsches Magazin* 50 (2012), http://sz-magazin.sueddeutsche.de/texte/anzeigen/39059.

35. Han, *Im Schwarm*, 65.

36. Taureck, *Überwachungsdemokratie*, 45.

37. This vision provides a perfect exemplification of Barth's analysis of human powers claiming quasi-divine attributes and thus absolute authority. In this volume, the intricate relation of political and divine sovereignty at the heart of Karl Barth's critique of political religion and their contrast to the aforementioned understanding of political theology by Carl Schmitt is developed in greater depth by the contributions of Devin Singh and Clifford B. Anderson.

38. Chris Anderson, "The End of Theory: The Data Deluge Makes the Scientific Method Obsolete," *Wired* (July 16, 2008), http://archive.wired.com/science/discove ries/magazine/16-07/pb_theory.

39. Cf. in this volume the contribution by Markus Höfner who rightly points out that Barth as a resource for political theology cannot be onesidedly read as a critique of the non-Christian world, but always against powers which are as much at work inside as outside of the church.

40. Ed Young, Video downloaded from: https://www.fellowshipchurch.com/ drones, accessed October 4, 2014.

41. *Living under Drones: Death, Injury, and Trauma to Civilians from US Drone Practices in Pakistan,* ed. International Human Rights and Conflict Resolution Clinic and Global Justice Clinic, Stanford Law School and NYU School of Law, 2012, vi.

42. Ibid., vii.

43. Jo Becker and Scott Shane, "Secret 'Kill Lists' Proves a Test of Obama's Principles and Will," *New York Times* (May 29, 2012), http://www.nytimes.com/20 12/05/29/world/obamas-leadership-in-war-on-al-qaeda.html.

44. For an extended reading of Ps 139 in a "panoptic" and "anti-panoptic" interpretation, see David Lyon, "Surveillance and the Eye of God," *Studies in Christian Ethics* 27, no. 1 (2014): 21–32.

45. (Cf. Delores Williams, /Sisters in the Wilderness: The Challenge of Womanist God-Talk/ (Maryknoll: Orbis,1990). Nevertheless, this God's vision.

46. For a more robust corrective vision of God's knowledge, this highly selective biblical material would have to be and could easily be expanded by more thorough discussions, for example, of the book of Job or even the Gospels.

47. Cf. Eric Stoddart, "(In)visibility and the Process of Public Theology," *International Journal of Public Theology* 7, no. 1 (2013): 45–64.

48. Karl Barth, *The Church Dogmatics III,3* (Edinburgh: T&T Clark, 1960), 519.

49. Barth, *The Christian Life*, 234.

50. Ibid.

51. Ibid., 260f.

52. Barth, *CD III,3,* 521f.

53. Karl Barth, *Epistle to the Romans [1922]*, trans. Edwyn Clement Hoskyns, 6th ed. (London: Oxford University Press, 1968), 483. This quote has been employed by Arne Rasmussen, "'Deprive Them of Their Pathos': Karl Barth and the Nazi Revolution Revisited," *Modern Theology* 23 (2007): 369–391 and Angela Dienhart Hancock, *Karl Barth's Emergency Homiletic, 1932–1933: A Summons to Prophetic Witness at the Dawn of the Third Reich* (Grand Rapids: Eerdmans, 2013) as a lens for Barth's attitude toward the political theology of National Socialism in Germany in the 1930s.

54. Barth, *The Christian Life*, 234. In this volume, Angela Dienhart Hancock explores how to develop practices and mechanisms from within Christian congregational life and pastoral training that can foster democratic discourse and conversation in such a pathos-freed understanding.

Chapter 10

Sino-Theology as Public Theology

The Reception of Karl Barth's Theology and Its Significance in the Chinese Context

Chin Kenpa

SINO-THEOLOGY AND CHINESE THOUGHT

The rejection of Christianity in traditional Chinese thought is essentially a theological issue. Beginning with Nestorianism during the Tang[1] dynasty, the fate of Christianity in China has always been closely linked to the prevailing political situation.[2] This became even more obvious by the later part of the Qing dynasty, a period in which Christianity had become closely linked with the question of modernization. By the time of the Anti-Christian Movement, which began in 1911 and continued until 1922, Christianity was widely perceived to be in direct conflict with Chinese political theology.[3] From that time forward, Christianity has been a highly sensitive issue in Chinese thought. In recognition of this dynamic, Christians in China have been making efforts toward indigenization, in other words, framing Christianity as a type of "public theology," in order to make it more compatible with Chinese thought. Despite these efforts, over the last century Christianity in China has made little progress with regard to influence in the public sphere.[4]

As a result, by the 1990s the question of "Sino-theology" had transformed into one of "public theology."[5] Furthermore, theologians in modern China are not necessarily Christians, though in their interactions with other intellectuals they naturally share what they have learned from Christianity. No doubt, many are highly surprised by the proposition that Sino-theology is really a form of non-Christian public theology.[6]

We have to keep in mind that Sino-theology originated with Liu Xiaofeng, whose theological perspective is essentially Barthian. Liu completed his PhD in theology in Switzerland under the guidance of Heinrich Ott, and it was there he came to admire Karl Barth and Barthian theology.

As Sino-theology emerged as a form of public theology in contemporary China, it was quite distinct from traditional Church theology. For, instead of focusing on traditional theological questions, Sino-theology mainly deals with issues central to contemporary Chinese thought. In other words, in entering the public sphere, theology has become an academic subject, just like philosophy, political science, or sociology. At the same time, it is often regarded as a religion-based intellectual tradition, similar to the traditions born of Confucianism, Daoism, and Buddhism. Alternatively, some see theology as a secular intellectual tradition, comparable to existentialism, Platonism, realism, or critical theory. Prior to the advent of Sino-theology, such a state of affairs was hard to imagine.

THE "SUBSTANCE" OF CHINESE CULTURE AND THE THEOLOGY OF KARL BARTH

Ever since the late Qing dynasty, the Chinese nation has been profoundly influenced by a distinctive approach to cultural borrowing which is often described as "Chinese culture as substance, Western culture as practice" (中體西用). In this way of thinking, Western modes of thought are adopted in such "practical" areas as science and political theory, but without completely discarding the essence of Chinese culture. Some have even argued that the knowledge and technology borrowed from the "barbarians" (夷) should first be "Sinocized," and then used to enhance the inherent superiority of Chinese civilization. Adherents of this perspective typically ignore the contradictory nature of such an approach or may argue that any contradictions which do exist can easily be solved by applying the famous Chinese principle of "harmony." This is why anyone keen on importing a new idea to China has typically put much emphasis on its Chinese characteristics.[7] In light of the prevalence of such an attitude, it is not surprising that Christianity has met with so much resistance in China. What does Beijing have to do with Jerusalem? It has to be one or the other, not both.

Because there is no concept of a single supreme being in traditional Chinese thought, the Chinese have always found it difficult to understand exactly what is meant by "God" in Christian doctrine. In Chinese political theology, the closest approximation to the Christian concept of God would be "deity" (公), yet deities are not seen as sacred. On the other hand, traditional Chinese thought does include a concept of the sacred—indeed, anything can become sacred. God belongs to all, but not to any one individual; God is my God and is also the God of others. God is the highest representation of what it means to be "public." God doesn't belong to any particular person, group, party, race, or nation. This is the true meaning of God. This affirmation is the starting point of both Barthian theology and Sino-theology.

In light of the history of reception of Barth's thought among Chinese intellectuals, it is not difficult to see why he has been understood as a "public theologian" rather than a scholar of Church doctrine. The earliest Chinese theologian to introduce Barth's ideas to China was T. C. Chao (1888–1979). In his 1939 book, *Bate de zhongjiao sixiang* 巴特的宗教思想 (*The Religious Ideas of Karl Barth*), Chao provides a comprehensive introduction to Barth's theology, yet points out that he doesn't consider himself to be a Barthian.[8] Published within two months of its completion in April 1939, the book is over 30,000 characters long, divided into 12 chapters, and includes a good number of highly germane quotations.

The issues which most concerned Chinese theologians in the early twentieth century were largely determined by the times they lived in, and Chao's introduction to Barth is no exception, having nothing to do with any academic interest per se. In this book, Chao is careful to avoid a number of topics, for, although this was a time when other Chinese theologians were grappling with the issues of imperialism, Chao himself was writing from Japanese occupied Beijing.

The book was published by the Shanghai Youth Association as part of its "Exception Era Series," with a clearly stated purpose: to publish works that specifically dealt with issues relating to the Japanese invasion. Thus, it is abundantly clear that Chao chose to introduce the ideas of Barth at this particular time because Barth was then facing the same issues in Europe: militarism and the appropriate Christian response to it.

In discussing Barth's political theology, Chao states:

> Barth's theology is a rendition; it's a type of protest. . . . Yet, both of these positions are fundamentally flawed, and can be seen as the Achilles' heel of the Church, viz., a man must make use of both religion and his own power to find God.[9]

In Chao's view, this is the standpoint on which Barth bases his opposition to all movements which are essentially political in nature, as well his critique of liberal theology. Thus, whether one regards Barth's theology as crisis theology or dialectical theology, its central idea is that of judgment, and this judgment comes from human beings, not God, yet it is also an act or desire of God. As Chao saw it, at the outbreak of World War II, Europe and the Far East were both suffering from the effects of Imperialism, and China was suffering from Japanese militarism, thus the theologians in both areas were confronting the same issues.

In 1988, under the pen name MouMou (默默), Liu Xiaofeng published an article titled "God is God: An Essay in Commemoration of the 20th Anniversary of Karl Barth's Death" in the influential literary magazine *Dushu*. The article appeared in a column titled "Western Christian Theology in the 20th Century" in which Liu introduced nine important theologians, including Karl Barth, Karl Rahner, Rudulf Bultmann, Dietrich Bonhoeffer, and Jürgen Moltmann.[10]

It should be noted that this series of articles appeared around the time of the Tiananmen Incident and that "God is God" begins and ends by raising questions on the topic of political power. In other words, Liu's article on Barth was addressed to the context of political theology in both the East and the West, using Barth's theological assertions to recast any secular statement into a verbalization of the sacred. The following quotes illustrate how Liu applies Barthian thought to the topic of "problematic" in modern Chinese thought, in the process of which he presents Barth not so much as a Church theologian, but rather as a public intellectual:

> The sanctification of secular authority, the historical idolization of political leaders, the mystification of political power—these are found in both the East and the West, in the past and in the present. It exists even in the present time. As a result, humanity has suffered dearly, we can only hope that we never forget the terrible suffering of the concentration camps, for no one can guarantee that humanity will not repeat the same terrible mistakes.[11]

Liu's starting point is political theology. In the Western context, he discusses Barth in relation to Nazism. In the Chinese and Eastern context, he discusses Barth in relation to autocracy and hero worship. Liu asserts that the traditional Chinese concept of "enforcing justice on behalf of heaven" (替天行道) is exactly what Barth criticizes. Despite the existence of such related concepts as heaven, the way, and the absolute principle, Chinese thought has always lacked the concept of God, as noted earlier. As a result, deified or mythologized individuals have served as substitutes for God. Yet, such a political theology of apotheosis has often led to totalitarianism and oppression. As Liu puts it:

> Despite the widespread acceptance of the traditional Chinese concept of "enforcing justice on behalf of heaven," neither heaven nor the absolute principle are God. For nobody has ever seen their compassion and grace. At present, we no longer believe in such fairy tales, and some have begun to revile God. But have such people ever actually perceived the word of God? Do they really know who God is?[12]

Christian fundamentalists and evangelicals in China regard Barth as neo-orthodox, and therefore reject his theology as a form of secular philosophy.

But because Chinese intellectuals understand Barth to be a "public" thinker, Barth is readily understood in terms of Sino-theology, inasmuch as Sino-theology is an intellectual movement outside the Church. The reception of Barth's thought among Chinese academics, therefore, is distinctive.

"God is God" was included in *Towards the Truth on the Cross*, Liu's introduction of eleven prominent Western theologians of the twentieth century, which was published in 1990 in Hong Kong and republished in Beijing the next year.[13] When Liu subsequently put forth his proposal for a Sino-theology, his theological position was not primarily Barthian, and was based not only on his intellectual understanding but also rooted in his personal experience.

ZHANG XU: KARL BARTH'S POLITICAL THEOLOGY IN A CHINESE CONTEXT

Zhang Xu's *Kaer Bate shenxue yanjiu* 卡爾・巴特神學研究 (*The Theology of Karl Barth*) is the first and only comprehensive treatment of Barth's theology in Chinese. According to the author, the book was strongly influenced by Liu's work. The essay "God is God" can be seen as the precursor of this book, as the author points out.[14] As a follow up to *Kaer Bate shenxue yanjiu*, five years later Zhang came out with *Shangdi sile, shenxue hewei?*上帝死了，神學何為 (*If God Is Dead, Then What Is Theology for?*) In this latter work, Zhang again presents Barth's ideas as public discourse.[15] From this perspective, Barth's ideas belong to neither the Church nor Christianity; rather, they belong to culture; they belong to all those who are honestly concerned with confronting the practical implications of the concept "God is dead."

Although both Liu and Zhang discuss the political issues that emerged after the First and Second World Wars, Zhang is less interested in the issue per se. Instead, Zhang is more concerned with the history of thought, especially the fundamental questions addressed by Christian theologians in the twentieth century. Thus in *Shangdi sile, shenxue hewei?* Zhang compares Barth's ideas with those of other theologians such as Bonhoeffer, Bultmann, and Moltmann. According to Zhang, he seeks to address the issues of modern criticism and the crisis of modernity.

In comparing Barth to Wittgenstein and Heidegger, Zhang clearly intends to bring Barth's ideas into the public sphere. For Zhang, all the theological issues Barth addresses are the same issues addressed by contemporary secular thinkers, and all have to do with the idea of the death of God, the subject of much discussion in the twentieth century. This is exactly what Barth means by "crisis"; for Barth sees crisis not as a purely theological issue, but also as a crisis of humanity and a crisis of faith. Above all, Barth is concerned with the crisis of political institutions, for this is the arena in which all the other crises are played out.

In the last chapter of *Kaer Bate shenxue yanjiu*, Zhang sums up his understanding of Barth's theology by stating:

> In order to fully appreciate the influence of Barth's revolutionary theology has had
> on the Protestant Church and European society in the 20th century, we have to first
> recognize that he was a public figure in the midst of a great controversy. Similarly,
> we must keep in mind Barth's experience during the two world wars if we are to
> fully understand the motivations behind his controversial theological ideas, for
> example, his scathing criticism of both liberal theology and natural theology.[16]

Zhang also states:

> In fact, the "non-political" stance of Barth's theology is itself a type of political
> stance. Such a theological politics is the primary means by which his theology
> produces an effect on political realities.[17]

This is the kind of issue addressed by public theology: the notion "God is
dead" is at the root of the political crisis. Similarly, the political crisis in China
begins with the similar notion that either "God is dead" or "God doesn't exist."

For the Chinese intelligentsia, Barth's theology is not a Church theology,
but rather a public theology which provides a formidable critique of traditional Chinese thought, especially on the issue of conflating the word of
God and the word of man. In other words, the Chinese intelligentsia accepts
Barth's theology not as Christian theology or Church doctrine, but rather as a
critique which provides a way of understanding God in a way not present in
traditional thought. God is not God in the Christian or theological sense, but
God is a public attitude. In this sense, God is not personal, but wholly other.
One of the main aims of Sino-theology is to offer a critique of the notion that
the emperor is the "Son of Heaven." A world without God is also a world
without a sense of a public sphere; the acceptance of such an idea amounts
to advocating political theology. The main reason for the Chinese intelligentsia's reception of Barth is precisely that Chinese thought has always lacked
the concept of a God who exercises a profound influence on the public sphere.

Zhang reiterates Liu's statement that "God is God," an assertion which is
meant to have a practical sociopolitical implication. As Zhang states:

> It was from Blumhardt that Barth learned to seriously consider the concepts
> "God is God" and the "Kingdom of God," and he did not initiate the religious
> socialist movement based on the expectation of a political theology which is
> secular in nature. . . .
>   As a theologian, Barth is primarily concerned with the question of how to
> apply the word of God in real life circumstances. Rather than being a merely

political question, this is a question of how to apply theology in pracitcal use, a question of "theological politics." Today the prevailing view is that politics has nothing to do with the soul and that theology has no interest in secular authority. In Barth's view, however, Christians should take an active interest in the realities of secular life. First, this is because the Gospel of the New Testament is revolutionary, not conservative; it's all about throwing off fetters and establishing a new order known as the Kingdom of God. For Barth, obeying the word of God entails an undeniable duty toward the prevailing political system, for no political system can exist independent of the grace of God and the redemptive power of Jesus Christ. Indeed, the political sphere is where Jesus Christ was sacrificed and where the people he has called live in, as pointed out in the Barmen Declaration. As Barth saw it, the reason Europeans didn't understand the Nazi threat was because they didn't understand the First Commandment as a political axiom.[18]

From this it can be seen that Zhao, Liu, and Zhang all regard Barth's theology as a type of political theology which provides a powerful critique of the endless ideological battles which have been going on in China for over a century. Both imperialism and communism have been disastrous for Chinese society. The main reason China has suffered such a fate is due to the lack of a concept of God, or perhaps due to the resulting attempts to make up for this lack by substituting various ideologies, such as nationalism or totalitarianism. The result has been to grant excessive power to secular authority, a situation in which criticism is not allowed, and in which confusion prevails.

In sum, the three main implications of Barth's theology for Sino-theology are as follows:

1. It provides a means of criticism of tradition, authority, and humanism.
2. It constitutes a non-Church-based approach to theology that is palatable to non-Christians.
3. It presents theological considerations in terms intelligible to the Chinese intelligentsia.

SINO-THEOLOGY AS PUBLIC THEOLOGY

Liu has much praise for Barth's commentary *The Epistle to the Romans* and sees his 1998 Chinese translation of the book as a major accomplishment in his academic career. First published in Hong Kong to commemorate the thirtieth anniversary of Barth's death, the book was republished in 2005 in mainland China in simplified characters. Another reprint came out in 2009 to commemorate the ninetieth anniversary of the publication of the German original. The Chinese translation has been widely quoted and has had an unprecedented impact not only in theological circles but also on the intelligentsia as a whole, just as the original had in Europe when it was published in 1919. Such reception is especially meaningful in China, where theology isn't widely recognized as an academic discipline.

Paul's First Epistle to the Corinthians might give us a better understanding why Barth's political theology caused such a stir in China. Indeed, if Paul had been aware of the existence of Indians and Chinese in the East, how would this have affected his First Epistle to the Corinthians? How might a Christian theologian refer to Paul's refutations of Jewish religion and Greek philosophy while attempting to respond to the great traditions of India and China? If Paul had been aware of the Chinese and Indian spiritual and philosophical traditions, First Corinthians might have read more like this:

> For the Jews require a sign, the Greeks seek after wisdom, and the Chinese speak of virtue. But we preach Christ crucified, aa stumbling block to the Jews, and foolishness to the Greeks, and barbaric to the Chinese. But to those who are called, whether Jews, Greeks, or Chinese, Christ is the power of God, and the wisdom of God. Because the foolishness of God is wiser than human wisdom; the weakness of God is stronger than human strength; and the barbarianism of God is nobler than human barbarianism.[19]

One of the reasons why the cross is such a powerful symbol in Christianity is that it inspires people's thinking. Similarly, Barth's ideas have caused a stir among the Chinese intelligentsia. Indeed, it is quite remarkable that a theologian could have such an impact on Chinese intellectuals. Although Barth is rejected by Christian fundamentalists in China, his theological perspective has posed a forceful and critical challenge to the concepts of empire and the Divine-emperor (天子皇權) in Chinese thought. This demonstrates that Sino-theology can be seen as a forerunner of public theology. It also shows that "the foolishness of God is wiser than human wisdom."

NOTES

1. All transliterations of Chinese characters are in Hanyu Pinyin. The only exception is "T. C. Chao" (趙紫宸 Zhao Zichen).

2. Chin Ken-pa, "Jingjiao under the Lenses of Chinese Political Theology," *Religions* vol. 551, no. 10 (2019): 1–22.

3. Chin Ken-pa 曾慶豹, "Sheme shi Hanyu shenxue?" 什麼是漢語神學？[From Chinese Theology to Sino-Theology: The Paradigm Shift], *Sino Christian Studies* 漢語基督教評論 no. 8 (2009): 81–112.

4. For an analysis of the Chinese State's stance toward Christianity cf. Kom-Kwong Chan, "The Ecclesiological Implications of the Political Attitude of the Chinese Authority toward Christianity," in this volume.

5. Liu Xiaofeng劉小楓, *Hanyu shenxue yu lishi zhexue* 漢語神學與歷史哲學 [Sino-Theology and the Philosophy of History] (Hong Kong: Institute of Sino Christian Studies, 2000).

6. For decisively Christian approaches to "public" or "political" theology with reference to Karl Barth, cf. Lai Pan-Chiu, "Religious Diversity, Democracy, and Public Theology: Conversing with Barth in Hong Kong Context," and Paul Daffyd Jones, "Karl Barth's *The Christian Life* and the Task of Political Theology," both in this volume.

7. See Chin, "From Chinese Theology," 107.

8. T. C. Chao 趙紫宸, "Bate de zhongjiao sixiang" 巴特的宗教思想 [The Religious Ideas of Karl Barth], in *T. C. Chao wenji* 趙紫宸文集 [The Collected Works of T. C. Chao] (Beijing: Commercial Publishing, 2004), vol. 1, 5–35.

9. T. C. Chao, *The Religious Ideas of Karl Barth*, 12. All translations of the Chinese works in this article are by the Author of this article unless stated otherwise.

10. This column appeared in *Dushu* (讀書) between 1988 and 1989. All the writings in this column were later expanded with footnotes and collectively published in 1990 as a single volume titled *Zou xiang shizijia shang de zhenli—ershi shiji shenxue yinlun* 走向十字架上的真理—二十世紀神學引論 [Towards the Truth on the Cross: A Survey of 20th Century Theologians] (Hong Kong: Joint Publishing, 1990).

11. See Liu Xiaofeng, *Towards the Truth on the Cross: A Survey of 20th Century Theologians*, 42.

12. Ibid., 70.

13. Liu Xiaofeng, *Zou xiang shizijia shang de zhenli—ershi shiji shenxue yinlun* 走向十字架上的真理—二十世紀神學引論 [Towards the Truth on the Cross: A Survey of 20th Century Theologians] (Hong Kong: Joint Publishing, 1990).

14. Zhang Xu張旭, *Kaer Bate shenxue yanjiu*卡爾·巴特神學研究 [The Theology of Karl Barth] (Beijing: Shanghai People's Publishing House, 2005).

15. Zhang Xu張旭, *Shangdi sile, shenxue hewei?*上帝死了，神學何為 [If God is Dead, Then What is Theology for?] (Beijing: Renmin University Press, 2010).

16. See Zhang Xu, *The Theology of Karl Barth*, 278.

17. Ibid., 279.

18. Ibid., 278.

19. Adaptation made by the Author of this article.

Chapter 11

Karl Barth on the Righteousness of God

The Attributes of God in Political Context

Alexander Massmann

In one of his most famous political statements, Karl Barth announced in 1938 that every Czech soldier who would fight and suffer in a battle against Germany would do so for the church of Jesus Christ.[1] This is remarkable, given that 16 years before, he had denounced the idea of a "war between good and evil."[2] "When would our worst enemies," he asked, "have been concerned subjectively with anything but—doing what is objectively right?"[3] While the battle between Czech and German forces ended up not taking place, another drastic political statement of Barth's from the same year was less hypothetical. His public call to remove Hitler from power was barely concealed.[4] At such points during his career Barth did not shy away from providing religious justifications to back up drastic political statements. Both of the political appeals mentioned involve violence to be committed in the name of God.

Today, however, Barth's earlier warning against a "war between good and evil" is likely to resonate more strongly. After all, the 21st century has witnessed an unexpected level of terror, unrest, and war, in the Greater Middle East, Europe, and the US, fueled on all sides by religious rhetoric. The use of force may or may not be necessary to restore peace, but one may ask whether there are no other norms, more rational, less emotional and arcane perhaps than religious thought, that might provide guidance in such conflicts.

BARTH ON GOD'S DISTRIBUTIVE JUSTICE

Just two years after bursting onto the public stage with strong religious rhetoric about the political use of force in 1938, Barth published the first part of his doctrine of God, as part of his multivolume *Church Dogmatics* (*CD* II/1, 1940). This subvolume had been in the making since the summer of 1937.[5] Certain factors stand out from the historical background in this period. In 1938, a synod of the German Confessing Church suddenly demanded an oath of allegiance to Hitler from its pastors, which provoked Barth's remark that a true Christian confession must even imply struggle against the Confessing Church.[6] In his view, even this group was woefully unaware of the conflict between loyalty to Hitler and the First Commandment.[7] Instead, he saw the Confessing Church as discovering a new love for spirituality—or "navel gazing," as it seemed to Barth.[8] The relations between the German churches and the National Socialist regime were the subject of a seminar he taught in the summer term of 1939, during the course of which he finished the manuscript for *CD* II/1.[9] The term came to an end when Germany invaded Poland (September 1939). Even after France and Great Britain declared war on Germany in response, the Allies did not engage in significant military operations against Germany for another six months.

As part of the doctrine of the attributes—or perfections—of God in *CD* II/1, Barth discusses God's *Gerechtigkeit* (justice, righteousness). Against this historical backdrop, it may seem surprising that he frames this issue in conjunction with God's mercy ("The Mercy and Righteousness of God," sect. 30.2) and that he begins the section with a strong assertion of God's grace. God is merciful, Barth argues, not because God adopts a merciful stance in order to relate meaningfully to the creature, as if God were inherently neutral. Instead, at the very core of God's being, God is merciful. This section is preceded by Barth's exploration of the two attributes of grace and holiness, which defines grace as

> the distinctive mode of God's being in so far as it seeks and creates fellowship by its own free inclination and favour, unconditioned by any merit or claim in the beloved, but also unhindered by any unworthiness or opposition in the latter—able, on the contrary, to overcome all unworthiness and opposition.[10]

God's power is not seen merely in the power to punish, but primarily in the power to bring about community. This communion, however, is not based solely on forensic justification. This brings Barth to the second attribute of *Gerechtigkeit* (justice/righteousness). Barth insists that God's holiness must not be compromised. The ecclesial and political backdrop of Barth's work suggests that this was his fear especially with a view to German politics and the role of the German Protestant churches.

CD II/1 draws on Protestant Orthodox theologians to argue that divine holiness combines both a communicative or effective aspect and a distributive aspect, both a salvific and a punitive dimension. In loving the creature, God does not turn a blind eye to the creature's sin. God is loving and just at

the same time. On the one hand, God's holiness brings forth justice in creatures, while, on the other, God hates and punishes sin.[11] It is of the utmost
importance to Barth that the communicative aspect neither compromises
God's holiness—which he considers the danger with the doctrine of the justification of the sinner—nor that the distributive aspect amount to the blind
violence of a tyrant with a short fuse.

In contrast, the standard position in twentieth-century German Protestantism,
at least as far as the influence of Lutheranism had prevailed, was a one-sided
emphasis on the salvific or communicative nature of God's righteousness.[12]
"This righteousness in God is pleasing, for it makes God not a just judge, but
a forgiving father who wills to make use of his righteousness not to condemn,
but to justify and acquit sinners."[13] What is new and remarkable in *CD* II/1 is
thus the abiding importance Barth attributes to God's *iustitia distributiva*.[14]
Barth's contemporaries no doubt felt the provocation in his statement that
God is "wholly and utterly—the Judge. His revelation is wholly and utterly
the Law, manifesting His will as righteousness, and distinguishing it from
all unrighteousness. His activity is wholly and utterly the execution of this
Law."[15] "He is merciful as He really makes demands and correspondingly
punishes and rewards."[16]

What was at stake in Barth's insistence on God's integrity and the requirements of justice in 1940 is evident from the recent discovery that the number
of ghettos and concentration camps established under Nazi rule was no less
than 42,500.[17] For Barth, in turn, there was a direct connection between
his concept of God's justice that is both distributive and salvific, which he
worked out between 1937 and 1940, and the fact that he joined the Swiss
army in April 1940, insisting that he be given not an office job, but be allowed
to train with a loaded rifle.

While the ethical case for a military reaction against National Socialism
seems clear from today's perspective, the question is whether the human
response to God's call for temporal justice should consist in taking up arms
even in the more varied political conflicts today. Does Barth charge the problem with a religious energy that is hard to control even if a more subtle course
of action is required by less clear-cut patterns of conflict? This is an important
question, but first the implications of Barth's theological case require exploration within his context.

THE POLITICAL PAYOFF OF BARTH'S
RECONFIGURATION

Luther's interpretation of God's righteousness in terms of distributive and
salvific righteousness contained the seeds of a trend that led toward the secularization of political justice.[18] Luther, and to a stronger degree Lutherans

after him, have argued that reality is to be perceived in two dimensions.[19] Reigning in the church, God governs affairs spiritually through the proclamation of the gospel. This needs to be distinguished from worldly matters that are to be guided by God's law, which again is reflected in natural law.[20]

While not without problems of its own, in historical perspective there is much to be said in favor of Luther's theory of two regiments, especially as religious views are never immune to sin and fanaticism. German jurists such as Samuel von Pufendorf were able to build upon the natural law tradition advocated by Luther, thus contributing to proto-democratic traditions in Germany.[21] The problem is, of course, that natural law is not immune to sin and fanaticism, either. Indeed, Hitler's initial electoral success would have been inconceivable without almost unified Protestant electoral support.[22] Protestant freelancers were the strongest NSDAP voting block among all socio-economic groups, and on average, Protestants voted twice as often for Hitler than Catholics. This should certainly not be taken as saying that a Lutheran esteem for natural law traditions was the main, or even sole, predictor of Protestant voting patterns. Apart from more local factors—even the wish to edge out Jewish business competitors—a widespread antipathy against Weimar pluralism and a nostalgic longing for the Wilhelmine association of throne and altar often inspired support for Hitler. Protestant churches also saw the new nationalist enthusiasm as an opportunity for a broader missionary appeal. Nonetheless, it was not difficult to dress up all these factors as a deep expression of the creator's intentions reflected in natural law.

In this context, Barth's 1938 lecture "*Rechtfertigung und Recht*," translated as "Church and State," is highly significant. Barth argued that the theology of the Reformers falls short of answering a crucial question:

> is there a connection between justification of the sinner through faith alone, completed once for all by God through Jesus Christ, and the problem of justice, the problem of human law? Is there an inward and vital connection by means of which in any sense human justice (or law), as well as divine justification, becomes a concern of Christian faith and Christian responsibility, and therefore also a matter which concerns the Christian church?[23]

In *CD* II/1 Barth responds: "As a matter of fact, from the belief in God's righteousness there follows logically a very definite political problem and task."[24] In the 1938 lecture Barth had not yet described divine righteousness explicitly in distributive terms, as the divine implementation of a just order, by force if need be. Nonetheless, a clear distinction to the Lutheran tradition is unavoidable if legal justice is supposed to be invested with punitive authority and to correspond to divine justice. Attributing fundamental soteriological relevance to distributive justice, Barth now reclaims the strong tradition of

God's partiality for the marginalized that, according to the Old Testament, must be reflected in the legal system. With the distributive aspect fully integrated into God's righteousness, a theological account of worldly justice needs to live up to those religious political traditions. Political justice must first of all look for a "restoration of justice in favour of the threatened innocent, the oppressed poor, widows, orphans and aliens."[25] More specifically, in 1940, Barth calls for solidarity with Israel: "When we encounter divine righteousness we are all like the people of Israel, menaced and altogether lost according to its own strength."[26] Justification by faith needs to coincide with political justice, unless the justifying God is thought of as turning a blind eye to sin. Thus, whoever trusts in God's righteousness spiritually "stands under a political responsibility" and "can only will and affirm a state which is based on justice [*sc. Rechtsstaat*, constitutional democracy]."[27]

Barth's reintroduction of the distributive aspect into the concept of God's righteousness is in effect a desecularization, or sacralization, of the notion of justice, motivated by the fact that natural law concepts had utterly failed to prevent National Socialist abuses of state power. In contrast, Protestant theologians in Germany have typically conceived of political power in the context of natural law because they have been particularly worried that a directly political interpretation of religious traditions would distort the true spirit of Christian piety. They operated under the paradigm of Luther's struggle against episodes of unspiritual, feudalistic Vatican power politics and of Luther's fear of an anarchic dissolution of the coercive measures of the state by Christian enthusiasts.

On the other hand, since Enlightenment times, German Protestant churches had also been wary of embracing rationalistic natural law with its potential democratic and secular implications. Instead, they opted for another particular tradition of natural law with divinely sanctioned estates under monarchic authority. Among theologians, the old liberal guard declined in prominence during the 1920s, roughly at the moment when it developed a constructive stance toward the new democratic system.[28] Against this backdrop, the importance of *CD* II/1 sect. 30 lies in the search for the religious life blood that would act as a cultural force to create and sustain a constitutional democracy.[29] Barth's argument implies in turn that a church oblivious of the political dimensions of its religious traditions will leave politics vulnerable to being turned into a travesty of justice in the hands of totalitarian forces.

However, we are left wondering what to make of the fact that neither natural law nor religious traditions are immune to authoritarian temptations. During the decade around Hitler's rise to power especially, both adherents and opponents of an authoritarian nationalist regime might even have agreed that political power must protect the weak. The disagreement would have come down, however, to the question of who the weak were who require and deserve political support: was it the German people, supposedly mistreated in the political system of Versailles, or was it other marginalized groups such as Jews and other minorities?

Presumably, neither a secularized natural law ethics nor an affirmation of religious goals is per se the right way to conceive of political justice. For all his merits in the fight against replacing the Weimar Republic with a totalitarian order,[30] at a certain point even Barth himself put a premium on a strong administration. Around 1930, he argued in his ethics lectures that, faced with the state as the divinely ordained "remedy against corrupt nature,"[31] the individual should first of all consider his or her own sinfulness rather than private rights: "the dogma of original sin is much better preserved by the police than by teachers and even by modern pastors." Reconciliation with Christ presupposes sin, which led Barth even to reverse the principle of presumed innocence: "It is well known that in the eyes of the law everybody is always a suspicious person, an unreliable citizen, until there is proof to the contrary, which needs to be produced at any moment."[32]

Since neither particular religious traditions nor a more general natural law approach are immune to ideological distortions, a lively interplay of these traditions within civil society is a worthy goal.[33] Many procedural requirements of a constitutional democracy have been shaped by Enlightenment thought, and Barth affirmed them at various places without hesitation—even if he was haphazard in the ethics lectures.[34] Nonetheless, as natural law tends to abstract from historical particulars, the concept may end up with blind spots that one might identify only when one has been shaped by particular historical experiences. A more general concept of rational natural law, which on the other hand aspires to a more comprehensive account of ethics and society, would prompt proponents of particular religious traditions to engage the empirical dimension in their statements on religion and society, rather than to invest in a vision that may have a prophetic ring to it but ignores differences of worldview in a pluralistic society, or that lacks pragmatic attention to workable solutions in functional spheres such as the economic or legal systems.[35]

At one point Barth expressed his own political vision saying that Christians will make their contributions to political debates from a christological point of view, while non-Christian partners in debate will have to make do scooping their water "from the porous wells of so-called natural law."[36] My own suggestion goes beyond this to the extent that such measured appreciation may also turn into condescension. In contrast, Christians should be ready to learn and also profit from natural law traditions and worldly expertise. While the factors that shaped Western political systems have included helpful secular influences, the way to inhabit them properly for Christians is not a self-imposed strict secularity, but a religious stance aware of its own perspectival position within a larger whole. This is the trajectory on which Barth's discussion of God's justice and God's righteousness makes some headway.

It is important to note at this point that reconciling religious and secular traditions is not a contradiction in terms. Neither is Barth's desecularizing move anti-modern, as the popular equation of secularity and modernity has it. On the contrary, among Barth's goals are some that are typically associated with the modern European project of secularization, the "specifically modern forms of socialization, the most prominent of which are the market economy,[37] the public sphere and the citizenship 'democratic' state, all being characterized in principle by immediate, direct and equal access."[38] Nonetheless, unable to rule out entirely forms of creaturely revolt against the creator which are more or less subtle, we will have to face the possibility that even the best balance between Biblical religious traditions and natural law may lead us astray. In the words of Barth's later work:

> The proper 'Grand Inquisitor' or 'Antichrist' who can commend his evil cause, and therefore the man of sin in the full power of his work, is a sympathetic and a seriously persuasive and convincing figure, not to be confused with such unsympathetic associates as Hitler, Mussolini or Stalin, and able to count upon finding many well-disposed people to applaud and follow him.[39]

GOD'S RIGHTEOUSNESS: PROBLEMS AND PERSPECTIVES

Barth's work on the theological foundations of a critique of injustice implies another significant problem, however. In putting the square peg into a round hole, his case for both the distributive and the salvific nature of God's righteousness comes at a steep price. Barth seeks to adhere to the strict gratuity of justification with the concept of a pedagogic use of violence. Sin is true misery,[40] and God's punishment will be complemented by the free gift of new obedience. Ultimately, the balance of God's grace and God's holiness culminated in the vicarious punishment of Jesus Christ. As God's righteous wrath ran its course, "really smiting and piercing human sin, . . . the righteousness of God which we have offended was really revealed and satisfied," Barth says, hinting at Anselm's theory of satisfaction.[41] Due to God's grace, sinners no longer need to bear the full brunt of God's wrath themselves.

In the same chapter of *CD* II/1 in which he analyzes God's grace and holiness (§30.1), Barth also discusses God's constancy and omnipotence (§31.2). Indeed, in the issue of divine righteousness, God's constancy and omnipotence are crucial:

> The salvation revealed and given by [God] to the world . . . does not in any sense consist in making concessions of any kind or withdrawing in face of [the

world], as if He had to take its defection seriously in the sense that, faced with a *fait accompli*, He could only be different, retracting or qualifying the law of His will, or letting mercy take the place of justice and the like.[42]

Another section highlights the interrelationship of God's justice and power even more strongly:

> the power of God is never to be understood as simply a physical possibility, a *potentia*. It must be understood at the same time as a moral and legal possibility, a *potestas*. God's might never at any place precedes right, but is always and everywhere associated with it. Like all true might, it is in itself and from the beginning legitimate power. . . . It is the power which is the origin of legitimacy and is always exercised in the fulness of this legitimacy. It is the power which never lacks or can lack the dignity of the Godhead, of the Creator, Reconciler and Redeemer. What God is able to do *de facto*, He is also able to do *de jure*, and He can do nothing *de facto* that He cannot also do *de jure*.[43]

Barth goes on to defend not only God's omnipotence and constancy but also God's universal efficacy, or God's omnicausality.[44] God is so powerful that God neither wants to nor needs to compromise God's holiness and God's mercy. However, as Barth affirms both God's omnipotence and God's universal efficacy, he struggles to avoid the inversion of his argument: on the one hand, God is so powerful and constant that God achieves God's purpose without tempering justice with mercy; on the other hand, this seems to imply that the sinfulness that is at issue here cannot come from any other source than the omnipotent and universally efficacious God. At one point—again, writing in 1940—Barth puts this with surprising bluntness: "whoever receives any power, they do not receive it from anywhere other than this source of power; Rom 13:1."[45] Already, Barth's strong notion of divine punishment at Golgotha may seem to be vaguely ennobling violence with the appearance of soteriological necessity. The notion of God's universal efficacy then comes full circle as it is hard to avoid the conclusion that all violence is in fact divinely sanctioned. Indeed, even in 1940, in the midst of World War II, Barth is willing to argue that, after Christ's crucifixion, God still achieves a pedagogical effect by bringing about a reflection of Christ's passion in our own suffering. God is lord even over the power that opposes God:

> Created powers, and above all the powers of opposition and therefore of powerlessness, are always distinct from God's power. He permits them to exist as powers apart from and beside His power. He gives them a place, and this applies not only to the powers created through His work but also to the powers of opposition and powerlessness, to the possibility of the impossible, of that which has

been excluded by His own act. Yet this does not mean that He abandons even part of His lordship over them, that He is even partially powerless over against them, or that they have even partially an independent position and function in relation to Him. On the contrary, it is by His power that He creates or at any rate tolerates other powers. In this His power is always power in and over them, and He is always first and last the only one who is full of power. . . . Thus none of them can escape Him, but all must serve Him and will definitely serve Him in one way or another.[46]

Barth conceives of God in both a critical and constructive relationship with the creature, with God exercising judgment and enabling a new life. In this relationship, God is so sovereign that competition and cooperation are equally excluded. "Whoever competes and co-operates also experiences competition and co-operation. What conditions is also conditioned."[47] Barth's doctrine of God does not see God and the creature in a correlation that is established by some larger third entity. The doctrine of the divine attributes intends to flesh out in greater detail the sovereignty of God that is implied in the categorical distinction between God and the creature. While Barth thinks of God and the creature as categorically distinct, the only way communion between the two can be thought of is in a christological approach: "God and the creature could never be thought of together under any other concept than in the name of Jesus Christ."[48]

Faced with this christological approach, however, we must ask why we should assume God's universal efficacy, as well as the idea that the creature can neither compete not cooperate with God. In fact, Barth's discussion of divine omnipotence is fundamentally driven by just the kind of metaphysical approach Barth often wishes to exclude. This is the reason why Barth conceives of God's attributes as each capturing two supreme achievements, which are not only distinct but even seem to be in tension: God justifies the sinner by grace and brings about justice in punishing injustice; God makes the sinner holy in an act of condescension and eliminates all sin that is in opposition to communion with the holy God.

However, if Jesus Christ is to be seen as the crucial revelation of God's self, in what sense can we still ascribe violent punishment to God at all? It is not Jesus Christ who uses violence to implement justice. His unflinching commitment to justice in a wider sense is the reason for the Passion. It is thus much more appropriate to speak of God's commitment to justice that does not exclude God's own suffering—in a way, however, that is more cautious about the immediate achievements of God's commitment to justice. Although God's justice is by no means powerless, and although, in the best of cases, human justice may give powerful testimony to God's righteousness, God's justice cannot be identified with human justice, nor should it be considered so powerful that any human act of injustice is always taking place within the immediate reach of God's justice.

In Barth's case, the issue becomes pressing with the National Socialist genocide. Barth repeatedly asserts that Israel's suffering is due to divine wrath, which supposedly works out for the best. Barth portrays Israel as the paradigmatic transgressor.[49] But if the Romans truly acted as "instruments of God"[50] when they crucified Jesus, then how can Barth escape lumping the Nazis with the Romans in this regard? In consequence, we may emphasize the rights of the weak as much as we like; as long as we continue to ascribe redemptive power to violence as such, we are implicitly lending it legitimacy, and a clean break with the politics of violence remains unlikely.

This does not mean that, from a Christian perspective, the legal system must be stripped of all recourse to the use of force, for example, if force is used in the service of protecting society from a convicted criminal. The criminal system may even use force to protect the criminal from some consequences of his or her own misdeeds. What must not happen is that religious violence oversteps the boundaries of due process. In contrast, it is the legal system itself that deserves protection und support for religious reasons, as long as the powerful do not enjoy a privilege before the law, as long as the legal system remains able to correct itself through democratic means, and as long as it supports the process in which democratic societies are engaged in constructive self-critique. Under these conditions, Christians should support the legal system by contributing to its improvement. What Jeffrey Stout says about the relation between Christianity and democracy also obtains in the relation between Christianity and the legal system:

> Under circumstances [such] as . . . ours, with potentially anti-democratic forces assembling allies and attempting to divide or co-opt their foes, the question of character attains utmost importance for friends of democracy. It becomes the question of whether the people can summon the spiritual wherewithal, the moral fiber, to act on behalf of democracy before democracy itself gives way.[51]

The constructive achievement of Barth's doctrine of God's righteousness is the search for a vital connection between God's soteriological activity and the legal system. Although his achievement is tarnished by assumptions about a fundamental divine use of violence, we can also discover helpful perspectives as we continue to trace Barth's development of the matter. In 1959, Barth reflected again on the issue of "The people of God in world-occurrence."[52] Worldly history, Barth says, takes place *providentia Dei et confusione hominum*, under God's providence and through human confusion. He then argues that eschatological truth can certainly not be extrapolated from this process, as this would lend legitimacy to human confusion and sin.[53] Indeed, exactly this is part of the problem with God's distributive righteousness in *CD* II/1. Either God also has a satanic side or the violent part of Good Friday is not God's work and revelation; it looks rather a lot like *hominum confusio*. In contrast, in *CD* IV/1, sect. 59.2, Barth argues that the cross represents "our judgment, end and death." With regards to justification, the emphasis shifts to the resurrection of Jesus Christ. Rather than being implied in the cross, the resurrection is "in distinctive contrast" to it, far from being its "predicate, or adjunct, or closer definition."[54] Rather than offering satisfaction to God or physically destroying sin, the cross actually adds to the bill of indictment, implying a "terrible 'against us.'"[55] The final paragraph of this section locates salvation not in the violence of the cross but in the saving act of the resurrection. It draws the conclusion, quoting an Easter hymn: "Jesus lives and I with Him."[56]

As Barth now envisions God's justice as restorative rather than retributive, this new development has various political implications. For the moment one conclusion to be drawn is that we do not need to affirm God's distributive punishment in order to hold on to Barth's integration of Judeo-Christian legal traditions into political discourse. In keeping with the *contra nos* of the violence of the cross and the *pro nobis* of resurrection, we can hold on to a divine judgment of reprobation that may be in contrast to historic events without identifying the violent side of the cross with God's action.

NOTES

1. Barth, "Brief an Prof. Dr. Josef L. Hromádka, Prag, 1938," in *Offene Briefe 1935–1942*, ed. D. Koch, Barth-Gesamtausgabe (Zurich: TVZ, 2001), 107–133, 114: "Every Czech soldier who then fights and suffers will do so also for us—and today I am saying so without reservations: he will do so also for the church of Jesus Christ, which in the sphere of Hitler's or Mussolini's influence can only become either a laughing stock or be wiped out" (all English texts with German bibliography translated by author, A. M.).

2. Barth, *Der Römerbrief (Zweite Fassung): 1922*, eds. Cornelis van der Kooi and Katja Tolstaja, Barth-Gesamtausgabe (Zurich: Evangelischer Verlag, 2010), 653.

3. Ibid., 634.

4. Barth, "Church and State," in *Community, State, and Church: Three Essays: With a New Introduction*, ed. David Haddorff, trans. Will Herberg (Eugene: Wipf & Stock, 2004), 101–148, 145 (trans. rev.): "Can we pray that the State shall be preserved, preserved as a *Rechtsstaat* [constitutional democracy], or that it will again become a *Rechtsstaat* [...] thus without, in certain cases, like Zwingli, reckoning with the possibility of revolution, the possibility, according to his strong expression, that we may have to 'overthrow with God' those rulers who do not follow the lines laid down by Christ?"

5. Eberhard Busch, *Karl Barth: His Life in Letters and Autobiographical Texts*, trans. John Bowden (Eugene: Wipf & Stock, 2005), 284.

6. Ibid., 288 ("in the struggle against the deception pursued by the synod of the Confessing Church," trans. rev.).

7. Ibid., 273.

8. Ibid., 273 f.

9. Ibid., 292 f.

10. *CD* II/1, 353.

11. Ibid., 359.

12. Before the twentieth century, Quenstedt can be named as an exception: "*Iustitia Dei* [...] [*est*] *vel remuneratrix* [...] *vel vindicatrix*," ibid., 377.

13. Martin Luther, "Erklärung des 51. Psalms," in *Galatervorlesung (cap. 5–6) 1531; Vorlesungen über Psalm 2, 45 und 51 1532*, ed. K. Drescher, Weimar Edition 40/2 (Weimar: Böhlau, 1914), 313–470, 444; Barth, *CD* II/1, 378 (trans. rev.). For Luther's distinction between *iustitia passiva* and *iustitia formalis/activa* see "Vorrede Luthers zum ersten Bande der Gesamtausgabe seiner lateinischen Schriften, Wittenberg 1545," in *Schriften 1543/46*, ed. K. Drescher, Weimar Edition 54 (Weimar: Böhlau, 1928), 176–187, 184.

14. *CD* II/1, 382, 391.

15. Ibid., 381.

16. Ibid., 383, see also 390.

17. Eric Lichtblau, "The Holocaust Just Got More Shocking," *The New York Times*, March 1, 2013, SR3 (New York edition), http://tinyurl.com/aqrzorn (last accessed July 22, 2021).

18. Luther's theory of God's two regiments can be called a step toward secularization, as a differentiation is increasingly made between ecclesial power and political power (institutional differentiation). Moral questions traditionally impinging on God's righteousness are increasingly left to private discretion (privatization), and religious practices such as the institution of penance or the celebration of religious holidays set off on their decline. For these criteria of secularization see José Casanova, "Religion in Modernity as a Global Challenge," in *Religion und die umstrittene Moderne*, eds. M. Reder and M. Rugel (Stuttgart: Kohlhammer, 2010), 1–16, 1. Reaching further back into intellectual history, the philosopher Otfried Höffe makes a case that Plato's philosophy of justice in *Politeia* was an important step toward the secularization of justice in comparison with religious notions of justice in Egypt, Mesopotamia, Israel, and pre-classical ancient Greece. Höffe, *Gerechtigkeit: Eine philosophische Einführung*, Beck Wissen (Munich: Beck, 2001), 20. See also Plato's Euthyphro. According to Höffe, Aristotle's account of justice will then go on to shed Plato's metaphysical framework.

19. See Luther's essay "On Secular Authority, How Far Does the Obedience Owed to it Extend?"/"Von weltlicher Obrigkeit, wie weit man ihr Gehorsam schuldig sei," in *Predigten und Schriften 1523*, ed. P. Pietsch, Weimar Edition 11 (Weimar: Böhlau, 1900), 245–81, 249, 251.

20. Ibid., 251.

21. Horst Denzer, "Samuel von Pufendorf," in *Theologische Realenzyklopädie*, vol. 28, eds. H. Balz et al. (Berlin and New York: de Gruyter, 1997), 3–6. On Luther, see John Witte, Jr., "Freedom of a Christian: Human Dignity, Liberty, and Equality in the Theology of Martin Luther," in *God's Joust, God's Justice: Law and Religion in the Western Tradition*, Emory University Studies in Law and Religion (Grand Rapids: Eerdmans, 2006), 49–62, 61: "Protestants over the centuries have often defied these founding ideals. . . . But an instinct for egalitarianism . . . is a Lutheran gene in the theological genetic code of protestantism."

22. Jürgen W. Falter, *Hitlers Wähler* (München: Beck, 1991), 169–188, 251–256.

23. Barth, "Church and State," 101.

24. *CD* II/1, 386. Barth makes an overt gesture to the 1938 lecture "*Rechtfertigung und Recht*," or "Justification and Justice" ("Church and State") (Ibid.).

25. Ibid. (trans. rev.).

26. *CD* II/1, 387.

27. Ibid.

28. See, for example, Ernst Troeltsch's Spectator Letters and his "Der Untergang des Abendlandes," in *Spectator-Briefe und Berliner Briefe (1919–1922)*, ed. Gangolf Hübinger, Kritische Gesamtausgabe 14 (Berlin and New York: de Gruyter, 2015), 53–588, and Friedemann Voigt, *Ernst Troeltsch Lesebuch* (Tübingen: Mohr Siebeck, 2003), 286–293.

29. In his contribution to this volume ("Democracy and Church: Barth and Yoder on Democratic Practice"), Kristopher Norris also highlights particular virtues Christians should bring to the democratic process. Furthermore, the momentous transitions between three epochs in Germany during the first half of the twentieth century also mirror Alexis de Tocqueville's uneasiness about the potential religious underpinnings of the democratic watershed in France and the United States. See the essay by David Haddorff in this volume: "American Democracy and Trinitarian Sovereignty: Lessons From Barth and Tocqueville."

30. At a local level, Barth cultivated an ethos of rational debate on political issues among his students. See the contribution by Angela D. Hancock in this volume, "Training for a Serious Game: Theo-Political Deliberation as a Christian Practice." In the wider public, the pamphlet *Theological Existence To-Day! (A Plea for Theological Freedom)*, trans. R. Birch Hoyle (Eugene: Wipf & Stock, 2012) or the open letter "An die Frankfurter Zeitung: 1932" stand out. In *Offene Briefe 1909–1935*, ed. Diether Koch, Karl-Barth-Gesamtausgabe (Zurich: Theologischer Verlag, 2001), 170–183.

31. Karl Barth, *Ethics*, ed. Dietrich Braun, trans. Geoffrey W. Bromiley (Eugene: Wipf & Stock, 2013), 444. The quotation is from the ethics lectures Barth held in winter 1928/1929 and which he repeated in roughly the same form in winter 1930/31. These statements are part of the larger chapter 3, "The Command of God the Reconciler."

32. Ibid., 378. "Wittingly or Unwittingly," police work rests on "a very theological presupposition." "In all who bear a human face it [i.e., the police] sees necessary objects of innumerable regulations and ordinances, and possible objects of civil or penal proceedings" (Ibid).

33. Secularization may even be complementary with religious revival. Casanova, "Religion in Modernity as a Global Challenge," 3.

34. In the ethics lectures, Barth's two versions of the subsection "Church and State" (in §13.4) even seem to defend constitutional democracy. The main problem is that in this tendency, they are contrary to the overall direction of §§12, 13, and that the individualistic emphasis on love and repentance undercuts the public claims required in a struggle for democracy.

35. Barth's essay "The Christian Community and Civil Community" is an example of the synthesis envisioned here. In *Community, Church, and State: Three Essays*, ed. David Haddorff, trans. Will Herberg (Eugene: Wipf & Stock, 2004), 149–189. This synthesis, not by itself immune to ideological distortions, already requires a functioning constitutional democracy. Nevertheless, Reinhold Niebuhr captured a significant aspect of the natural law tradition in 1935: "The obligation to affirm and protect the life of others can arise at all only if it is assumed that life is related to life in some unity and harmony of existence. In any given instance motives of the most calculating prudence rather than a high sense of obligation may enforce the standard. Men may defend the life of the neighbor merely to preserve those processes of mutuality by which their own life is protected. But that only means that they have discovered the inter-relatedness of life through concern for themselves rather than by analysis of the total situation. This purely prudential approach will not prompt the most consistent social conduct, but it will nevertheless implicitly affirm what it ostensibly denies— that the law of life is love." Niebuhr, *An Interpretation of Christian Ethics* (London and New York: Harper, 1935), 106 f.

36. Barth, "The Christian Community and Civil Community," 170.

37. Here a caveat needs to me made. A strengthening of the market economy is only among Barth's goals insofar as he also reacts against the exclusion of some from economic participation in society due to marginalization; his case for the Old Testament *personae miserae* also has an economic edge. On the whole, Barth's stance toward market economies was at least ambivalent as he perceived it to be less than ideal in providing equal access to economic resources. I am not suggesting that Barth endorses the most diverse aspects of economic life associated with modern market economies; the crucial point is protest for fair and equitable participation in economic life.

38. Casanova, "Religion in Modernity as a Global Challenge," 4.

39. *CD* IV/3, 438 (trans. rev.).

40. *CD* II/1, 371.

41. Ibid., 398.

42. Ibid. 504 (trans. rev.).

43. Ibid., 526 (trans. rev.) See also Haddorff, "American Democracy and Trinitarian Sovereignty," in this volume.

44. *CD* II/1, 527 f.

45. *CD* II/1, 526.

46. Ibid., 538. This argument will be resumed in *CD* III/3, 289: "God determines the sphere, the manner, the measure and the subordinate relationship to His Word and work in which it [i.e., *das Nichtige*, or evil] may still operate."

47. *CD* II/1, 580.

48. Ibid., 580.

49. Ibid., 367, 384, 396.

50. Ibid., 396.

51. Jeffrey Stout, *Democracy and Tradition* (Princeton and Oxford: Princeton University Press, 2004), 23.

52. *CD* IV/3, sect. 72.1: *Das Volk Gottes im Weltgeschehen.*

53. Ibid., 705.

54. *CD* IV/1, 297.

55. Ibid., 296: a *contra nos* rather than a *pro nobis* (for us).

56. Ibid., 356.

Chapter 12

Religion, Democracy, and Globalization

Schmitt and Barth in the Shadow of Political Theology

Oliver Hidalgo

INTRODUCTION

This article is a contribution on the complex relationship between religion, democracy, and globalization with regard to the theological-political approaches by Karl Barth and Carl Schmitt. As I want to show from the perspective of political science, the deep antagonism between both thinkers can help us to identify the main challenges a possible formation of global democracy is inevitably confronted with. The crucial question in this respect is whether the evident tensions between religion, democracy, and globalization must be seen as an insurmountable obstacle to the rise and emergence of global democracy or, nevertheless, if they might be able to provide the three pillars of a universal building.

In order to answer this, basically we have to identify the particular level of discussion we are facing when thinking about the difficult relationship of the three topics. Apparently, the question about religion, democracy, and globalization demands both a distinction from domestic and international affairs. In the latter respect, it can be assumed as the main problem what kind of challenge religion implies for politics and democracy. However, a global perspective on religion and democracy seems to be different. As long as we look at democracy from a domestic or even from an international point of view, it likewise offers us a benchmark for judging the connections between religion and politics we are observing. Then, democracy can function as a criterion for the political-theological complex, which means distinguishing these connections between religion and politics as far as they are compatible with democracy (e.g., religion as a pre-political resource for guiding citizens in civil society; civil religion; religious parties on the basis of the democratic constitution and the rule of law) from those not being compatible (e.g., theocracy, God's political sovereignty and religious governance; political religion in the sense of Eric Voegelin[1] and Raymond Aron,[2] etc.). Against the background of globalization, democracy must necessarily lose this quality as long as a global democracy does not exist at all. Hence, the orientation we can draw from the concept of democracy in order to evaluate the risks and chances of religion and politics does hitherto not work in a global context.

Of course, this brief outline may not lead to the assumption that—at a global level—things could reverse, so that vice versa religion becomes the criterion for democracy. Moreover, regardless of every envisaged level of discussion, the relation between religion and politics will always retain its own ambiguity. On the other hand, considering the particular role of religion beyond domestic or international issues must leave the usual style of conversing and must ask precisely to which extent it is just the ambiguity of "theo-politics" that could help us to grasp the proper problem of global democracy and, as a next step, what is crucial in supporting the endeavor to get a kind of normative foundation for global or transnational democratic structures. To demonstrate this, my contribution will sketch once again the unsolved questions of global democracy, before showing what is supposed to be the part of religion(s) within the whole game. Proceeding from this, I will refer to Carl Schmitt and Karl Barth to acknowledge the impacts and dilemmas of such global and democratic theo-politics.

THE CHALLENGE OF GLOBAL DEMOCRACY

Today, it seems to be obvious that the globalization of economy and communication implies the necessity of global politics as well. Since long, poverty, climate change, energy resources and consumption, migration, proliferation or also the regulation of worldwide financial markets have become issues that can be tackled only by way of political interaction and cooperation of transnational actors, that is by way of—as we call it—*global governance*. Thus, it is not a surprise that there are several attempts to designate regulations on a worldwide scale, like the UN Millennium Development Goals (MDGs), the world climate conferences, proposals for the global governance of peace, security, and conflict resolution, and so on. However we are, now as before, far away from a kind of *global governance* that could be more than a sort of fraudulent labeling. For this, there are noticeably two main reasons: The first one is the fact that the just mentioned "world problems" concern human beings in general and the responsible political actors in particular in a very unequal degree of intensity. For example, the various effects of climate change will make the situation in the southern hemisphere with all its developing countries much worse than in the northern industrialized countries. And, the inequality of concernment obviously provokes a diversity of interests at the same time. The second problem is that even if there was a shared global responsibility, it would have to be channeled into some institutions and processes of collective decision-making to achieve a concrete praxis of world governance. In terms of this, we are confronted with the empirical lack of democratic legitimacy and control of international organizations as well as with the lack of a transnational community that would be able to create synallagmatic decisions—decision based on mutual agreement.

Meanwhile, both reasons together have created some serious doubts that the phenomena and processes of globalization and also the acceleration of global interdependences will finally lead us to global governance and democratically structured international organizations. Therefore, the optimism expressed by models of global democracy (formulated by thinkers like David Held,[3] Daniele Archibugi,[4] Otfried Höffe,[5] and others) during the 1990s have gradually been replaced by rather pessimistic positions, like Robert A. Dahl's that cherished the inevitable national boundaries of democracy.[6] Accordingly, it is primarily the pattern of a cosmopolitan democracy that is increasingly assumed as an illusion[7]—and sometimes even as an instrument to maintain the existing global exploitative economic and social structures by suggesting just a superficial common interest that is actually assumed to be the exclusive interest of the Western World.[8]

Thus, if still one sticks to the prospect of a democratic future at a global level, the majority of contemporary political thinkers—for example, Larry Diamond,[9] Fred Dallmayr,[10] or James Bohman[11]—rather propose an *international* option that avoids a democratization across national borders at the price of a dangerous and—in consequence—anti-democratic concentration of power. This means that all different countries, cultures, and civilizations in the world must find their own particular approach to achieve the universal values of democracy:[12] not by adopting only Western ideas but by understanding and realizing the global roots of the concept.[13] Indeed, a spillover of democratic norms from their historical origins in the Western World to non-Western societies cannot be ruled out but would in reality be an intricate process of diffusion, that is a sort of "vernacularization,"[14] of "reiterative universalism"[15] or to a certain degree "democratic iteration."[16] As a consequence, the relation and intellectual exchange between Western and non-Western democracies is one of the most important debates in contemporary political theory.[17]

In this realm, religion obviously plays a key role: first, because more than twenty years after Samuel P. Huntington's influential thesis of a *Clash of Civilizations* there is still the widespread prejudice in the Western World that certain religions, cultures, and societies might be incompatible with the Western idea of democracy. Therefore Islam, Confucianism, Buddhism, and other religious convictions are frequently estimated as serious obstacles to a successful promotion of international democratization.[18] Second, because there is another prevalent opinion that the plurality of world religions might even offer the opportunity to establish different kinds of democracy but not at all a global *overlapping consensus*.[19] However, the latter might become necessary for a practice of global governance based on the idea of public reason and on a subsequent canon of shared values both religious and non-religious people are able to confirm and to support.[20] On this note, the plurality of (world) religions is discovered to be crucial for the question of global democracy to the whole extent.

RELIGION AND DEMOCRACY IN THE ERA OF GLOBALIZATION

Regarding the partial structures of global governance, which have been hitherto applied, we may state that religious organizations predominantly work on policy fields traditionally belonging to the *transnational* public sphere: war and peace, environment, poverty, development. The reason for that might be that religious organizations try to close the existing gaps within global politics. In this respect, it seems to be plausible that often religious organizations have a significantly higher interest in that field of politics than the majority of political actors who are first of all elected in order to represent and to achieve national objectives and therefore depend on results rather beyond the problems of the world.

In contrast, the political and ethical claims of religious communities usually seek for an idea of justice that cannot be reduced to national affairs. This might explain why they are more engaged in transnational and global projects than other actors in the field of international relations. Moreover, it is not only their altruism but also their special interest that enforce (world) religions and religious communities to think global, not national.

While religious identities, the missionary work of religions and also the request to represent all members and followers of one religious group do not stop at state borders, religious communities are almost predestined to play an important role in global politics. This could also elucidate the high number of religious organizations who definitely aim to support global interests, first of all the *Vatican,* but furthermore the *World Evangelical Alliance* (WEA), the World Jewish Congress (WJC), the Muslim World League (MWL), the World Hindu Congress (WHC), the International Network of Engaged Buddhists (INEB), and many more.

The difference between transnational religions and national states can be traced back to the origins of nationalism itself. As Benedict Anderson pointed out in *Imagined Communities* (1991), the modern concept of "nation," which is defined by its territorial borders, has to be understood as being opposite to the former religious communities which were connected by sacred languages.[21] In this context, Anderson did by no means assert that the "appearance of nationalism was 'produced' by the erosion of religious certainties"[22] or that the attainment of nationalism was an overcoming of traditional religions. But indeed he emphasized that the concept of *nation* primarily came "to maturity at a stage of human history when even the most devout adherents of any universal religion were inescapably confronted with the living pluralism of such religions, and the allomorphism, or mismatch, between each faith's ontological claims and territorial stretch."[23] In this particular historical situation—in the course of the seventeenth and eighteenth centuries—the modern national state demonstrated its sovereignty by becoming independent from religion. Reversing this logic, it could be attractive for religious communities today to demonstrate vice versa their independence and emancipation from the national state by taking global responsibility.

Additionally, this role of religious communities in the era of globalization corresponds to the special conditions for religion and politics in the modern era against the infamous diagnosis by Jean-Jacques Rousseau in 1762 that religion is only politically effective if connected with state policy.[24] As Alexis de Tocqueville has analyzed in the two volumes of the impressive study on *Democracy in America* (1835/1840), it could be—in modern times—even beneficial for the legitimacy of the political claims by religious communities if they were *not* connected and associated with ethically sometimes very problematic and always contingent state interests.[25] Hence, even more the often neglected global aspects of politics could be estimated as a particular domain and capability of religions, due to the democratic separation of state and church. From this point of view, optimists might even proceed with the assumption that a successful common political engagement of world religions (which can be actually observed by the projects of *Religions for Peace*,[26] of the *World Parliament of Religions*[27] and further interreligious organizations) will contribute to blaze the trail for a substantial global governance and global democracy in the future. In this respect, it would be most favorable if the progress of interreligious dialogues, the further formulating of shared goals and common normative convictions were able to activate special spillover effects to the arena of world politics. And although this might look rather illusionary at the present time, it is evident that every chance for global democracy at least depends on an enhancement proving that the unchangeable fact of the plurality of world religions is not equivalent to the impossibility of developing a transnational or global political identity.

On the other hand, even a successful intercultural and interreligious dialogue may not be confused with a new project of cosmopolitism. Coming to
terms with different religious communities and identifying such a thing as
a common denominator between them does not mean ignoring the remaining differences and conflicts. In this respect, the main problem of cosmopolitanism is neither that this project seems to be unrealistic nor that its
results could never be reliable. On the contrary, for global democracy (like
for every democracy) the commitment must always be to keep the balance
between unity and plurality, common sense and conflict. Certainly, the aim of
democracy is not to solve all conflicts but only to find a way to handle them.
Therefore, global democracy would need both sides—the one stressed by
Chantal Mouffe[28] and other exponents of an agonistic theory[29] who—partly
referring to Carl Schmitt' *Concept of the Political*[30]—insist on the inevitable
contrariness of political entities; and the other one stressed by Immanuel
Kant,[31] Robert Keohane, and Joseph Nye[32] who drew attention to the general
interest in cooperating within the international relations. If we ignore one of
these two necessary sides of global democracy, the consequence would be
either that the underestimation of political conflicts leads to the misunderstanding that global democracy means nothing but a stabilizer for the present
Western-dominated world order or that the overestimation of conflict fails to
understand democracy as a political system that requires the general consensus that the results of democratic decision-making have to be accepted not
only by the superior but also by the inferior: As democracy *is* conflict, but
only a kind of conflict that shows respect to the interests of all citizens and
does not degenerate into a tyranny of majority. So if a shared foundation of
values and a common democratic identity are missed, the hasty implementation of elections would even force the existing ethnic, cultural, social, and
religious antagonisms, as Paul Collier has pointed out in *War, Guns, and
Votes: Democracy in Dangerous Places* (2009).[33]

This relevant synchronicity between consensus and conflict in democracy
can be illustrated best by an example we have already mentioned earlier:
the climate change. Here, the trouble is that, concerning contemporary
ecological problems, there is no common interest available in the sense of
Kant, Keohane, or Nye. Instead, what we face is a conflict that shows several
legitimate but nevertheless incommensurable positions which, corresponding to this, cannot be solved by rational consideration. So the only way to
handle the conflict in a constructive manner is to argue out the differences, to
deal with the problem and then to decide a modus vivendi[34] without fostering the illusion that the problem can be solved by a just compromise or by
a solution that advantages or disadvantages every affected country or actor
equally. Democracy does not mean that everything is just and that there
are no winners and losers. On the contrary, democracy is, simply spoken,
a way of making even unjust decisions acceptable for the discriminated

actors and agencies; acceptable because they maintain the chance to achieve another result in the future, which makes democracy as difficult as it is.

However, the "clash" of (world) religions or better: of religious-political identities,[35] offers us at least a kind of *theo-political* pattern to understand the crucial questions and challenges of global democracy. The plurality of religions symbolizes and represents both the existence of equally legitimated though incommensurable positions and the prospect that these positions might nevertheless be able to coexist (which is the political reality in consolidated democracies). We are even able to figure that different religious convictions imply the chance for a common identity: as *believers*. Concerning democracy, particularly global democracy, the situation is—at least in theory—very similar: As democrats, we believe in the same thing—democracy—although we might belong to very opposing political camps. So the adherents of diverse religious communities and the supporters of various political parties have in common that they are united and divided at the same time. This seems to make it also conceivable that a progress in the field of interreligious dialogue will be joined by further steps toward a global democracy.

Indeed, this is a very theoretical approach and much more complex than presented in this chapter. For example, in democracy the necessary arrangement between the adherents of different religions includes "non-believers" in the religious sense, whereas democracy has to defend itself against its enemies like every political system has to do in order to survive. So the similarities between believers and democrats are apparently limited. Moreover, the peaceful coexistence of different religious communities in consolidated democracies cannot be easily transferred into the global system. At a global level, there is no democratic Super-State and no rule of law that guarantees religious freedom and plurality. Correspondingly, the probability that the general political ambiguity of religious identities might turn toward its destructive side in the field of international and global politics becomes even higher. Finally, it might develop into a dilemma between cause and effect. It needs a common theo-political identity in order to install global democratic structures; but without a global democracy, a shared canon of religious and cultural values is hardly to achieve. Nevertheless, it is important to recognize that global democracy stands and falls with answering the theo-political question.

THE THEORIES OF CARL SCHMITT AND KARL BARTH—A FRAMEWORK FOR CONTEMPORARY INTERNATIONAL POLITICAL THEORY?

Although the following remarks might insinuate a still preliminary perspective, Schmitt and Barth are obviously relevant in the realms of religion, democracy, and globalization—under the premise that we take a rather unbiased approach toward both thinkers.

As is well-known, we can find in Schmitt a radical critique of political liberalism.[36] For Schmitt, the liberal request for a peaceful and democratic universal order is both a raw illusion and a fundamental peril. Since all international and global politics have to be characterized as relations between friends and enemies, any attempt to escape war is not a realistic option,[37] while the liberal assertion to install a universal world order will produce the "enemy" only in a different way than hitherto: not as a *relative* one among many others but as an *absolute* enemy of mankind who is blamed by liberal thinkers and politicians for working against the liberal hegemony and for apparently denying universal values like the human rights. Proceeding from this, it becomes evident why Schmitt did estimate the League of Nations, the Geneva protocol, and particularly the agreement to outlaw war in the course of the Kellogg-Briand Pact (1928) as instruments in order to destroy state sovereignty[38] and to provoke the totality of war. Most notably, Schmitt insisted that the German Reich as a declared *hostis injustus* was forced to use every occasion to overcome its discrimination, which in turn would necessarily provoke a fiercely determined reaction by its enemies and finally to trigger a spiral of violence—similar to the religious wars in Pre-Westphalia Europe.[39] In contrast to this, the limitation of war (*ius in bello*) could be achieved only by unrestricted state sovereignty including the *ius ad bellum*.

During the interwar period, Schmitt's argument could function as a justification for Nazi imperialism.[40] However, as Chantal Mouffe worked out, the major relevance of Carl Schmitt's thought for contemporary international politics is not the problem of imperialism but the general emphasis on legitimate ways of expressing existing political antagonisms.[41] The end of the bipolar system after 1989 and the rise of the liberal model of global democracy and civil society will not put an end to the pluralistic nature of world politics as such. Instead, antagonisms between political entities will inevitably remain, even more since states are declining while non-state-actors are gaining importance in the political sphere, as Schmitt foresaw in *Theorie des Partisanen* (1963) by anticipating the deep connection between spaceless universalism in theory and global terrorism in practice. Hence, the liberal illusion of a worldwide consensus is expected to be joined by the occurrence of a new form of hostility and by the logic of escalating political conflicts.[42] In sum, Schmitt made the liberal defamation of the political relation between friend and enemy responsible for producing unintended, brutal consequences. In his eyes, the Post-Westphalian era beyond the sovereignty of national states and with the Western enforcement of a unipolar world order must produce horrible collateral damages, particularly the appearance of an illegal and existential (not conventional) enemy resisting unipolarism without knowing any compromise.[43] It does not take much to notice the analogies with present debates about new wars[44] and transnationally operating terrorism.[45]

Moreover, we may not overlook the theo-political background of the Schmittian distinction of friends and enemies. Since all significant political concepts are secularized theological ones,[46] theology does precede all politics. In this respect, the antagonistic nature of the politics assumed by Schmitt corresponds with the opposing reactions to the "truth" of revelation in human history, where the pluralism of religions, cultures, and civilizations seems to follow the distinction between "believers" and "non-believers." Thus, the logic of *us* and *them* or *who is not for us, is against us* emerges in political domains because the peoples' metaphysical view determines their patterns of thinking and organizing the politics.[47] Accordingly, Schmitt's remarks on the *katechon*[48]—the historical power to restrain the appearance of the Antichrist and to prevent him from becoming fully manifest—as well as the interpretation of human history as an interim period influenced by the anthropology and political philosophy of St. Augustine[49] can be reconstructed as components of a consistent political theology of international relations. And although the latter rather marks the observation that the relevance of theo-political thinking in foreign policy is in providing a theoretical framework, for which the "reference to a transcendent commandment of God coming from the absolute outside"[50] is not necessary, Schmitt's radical position and conceptual absolutism cannot be understood adequately without referring to the applied political-theological vocabulary. In this respect, we should remember the context within which the concept of *political theology* was originally introduced. In the eponymous work from 1922, Schmitt attempted to dispense the concept of sovereignty from all theological, moral, or institutional boundaries by comparing the political sovereignty to create law and order with God's ability to create the world *ex nihilo*. To a certain extent, Schmitt's political decisionism even requests to surrogate the power of God on earth, which had the logical consequence that there are neither institutional controls nor elements of moral restraint, conciliation, and reasoning to be discovered in Schmitt's political thought.[51] Despite proclaiming the relativism of hostility and the de-escalation of warfare, Schmitt's concept of the political and in particular the pertinent idea of sovereignty are rather in the danger of leading to very extreme conclusions. In order to identify the conceivable radicalism of Schmitt's political theology, we have to acknowledge that he presumes the high intensity of politics as a sort of objective truth in human history. At the same time he promotes the political as the decisive norm for each individual domain of human life, instead of being able to regulate the political by way of valid ethical standards.[52] In fact, the political is "total" to the extent that, whenever a political conflict breaks out, no other criterion for decision-making could claim priority.[53] According to Schmitt, there is no escape from the political struggle for existence. The instruments and agencies may change, but the existential menaces will always remain, which reveals the political as being nothing but "the fate of human beings."[54]

Nevertheless, this radicalism based upon figures such as truth, belief, objectivity, friend and enemy, is precisely a view that promises orientation for contemporary International Relations theory. Considering the current crisis of world order, the phenomenon of failing states, the challenge of transnational terrorism or even the (possibly self-fulfilling) prophecy of the clash of civilizations, Schmitt's political existentialism could still advance to becoming a dominating paradigm, as it can be read as an essential criticism of globalization[55] including a warning about the dangers of a unipolar world. The problem therefore lies less in the quality of the diagnosis than in the proposal for its therapy. Schmitt is apparently convincing when identifying the problems of liberalism, universalism, and cosmopolitanism to stress that the reality of conflicting political identities must be part of every theory of the political and of democracy and that a global order ignoring this impact is in danger to trigger rather the opposite. On the other hand, he shows no consciousness at all that common values are needed as well to de-escalate conflicts in the way he provides. The *Nomos of the Earth* that is enforced only due to the idea of state sovereignty lacks the perspective of a transnational moral consensus as a crucial resource for the global acceptance of international laws. In consequence, Schmitt was not able to deduce a consistent political theory from his own premises.

With regard to this, it is very fascinating to come to terms with the theo-political thought of Karl Barth who is the classical counterpart of Carl Schmitt concerning many aspects that have been discussed earlier.[56] Like Schmitt, Barth considered the theological and the political as a zone of indistinction.[57] Moreover, both thinkers were skeptical toward liberalism. However, Barth's relevant critique is not directed against political liberalism but against liberal theology. The relativism of liberal hermeneutics of the religious sources is accused of being responsible for, during the Third Reich, the Christian belief not providing (the majority of) Christians with the power and capacity to resist and fight against the Nazi system. In contrast to this, Barth's own opposition against Hitler's Germany, which forced him into exile after 1935, had a specific anti-liberal-theological foundation: a strict universalism that binds all humanity in a solidarity of sinfulness.[58]

In comparison to Schmittian theo-political terms, we can draw the assumption that, for Barth, the liberal-theological examination and attenuation of revelation made Christians avoid the necessary (and commanded) political conflict with a criminal regime. Against Max Weber and the thesis of a global disenchantment, both Barth and Schmitt reveal the perception that the decisive battles of the modern world still occur in the field of political theology, while the secular means are nothing but an intra-metaphysical phenomenon.[59]

Hence, the decision of what is (theologically) true or false is the fundamental problem of mankind and therefore determines each concept of the political. However, it was just theology what made Barth develop a completely different political doctrine.[60] On the one hand, the theo-politics formulated in *Barmer Theologische Erklärung* (1934) and essentially inspired by Barth emphasized the duty of Christians to engage in politics against an apolitical interpretation of the Lutheran two-kingdoms-doctrine (Thesis two). But, on the other hand, the *Confessing Church*, which was to object Nazi politics on theological and moral principles, was aimed against any political usurpation of theology as well. As state sovereignty is not launched in the Schmittian manner as the only source of political legitimacy, the constitution of the Church does not at all depend on state power (Thesis three), which guarantees both the autonomy of the Church (Thesis six) and the theological delegitimation of the total state (Thesis five). Obviously, the latter arguments demonstrated the opposition of the declaration to the government-sponsored efforts in order to Nazify the German Protestant Church at that time.

Accordingly, the Anti-Schmittian impact of Barth's theo-politics promoting the Church exactly as that kind of *potestas indirecta* Schmitt identifies as a fatal contradiction to the doctrine of sovereignty[61] was based on the same cornerstone that had already characterized the commentary on the *Epistle to the Romans*. There, the "infinite qualitative distinction" between God and man, which Barth had adopted from Søren Kierkegaard emphazising the highly different attributes of temporal man and the eternal qualities of a supreme being,[62] required a strict separation of the theological from the political sphere and, consequently, between Barth's own theo-politics and all forms of political religion and ideology. For Barth, theology must always remain theology and may never become political itself, even if being confronted with politics and although theology basically provides a deep relation with politics. By doing so, theology as theology finally acts for the sake of politics.[63]

"Theo-politics" in this sense means neither a political program based on theological dogmas nor a structural analogy between theological and political patterns or concepts. On the contrary, theo-politics demands keeping away from real-politics.[64] For that matter, Schmitt indicated Barth's theo-politics basically as depoliticization (*Entpolitisierung*) of theology,[65] whereas there are contrary voices who called Barth's work the first-ever authentic contribution to political theology.[66] As a result, we can detect as the crucial difference between the two thinkers that politically anti-liberal Schmitt was undecided about theological and ethical questions because, after all, he considered theology only in terms of politics, while theologically anti-liberal Barth was passionately committed to democratic politics treating theology and politics as divided spheres,[67] although the theo-political statements suggested a clear primacy of church over state and of theology over politics.[68] Therefore, the critique of Barth's illiberal theological positions as being part of an autocratic ideal of politics[69] is apparently not convincing.[70] The Schmittian critique of the powerlessness of the democratic parliament when it comes to deciding the exceptional case and to withstanding its enemies has definitely no equivalence and not even a link in Barth. Instead, the missing link in Schmitt's own theory becomes the clearer the more we are considering, with Barth, that the scope of religious convictions (which are and must be pluralist from the perspective of global politics) must allow for something else than only an "arbitrary" distinction without being able to say subsequently what is *politically* right and what is wrong.[71]

But what is about Barth's theologically illiberal position? Is the "wishful" theo-political conflict with unjust regimes resulting from the critique of liberal theology accompanied by a rather problematic theo-political conflict, as the material distinction between truth and heresy could force a political fight against "unjust" religions and the persecution of non-believers? So, does Barth's position imply the logic of escalating theo-political conflicts Schmitt's position avoids more or less successfully? At this point, it has to be said that Barth was definitely not blind to the dilemma that the theologically necessary distinction between truth and heresy might find its political correlation in intolerance and persecution. For Barth, that makes religion becoming a permanent theo-political problem itself. He even called religion to be *unbelief*, since only God is able to reveal the truth; men must inevitably fail.[72] Hence, Barth just reflected on the perils of the theological-political complex which Schmitt most of all neglected.

CONCLUSION

Domestically, internationally and globally seen, theo-political impacts and connections between religion and politics are never without risks. But likewise, this special awareness might serve as an adequate starting point for theorizing the positive potentials theo-politics provides as well. With regard to global politics, our reflections concerning democracy and theo-politics show a kind of speculative character because the configuration of global democracy and global governance is theoretically still underexposed and practically very incomplete.

Nevertheless, the theo-political pattern of coexisting world religions with its characteristic synchronicity of conflict and consensus could provide us with at least a preliminary orientation. Correspondingly, the theo-political reflection of global democracy might help us to understand what balances are apparently needed and what extremes must be avoided. In this respect, the plurality of world religions in practice can be assumed as being both an obstacle and an expedient for global democratic structures in the future.

The final recourse on Karl Barth and Carl Schmitt has confirmed that political conflict is a necessary implication of all theo-politics and of theo-politics to a global extent in particular. However, the comparison of both thinkers additionally suggests that the theological *and* political distinction of what is *right* and *wrong* anticipates whether theo-politics may support democracy (Barth) or rather undermines it (Schmitt). The main problem is that the human claim to find the *truth* in theo-political matters is never beyond errors. Nonetheless, this is no reason to surrender.

NOTES

1. Cf. Eric Voegelin, *Die politischen Religionen* [1938] (Munich: Wilhelm Fink, 1996).

2. Cf. Raymond Aron, "L'avenir des religions séculières," *La France libre* 4, no. 8 (1944): 210–217.

3. Cf. David Held, *Democracy and the Global Order: From the Modern State to Cosmopolitan Governance* (Cambridge: Polity Press, 1995).

4. Cf. Daniele Archibugi and David Held, eds., *Cosmopolitan Democracy: An Agenda for a New World Order* (Cambridge: Polity Press, 1995); Daniele Archibugi, *The Global Commonwealth of Citizens: Toward Cosmopolitan Democracy* (Princeton: Princeton University Press, 2008).

5. Cf. Otfried Höffe, *Demokratie im Zeitalter der Globalisierung* (Munich: Beck, 1999).

6. See Robert A. Dahl: "Can International Organizations be Democratic? A Skeptic's View," in *Democracy's Edges*, ed. Ian Shapiro and Casiano Hacker-Cordón (Cambridge: Cambridge University Press, 1999), 19–37. Further skeptical comments on the chances of global democracy can be found in Markus Lederer and Philipp S. Muller, eds., *Criticizing Global Governance* (New York: Palgrave Macmillan, 2005); Jim Whitman, *The Limits of Global Governance* (London et al.: Routledge, 2005); Klaus Dingwerth, *The New Transnationalism: Transnational Governance and Democratic Legitimacy* (Basingstoke et al.: Palgrave Macmillan, 2007); Jean Grugel and Nicola Piper, *Critical Perspectives on Global Governance* (Milton Park et al.: Routledge, 2007).

7. David Held reflects on such growing pessimism concerning global and cosmopolitan democracy in the more recent publications *Cosmopolitanism: Ideals and Realities* (Cambridge et al.: Polity Press, 2010) and *Global Governance at Risk* (Cambridge: Cambridge University Press, 2013).

8. For this critical perspective, see, for example, Susanne Soederberg, *Global Governance in Question: Empire, Class, and the New Common Sense in Managing North-South Relations* (London: Pluto Press, 2006); Deen K. Chatterjee, ed.,

Democracy in a Global World: Human Rights and Political Participation in 21st Century (Lanham: Rowman & Littlefield, 2007).

    9. Cf. Larry Diamond, *The Spirit of Democracy: The Struggle to Build Free Societies Throughout the World* (New York: Time Books, 2008), 17ff.

    10. For Dallmayr's "apophatic" perspective on democracy see the books *Achieving Our World: Toward a Global and Plural Democracy* (Lanham: Rowman & Littlefield, 2001) and *The Promise of Democracy* (Albany: State University of New York Press, 2010).

    11. Cf. James Bohman, *Democracy across Borders: From Dêmos to Dêmoi* (Cambridge: MIT Press, 2007). See also Cristina Lafont, "Can Democracy Go Global?" *Ethics and Global Politics* 3, no. 1 (2010): 13–19.

    12. To illustrate a particular Asian or Confucian context of democracy we can take into account the reflections by Ralph Ketcham, *The Idea of Democracy in the Modern Era* (Lawrence: University Press of Kansas, 2004); Alan T. Wood, *Asian Democracy in World History* (New York/London: Routledge, 2004); Brooke Ackerly, "Is Liberalism the Only Way Toward Democracy? Confucianism and Democracy," *Political Theory* 33 (2005): 547–576; Daniel Bell, *Beyond Liberal Democracy: Political Thinking for an East Asian Context* (Princeton/Oxford: Princeton University Press, 2006); Sungmoon Kim, *Confucian Democracy in East Asia: Theory and Practice* (Cambridge: Cambridge University Press, 2014). For the characteristics of African Democracy, see Lioba Moshi and Abdulahi A. Osman, *Democracy and Culture: An African Perspective* (London: Adonis & Abbey, 2008); Ademola Kazeem Fayemi, "Towards an African Theory of Democracy," *Institute of African Studies Research Review* 25, no. 1 (2009): 1–21; Saliba Sarsar and Julius O. Adekunle, eds., *Democracy in Africa: Political Changes and Challenges* (Durham: Carolina Academic Press, 2012); Nic Cheeseman, *Democracy in Africa: Success, Failures, and the Struggle for Political Reform* (Cambridge: Cambridge University Press, 2015). The case of democracy in Latin America is discussed in Larry Diamond, Marc F. Plattner and Diego Abente Brun, eds., *Latin America's Struggle for Democracy* (Baltimore: Johns Hopkins University Press, 2008); Jorge I. Dominguez and Michael Shifter, eds., *Constructing Democratic Governance in Latin America*, 3rd ed. (Baltimore: Johns Hopkins University, 2008); Donna Lee Van Cott, *Radical Democracy in the Andes* (Cambridge: Cambridge University Press, 2009). Most notably for the debate on a specific Islamic pattern of democracy are Muqtedar Khan, ed., *Islamic Democratic Discourse: Theory, Debates and Philosophical Perspectives* (Lanham: Rowman & Littlefield, 2006); John Donohue and John Esposito, eds., *Islam in Transition: Muslim Perspectives* (New York/Oxford: Oxford University Press, 2007); Shireen Hunter, ed., *Reformist Voices of Islam: Mediating Islam and Modernity* (Armonk: M. E. Sharpe, 2009); Ingrid Mattson, Paul Nessbitt-Larking and Nawaz Zahir, eds., *Religion and Representation: Islam and Democracy* (Newcastle Upon Tyne: Cambridge Scholars, 2015).

    13. Cf. Amartya Sen, "Democracy as a Universal Value," *Journal of Democracy* 10, no. 3 (1999): 3–17; Amartya Sen, "Democracy and Its Global Roots: Why Democratization is not the same as Westernization," *The New Republic* 229, no. 14 (2003): 28–35.

14. Sally Engel Merry, *Human Rights and Gender Violence: Translating International Law into Local Justice* (Chicago: University of Chicago Press, 2006).

15. Michael Walzer, *Thinking Politically: Essays in Political Theory* (New Haven: Yale University Press, 2007).

16. Seyla Benhabib, "Democratic Iterations: The Local, the National, and the Global," in *Another Cosmopolitanism*, ed. Seyla Benhabib et al. (Oxford: Oxford University Press, 2004), 45–81.

17. For a history of democracy in such a "global" provenance stressing the non-Western characteristics of democracies worldwide, see John Keane, *The Life and Death of Democracy* (New York: Simon & Schuster, 2009); Benjamin Isakhan and Stephen Stockwell, eds., *The Secret History of Democracy* (London: Palgrave Macmillan, 2012); Benjamin Isakhan and Stephen Stockwell, eds., *The Edinburgh Companion to the History of Democracy: From Pre-History to Future Possibilities* (Edinburgh: Edinburgh University Press, 2015).

18. From the wide range of publications examining that matter of research I want to mention only Bernard Lewis, *What Went Wrong? The Clash between Islam and Modernity in the Middle East* (London: Weidenfeld & Nicholson, 2002); Dan Diner, *Lost in the Sacred: Why the Muslim World Stood Still* (Princeton: Princeton University Press, 2009); Richard W. Mansbach and Edward J. Rhodes, eds., *Global Politics in a Changing World* (Boston: Houghton Mifflin, 2009); David Elstein, "Why Early Confucianism Cannot Generate Democracy," *Dao* 9, no. 4 (2010): 427–443; Timur Kuran, *The Long Divergence: How Islamic Law Held Beck the Middle East* (Princeton: Princeton University Press, 2011); Monica Mookherjee, ed., *Democracy, Religious Pluralism and the Liberal Dilemma of Accommodation* (Dordrecht: Springer, 2011); Carsten Anckar, *Religion and Democracy: A Worldwide Comparison* (New York: Routledge, 2011); Monica Duffy Toft, Daniel Philpott, and Timothy S. Shah, *God's Century: Resurgent Religion and Global Politics* (New York: W.W. Norton, 2011); Matthew J. Walton and Susan Hayward, *Contesting Buddhist Narratives: Democratization, Nationalism and Communal Violence in Myanmar* (Honolulu: East West Center, 2014).

19. For this concept as a rational and political basis for liberal justice and public democracy in both domestic and international affairs, see John Rawls, *Political Liberalism* (New York: Columbia University Press, 1993) and John Rawls, *The Law of Peoples* (Cambridge: Harvard University Press, 1999).

20. Cf. John Rawls, "The Idea of Public Reason Revisited," *Chicago Law Review* 64, no. 3 (1997): 765–807.

21. Benedict Anderson, *Imagined Communities: Reflections on the Origin and Spread of Nationalism* (London/New York: Verso, 1991), 13ff.

22. Ibid., 10.

23. Ibid., 7.

24. In this respect, we can refer to Rousseau's sketch of a modern *civil religion* implemented by the people's sovereignty, which should be adequate to function as the Republic's moral foundation, thus avoiding the defects of all alternative types of religion: the "religion of man" as the "pure and simple religion of the Gospel," which must inevitably fail to stabilize the community because of its politically indifferent

nature; the (ancient) "religion of the citizen," "established in one country," which was politically effective but always tended to violence and intolerance toward other denominations; finally, the (Catholic) "religion of priests" as the most negative political religion because of giving men two orders, one for society and one for religion, and therefore preventing from being both clerics and citizens at the same time (Jean-Jacques Rousseau, *The Social Contract or Principles of Political Rights* (London: Penguin, 2004), book 4, Ch. 8, 160).

25. For the Tocquevillean approach to a politically vital democratic republic, see Mark Chaves and David E. Cann, "Regulation, Pluralism, and Religious Market Structure," *Rationality and Society* 4, no. 3 (1992): 272–290.

26. Cf. Roland Czada, Thomas Held and Markus Weingardt, eds., *Religions and World Peace: Religious Capabilities for Conflict Resolution and Peacebuilding* (Baden-Baden: Nomos, 2012); Günther Gebhardt, "Interreligiöse Zusammenarbeit in Konfliktsituationen: Die Tätigkeit von *Religions for Peace* (RfP)," in *Religionen— Global Player in der internationalen Politik*, ed. Ines-Jacqueline Werkner and Oliver Hidalgo (Wiesbaden: Springer VS, 2014), 195–213.

27. Cf. Council for a Parliament of the World's Religions, "A Call to Our Guiding Institutions," in *Threshold 2000: Critical Issues and Spiritual Values for a Global Age*, ed. Gerald O. Barney (Grand Rapids: CoNexus Press, 1999), 121–144; Martin Bauschke, "Das Weltparlament der Religionen und das Projekt Weltethos als Beispiele für die Macht der Moral in der Politik," in *Religionen—Global Player in der internationalen Politik*, ed. Ines-Jacqueline Werkner and Oliver Hidalgo (Wiesbaden: Springer VS, 2014), 87–108.

28. Cf. Chantal Mouffe, *On the Political* (London/New York: Routledge, 2005); Chantal Mouffe, *Agonistics: Thinking the World Politically* (London/New York: Verso, 2013).

29. See, for example, William E. Connolly, "A World of Becoming," in *Democracy and Pluralism: The Political Thought of William E. Connolly*, ed. Alan Finlayson (London/New York: Routledge, 2010), 222–235. Connolly, however, recognizes politics not only as a taming of conflicts but also as a requirement to overcome the tendency to interpret political identities merely as mutual threats (ibid., 226ff.).

30. Cf. Chantal Mouffe, "Carl Schmitt's Warning on the Dangers of a Unipolar World," in *The International Political Thought of Carl Schmitt: Terror, Liberal War and the Crisis of Global Order*, ed. Linda Odysseos and Fabio Petito (London: Routledge, 2007), 147–153.

31. See most of all Immanuel Kant, *Über den Gemeinspruch/Zum ewigen Frieden* (Hamburg: Meiner, 1992).

32. Cf. Robert O. Keohane and Joseph S. Nye, *Power and Interdependence: World Politics in Transition* (Boston: Little, Brown & Co., 1977); Robert O. Keohane, *After Hegemony: Cooperation and Discord in the World Political Economy* (Princeton: Princeton University Press, 1984); Joseph S. Nye, *Understanding International Conflicts: An Introduction to Theory and History*, 6th ed. (New York: Pearson/ Longman, 2007).

33. Paul Collier, *Wars, Guns, and Votes. Democracy in Dangerous Places* (New York: Harper & Collins, 2009).

34. For the correlation between modus vivendi theory and the theory of agonistic democracy, see Chantal Mouffe, *Deliberative Democracy or Agonistic Pluralism* (Political Science Series 72) (Vienna: Institute for Advanced Studies, 2000); Enzo Rossi, "Modus Vivendi, Consensus, and (Realist) Liberal Legitimacy," *Public Reason* 2, no. 2 (2010): 21–39; Ed Wingenbach, *Institutionalizing Agonistic Democracy: Post-Foundationalism and Political Liberalism* (Farnham: Ashgate, 2011), passim.

35. By referring to Samuel Huntington's infamous concept I do not claim that there is really a kind of substantial or ontological conflict between world religions such as Christendom, Islam, Confucianism, Hinduism, Shintoism, and so on. But I do endorse that political conflicts are frequently structured along religious identities, convictions, and values. Hence, religion is not at all the reason for political conflicts but often shifts existing social, economic, and political conflicts into a specific form overwhelming the actual pluralism of identities (cf. Amartya Sen, *Identity and Violence: The Illusion of Destiny* (London/New York: Penguin Books, 2006), therefore allowing for simple distinctions between friends and enemies. For my argument, see Ines-Jacqueline Werkner and Oliver Hidalgo, eds., *Religiöse Identitäten in politischen Konflikten* (Wiesbaden: Springer VS, 2016).

36. An overview of Schmitt's general position is presented in David Dyzenhaus, ed., *Law as Politics: Carl Schmitt's Critique of Liberalism* (Durham/London: Duke University Press, 1998).

37. Cf. William Scheuerman, *Carl Schmitt: The End of Law* (Lanham: Rowman & Littlefield, 1999), 225–251.

38. See Carl Schmitt, *Der Begriff des Politischen*, 7th ed. (Berlin: Duncker & Humblot, 2002), 50–59.

39. See Carl Schmitt, *Die Wendung zum diskriminierenden Kriegsbegriff* (München: Duncker & Humblot, 1938).

40. Cf. Carl Schmitt, *Völkerrechtliche Großraumordnung mit Interventionsverbot für raumfremde Mächte: Ein Beitrag zum Reichsbegriff im Völkerrecht* (Berlin: Deutscher Rechtsverlag, 1939).

41. Chantal Mouffe, "Carl Schmitt's Warning on the Dangers of a Unipolar World," in *The International Political Thought of Carl Schmitt: Terror, Liberal War and the Crisis of Global Order*, ed. Linda Odysseos and Fabio Petito (London: Routledge, 2007), 152.

42. For this see Gary Ulmen, "Partisan Warfare, Terrorism and the Problem of a New Nomos of the Earth," in *The International Political Thought of Carl Schmitt: Terror, Liberal War and the Crisis of Global Order*, ed. Linda Odysseos and Fabio Petito (London: Routledge, 2007), 97–106 and Linda Odysseos, "Crossing the Line? Carl Schmitt on the *Spaceless Universalism* of Cosmopolitanism and the War on Terror," in *The International Political Thought of Carl Schmitt: Terror, Liberal War and the Crisis of Global Order*, ed. Linda Odysseos and Fabio Petito (London: Routledge, 2007), 124–143.

43. Cf. Carl Schmitt, *Die Theorie des Partisanen: Zwischenbemerkungen zum Begriff des Politischen*, 6th ed. (Berlin: Duncker & Humblot, 2006): 91–96.

44. Cf. Mary Kaldor, *New and Old Wars: Organized Violence in a Global Era* (Stanford: Stanford University Press, 1999); Herfried Münkler, *Die neuen Kriege* (Bonn: Bundeszentrale für Politische Bildung, 2002).

45. See e. g. Steven Chermak and Joshua Freilich, eds., *Transnational Terrorism* (Farnham et al.: Ashgate, 2013).

46. Carl Schmitt, *Politische Theologie: Vier Kapitel zur Lehre von der Souveränität,* 7th ed. (Berlin: Duncker & Humblot, 1996), 49.

47. Ibid., 50–51. For an analysis of this relation, see Heinrich Meier, *Die Lehre Carl Schmitts: Vier Kapitel zur Unterscheidung Politischer Theologie und Politischer Philosophie* (Stuttgart: Metzler, 2004), 107–186.

48. Carl Schmitt, *Der Nomos der Erde im Völkerrecht des Jus Publicum Europaeum,* 4th ed. (Berlin: Duncker & Humblot, 1997), 28–32.

49. Carl Schmitt, *Politische Theologie II: Die Legende von der Erledigung jeder Politischen Theologie,* 4th ed. (Berlin: Duncker & Humblot, 1996), 74–98.

50. Mika Ojakangas, "A Terrifying World Without an Exterior: Carl Schmitt and the Metaphysics of International (Dis-)Order," in *The International Political Thought of Carl Schmitt: Terror, Liberal War and the Crisis of Global Order,* ed. Linda Odysseos and Fabio Petito (London: Routledge, 2007), 208.

51. In support of this argument, see further works and articles as *Verfassungslehre* (1928), *Der Hüter der Verfassung* (1931), *Legalität und Legitimität* (1932), and *Der Führer schützt das Recht* (1934).

52. Cf. Oliver Hidalgo and Christo Karabadjakov, "Der Andere als Freund oder Feind? Emmanuel Levinas, Carl Schmitt und die verweigerte Vermittlung zwischen Ethik und Politik," *Philosophisches Jahrbuch* 116, no. 1 (2009): 118–121.

53. Cf. Michael Hollerich, "Carl Schmitt," in *The Blackwell Companion to Political Theology,* ed. Peter Scott and William T. Cavanaugh (Malden/Oxford: Blackwell, 2004), 116. See also Oliver Hidalgo, "Carl Schmitt, Immanuel Kant, and the Theory of International Relations: Reflecting the Problems of Just War Theory, Unipolarism and Political Realism," *Philosophy Study* 3, no. 3 (2013): 180–192.

54. Schmitt, *Der Begriff des Politischen,* 77.

55. Cf. Harald Kleinschmidt, *Carl Schmitt als Theoretiker der internationalen Beziehungen* (Hamburg: Universität der Bundeswehr, 2004), 11.

56. In the following passage, I will renounce on a comparison between the Catholic heritage in Schmitt and the Protestant sources in Barth. Although such a comparison implies significant insights to understand both authors generally, it would be rather misleading for grasping our subject of political theology and globalization.

57. For this, see particularly Devin Singh, "A Tale of Two Sovereignties: Karl Barth and Carl Schmitt in Dialogue," in this volume.

58. Cf. Mark R. Lindsay, *Covenanted Solidarity: The Theological Basis of Karl Barth's Opposition to Nazi Anisemitism and the Holocaust* (New York et al.: Peter Lang, 2001), 260. For this, see most of all Barth's Commentary *The Epistle to the Romans* (London: Oxford University Press, 1933).

59. For Barth's position in this respect, see Rudy Koshar, "Demythologizing the Secular: Karl Barth and the Politics of the Weimar Republic," in *The Weimar Moment. Liberalism, Political Theology, and Law,* ed. Leonard V. Kaplan and Rudy Koshar (Lanham et al.: Lexington Books, 2012), 313–334.

60. For a brief outline of Barth's theo-politics in its opposition to Carl Schmitt's political theology, see Haddon Willmer, "Karl Barth," in *The Blackwell Companion to Political Theology*, ed. Peter Scott and William T. Cavanaugh (Malden/Oxford: Blackwell, 2004), 123–135.

61. Carl Schmitt, *Der Leviathan in der Staatslehre des Thomas Hobbes: Sinn und Fehlschlag eines politischen Symbols* [1938], 3rd ed. (Stuttgart: Klett-Cotta, 2003), particularly 99–118, 131.

62. "If I have a system, it is limited to a recognition of what Kierkegaard called 'infinite qualitative distinction' between time and eternity, and to my regarding this as a possessing negative as well as positive significance: 'God is in heaven, and thou art on earth'" (Barth 1933, 10).

63. See Barth's open letter to Emanuel Hirsch from April 17, 1932 (Karl Barth, *Offene Briefe 1909–1935. Gesamtausgabe Vol. 5* [Zürich: Theologischer Verlag, 2001], 202–203).

64. Accordingly, we have also to distinguish Barth's personal sympathy for social democratic policies from a socialist political doctrine.

65. Carl Schmitt, *Glossarium: Aufzeichnungen der Jahre 1947–1951* (Berlin: Duncker & Humblot, 1991), 228. As far as I see, this is the only explicit reference on Karl Barth we can find in Schmitt's work.

66. Cf. Daniel Cornu, *Karl Barth und die Politik: Widerspruch und Freiheit* (Wuppertal: Aussaat, 1969), 58. As a proof the thesis, Cornu mentions the study *Rechtfertigung und Recht* (1938).

67. Cf. Mathias Eichhorn, *Es wird regiert! Der Staat im Denken Karl Barths und Carl Schmitts in den Jahren 1919 bis 1938* (Berlin: Duncker & Humblot, 1994), 276.

68. Cf. Koshar 2012, 330.

69. Cf. Friedrich Wilhelm Graf, "Der Götze wackelt? Erste Überlegungen zu Karl Barths Liberalismuskritik," *Evangelische Theologie* 46 (1986): 422–441.

70. Cf. Eberhard Jüngel, "Zum Verhältnis von Kirche und Staat nach Karl Barth," in *Ganz werden: Theologische Erörterungen Vol. V* (Tübingen: Mohr Siebeck, 2003), 214–215, note 169. See also Clifford B. Anderson's defending of Barth's Christological approach to legitimating the rule of law in his "Constitutional Theology: Karl Barth and Carl Schmitt on Legitimacy and the Rule of Law," in this volume.

71. Another promising perspective to distinguish the political theologies of Barth and Schmitt is to examine the Jewish heritage in the theo-political thinking of Karl Barth who was deeply influenced by Hermann Cohen. On this foundation, Barth evolved the basis for a philosophically justified theo-politics together with Franz Rosenzweig rejecting modern efforts to combine religion and rationalism and, moreover, religion and the state. See Randi Rashkover, *Revelation and Theopolitics: Barth, Rosenzweig and the Politics of Praise* (London/New York: T&T Clark International, 2005).

72. For a comprehensive analysis of Barth's theological critique of (the idolatry of) religion, see Tom Greggs, *Theology against Religion: Constructive Dialogues with Bonhoeffer and Barth* (London/New York: T&T Clark, 2011).

Part III

CHRISTIAN PRAXIS AND THE CHURCH

POLITICAL DIMENSIONS OF CHRISTIAN EXISTENCE

Chapter 13

Neither Self-Evident Frame nor Self-Enclosed Sect

The Christian Church in Barth's Political Ecclesiology[1]

Markus Höfner

INTRODUCTION

Political theology comes in a rich variety of flavors. Generally, it refers to the intellectual endeavor to analyze or promote a specific relation of religion and politics or religion and society, with the instruments provided by political science or sociology, from the standpoint of a scientific observer. The term "political theology" can also designate the effort of critical self-reflection, undertaken by participants of a specific religious language-game and praxis that aims to understand and define the role and function a specific religion can and should pursue within a larger social and political setting. When it comes to political theology, there is thus a difference in perspective. Political theology can also serve different aims. It can be undertaken in order to stabilize and give legitimation to the political *status quo* or it can aim at transforming or even revolutionizing an existing political order. Various types of political theology can be differentiated by asking which actors or media of political engagement they presume and address: Individuals, communities, or organizations? If the primary actor and medium addressed is the Christian church—as a community and organization—we can call this political theology a political *ecclesiology* as it presupposes and profiles the Christian church itself being a political entity.

The option to develop political theology *as* political ecclesiology is attractive in late modern Western contexts wherein the Christian church no longer serves as a self-evident frame for the whole of society, but instead emerges as one societal factor among others. Under these conditions, the very being of the church is a matter of debate and conscious formation.[2] This is especially true of the German context in which the long-lasting effects of a state church tradition coalesce with processes of secularization.[3] In such a situation, political ecclesiology can serve as a means to promote a shift in the Christian church's self-understanding from being a (all-encompassing) church toward being a (self-enclosed) sect, to use the typology developed by Ernst Troeltsch.[4] This, however, is not the only option available, as this chapter tries to show.

Given the differentiations just sketched, the political theology proposed by Karl Barth clearly is constructed from the theological perspective of a participant in the Christian language-game. It clearly aims not at the stabilization, but the transformation of the given political *status quo*. And Barth clearly construes his political theology as a political ecclesiology, reflecting on the political being of the Christian church itself. Karl Barth's political ecclesiology, however, does *not* promote a "church-to-sect" movement[5] in the self-understanding and the theological orientation of the Christian church. For while Barth presupposes and profiles the particularity of the Christian church as one societal entity among others, he does so in a decisively non-sectarian manner. And this, I believe, is what makes Barth's political ecclesiology a valuable resource for addressing the challenge of reflecting on and theologically orienting a Christian church which no longer is a self-evident institution, but wants—and *should* want—to resist the temptation to become a self-enclosed sect.

In order to substantiate this claim, I will first look at John Howard Yoder's interpretation of Barth's political theology, which portrays Barth as an exponent of sectarian Protestantism. In order to challenge Yoder's interpretation, I will then analyze what I will call Barth's shift from "gathering" to "sending" and the nonsectarian notion of the church's particularity this shift promotes. Against this backdrop, I will explicate the consequences that this ecclesiological deep grammar has for Barth's political theology which is in fact different—and more interesting—than what Yoder's interpretation suggests.

BARTH'S POLITICAL THEOLOGY
ACCORDING TO JOHN HOWARD YODER:
SECTARIAN PROTESTANTISM?

In his interpretation, John Howard Yoder[6] portrays Barth as a "post-Christendom theologian"[7] who profiles a free church ecclesiology. Thus, in Yoder's view, Barth affiliates with the radical wing of the reformation tradition and develops a picture of the Christian church much in line with Troeltsch's sect as opposed to the established, institutionalized church. And this concept of a sect-like Christian church, Yoder holds, is the basis for Barth's political theology which really is a political *ecclesiology* as it is centered on the church itself being a political entity—and not on Christian political engagement based on general ideas and values the Christian community shares with the wider society.[8]

This take on Barth's theology has the merit of not only highlighting some obvious free church elements in Barth's ecclesiology, like Barth's critique of infant baptism or his stress on confession as a mark of the Christian community. Above all, Yoder's analysis profiles the important insight that Barth conceives of the Christian church not as a frame for the whole of society, but of a *particular* social entity among others. Like Yoder himself, Barth thereby combines his theological reflection on the Christian church with a specific diagnosis of the church's factual situation in society.[9] While there are differences between Yoder's diagnosis of an emerging post-Constantinian or post-Christendom situation in late modern societies and Barth's perception of the factual societal role of the Christian church,[10] it is clear that Barth, like Yoder, rejects the idea of the Christian church (still) being the comprehensive medium of a Christian society. Modern society, Barth holds, is not a *corpus Christianum*,[11] because processes of modernization have led and are still leading to the world becoming independent of the church: "The Church in the modern period has slowly but relentlessly lost its position in the world [its 'Weltgeltung'] in the form in which it could previously enjoy it,"[12] so that, in Barth's view, the "diastasis between the Church and the world,"[13] which makes the church a particular social entity, is a sign of modernity not to be overlooked.

In his interpretation of Barth's theology, however, Yoder reads Barth's notion of the particularity of the church with a certain twist. One can debate whether it is fair to call this twist outright sectarianism, but using Troeltsch's sociological type of the sect as a basis, at least two sectarian features are obvious in Yoder's take on Barth's ecclesiology[14]: *First*, Yoder emphasizes that the particularity of the church within society not only *implies* its otherness from secular communities and organizations in the world. Rather, he holds—and attributes to Barth—that this otherness of the church is and should be a central *goal* of its very existence. For Barth, as Yoder reads him, the Christian church stands in a "polar encounter with the world."[15] And as it is in constant danger to fall into conformity with the wider society, the Christian church must strive to uphold its otherness in the movement of sanctification.[16] The picture of the Christian church Yoder thus derived from his reading of Barth is the picture of a "contrast society."[17] *Second*, Yoder assumes that for Barth—as for Yoder himself—the Christian church represents and mediates God's salvific work in Jesus Christ to the world and thus has a priority over the word in the order of salvation. The church's task, Yoder writes in his Barth interpretation, is to "re-present the story and the historicity of Jesus"[18] to the world, thus furthering the coming of the kingdom of God. Therefore, in Yoder's view, the "meaning of history [. . .] lies in the creation and the work of the church"[19] and the full eschatological realization of the kingdom of God "will mean the victory of the church and the overcoming of the world."[20]

It is against the backdrop of this sectarian reading of Barth's ecclesiology and its emphasis on the particularity of the church that Yoder constructs Barth's political theology as a political *ecclesiology*. What Yoder claims we should learn from Barth is that the "access to social ethics should consist in the *exemplarity* of the church as foretaste/model/herald of the kingdom."[21] Following this line of thought, Yoder holds, does not lead to quietism and the Christian's withdrawal from wider society.[22] The consequence of developing political theology as political ecclesiology, however, in Yoder's view is that the church's exemplary being—and not categories taken from the wider wisdom of the world—must be prior in orienting Christian political engagement in church and society.[23] Consequently, for Barth, as Yoder reads him, Christian political theology should be "the non-conformist ethic of the confessing community."[24] Now as indicated earlier, I think this take on Barth's political theology is one-sided, to say the least. Barth's own position is different—and more interesting—than Yoder's interpretation.[25] In order to substantiate this claim, I will not directly turn to what I see as Barth's political theology, but first consider its formative background in what I think should be described as a shift from "gathering" to "sending" in ecclesiology.

BARTH'S SHIFT FROM GATHERING
TO SENDING: THE NONSECTARIAN
PARTICULARITY OF THE CHURCH

It is a basic trait of Barth's mature ecclesiology that he shifts emphasis from the "gathering" of the Christian community to its "sending" into a non-Christian world. Recognizing this shift from gathering to sending is crucial to critically assess Yoder's sectarian interpretation of Barth's ecclesiology. For it is on this basis that Barth develops an ecclesiology that acknowledges the particularity of the Christian church within society—as Yoder rightly sees—but he does so in a decisively nonsectarian manner—and thus Barth's position is contrary to Yoder's interpretation. This shift from gathering to sending finds its clearest expression in §72 of his *Church Dogmatics* entitled "The Holy Spirit and the Sending of the Christian Community."[26]

Here, Barth writes, that "the true community of Jesus Christ is the community which God has *sent out* into the world in and with its foundation. As such it exists *for* the world."[27] What Barth claims with this statement is not simply that the Christian church should act toward a non-Christian world, that it has a task and a mission to fulfill toward those who remain outside the Christian community. There is hardly one Christian ecclesiology denying this. Rather, Barth's more fundamental—and original—thesis is that this being sent out into the world defines the very being of the Christian church. The church for Barth thus is an apostolic community not just in listening to and following the apostles' witness to the Gospel represented in the texts of the biblical canon; the apostolicity of the church at the same time means that is partakes in the "apostolic movement,"[28] the "implicit and explicit outward movement to the world"[29] that characterized the apostles' being and actions. In Barth's view, the church's sending out into the world thus represents the one *nota ecclesiae* without which the church would not be and could not be recognized as the church.[30] By making the sending of church central to its very existence, Barth speaks out against the "holy egoism"[31] he perceives in the tradition of Christian ecclesiology: Contrary to the traditional view, the existence of the Christian church for Barth is not an end in itself. Rather, the church's existence is *ec*-centric, it exists in its function for the non-Christian world and thus always points beyond itself. This precedence Barth gives to sending over gathering in his notion of the Christian church does *not* mean that the gathering of the Christian church is irrelevant in his view; his intention is not to replace the gathering of the church by her sending. The analyses of the church's constitution as a particular and distinct community within society which Barth unfolds in *Church Dogmatics* IV/1-2 are not negated by his elaboration of the concept of sending in *Church Dogmatics* IV/3.[32] It does mean, however, that the gathering of the Christian church is not the *ratio* of its being and not the determining center of God's reconciling work. As for Barth, the Christian church is not *first* gathered as a community of believers enjoying the gift of salvation and *then* bestowed with the additional task of being sent into a yet unreconciled world. Rather, the gathering of the church according to Barth takes places on behalf of her sending out into the world, the gathering is (just) the *conditio* sine qua non for the sending as the *ratio* of the Christian church.[33] Consequently, Barth's shift from gathering to sending is a shift in the *logical order* of these two dynamics indispensable for the being of the Christian church.

In order to further profile this shift from gathering to sending in Barth's ecclesiology, let me point to three theological claims Barth makes as its backdrop and context.

(i) First, one central precondition of Barth's shift from gathering to sending in ecclesiology is his *universalism* with respect to salvation. This universalism finds expression in Barth's doctrine of election in *Church Dogmatics* II/2 where he substantiates the claim that salvation is not a possibility, but a reality grounded in the unique history of Jesus Christ who, Barth affirms, is both the electing God *and* the elected human being.[34] Salvation, Barth holds, is not an offer God makes to human beings which has to be realized by a human response in faith, love, and hope. Rather, salvation in Barth's view is already realized objectively in the election of Jesus Christ. To be sure, positing salvation as an objective reality, does not make the human response to God's salvific action in faith, love, and hope irrelevant. But the point of this response, Barth holds, is not the realization of a mere possibility, but the acknowledgment of a reality always already established in the unique history of Jesus Christ.[35] Now saying this for Barth means that, as an objective reality, salvation is truly universal. Each and every human being always already is involved in the unique history of Jesus Christ and thus, to use one of Barth's favorite terms, *de iure* always already reconciled with God. And as *de facto* acknowledging this reality of salvation in faith, love, and hope for Barth is the only appropriate human response to the objective reality of salvation, the human refusal to do so in his view does not only contradict God's salvific work, but inevitably results in human self-alienation.[36] *De facto* living in contradiction to what is real and true *de iure*, however, does not negate the objective reality of salvation itself. There is thus no way the—positive or negative—human response to God's salvific work could turn the universal reality of salvation into a particular reality encompassing only some human individuals. For according to Barth's reformulation of the reformed doctrine of a double predestination or election, in the election of Jesus Christ, God chooses salvation for all human beings and damnation exclusively for himself in the human person of Jesus.[37]

Now, of course, this soteriological universalism has far-reaching consequences for a theological take on the Christian church. For one of the challenges Christian ecclesiology has to meet is working out a sound differentiation between church and non-church. This challenge remains irrespective of the decision to use or not use the traditional theological language of church and world, and irrespective of the need one may see to design the dividing line between church and non-church more or less "porous." You cannot say what the Christian church *is* if you cannot say what it is *not*. Now the most prominent strategy to answer this challenge in the tradition of Christian theology has been—and still is—to model the difference of church and non-church following the pattern provided by the difference of salvation and condemnation. One may point to Augustine's differentiation of *civitas Dei* and *civitas terrena* (or even: *civitas diaboli*) as a classic example[38] or to the divide of "Collective Life of Salvation" ("Gesamtleben der Erlösung") and "Collective Life of Sin" ("Gesamtleben der Sünde") in Schleiermacher as a modern version of this strategy.[39] This strategy, however, does not work for Barth's ecclesiology but is rather ruled out from the beginning by his soteriological universalism: There is no other to salvation Barth can use to define the other to the church.[40] Barth therefore needs an alternative strategy to differentiate between church and non-church. And this alternative strategy, I hold, is what is provided by Barth's shift from gathering to sending in ecclesiology. For in making the sending of the church out into the world central to its very being, Barth can define the difference between church and non-church in terms of the church's specific function: What makes the church distinct from other social entities is the conscious commitment to its sending out into the world, a commitment based on the universal reality of salvation which is already acknowledged in the church but not (yet) in the non-Christian world.[41]

(ii) This brings me to a second point. Barth further profiles the sending of the church out into the world by describing its specific task as *witness*. The church, Barth holds, is called to witness to the world. Now the concept of witness in Barth's reflections is both comprehensive and limited. It is *comprehensive* as the task of witness in Barth's view does not only apply to what the Christian church and individual Christians say but also to what they do—in sermons, rituals, and pastoral counseling as well as in Christian social work—and notably even to the order of the Christian community itself.[42] As he formulated in the *Barmen Declaration* (1934): The Christian church is to witness "with its *faith* as with its *obedience*, with its *message* as with its *order*."[43] As I will try to show more fully later, this comprehensive understanding of witness is essential for the ecclesial dimension of Barth's political theology as it profiles the political nature of the church's being in its visible particularity. At the same time, however, the notion of witness is used by Barth to express a *limitation* to what the sending of the church amounts to. For witnessing in Barth's view is a human praxis that is open to better or worse performance—but must never be identified with the salvific action of God. Describing the church's sending as witness thus gives expression to Barth's moral ontology which presupposes a parallelization in distinction of divine and human action.[44] Witness as the concrete form of the church's sending thus for Barth poses the ethical challenge of the human praxis of the church to correspond to the salvific work of God. It does not, however, mediate this salvific work toward the world, but is sustained and surrounded by the self-witness of Christ. Which brings me to my third point.

(iii) In being sent into the world and engaging in the task of witness, the Christian church according to Barth, partakes in what he calls the prophetic office of Christ. Barth uses the notion of a prophetic office of Christ to express his conviction that the person and history of Jesus Christ is not merely a fact of the past, but is present in all times and places. Thus, in Barth's view, it is not only the case that the universal reality of salvation has been established once and for all in Jesus Christ in a particular time and place, but that the communication of this reality *in all times and places* must be considered the self-communication of the person and history of Jesus Christ.[45] In his prophetic office, Jesus Christ is "His *own* authentic Witness."[46] This conviction has two important consequences for Barth's understanding of the church's sending: *First*, the sending of the church and its concrete enactment in the praxis of witness for Barth does not aim at representing the person and history of Jesus Christ as an event of the past, but rather points to the presence of Christ and to his self-communication in his prophetic office. It is for Barth a privilege of the Christian church—but never a possession it can get hold on— that in his prophetic office, Jesus Christ *uses* the church's witness for this self-communication. The Christian church thus for Barth really can partake—but *only* partake—in Christ's prophetic office.[47] *Second*, Barth maintains that this self-communication of Jesus Christ is not confined to the boundaries of the church. In its sending out into the world, the Christian church has to expect to find "true words, genuine witnesses and attestations of the one true Word"[48] and "parables of the kingdom of heaven"[49] of God *extra muros ecclesiae*. In its witness to the world, the Christian church may thus encounter—and learn from—the (unconscious) witness of the world itself.

Soteriological universalism, the concept of witness, and the prophetic office of Christ—these three theological topoi form the decisive context and backdrop of the shift from gathering to sending characteristic for Barth's ecclesiology. These reflections not only indicate that Barth views the Christian church as an essentially *particular* entity within a larger societal setting, rather than as a frame encompassing the whole of society. They also underline that the kind of particularity of the church implicit in Barth's shift from gathering to sending is a decisively *nonsectarian* one. Contrary to Yoder's interpretation, depicting the Christian church as a particular social entity among others does not lead Barth to focus on the *otherness* of the church and its distinction from the non-Christian world as a goal in itself nor does Barth ascribe to the church a priority over against the world in the order of salvation. Rather, Barth's notion of the church's particularity as implicit in his shift from gathering to sending is highly dialectical: On the one hand, Barth emphasizes the church's existence not as a self-evident frame for the whole of society, but as a distinct and particular social entity within it and thus accentuates her otherness from her non-Christian environment. On the other hand, however, Barth constantly undermines any dichotomy of church and non-Christian world by insisting that the boundaries between them are both relative and provisional: They are *relative*, Barth holds, because the difference of church and world is not to be equated with the difference of salvation and damnation. Rather, in Barth's view, the church is distinct from a non-Christian world only in acknowledging universal reconciliation and witnessing to it in its sending into the world. Furthermore, the boundaries between the Christian community and her secular environment are *provisional* as the Christian hope for universal reconciliation becoming universally effective is directed toward the kingdom of God and *not* toward an eschatologically completed church. For neither can the church bring about this universal effectiveness of reconciliation herself nor is the coming of God's kingdom paralleled by an *expansion* of the church into the world: The eschatological vision guiding Barth's ecclesiology is not the eventual integration of a non-Christian world into the church. The Christian hope for Barth is not for "the victory of the church and the overcoming of the world,"[50] as Yoder has it, but the coming of the kingdom of God to both church and world. The particularity of the church vis-à-vis a non-Christian world thus for Barth is not a problem to be overcome, but the positive prerequisite of the church's existence in her sending into the world. Barth thus offers a positive theological assessment of the particularity of the church in modernity which moves beyond the illusion of establishing—or re-establishing—a Christian world. In the horizon of universal salvation, in her task of witness, and in her partaking in the prophetic office of Christ effective both inside and outside the Christian church, the church's task is to witness to God's salvific work encompassing both church and world, acknowledging its own particularity as both relative and provisional. This dialectical notion of the church has consequences for Barth's reflection about her relation to the political sphere.

BARTH, POLITICAL ECCLESIOLOGY, AND CHRISTIAN RESPONSIBILITY FOR SOCIETY AND STATE

Having sketched Barth's shift from gathering to sending and the nonsectarian notion of the church's particularity this shift promotes, we are now in a position to critically assess the merits and limits of Yoder's interpretation of Barth's political theology.

Now, to my mind, Yoder not only rightly points to the fact that Barth conceives of the church as a particular social entity but also sees clearly that this notion leads Barth to have his political theology at least include a political *ecclesiology*. That is to say that the political relevance of the Christian faith for Barth does not start with the church addressing issues of state politics and engaging in political discussions going on in its non-Christian environment. The Christian community as a particular social entity among others, Barth holds, *is* political in its very nature. Barth thus highlights that the "very term *ekklesia* is borrowed from the political sphere" and that the "Christian community exists at all times and places as a *politeia*."[51] This ecclesial dimension of Barth's political thought clearly flows from his notion of the particularity of the church. For this particularity in Barth's view is not to be identified with a process of functional differentiation resulting in a distinction between the political, economic, juridical, and religious spheres or dimensions of society, inhabited at times by all individual citizens. Rather, Barth holds, the church is particular as not all, but only some members of society are gathered into the Christian community—which is the special theme of *CD* IV/1 § "The gathering of the Christian Community"—and engage in a particular praxis not shared by other members of society—which is the special theme of *CD* IV/2 § "The upbuilding of the Christian Community." It is this visible particularity of the Christian church which makes it political in its very nature, according to Barth.

Now while this ecclesial dimension of Barth's political theology is adequately captured in Yoder's interpretation, its focus and horizon are not. Based on his nonsectarian understanding of the church's particularity, Barth is not, as Yoder thinks, advocating a political theology focused on the *exemplarity* of the church's being nor is he advocating the idea that a political theology developed as political ecclesiology is essentially *nonconformist*.

To start with the question of non-conformity, there are certainly many instances to be found in Barth's political theology where Barth is critical of the political and economic *status quo*. His support of a democratic socialism and his emerging pacifism are the most prominent examples, and are widely used by Yoder in his interpretation of Barth.[52] His plea for a Christian "revolt against disorder" and his critique of the "lordless powers" in his *The Christian Life* §78 would be another, including his insightful diagnosis and critique of political absolutism, economic power, and ideology.[53] Thus, one important lesson Barth's political theology aims to convey is that Christians "have to swim manfully against the stream."[54] This critical stance toward the political and economic *status quo* and the demand for Christians to "swim manfully against the stream," however, is not modeled along a supposed divide between the Christian church and the non-Christian world. It is here, I believe, that Barth's nonsectarian understanding of the particularity of the church becomes effective in his political theology. The critical impetus of Christian political theology and political action is not to be equated with a critical, nonconformist stance of the church over against the world in Barth's thinking for both negative and positive reasons. The negative reason, so to speak, is that the Christian "swimming against the stream" for Barth not only implies the necessity of watchfulness and critique with regard to non-Christian society, but equally so with regard to the church itself. The stream to swim against is not the non-Christian world, but the powers of injustice, oppression, and "nothingness" operative outside as well as inside the Christian church. To cite just one example: It is clear from Barth's analysis that he sees the "lordless power" of ideology as a danger not only for non-Christian society, but for the church as well: Not only the slogans "Germany, wake up" or "The American way of life" in Barth's view can be signs of ideology, this "lordless power" can manifest as well in catchwords like "biblical reformed insight" or "relevant preaching."[55] The positive reason why Barth's political theology is decidedly not nonconformist is that Barth presupposes and promotes a process of *mutual* learning between Christian church and non-Christian society. As indicated earlier, the Christian church for Barth cannot claim the role of a prophet giving moral and political orientation to a non-Christian society. The church, Barth holds, only *partakes* in the prophetic office of Christ and thus has to reckon with and be attentive to signs of Christ's prophetic work *extra muros ecclesiae*. As noted earlier, for Barth there are "true words"[56] and "parables of the kingdom"[57] outside the Christian church which signify that, though the church *de facto* is a particular social entity, salvation *de iure* already is a universal reality and it is in this universal scope that Christ is operative in his prophetic office. The "essence of Christian politics," Barth therefore can write, is "a continuous line of discoveries *on both sides* of the boundary which separates the political from the spiritual spheres."[58] And it is important to note that, on this basis, the Christian church and individual Christians for Barth have a responsibility for the non-Christian society which can only be responded to where "Christians apply themselves to the same task with non-Christians and submit themselves to the same rule."[59]

A similar critique, to my mind, has to be raised against the role Yoder ascribes to the *exemplarity* of the church in Barth's political theology. Again, it is certainly true that Barth, given his conviction that the very being of the church participates in witness and has to be ordered according to this task, does describe the Christian community as exemplary. Barth can thus write that the "real church must be the model and prototype of the real state" and must "set an example" for the state "by its very existence."[60] And Barth further elaborates this exemplary function of the church's very being in his discussion of church law, which, he holds, is "exemplary law" and can and should serve as "a pattern for the formation and administration of human law generally."[61] These claims, however, are set into perspective and counterbalanced by Barth following the deep grammar of his nonsectarian notion of the church's particularity.[62] The exemplary function of the Christian church toward the non-Christian society is only a relative one, according to Barth, for at least two reasons. *First*, Barth locates the exemplary function of the church not in the two-sided relation of the Christian church and the non-Christian society, but rather in a three-sided relation of church, society, and the kingdom of God. Thus while in its exemplary function the church should serve as a reminder of the Kingdom, it is never to be identified with it—and it has to reckon with the fact that the non-Christian society itself is "an exponent of [God's] kingdom."[63] This means that the primary context within which theological thought about state and non-Christian society for

Barth is not sin—not even creation—but salvation. This results in a picture of state and non-Christian society not at static entities but as social configurations open to and in need of transformation. That Barth positively relates *both* church *and* non-Christian society to God's coming kingdom is reflected by the fact that the knowledge of God the church witnesses to is not totally absent from non-Christian society[64] and that even sanctification—the modeling of the church into correspondence with reconciliation and consequently it's becoming an *exemplary* social entity—is paralleled within non-Christian society.[65] Against this backdrop, the exemplary function of the church can never result in what Yoder calls the "priority of authentic identity"[66] of the church over its engagement in worldly affairs. The authentic identity of the Christian church, according to Barth, consists in its sending into the world, in the horizon of which the church—including its exemplary being—can never be an end in itself. The *second* reason the exemplary function of the church is only a relative one in the context of Barth's political theology is that, contrary to Yoder's interpretation, Barth does not combine this exemplary role with a mediating one. The exemplary being of the Christian church, in Barth's view, does not constitute a priority of the church in the order of salvation. This, I think, is already clear from Barth's universalism with regard to salvation and his non-sacramental concept of witness I outlined earlier. It may be useful, however, to add an additional observation. In the opening sections of the ecclesiological paragraphs in the doctrine of reconciliation in his *Church Dogmatics*, Barth describes the Christian church as the "provisional representation of the whole world of humanity justified [sanctified/called] in Him."[67] Now it is clear from Barth's analysis that in its being a "provisional representation" of the whole world humanity reconciled with God, the church is to *witness* to God's salvific work vis-à-vis a non-Christian world. This, however, does not mean for Barth that church is to *mediate* God's salvific work in terms of making it present, available and effective in the first place. This is why Barth's linguistic strategy in his doctrine of reconciliation is to avoid the German term *Repräsentation*—which carries the overtone of mediation—and uses the term *Darstelllung* instead, as in the phrase quoted earlier where the German text speaks of the church being a provisional *Darstellung*, not *Repräsentation* of humanity reconciled with God.[68] And this linguistic strategy underlines that the exemplary function of the church is not only limited as it is non-sacramental and non-mediating. It is also limited because, in Barth's view, the Christian church, being the "provisional representation" of reconciled humanity, is not only a model *for* the world, but at the same time a model *of* the world, given that the Christian church in faith, love, and hope vicariously gives the human response correspondent with the universal reality of salvation on the part of the non-Christian world not (yet) prepared to do so.

CONCLUSION

In his contribution on *State and Civil Society* for *The Blackwell Companion to Political Theology* (2003), Daniel M. Bell differentiates between two types of Christian political theology[69]: The *first* type, which he calls the "dominant tradition," comprises Moltmann's political theology as well as the project of public theology advocated by Ronald Thiemann and Max Stackhouse. This type is characterized, according to Bell, by seeing the secular state as the principal political agent and civil society as a realm of freedom, balancing and controlling state power, while the church is primarily regarded as a proponent of ethical values, acting within civil society. The *second* type, labeled the "emergent tradition" by Bell, stand in opposition to the first and is exemplified by authors like Yoder, Hauerwas, and Milbank. According to Bell, this second type focuses on the church as a political entity of its own, shaped by a specifically Christian narrative, such that it forms a contrast to both state and civil society. According to this view, the state and civil society are both seen as hegemonic forces, driven by the narrative of secularism that the church has to resist and overcome. Now, as David Haddorff suggested, a good way to characterize Barth's political theology is to say that it does *not* fit into this scheme, but cuts across both of Bell's types.[70] For Barth's approach, which interestingly enough, Bell does not mention, is in line with the emergent type that Barth, also, emphasizes the political *being* of the Christian community as a distinct social entity. At the same time, however, Barth agrees with the dominant type by advocating Christian responsibility for state politics and Christian engagement in civil society. And he does so, I tried to show, following the deep grammar of a nonsectarian notion of the church's particularity based on a shift from "gathering" to "sending." It is this specific profile which makes Barth's political theology more interesting than Yoder's interpretation suggest, and a valuable theological resource for any theological reflection which wants to interpret and orient a Christian church which is no longer a self-evident *frame,* while preventing it from becoming a self-centered *sect.*

NOTES

1. I wish to thank the participants of the Theo-Politics project for critical discussions of earlier versions of this chapter. A special thanks goes to Angela Dienhart Hancock for a lucid response to my analysis.

2. One can thus argue that political ecclesiology is a specifically modern phenomenon, provoked by processes of functional differentiation and secularization. Cf. Georg Pfleiderer, "Politische Ekklesiologie in der Neuzeit: Ein einführender

Bericht," in *Protestantische Kirche und moderne Gesellschaft: zur Interdependenz von Ekklesiologie und Gesellschaftstheorie in der Neuzeit*, ed. Albrecht Grözinger (Zürich: Theologischer Verlag, 2003), 21–44.

3. For an in-depth analysis of church and religion in Germany from the perspective of political science and sociology cf. the contribution of Gert Pickel in this volume.

4. Cf. Ernst Troeltsch, *The Social Teaching of the Christian Churches*, 2 vols. (Lousville: Westerminster John Knox Press, 1992), esp. 331–343.

5. For a sociological assessment of "church-to-sect" movements and their attractiveness from the perspective of religious economy cf. Rodney Stark and Roger Finke, *Acts of Faith: Explaining the Human Side of Religion* (Berkeley: University of California Press, 2000), 193–217.

6. Every present discussion of Yoder's theology is inevitably overshadowed by his sexual behavior for decades the many women affected clearly identified as abusive. The extent of Yoder's sexual assaults—and the failures of institutional control in that respect—have only become visible in recent years. Cf. for a clear and nuanced assessment Rachel Waltner Goossen, "'Defanging the Beast': Mennonite Responses to John Howard Yoder's Sexual Abuse," *Mennonite Quarterly Review* 89 (January 2015): 7–80.

7. Cf. John Howard Yoder, "Karl Barth, Post-Christendom Theologian," in *Karl Barth and the Problem of War & Other Essays on Barth*, ed. John Howard Yoder (Eugene, OR: Wipf & Stock Publishing, 2003), 175–188.

8. John Howard Yoder, "The Basis of Barth's Sodal Ethics," in *Karl Barth and the Problem of War & Other Essays on Barth*, ed. John Howard Yoder (Eugene, OR: Wipf & Stock Publishing, 2003), 133–147.

9. Both Barth and Yoder thus affirm Troeltsch's thesis of an interdependence of theological reflection and social and historical location (explicitly so in John Howard Yoder, "The Kingdom as Social Ethic," in *The Priestly Kingdom: Social Ethics as Gospel*, ed. John Howard Yoder [Notre Dame: University of Notre Dame Press, 1984]), 80–101, 80.

10. Cf. esp. *John Howard Yoder*, "Why Ecclesiology is Social Ethics: Gospel Ethics Versus the Wider Wisdom," in *The Royal Priesthood: Essays Ecclesiological and Ecumenical*, ed. John Howard Yoder (Grand Rapids: Herald Press, 1994), 102–126 and Barth, Church Dogmatics (Edinburgh: T&T Clark, 1936–1977) [CD], 18–38. The most striking difference, it seems to me, is that Yoder tends to picture the Constantinian era as a historical meander so that living in *pre-* or *post*-Constantian times does not seem to make that great a difference, while Barth portrays the societal particularity of the church as a distinctively *modern* phenomenon.

11. Cf. for example Barth, *CD* I/2, 334; *CD* IV/3, 21.

12. Barth, *CD* IV/3, 19.

13. Barth, *CD* IV/3, 21.

14. In my diagnosis and critique of these sectarian features, I draw on the analysis offered by George Hunsinger, "Karl Barth and the Politics of Sectarian Protestantism: A Dialogue with John Howard Yoder," in *Disruptive Grace: Studies in the Theology of Karl Barth*, ed. George Hunsinger (Grand Rapids: Eerdmans, 2000), 114–128. While Hunsinger offers a lucid interpretation of Barth and a sound critique of Yoder's

interpretation, he does not explicate what I believe is the ecclesiological deep grammar of Barth's political theology.

15. Yoder, "The Basis of Barth's Sodal Ethics," 143.

16. Cf. ibid., 142–144.

17. Cf. John Howard Yoder, "The Otherness of the Church," in *The Royal Priesthood: Essays Ecclesiological and Ecumenical*, ed. John Howard Yoder (Grand Rapids: Herald Press, 1994), 53–64.

18. Yoder, "The Basis of Barth's Sodal Ethics," 144.

19. John Howard Yoder, *The Christian Witness to the State* (Newton: Herald Press, 1964), 13.

20. Ibid., 17.

21. Yoder, "Why Ecclesiology is Social Ethics: Gospel Ethics Versus the Wider Wisdom," 106; emphasis mine.

22. Cf. ibid., 119–122 and Kristoffer Norris' contribution to this volume.

23. Cf. ibid., 118f.

24. Yoder, "The Basis of Barth's Social Ethics," 145f.

25. As Kristoffer Norris convincingly argues, Yoder in other respects moves beyond Barth in ways productive for contemporary theological reflection, for example, in his differentiation of democratic practices and the state apparatus which is much clearer than what Barth's texts offer. Cf. Kristoffer Norris, "Democracy and Church: Barth and Yoder on Democratic Practice," in this volume.

26. Barth's shift from "gathering" to "sending," however, is already clearly present in *CD* II/2 and governs the ecclesiological reflection in *CD* IV/1-2. It is prefigured in Barth's insistence on the difference between the Christian church and the kingdom of God from his earliest theology.

27. Barth, *CD* IV/3, 768; emphasis mine.

28. Karl Barth, *Die kirchliche Dogmatik: Die Lehre von der Versöhnung* (IV/3), Zürich, 1959, 798; translation mine; cf. Barth, *CD* IV/1, 715.

29. Barth, *CD* IV/1, 724.

30. Cf. Barth, *CD* IV/3, 771f.

31. Barth, *CD* IV/3, 767.

32. I here differ from the analysis presented by John Flett, who, I think, lucidly profiles the motif of sending in Barth, but does so on the expense of the gathering of the church (Cf. John G. Flett, *The Witness of God: The Trinity, Missio Dei, Karl Barth and the Nature of Christian Community* (Grand Rapids: Eerdmans Publishing Company, 2010).

33. Cf. Barth, *CD* IV/1, 606.

34. Cf. Barth, *CD* II/2, 94–145.

35. Cf. George Hunsinger, *How to Read Karl Barth: The Shape of his Theology* (New York: Oxford University Press, 1993), 35–39. Hunsinger convincingly shows that this "soteriological objecivism" for Barth is a complement to his "revelational objecivism": Just as God is objectively involved in—and thus defined by—the unique history of Jesus Christ, so for Barth is humanity. A human existence without the acknowledgment of salvation in faith, love, and hope thus for Barth is a human existence lived in abstraction from its true reality.

36. Cf. Barth, *CD* IV/3, 662–680.

37. "When we say that God elected as His own portion the negative side of the divine predestination, the reckoning with man's weakness and sin and inevitable punishment, we say implicitly that this portion is not man's portion. In so far, then, as predestination does contain a No, it is not a No spoken against man. In so far as it does involve exclusion and rejection, it is not the exclusion and rejection of man. In so far as it is directed to perdition and death, it is not directed to the perdition and death of man." (Barth, *CD* II/2, 166). Barth's universalism, it should be noted, is bound to the unique person of Jesus Christ and not be confused with a principle, e.g., that of a "triumph of grace" as G.C. Berkouwer had it (Cf. G.C. Berkouwer, *The Triumph of Grace in the Theology of Karl Barth* (Grand Rapids: Eerdmans Publishing Company, 1956). Barth's reservations against the *doctrine* of universal salvation (or *apokatastasis panton*) voiced in his defence against Berkouwer's critique underline this point, but do not revoke the specific universalism Barth does promote (Cf. Barth, *CD* IV/3, 173–192). For a lucid analysis of Barth's universalism cf. Tom Greggs, "'Jesus is Victor': Passing the Impasse of Barth on Universalism," *Scottish Journal of Theology* 60, no. 2 (2007): 196–212.

38. Cf. Aurelius Augustinus, *The City of God against the Pagans* (Cambridge: Cambridge University Press, 1998).

39. Cf. Friedrich Daniel Ernst Schleiermacher, *The Christian Faith* (London: Continuum International Publishing, 1999), §114.

40. With regard to political theology, this move leads to a radical "de-dramatication": The horizon in which the polical sphere is to be reflected on theologically for Barth can never be the battle between good and evil, but always is the story of the universal reality of salvation becoming effective in both church and non-Christian world. Cf. Günter Thomas, "Karl Barth's Political Theology: Contours, Lines of Development and Future Perspectives," in *Dogmatics after Barth: Facing Challenges in Church, Society and the Academy*, ed. Günter Thomas, Rinse H. Reeling Brouwer, and Bruce McCormack (CreateSpace Independent Publishing Platform, 2012), 181–197. 187f.

41. As will become clear later in the text, this distinction of church and non-church for Barth remains a relative and provisional one.

42. Cf. Barth, *CD* IV/3, 830–901.

43. "The Theological Declaration of Barmen 1934," in *Reformed Confessions of the 16th Century*, ed. Arthur C. Cochrane (Philadelphia: Westminster Press, 1966), 332–336, 335; my emphases.

44. Cf. John Webster, "'The Grammar of Doing': Luther and Barth on Human Agency," in John Webster, *Barth's Moral Theology: Human Action in Barth's Thought* (Edinburgh: T&T Clark, 1998), 151–178.

45. Cf. Barth, *CD* IV/3, 3–38.

46. Ibid., 46.

47. Cf. ibid., 792–795.

48. Ibid., 122.

49. Ibid., 114. For a theological interpretation of this topic informed by cultural studies cf. Günter Thomas, *Medien, Ritual, Religion: Theologische und*

sozialwissenschaftliche Untersuchungen zur religiösen Funktion des Fernsehens (Frankfurt: Suhrkamp, 1998), 110–117.

50. Yoder, *The Christian Witness to the State*, 17.

51. Karl Barth, "The Christian Community and the Civil Community," in *Community, State, and Church*, ed. Karl Barth (Eugene: Wipf & Stock Publishing, 2004), 149–189, 153.

52. Cf. Yoder, "The Basis of Barth's Sodal Ethics," 130–140.

53. Cf. Karl Barth, *The Christian Life (Church Dogmatics IV, 4)* (Grand Rapids: Eerdmans Publishing Company, 1981), 205–213. 213–233. In her contribution to this volume, Hanna Reichel convincingly shows how Barth's analysis of the "Lordless Powers" can be applied for a theological interpretation of the Surveillance Society and the political theology it implies.

54. Barth, *Christian Life*, 267.

55. Ibid., 226.

56. Barth, *CD* IV/3, 122.

57. Ibid., 114.

58. Barth, "The Christian Community and the Civil Community," 180; emphasis mine.

59. Ibid., 159. It is noteworthy that for Barth, the individual Christian's political activity is to be done "anonymously" (cf. ibid., 187).

60. Ibid., 186.

61. Barth, *CD* IV/2, 719.

62. One still, I think, has to ask whether Barth himself does not push the exemplary function of the church too far. My argument here is that he does not push it as far as Yoder believes.

63. Barth, "The Christian Community and the Civil Community," 156.

64. Barth, *Christian Life*, 115–153.

65. *Barth*, "The Christian Community and the Civil Community," 157.

66. Yoder, "Why Ecclesiology is Social Ethics," 119.

67. Barth, *CD* IV/1, 643; cf. *CD* IV/2, 614; IV/3, 681; the exact wording is slightly different each time.

68. Cf. Karl Barth, *Die Kirchliche Dogmatik: Die Lehre von der Versöhnung* (IV/1) (Zürich: Theologischer Verlag, 1960), 718.

69. Daniel M. Bell, "State and Civil Society," in *The Blackwell Companion to Political Theology*, ed. Peter Scott and William T. Cavanaugh (Blackwell Reference Online, 2003).

70. Cf. David Haddorff, "Barth and Democracy: Political Witness Without Ideology," in *Commanding Grace: Studies in Karl Barth's Ethics*, ed. Daniel L. Migliore (Grand Rapids: Eerdmans Publishing Company, 2010), 96–121.

Chapter 14

Democracy and Church

Barth and Yoder on Democratic Practice

Kristopher Norris

INTRODUCTION

Democracy is in trouble.[1] At least this is the message emanating from some prominent American political and religious circles. From Stanley Hauerwas's warning that "majority rules" ideology produced Adolf Hitler[2] to Jeffrey Stout's exclamation regarding democracy's production of an economic-imperialist oligarchy—that is, "We're fucked!"[3]—many recent observations suggest that democracy has generated a form of public "discontent."[4]

Liberal Democracy in Critique

It has become fashionable in certain theological circles to criticize democracy as dangerous for, or even a rival of, the church. These critiques, offered most prominently by American post-liberal theologians like Hauerwas and William Cavanaugh, propose that current democratic practice presumes a neutral government that does not affirm any vision of the good life. Rather democracy merely provides a procedural framework of individual rights that respects persons as independent subjects capable of choosing their own values and ends. Due to its inherently individualistic nature, Hauerwas contends, democracy inflicts a leveling effect on society that fragments tradition and atomizes individuals. Furthermore, democracy posits a consumeristic and autarchic conception of freedom, employs violence to sustain its legitimation, and poses an existential threat to the church's integrity by convincing the church to underwrite the democratic project.[5]

In light of these critiques, this chapter looks to Karl Barth and his student, John Howard Yoder, to examine the question: Should Christians faithfully support democracy? To many global readers this may seem an odd question.[6]

However, in the Western, and perhaps especially American context, this has been a live and hotly debated question—in some ways since the warnings of Tocqueville in the early nineteenth century, but especially over the last forty years. I will argue that Christians should support democracy, of a certain sort and with some important qualifications, by drawing on Barth's and Yoder's respective conceptions of democracy and understandings of the church's relationship with democracy and the democratic state.

Post-liberal critiques like Hauerwas's, I believe, are insightful and forceful enough to deserve attention, especially as they resonate with critiques posited by other religious and political theory scholars like Jeffrey Stout and Romand Coles. The key distinction between these two sets of critiques is that the contentions of the latter are positioned, explicitly, against a procedural vision of democracy, attributed to political philosopher John Rawls, marked by pretensions to government neutrality and libertarian freedom.[7] While perhaps this is still the dominant form in current American political practice, it is not the only available vision of democracy. This insight suggests that the critiques of theologians like Hauerwas are directed more precisely toward Rawlsian liberalism than democracy as such, leaving open the door for faithful Christian support of democracy.

An Alternative Vision of Democracy

Stout and Coles offer more than critique; instead they seek to "redeem" democracy by generating an alternative, substantive vision that they call *democracy as tradition* or *radical democracy*, respectively.[8] At the risk of masking distinctions between their two proposals, I'll highlight a few key elements of this alternative vision, which I'll call *civic democracy* for shorthand.

This vision dismisses the notion of government neutrality toward particular visions of the good and charges the state with the task of cultivating particular civic virtues among its citizens in order to achieve the common goods of self-government. Political deliberation occurs through common practices that welcome normative commitments, especially the practice of giving and asking for reasons in the public square, including reasons animated by and expressive of one's own religious commitments. This, then, requires a posture of receptive listening, inclusivity, and social engagement that spans across cultural and religious differences and works to cultivate—rather than bracket—the tensions present in these different conceptions of the good. Civic democracy, therefore, calls citizens to share in responsibility for the arrangements and policies undertaken by the republic. This shared responsibility highlights collaboration over competition and building relationships over achieving predetermined results.

The aforementioned proposals circumvent much of Hauerwas's critique. Therefore, to obtain a more nuanced theological assessment of democracy, since most theopolitical critiques largely evade this alternative vision, I will offer an analysis that draws on the work of Karl Barth and John Howard Yoder. Both theologians offer serious appraisals of democracy and the church's relationship with democracy, but ones that have been largely ignored in this debate. I hope to show that Barth and Yoder can propel the conversation forward and more adequately address the question of whether Christians can faithfully support democratic vision and practice.

BARTH ON DEMOCRACY

Karl Barth addresses the topic of democracy sparingly throughout his extensive corpus, and always within the context of his broader treatments of the state. This suggests that for Barth democracy does not entail a set of practices, as it seems to do for the aforementioned thinkers. Rather democracy is a particular form of governmental rule, inseparable from the apparatus of the state.

In this section, I will begin to make a case for a faithful Christian posture toward a civic conception of democracy by engaging Barth's treatment of democracy and the church's relationship with state government. I will first outline Barth's conception of the state, then move more specifically to his direct thoughts on democracy as a form of government, and finally examine his views on the church's relationship with the democratic state.

Barth's Conception of the State

For Barth, the state bears two primary theological markings. First, it exists as a divinely appointed institution for earthly rule, the human representative of Christ's lordship over the world, outside the church.[9] It serves as an instrument of divine grace, offering physical protection for its citizens "from the invasion of chaos" in the world, and even contributes to God's plan of salvation by offering humans the gift of time through the protection of their lives—time to hear the gospel, repent, and have faith.[10] In this way the state is the church's "worldly partner,"[11] purposed toward the same divine ends by protecting human life for salvation and securing a worldly space for the church and its work.

Still, Barth clearly asserts that the state is not to confuse itself with the church; it is outside the church, but not Christ's dominion. In fact, Barth employs a litany of striking descriptions of the relation of the state to Christ's rule, labeling the state an "exponent," "allegory," and "analogue" to the Kingdom of God.[12]

And second, though part of the sacred order, the state can often become, in Barth's terms, "demonic": "The New Testament makes no attempt to conceal the fact that at all times the church may, and actually does, have to deal with the 'demonic' State," he claims, though it is not inevitable that any particular state will become demonic.[13] For Barth, this demonic form means that the state has renounced its divinely appointed purpose. This demonism seems to consist primarily in inhibiting the free preaching of the gospel, though it may also refer to a state that perpetuates disorder, injustice, and subjugation. Demonism occurs when the state "no longer protects the right, nor finds in it its determination and limit. It subjects the right to itself and makes triumphant use of it. The state no longer serves man [*sic*]; man, both ruled and ruling, has to serve the state."[14] It is significant however, that even in its perverted form, the state retains divine power; in its most demonic moment, the state cannot help but render the service it is meant to render.

It is also important to note that Barth's claim that God ordains the institution and earthly authority of the state, as such, is not a claim that God ordains any particular form of state governance. In positing that states are always tempted toward perversion, ruling in a corrupt or unjust manner, Barth suggests that the church is free to participate in the "human search for the best form, or most fitting system of political organization."[15] Thus there is "no cause for the Church to act as though it lived, in relation to the State, in a night in which all cats are grey."[16] The church is free to make judgments about "the better political system in any particular situation," to discriminate between just and unjust states and better and worse political forms, recognizing the divine ordination of all states but offering different levels and forms of support and criticism as expressions of its political responsibility toward the state.[17] This freedom of discrimination of forms of state government opens the door for his more direct analysis of democracy.

Democracy: Preferable, but Relativized

While Barth embeds his discussions of democracy within the general topics of church and state or the protection of human life, his belief that the church should prefer a democratic form of state governance emerges at several points: "Christian choices and purposes in politics tend on the whole towards the form of State, which, if not actually realized in the so-called 'democracies,' is at any rate more or less honestly clearly intended and desired."[18] He seems to oscillate between claiming democracy as the closest form of government to the Christian vision—at one point calling it "a justifiable expansion of the thought of the New Testament"—and suggesting that it is not necessarily the most Christian form at other points.[19] In the end he seems to settle here: while no one political concept or form is *the* Christian concept, the democratic form "shows a stronger trend in this direction than any other."[20] While he rarely offers any substantive justification for this claim—theological or empirical— when he does, he associates democracy with the form of life portrayed in the gospel.[21] This seems to consist in the corresponding virtues of freedom, equality or mutuality, and common responsibility inherent in both the gospel life and democracy.

While extolling the relative virtues of the democratic state, Barth was under no pretensions of democracy's purity. All political forms and systems have their limits, he contends, and democracy is no different. He is clear that all forms of political organization are tempted to become what he calls a "lordless power," and the "demonic" is at work in all forms of politics, be they "monarchical, aristocratic, democratic, nationalistic, or socialistic."[22]

Barth further relativizes all forms of government under the dominion of Christ and the presence of the church, though as Markus Höfner correctly notes,[23] neither the church nor the civil order are to be identified with the Kingdom of God. In his 1946 essay, "The Christian Community and the Civil Community," Barth employs the image of two concentric circles, the inner circle of the church and outer circle of the state, or civil community, surrounding the kingdom of God in the center.[24] Therefore, it is the church that legitimizes the state, he claims; the state has no independence apart from or over-against the church.[25] The church is the center and constitution of the state, though the state will not understand itself as subordinated to the church in this way. Barth ascribes a theological, political, and practical priority to the church over the state; the state's ultimate divine purpose is to create opportunities for the preaching and hearing of the Word and to secure the existence of the church.[26]

Barth offers three reasons for this ecclesiological priority. First, the church embodies a higher form of politics. Its governance is ecumenical and therefore "resists all abstract local, regional, and national interests in the political sphere" as well as parochial politics.[27] Second, the church maintains a practical separation from the state. It can never allow the state to determine its identity and purpose.[28] In other words, "The Church must remain the Church." While both are ultimately directed to the soteriological designs of God, each is given separate tasks in that plan and neither should infringe on the identity or work of the other. And third, the church reminds the state of the Kingdom of God, and it would lose its ability for criticism if aligned too closely with the state.[29] The church is bound in responsibility both to support and to criticize the state.

In the end, while the democratic state may tend more closely to the Christian view of proper human authority, it is still one among many forms of state government, susceptible to perversion like any other form, and always subordinate to the rule of Christ and earthly presence of the church.

The Church's Relationship with the State

Since the church maintains this theological and practical priority over the state, its relationship with the state is one of responsibility. The church, by virtue of its earthly, human existence owes support and loyalty to the state. Barth claims that Christians "bear responsibility for its condition, and for what is done or not done by it. They are in the same boat with its government, whatever its constitutional form."[30] In other words, the church is always to be *for* the state, in service of the state, never *against* it—even if the state falls into corruption.[31] Barth frames the church's loyalty to the state in terms of responsibility, and this responsibility takes four concrete forms: intercession, political action, criticism, and example.

The church's first task toward the state is prayer. The state has the power to protect and guarantee the freedom of the church, so in some ways, the church's prayer for the state is also instrumental for its own benefit. At the same time, intercession belongs to the essence of the church and is thus, the "essential service which the Church owes the State."[32]

But, the church would not be taking its responsibility seriously if it did no more than pray. Barth writes that Christians cannot pray aright without also being projected into corresponding action.[33] The proper outworking of its intercession for the state, therefore, consists in working actively on behalf of the civil community through direct political action: "responsible choice of authority, responsible decision about the validity of laws, responsible care for their maintenance, in a word, political action."[34] Moreover, the content of this political action and work on behalf of the civil community consists in work for social justice. Barth also notes that living under democracy only increases the political duties incumbent upon Christian citizens, since the democratic state allows for greater political involvement from its citizens.

This loyalty and action on behalf of the state, however, does not mean the church should adopt a blind obedience or attitude of "unquestioning assent to the will and action to the State."[35] Rather, the church honors the state through both its support *and* its criticism when necessary: the church reminds the state of things of which it is unable to remind itself. When a state becomes "demonic," or turns against God's purpose, the church—as part of its responsibility to the state—will refuse to cooperate, and will publicly express its resistance, even to the point of "revolt" against lordless powers.[36] This is not done "against the State, but as the Church's service for the State!"[37] Even the most "brutally unjust State" only increases the church's imperative of responsibility—even if this duty can only be fulfilled by suffering at its hands.[38] Through its resistance, the church acts in responsibility for the state, reminding it that its ultimate power is from God—"that it does not exercise an intrinsic but a transmitted authority."[39] Thus even if ecclesial responsibility becomes limited to enduring suffering from an unjust state, the state will still act as a servant of divine justification. By sometimes affirming and sometimes opposing the state's actions, the church provides the "frontier" for the state and its best support.[40]

Finally, I would argue that Barth offers another case for democracy through a fourth form of the church's responsibility for the state: providing it a political example. "The real Church must be the model and prototype of the real State," Barth writes. "The Church must set an example so that by its very existence it may be a source of renewal for the State."[41] The church offers this example simply by "maintaining and occupying its own realm as Church" because the church itself is the primary political reality.

More specifically, the church owes the example of its organization—its law and order—to the world.[42] Its patterns of life together, community law and order, and offices of governance all serve as a model to the state of the true order of politics. For Barth, a reflection of his Free Church sensibilities, this "brotherly Christocracy" of the church's law and order is predicated on the biblical notion of the priesthood of all believers, and thus is tethered to the act of communal worship. It is in worship that the community of believers affirms and confesses the lordship of Christ; the lordship of Christ actually "takes place" in the practices of worship.[43] In fact, Barth arranges his discussion of Christian life liturgically, pivoting on the themes of Baptism, the Lord's Prayer, and the Lord's Supper.[44] In his discussion of the order of the community in *Church Dogmatics*, Barth outlines the social and political implications of four liturgical practices:

1. The common *confession of sin and faith* is the primary communal and ecumenical response to the Word of God and recognition of the true lordship of Christ.
2. In *baptism* the community emphasizes the mutual trust inherent in its order, recognizing one another as fellow priests, equals, and members of the same body.
3. In the *Lord's Supper*, the community affirms its commitment to no distinction of persons under Christ. The gathering at the table orders the community by making the strong responsible for the weak, the healthy for the sick, the rich for the poor.
4. Finally, in *communal prayer* the congregation surrenders itself to God in obedience. This constitutes the community, "makes it a 'we,'" and unites the members in equal dependence upon and access to God.[45]

Barth sums up his discussion of church order as a political model to the state by identifying six ways it serves as an example. It: (1) is ordered to service, (2) practices mutual trust, (3) is united in fellowship and common responsibility for one another, (4) treats everyone as a family member, (5) opens itself to others, and (6) proclaims that humanity is not the ultimate subject of the law but is always under the authority of Christ.[46] These items correspond to the themes and elements of civic democratic ideals noted previously, such as trust, relationship, and inclusivity, and also serve to further relativize all government systems in their subordination to and constitution in the rule of Christ.

In light of this exemplary view of the church, it is important to note that Barth still offers a cautious and realist account of both the church and politics: *both* at best tender modest, situational, and incremental prospects for faithful action (see Paul Jones' on Barth's "realism" and Höfner's account of the provisional nature of the church's distinction from the world in Barth's view).[47] Still, his measured proposals suggest that this ecclesio-political order, manifest in the event of worship, models a form of political order resonant with the civic form of democracy proposed by Stout and Coles. While Barth does not explicitly draw a connection to democracy in his discussion of church order, the four social implications of worship practices noted earlier contain parallels to the vision of democracy outlined by these thinkers.

In the end, it seems for Barth, Christians can faithfully support and practice democracy. While he understands democracy as a form of state rule rather than a set of practices, his description of church order as an example of state governance offers a rich palette of "democratic" practices emerging from the "priesthood of all believers," with strong parallels to the civic vision of democracy advocated for in this chapter.

YODER ON DEMOCRACY

John Howard Yoder was a student of Barth's at Basel. While Barth's influence is evident in many elements of Yoder's work, Yoder also provides an important Anabaptist inflection that nuances Barth's analysis of democracy.[488] In other words, Yoder provides a useful interlocutor for Barth since Barth's claims provide the theopolitical foundation for Yoder's more direct and expansive assessment, while also complementing and amending Barth's work on this topic. Working within this Barthian framework, Yoder's Anabaptist perspective helps him to animate to new ends the important theological elements that Barth introduced into this question, especially advancing the theopolitical significance of the "priesthood of all believers." I argue that this move allows Yoder to better delineate between democratic practice and the apparatus of the state in a way that Barth could not. Yoder thus builds on Barth's work, and fills some of the recesses in Barth's assessment. Yoder's views on democracy can be found in two places: his direct treatment of democracy and his "free church" (and democratic) account of ecclesiology, which seems to offer much continuity with both Barth's treatment of the church as a political exemplar and the democratic vision described earlier.

Yoder's Appraisal of Democracy

Yoder is concerned about any ecclesial attempt to discriminate between and choose a form of state governance. He says: "To ask, 'What is the best form of government?' is itself a Constantinian question. . . . It assumes that the paradigmatic person, the model ethical agent, is in a position of such power . . . that it falls to him to evaluate alternative worlds and to prefer the one in which he himself (for the model ethical agent assumes himself to be a part of 'the people') shares the rule."[49] Yet, for the sake of argument, it seems, Yoder does entertain this Constantinian question, though with trepidation and humility, walking a fine line of refusal to develop accounts of government legitimacy while maintaining that the church can make discriminating judgments about the possibilities and limits of a particular civic order. For example, in his short work, *Discipleship as Political Responsibility*, he suggests that while the idea of a just state is useful and in no way to be equated with God's justice, Christians should still demand the state to be just.[50]

Despite this epistemological concern, Yoder concludes with Barth that democracy can be preferable over other more totalitarian forms. While the democratic state presents its relatively open form of rule as legitimation for its existence as a form of government, this allows for a degree of "immanent critique" from its citizens. That is, democracy provides Christians as "subjects" with an opportunity to call the state to be more just in its ways of governing. The proper Christian witness to the state asks how the state can best fulfill its responsibilities in a fallen society, addressed in specific criticisms.[51] This social critique always speaks in terms of specific alternatives or the elimination of specific abuses, but should never appeal to a "doctrine of lesser-evil." Still, democracy is more benevolent by Christian standards simply because its language of legitimation opens the door for critique and some degree of accountability. Democracy is still the least oppressive form of government since it "provides the strongest language of justification and therefore critique."[52]

Additionally, democracy is preferable because of the idea of "minority leverage." Yoder insists that real democracy does not lie in the idea of majority rule but in minority leverage, the idea that in a democracy even the minority voice is to be protected and not silenced violently. "The crucial need is not to believe that 'we, the people' are ruling ourselves," he claims. "It is to commit ourselves to defending *their* right to be heard."[53] (It is especially appropriate here to name Yoder's failure and hypocrisy on this point, in light of his sexual abuse of female graduate students and colleagues. As new reports have emerged over the past few years, the scope of Yoder's abuse has become even more apparent, as well as his use of power and prestige to degrade his accusers and obfuscate his own institutional process of discipline and reconciliation. This surely only further silenced these "voiceless" victims.)[54]

At the same time he offers praise for democracy, however, Yoder, like Barth, quickly qualifies it by relativizing all forms of government. Yoder places them all under the category of dominion or coercion—and here it matters most that Yoder conceives of democracy in terms of a form of government. Even in democracy, he claims, coercive control is still prior to any justifications for or qualifications of that control. Democracy is not sui generis, but a particular form of justification or legitimation offered for coercive rule. By relativizing all forms of government in claiming that coercive power precedes the justification that a particular realm's government offers for its power, he highlights the priority of coercion—"the facticity of the sword"—over theories of legitimation.[55] This means that myths such as "social contract" or "rule of the people" can be useful abstractions but should give Christians no pretensions that it is their responsibility to take over the government. Christians should take a cautious approach to democratic government in a sense, because democracy is really only a form of legitimation that operates according to an ethic of domination.

The Anabaptist influence of a dual morality and skepticism toward the state persist despite his qualified advocacy. He approves of the "Barthian" logic, which suggests that all powers are fallen and distorted reflections of the "true politics" of God. Therefore, the church denies the government's claim to autonomy and clarity of vision.[56] From this logic, the reason democracy is the best form among all fallen powers is that its mode of legitimation opens the way for the possibility of Christian immanent critique whereby the church can attempt to hold government accountable to its own standards by appropriating the language (and ethic) of democracy itself.

Yoder's Democratic Ecclesiology

Beyond his direct theological assessment of democracy as a form of government, Yoder, like Barth, suggests that another case for democracy can be made by examining the form of Christian community as a model for civil society. Expanding on the brief links Barth draws between liturgy and political organizing, Yoder suggests the church may serve as a prototype for the structure and practice of democratic polity. In one of his earlier works, Yoder notes an "egalitarian thrust" within the Christian community that casts light beyond the borders of the church to the wider society.[57]

The church is constituted by its practices, the ordering of a particular way of life together, and one could easily extrapolate these communal practices into a secular or pluralistic setting. These are political ideas and practices, he suggests, not only in their ecclesiological formulation of the church as a sociopolitical body, but also in that they can be commended to most any society as a "healthy way to organize." Because of their political nature, "these practices can be prototypes for what others can do in the wider world" since none of the concepts is "religious or esoteric in the regular, narrower sense of the terms."[58] If the church, then, can serve as a paradigm for the social and political structure of the larger society, then the question becomes, "What form of political order do these ecclesiological practices suggest for the wider society?"

Yoder follows Barth in ascribing social significance to the liturgical practices of the Lord's Supper and baptism: the Lord's Supper demanding economic solidarity, egalitarian sharing, and even a privileging of the poor; and baptism signaling a leveling of the dividing wall of earthly identities and calling for radical egalitarianism and inclusivity.[59] These practices parallel similar notes of egalitarianism and solidarity in Barth, while Yoder's concepts of "binding and loosing," "open meeting," and "moral practical reasoning" provide a fuller vision of (civic democratic) communal moral deliberation.[60]

The communal practice of "binding and loosing," based on Christ's injunctions in Matthew 18, is the ecclesial process of judging and correcting for wrongdoing, as well as reconciling wrongdoers back into the community. This deliberation leads to an examination of the community's rules and teaches the members to resolve their differences dialogically. In such cases, conflict becomes useful because it teaches the community how to best process conflict, learn appropriate resolution skills, tend to differences, and trust in one another since the community's decision is binding on all parties. In his communal hermeneutic of practical moral reasoning, "people make particular choices which are illuminated by their general faith commitments, but which still need to be worked through by means of detailed here-and-now thought processes."[61] This process applies not only when a community member wrongs another, but whenever there is intellectual, spiritual, social, or moral conflict.

Yoder outlines the elements of proper communal "moral practical reasoning" as an open context, freedom of speech for both parties, inclusion of external voices from outside the community for mediation, the intention of reconciliation, and an expected outcome "that God can stand behind."[62]

This process correlates closely to his later description of the practice of the open meeting for scripture interpretation or to discern God's guidance for the community (and similar to Barth's practice of "open evenings" in which he would invite students to his home to discuss politics and encourage "deep listening," an ethos of openness, as described by Angela Hancock[63]). Yoder cites the primary elements of that practice to be freedom of speech, orderliness of dialogue, and non-coercive deliberation, as well as special attention to minority opinions and the "voiceless"[64]—those who are perpetually underprivileged (though again, we must acknowledge Yoder's personal and theological failures on this point).

These visions parallel the central elements of Stout's concepts of public discourse and responsible citizenship: close listening, cooperation, speaking openly in one's own form of language, discerning lines of convergence toward a common good, and holding one another accountable.[65] In fact, Yoder anticipates such connections, acknowledging that since the process includes a variety of roles and perspectives, it is ideal for use in a pluralistic setting. He suggests, "In a healthy democracy it can function as an alternative to civil litigation or to criminal prosecution."[66] The practice also offers an alternative vision of dialogical procedure for evaluating laws and policies as well as governmental and political behavior. In addition to the parallels with Stout, Yoder's ecclesial practices also connect to the "liturgies and body practices of democratic life" that Coles notes. Coles' conception of democracy as constituted by practices of receptive movement, attentive listening, collaboration, and dwelling (nonviolently) within the tensions of a community certainly echo the vision of Yoder.

EVALUATIONS: CAN CHRISTIANS FAITHFULLY SUPPORT DEMOCRACY?

After examining this promising alternative vision of democracy and investigating a faithful Christian approach to democracy with the help of Barth and Yoder, I will now briefly analyze these two sets of concepts and practices, noting both important continuities and points of divergence between ecclesiology and democracy. I claim that democracy does not necessarily pose the threat to Christianity that worries Hauerwas. In fact, Christians can faithfully support this alternative vision and practice of democracy, and perhaps even sharpen their own practices in light of it. I will make my case by identifying three continuities between a "civic" model of democratic practice and Christian ecclesiology. I will then qualify this claim by addressing three distinctions that prevent Christianity from unreservedly supporting democracy, and conclude with a note about what the church may in fact learn from this vision of democracy.

Continuities

The first continuity between civic democracy and an ecclesiology framed by Barth and Yoder is the accent on constitutive practices directed to a particular vision of the good. Far from the naïve attempt of Rawlsian liberalism to delimit public discourse within the bounds of a mythical "public reason" by bracketing conceptions of the good,[67] this democratic vision offers a particular conception of the good and attempts to form the social body through its practices, similar to Yoder's vision of "body politics" and Barth's coupling of liturgical practices and the Christian life. Both visions—democratic and ecclesiological—involve a self-conscious "hermeneutic of peoplehood" whose practices include attentive listening, giving and receiving reasons in public, peacefully deliberating about moral issues, and including all voices along with their confessional commitments, all oriented toward the proper ends of that community.

Second, the language of witness persists throughout Barth and Yoder's ecclesiologies, as well as this alternative vision of democracy, most explicitly in Coles' notion of radical democracy. Coles uses the term witness to express the receptive practices essential to democracy—attentive listening, traveling to others to hear their stories, non-coercive dialogue, the openness and vulnerability of risking one's own confessional reasons in public while receiving those of others and allowing those to transform one's own tradition. Likewise, as Höfner notes, Barth presupposes and promotes a process of *mutual* learning between the church and non-Christian society,[68] while Yoder's ecclesiology is constituted by patience in listening and discernment, granting a voice to everyone, and allowing those voices to help reshape the community. This inclusive epistemology of witness calls for vulnerable encounters and the giving and receiving of reasons with others without coercion or exclusion, an "epistemological nonviolence."[69]

Thirdly, once the atomizing threats of liberal procedural democracy are removed, the remaining Barthian and neo-Anabaptist critiques (including those of Hauerwas) are directed at the state rather than the practices of democracy itself. The ethic of domination and coercion of the state, bound to its violent, coercive, and allegiance-garnering activities, as Yoder has it, is antithetical to the "ethic of discipleship" that ought to shape the community of the faithful. An alternative democratic vision exists, in part, independently of the state and its coercive violence. Civic democratic proponents accent "bottom-up" work and focus on democratic practice within the wisdom of small, localized communities. Attention to grassroots democratic activism and the American Civil Rights movement as exemplars of this vision creates a significant distance between democracy as a communal practice and the legitimating "use" of democracy by the state.

Distinctions

These continuities appear promising, enabling a faithful Christian participation in democracy. Still, my own Anabaptist misgivings persist, and I worry that any advocacy that too closely aligns the two traditions runs the risk of civil religion that instrumentalizes Christianity as support for the state—or worse, idolatry. Here I note three important distinctions: the results-oriented *telos* of democracy, pneumatology, and the confessional nature of the church. Here it is necessary to distinguish between Coles and Stout, with Coles' account more amenable to Christian concerns. Stout's idea of democracy as a tradition is oriented toward the end of responsible "citizenship," the moral formation of American citizens in "democratic piety." Stout argues that activities embody the ideal of democratic citizenship "to the extent that the activities are successful."[70] Coles, on the other hand, shares Yoder's anti-Constantinian worries about attempting to "handle the world," or using positions of power to engender particular results. The radical openness of his vision and Yoder's ecclesiology precludes predetermined or limited outcomes, cultivating relationships rather than results. "Nothing is more important to radical democracy," Coles claims, "than cultivating relationships through which more and more people might become a 'we' of more resonant bodies."[71]

Secondly, in the church the practice of communal moral deliberation is tethered to consensus;[72] there is no voting or majority rule because the purpose is to discern the will of the Spirit and not the "best," "most effective," or "most popular" course of action or policy. Yoder notes that while one can derive secular analogies, the pneumatological aspect of this process—both the guidance of the Holy Spirit and the practical significance of spiritual gifts—results in an indefeasible distinction between the ecclesial construction and a secular analog.

Thirdly, any theological support of democracy must acknowledge the provincial and particular nature of the church and its language and not elide the Christological and moral distinction that persists between ecclesiology and democracy. Democracy, even of the civic or radical type, promotes a different set of virtues than does Christianity. This is not to say that there may not be significant overlap in common virtues like listening, egalitarian dialogue, or attention to minority voices. But it does mean that these virtues in democratic community will be oriented to a different end—often democracy itself—than that of Jesus Christ as Lord.[73]

The best Christians can say of democracy, unlike its best "secular" proponents, is that democracy is the process but Christ is the goal—one should never be confused for the other.[74] As Yoder and Barth continue to remind us, it is the worship of Christ as Lord that provides the most significant barrier between ecclesiology and democracy. The Church's foundational confession that "Christ is Lord" is a claim that communities outside the church cannot make. While the church's Christological center of gravity does not limit whom the community will listen to, it does establish epistemological and moral limits bound by its confession. Yoder insists this "ethics of discipleship" is distinct from "an ethic of justice within the limits of relative prudence and self-preservation, which is all one can ask of the larger society."[75]

Learning from Democracy

On the other hand, many of the democratic practices prescribed by these theorists may indeed expand and enrich the ecclesiologies of Barth and Yoder and push them toward greater faithfulness. I'll mention one example. Building on Barth's liturgical movements toward social egalitarianism, Yoder more specifically emphasizes the church's attention to minority voices within the community and willingness to listen to their guidance (linking this to democracy's protection of minority voices). The radical openness prescribed by Cole's account of grassroots organizing may push this church practice to even attend to voices that are not represented in the ecclesial community— to offer an external corrective to misguided church practices or omissions, such as calls for racial reparations from white American denominations and congregations due to their historical complicity in white supremacy, a type of secular "parable of the kingdom" to use Barth's term.[76]

Congregations tend toward social homogeneity, a phenomenon that usually circumscribes their social imaginations and practices of justice. A greater vulnerability to and inclusivity of minority and external voices—of the type Coles proposes—may extend into a "preferential option for the poor" or preferential option for the minority opinion in community deliberations, similar to the challenges of liberation theology.[77] This practice may shape the church into a place for the "crosscutting" conversations that Angela Hancock discusses[78] and imbue Yoder's notion of moral practical reasoning, a form of democratic deliberation, with more vulnerability by including those unlike ourselves and granting a preferential option to their case. This requires a greater openness to change and correction, greater sense of risk-taking, and greater faith in the endurance and ultimate truth of one's tradition than most congregations are willing to maintain.

CONCLUSIONS

In conclusion, I answer the driving question of this essay—with appropriate caution regarding the Constantinian presumptions of the question—in the qualified affirmative. Christians can and should faithfully support democracy, insofar as democracy is conceived of and practiced in an alternative civic and radical form. This means that democracy exists independently of the violent dominion of the state and is practiced in small, local communities seeking to cultivate a life directed to common ends guided by the virtues and habits of inclusivity, hospitality, listening, and receptive witness. In agreement with Yoder, the church has sufficient reason to call the state that uses democracy as a form of legitimation to account, using the state's own terms and ethics. It may even prefer democracy to other forms of government.

Still, while important and beneficial aspects of "democratic" ecclesiology can be informative as a prototype for civic democratic practice, one can never forsake the church's Christological particularity. Some elements simply cannot be transplanted or translated and others restrict the degree to which faithful Christians can support democratic practice and ideology. This means that Christians can support democracy only to the degree that this support does not become a "competitive revelation claim" of any sort (a common trope for Yoder), requiring rival allegiance or attempting to inculcate virtues of citizenship at odds with the virtues of the gospel. In Barth's words, democracy can make a claim on the actions of its citizens but it cannot claim their hearts. Democracy cannot impede the Christian's claim and witness to the fact that Christ is Lord. This means that provisional support is to be granted with the recognition that democratic community cannot be collapsed into the church. That said, the church would do well to learn from the example of radical democratic communities, affirm the work and goals they share, and, as Coles hopes, open themselves to radical possibilities and commit themselves to the mutual vision that "another world is possible."[79]

NOTES

1. This chapter was completed prior to the election of Donald Trump as president of the US. That administration and its aftermath have presented even more serious challenges to democracy in the US context and beyond that cannot be discussed in this essay, but suggest even greater importance to churches supporting the civic task of democracy.

2. Stanley Hauerwas, *The Hauerwas Reader*, ed. John Berkman and Michael Cartwright (Durham: Duke University Press, 2001), 527.

3. Jeffrey Stout, *Blessed Are the Organized: Grassroots Democracy in America* (Princeton: Princeton University Press, 2010), 245.

4. See Michael Sandel, *Democracy's Discontent: American In Search of a Public Philosophy* (Cambridge, MA: Harvard University Press, 1996).

5. These critiques run throughout the Hauerwas corpus, but see especially *Resident Aliens: Life in the Christian Colony*, with William Willimon (Nashville: Abingdon, 1989), *The Peaceable Kingdom* (Notre Dame: University of Notre Dame Press, 1983), *Dispatches from the Front: Theological Engagements with the Secular* (Durham: Duke University Press, 1994), and *The Hauerwas Reader*.

6. I acknowledge that this may be an especially privileged question to some of the Asian readers of and contributors to this volume, who are in the midst of struggles for democracy in light of more oppressive forms of governance.

7. John Rawls's democratic vision is predicated on notions of justice and fairness that require reasons embedded in any "comprehensive doctrine"—especially religious ones—to be (at least eventually) translated into "public reason," or ideals and principles that no reasonable person with another point of view could reasonably reject (*Political Liberalism* [NY: Columbia University Press, 1993], 49). "In discussing constitutional essentials and matters of basic justice we are not to appeal to comprehensive religious and philosophical doctrines . . . [but] to rest on the plain truths now widely accepted, or available, to citizens generally" (224–225).

8. This section draws on the following texts: Stout, *Blessed Are the Organized* and *Democracy and Tradition* (Princeton: Princeton University Press, 2004) and Coles, *Beyond Gated Politics: Reflections for the Possibility of Democracy* (Minneapolis: University of Minnesota Press, 2005).

9. Karl Barth, *Church Dogmatics* IV/2, ed. G. W. Bromiley and T. F. Torrance (Peabody, MA: Hendrickson Publishers, 2010), 687 (henceforth cited as *CD*).

10. Barth, *Community, State, and Church* (Eugene, OR: Wipf & Stock Publishers, 2004), 156 (henceforth cited as *CSC*).

11. *CD* IV/2, 688.

12. *CSC*, 156, 169.

13. While the term demonic seems antiquated, Barth clarifies his choice of the term by explaining that the same word (*exousiai*) is used to indicate both state and angelic power. If the form of power is the same, then the state may also succumb to the demonic temptations of its authority in the same way as the fallen angels (*CSC*, 114, 118, 135).

14. Barth, *The Christian Life* (New York: T & T Clark, 2004), 220.

15. *CSC*, 161.

16. *CSC*, 119.

17. *CSC*, 163.

18. *CSC*, 182.

19. *CSC*, 145, 181.

20. *CSC*, 182.

21. *CSC*, 181.

22. *The Christian Life*, 220. While significant, the "demonic" state (what he calls Leviathan) is not the only "lordless power," but along with Mammon and ideology

form "interlocking patterns of behavior that uphold and reinforce injustice" (Paul Jones, "Karl Barth's *The Christian Life* and the Task of Political Theology," in this volume).

23. Cf. Markus Höfner, "Neither Self-Evident Frame nor Self-Enclosed Sect: The Christian Church in Barth's Political Ecclesiology," in this volume.

24. *CSC*, 169.

25. *CSC*, 140, 169.

26. *CSC*, 166.

27. *CSC*, 178, 165.

28. *CD* IV/2, 689.

29. Here again, Barth seems to oscillate between two positions. He clearly notes that the church should not expect the state to become the Kingdom of God, "it belongs to the very nature of the State that it is not and cannot become the Kingdom of God" (*CSC*, 167). On the other hand, he admits that the church "sets in motion the historical process whose aim and content are the moulding of the State into the likeness of the Kingdom of God" (*CSC*, 171).

30. *CD* III/4, 464; also *The Christian Life*, 267.

31. *CSC*, 139.

32. *CSC*, 129, 136.

33. *The Christian Life*, 213.

34. *CSC*, 144, 173.

35. *CSC*, 139.

36. *The Christian Life*, 210–213.

37. "Jesus would have been an enemy of the State if He had *not* dared, quite calmly, to call King Herod a 'fox,'" *CSC*, 139, see also 170.

38. *CSC*, 136.

39. *CD* IV/2, 689.

40. *CD* III/4, 469 and *CSC*, 131.

41. *CSC*, 186.

42. *CD* IV/2, 721.

43. See *CD* IV/2, 694, 698, and 707. This offers an interesting contrast to the minimal attention Barth gives to the church's *gathering* compared to its *sending*, addressed in Jones' chapter.

44. *The Christian Life*, 46.

45. See *CD* IV/2: (a) 699, (b) 701, (c) 708, (d) 704, 708.

46. *CD* IV/2, 722–724.

47. As Jones quotes from *The Christian Life*, "As a rule, the steps will only be little ones, or apparently little ones, made with no particular elevation on the way in our present" (Barth, *The Christian Life*, 172; cf. Paul Jones, "Karl Barth's *The Christian Life* and the Task of Political Theology," in this volume).

48. Yoder did not write his dissertation under the direction of Barth, but claimed to have studied with him more than some of Barth's own doctoral students, taking ten seminars. He always acknowledged a debt to Barth for his theological formation and dedicated a book of essays to analyzing and critiquing the work of his teacher [now in the form of *Karl Barth and the Problem of War, and Other Essays on Barth*, ed. Mark Thiessen Nation (Eugene, OR: Cascade Books, 2003)].

49. Yoder, *The Priestly Kingdom: Social Ethics as Gospel* (Notre Dame: University of Notre Dame Press, 1984), 154.

50. *Discipleship as Political Responsibility* (Scottsdale, PA: Herald, 2003), 24.

51. Yoder, *The Christian Witness to the State* (Scottsdale, PA: Herald, 2002), 32.

52. Yoder, *The Priestly Kingdom*, 160.

53. Ibid., 167.

54. The degree to which this undermines his work in theological ethics, especially as it relates to "Body Politics," will surely be the topic of many works to come. The fullest accounts and theological assessments of these events can be found in Rachel Waltner Goosen's "'Defanging the Beast': Mennonite Responses to John Howard Yoder's Sexual Abuse," *Mennonite Quarterly Review* 89 (2015): 7–80 and Karen V. Guth, "Moral Injury, Feminist and Womanist Ethics, and Tainted Legacies," *Journal of the Society of Christian Ethics* 38, no. 1 (2018): 167–186.

55. Yoder, *The Priestly Kingdom*, 159, 165.

56. Ibid., 163. This reinforces his position from *The Politics of Jesus* where he wrote of the powers as fallen entities, "seeking to separate us from the love of God," and "holding us servitude to their rules." It is the responsibility of the church to make the proclamation of God's ultimate purposes known to these powers (*The Politics of Jesus* [Grand Rapids, MI: Eerdman's, 1994], 141, 156)

57. Yoder, *The Christian Witness*, 18.

58. Ibid., 45, 46. It seems Yoder intends this on two registers, both immanently—society can constitute itself according to these same practices—and eschatologically—"The pattern we shall discover is that the will of God for human socialness as a whole is prefigured by the shape to which the Body of Christ is called" (ix).

59. *Body Politics: Five Practices of the Christian Community Before the Watching World* (Scottsdale, PA: Herald, 2001), 22, 33.

60. Binding and loosing and open meeting come from *Body Politics*, while his idea of "moral practical reasoning" comes from his essay "A Hermeneutics of Peoplehood," which appeared several years prior, laying the theoretical foundation for these practices.

61. Yoder, *The Priestly Kingdom*, 17.

62. Ibid., 28.

63. Cf. Angela Hancock, "Training for a Serious Game: Theo-Political Deliberation as a Christian Practice," in this volume.

64. *Body Politics*, 61, 66.

65. Stout, *Blessed Are the Organized*, xvi, 231, 14, 235, 231, 14.

66. *Body Politics*, 11.

67. See Stout, *Democracy and Tradition*, 63–91. Stout argues that Rawls is too optimistic that pluralistic communities can actually achieve some consensus about what is commonly acceptable to others: "He has underestimated what a person can reasonably reject, I suspect, because he has underestimated the role of a person's collateral commitments" (70). Therefore, Rawls' sphere of public reasons is too small to actually work. In addition Stout argues that Rawls' concept of public reason is not a neutral concept that hovers above all comprehensive doctrines. According to Stout and others, the concept itself relies on a comprehensive doctrine, a particular

conception of who a reasonable person is. For Rawls, to be reasonable is to accept this need for a social contract and the willingness to deliberate based on it; anyone who rejects Rawls's view is unreasonable from the start.

68. Cf. Markus Höfner, "Neither Self-Evident Frame nor Self-Enclosed Sect," in this volume.

69. Coles, *Beyond Gated Politics*, 126, 133.

70. Stout, *Blessed Are the Organized*, 13.

71. Coles and Hauerwas, *Christianity, Democracy, and the Radical Ordinary: Conversations Between a Radical Democrat and a Christian* (Eugene, OR: Cascade Books, 2008), 2, 81.

72. Ibid., 68.

73. See Markus Höfner's contribution in this volume for an account of the differences between Barth and Yoder on ecclesial distinctiveness.

74. William T. Cavanaugh, *Migrations of the Holy: God, State, and the Political Meaning of the Church* (Grand Rapids, MI: Eerdman's, 2011), 193.

75. Yoder, *The Christian Witness*, 23.

76. See *CD* IV/3, 114.

77. See Gustavo Gutierrez, *A Theology of Liberation* (Maryknoll, NY: Orbis, 1973), among others.

78. Cf. Angela Hancock, "Training for a Serious Game: Theo-Political Deliberation as a Christian Practice," in this volume.

79. I want to thank all the members of the "Barth and Theopolitics" Symposium in Bochum, Germany who offered helpful feedback on this contribution, but especially Thomas Xutong Qu, Paul Jones, Markus Höfner, and Charles Mathewes, for their thorough edits.

Chapter 15

Training for a Serious Game

Theo-Political Deliberation as a Christian Practice

Angela Dienhart Hancock

INTRODUCTION

There are two primary ways Christian communities in the United States relate to the rhetorical world of politics. On the one hand, they may embrace absolutist political rhetoric themselves, skillfully wielding it in concert with like-minded others to achieve particular political ends. On the other hand, leaders of Christian communities in the United States may withdraw from participation in political discourse altogether in protest or resignation, overtly or tacitly encouraging congregants to avoid politics and stick to faith.[1] This essay argues that Karl Barth offers a much-needed third way for political discourse in and between Christian communities in the context of a Western-style democracy. Barth's contribution to an ethos of theo-political deliberation in the context of Christian communities can be discerned not only in his systematic writings, but perhaps most directly in his practice in the early 1930s—as a theologian of the church, as a thoughtful student of history, and as a teacher of young Protestants in the context of Weimar Germany, a struggling democracy where absolutist political rhetoric was pressing in on all sides.

The essay is structured as follows: first, a brief account of the relationship between politics and "sacred rhetoric" in North America; second, a description of Barth's rejection of absolutist pathos and his corresponding "positive possibility" for human interaction, grounded in his thick description of human being as thoroughly relational; third, an exploration of two instances in the early 1930s in which Barth's ethos vis-à-vis deliberation is evident: the so-called "open evenings" and his lectures on Protestant theology in the nineteenth century; fourth, a brief analysis of the factors which hinder "crosscutting" political conversation among citizens in general and Christians in particular in the United States; and finally, after identifying the features of political speech that leaves room for the Godness of God and exemplifies a "critical and comprehensive generosity" toward others, I offer a constructive proposal to facilitate Barth's third way of theo-political deliberation in the context of the North American church.

SACRED RHETORIC

Democracy entails conflict: conflicts involving interests, rights, conceptions of the good, and the nature of justice, among other things. Democracy also entails conflicts about the very form its conflicts should take. Proponents of deliberative democracy argue that when citizens disagree about public issues, they should reason together in an effort to reach a mutually acceptable deci-sion.[2] But this ideal—citizens reasoning together—bears little resemblance to the primary way political conflict is manifest in the United States. Rhetoric is the tool or weapon politicians and engaged citizens wield to demonize opponents and garner votes. The power struggles and culture wars endemic to the North American political habitat are enjoined in a sea of slogans, buzz words, sound bites, blog posts, tweets, and talking points. The more optimis-tic among us might see this constant roar as evidence of robust engagement, a healthy bluster that harms no one. But there is strong evidence that this war of words cripples the kind of dialogue many consider vital to the democratic process, making reasoned discourse and political compromise less likely.

Why is this the case? Political scientist Morgan Marietta argues that the kind of speech that sustains this state of affairs is what he calls "sacred rheto-ric." "Sacred" as Marietta understands the word does not mean "holy" per se, but absolute. To claim a value or idea as sacred in this sense means it is non-negotiable. In defense of a sacred value no political compromise is possible and anyone who disagrees is not just an opponent but an enemy.[3] Sacred rhet-oric, then, links a particular political position with a non-negotiable value—a very persuasive strategy, especially if the sacred value is widely shared.[4]

While the use of sacred rhetoric has been shown to increase the degree of political participation on the part of those who consume it, it also not sur-prisingly has a detrimental effect on the character of public debate overall. According to Marietta, it is the absolutists and their way with words—right and left, religious and secular—who paralyze and polarize the American electorate.[5]

Christian churches in the United States have reacted to the rhetorical strug-gle inherent in democracy in different ways over the course of their history, sometimes taking up the weapon of sacred rhetoric to advocate for a political or social cause, other times withdrawing into a private theo-linguistic world, warily eyeing democratic practices themselves. This pattern has continued in recent decades: there are pastors, right and left, who use the language of holy absolutes to mobilize congregations of the like-minded to political action, while influential post-liberal theologians direct their fire at the state and its traditions, urging church leaders to cultivate countercultural communities who refuse to participate in the language games of liberal democracy.[6] Is there a third way for the church to relate to the world of democratic discourse? One that leads to robust political engagement without the stridency borne of religious or anti-liberal absolutism?

KARL BARTH AND THE "GREAT POSITIVE POSSIBILITY"

Karl Barth was keenly aware of the dangers of "sacred rhetoric" in political speech and thought. As early as the second edition of his Romans commentary he worried about "pathos" as a rhetorical characteristic of reactionaries and revolutionaries alike. At the time Barth was writing the second edition of the commentary, in 1921, the German church's endorsement of the war, the grim aftermath of the Bolshevik revolution, and the potential for similar bloody revolutions elsewhere weighed heavily on his mind. These concerns are evident in Barth's exegesis of Romans 12–13, in which both the relationship of church and state and the question of the ethics of revolution come to the fore. Because Barth's reading of Paul leaves no room for either reactionary conservatism or left-wing revolution—although he affirms that the "Red" revolutionary is more dangerous because "nearer to the truth"—he concentrates on the proper form that the Christian's resistance to absolute claims on the part of the state (or any other human institution, including the church as an institution itself!) should take:[7]

> It is evident that there can be no more devastating undermining of the existing order than the recognition of it which is here recommended, a recognition rid of all illusion and devoid of all the joy of triumph. State, Church, Society, Positive Right, Family, Organized Research, and so forth live off of the credulity of those who have been nurtured upon vigorous sermons-delivered-on-the-field-of-battle and other suchlike solemn humbug. Deprive them of their PATHOS, and they will be starved out; but stir up revolution against them, and their PATHOS is provided with fresh fodder.[8]

Barth uses the word "pathos" in describing human "passions" whether erotic, political, ethical, or aesthetic, but most particularly, religious.[9] It is religion which is the "crowning of all other passions [*pathos*] with the passion [*pathos*] of eternity, the endowment of what is finite with infinity, the most exalted consecration of the passion [*pathos*] of men, and their most secure establishment."[10]

Barth later argues that religion has been invoked ("triumphantly") in connection with science, art, ethics, socialism, the State, the youth movement, and race, "as though we had not had abundant experience of the waste land of 'Religion and . . .'"[11] It is difficult not to think ahead to the situation at the end of the Republic as Barth continues:

> Is it possible to justify these strange prophets [*Führers*], when we see hosts of men and women flocking to enlist willingly under their banners, eager to lay hold of religion, in order that their complacent capacities may be sanctioned, developed, and consecrated; when we behold them zealous to add to their passions [*pathos*] one further emotion, the emotion [*pathos*] of eternity . . . ?[12]

People who seek to improve the world, Barth explains, will instead do their best to prevent the intrusion of religion into that world. They will lift up their voices to warn those careless ones, who, for aesthetic or historical or political or romantic reasons, dig through the dam and open up a channel through which the flood of religion may burst into the cottages and palaces of men.[13]

To deprive the state of its pathos, then, means to keep eternity out of it. Deny its ultimacy. Starve it ideologically. It is a strategy of nonviolent resistance that meets the pathos of conservatism with what Barth calls the "Great Positive Possibility"—love of the other—and not with the pathos of revolution, which returns evil for evil and incites ideological warfare.[14]

Here, as in his later lectures on ethics at Münster and Bonn, political activity, while important and necessary, does not have *eternal* significance and should not be baptized as such. It is a *game* that is played in full and vigilant awareness of its relativity:

> Calm reflection has thus been substituted for the convulsions of revolution— calm, because final assertions and final complaints have been ruled out, because a prudent reckoning with reality has outrun the insolence of warfare between good and evil, and because an honest humanitarianism and a clear knowledge of the world recognize that the strange chess-board upon which men dare to experiment with men and against them in State and Church and in Society cannot be the scene of the conflict between the Kingdom of God and Anti-Christ. A political career, for example, becomes possible only when it is seen to be essentially a game; that is to say, when we are unable to speak of absolute political right, when the note of "absoluteness" has vanished from both thesis and antithesis, and when room has perhaps been made for that relative moderateness or for that relative radicalism in which human possibilities have been renounced.[15]

But it is not only the state that is to be denied religiously funded *pathos*. The second Romans commentary also argues that would-be revolutionaries should also be deprived of the holy legitimation they need to "storm the heavens."[16] Any political ideology that claims divine sanction is denied it.

When it comes to political questions, then, "pathos" in substance or in style would not be a faithful witness to the Godness of God. Barth claimed that when political views are held with deadly "eternal" seriousness, neither critical distance nor reasoned conversation about politics is possible. Instead, the language game of politics should be played in light of its relativity. But Barth is clear that, in spite of its provisionality, politics is a serious game—one that the Christian community is unreservedly called to play. Paul Dafydd Jones' essay in this volume vividly describes the nuanced approach Barth advocates: an abiding confidence in the ultimate outcome of the "covenantal drama" and the relative, but important political "moments" within it, in which Christians are called to make decisions and act, "going to meet" God's good future by revolting against the power of sin and death.[17] For Barth, then, the church is called to be a witness in the political realm, to participate in public conversation with "a critical yet comprehensive generosity," not from "outside" the world but from within, because both church and world are sustained by God's reconciling grace.[18]

But to press Barth further, what does political conversation sound like when Christians wholeheartedly play the game of politics without "sacred rhetoric," particularly in the context of a democracy? What resources does Barth offer those seeking to cultivate and guide political deliberation in Christian communities?

One place to get our bearings would certainly be Barth's thick description of human being in §45 of the *Church Dogmatics*. Not surprisingly, Barth grounds his discussion of theological anthropology in Christology. Only by looking at Jesus can we learn what it is to be human, that is, to be beings created by God and in God's image. Barth argues that, as such, human being is thoroughly relational—a being in encounter; a being in a history with God and with others. Barth's anthropology is grounded not only in his understanding of Jesus as the one who lives "for others" but in the relational dynamics of the Triune life itself. For Barth, there is no genuine humanity without the existence of others.[19] This conception of co-humanity (*Mitmenchlichkeit*) does not remain an abstraction in Barth's account but leads to certain practices and attitudes. These practices and attitudes are not inevitable—indeed, Barth thinks it is very difficult for us to be human. Inhumanity is a constant temptation. But when we are the beings we were created to be, certain things happen. First, being human involves open, direct, face-to-face interaction with others; seeing and being seen, moving out of ourselves, looking each other in the eye. Second (and most significant for the question at hand), being human involves mutual speech and hearing, a speaking and listening characterized by honest, non-defensive dialogue. Even when another has succumbed to inhumanity, Barth thinks, each person is responsible for the humanity of his or her own speaking and hearing, accepting the obligation of making himself or herself known and listening to the other without suspicion, though it is a struggle.[20] Third, genuine encounter results in a summons to action on behalf of the other. If we truly see and speak and listen it will lead us to offer mutual help and support. Finally, being human means all of the aforementioned is undertaken without reluctance or neutrality, but freely and gladly, with each person encountering the other not as "tyrant or slave," but as "companion, associate, comrade, fellow, and helpmate."[21] In Barth's description of humanity as being in encounter the beginnings of a habitus for the practice of theo-political deliberation can be easily discerned.

But it is not only Barth's systematic writings that hold promise in this regard, it is also his *practice* as a teacher of young Protestants in the context of Weimar Germany in the early 1930s.[22] Why? Because the Weimar Republic was a struggling democracy where sacred rhetoric was pressing in on all sides. The outrage over the outcome of the war, the trauma of hyperinflation, rapid cultural change, fear of a Russian-style revolution, brutally high unemployment rates, and the advent of democracy itself intensified the language of political debate as the 1920s unfolded. Military metaphors, hyperbole, slogans, insults, dire predictions and threats were everywhere, mixed with sweeping utopian promises and punctuated by the politically motivated violence that broke out in the back alleys and beer halls of Germany's cities. From 1931 to the end of the Republic, as the depression deepened and the violence escalated, politicians, the press, and the public engaged in an all-out war of words.[23] Public spaces were plastered and re-plastered with campaign posters, party "gangs" looked for trouble in the alleyways, uniformed party militias marched through the streets as if to war, and the papers screamed partisan accusations. Nearly every public venue was a breeding ground for agitation, demonstration, or proselytizing. Pathos was everywhere.

How could anyone secure a place for rational discourse about politics amid this onslaught of posters, rallies, slogans, parades, insults, banners, visions, and threats? The Protestant church, in spite of its avowed position "above parties" had not managed to resist the rhetoric of *Volk* and *Kampf*, and the "sacred" speech that dominated the public square had become a feature of the church's life as well.[24]

How did Barth react to this rhetorical situation? How did he seek to form his students to participate in the serious game of politics with the "critical and comprehensive generosity" he promotes? We will consider two representative examples in which Barth's strategy *vis á vis* formation for theo-political conversation can be discerned, one direct, one indirect. The first is his practice of hosting "open evenings" for his students; the second, the way he cultivated an ethos of openness to others in his 1931–1932 lectures on Protestant theology in the nineteenth century.

OPEN EVENINGS

When Barth arrived at the University of Göttingen in 1921, fresh from the pastorate in Switzerland, he found the political views of his nationalistic faculty colleagues jarring. But while it became clear he would not make much headway with them, Barth did not abandon efforts to contribute to the future of Weimar democracy. He turned his attention to what he hoped was the more receptive ground of the students themselves, hosting open evenings at his home which were often devoted to the discussion of politics and cultural events, something he continued when he left Göttingen and went to Münster. There Barth led the students through a series of biographies and autobiographies of many contemporary political figures (including the Kaiser). And in the following semester they turned to the question of the motives and commitments that underlay the various political positions. Through the course of such meetings, Barth modeled both a theologically grounded critique of politics and the civil discourse so vital to sustaining a democracy.[25] Barth continued the tradition of open evenings at Bonn in the tumultuous winter of 1930–1931. The open evenings he held at that time were all about politics, and large crowds of students would gather for discussion of the platforms and ideologies of the Weimar parties.[26]

Why would a professor of systematic theology do this? Why go to such lengths to make sure young Protestant pastors-to-be had intentional, thoughtful, theologically grounded conversations about politicians and political parties and political positions and not just discuss theologians and doctrines and church matters? To cultivate in them the capacity to think deeply, theologically, critically, comprehensively, and generously about politics, but perhaps also to equip them to go out into the parish and to host such discussions themselves.[27]

AN ETHOS OF OPENNESS

The open evenings are just one example of Barth's broader pedagogical approach, one that encourages deep listening and thoughtful discussion. Alexander J. McKelway, a former student of Barth, describes Barth's reaction to the aggressive partisan debates that sometimes erupted in the classroom. Barth was more than willing to express criticism of other theological positions, yet he was unhappy when students were unwilling to listen earnestly and well to the positions of others before venturing a response. He was constantly asking them to consider what might be worthwhile among the grand sweep of the theological tradition right down to their contemporaries, to be open to what they might learn, even from unlikely sources. Barth modeled this attitude of expectation himself, something Dietrich Bonhoeffer observed after participating in Barth's Schleiermacher seminar in Bonn: "He has an openness, a readiness to listen to any pertinent criticism, and at the same time an intense concentration on the subject, whether a suggestion is made proudly or modestly, dogmatically or quite tentatively."[28]

This ethos of openness to the other is explicitly named and implicitly practiced in Barth's lectures on Protestant theology in the nineteenth century—lectures he delivered first in Münster and then again in revised form in Bonn in the early 1930s. In his opening lecture, Barth exhorts his students to listen well even to those they might consider "arch-heretics," for

> we are in no position to identify such arch-heresy. Not even among avowed pagans, much less among Jews or suspect, even very suspect, Christians. All heretics are relatively heretical, so even those who have been branded heretics at one time or another and condemned for their avowed folly and wickedness must be allowed their say in theology.[29]

Notice that Barth deprives even anti-heretics of their pathos! Heresy is itself only relative, not absolute. No sacred rhetoric is needed. Barth goes on to tell the students they must be "strong and free enough to give a calm, attentive, and open hearing" not only to their favorite voices but to "all the voices of the past."[30] Because God is God, Lord of the church, Lord of theology,

> we cannot anticipate which of our fellow-workers from the past are welcome in our own work and which are not. It may always be that we have especial need of quite unsuspected (and among these, of quite unwelcome) voices in one sense or another.[31]

What is needed if one is to listen well even to "unwelcome" voices? "To hear someone else always means to suspend one's own concern, to be open to the concern of the other."[32] This then is the ethos Barth seeks to form in his students: to listen empathetically, even when they disagree. Or as Barth puts it in his discussion of *Mitmenschlichkeit* some years later, to really hear others means "to interpret or even to discern the dream with which they are occupied when they say it."[33]

As the lectures on Protestant theology unfold, Barth models the engagement he advocates. As Paul Tillich observed, in these lectures Barth "evaluates with fairness and appreciation those men against whose theological influence Barth fought all his life."[34]

So what might Barth's practice of formation for theo-political conversation—the implications of *Mitmenschlichkeit*, the open evenings, the ethos of openness—have to offer the North American church in the context of a well-established democracy abounding in sacred rhetoric?

BEYOND THE LEGACY OF MALFORMATION

In his book, *The Mighty and the Almighty: An Essay in Political Theology*, Nicholas Wolterstorff argues that, among other things, God exercises moral governance of human life through two features of human nature, the impulse toward caring for others and the capacity for moral judgment and action. Yet these gifts are "all too commonly subject to inhibition and malformation."[35] While more could be said with regard to Wolterstorff's broader theological claims, he is certainly right that becoming a Christian does not mean an immediate infusion of the capacity for "a critical and comprehensive generosity" toward others. Our ability to practice openness in the realm of theo-political discourse does not arise automatically in the Christian community, particularly in the rhetorical situation of North America, with absolutist pronouncements streaming live 24/7.

The omnipresence of sacred rhetoric about politics is not the only factor that makes it difficult for American Christians to talk deeply with each other about public issues. Political scientist Diana Mutz explains that in relation to the citizens of other countries, Americans have less exposure to "cross-cutting" conversations, that is, conversations with people whose political views differ from our own.[36] While we are exposed to an enormous amount of political rhetoric via media outlets, citizens rarely engage in such debate themselves. This is not to say Americans don't talk about politics, but the empirical evidence strongly suggests we talk about politics with people who in large part share the views we already hold, where deliberative skills are relatively unnecessary. However, Mutz sees great potential for crosscutting conversation in voluntary associations like churches, precisely because they are gatherings of people with what she calls "weak ties"—people who are not as intimate as family members but with whom we share some commitments.

So why don't such conversations happen? Because Americans avoid political talk in contexts where they value community and harmony above all else, places like churches. In those contexts, "putting differences aside means either avoiding politics or having like-minded neighbors."[37] The leaders of a given congregation might pursue a controversial political goal, for example, but this is most likely to result in a congregation who self-selects on the basis of their commitment to this political goal, not in a politically diverse congregation where the practice of communal deliberation might flourish.[38] So, not only are American Christians ill-suited for deliberation due to the malformation that comes with sacred rhetoric, they also are unlikely to have much experience of the kind of conversation in which critical and generous deliberative skills might be honed—they either choose to worship with like-minded others, or they don't talk about politics at church because the potential risk to what is most valued (harmony) is too high.[39]

Practically speaking, there are two primary ways congregations relate to the rhetorical world of politics. As noted earlier, Christians in the United States can (and often do) embrace sacred rhetoric themselves, learning (often from clergy) to skillfully wield it in concert with like-minded others to achieve their chosen political ends.[40] Christian opinion leaders in the United States can (and sometimes do) pronounce democracy dead in the water and withdraw from the game altogether in protest (or apathy), overtly or tacitly encouraging congregants to avoid politics and stick to theology. But there is a third way: cultivating the practice of critical, comprehensive, and generous theo-political conversation in North American congregations. But on what theological basis might such deliberation be explicitly claimed as a Christian practice? Is there any biblical warrant for embracing this third way, a key question for those thinking after the Reformed Barth?

While the idea of theo-political discourse within congregations as a Christian practice appears to be a novel one, theologians of various sorts have argued for the importance of "crosscutting" conversations. Public theologians write extensively about the need for dialogue among people with different political, cultural, and ethical convictions. Pastoral theologians write about the skills needed to seek peace in situations of conflict within and among congregations and denominations. Ecumenical theologians discuss how Christians of varying traditions can seek common ground despite vast theological and cultural differences. In this rich and sometimes overlapping conversation, a variety of biblical texts are cited as warrants for engagement with those who disagree, and for the ethos or character of that engagement.[41]

But the biblical warrant that is perhaps most persuasive when it comes to grounding theo-political deliberation as a Christian practice in the context of the church in the United States is rooted in Jesus' response to a question about taxation, included in all of the synoptic gospels: "Render unto Caesar the things that are Caesar's, and unto God the things that are God's." As Franklin Gamwell argues, the question Christians today should ask in response to this text is not "What belongs to Caesar and what belongs to God?" but, "How should someone who seeks always to serve the divine purpose relate to the political order?"[42] What belonged to "Caesar" in the context of the Roman Empire was limited by the nature of its form of government: obey the law, pay your taxes. But in a democracy? Is it not the case that one of the things we render is our participation, our voice, our deliberation, and hence the cultivation of the skills and habits that make such deliberation possible in a context where it is often enfeebled? Our attention to learning to play the game of political conversing seriously and well is itself a witness to God's determination to be with and for all people, including our fellow citizens.

But this third way will not be an easy one. Learning to play the serious game without pathos requires training. We need to practice something like Barth's "open evenings" in Christian communities—hosting regular intentional theologically grounded discussions about political issues, politicians, and political ideologies, discerning the dreams that drive them, not occasionally but habitually. But how?

TRAINING FOR THE SERIOUS GAME

Cultivating strong deliberative skills in local congregations will take sustained and intentional practice. Jeffrey Stout and Stanley Hauerwas agree that "ethical and political reasoning are creatures of tradition and crucially depend on the acquisition of such virtues as practical wisdom and justice."[43] But in the context of rhetorical malformation and given our inexperience when it comes to listening deeply to the other side, especially in church, deliberative virtues may be in short supply in American congregations. So, on the way to those virtues, a few guidelines for those interested in cultivating crosscutting theo-political conversations in local congregations in the United States are offered as a place to start.

First, the trust essential to ongoing dialogue between non-like-minded others arises from a form of life together; it emerges from the web of practices that constitute the common life of a Christian community: worship, prayer, Eucharist, sharing of material possessions, spending time together, learning together. The relationships that are formed and reformed by regular participation in such practices are crucial in the effort to overcome the fears that cause Americans to keep their political views to themselves when conflict may result. In his book, *A Brutal Unity: The Spiritual Politics of the Christian Church*, Ephraim Radner explains that in the earliest Christian communities, the ability to reason together and come to common decisions was presumed to be the fruit of a particular kind of life, and that the practice of communal discernment was central to that life, not just a means to some other end.[44] The effort to cultivate ongoing crosscutting theo-political conversations, then, begins with, and is sustained by, attention to the health and vitality of the practices that constitute the wider habitat and habitus of a given Christian community.

Second, the conviction that an ideal Christian community is one of harmonious agreement must be relentlessly challenged in local congregations via preaching, teaching, and regular exposure to Christians who model a critical and comprehensive generosity as they disagree with one another. As Kathyrn Tanner argues, efforts to prevent disagreement in Christian communities are misguided, for the fact that Christians disagree is central to their identity, and it always has been. Instead, Christian communities should work to avoid divisiveness by encouraging what she calls a "genuine community of argument," for

> despite their disagreements, Christians are united in argument in that they believe that the project of interpretation, which leading a Christian way of life requires, is properly pursued by way of an extended argument with everyone else engaged in the same project. If sin does not rule out one's own contributions to the enterprise, it can never entirely rule out anyone else's either. . . . Even without agreement in results, unity among Christian practices is therefore sustained by a continuity of fellowship, by a willingness, displayed across differences of time and space, to admonish, learn from, and be corrected by all persons similarly concerned about the true meaning of Christian discipleship. All Christians are in this project together.[45]

Replacing the deep-seated longing for harmony in church with a zeal for the camaraderie forged through gracious conflict will take careful and imaginative pedagogical strategies.

Third, the practice of crosscutting theo-political conversations in congregations requires a particular kind of facilitator. Generally speaking, clergy in the United States have a spotty track record when it comes to equipping congregations with deliberative skills and habits. On both the right and the left, some ministers have proven very effective in mobilizing voters, often with a hearty dose of sacred rhetoric, but understandably those focused on rousing the like-minded to action are not very interested in teaching a practice that involves deep listening, self-criticism, and openness to unlike-minded others. Some clergy find themselves in the midst of crosscutting conversations with the minister on one side of a host of political issues and the congregation—by and large—on the other.[46] Other clergy are understandably leery of the whole enterprise, and keep their politics to themselves. While there are certainly examples of clergy encouraging dialogue about public issues, say, arranging a forum on a controversial topic, these are typically occasional and "top-heavy" rather than participatory and ongoing.

Yet clerical leadership can play a key role in forging a new practice.[47] Clergy who can serve as a catalyst for regular intentional theologically grounded discussions about political issues, politicians, and political ideologies in a congregation will need to be brave enough to face the risks conflict will bring, humble enough to model genuine openness to non-like-minded others, and be well-equipped with deliberative skills themselves.[48]

Finally, it is vital that participants in theo-political conversation not just consent to, but embrace, a set of ground rules for their interactions with each other. There are a number of worthy models to choose from, indeed, "rules of art" could be easily be developed or adapted with reference to Barth's discussion of human being in encounter. There are certain elements common to many of these lists: the priority of face-to-face encounters, strategies for listening well, skills to discern the underlying convictions and longings of interlocutors, an ethos of openness, a commitment to remain in relationship, and so on. Particularly helpful in the context of deliberation in congregations are Iris Marion Young's inclusion of the practices of hospitality (care-taking) and storytelling to what have been considered standard norms of delibera-tion.[49] Which slate of ground rules is adopted is perhaps less important than their hearty endorsement by participants. In some congregations the ideal would be for a group to begin by examining some of these examples and then craft their own "rules of art" for their deliberative gatherings; others would benefit from more initial guidance from a wise facilitator.

CONCLUSION

Sacred rhetoric is here to stay, and the temptation to join in is a powerful one. In the rhetorically charged context of the United States, Karl Barth offers churches resources for resistance and reformation. A genuinely countercul-tural rhetoric does not consist in taking up absolutist speech to defeat abso-lutism but precisely in depriving both of their pathos. This counter-speech begins in a web of modest practices, slowly, patiently, cheerfully; with groups of ordinary Christians on folding chairs in church basements, say-ing their prayers and trusting one another enough to talk about the two most dangerous things in the world: religion and politics. Such conversations begin in local congregations, but if they happen the way they should, they will not end there. Over time participants in these local discussions will be prepared to practice politics without pathos beyond the boundaries of the church as well.[50] Indeed, this outward movement is necessary if we are to think after Barth, for, as Markus Höfner argues, Barth claims God's gathering of the church is never an end in itself, but always takes place for the sake of its sending out into the world.[51]

Individuals and congregations can only be formed in the ethos of criti-cal generosity by practicing it, not for its own sake, nor even for the sake of a healthy democracy in the United States of America, but because in its enactment of *Mitmenschlichkeit*, it is a faithful witness to the God who is God, the God for the world.

NOTES

1. Examples of the former abound, from the early activism of the Social Gospelers to the political advocacy of the Christian Right, many mainline Protestant denominations, and the evangelical Left, to name a few. The latter ranges from isolationist communities like the Amish to the recent arguments of influential post-liberals like Stanley Hauerwas, who openly worry that any involvement by the church in public debates is to serve American-style democracy, not God. See Martin Toulouse, *God in Public: Four Ways American Christianity and Public Life Relate* (Louisville: Westminster John Knox, 2006), 191. Sometimes church leaders migrate dramatically from one camp to the other. Jerry Falwell, who later founded the Moral Majority and is credited with the rise of conservative Christian influence in American politics, said in a 1964 sermon (denouncing pastors for speaking in favor of civil rights), "Preachers are not called to be politicians, but soul winners." Peter Applebone, "Jerry Falwell, Leading Religious Conservative, Dies," *The New York Times*, May 15, 2007.

2. Amy Gutmann and Dennis Thompson, *Democracy and Disagreement* (Cambridge: Harvard University Press, 1996), 1.

3. Morgan Marietta, *The Politics of Sacred Rhetoric: Absolutist Appeals and Political Persuasion* (Waco: Baylor University Press, 2012).

4. Marietta cites constitutionalism as a nearly universal sacred value in the United States. Ibid., 18.

5. William Simon argues that both religious fundamentalists and those engaged in identity politics reject deliberative democracy as an ideal and prefer bargaining, not deliberation, as the means to pursue political ends. "Three Limitations of Deliberative Democracy: Identity Politics, Bad Faith, and Indeterminacy," in *Deliberative Politics: Essays on Democracy and Disagreement*, ed. Stephen Macedo (Oxford: Oxford University Press, 1999), 50–51.

6. Cf. Jeffrey Stout's claim regarding the influence of Stanley Hauerwas: "There is no doubt that the main effect of his antiliberal rhetoric, aside from significantly widening his audience, is to undercut Christian identification with democracy. No theologian has done more to inflame Christian resentment of secular political culture." Jeffrey Stout, *Democracy and Tradition* (Princeton: Princeton University Press, 2004), 140.

7. Karl Barth, *The Epistle to the Romans*, 6th ed., trans. Edwyn Clement Hoskyns (London: Oxford University Press, 1968), 478.

8. Barth, Ibid., 483. Barth's interpretation challenges the ultimacy of every state, including that of Weimar. That Barth was *not* thinking of the Republic but of Imperial Germany in this text is clear from the reference to the battlefield sermons, but it is certainly true that the Weimar state would not be exempt from Barth's critique. No state is to be identified with the Kingdom of God.

9. Ibid., 235.

10. Barth, Ibid., 236.

11. Ibid., 267.

12. Ibid.

13. Ibid.

14. This love of the other "ought to be undertaken as the protest against the course of this world, and it ought to continue without interruption." Barth, Ibid., 492.

15. Barth, Ibid., 489.

16. Barth, Ibid., 485. Barth makes a similar argument with regard to any number of movements and causes that take themselves with ultimate seriousness: "Deprive a Total Abstainer, a really religious Socialist, a Churchman, or a Pacifist, of the PATHOS of moral indignation, and you have broken his backbone." Barth, Ibid., 509.

17. Paul Dafydd Jones, "Karl Barth's *The Christian Life* and the Task of Political Theology," in this volume.

18. Karl Barth, *Church Dogmatics* IV.3.2, ed. G.W. Bromiley and T.F. Torrance (Edinburgh: T&T Clark, 1956–77), 771.

19. *CD* III/2, 229.

20. "Most of our words, spoken or heard, are an inhuman and barbaric affair because we will not speak or listen to one another. We speak them without wanting to seek or help. And we listen to them without letting ourselves be found or helped. . . . What we speak and write and hear and read is propaganda. And the result is that our words are emptied and devalued and become mere words. We live in a constant deflation of the word. Yet we have to realize that suspicion and disillusionment are not the way to improve things either here or anywhere. . . . With suspicion and disillusionment in relation to the word we basically turn our back on humanity. For this reason, although suspicion and disillusionment are no doubt justified in practice, we must not in any circumstances allow them house-room." Ibid., 260.

21. Ibid., 274. The full discussion of these four dimensions of being in encounter may be found in Ibid., 250–85.

22. Kristopher Norris may be correct in his observation that Barth does not explicitly discuss democracy as a set of practices in his systematic writings, but on this question it is Barth's own practice as a citizen and a teacher in the context of a democracy that it particularly illuminating. See Kristopher Norris, "Democracy and Church: Barth and Yoder on Democratic Practice," in this volume.

23. Bernhard Fulda, *Press and Politics in the Weimar Republic* (Oxford: Oxford University Press, 2009), 169. The political environment was so volatile that President Hindenburg tried to diffuse the situation by ordering a political cease fire for Christmas 1931. Hindenburg's "Schutz des inneren Friedens" forbade all public political gatherings, posters, flyers, and pamphlets from December 10, 1931, to January 3, 1932. Barth refers to the ceasefire in his Christmas meditation published in a Munich newspaper in 1931. See Karl Barth, *Gesamtausgabe*, ed. Hinrich Stoevesandt and Hans Anton Drewes (Zürich: Theologischer Verlag, 1971), V.I.8, 632.

24. Diana Mutz notes that the dense homogenous political networks characteristic of late Weimar did not support the practice of "crosscutting" dialogue, that is, conversation with those holding contrasting views. Diana C. Mutz, *Hearing the Other Side:*

Deliberative versus Participatory Democracy (Cambridge: Cambridge University Press, 2006), 134.

25. Barth describes his open evenings in May of 1924 in a letter to Thurneysen, noting that they had read the political autobiographies of Alfred von Tirpitz und Karl Liebknecht, and would continue with Georg Michaelis, the Kaiser, Philipp Scheidemann, the Crown Prince, Erich Ludendorff, Theobald von Bethmann-Hollweg, and Matthias Erzberger. Barth explained that he encouraged the students to question the motives behind the actions of the various politicians, and to explore their political relationship to one another. Barth, *Gesamtausgabe*, V.4, 252.

26. Eberhard Busch, *Karl Barth: His Life from Letters and Autobiographical Texts* (Philadelphia: Fortress Press, 1976), 203. Barth, *Gesamtausgabe*, V.34, 47–48.

27. We also see evidence of this commitment to conversation with congregants about public issues in Barth's practice as a parish pastor in Safenwil: he held evening classes for working women and men on issues related to the labor movement and social democratic policy and hosted a book group on "Socialism and the Social Movement" in the manse. Frank Jehle, *Ever against the Stream: The Politics of Karl Barth, 1906–1968* (Grand Rapids: Eerdmans, 2002), 30.

28. Dietrich Bonhoeffer quoted in Busch, *Karl Barth*, 215.

29. Karl Barth, *Protestant Theology in the Nineteenth Century: Its Background and History*, new ed. (Grand Rapids: Eerdmans, 2002), 3.

30. Ibid.

31. Ibid.

32. Ibid., 10.

33. *CD* IV/3.2, 472–473.

34. Paul Tillich, quoted in "Preface to the First Edition" of Barth, *Protestant Theology*, ix. Lest we dismiss the relevance of these lectures to the task at hand because they focus on the interpretation of the ideas of the dead, it is critical to remember that for Barth, these theologians are not dead—"they still speak and demand a hearing as living voices. . . ." Barth, *Protestant Theology*, 3. The ethos Barth advocates in this particular classroom has implications for engagement with all others, living and dead.

35. Nicholas Wolterstorff, *The Mighty and the Almighty: An Essay in Political Theology* (Cambridge: Cambridge University Press, 2012), 110.

36. Mutz, *Hearing the Other Side*, 51.

37. Ibid., 138. This is not to suggest that no deliberation occurs at all: denominations publish position papers that usually emerge from a deliberative process, albeit a high-level one. There are also clergy-driven conversations about public issues in local congregations that can include "crosscutting" dialogue. Sometimes these are designed to convert participants to the minister's point of view, sometimes to mobilize a congregation for political action, sometimes to educate about an issue more generally, and sometimes such forums are a strategy for crisis management in the aftermath of a controversial vote or incident. What these sorts of events have in common is their occasional (v. sustained) nature.

38. Ibid., 139. Americans have abundant options when it comes to choosing a church community, making it more likely "church shoppers" can find a congregation

of like-minded others if they so desire. For an account of how this robust religious diversity emerged in the American context, see Nathan O. Hatch, *The Democratization of American Christianity* (New Haven: Yale University Press, 1991).

39. The consequences of open disagreement are all too visible in recent years in the Protestant mainline in the United States, as debates over sexuality, Israel, and so on have led to a mass exodus by conservative Presbyterians, Episcopalians, and Lutherans, with others threatening similar actions in other denominations. The message: disagreement about public issues = the loss of members, money, and (at least the appearance of) harmony. Why risk it at the local level?

40. In his study of the Christian Right, Jon Shields explains that religious leaders in the movement have little interest in instilling a deliberative ethos because strident appeals are more effective in rousing and mobilizing activists. They do not encourage activists to question their own assumptions. There is, however, a widespread embrace of an ethos of civility in public forums, but Shields notes that this embrace is strategic, not ethical: stridency does make for good press. Jon A. Shields, *The Democratic Virtues of the Christian Right* (Princeton: Princeton University Press, 2009), 15–25.

41. Texts regularly invoked include: Eph. 4:12–13 (equipping the saints), 1 John 4:1 (test the spirits), Jer. 29:7 (seek the welfare of the city), Rom. 12:17–18 (live peaceably with all), Phil. 2:2–14 (look not to your own interests), and the stories of Joseph, Daniel, and Esther.

42. Franklin I. Gamwell, *Politics as a Christian Vocation: Faith and Democracy Today* (Cambridge: Cambridge University Press, 2005), 9.

43. Stout, *Democracy and Tradition*, 11.

44. Ephraim Radner, *A Brutal Unity: The Spiritual Politics of the Christian Church* (Waco: Baylor University Press, 2012), 214–16.

45. Kathryn Tanner, *Theories of Culture: A New Agenda for Theology* (Minneapolis: Fortress Press, 1997), 154–55.

46. Peter J. Thuesen describes the pervasiveness of this dynamic in the context of mainline Protestantism in the second half of the twentieth century and beyond, noting "an enduring rift, confirmed by sociological studies, between a generally liberal socially conscious clergy and a more politically and socially conservative laity." Peter Thuesen, "The Logic of Mainline Churchliness," in *The Quiet Hand of God: Faith-Based Activism and the Public Role of Mainline Protestantism*, ed. Robert Wuthnow and John H. Evans (Berkeley: University of California Press, 2002), 46.

47. In his study on moral deliberation in congregations, Brent Coffin found that Protestant clergy exercised four kinds of authority in relation to the practice of deliberation: moral authority (by virtue of office and to the degree they embodied the community's values), invitational authority (deciding which voices to include and which issues to discuss), convening authority (deciding to gather group[s] for deliberation), and constraining authority (intervening to prevent certain activities). Brent Coffin, "Moral Deliberation in Congregations," in *Taking Faith Seriously*, ed. Mary Jo Bane, Brent Coffin, and Richard Higgins (Cambridge: Harvard University Press, 2005), 133–34.

48. This is not to say that lay leaders cannot and should not play a similar role, indeed some laypeople may bring superior deliberative skills to the table. A wise pastor will play a supporting role in such cases.

49. Iris Marion Young, "Communication and the Other: Beyond Deliberative Democracy," in *Democracy and Difference: Contesting the Boundaries of the Political*, ed. Seyla Benhabib (Princeton: Princeton University Press, 1996), 129–32.

50. Jeffrey Stout argues that this kind of "internal" practice is critical in relation to "external" performance: "The discursive exchange essential to democracy is likely to thrive only when individuals identify to some significant extent with a community of reason-givers." Stout, *Democracy and Tradition*, 293.

51. Markus Höfner, "Neither Self-Evident Frame nor Self-Enclosed Sect: The Christian Church in Barth's Political Ecclesiology," in this volume.

Chapter 16

"Gleichnis wagen"[1]

Karl Barth's Political Theology and Its Meaning for the Church-State Relationship in Mainland China Today[2]

Thomas Xutong Qu (瞿旭彤)

PRELIMINARY REMARKS AND OUTLINE

Karl Barth is indeed a theological giant. He is not, however, a quasi-religious founder of a theological school and should not be followed without being questioned and criticized. His theology, especially his political theology, offers important insights, but also exhibits significant limits.[3]

First, we will clarify the term "political theology" as used in this chapter.[4] Compared to descriptions such as "political ethics," "social ethics," and "theological ethics,"[5] the term "political theology" indicates that we will be talking primarily about theology. As such, we will be discussing Barth's political theology as consequence, explication, and application of his theological principles in a concrete political situation.[6]

Barth is a theologian and remains a theologian even when he speaks about politics and acts as a political person. This theological perspective is also consistent with his famous christological concentration on the so-called theological "matter" ("Sache").[7]

Based on my dissertation about Barth's reception of Goethe's writings,[8] this essay will focus on a significant concept of Barth's theology, namely, the concept of "Gleichnis." We do this in order to understand and expound his political theology and, especially, his understanding of the church-state relationship with its meaning for the current situation in Mainland China.

Unfortunately, the German term "Gleichnis" can only be partly translated into English as "parable," "analogy," or "allegory."[9] The first section of this chapter will give an account of Barth's trinitarian and dialectical understanding of "Gleichnis." This is based on a reading of his influential lecture "The Christian's Place in the Society" in 1919. The second section will focus on Barth's understanding of the church-state relationship with the help of the concept of "Gleichnis" in one of his most important and comprehensive political-theological texts: the "Christian Community and Civil Community" lecture of 1946.[10] The third section will then describe three representative ideal types of the church-state relationship concerning protestant churches in Mainland China. Some basic critiques and preliminary proposals from the viewpoint of Barth's political theology will also be provided.

BARTH'S TRINITARIAN AND DIALECTICAL UNDERSTANDING OF "GLEICHNIS"[11]

"The Christian's Place in Society" lecture of 1919 is one of the most important texts of Barth's political theology. It marks the beginning of his theological influence in Germany. This lecture, given at a conference of religious socialists in the small town of Tambach in northern Germany, transformed the nearly unknown young country pastor from Switzerland into a well-known and influential theologian in German church and theological circles (2).[12] According to Eberhard Busch, this lecture has "in a nutshell many thoughts, which Barth has elaborated then in the coming years."[13] It is also the case with respect to Barth's concept of "Gleichnis."

In this lecture, Barth mentioned the name of Goethe explicitly only two times (27), and cited Goethe's verse implicitly at least seven times (4, 5, 7, 14f., 24). Among these implicit citations, the most significant one is "Noch deutlicher aber auch: Alles Vergängliche ist *nur* ein Gleichnis" (24). This verse is one of Barth's favorite Goethe citations and comes from Goethe's masterpiece *Faust*.[14] Translated literally into English it means: "Everything perishable is only a parable."[15]

This citation is found in the third section of the lecture. However, it is in the major part of the lecture, sections three through five, that Barth describes the so-called "priestly movement" of Christians in society from three viewpoints: creation, redemption, and fulfillment. Stated another way, Barth's description comes from the three dimensions of the Kingdom of God: *regnum naturae*, *regnum gratiae*, and *regnum gloriae*. In this kingdom, Jesus Christ is the same yesterday, today, and for all eternity (Heb. 13:8).[16] This description can be reconstructed with the help of a threefold accentuation of the above-mentioned Goethe citation.[17] Doing so also allows us to explore Barth's understanding of the church-state relationship.

Everything Perishable *IS* only a "Gleichnis"

This accentuation on thc copula "is" implicates the so-called *analogia entis* in the Barthian sense and correspondingly his liberal theological phase. One of the most important examples is his first commentary on the Epistles to the Romans (1918) with the emphasis on unity or identity—for instance, the identification between the eternal spirit and the biblical spirit.[18]

In the third section of "The Christian's Place in Society," Barth acknowledges that the "priestly movement" of the Christians is an affirmation of life and the world from the viewpoint of creation. The movement wants to "see the imperishable in the 'Gleichnis' of the perishable" (24).

God is the creator of human beings and the world. He has created everything by and for Jesus Christ (Col 1:16). With the help of the accentuation on "is," we come to the point concerning the possibility and the qualification of the life and the world. Everything in this world, everything both natural and human, is perishable and even absolutely in vain, but not totally unimportant (21).

Although the world is fallen, God is still, and remains always, the creator of this fallen world. In the kingdom of nature, everything perishable is a "Gleichnis," which points to something imperishable. In worldly things, we can recognize the analogy of the divine. These worldly things do not remain by themselves, but point to the original creation of God and the original, immediate relationship with God. The perishable has therefore the original possibility of knowing the imperishable.

Concerning the political attitude of Christians in society,[19] Barth claims that they are not allowed to escape from the world and society. They should therefore practice their "grateful, smiling and understanding patience" (22).

Everything Perishable is *ONLY* a "Gleichnis"

This accentuation on the adverb "only" emphasizes that it is impossible for the perishable to know the imperishable from the viewpoint of redemption. It implicates the dialectical phase of Barth's theological development. An example of this is his second commentary on the Epistles to the Romans (1921) with the emphasis on the difference or diastase that appears in "the infinite qualitative difference" between God and human beings.[20]

In the lecture's fourth section, Barth changes his viewpoint from the kingdom of nature to the kingdom of grace. From this viewpoint, God is not only the creator but also the redeemer. He has redeemed human beings, and brought them into the kingdom of his beloved son, "where in Christ the whole life is problematic, precarious, and full of promise" (29, cf. Col 1:13).

From this viewpoint, everything perishable is for Barth *ONLY* a "Gleichnis." The imperishable lets itself be seen in the "Gleichnis" of the perishable. But it also hides itself through the "Gleichnis." The perishable, for example the human action, is a "Gleichnis," which stays in analogy to the divine action, but is not in continuity with it. This is because the "Gleichnis" is not the thing itself, to which the "Gleichnis" points. We should not "confuse the 'Gleichnis' with the thing" (28).

In this confusion of the perishable and the imperishable, Barth has seen the essential reason for the wrong and even dangerous ways of the different human actions.[21] Christians should therefore turn away from the confirmation of the world and see in the perishable only a "Gleichnis." They should go further with the movement of God and in so doing go "from defense to attack, from yes to no, from naivety to critique on the society" (31). For the purposes of this chapter, this critique will also be applied to both the church and the state.

Everything Perishable is only a "Gleichnis" *[OF THE IMPERISHABLE]*

This accentuation emphasizes that the imperishable can and will let the perishable know itself from the viewpoint of fulfillment. It implicates the church-dogmatic phase of Barth's theology. Examples in his works include his understanding of *analogie fidei* and his teachings about lights in *Church Dogmatics* (1932ff.).

Neither the confirmation nor the critique is for Barth the ultimate and proper attitude for Christians in society. From the third and last viewpoint of fulfillment, Barth speaks in the fifth and last part of his lecture about "the *totally* other of the kingdom" of God, which is the kingdom of glory (33).

Only in God and his fulfillment for all eternity, the synthesis between the confirmation and the critique could be found, so that both of them could be placed in proper relation to each other. Therefore, the only action the Christian in society could take is "to follow attentively what is done by God" (37). This is for Barth the whole "priestly movement" of the Christian in society from the viewpoint of fulfillment.[22]

With respect to this aspect of the eternal, the accentuation of the Goethe citation lies now on the missing *genitivus sujectivus*, namely, "the imperishable." The absence of this subjective genitive implies that the imperishable is not only other than "what we suggest with our thought, speech and action in 'Gleichnissen'" [from the viewpoint of creation] or "which appearance we, tired of 'Gleichnisse,' wish for us" [from the viewpoint of redemption]. "There is no continuity from the analogies to the divine reality" (33f.).

Only in God could the synthesis between the thesis and the antithesis be found in the fulfillment of the promise suggested by the confirmation of the "Gleichnis" and sought by the negation of the "Gleichnis." All of which leads to the idea that the church and the state can find their respective places in relation to each other but only through the synthesis of God himself in his coming kingdom.

Some Philosophical-Theological Dimensions of the Concept of "Gleichnis"

Based on this reading of "The Christian's Place in Society," which counts as one of the birthplaces of Barth's thought about "Gleichnis,"[23] we will now sketch some crucial dimensions of this concept from a philosophical-theological viewpoint.[24]

First, "Gleichnis" means a kind of *comparison* ("Vergleich") between human beings and God. The referential point of comparison is Jesus Christ in the *eschatological* horizon (Hebr 13:8) from the above-mentioned trinitarian perspective. In this sense, the concept of "Gleichnis" is basically a *christological* one. Only in this christological and eschatological horizon can we understand the starting point of Barth's concept of "Gleichnis."

Second, this concept also implies that the perishable has an *ontological* relationship to the imperishable, and is therefore different from the concept of sign. This corresponds with Barth's so-called actualism. A "Gleichnis" originates contingently and unexpectedly from the grace of God, and should be given or should become a "Gleichnis" again and again, here and now (namely, "Gleichnis" as event [Ereignis]).[25] In this sense, a "Gleichnis" is different from symbol. Moreover, a "Gleichnis" is much more than a language event, and therefore different from the concept of metaphor.

Third, the concept of "Gleichnis" has a *hermeneutical* dimension as well. It both destructs and constructs. The *destructive* dimension can be understood with the help of Heidegger's critique of traditional metaphysics or with the help of the negative theological tradition. For example, if one might say of the human "Gleichnis" that humanity's knowledge and thoughts about God are, in fact, incorrect and have obstructed humanity's proper knowledge of God.

For Barth, the *constructive* moment is to be found only in God himself. What we should do is become an indication or witness of God and his revelation in Jesus Christ, even in very tough political situations.

The fourth dimension is the *deictic or referential* moment of a "Gleichnis."[26] This moment implies a "Gleichnis" should not remain by itself and for itself, but point to another thing. It relates to Barth's so-called theological thing, namely, God's (self-) revelation to human beings and the world through Jesus Christ.

In order to describe this relationship of "Gleichnis" to the theological thing, Barth uses at least two concepts in different theological contexts. One is the concept of *reminder* and the other is the concept of *witness*. As reminder or witness, a "Gleichnis" should play an exemplary role.[27] As relates to Barth's understanding of the church and the state, we can say in advance: Every human existence and form, including both the church and the state, is or should become a "Gleichnis" of the kingdom of God. And, for Barth, this means the kingdom of Jesus Christ. As a witness of God's revelation in Jesus Christ, the church should become exemplary and remind the state of the kingdom of Jesus Christ.

"CHRISTIAN COMMUNITY AND CIVIL COMMUNITY" (1946)[28]

Among Barth's writings about politics, this lecture is the most famous and comprehensive.[29] According to Barth himself, this lecture is actually a detailed explication of Thesis 5 of the Barmen Theological Declaration of 1934.[30] Barth has mentioned this thesis explicitly six times in the lecture (92, 97, 98, 103, 111, and 136).[31] At the end, he cites this thesis and states that he has delivered his lecture in the sense of Barmen V and therefore also in the tradition of the Confessing Church (136).[32]

Before taking up the main topic of this article, we need to describe the reconstructed picture[33] of Barth's understanding of the relationship between the church and the state as offered by Oscar Cullmann (cf. 96).[34] The church and the state form two concentric circles (cf. 96 and 112): the church is the interior circle. The essential task of the church is to live out the Christian faith and to preach the name of Jesus Christ to all humankind. The state is the external circle. Its essential task is to ensure freedom, peace, and humanity (cf. 90, 97, 102 and 108). Jesus Christ is their common center, principle, and origin. This differs from the neo-platonic-theological tradition after Augustine (cf. 89).[35] For Barth, there are not two kingdoms, only one kingship of Jesus Christ with two regimes, namely, the church and the state.[36]

With this basic idea we come to the fourteenth section of the "Christian Community and Civil Community." For Herbert Lindenlauf, this section is "the center of the whole lecture," since Barth introduces the criterion of the knowledge and action of his political ethics.[37] For the well-known Lutheran theologian Oswald Bayer, this same section is the "most important" and "the systematic foundation" of the lecture, since it is here that we find not only "the constituting principle"[38] of this classic political-theological text, but "of the whole theology of Barth."[39]

Upon examination, however, this political-ethical criterion, or the constituting principle is not the concept of analogy, as suggested by Lindenlauf, Bayer, and many other scholars,[40] but rather the concept of "Gleichnis."[41]

With the help of the concept of "Gleichnis," Barth provides in this fourteenth section (112–115) a clear description of the essence of politics as it relates to the church and to the kingdom of God. The state should become "a *'Gleichnis,'* a correspondence, an analogy to the kingdom of God, which is believed in the church and preached by the church" (112; cf. the church as a "Gleichnis," 114). But what is the layered meaning of "Gleichnis" when applied to the essence of politics and its relationship to the church and to the kingdom of God? Using the fourteenth section, with reference to other sections as well, we will analyze and explore its multifaceted meanings.

To clarify at the outset, "Gleichnis" doesn't mean *"Gleichung"* (112). It doesn't mean identification or identity. By accentuating the passage from Goethe ("Everything perishable is *ONLY* a 'Gleichnis'"), the emphasis is on the difference in a united identity. As viewed within the first dimension of "Gleichnis" mentioned earlier, the state is ontologically or substantially different from the church and from the kingdom of God.

As an instrument against the sin of human beings,[42] the state is the graceful decree ("Anordnung") of God on the behalf of human beings in a christological and eschatological horizon (96, 98, 106, 108, and 112).[43] In this sense, the state is for Barth a practical and necessary legal order to ensure freedom, peace, and humanity.[44] The state should also, in Barth's view, implement the classical principle of the separation of the three (legislative, administrative, and judicial) powers (cf. 90f.).[45]

The state is neither subordinate to the church, nor the duplicate of the church in the political area (102). As a legal order, the state doesn't have its own autonomous laws ("Eigengesetzlichkeit"), because it is still within the circle of the kingship of Jesus Christ (97, 112). Compared with the church, the state is "spiritually blind and ignorant" with respect to the kingdom of God and its own origin, center and principle (91, cf. 99).

Moreover, the state should not be confused with the kingdom of God,[46] and the church should not take any political concept of the state, even when it is a democratic one,[47] as the only true Christian concept against all others. The church should only believe in and obey the word of God in Jesus Christ and not believe in or obey any political form or political reality (102f.). This is the hermeneutical, destructive dimension of the concept of "Gleichnis."

"Gleichnis" doesn't mean *"Ungleichung,"* or difference, either (112). With the help of another accentuation of the Goethe passage: "Everything perishable is a 'Gleichnis' *[OF THE IMPERISHABLE].*" Barth emphasizes here both unity and difference. As noted earlier, as there is only one kingship of Jesus Christ, there is no absolute difference, but rather an eschatological and ontological difference in unity between the church and the state, on the one hand, and between them and the kingdom of God, on the other.

This is one of the important reasons[48] why Christian community (church) and civil community (state) have the same name: "community."[49] The same name indicates the positive and constructive relationship between them, while both of them relate themselves primarily not to institutions and offices, but to concrete human beings in a common concrete community ("in einem gemeinen Wesen," cf. 89f. and 93f.). The existence of the church is therefore "highly political" and has "highly political" significance.

For Barth, there is no "apolitical" existence of the church, especially with reference to the kingdom of Jesus Christ, namely the "polis," which is essentially political and established by God and coming from heaven to earth (94, 98, and 131). This is the above-mentioned eschatological horizon and the constructive dimension of Barth's political theology. In this horizon, there is neither an eternal church (94)[50] nor an eternal state (cf. 111), but only the one eternal kingdom of Jesus Christ (95). Consequently, in keeping with the destructive dimension of "Gleichnis," the church should not become a theocracy.[51] Likewise, the state should not become a church as a political religious system or church-state (102, 108, and 109).[52]

The third dimension of "Gleichnis" means the "*Gleichnisfähigkeit*" (112f.). That is, the state can become a "Gleichnis" of the kingdom of God and reflect the Christian truth and reality indirectly. However, this reflection should not be taken for granted. It is not given once and for all like an ontological necessity, but always in an ontic way endangered and questionable. In this context, if someone talks about the legitimacy of the state, it perhaps wouldn't be consistent with Barth's theological intention. He never provided any legitimation for any form of the state. For him, the existence of the state, as we already said, is only a contingent and practical necessity, but not an ontological necessity. [53]

The fourth dimension shows that the state as "Gleichnis" has a kind of "*Gleichnisbedürtigkeit*" (113). That means: the state needs to be formed and transformed into a "Gleichnis" of the kingdom of God,[54] because it doesn't know its own origin or center and its intrinsic goal or task. The state cannot remind itself of its own principles by an appeal to a natural right.[55] Therefore, the state is dependent on the church.[56] The state should be *reminded* by the church because the church knows what the essence of the state is and what the state should do (cf. 95, 110).

As we have already analyzed, the church itself is, for Barth, not the kingdom of God, but instead knows this kingdom (110f.). The church must remain a church (98, 134), and preach the kingship of Jesus Christ and the hope of the coming kingdom of God (99).[57] In relation to the state, it is crucial for the church to provide an orientation and guideline to be recognized and adhered to in every circumstance (105, 112 cf. 125).[58]

The church should also *distinguish* the just state from the unjust state. It should engage itself to implement the constitutional state ("Rechtsstaat") and social justice but avoid siding with anarchy, tyranny, or the totalitarian state (104, 116, and 118). In accordance with the distinguishing and engaging actions, the church should (from case to case and from situation to situation) make concrete *judgments* on questions concerning the foundation, maintenance, and implementation of the order of the state (104) that touch on the guarantee of freedom for every citizen. This orientation and guideline, however, doesn't come from a so-called natural right (105f, cf. 126) (or from the popular vocabulary of the moment: human rights, human freedoms, or human dignity, etc.),[59] but from the "dei providential hominum confusion" (namely, "the providence of God and the human confusion," 105–107).

By taking up this orientating and guiding role, the church becomes a *deictic or referential* witness of the kingdom of God, with engagement not only in word but also in deed.[60] The "implicit, indirect, but none the less real" witness of the church is for Barth "its political action" (114)[61] because the church demonstrates as, an engaging witness, its political responsibility and solidarity and provides a help to the transformation of the state into a "Gleichnis" of the kingdom of God (cf. 113f. and 135).

The church itself must also dare to become a "Gleichnis" of this kingdom again and again, here and now.[62] In this sense, the existence of the church is exemplary for the state, that is to say, its existence is the source of the renewal of the state and also the preserving power of the state.[63] For Barth, this exemplary existence is perhaps the most decisive contribution of the church to the construction of the state (133).[64]

THREE REPRESENTATIVE IDEAL TYPES OF THE CHURCH-STATE RELATIONSHIP IN MAINLAND CHINA AND THE MEANING OF BARTH'S POLITICAL THEOLOGY

Now, we turn to deal with the church-state relationship in Mainland China today.

A Preliminary Analysis of the Situation in Mainland China in a Postcolonial and Globalizing Context

Mainland China is full of complexities, inconsistencies, and even contradictions. Many of the more than 1.3 billion people in Mainland China are living neither at the same time nor in the same world as their fellow citizens. China was and is a continent in itself, and is actually on its way to becoming a modern nation- or civilization-state (or, perhaps, to find its own unique cultural and political form).

For more than a thousand years, "the Middle Kingdom" was culturally and economically one of the leading countries in the world. It was only in the last 200 years, beginning with the opium war with the British Empire in 1840, that the largely agrarian China was endlessly attacked and exploited by different industrialized and imperialistic nations. The enormous contrast between ancient glory and modern humiliation has been very influential to the formation of the Chinese mentality today.

After decades of struggle the colonialists and their local collaborators were defeated. This led to the independence and sovereignty of the Chinese people. The peace and development that followed was brought about by the Chinese Communist Party (CCP) after the People's Republic of China was founded in 1949.

With the ever-present memories of China's ancient glory and modern humiliation operating in China's consciousness, the CCP endeavors to make China a "wealthy, democratic, civilized and socialist modern country." These have been the central goals of successive Chinese leaders since Deng Xiaoping started the economic reforms of the late 1970s. In this context, the CCP regime should not be seen as a dictatorship. Instead, the common political conception of the CCP is that it is an elitist and authoritarian regime.

The long history of China, when taken into account, finds the CCP regime to be most like an imperial dynasty with its pragmatic practices but in a time of post-colonialism and rapid globalization rather than in ancient times. Furthermore, Mainland China is now at a time of profound transition and transformation. It also faces serious problems: social injustice, environmental pollution (e.g., air and water), and so on, which would be daunting tasks even in relatively stable times.

Within this highly complex historical constellation, the various iterations of the church in Mainland China can be seen as colors on a huge spectrum. No one sees all the colors at once. In what follows, we will only discuss three representative ideal types of the protestant churches in Mainland China. This will only include their theological understanding of the church-state relation-ship[65] and will not deal the many other understandings, political or cultural, that differentiate the three.

"The Three-Self Patriotic Movement of the Protestant Church"

The "Three-Self Patriotic Movement" movement originated theologically primarily from the liberal stream of Chinese Christianity. It is somewhat similar to the religious socialists of Western Europe with whom Barth was associated for some time.

This movement was established in 1954 immediately after the Korean War and was directed against the United States and its allies. Within this politically motivated anti-American or anti-Western context, "three-self" means self-governance (independent from the governance of foreign missionaries and denominations); self-support (financial independence from foreigners); and self-preaching (indigenous missionary work without the foreigners).

For this type of Chinese Christian, the legality of the CCP regime comes from its legitimacy as mentioned earlier in the Party's historical contributions and achievements.[66] In socialism and the CCP, these Christians, or some part of them, see the hope of an independent and modern China. In the postcolonial context, this partially explains why the movement wants to cooperate with the regime and pursue a so-called "accommodation into the socialist society." For this movement, this means there is at least a certain anticipation of the kingdom of God.

The Politically Engaged Christians

However, for politically engaged Christians, particularly during the past few years, the CCP may be (more or less) legal, but it has either lost, or never really had, any legitimacy. In the context of globalization, especially as compared to the western developed and democratic nations, most of which have a strong Christian tradition, the CCP and the Chinese political system are seen as the fount of all of China's problems be it corruption, social injustice, environmental pollution, and so on. Democratically active, these Christians often criticize the regime in private but also in public (for example, on the Chinese Twitter—Weibo). Some of them even try to overturn the regime whenever possible.

The Apolitical Mainstream

Distinct from these two politically engaged groups, mainstream Chinese Christians have very little interest in politics, the state or the CCP. For them, personal evangelization and the redemption of the soul are the most important factors of genuine Christian life. A Christian of this type emphatically practices a moral and faithful life, and tries to improve his or her personal relationship with the Lord Jesus Christ. A significant example for this theological emphasis is the Chinese translation of the word for "peace": "ping'an." This translation connotes a personal interior peace much more than social and political peace. (Barth, on the contrary, would have the word "peace" connote social and political peace.) These Christians come mostly from the evangelical and fundamental traditions and are highly indifferent to politics.

Basic Critiques and Preliminary Proposals from the Viewpoint of Barth's Political Theology

Based on the concept of "Gleichnis," we have sketched Barth's basic understanding of the relationship between the church and the state in the christological and eschatological horizon of the kingdom of God. Both the church and the state should be understood as "Gleichnis" of the kingdom of God. Concerning the three representative ideal types of the protestant churches in Mainland China and their different attitudes toward politics and the state, we conclude this chapter with some basic critiques and preliminary proposals from the viewpoint of Barth's political theology.

First, a church may try to accommodate itself to a certain political system and even pin its hopes on the state and its system much like the Three-Self Patriotic Movement of the Protestant Church in China does. This church tends to see a utopian ideal society, envisioned in the CCP regime, as (at least partly) a "Gleichnis" of the Christian eschatological hope for the kingdom of God. In this case, Barth would remind us that any utopian ideal society is *only* a "Gleichnis." We should not confuse this society with the kingdom of God, which should be believed in the church and preached by the church. Consequently, this church should not become an institutional organ of the state and lose its Christian identity. The church should also keep a critical distance from the state or the regime and try to become a church again and again. It should return to its own task which is to preach the Gospel of God and to hope for the coming kingdom of God. The state is no substitute for the kingdom of God. The state cannot act to provide the orientation and guidelines for the church. The church itself should become a "Gleichnis" of the kingdom of God, and remind the state of its essence and task to ensure freedom, peace, and humanity.

Second, a church may want to advocate a political concept. And politically engaged Christians in China try to do this. But even if the political concept is a democratic one, a church should not identify the democratic concept as the only Christian concept of the kingdom of God. This confuses the possible instrument with the essential end. Barth would admit the affinity between democracy and the Christian political orientation and guideline. However, he would still remind us that the democratic concept is only a "Gleichnis" of the kingdom of God.[67]

Third, the apolitical mainstream Christians in China want nothing to do with politics. This church escapes from political life and abandons its political responsibility for, and solidarity with, society. The church in China, avowedly apolitical or not, is actually highly political. This is not only because of its essence as a "Gleichnis" of the kingdom of God which, as noted earlier, is highly political, but also because of the historical and current context in Mainland China. For example, in China's history, many religious faiths and practices, including Christianity, have been instrumentalized as tools to overturn the ruling dynasties. The different dynasties in Chinese history have tended to be on guard against any religious group with a considerable number of believers. The CCP regime has a similar concern about the great number of Chinese Christian believers.[68] Moreover, because of China's humiliating history of foreign subjugation, the CCP and many ordinary Chinese citizens have a suspicious and even hostile attitude to the Christian church. It is for these reasons that mainstream Chinese Christians must face their political situation directly and reflect honestly and deeply their political responsibility for, and solidarity with, the larger Chinese society.

The political responsibility and solidarity of Chinese Christians requires them to not only become a good, politically engaged citizen but also to be exemplary in word and deed in order to change the suspicious and hostile attitudes toward the Christian church in China. Moreover, they should become a church with its political manifestation in the public sphere. However, since the CCP's religious policy needs to be developed, the Christian church should also find pragmatic and realistic ways to act politically, but not in direct contradiction to the regime.

Recently in Chinese intellectual circles, disputes have arisen about the role of the church in Mainland China. Should the church criticize the regime as the *prophets* did in the Old Testament? Should the church even try to overturn the regime by *revolutionary* means? Should the church take a part in the modernization of China as *servant* of the people and the country? Should the church play the role of a *consultant* for the regime in different issues concerning the further development of China?

From the viewpoint of Barth's political theology, the church should first become a church and above all develop a critical relationship with the state. The church should have its own judgment concerning the orientation and guidelines of the state and also remind the state of its genuine and essential goals and tasks. If there is direct conflict with the Christian hope of the kingdom of God coming from a state program, the church should speak out. Constructively, the church should be subordinate to the state and its legal order but dare to become a true witness of the kingdom of God and show its exemplary existence in word and deed for the benefit of the state. It is in this way that the church can provide the state with the correct orientation and guidance to achieve freedom, peace, and justice for the Chinese people.

NOTES

1. Karl Barth, "Christengemeinde und Bürgergemeinde," in: ders., *Texte zur Barmer Theologischen Erklärung*, mit einer Einleitung von Eberhard Jüngel und

einem Editionsbericht hrsg. von Martin Rohkrämer (Zürich: Theologischer Verlag, 1984 [1946]), 89–136, 121.

2. This article is a revised version of my presentation at the Second Symposium of International Research Conference "Theo-Politics? Conversing with Barth in Western and Asian Contexts," March 13–16, 2014, in Bochum, Germany. I am grateful for the insightful and critical comments of the participant scholars, especially Kristopher Norris.

3. For the "conceptual limits" and "some lasting impulse" concerning Barth's political theology, cf. Günter Thomas, "Karl Barth's Political Theology: Contours, Lines of Development of Future Perspectives" in Dogmatics after Barth: Facing Challenges in Church, Society and the Academy, ed. Günter Thomas, Rinse H. Reeling Brouwer, and Bruce McCormack (CreateSpace Independent Publishing Platform, 2012), 181–197. 182f.

4. For Günter Thomas ("Political Theology," 181), Barth's political theology could be regarded "as a key subject area in the international discourse inspired by his theology."

However, the term as used in this chapter is different from Gerald A. Butler's conception of Barth's political theology. Butler's view comes from a different aspect, namely, the aspect of the hermeneutical role of the sociopolitical reality in Barth's life and work. As Butler has correctly stated, "Barth chose to keep socio-political reality under the firm control of his own focus and norm," Gerald A. Butler, "Karl Barth and Political Theology," *Scottish Journal of Theology* 27 (1974): 441–458, 458. Similarly, Karl Barth's theology in its reception by the so-called "Sino-Theology" in China has been interpreted as a public theology which could be compatible with Chinese thought; see further Chin Ken-pa, "Sino-Theology as Public Theology: The Reception of Karl Barth's Theology and Its Signification in the Chinese Context," in this volume.

5. Jürgen Moltmann has used the specific term "christocratic ethics," in *Ethik der Hoffnung* (Gütersloh: Gütersloher Verlagshaus, 210), 40.

6. Cf. Thomas, "Political Theology," 186: "I take as my methodological starting point Barth's own opinion that ethics, and thus also a political theology, are inseparably connected with, and indeed rooted in, theological dogmatics." With reference to the lecture "Christian Community and Civil Community," "So wird nunmehr deutlicher als zuvor, daß es sich in der 'Lehre' von der Herrschaft Christi nicht um eine christliche Staatslehre, sondern einzig um die theologische Explikation eines Bekenntnisinhaltes handeln kann," as Herbert Lindenlauf writes in his book *Karl Barth und die Lehre von der "Königsherrschaft Christi." Eine Untersuchung zum christozentrischen Ansatz der Ethik des Politischen im deutschsprachigen Protestantismus nach 1934* (Spardorf: René F. Wilfer, 1988), 218.

7. In other words, when we deal with Barth's political theology, we should speak first of his words about the theological matter (Wort zur Sache) and then of his words about concrete political situations (Wort zur Lage).

8. Cf. Thomas Xutong Qu, *Barth und Goethe. Die Goethe Rezeption Karl Barths 1906–1921* (Neukirchener-Vluyn: Neukirchener, 2014).

9. It is the reason why we will use this word in German throughout this chapter. For instance, William Werpehowsik ("Karl Barth and Politics," in *The Cambridge Companion to Karl Barth*, ed. John Webster [New York: Cambridge University Press, 2000], 228–242) has translated this word with "allegory" (232) and also "parable" (232, 233).

10. About "a conceptual re-description of the relation between church and state" in Barth's another important political-theological text *Rechtfertigung und Recht* (1938), see Clifford Anderson, "Constitutional Theology: Karl Barth and Carl Schmitt on Legitimacy and the Rule of Law," in this volume.

11. Cf. Qu, *Barth und Goethe*, 189–194.

12. In the first section, the citations without bibliographic detail come from Karl Barth, "Der Christ in der Gesellschaft," in *Anfänge der dialektischen Theologie, Teil I: Karl Barth—Heinrich Barth—Emil Brunner*, hrsg. von Jürgen Moltmann, 2. um einen Anhang erweiterte Auflage (München: Chr. Kaiser, 1966 [1919]), 2–37.

13. Eberhard Busch, *Karl Barths Lebenslauf nach seinen Briefen und autobiographischen Texten*, 4. durchgesehene Auflage (München: Chr. Kaiser, 1986), 123.

14. The following verse is: "Das Unzulängliche, / Hier wird's Ereignis" (The deficient/Here it becomes event), cited from Johann Wolfgang Goethe, *Werke, Band 3: Dramatische Dichtungen I [Faust]*, textkritisch durchgesehen und kommentiert von Erich Trunz (München: Deutscher Taschenbuch Verlag, 1998), 364. It seems to us that the two words in this Goethe citation, namely, "Gleichnis" and "Ereignis," are two crucial concepts to understand the theological thinking of Karl Barth.

15. Cf. Qu, *Barth und Goethe*, 55–58, 189–194, 196–198, and 245f.

16. It should be noted here that the biblical verse from Heb. 13:8 is one of the most cited in Barth's theological works. In this context, we could understand this verse as an important key to interpreting the theological existence of Karl Barth and his theological development.

17. Admittedly, Barth seems to have made no clear distinction between "Gleichnis" and analogy. What we are trying to explore and explain is actually more implicit than explicit in his theological thinking in this lecture. This observation also applies to his 1946 lecture "Christian Community and Civil Community."

18. Cf. Xutong Qu, "Geist und Wort. Die biblisch-hermeneutische Entscheidung Karl Barths aus dem Blickwinkel seiner Goethe-Rezeption 1918–1922," in *Gottes Geist und menschlicher Geist*, hrsg. von Gregor Etzelmüller und Heike Springhart (Leipzig: Evangelische Verlagsanstalt), 81–89, 81–84.

19. It is interesting that Barth talks seldom about the church in society and the state in this lecture.

20. Karl Barth, *Der Römerbrief (Zweite Fassung) 1922*, hrsg. von Cornelis van der Kooi und Katja Tolstaja (Zürich: Theologischer Verlag, 2010), 17; cf. Qu, "Geist und Wort," 84–88.

21. Cf. Barth's critique of the human eagerness is explained in his lecture "Die Grechtigkeit Gottes" (in: ders., *Das Wort Gottes und die Theologie. Gesammelte Vorträge* [München: Chr. Kaiser, 1924, 1916], 5–17, 14f.), since human beings have confused human justice with the justice of God.

22. Therefore, the cited word of Barth shouldn't be understood as the summary of the threefold priestly movement of the Christians, cf. Bruce L. McCormack, *Theologische Dialektik und kritischer Realismus. Entstehung und Entwicklung von Karl Barths Theologie 1909–1936*, aus dem Englischen (1995) übersetzt von Matthias Gockel (Zürich: Theologischer Verlag, 2006), 182f. This suggestion would be confirmed by the question of Barth in the near context, while he emphasizes clearly the viewpoint of fulfillment with italic script: "Because where and when should we cannot know *sub specie aeternitatis*, what is to do?" (Barth, "Der Christ in der Gesellschaft," 37). [The English translation of this passage reads, "After All, why should we not know what to do, *sub specie aeternitatis*?" (p. 68)].

23. Cf. Lindenlauf, *Barth und "Königsherrschaft Christi,"* 228 with footnote 559.

24. We cannot give a detailed explanation of the related concepts, which would go beyond of the frame of this chapter and become another research subject.

25. In this sense, we would ask, whether this concept could be still understood in the framework of the platonic tradition, cf. Oswald Bayer, "[Chapter] III. Karl Barth," in: ders., *Theologie* (Gütersloh: Gütersloher Verlagshaus, 1994), 310–388, 367. Or we should search for another thinker to make a more proper understanding (of course still with reference to the platonic tradition). Perhaps Bayer's possible affinity for the platonic tradition is the reason why he suspects there is a gnostic character to Barth's theology about knowledge (Bayer, "Barth," 366), and criticizes that Barth's conceptions at this point are in need of distinguishing skills (368).

26. See Bayer's analysis about this moment, Bayer, "Barth," 366 and 369f.

27. There may be a temporary, but at the same time eternal, moment of a "Gleichnis." A "Gleichnis" could be dialectical, both successful and unsuccessful, depending on the change of viewpoints.

28. For a detailed and structured analysis of this text from the Christocentric viewpoint, see Lindenlauf, *Barth und "Königsherrschaft Christi,"* 211–264.

29. Cf. Daniel Cornu, *Karl Barth und die Politik. Widerspruch und Freiheit*, aus dem Französischen übersetzt von Rudolf Pfisterer (Wuppertal: Aussaat, 1969), 96; Lindenlauf, *Barth und "Königsherrschaft Christi,"* 211.

30. Cf. Lindenlauf, *Barth und "Königsherrschaft Christi,"* 212; Thomas, "Political Theology," 194.

31. In the second section, the citations without bibliographic details come from Barth, "Christengemeinde und Bürgergemeinde."

32. Cf. Bayer, "Barth," 365.

33. Barth hasn't taken a special part to describe this picture and just uses it through this lecture (for example 96, 97, 98, 112, 133), cf. Bayer, "Barth," 365f; Lindenlauf, *Barth und "Königsherrschaft Christi,"* 218–223.

34. Bayer, "Barth," 365f with footnote 208.

35. Different from "the long shadow of Augustinian theology," the "framework for history is not God's struggle against sin, but the revelation of His fidelity and partnership" (Thomas, "Political Theology," 188).

36. Concerning Barth's dissatisfaction with the Lutheran teaching of two kingdoms, see Daniel Lee, "On Becoming Citizen: Reading Barth in the Midst of Political Change," in this volume.

37. Lindenlauf, *Barth und "Königsherrschaft Christi,"* 226.

38. Bayer uses also another similar expressions such as "das Denken regierende Figur" ("Barth," 368), "Herrschaft des Analogiemodells" (370), or "Schlüsselbegriff der ganzen Theologie" (371).

39. Bayer, "Barth," 365f.

40. Cf. Cornu, *Barth und Politik*, 99; Lindenlauf, *Barth und "Königsherrschaft Christi,"* 226ff. with footnote 547. Bayer has seen the significance and distinctiveness of the concept of "Gleichnis" because for him it is "das Wort, das es Barth erlaubt, Zusammenengehörigkeit und Differenz, Ähnlichkeit und Unähnlichkeit zugleich zu denken" (Bayer, "Barth," 367, and cf. his description of the two moments of "Gleichnis" at 368). However, Bayer seems to have equated this concept with the concept of analogy, and neglected the third trinitarian and dialectical dimension of the "Gleichnis," namely, the moment of identity of difference and identity. This is perhaps the reason why he criticizes Barth's approach—he is starting from a totally different standpoint. His critique of Barth also results perhaps from his Lutheran-theological background and its latent affinity with the classic neo-platonic tradition, which emphasizes unity more than difference and would not allow difference in the sense of postmodern philosophy to be the starting point of metaphysical or ontological thinking.

41. In Barth's political theology, Thomas ("Political Theology," 195) sees a "multifaceted [. . .] model of so-called 'parables,'" which is for him "not fully developed." According to his interpretation, a *performative dimension* means that even in its being, taking and acting, the church should be a parable for God's turning to the world, a sign of the kingdom of God, a 'depiction and parable' (*KD* IV/3, 909) of God's community with humanity. [. . .] In short, the church should not only talk, but work and act as parable—without pretending to be the kingdom of God" (196).

42. About the rule of law as a necessity in a sinful world, see further see Clifford Anderson, "Constitutional Theology: Karl Barth and Carl Schmitt on Legitimacy and the Rule of Law," in this volume.

43. For a different opinion, see Thomas ("Political Theology," 190): "They are completely contingent human invention. In the final analysis, they must be measured by their subservience to human life, not by how they correspond to a supposed natural right elevated to a biblical status."

44. For Barth, it is factually the divine service of the state, although this service would be perverted, cf. Barth, "Christengemeinde und Bürgergemeinde," 97.

45. Jürgen Moltmann has correctly noticed that the foundation of the state as the political community is neither power nor the monopoly of power, but the law or the legal order, *Ethik*, 40.

46. "Essentially, the state is not the kingdom of God and cannot become the kingdom of God" Barth, "Christengemeinde und Bürgergemeinde," 111.

47. However, Barth sees "A Remarkable Affinity" of the Christian political orientation and guideline with the democracy, Barth, "Christengemeinde und Bürgergemeinde," 127f.

48. With reference to the common features of the church and the state, Barth has emphasized the two following aspects. First, both are in "the not yet redeemed world" (cited by Barth from the Barmen V, cf. Barth, "Christengemeinde und Bürgergemeinde," 92). Second, neither of them is the kingdom of God.

49. Barth learned these two terms from the contemporary political and church life in Swiss villages, namely, "die Einwohner-, die Bürger- und die Kirchengemeinde," cf. Barth, "Christengemeinde und Bürgergemeinde," 90. He used the latter two terms for the political community (the state) and the Christian community (the church), cf. Lindenlauf, *Barth und "Königsherrschaft Christi*," 213f. Lindenlauf has expressed correctly that Barth does not advocate here the Swiss political practice as the constitutional form that corresponds best to the gospel.

50. Cf. Cornu, *Barth und Politik*, 97. It signifies for Thomas the temporary character of the church: "The church does not transmit some eternal truth, but—by concentrating on the living Christ—constantly learns in changing social, cultural and political environments," Thomas, "Political Theology," 197.

51. In this sense, we disagree with the following opinion of Ulrich Dannemann (1977, 142): "ebenso hat die statische Zuordnung von Christengemeinde und Bürgergemeinde den Eindruck hinterlassen können, Barth falle in neuer Form in alte theokratische Konzeptionen zurück," *Theologie und Politik im Denken Karl Barths* (München / Mainz: Chr. Kaiser / Matthias-Grünewald-Verlag, 1977), 142; and the statement of Günter Thomas: "In this context, a political theology does not aim at the Christianization of society or at the expansion of the church's direct influence," "Political Theology," 193, cf. 194.

52. Cf. Thomas, "Political Theology," 194.

53. Concerning a different interpretation of two biblical verses about political authority (Rom. 13:1–7 and 1 Pet. 2:13–17), see Clifford Anderson, "Constitutional Theology: Karl Barth and Carl Schmitt on Legitimacy and the Rule of Law," in this volume, especially the following statement: "The legitimacy of secular authority is theological, not political."

54. In this context, Barth emphasizes clearly the important of the history: "Es bedarf immer wieder einer Geschichte, die ihre Gestaltung zum Gleichnis des Reiches Gottes und also die Erfüllung ihrer Gerechtigkeit zum Ziel und Inhalt hat," Barth, "Christengemeinde und Bürgergemeinde," 113; cf. Lindenlauf, *Barth und "Königsherrschaft Christi*," 234. Therefore, we are against Dannemann's critique (*Theologie und Politik*, 142): "In der Tat fehlt auch bei der Bestimmung der Analogie von Christengemeinde und Bürgergemeinde großenteils die geschichtliche Dimension."

55. With reference to the Goethe citation, it is the accentuation of "Everything perishable *is* only a Gelichnis" from the viewpoint of creation.

56. However, this dependence doesn't mean the church is superior. It is actually the solidary responsibility of the church for the state; the church remains subordinate to the state and its legal order, cf. Barth, "Christengemeinde und Bürgergemeinde," 100f. Besides its reminding responsibility and solidarity, the church should pray for the state, respect and obey the legal order and the power of the state, and participate together with non-Christians in the various tasks of the state.

57. Therefore, the church is for Barth not the end in itself and for itself, and should serve God and then human being, cf. Barth, "Christengemeinde und Bürgergemeinde," 108.

58. Cf. Werpehowsik, "Barth and Politics," 234.

59. Barth speaks explicitly against the formation of a Christian party (with the German Christian Democratic Party [CDU] as a concrete example), because this kind of party, if it calls itself Christian, has (mis)understood "the kingdom of God once again as a great humane goal, which is based on the ground of the natural right." Besides the gospel, something additional is placed into the political area, which is "a supposedly Christian, but in reality out of humane world-view and morality agglutinated law," Barth, "Christengemeinde und Bürgergemeinde," 131, 134; cf. Thomas, "Political Theology," 195 with footnote 44.

60. Thomas ("Political Theology," 193) has correctly stressed that the church is "only one collaborator in a much larger, wider, and no less effective process of witnessing to the resurrected Christ."

61. Cf. Werpehowsik, "Barth and Politics," 233. In this context, Barth regard the confession of the church as its political action, cf. Cornu, *Barth und Politik*, 100.

62. Barth, "Christengemeinde und Bürgergemeinde," 121: "Sie muß das Gleichnis wagen." For Thomas ("Political Theology," 15) the *"productive and intervening dimension* means that the church itself is instructed to form parable for the kingdom of God." Also with respect to the fact that the exemplary church is rarely in history to be found, as Jürgen Moltmann (*Ethik*, 41) has correctly noticed that the church must dare to become a "Gleichnis." However, this truly rare existence of the exemplary church should not be taken as a critique of Barth's emphasis on the guiding and exemplary role of the church, as Moltmann (*Ethik*, 41) does. Barth is talking not about the indicative of the factual status of the church, but about the imperative of the contingent event of the church. Barth himself knows very well that "the Christian community also takes a part in the human illusions and confusions," Barth, "Christengemeinde und Bürgergemeinde," 107. Moreover, Barth emphasizes that the church should offer individual Christians as political actors to the state; aspiring to fulfill their political responsibility and do the best for the state, they give the state an impulse to observe the Christian orientation and follow its guidelines. (134f.).

63. In other words, the consistent orientation and the continuous guideline of the church should provide the explicated principles again and again, which could be respectively applicable, Barth, "Christengemeinde und Bürgergemeinde," 125. Therefore, "the just state must have its prototype and example ('Urbild und Vorbild') in the church" (Ibid., 133).

64. Barth has given numerous examples of the exemplary existence of the church in the state in his lecture (124–135, cf. the brief summary of Cornu, *Barth und Politik*, 10f. Thomas ("Political Theology," 197) has seen a moment which is not explicitly expressed in "Christian Community and Civil Community": "The receptive dimension refers to the church's thoughtful expectation that it will encounter parables of the kingdom of God in the world of politics, in civil society, and in all the spheres outside of the church."

65. We I have omitted here the new emerging city-churches in the big cities, since the more investigations should be done.

66. About the distinction between legality and legitimacy, and also contemporary conversation in Mainland China over the legitimacy of its constitution, see further

Clifford B. Anderson, "Constitutional Theology: Karl Barth and Carl Schmitt on Legitimacy and the Rule of Law," in this volume.

67. However, there are still many scholars who would talk about Barth's theological support for democracy, see for example, David Haddorff, "American Democracy and Trinitarian Sovereignty: Lessons from Barth and Tocqueville," in this volume. It seems to us that David Haddorff has overemphasized the affinity between the Christian community and democracy.

68. Concerning the suspicious, and even hostile of CCP regime toward Christian religion, see Kim-kwong Chan, "The Ecclesiological Implications of the Political Attitude of the Chinese Authority towards Christianity," in this volume.

Recently this kind of suspicion and hostility would have been increased to a certain extent by the so-called "Occupy the Central Movement in Hong Kong," or "the Umbrella Movement," which was formally launched by a lay Christian, a Baptist pastor, and a professor with a Christian background. About this movement, see further Lai Pan-chiu, "Religious Diversity, Democracy, and Public Theology: Conversing with Barth in a Hong Kong Context," and Kin Yip Louie, "Public Theology and Christian Social Action in Hong Kong: From the Past to the Present," in this volume.

Chapter 17

Religion, Politics, and the Christian Church in Germany

Perspectives from Sociology

Gert Pickel

INTRODUCTION: RELIGION FROM A
SOCIOLOGICAL PERSPECTIVE

When we look as sociologists at an object, issue or development, then we try to adopt a down-to-earth view. Deriving from the ideas of Max Weber, the perspective of a sociologist should be objective or at least intersubjective.[1] The task is to have no value judgment. This perspective sometimes seems to puzzle theologians, since they assume normative positions. If there are different interpretations of the same results, then theologians often see the reason for this as lying more in normative differences than in analytical theories. Sociologists, in contrast, take theories as the object of their interest. They need these theories to be able to make more than simple ad hoc statements about the current situation. They try to identify patterns in the behavior, attitudes, and values of people—more precisely, in society. On the other hand, empirical research and empirical results are necessary to say something about society. Empirical research in general does not determine results; rather, empirical research can only provide results that are open to different interpretations. Differences in interpretation arise from reference to different theories and data. The same is the case in the sociology of religion. The case is that not every interpretation (or theory) is as plausible and as supported by the data as another. Therefore, some interpretations are more "true" than others—or more plausible in the light of the data. Therefore, only working with empirical data can determine the plausibility of theories and statements concerning the connections between religion, politics, and the Christian Church in Germany.

The last few decades in Germany have been driven mostly by discussions about a *decline of Christian religiosity*. The process of secularization in particular has shaped the development of religion in German society.[2] This will remain the case in the near future, too. There are nevertheless discussions about the consequences of this development for individual religiosity as well as for the role of religion in the political process—or in politics as a whole. The first discussion refers to narratives such as the return of religion or the so-called *"post-secular age."*[3] The picture of religious development painted by these narratives seems at first to contradict the narrative of secularization: not less, but more, religion in the public sphere is the reason for rejecting the secularization thesis. The second discussion of a *post-secular age* refers to the idea that, with an ongoing, universal and widespread process of secularization, it is no longer necessary for politics and politicians to deal with religion—in Europe or in Germany.

Responding to the criticisms of secularization theory, its proponents make their own criticism,[4] arguing that what drives the opponents of secularization theory is nothing more than a fond hope. Empirical data show the decline in many indicators of religiosity—and the decline has been constant for the last few decades in Germany, the United Kingdom, Sweden, and Spain. If we look at the ties that people have to the Christian churches and Christian practices in Europe, then the picture is clear—secularization. But secularization happens in different ways and in different dimensions. Following Dobbelaere, we should differentiate between social, individual, and organizational secularization.[5] Jose Casanova, who is by no means a supporter of secularization theory, also points out the different possible dimensions that secularization can have.[6] Besides the fact that some dimensions can occur while others do not, looking at non-European countries often seems to contradict the theory of secularization. Religion and religiosity are widespread in Africa, Asia, and the United States.[7] Especially the high level of religiosity in the United States is a useful argument against secularization theory, and particularly so for supporters of the market model of religion.[8] Many scholars have stressed in the last few years the narrative of a return of religion for Europe, too. The two pictures differ and seem to constitute a paradox. Which picture is now the right one?

This question is connected to the question of the *relation between religion and politics* in modern societies today. The relation between church and state used to be of great importance for Europe. Today, though, the situation is more complicated. Religious freedom, migration, and individualization have brought *religious pluralization*. More people from religions other than the traditional Protestant and Catholic religions are now living in Germany, and members of Christian churches have plural religious positions and attitudes—and the group of non-church members and perhaps of non-religious people has grown rapidly in the last few decades.[9] This has led to new debates on the relation between politics and religion. Other religions and conflicts of identity are now the focus of public interest, and especially so with the increase in immigration of mostly Muslims to Germany and other European countries since 2015. Religion is now often seen as a cause of conflict and of problems in society.[10] Christian churches have to deal with this problem, and to find political solutions to the problems of Islamophobia and secularism.

My thesis is simple: despite the substantial process of secularization at different levels of German society, the role of religion in politics has grown. One central reason is the shift undergone by religion in modern societies to the *sphere of conflict*. Arguments about religion are increasingly arguments about whether it is a source of conflict and danger for modern societies. In addition, it is no longer "normal" for a person in society to be religious and for religions to enjoy special privileges in society. Consequently, the role of religion has increasingly become the object of debate, and new arrangements are necessary. There is therefore secularization at the social, individual, and organizational level—and at the same time an increase in the relevance of religion in political conflicts. This poses a problem to those (such as Karl Barth) who see the church as performing a strong role in a civil community,[11] since, if religion is a source of *conflict*, then what might appear an easy option for modern societies is to separate religion and politics.

RELIGIOUS DEVELOPMENTS IN GERMANY—THEORETICAL REMARKS

We should first of all gain clarity concerning religious developments in Germany. For a substantial interpretation of the data used to illustrate this, theoretical assumptions of the potential development are very helpful. Current theoretical discussions in the sociology of religion mainly use *three theoretical approaches*, with all three providing different interpretations of the social changes undergone by religion. The first approach is the classic *secularization theory*, which points to the continual *loss of social relevance* of religion in modern societies in the process of modernization.[12] This development arises from the *tension* between modernization and religion, and is manifested in processes such as *rationalization, increasing welfare, urbanization*, the *functional differentiation* of modern societies, and the ousting of religion from public life (*privatization*). In addition, religious norms find it increasingly difficult to gain support among members of society, and their institutional and communal bases disintegrate. The situation in *East Germany* and its development since 1990 can sometimes be interpreted almost as *premature secularization*. It is certainly something like *forced secularization*.[13]

The communal basis of religion was eroded extensively during the socialist period, and, as a result of this, as well as of the simultaneous process of
accelerated modernization that took place, we can hardly expect religious
revitalization to make any headway in Eastern Germany in the future. We can
perhaps expect at most some brief moments of revitalization, which will then
revert fairly quickly to the general European trend of secularization.

The *religious market model* is rather indeterminate as to the development
of religiosity and people's ties to the church. According to this model, the services offered by churches, as well as the degree to which the religious market
is regulated, determine a country's religious vitality.[14] The main churches can
no longer satisfy the ever-diversifying interests of individualized believers,
and the market model sees every citizen as in some way being an individualized believer. If the religious market continues to be limited to the established
suppliers (churches), then this will certainly result in a decrease in people's
religious vitality. Only the emergence of *competition* on the religious market
will revive people's interest in religion. What differentiates the market model
from secularization theory are three assumptions: (1) Religious *pluralism*
has a positive effect on religious vitality. (2) Modernization does not necessarily lead to religion losing its relevance in society. (3) Every individual
is in search of a religious model that will provide an answer to the ultimate
question of meaning. According to the market model, this applies to every
believer. There is therefore a continuous *demand for religion*, but never the
right supply.

A consistent application of the explanatory model of the religious market
approach promises a *revitalization* of all kinds of religion with respect to *East
Germany*. Thus, on the one hand, the new situation on the market is characterized by the cessation of political repression; and, on the other, the market
is largely freed from the restrictions hitherto imposed on it by the Christian
churches. Hence, traditional affiliations to the Christian churches have loos-
ened, which provides believers who are looking for religious ideas with a new
range of religious approaches. This should in turn bring about an increase in
both religious plurality and vitality. Froese and Pfaff (2009: 137; 2005) qualify this general statement, as they believe that the religious market has only
opened up to a very limited extent since 1990. In addition, the changes that
have taken place in East Germany since then have entailed an even greater
involvement of the state, such as the introduction of a church tax. Froese and
Pfaff also point to additional reasons for the absence of religious revitalization in East Germany, such as the tarnished image of the Protestant Church
since the Nazi regime and its involvement with Stasi surveillance practices.[15]

The *thesis of religious individualization*, which is discussed in particular
in the European realm, sees a link between the personal level of faith and
an individual's affiliation to the church.[16] Individual religiosity is seen as an

Table 17.1 Fundamental Lines of Thought in the Contemporary Sociology of Religion

	Secularization Theory	*Theory of Individualization*	*Theory of Pluralization and Vitalization*
Authors	Brian Wilson Steve Bruce Peter L. Berger	Thomas Luckmann Grace Davie	Rodney Starke Roger Finke Laurence Iannaccone
Basic Thesis	General differences between modernity and religion lead to a constant decline in the social significance of religion	Institutionalized religion can lose significance, but, because people's religious beliefs are an anthropological constant, only a change in the forms of religiosity appear	There is a constant demand for religiosity and religious beliefs. The level of religious vitality therefore depends on the supply of religious products on the religious market
Relation to General Theory	Modernization Theory	Theory of Individualization	Rational-Choice and Market Theory
Explanation for Western Europe	Continuous decline of all forms of religiosity	Decline of involvement in the churches, but consistent individual religious beliefs	Development of religiosity depends on the level of pluralization in society
Explanation for Europe and Germany	Continuous decline of all forms of religiosity, perhaps after a period of revitalization until a certain point	Decline of involvement in the churches, but increasing individual religious beliefs	Revitalization of religiosity after the end of repression, and the rebuilding of a religious market

Source: Author's own composition. Gert Pickel, "Secularization as a European Fate? Results from the Church and Religion in an Enlarged Europe Project 2006," *Church and Religion in Contemporary Europe: Results from Empirical and Comparative Research,* ed. Gert Pickel and Olaf Müller (Wiesbaden: VS Verlag, 2009), 89–122.

anthropological constant, something inherent to the human being. Religious needs will therefore never cease entirely. This does not apply equally to public manifestations of religion, since particular social forms of religion that occur in certain regions may indeed lose their relevance. In that case, individual religiosity modifies its form, resulting either in new types of religious practice and affiliation, or in "*invisible religiosity.*" Proponents of the thesis of religious individualization criticize secularization theory for focusing too narrowly on questions related to the sociology of the church, as well as for its substantive concept of religion, which no longer reflects society adequately, since it is mostly limited to a Christian concept of religion. With respect to *East Germany*, supporters of the individualization thesis claim that new forms of religion will spread substantially. They expect these forms to be highly diverse and to manifest themselves more in *private* than in institutionalized forms. In this respect, the expansion of the right to self-determination is crucial, as it prepares the ground for religious individualization alongside the loosening of traditional affiliations to the predominant Christian religion.

The latter two theoretical approaches both reject secularization theory as a model unsuited to explaining religious vitality in modern societies. They consider the claim that there is a tension between modernity and religion that leads almost inevitably to the decline in the relevance of religion to be both outdated and inadequate with respect to the reality in the world as a whole. Processes of secularization do not necessarily proceed in a linear fashion, with alternative factors or social conditions affecting or even interrupting these processes—or producing *path dependencies*. Overall, the line of reasoning used by secularization theory continues to be instructive due to its complexity, and it can help to structure further empirical analyses. The analyses base on Dobbelaere's ideas: he differentiates between social secularization and individual secularization.[17] At the same time, with the focus on secularization the relation between religion and politics can be analyzed.[18] If we wish to gain insights into the relations between politics, society and the Christian church, then we should begin by looking briefly at how religiosity has developed in Germany in the last few years.

THE DEVELOPMENT OF RELIGION IN
GERMANY: EMPIRICAL FINDINGS

Secularization at the Social Level: The Relation between
Religion and Society

Theoretical approaches enable us to interpret the situation of religion in Germany. We will now look at the empirical findings and see which approach is more suited to interpreting current developments. We will first focus on secularization at the social level. This level of secularization has taken root in Germany in the last few decades. The underlying process of functional differentiation has diminished the areas in which religion plays the primary role. The decisions made in politics, society, and sometimes in everyday life are related less and less to religion and religious beliefs. This is something like a "common sense" in Germany, besides the existing legacies. Only 25 percent of Germans think that there should be some reference to God in the

European constitution, and almost the same proportion have the same attitude when it comes to the influence that religious leaders should have on politics. This figure is stable, being the same for both 2006 and 2013, and other studies conducted in the last few decades show a similar trend.[19]

The separation of religion and politics is well established not only in Germany; results of the Bertelsmann Religionsmonitor 2013 underline that there is a widespread understanding of modern societies in Europe as being secular societies at the social level. Religion should in general not interfere with politics or science. This means that the *idea of functional differentiation is widespread in Europe*, and especially so in Western Europe. As a consequence, debates about the interaction between the religious and the secular sphere, especially in schools, universities and the economic sector, produce controversies in public debate. Even Jose Casanova, who is in general critical of the ideas of secularization theory, sees secularization as well as functional differentiation as processes that are present in modern societies. But, Casanova also points out that this process is only one dimension of secularization, and that processes in the other dimensions can differ.

Individual Secularization

The starting point here are the different situations in West and East Germany. We find in West Germany a *culture of membership* when it comes to religion, which is a result of long historical processes. In contrast, we find in East Germany a *culture of non-membership*, if not of non-religiosity. What is important here are the legacies from the GDR's socialist period. Besides the clear differences between the two areas, the most interesting finding is that the Christian churches have experienced the same trend in both East and West—namely, a decline in membership since 1989. Sometimes, the development in West Germany now is faster, than in East Germany, where most of the decline happened in former times. Monika Wohlrab-Sahr speaks here of a situation of "*forced secularity*" in East Germany.[20] The decline has taken place in West Germany at a completely different level, though: 80 percent of West Germans are still members of a Christian church. But the situation has changed in the last few years, and not in the way that members of the churches in West Germany thought that it would. The Protestant and the Catholic Church have together lost almost 3 million members in all. Meanwhile, the group comprising those not affiliated to a church now constitutes the largest group in Germany as a whole.

But this apparent evidence for secularization is not the only development that can be seen in table 17.2. *Secularization* is not the only development in the area of membership. A process of *religious pluralization* has also occurred, with members of Muslim communities and the orthodox Christian

Table 17.2   Widespread Secularization in German Society

	West Germany	East Germany
Religious leaders should not influence government decisions (C&R 2006)	70	70
Religious leaders should influence government decisions (RM 2013)	32	21
Only politicians who believe in God are suitable for public office (RM 2013)	9	11
The European constitution should include an explicit reference to God (C&R 2006)	27	20
Science should not be influenced by religion (C&R 2006)	72	74
Education should be free from religion (C&R 2006)	42	60
Religious symbols such as crucifixes should not be present in schools (C&R 2006)	31	55

Source: Author's calculations based on "Church and Religion in an Enlarged Europe" (C&R 2006); European Values Study (EVS 2008); Bertelsmann Religionsmonitor (RM 2013), positive answers in percent.

church growing recently in Germany, and mostly in West Germany. The dominant process, though, is that of the clear increase in the number of those without religious affiliation.[21]

Membership is only one dimension of religiosity, however. We also have to look at practice and attitudes. The problem is that developments in religious practice do not differ from developments in membership. Different forms of religious practice, whether church attendance (a collective religious practice) or the individual practice of praying, are in decline in both West and East Germany. As result, there is a slow but continuous shift from active Christians and regular churchgoers to more secular people without any religious practice. They are often called religiously indifferent today to demonstrate their disinterestedness in Christianity, but they could just as well be classified as non-religious.

Membership of or belonging to a church is not the same as believing.[22] The concept of religious individualization in particular interprets the development more as a *transformation of religiosity* than as secularization,[23] and sees modern societies as moving increasingly toward a patchwork religiosity.[24] Different forms of private religiosity, sometimes invisible and sometimes visible, are the signs of the times. Supporters of secularization theory are skeptical of such an interpretation and argue instead that the decline of religious practices points in a different direction. Belief in God has also dwindled in the last few decades, with only 25 percent of West Germans now believing in a personal God as preached by the Christian churches. This is a further indicator of religious indifference or non-religiosity.[25] It is important to know that the non-religious do not oppose religious belief or religion aggressively,

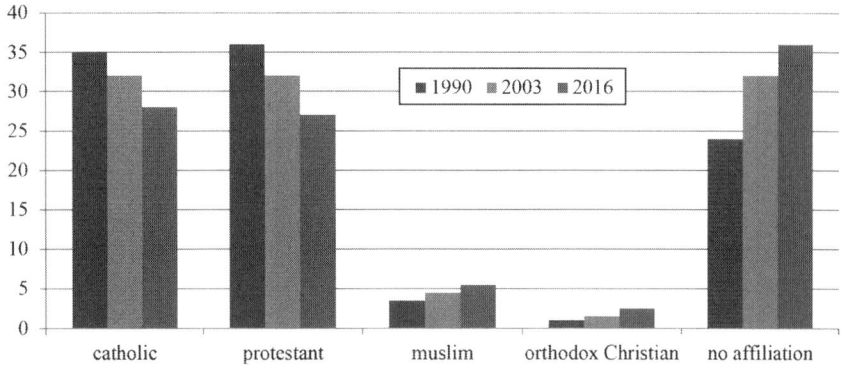

Figure 17.1 Changes in Church Membership. *Source: Fowid 2016 and author's own calculations from different data sources ad surveys.*

with only 1 percent in the Bertelsmann Religionsmonitor 2013 saying that they try to convince others not to be religious. The point is that religion is becoming more and more diffuse and abstract for most Germans and, in the end, it has taken a subordinate role in the everyday lives of most citizens. The growing disinterest in religiosity and religious issues are attributes of religious indifference.

Despite the fact that West and East Germany are both witnessing a growing disinterest in religion, there are differences between the two regions. Even if West Germans are diffuse in their beliefs, the majority see themselves as religious or are even members of a church. In contrast, more than half the population in East Germany do not believe in God or in some higher being at all, and, in surveys, 25 percent describe themselves as atheists. There is a strong correlation between membership, religious practice and belief. At the heart of the process is socialization, and the fact that fewer people are being brought up with religious traditions and knowledge. People do not lose their religiosity from one day to the next. People who have not been brought up with religion will remain areligious for more or less their entire lives. Nevertheless, religious socialization is entangled with social circumstances. As Ronald Inglehart has pointed out, people acquire their (religious) social-ization at the beginning of their lives according to the social surroundings. The values acquired in childhood remain more or less stable throughout life. What we can see nowadays is that the social surroundings are shifting from an understanding of religiosity as normal to the idea of secularity as normal. People do not necessarily now need religion to live, unlike the case with work, family, or recreation. This is transported through the process of socialization, with its contents changing over the generations. The relevance of religious socialization in families declines from generation to generation, and over the course of time. Almost twice as many people in the oldest birth cohort than in the youngest cohort see themselves as having been brought up religiously. The same "steps" are visible across the generations if we look at a similar chart depicting subjective religiosity (not presented here).

This process was forced by socialism in East Germany and led to a situation that is different from West Germany. Hence, the culture of irreligiosity in East Germany and of religious affiliation in West Germany. But there are more indicators in the last two decades that suggest that West Germany is moving in the same direction as East Germany than the other way around. A person's own socialization affects the way that he or she will then bring up his or her own children. If a person is socialized in a faith, then there is a greater likelihood that he or she will bring up his or her children in the faith than is the case if a person has had no religious socialization (see figure 17.2). Differences between West and East Germany result mainly from different historical and cultural paths and legacies.[26] These shape the level of religiosity, but not the direction that developments have taken since 1989—namely, secularization in both East and West.

What is Going on in the Protestant Church?

The findings are relatively clear: in Germany, as in most other European countries, secularization is taking place.[27] Perhaps accompanied by

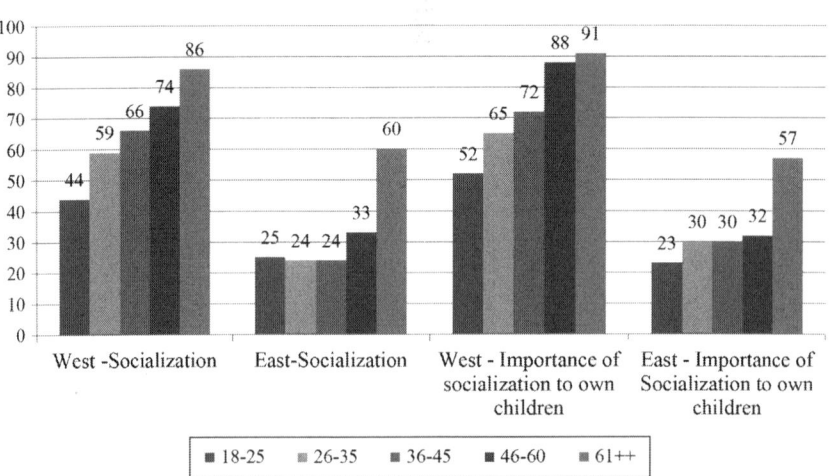

Figure 17.2 Religious Socialization of Generations. *Source: Author's own calculations based on Church and Religion in an Enlarged Europe (C&R) 2006 (West: n = 717; Ost: n = 563); Socialization = brought up in a faith; Importance of socialization = would bring up or have brought up my children in a faith.*

individualization and some factors pointed out by the market model, secularization seems to be the dominant effect in the development of religion. We can take a closer look at the changes by looking specifically at the movements among members of the Protestant Church in Germany. What does it mean for the Protestant Church in Germany? Here we have some specific data that indicate that secularization begins inside the church (figure 17.3). Nearly one-third of members of the Protestant Church in West Germany feel little or no connection to their church. The level of connection is a little higher in East Germany, but we have to assume that most people there have left the church in the past few decades in the process of a forced secularization, which leads to a forced secularity.

More importantly, there are clear differences between the age cohorts. Affiliation is much lower in the younger than in the older generations. This is a consistent trend. We can interpret this as showing that a process of secularization among members is taking place inside the church and will lead to a further erosion of church membership in the near future. Drawing on theories from developmental psychology, we can also claim that people become more religious as they grow older; and, indeed, this sometimes happens as people near their death. In general, though, there is a generational process of decline and erosion. If people become distant from the church, then most will leave the church over the course of their lives—usually during the stage of post-adolescence (between the ages of twenty-five and thirty-five), when there occur many benchmarking experiences (leaving home, first employment, establishing a partnership, and perhaps a family).

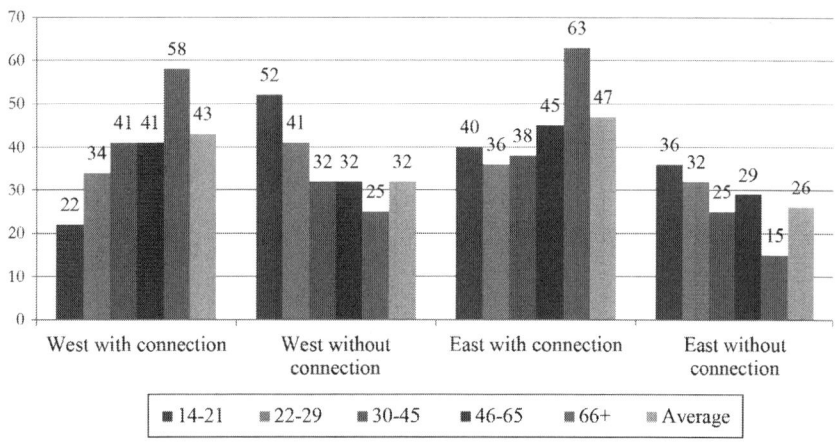

Figure 17.3 Connection to the Church among Protestants. *Source: Membership study of the Protestant Church; feel myself connected to the Protestant Church; connection = strong and some connection; no connection = weak and no connection.*

This can be underlined by another empirical finding: not only the church but also religiosity is under pressure in younger ages. Not even half the members of the Protestant Church between 14 and 21 describe themselves as religious (82 percent describe themselves as religious in the oldest cohort in West Germany). The picture of a staircase leading from young to old is visible in both West and East Germany (figure 17.4). If we assume that only a minority of young people will "learn" to be religious, then the *erosion of church membership is strongly connected to an erosion of subjective religiosity*. The very low level of subjective religiosity among the non-affiliated points in the same direction. Not only does the self-attribution of subjective religiosity sink over the generations (as well as the self-proclaimed belief in God); there is also a close correlation (Pearson's $r > .50$) between connection to the Protestant Church and subjective religiosity. If we recall the main idea of the secularization thesis, which is that there has been a generational decline in the social relevance of religion as a result of falling religious socialization, then the result seems clear. Supporters of the individualization thesis would not be impressed at all. They understand religiosity as a much wider concept, one that includes almost every form of spiritual living and every form useful to reducing situations of uncertainty in life. Besides the problem of identifying these forms empirically, it is not clear ultimately what religiosity is. In addition, the potential forms of patchwork religiosity are fluent. But now fluid processes can also simply ebb away.

Let us return to the Protestant identity. Being a member of, and baptized into, the Protestant Church are the central factors in people's identification of themselves as Protestant. The social component of identity seems to

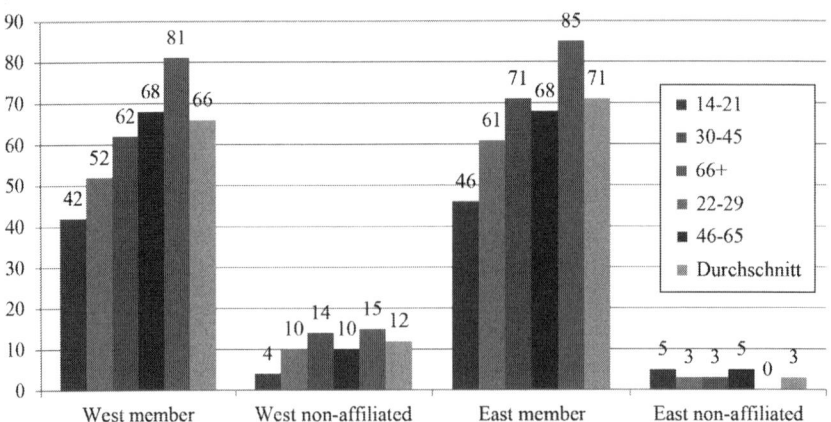

Figure 17.4 The Subjective Religiosity of Protestants and the Non-Affiliated. *Source: Membership study of the Protestant Church; see myself as a religious person, positive answers on a 4-point scale.*

dominate Protestant identity—and not so much a personal religiosity (figure 17.5). Together with the empirical finding that the main reasons for belonging to the Protestant Church are the opportunity to have a church marriage and funeral, the component of social membership and affiliation seems to be more relevant than is sometimes mentioned in theology—especially in liberal Protestant theology. Both rites and social affiliation play a crucial role in the relationship that people have to religion. Rites and official acts have their central power in their social meaning and in their ability to build up community, too. For the majority of "simple" church members, the feeling of belonging and the sense of identity are the central resources in being a Protestant. It seems that the social organization of religion is more important than some scientists mean. At least, to be a member is important, sometimes without being a religious person.

It is therefore not surprising that many Protestants should demand social activities from the institution and invest a great deal in the social groups around the church. Much social capital for society is produced in the church today.[28] This is confirmed by other results, too. Thus, trust in fellow human beings is 20 percentage points higher among Protestants than among the non-religious. And among visitors to the congresses of the German Protestant Church, who are mostly Protestants actively involved in their church, that figure rises to an almost unbelievable 80 percentage points. It seems as

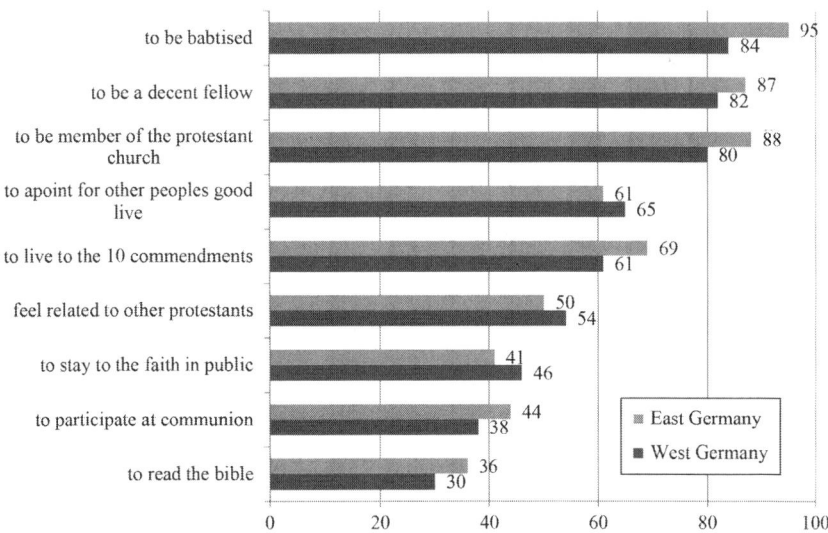

Figure 17.5   Protestant Identity—and What Leads to It. *Source: Membership study of the Protestant Church; what is relevant to be a Protestant (positive answers on a 4-point scale).*

though affiliation—or, more precisely, the sense of belonging—has an almost autonomous significance for "being a Christian."

The Theoretical Explanation of the Empirical Findings

I pointed out in the second section the possibility of explaining the empirical findings using three theoretical approaches. Most indicators are consistent with the ideas of secularization theory. Individual attachment to Christian religiosity declines in all indicators. The spread of religious indifference is not as rapid as the spread of indifference to the institutionalized church. Processes of individualization moderate this. But the tendency of secularization is clearly visible. Religious socialization declines, fewer people practice religion, and hardly anybody speaks about religion in public (besides the conflicts with and between religions). If a person loses his or her integration into a religious community, then religiosity will vanish as an individual passion in the following generations. The cause is simple: if children see that religion is only something additional and is less important in everyday life than many other phenomena, then they will see it as not being relevant for their own lives. Religious knowledge then vanishes along with the obligation to take part in religious practices, and the individualization of religion is only a bridge between religious grandparents and religiously indifferent children.

If we summarize the empirical results presented, the following becomes clear: (1) There is only limited religious potential among the non-religious, at least if we take a Christian-oriented view. Not being a member of a religious community also usually means not being religious. (2) Strictly speaking, the process of secularization is even more advanced. Thus, there are (especially in West Germany) many people who still belong to a Christian church—but who are no longer religious. (3) Social identity as a Protestant (or presumably also as a Catholic) has an autonomous significance that sometimes extends beyond subjective religiosity. It is perhaps the case that the social power of religion is underestimated in individualized societies. And perhaps it is the case also that social affiliation shapes subjective religiosity, and not only that religiosity shapes affiliation.

RELIGION AND POLITICS

What are the consequences for the relationship between religion and politics taking into account a Barthian perspective, which advocates a strong role of the Christian church in society and politics? If we look at the traditional relationships of religion to parties, electoral behavior and direct political influence, then it looks first of all as though secularization also entails for religion a loss of influence on politics. The discrimination of people from different religions and religious minorities can't also be seen in Germany, like in some other areas of the world.[29] Classic political lines of conflict becoming blurred, and the statements made by Christian churches are being heard to only a limited extent.[30] Religiosity may be in decline, but that does not necessarily mean that the impact of religion on politics is diminishing. Looking at the public debates, we can see that such a relation is becoming increasingly important for political culture. It is here that the narrative of a return of religion has its origins. However, less important is the Christian religion for political decisions, with people not seeing it as relevant that members of the German parliament be religious. Here applies the preference of citizens for a clear functional separation of religion and politics. This makes the following tendency quite clear: the increasing number of discussions about religion is mostly about *religion as a factor of conflict*. Unlike in the times of Georg Simmel, when religion was seen as a central factor of integration, the opposite view is now spread among large sections of the population across the whole of Europe. People not only view Christianity as old-fashioned and outdated in modern societies; the process of religious pluralization also encourages them to see religion as a factor of conflict. In 2012, 60 percent of Germans said that the conflict between Christians and Muslims would be one of the most significant conflicts in the near future. Therefore, the enemy is visible —Islam and Muslims. The current "refugee crisis" in Europe has only encouraged this critical view of Muslims and motivated people to express their attitudes. A survey conducted by the University of Münster in 2010 showed that almost 60 percent of Germans have a negative attitude toward Muslims in general (figure 17.6).[31] Members of all other religions, including atheists, are not seen in such a negative light.[32] What is behind this negative attitude toward a particular religious group?

It would not be wrong to conclude that it is a *stereotype* formed by different perceptual mechanisms. Thus, in the new federal states, where the number of Muslims is very low, the largely negative view of members of this particular social group cannot be based on personal experience. The attitudes must arise in other ways than through contacts, a central explanatory motive here being perceptions of threat. For example, it is known from research on stereotypes that it is precisely the perception of a threat posed by another group that causes people to reject that group. And this is the case when it comes to people's attitudes to Muslims. Many people consider Islam as a threat at least since September 11, 2001. Differences in how people judge different religions correspond to the attitudes presented earlier. Only when it comes to Islam does the proportion of those who regard religious pluralization as a threat exceed the proportion of those who value pluralization as enriching society. All other religions are perceived more often as enriching than posing a threat.[33]

	Muslims		Jews		Hindus		Buddhists		Atheists		Christians	
	D-West	D-East	D-West	D-East	D-West	D-East	D-West	D-East	D-West	D-East	D-West	D-East
Very positive	5.8	2.7	8.2	6.1	5.4	4.1	13.4	8.0	11.0	27.7	35.1	23.1
Positive	28.4	23.2	50.4	47.7	45.0	33.4	51.8	41.6	43.2	46.2	54.9	55.8
Negative	40.7	40.2	23.1	19.8	19.5	21.5	14.2	18.9	22.5	10.1	6.1	10.6
Very negative	17.1	22.0	5.1	9.7	4.6	9.5	3.8	7.9	8.4	3.7	0.9	3.7
Do not know	4.8	8.8	8.9	13.4	20.4	27.3	13.2	19.0	10.5	9.4	1.3	4.5
No answer	3.3	3.2	4.3	3.4	5.2	4.2	3.7	4.7	4.5	2.9	1.8	2.4
Total	100	100	100	100	100	100	100	100	100	100	100	100

Figure 17.6 Personal Attitudes toward Members of Religions in Germany. *Source: "Wahrnehmung und Akzeptanz religiöser Vielfalt in der europäischen Bevölkerung 2010," "What is your personal attitude towards . . ." (in percent).*

Figures 17.6 and 17.7 reveal a further finding: on the one hand, skepticism about *atheism* is still stronger in West Germany than in East Germany; on the other, Christianity is more often identified as a threat in East Germany. These findings are not surprising given the different religious cultures in West Germany and East Germany. What is more surprising is the extent of the differences. Thus, the tension between West German Christians and East German non-religious people seems to be becoming ever more relaxed, and the mutual rejection between the two groups based on religious or non-religious aspects seems to be finding resolution. For the greater part of the German population, affiliation to Christianity or its absence only plays a very subordinate role in their everyday lives. Perceptions of threat such as in the United States, where a majority of the population identify atheism as a concrete threat, do not exist in Germany. This easing of tensions also has consequences for how the demands of the new atheism are dealt with politically. For, the demands of organized atheism seem to have only limited legitimacy in the population. On the one hand, broad sections of the population are barely actively behind the anti-religious politics of these organizations; and, on the other, the majority of Germans see no essential conflict at this point. Although many West Germans perceive the culture of non-religiousness in the East of Germany as alien, this does not have a central significance for their political decisions and for their living together in a political community. This can also be seen in the light of a society that is seen as being largely secular by almost all citizens, a society based on largely accepted processes of functional differentiation. If religion is located more in the private sphere and representatives of religious groupings stay away from politics, then

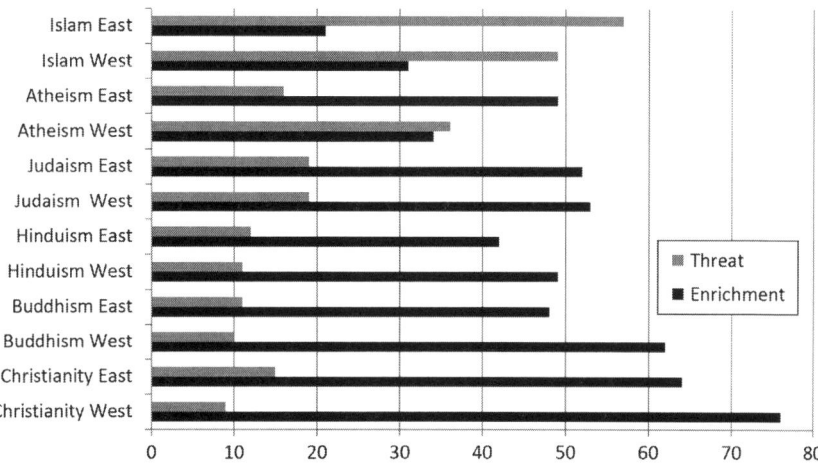

Figure 17.7 Perception of Religious Pluralization in Germany. *Source: Author's own calculations, Bertelsmann Religionsmonitor 2013; when you think about the religions that exist in the world, how threatening or enriching do you perceive the following to be? Proportions: very threatening/rather threatening; very enriching/enriching.*

there is no basis for conflict in this regard—and representatives of a (sometimes apparently ideological) atheism should also from the point of view of citizens stay out of politics. The acceptance by German citizens of a far-reaching secularity in society therefore by no means implies a turn to political atheism.

The situation is different with regard to Islam. Here, there is remarkable unanimity between West and East Germans, with both having a *skeptical to negative attitude*. In principle, denoting the corresponding public controversies as a debate about integration is more a euphemism than a description of reality. In reality, it is more a definite *debate on Islam*. Not only that about three in five respondents in West and East Germany profess a negative attitude toward Muslims; over half of the citizens in both areas also feel threatened by Islam.[34] Perceptions of threat, cultural otherness, and fear of foreigners come together in these statements. The fact that Islam is presented relatively consistently in the media as violent and hostile does the rest in constructing the corresponding stereotypes. The media usually presents Islam to German citizens as violent, fanatical, and above all as anti-women.[35] It is no wonder, then, that three-quarters of citizens in West and East Germany tend to agree or even agree strongly with the statement that the increasing number of Muslims should be regarded as a source of conflict. Perceptions of threat and the resulting fear of conflict are closely linked. Islam is regarded by most people as a religion that is not compatible with Western, and therefore also German, society.

This notion has serious consequences for the level of political decision-making. If Germans were to vote on the building of mosques or minarets, then up to three quarters would vote against. The introduction of a Muslim public holiday finds support from not even a fifth of Germans. Behind such stances are considerable fears of "over-foreignization" and perceived cultural threat. They are independent of concrete threats—and they need a group to be afraid of. This group can be found in the religious affiliation of Muslims. The fear of Islam outlined here can have far-reaching, indirect effects, since the demands to take action are directed at political parties. Not fulfilling these demands can result in the withdrawal of political support and electoral votes. In the long run, however, these attitudes can go beyond demands for specific support and damage the legitimacy of German democracy as a whole. One thing is clear: it is not so much religious pluralization itself that causes problems. Rather, it is the consequences in the minds of citizens that pose challenges to the political system of the Federal Republic.

Consequences: Secularization and More Discussions about Religion and Politics

What are the consequences, also from a Barthian perspective? One that is perhaps not entirely expected: religiosity may be in decline, but that does not mean that the relevance of religion for political discussions is on the wane. It seems to be the case that in Europe the end of a naturally occurring religiosity

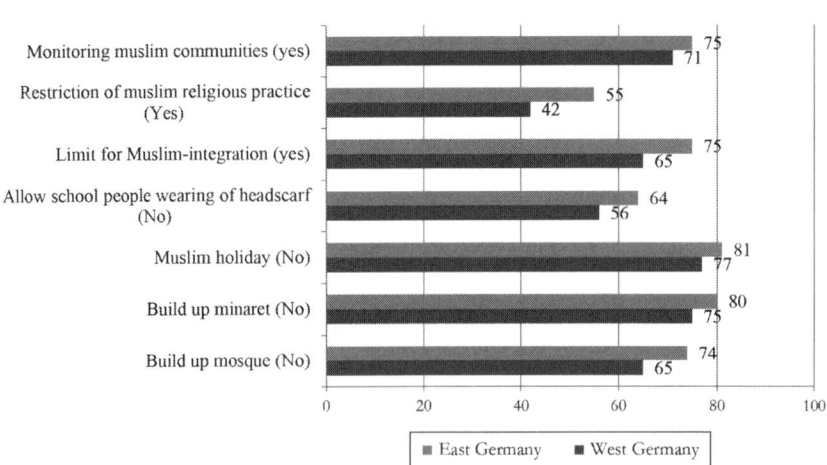

Figure 17.8   Attitudes toward Muslims, with Political Consequences. *Source: Perception and acceptance of religious diversity in the European population, 2010; Allbus 2012; Bertelsmann Religionsmonitor 2013.*

and social significance of religion make religion and religious people increasingly involved in public conflicts. Whether it is assisted suicide, the burka or headscarves, there is a greater polarization of attitudes when it comes to religious-social issues. On the other hand, discussions about religion and religiosity are not exactly the same as for individual religiosity. People can have a position on many issues, without their being involved in them. Social change and especially the ongoing process of modernization drive the process of secularization, and being religious is no longer "normal." In contrast, people without religion see their own lives as "normal" and feel no need to be religious at all. However, secularization can also be a driving force behind more polarization in society and more controversies between religious and secular people—or between members of different religious groups.[36] Results from surveys show that, in the eyes of Germans, one of the most significant conflicts is that between Muslims and Christians, with 60 percent predicting that this conflict will be significant in the future. These observations lead to new fields of policy, such as the policy of morality and the policy of religion. Politicians and parties have to deal with religion and questions related to religion—and this will increasingly be the case in the near future.

Why are ideas of a return of religion so present in the media? Mostly because there is a strong interest in the public discussion on religion. This is a result of the growing relevance of religion in politics. The evidence that religion is playing a role in politics contradicts secularization theory. Or perhaps not? Religion is certainly present in everyday life, but in the form of criticism and conflict. And another point becomes visible: religion must be understood in modern societies as something social. This also means that affiliation may play a larger role than we might often think from a theological perspective. On the one hand, with regard to people's own affiliation to a religion as part of their own social identity. But, on the other, also as an identifying feature for group attributions, as becomes clear in the case of Islam. At the same time, there can be consensus here between secular and religious Germans when it comes to rejecting a religion and its members, but also to being willing to enter into dialogue and live together with them. So it is hardly surprising that the most important current debates on religion and politics directly affect not Christianity but Islam. Retreating to a private religiosity (or nonreligiosity) is not enough here. Rather, every single Christian has to question how he or she behaves in such decisions or in other political decisions. And especially so if we bear in mind that in modern civil societies it is precisely this level of civil society in which a political culture and a secular community emerges and exists. We can therefore only agree with Karl Barth: "The way Christians can help in the political sphere is by constantly giving the state an impulse in the Christian direction and freedom to develop on the Christian line."[37] And this is best suited in a modern democracy to both pluralism of opinion and Christian plurality, even if these will be advocated over time by fewer and fewer Christians.

NOTES

1. Max Weber, *Wirtschaft und Gesellschaft* (Tübingen: Mohr, 1972).
2. Gert Pickel, "Religiosität in Deutschland und Europa—Religiöse Pluralisierung und Säkularisierung auf soziokulturell variierenden Pfaden," *Zeitschrift für Religion, Gesellschaft und Politik* (ZRGP) 1, no. 1 (2017): 37–74.
3. Martin Riesebrodt, *Die Rückkehr der Religionen* (München: Beck, 2001); Charles Taylor, *A Secular Age* (Harvard: Harvard University Press, 2007).
4. Steve Bruce, *God is Dead: Secularization in the West* (Oxford: Oxford University Press, 2002) or Pippa Norris and Ronald Inglehart, *Sacred and Secular: Religion and Politics Worldwide* (Cambridge: Cambridge University Press, 2004).
5. Karel Dobbelaere, *Secularization: An Analysis on Three Levels* (Brussels: Euraton, 2002).
6. Jose Casanova, *Public Religions in the Modern World* (Chicago: Chicago University Press, 1994).
7. Pippa Norris and Ronald Inglehart, *Sacred and Secular: Religion and Politics Worldwide* (Cambridge: Cambridge University Press, 2004).
8. Rodney Stark, "Secularization, R.I.P.," *Sociology of Religion* 60 (1999): 249–273; Rodney Stark and William Sims Bainbridge, *A Theory of Religion* (New Brunswick, 1987); Rodney Stark and Roger Finke, *Acts of Faith: Explaining the Human Side of Religion* (Berkeley: University Press, 2000).
9. Detlef Pollack and Gergely Rosta, *Religion and Modernity. An International Comparison* (Oxford: Oxford University Press, 2018).
10. Jonathan Fox, *A World Survey of Religion and the State* (Oxford: Oxford University Press, 2004).
11. Cf. the contribution of David Haddorff in this volume.
12. Steve Bruce, *God is Dead: Secularization in the West* (Oxford: Oxford University Press, 2002).
13. Monika Wohlrab-Sahr, Uta Karstein and Thomas Schmidt-Lux, *Forcierte Säkularisierung. Religiöser Wandel und Generationendynamik im Osten* (Frankfurt/Main: Campus, 2009).
14. Rodney Stark and William Sims Bainbridge, *A Theory of Religion* (New Brunswick, 1987); Rodney Stark and Roger Finke, *Acts of Faith: Explaining the Human Side of Religion* (Berkeley: University Press, 2000).
15. Paul Froese and Steven Pfaff, "Explaining a Religious Anomaly: A Historical Analysis of Secularization in Eastern Germany," *Journal for the Scientific Study of Religion* 44, no. 4 (2005): 397–422.
16. Grace Davie, *Religion in Britain since 1945: Believing without Belonging* (Oxford: Oxford University Press, 1994); Thomas Luckmann, *The Invisible Religion: The Problem of Religion in Modern Society* (New York: Penguin, 1967).

17. Karel Dobbelaere, *Secularization: An Analysis on Three Levels* (Brussels: Euraton, 2002).

18. Oliver Hidalgo, "Die 'säkulare' Demokratie. Theoretische Überlegungen mit einer speziellen Perspektive auf das Beispiel Deutschland," in *Religion und Politik im vereinigten Deutschland. Was bleibt von der Rückkehr der Religionen?* ed. Gert Pickel and Oliver Hidalgo (Wiesbaden: Springer VS, 2013), 165–193.

19. Like data of the Allbus-Studies: Heiner Meulemann, *Nach der Säkularisierung. Religiosität in Deutschland 1980–2012* (Wiesbaden: Springer VS, 2015) or Gert Pickel, "Die Situation der Religion in Deutschland—Rückkehr des Religiösen oder voranschreitende Säkularisierung?" in *Religion und Politik im vereinigten Deutschland. Was bleibt von der Rückkehr der Religionen?* ed. Gert Pickel and Oliver Hidalgo (Wiesbaden: Springer VS, 2013), 65–102.

20. Monika Wohlrab-Sahr, Uta Karstein and Thomas Schmidt-Lux, *Forcierte Säkularisierung. Religiöser Wandel und Generationendynamik im Osten* (Frankfurt/ Main: Campus, 2009).

21. Detlef Pollack, Olaf Müller and Gert Pickel, *The Social Significance of Religion in the Enlarged Europe. Secularization, Individualization and Pluralization* (Burlington: Ashgate, 2012).

22. Grace Davie, *Europe: The Exceptional Case. Parameters of Faith in the Modern World* (London: Routledge, 2002).

23. Thomas Luckmann, The Invisible Religion: The Problem of Religion in Modern Society (New York: Penguin, 1967); Detlef Pollack and Gert Pickel, "Religious Individualization or Secularization? Testing Hypotheses of Religious Change—The Case of Eastern and Western Germany," British Journal of Sociology 58, no. 4 (2007): 603–632.

24. David Martin, *A General Theory of Secularization* (New York, 1978).

25. Johannes Quack and Cora Schuh, *Religious Indifference: New Perspectives from Studies on Secularization and Nonreligion* (Heidelberg: Springer, 2017).

26. Gert Pickel, "Secularization as European Fate? Results from the Church and Religion in an enlarged Europe project," in *Church and Religion in Contemporary Europe: Results from Empirical and Comparative Research*, ed. Gert Pickel and Olaf Müller (Wiesbaden: Springer VS, 2009), 89–122.

27. Gert Pickel, "Religiosität in Deutschland und Europa—Religiöse Pluralisierung und Säkularisierung auf soziokulturell variierenden Pfaden," *Zeitschrift für Religion, Gesellschaft und Politik* (ZRGP) 1, no. 1 (2017): 37–74.

28. Robert Putnam and David E. Campbell, *American Grace. How Religion Divides and Unites Us* (New York: Simon & Schuster, 2011); Gert Pickel and Anja Gladkich, "Religious Social Capital in Europe. Connections between Religiosity and Civil Society," in *Transformations of Religiosity. Religion and Religiosity in Eastern Europe 1989–2010*, ed. Gert Pickel and Kornelia Sammet (Wiesbaden: Springer VS, 2012), 69–94.

29. Jonathan Fox, *The Unfree Exercise of Religion. A World Survey of Discrimination against Religious Minorities* (Cambridge: Cambridge University Press, 2016).

30. Susanne Pickel, "Do Religious People also in Modernity Elect Religious Parties? The Impact of the Religious Cleavage in Eastern Europe and Western Europe in Comparison," in *Transformations of Religiosity: Religion and Religiosity in Eastern Europe 1989–2010*, ed. Gert Pickel and Kornelia Sammet (Wiesbaden: Springer VS, 2012), 111–134.

31. Pollack, Detlef, Olaf Müller, Gergely Rosta, Nils Friedrichs and Alexander Yendell, *Grenzen der Toleranz: Wahrnehmung und Akzeptanz religiöser Vielfalt in Europa* (Wiesbaden: Springer VS, 2014).

32. See also the contribution of Oliver Hidalgo in this volume.

33. Detlef Pollack and Olaf Müller, *Religionsmonitor 2013. Verstehen was verbindet. Religiosität und Zusammenhalt in Deutschland* (Gütersloh: Bertelsmann Stiftung, 2013); Gert Pickel, *Religionsmonitor 2013. Religiosity in International Comparison* (Gütersloh: Bertelsmann Stiftung, 2013).

34. Gert Pickel and Alexander Yendell, "Islam als Bedrohung? Beschreibung und Erklärung von Einstellungen zum Islam im Ländervergleich," *Zeitschrift für Vergleichende Politikwissenschaft* (ZfVP) 10, no. 4 (2016): 273–309; Zan Strabac and Ola Listhaug, "Anti-Muslim Prejudice in Europe: A Multilevel Analysis of Survey Data from 30 Countries," *Social Science Research* 37 (2007): 268–286.

35. Pollack, Detlef, Olaf Müller, Gergely Rosta, Nils Friedrichs and Alexander Yendell, *Grenzen der Toleranz: Wahrnehmung und Akzeptanz religiöser Vielfalt in Europa* (Wiesbaden: Springer VS, 2014).

36. Oliver Roy, *La Sainte ignorance. Le temps de la religion sans culture* (Paris: Editions du Seuil, 2008).

37. Karl Barth, Community, *State, and Church. Three Essays* (Eugene: Wipf & Stock), 188; see also the contribution of Jeffrey Haynes in this volume.

Chapter 18

Karl Barth's *The Christian Life* and the Task of Political Theology

Paul Dafydd Jones

Four fairly recent books—Bernd Wannenwetsch's *Political Worship*, Mark Lewis Taylor's *The Theological and the Political*, Charles Mathewes's *The Republic of Grace*, and Monica Coleman's *Making a Way Out of No Way*—suggest that English-language political theology is undergoing an intriguing transition.[1] At first sight, each work stands within an easily identifiable tradition of thought. Wannenwetsch aims to deepen the "ecclesial turn" taken by Stanley Hauerwas, John Milbank, and others; Taylor stands among the growing number of North American thinkers who draw inspiration from continental philosophy in a post-Marxist key; Mathewes positions himself in the world of Christian realism; Coleman is indebted to process thinkers like Alfred North Whitehead and Charles Hartshorne. Upon closer inspection, however, each author seeks to overhaul the tradition of which she or he is a part, and does so by adding novel elements to it. The result is a collection of hybridized perspectives—creative alliances, "constructive" in the best sense, that overturn expectation and launch new trajectories for the field. Wannenwetsch, for instance, reconceives "the new traditionalism"[2] by way of a deft reading of Luther and an ecumenically nuanced liturgical sensibility. Taylor links his appreciation for open-ended materialism to a liberationist ethic, while trading on a Tillichian account of art as a vehicle of sociopolitical protest. Aware of the limitations of Reinhold Niebuhr's outsized doctrine of sin, Mathewes nests his brand of realism within an eschatologically charged reading of Augustine. Coleman, finally, combines a grand metaphysical vision with a frank affirmation of religious syncretism and a womanist ethic.

Now if one considers these texts representative, to some degree, of Anglophone political theology[3] in the last ten years or so, one can hardly say that the "old verities and truths of the heart" are being rejected.[4] The later Barth's wistful memory of the first phase of dialectical theology—"How we cleared things away! And we did almost nothing but clear away!"—would also be out of place.[5] In different ways, each of these works is somewhat cautious. There is a reluctance to strike out toward uncharted territory, and a concern to use extant resources to negotiate difficult terrain. Yet cautiousness goes hand in hand with a determination to innovate. Contrary to the bombastic tone of some ventures at the turn of the century (Exhibit A being the failed experiment of "Radical Orthodoxy"), these authors are fully aware that constructive advances depend, typically, on the patient analysis, evaluation, and integration of diverse discourses—and are more than willing to work toward that end. In the same moment that some familiar twentieth-century conventions ("liberal," "postliberal," "evangelical," etc.) are nearing the point of obsolescence, the field of political theology is delighting in the opportunities that arise in an unsettled intellectual context, and is making confident and valuable advances.

Given this context, it is worth asking: What role could Karl Barth play in the development of political theology today?[6] In a British and North American context, the question is not posed as frequently as one might suspect. While a previous generation of writers were clearly indebted to Barth— think of John Howard Yoder, Donald Mackinnon, and James Cone; think also of Stanley Hauerwas and Oliver O'Donovan—many at the cutting-edge of scholarly discussion show relatively little interest in his work. Mathewes and Wannenwetsch engage Barth only passingly; Taylor and Coleman, not at all. Given that the "Barth renaissance" in Anglophone circles continues apace, this lack of interest is somewhat odd.[7] Still odder is the fact that the very issues that exercise many contemporary political theologians—the relationship of church, state, and civil society; diverse disciplinary regimes, the balance of which often degrade critical reflection and religious commitments; the distribution of wealth; the meaning of sex, gender, and sexuality; the nature of work and leisure; and, last but not least, the relationship between Christian thought and progressive politics—were treated at length by Barth, and in a decidedly sophisticated way.

The relatively insular character of Barth scholarship is somewhat responsible for this state of affairs. For better or worse, the *Church Dogmatics* is a peculiarly addicting text, and it can exert a powerful grip on the imagination of some readers. One consequence of this is that "Barthians," of various stripes, huddle together; and as that happens, they become viewed as a group best left to itself. It is important, too, for those of us who remain hooked on the *Dogmatics* to consider Barth's absence from much theopolitical discourse without haughtiness. It is an obvious point, but one that some are liable to forget: no one working in the field of political theology is *obliged* to draw inspiration from this (or any other) "great thinker." Indeed, there are valid reasons for Barth being treated circumspectly. Certainly his reactionary treatments of sex and gender cast a troubling shadow over his work. And in a context in which various communities, historically excluded from academic discussion, continue to be denied the hearing that they deserve, it is understandable that those same communities do not turn to a European "authority," but focus on theological resources that have been undervalued or ignored.[8]

Yet I am still inclined to view the slight role that Barth plays in contemporary political theology as a missed opportunity. It is not just that Barth's writing has value in and of itself; it is also the case that it stands ready to enrich contemporary political theology, especially when its author is viewed less as a peerless sage, more as a participant in a fast-moving, pluralistic conversation. One need not view Barth through the restrictive prism of Anglo-American neo-orthodoxy, nor need one suppose that his genius requires that scholarship be limited to an endless stream of interpretative dissertations, monographs, and articles. One can read Barth differently: as one voice among many; as a pilgrim whose involvement in the liberal art of Christian theology obliges him to be "open" to diverse viewpoints, while also "thinking and speaking in responsibility and openness"; as a resource for constructive reflection in the present.[9]

To make the case for Barth's inclusion in the contemporary world of theo-politics, I focus on a late and incomplete text: *The Christian Life*.[10] I detail Barth's perspective gradually, and with an eye to connecting his thought with contemporary concerns. My first section tackles Barth's account of the covenantal relationship between God and humankind; the second considers Barth's distinctive brand of "Christian realism"; and the third engages Barth's anticipation of the post-Marxist sensibility exemplified by Ernesto Laclau, Chantal Mouffe, and others, as well as Barth's suggestion that "revolt" should define Christian political activity. As will become clear, I hope to do more than supply a persuasive outline of the political drift of Barth's late theology. I want also to identify concrete ways in which Barth's work is relevant to and beneficial for a range of theopolitical projects currently under development.

COVENANTAL RELATIONSHIP AS A
FRAMEWORK FOR POLITICAL THEOLOGY

While the charge of "occasionalism" continues to be raised against Barth's ethics,[11] it amounts to a drastic misreading of the *Dogmatics*, and one that must be corrected for Barth's (possible) contribution to political theology to be appreciated.

Certainly, for Barth, right action is a matter of responding obediently to God's concrete injunctions, the precise character and force of which cannot be foreknown. This is a particular concern of *CD* II/2, and it shapes all of

Barth's subsequent treatments of ethical and political issues. Christians have no recourse to a fixed "code" when it comes to ethical and political matters, and, in fact, all attempts to establish such a thing drift in the direction of "religious" evasions of God's sovereign direction of human life. Granted Barth's insistence that "the command of God encounters the ethical agent vertically," it does not follow, however, that Barth provides no support for the "horizontal" work of ethicists and political theologians.[12] While God's commands may be unanticipatable, they are not arbitrary. They are issued—and, in a basic sense, defined by—the covenant fulfilled by Jesus Christ. In this person and history, it becomes clear who God is and what God does. God is the one who loves in freedom; God is the one whose election of humankind assures us of God's favor. And in this person and history, it becomes clear who we are and what ought to distinguish our lives. We are those creatures that God has reconciled to herself; we are those creatures who have been granted the capacity and obligation to honor the act of God in Christ. Worries about "occasional" dictates, issued by an inscrutable deity, are therefore impossible. Barth provides a carefully contoured description of the "space . . . within which meaningful human action"—and, yes, meaningful *political* action—"can take place."[13]

Building on this foundation, I would suggest that Barth's work could make three fairly general contributions to political theology. First and most obviously, it provides a salutary reminder that Christian life has God's ways and works as its principal point of reference, with the economy of God's action, the centerpiece of which is Christ's fulfillment of God's covenant with Israel, being the "environment" in which Christians attempt to think faithfully and act politically. Those who worry, then, about an overinflated ecclesiology, which often carries an oppositional binary of church and world in its wake (a "neotraditionalist" tendency, which Wannenwetsch aims to check), and those who worry about disproportionate attention being given to the immediate contexts in which Christians exist (a risk run by Christian realists, which Mathewes aims to check), find in Barth a worthy ally. It is not that the church or the quotidian in which we exist is unimportant. It is simply that both "local" contexts must be viewed as parts of a whole, and their meanings subordinated to, and relativized by, a wide-angled account of God's creative, reconciliatory, and redemptive work. But does the unusual force of Barth's account of God's ways and works wash away the very particular contexts and locales in which we find ourselves, rendering them so much ephemera? Does Barth's Christo- and theocentrism effectively discredit studies that attend to the workings of particular church communities (Mary McClintock Fulkerson's *Places of Redemption*, or Jennifer Harvey's *Dear White Christians*, for instance) or the character of a particular sociopolitical and cultural moment (Brian Bantum's *Redeeming Mulatto*, or Luke Bretherton's *Christianity and Contemporary Politics*, for instance)?[14] No. Granted that all contexts, ecclesial and otherwise, must be viewed in light of God's saving work, these same contexts have their own particularity, distinction, and relative dignity. They are integral moments in a covenantal drama, elements of the created stage on which God's saving works are played.[15] Their status as "proximate" is not exclusive of their being caught up in what is "ultimate"—namely, the communicative activity of Christ and Christ's Spirit, and humanity's shifting reception of that same activity, as God draws all things to himself.[16] Barth's claim that God effects "the liberation of . . . *specific* people for free, spontaneous, and responsible *cooperation* in [God's] history" (102) can, then, be taken at face value. It is not an overdue dialectical complement to an outsized account of God's ways and works, but a straightforward statement about our responsibilities in an unfolding *Heilsgeschichte*.

Second, and in a related vein, *The Christian Life* challenges an approach to ethics and political reflection that Barth describes as an "indefinite ethics of the *kairos*" (6)—that is, a perspective whose investment in the particulars of any given concrete situation runs alongside a marked agnosticism about, if not hostility toward, "classical" and "realistic" descriptions of God's creative and saving work. Mark Lewis Taylor's *The Theological and the Political* might be read as a contemporary instance. Taylor's principal concern is to connect Jean-Luc Nancy's motif of "transimmanence" with reflection about the "weight of the world"—the first term being an artful rejection of those who treat immanence and transcendence, and materiality and spirituality, as mutually exclusive; the second phrase serving to identify oppressive structures and to affirm human agency—and thereby to provide a theopolitical commentary on resistance to wrongdoing. The book functions, too, as an exercise in conscientization. Its engagement with Nancy, Bourdieu, and others blurs the line between interpretation and activism: each reader is pressed to reckon with the responsibilities she ought to take up, in view of dehumanizing "systems of global capital, neocoloniality, imperial dominance."[17] So far, so good. But problems arise when one asks for a more nuanced account of the constructive framework Taylor commends, and when one tries to ascertain what the next step of the theopolitical task actually entails. Even if one grants (as I would) that the enterprise of "systematic theology" has often provided ideological cover for injustice and the maldistribution of opportunity, the absence of clear claims about the identity of God and the human has as its corollary a worryingly vague sense of what Christians ought actually to think and do, in order to relieve the "weight of the world." What orients us, once "doctrinal cognition" has been thrown overboard as so much unnecessary and outdated ballast?[18] We are left with little more than a "teeming singular plurality"[19]—a lively but somewhat elusive brand of theological materialism that, yes, ought to be artfully "haunted" . . . but to what end? Since the theological and the political are firmly tethered to the here-and-now, theopolitics seems now to be *limited* to a "sense of expectation" and a "cultivation of transformative possibility as carried in spectral practice."[20] It is not that people of faith might spearhead the world's transformation; it is more that we must *react* to a world that shifts and changes shape of its own accord.

This is, admittedly, a sharp critique of *The Theological and the Political*, and one that risks obscuring Taylor's talents for consciousness-raising, on the one hand, and astute interpretive work, on the other. But I do not offer it in hopes of invalidating transimmanental reflection, nor because I view the non-reductive materialist framework within which Taylor works to be necessarily antithetical to longstanding Christian convictions. I offer it in order to propose that Barth might serve as a critical interlocutor: a "specter" whose "haunting" of Taylor involves very different theological commitments, but (most likely) proximate political convictions, and therefore someone who might lend this project greater constructive clarity. Put in terms of a bundle of questions: Should the belief that a "thick description" of God and humankind provides a necessary basis for theopolitical reflection be jettisoned so quickly? Might not some aspects of so-called "guild Theology"[21] enhance Taylor's transimmanental project—particularly those that refuse to partition doctrine and the "artful signs" of "symbolic force,"[22] preferring instead to understand doctrine as a dialectically charged network of claims and narratives, the coherence of which is secured not by recourse to a discrete set of principles but by reference to the history of Jesus Christ? Might the *Dogmatics* enable Taylor to identify points of contact between the project of transimmanence and systematics, even granted that the latter mode of reflection is not one that Taylor supports? If it is fair to worry that *The Theological and the Political* risks a certain kind of occasionalism—a *genuine* "indefinite ethics of the *kairos*," and one that forecloses the possibility of ad hoc alliances with those who are not so enthralled with the open-ended materialism of Nancy et al.—these questions seem fairly urgent. And even if Taylor were to answer them in ways that Barth would deem inadequate, the very fact of posing and answering them, and doing so in conversation with an author whose work does not easily conform to Taylor's critique of "guild theology," could well pay dividends.

Barth's third contribution to contemporary discussions is a rhetorical strategy that engages political issues "without direct allusions":[23] a style of writing that offers relatively few contextual markers and eschews the conventions of political discourse, while *also* making theological reflection ingredient to the formation of political consciousness. While this rhetorical strategy does not feature in many contemporary works of political theology, any neglect of its role in Barth's writing sends interpretation off track very quickly. What falls from view is Barth's abiding concern to describe how human thought is transformed when it is brought, by grace, into the time and space of God's self-revelation, and Barth's belief that God's transformation of our thought enables a praxeaological response, the likes of which will be supplied outside of the margins of the text. What falls from view, to put it more simply, is the fact that Barth writes in ways that steel his readers to *act*. The *Dogmatics* is not only a teasing out of the *ratio* of Christian faith as it thinks about who God is and what God does is (although it is no less than that); it is also an extended attempt to cultivate a sensibility that helps Christians to participate—ecclesially, socially, and politically—in God's covenantal drama.

Lest this seem too abstract, some words from §78, "The Struggle for Human Righteousness," help to illustrate what I mean.

> The decisive action of their revolt against disorder—which, correctly understood, includes within itself all others—is their *calling upon God* in the second petition of the Lord's Prayer: *"Thy kingdom come!"* . . . The Kingdom of God is God himself in the act of normalizing human existence, and God himself in the victorious act of overcoming the disorder that still rules humanity. . . . To pray this prayer about the coming of the Kingdom does not excuse Christians from revolting and engaging in conflict with disorder in their own human thoughts, words, and works in a provisional way. On the contrary: they cannot rightly pray this prayer without being propelled towards a corresponding action of their own—action that is provisional but nonetheless serious. Oriented in this prayer to the coming of the kingdom, and thus made "comrades of the Kingdom," Christians cannot possibly refrain from a "coming" of their own. Which means: *going to meet the coming kingdom of God* [my emphasis], seeing and grasping the possibilities which are provisionally present or which offer themselves not for divine but for *human righteousness* and order, by being concerned for the actualization of these possibilities within the limits of their certainly weak ability and, above all, of their continually errant and corrupted will. (212-3, rev.)

Key to this passage is the movement between political allusion and the suggestion that human beings are now empowered to act, novelly and decisively, in the context of a covenant that is soteriologically fulfilled yet temporally open. On the one side, there is a strong emphasis on political responsibility, underscored through the use of words like "revolt" (*Aufstand*) and "disorder" (*Unordnung*), and with talk about the need to become "comrades of the Kingdom" (*Reichsgenossen*). Such allusiveness is not assimilable to any particular political program, even though it exhibits a leftward tilt. Barth's goal is otherwise: pressing readers to take up residence in the space between prayer and political action—or, more precisely, helping readers to understand that God elides the distinction between prayer and political action, such that "going to meet" the Kingdom is simultaneously a Christian intervention in the political sphere, and a political action that arises "spontaneously," given God's initiation and sustenance of faith. On the other side, in that reconciliation between God and humankind is an objective reality, human life in the here-and-now *gains* in meaning. Political activity may not be deemed inconsequential, a mere spinning of one's wheels, prior to the apocalypse. Even as Christians wait for the consummation of the Kingdom, this waiting should be an active affair. The prayer, "thy Kingdom come," has as its corollary the decision to move toward and into the future in conscious, discrete, and effective ways. Such movement ends up, in fact, being as "irresistible" as the grace that animates it. "Christians cannot possibly refrain from a 'coming' of their own" precisely because inclusion in the covenant of grace has as its concrete outworking the liberation of human beings to act, inside and beyond the church, in ways that bear witness to Christ's victory over sin and death.

I would certainly acknowledge that this rhetorical strategy has not always borne fruit. The prose of the *Dogmatics* can sometimes be a bit *too* intoxicating, and not a few interpreters have shown themselves resistant to reading it as a political document—or, more precisely, as a prolegomenon to the enactment of political agency.[24] It should also be noted that rhetorical reticence might be deemed a luxury that precious few can afford. Indirection can easily be construed as indifference, especially when voices that respond plainly to wrongdoing and express clear support for liberative social, political, and economic ventures are in short supply. Yet a case can still be made for Barth's approach. If one accepts that right action depends on God's gracious address, there is a value to styles of reflection that do not presume what we ought to do, but rather encourage us to wait, to dispose ourselves as individuals and communities who do not engage political issues with a preformed sense of what is required. It might even be that Barth's rhetoric is well suited for the present moment. One can imagine an unusual dialectic: on the one side, Barth's account of God's ways and works, the energy of which alerts a reader to her concrete responsibility and freedom to live into the covenant that Christ has fulfilled, but demurs with respect to specifics; on the other side, texts that insist, very directly, on the abiding connection between Christian faith and active solidarity with "those who stand with their backs to the wall."[25] We need not suppose that Barth's concerns about "religion" and experiential styles of reflection debar engagement with contemporary modes of contextual theology; there is obviously a world of difference between *Kulturprotestantismus* and projects that apply the motto of "faith seeking understanding" in subversive ways. I am proposing something more interesting: a coalition between Barth and an array of liberationist projects, the vitality of which might lend intellectual support to struggles for justice and peace.[26]

BARTH'S "REALISM"

Were this the sum total of Barth's contribution to political theology, Oliver O'Donovan's description of the *Dogmatics* as "a magnificent, but incomplete, beckoning movement"—a text that never quite gets beyond prolegomena—might be justified.[27] The ad hoc quality of Barth's theopolitical endeavors could support the point, showing Barth to be a systematician with occasional interests in politics, not a systematician for whom political concerns are inseparable from theology proper. Might one not say that Barth encourages a new kind of political consciousness, but offers scant advice as to how Christians should negotiate concrete political matters? Does not Barth demur when it comes to providing an agenda for political theology—"agenda" being something less than a platform, but something more than an invigorating run-up to political action? I would answer both questions negatively, and would argue that *The Christian Life*, as well as being an invaluable statement in its own right, helps one to attend to theopolitical concerns latent in earlier volumes of the *Dogmatics*. This section considers Barth's sense of how Christians should dispose themselves as political agents, identifying affinities between Barth's late work and the tradition of Christian realism.[28] The next section focuses on what Christians ought to be doing: it suggests that Barth's writings have particular value for those who support leftwing and/or progressive political projects.

Identifying a realist subtext to *The Christian Life* is important because it shows that Barth's grand dogmatic vision does not have as a complement grandiose and potentially hubristic political programs. The fact that humanity is situated in and determined by Christ may make sin baffling, but it does not render it unreal—much less easily combatable. Equally, it cannot be said that a joyous apprehension of God's favor exempts Christians from the hard task of differentiating between political options that can function *both* as vehicles of all-too-human self-interest *and* occasions for effecting a "little righteousness." Barth recognizes this, and he treats the negotiation of concrete political issues as a matter of dogmatic interest. He writes in ways that aim to help Christians "do politics" *better*—that is, with a bit less naïveté and/or cynicism, a bit more good cheer, and a bit more efficacy. Three points have particular importance: wariness toward preformed ethical or political codes, acceptance of the necessity of incremental change, and an acknowledgement of the ambiguity of all human endeavors. Taken together, these points show a surprising affinity between Barth's later work and the perspective developed by one of Barth's most astute critics: Reinhold Niebuhr.[29]

Recall, first, that Barth considers the initial petition of the Lord's Prayer—the vocative, "Father!"—as including, *per definitionem*, the question, "What shall I do?" (31ff.). When offered in good faith, the question is never idle.

It is a genuine plea for guidance: a kenotic act whereby the human being weighs her situation, embraces perplexity, and waits to be instructed. Indeed, insofar as this question troubles every passing moment of the Christian's life, recourse to conventional wisdom, whether that be understood in terms of a preexisting scheme of ethics or a political "game plan," is disallowed. In praying the Lord's Prayer, Christians press themselves to become critical toward putatively virtuous modes of behavior, and to reckon with the possibility that God might commend unusual courses of action—or, for that matter, deft and perhaps unsavory negotiations of complex political situations. Barth is blunt: the Christian must never suppose that "a trained and mastered routine . . . a learned and practiced art" (79) readies her for life in the public square. Political judgment is a situational, not habitual, affair; and the reality of grace is such that she must accept that the "ground beneath his feet is on fire" and that "the unrest that the Word of God has brought into his life will never leave" (187).

Second, Barth envisages Christian political action as a typically modest endeavor. The perspective of *The Christian Life* builds on Barth's discussion of the "limits" of human life in *CD* III/2; what Barth adds is a sense that these "limits" have political import, and should serve as a check against hubris. To be sure, political action might sometimes need to be dramatic, even revolutionary: a matter of "zeal and burning passion" (169). If God's zeal motivates God's saving actions, it stands to reason that we are called, on occasion, to act analogously. For the most part, however, political action is a matter of "little steps." A key passage:

> As a rule, the steps will only be *little* ones, or apparently little ones, made with no particular elevation. . . . We may simply say . . . that it is a matter of steps that . . . we are freed and required to take . . . as *people* of our time in what is (even in the most extraordinary case!) the fairly small space and frame of the opportunities we are offered and the possibilities that we are given, and in the fairly narrow view of our situation and problems that we usually have, yet still, be that as it may, as the *people* we now *are*, as God's *children* and not as gods! (172 rev.)

The rhetoric may not be Niebuhrian, but the counsel is very much so. Put as a maxim: granted the appeal of lofty political visions, do not lose sight of the fact that political progress requires the pursuit of proximate, achievable goals. And might we not say that advice of this kind has especial value in the present? In a situation characterized by the excesses of a relatively unregulated global market, the paroxysms of which serve only to concentrate wealth in the hands of an increasingly small number of people, the continued degradation of the ecosphere, and newly invigorated efforts to maintain racial, gendered, sexual, and religious privilege (both the "Tea Party" movement and the election of Donald Trump in the United States being one instance of a global tendency), it becomes ever-more tempting to exchange measured protest and strategic involvement in political processes for the thrill of moral indignation. The dynamics are familiar to us. The advent of "crisis capitalism," characterized by lavish bailouts to banking giants and the continuing dominance of multinational corporations, is met with impassioned, but politically inchoate, demands for "antiglobalization" and an "anti-austerity" platform; activism around Israel and Palestine devolves into splenetic, in-house exchanges over the legitimacy or illegitimacy of academic boycotts and divestment; discussions about the legacy of racism in the United States are reduced to tirades against Fox News, the Murdoch Empire, and Facebook slacktivism. And Barth would have none of it. While holding fast to a wide-angled account of God's ways and works, and while remaining clear about the values that ought to underwrite political action (on which, more later), he requires that Christians continue to press for incremental changes in the here-and-now. One can have one's sights firmly fixed on the Kingdom's lofty peaks while negotiating the "foothills where human life must be lived."[30]

Third, Barth joins with realists in emphasizing the ambiguity of political undertakings, while refusing to give this emphasis a leading role in his thought. In this he stands in contrast to Niebuhr, who often struggled to differentiate the doctrine of creation (which, when functioning well, treats the limits of human life as non-pernicious aspects of God's good work) and an account of sin (which, when functioning well, identifies corruption as an adventitious distortion of human life). On one level, Barth acknowledges frankly that human existence is shaped by multiple commitments. The "precedence of the Word of God" (§77.4) does not render mundane factors (familial responsibilities, economic endeavors, etc.) questionable, nor does it wrench an individual out of the context in which she finds herself. It is a precedence that intervenes in utterly particular circumstances and, to employ an overused colloquialism, "meets us where we are." It is a precedence, in fact, that *affirms* the goodness of the quotidian in which we find ourselves, even as God transforms our perception of that quotidian and asks us to act upon it—pressing us to give "greater weight . . . to one of the factors over one or all of the others (ambivalent as they all are in themselves)" (180). On another level, Barth knows well that human conduct is never perfectly correspondent to, much less purely iterative of, the divine command. Ethics can never be bought "at the price of absolute purity";[31] we always live in a "sphere of ambivalence" (181). There is only "an imperfect, fragile, and highly problematical righteousness" (265) available to us; our actions "at worst . . . will not be demonic, and . . . at best . . . will not be angelic" (185). Or, to put it differently, insofar as we are "mediocre believers,"[32] we are also mediocre political agents. Our apprehension of God's command occurs on a spectrum that is, on a good day, shaky, and, on a bad day, perversely misguided; likewise, our implementation of that command. With that said—and here is another turn that Niebuhr could not make—it does not follow that the actions that we undertake are only mitigatory, temporary bulwarks against a tide of wrongdoing, whose contradictory qualities can only be reconciled at the eschaton.[33] Granted that the Christian cannot suppose that she is *truly* doing God's works, political ventures can be undertaken in good cheer, and in the hope that our attempts to work a "little righteousness" are part of a covenantal history that is moving toward God's future.

"REVOLT": THE HEART OF CHRISTIAN POLITICAL ACTION

While I hope to have shown the value of Barth's approach to political theology and demonstrated common ground between Barth and the tradition of Christian realism, the idea that there is a positive and, indeed, *relevant* political agenda in Barth might still seem far-fetched. Even if Barth makes headway with certain ethical issues (as is clear, of course, from even a cursory reading of *CD* III/4), can one extrapolate something akin to a concrete theopolitical stance from *The Christian Life*, given Barth's reticence about specific courses of action? I think so. Barth offers a clear account of the values that must guide political action, whenever a community acclaims and orients itself to God's ways and works. He supplies, more particularly, a rough draft of the (likely) shape of Christian political action in the context of late modernity.[34]

The most conspicuous characteristic of this rough draft is a starkly negative appraisal of the modern political order. The remarkable second subsection of §78, in which Barth discusses the "lordless powers," is pivotal. The principal scriptural reference is Eph. 6:12, read by way of a Feuerbachian account of the human production of "pseudo-objective realities" (216). At this point, in contrast to the second edition of *Romans* and *CD* I/2, Barth is no longer concerned to appropriate Feuerbach's insights to support a critique of "religion." At issue is something akin to ideology critique:[35] a politically vital account of the ways in which material factors and all-too-human discursive processes gain a semidivine status, and thereby consolidate human beings' alienation from God and mistreatment of each another in the overlapping spheres of society, economy, and culture. The fact that Barth explicitly *names* "the hidden wirepullers in man's great and small enterprises, movements, achievements, and revolutions" (216) is, further, a point of terrific importance. Barth does not risk a strategy of rhetorical indirection when the stakes are this high: he writes plainly about the mythology of the nation-state and absolutist forms of rule, about the operations of capital and the "very mobile demon" of commodity fetishism, about ideologies that degrade critical thought and inhibit autonomous reflection, and about "chthonic forces" (227ff.) that, by way of subtle disciplinary regimes, divert us from the possibility of participating in the covenant of grace. This treatment of "hidden wirepullers" may be brief, but it is not perfunctory. Barth identifies large-scale dimensions of late modernity that he adjudges to be consistently inimical to Christian political action as manifestations of sin that the Christian must discern, wrestle with, and, as will become clear, *resist*.

It is also significant that Barth writes about lordless *powers*. While a lifelong commitment to democratic socialism haunts *The Christian Life* (and, indeed, the *Dogmatics* as such), Barth here anticipates the challenge to Marxist economism pioneered by Ernesto Laclau, Chantal Mouffe, and others, and embraced in Taylor's *The Theological and the Political*, Coleman's *Making a Way Out of No Way*, and other texts of a liberationist bent. Barth recognizes, in other words, "a *variety* of possible antagonisms in the social"[36] that converge to establish, support, and obscure structures of injustice, and Barth acknowledges that there is a pantheon of hypostasized "gods" that human beings have generated and sustain, and which corrupt our every thought, word, and deed. Now this does not amount to a denial that the operations of capital are decisive for much social and political life. Barth would likely share Laclau and Mouffe's cautions about an *under*valuation of economic forces: in the sketchy conclusion to §77.2, "The Known and Unknown God," he notes that there is "no greater deceiver, no one less worthy of our respect, than King Mammon" (151). Yet a king alone does not hegemony make, and Barth is as deft as the best post-Marxists in describing the interlocking patterns of behavior that uphold and reinforce patterns of discrimination. Indeed, striking a remarkably Foucauldian note, Barth indicates that what makes the lordless powers so effective is precisely their inconspicuousness, their "normalcy"; the fact that their influence is mediated through mechanisms of "wraithlike transitoriness . . . one appearing here and another there, then disappearing or retreating to give place to another, then appearing again" (215).[37]

Political theology can and should build on these suggestions. Exemplified here is a style of theological reflection that (*pace* Taylor, again) does not retreat from strong dogmatic claims, yet is comfortable in appropriating "materialist" modes of reflection developed by Foucauldians, radical democratic theorists, feminists and womanists, queer activists, and so on. Ideology critique is not "tacked on" to systematics; systematic theology, precisely because it is concerned with the ways in which human sin continues to disrupt God's good creation, and precisely because it is obliged to describe human life in a far-reaching and holistic way, gratefully receives insights from all quarters, and renders those insights integral to the theological task. There is a sense, too, in which this line of thought can be intensified, such that political theology, in its various idioms, might embrace the idea that the wide world of critical theory can be for *us* what Feuerbach was to Barth: a diagnostic tool that exposes, with an admirable lack of sentimentality, new forms of unfaithfulness and idolatry. What is gained is an account of sin whose adequacy is proven not only by its depth and richness, but also by its suppleness—its capacity to uncover and interpret the diverse ways in which human beings distort the "proximate" contexts in which we are placed. No doubt, the rhetoric used by secular thinkers will be transposed into a different register. Barth knew as much: when he drew on Feuerbach, he dispensed with materialist presuppositions, while freely appropriating Feuerbach's accounts of projection and wish fulfillment. Comparably selective appropriations of a Judith Butler, a Hortense Spillers, or even a Lee Edelman are required of us—as is the humility to explain why our "selectivity" is not a mark of disrespect, but a grateful receipt of insights that Christian communities, for various reasons, have failed to develop for themselves.

Barth's positive account of political action crystallizes around the motif of *revolt*—"not just rejecting . . . a bad possibility but . . . rising up and revolting against its actualization . . . affirming and grasping [another possibility] and entering into battle for its actualization" (207). Within *The Christian Life*, this motif emphasizes how struggle against "lordless powers" goes hand in hand with action *for* the Kingdom. Revolt is that quality of Christian action that arises when a "realist" appraisal of what God commands is matched with concrete actions in support of human righteousness. Beyond *The Christian Life,* this motif could serve as a point around which diverse theopolitical projects, typically of a leftist or progressive drift, can be seen to orbit.

For Barth, the category of revolt is, in a strict sense, derivative of and ordered to his account of God's identity and activity. God's free and loving revolt against sin is the analogate for which Christian action, ecclesial and political, must be the analogy; our task is live and act in ways that correspond to God's ways and works. "Christians may and can and should reflect and practice God's being and acting for man . . . making man the special object of their own interest" and being eager to "swim manfully against the stream regardless of the cost or consequences" (267). Is such "swimming" really possible, given the influence of "demonic factors in world occurrence" (267)? Well—*yes*. What Barth shares with scholars like Monica Coleman is a startling sense that "God offers possibilities that were previously unforeseen, a way . . . out of no way."[38] Political change need not be an ever-deferred hope against overwhelming odds—even granted, say, the seemingly inexorable operations of international capital and, less impressively but no less decisively, the extensive effects of restrictive disciplinary regimes. Political change is something that God enables in the here-and-now. It is something that God does, and therefore a pattern of action in which we can participate. Urgently so: the petition "Thy Kingdom Come" means that one can and must "run towards" the Kingdom "with all one's soul and all one's powers like one who is running a race" (so 1. Cor. 9:24ff. and Phil. 3:12ff.), "bravely following this movement and turning, having no other choice but to look ahead and also to live and speak and act ahead, to run from the beginning, the history of Jesus Christ first revealed in his resurrection" (262). In a manner that is doubtless quite different from anything imagined by the bombastic, frustrating, but nevertheless astute "Invisible Committee," Barth himself could say: "The real is what resists."[39] There is here a *definite* "ethics of the *kairos*": a belief that God's sanctification of Christian life enables political possibilities that admit of concrete actualization.

"Concrete actualization"? Exactly that. Granted that Barth's confidence in God's gracious sovereignty is can sometimes appear overwhelming, he is keenly aware that God's action, in many cases, is inclusive of human action. So much is well known in the world of Barth studies: a vital depiction of the integrity and efficacy of human action cuts across Barth's doctrine of creation, his theological anthropology, his doctrine of reconciliation, and his ecclesiology. Somewhat neglected, however, is the way in which Barth's "moral ontology" forms an integral part of his theopolitical vision. *The Christian Life* makes it clear: Christians may not "wait" for the Kingdom in a passive or timid way. They must move toward it; they must be willing to "snatch the available possibilities of doing what is commanded and thus catching up God's name where they are in arrears" (265); they must ascertain and realize, against the odds, forms of life that approximate God's covenantal design. Why the urgency? Because—and here again Barth and Coleman, and also Barth and Mathewes, find themselves unexpected stable-mates—God is actually *holding history open*, waiting for human beings to practice "a little righteousness" in church and world, before bringing the covenantal drama over which God presides to its glorious end. A passage from IV/1 makes the point dramatically:

> God will not allow his last word to be fully spoken or the consummation determined, accomplished, and proclaimed by him to take place in its final form until he has heard a human *answer* to it, a human *Yes*; until his grace has found its correspondence in a voice of *human thanks* from the depths of the world reconciled with him; until here and now, before the dawning of his eternal Sabbath, he has received praise from the midst of his human creature. So great is his grace, so broad is the reach of condescension, so serious is the solidarity in which he has committed himself with us human beings in the person of his Son . . . [that] God wills a body, an earthly and historical form of the existence of this Head. . . . In order that this may happen, God still gives the world space, time, and existence; he allows the end-time to dawn and to persist. (IV/1, 737-8 rev.)

A startling claim in and of itself; also a tantalizing hint as to what Barth's doctrine of redemption, in its eschatological dimensions, might have entailed. God's graciousness is so far-reaching that, because of *and in addition to* Christ's atoning history and the sending of the Spirit, humanity is given a role to play in bringing salvation to its conclusion.

What might this mean for political theology? Generally, it shows that even the most "theocentric" of theological perspectives, when framed in terms of a covenant soteriologically fulfilled but not temporally closed, can esteem human activity as having a transformative, even world-altering, effect. The election of grace is not reducible to our being liberated from sin (although it is never less than that); it is inclusive of God *capacitating* us to live and act, obediently and freely, with God. In the church? Well, yes, of course. But not only there.[40] The more particular application of Barth's perspective is this: If it is indeed the case that God waits on and for us, and if it is the case that such waiting entails the provision of time and space, wherein human beings are enabled and asked to express gratitude for grace, it is *also* the case that our gratitude will have, *as a necessary ingredient*, the articulation of a "little righteousness"—and therefore some measure of struggle against the lordless powers. The motif of revolt, then, is one way to interpret and honor some of the most important theological developments of the last half-century. An "ethics of impatience," expressed by "turbulent bodies" who refuse to pay homage to the "principalities" and "powers" (Eph. 6:12, KJV), and who demand economic, sexual, racial, and social justice: the messy and unfinished project of liberation theology, in various forms, hangs on the possibility that these same impatient bodies are, in a parabolic sense, "revolts" that anticipate the Kingdom itself.[41] If it is indeed true that what God waits for, and what God waits on, is a bundle of historical projects that participate in God's own revolt against sin—projects that *fill up* the time and space that we are given, and which demonstrate that gratitude for grace must be matched with the pursuit of a "little righteousness"—there is yet one more reason to connect Barth and political theology today.[42]

CONCLUSION

To return to a point made earlier: in no sense do I suppose that Barth's work is compulsory reading for anyone working in the field of political theology today. Barth must be read critically: not so much an indispensable sage, more as a resource. And if, as I hope, the good health of political theology continues, then *The Christian Life* in particular, and the *Dogmatics* in general, merit our attention. There is here, to give Barth the last word, something of value for those who hope for, and labor toward, a "'theology of freedom' that looks ahead and strives forward."[43]

NOTES

1. Bernd Wannenwetsch, *Political Worship*, trans. Margaret Kolb (New York: Oxford University Press, 2004); Mark Lewis Taylor, *The Theological and the Political: On the Weight of the World* (Minneapolis: Fortress Press, 2011); Charles Mathewes, *The Republic of Grace: Augustinian Thoughts for Dark Times* (Grand Rapids: Eerdmans, 2010); Monica Coleman, *Making a Way Out of No Way: A Womanist Theology* (Minneapolis: Fortress Press, 2008). While Wannenwetsch's text is a translation from the German, its reception on both sides of the Atlantic (and the author's erstwhile standing within the British academy) justify its inclusion in a discussion of Anglophone political theology.

2. Jeffrey Stout, *Democracy and Tradition* (Princeton: Princeton University Press, 2004), esp. 92–179.

3. Granted the problematic history of the term "political theology," in what follows I use it to refer simply to texts that connect Christian and post-Christian convictions with political economy, government, participation in the democratic process, economics, social justice, etc.

4. William Faulkner, "Nobel Prize Address," in *The Faulkner Reader* (New York: Modern Library, 1959), 3.

5. Karl Barth, *The Humanity of God*, trans. Thomas Wieser and John Newton Thomas (Richmond: John Knox Press, 1960), 43.

6. It is of course the burden of this volume to make some headway on this issue, and I would particularly commend the insights advanced by Pan Chiu Lai, Alexander Maßmann, Charles Mathewes, Hanna Reichel, and Günter Thomas as they relate to the political contexts of Germany, the United States, and Hong Kong.

7. I borrow this phrase from Bruce L. McCormack. See *Orthodox and Modern: Studies in the Theology of Karl Barth* (Grand Rapids: Baker, 2008), 281–284.

8. See here, for instance, James H. Cone, *The Spirituals and the Blues: An Interpretation* (Maryknoll: Orbis, 1972) and *God of the Oppressed*, rev. ed. (Maryknoll: Orbis, 1997), esp. 1–14.

9. Karl Barth, *Final Testimonies*, ed. Eberhard Busch and trans. Geoffrey W. Bromiley (Eugene: Wipf & Stock, 2003), 34.

10. I use the standard translation: *The Christian Life: Church Dogmatics Volume IV, Part 4: Lecture Fragments*, trans. Geoffrey W. Bromiley (London: T&T Clark, 2004). For the German original, see *Das christliche Leben: Die Kirchliche Dogmatik IV/4, Fragmente aus dem Nachlaß, Vorlesung 1959–1961*, ed. Hans-Anton Drewes and Eberhard Jüngel (Zürich: TVZ, 1999). Additional quotations are from *Church Dogmatics*, ed. G. W. Bromiley and T. F. Torrance (31 vols) (London: T&T Clark, 2009). In-text quotations are from *The Christian Life*, unless indicated. "Rev." indicates a revised translation, for which I am responsible. I have also restored Barth's emphases.

11. Most recently, see Stephen J. Gabrill, *Rediscovering the Natural Law in Reformed Theological Ethics* (Grand Rapids: Eerdmans, 2006), 23. See also Robin Lovin, *Christian Faith and Public Choices: The Social Ethics of Barth, Brunner and Bonhoeffer* (Philadelphia: Fortress, 1984).

12. Paul T. Nimmo, *Being in Action: The Theological Shape of Barth's Ethical Vision* (London: T&T Clark, 2007), 45. With respect to Barth's (possible) contribution to public discussions of ethical and political matters, and a particularly valuable treatment of claims advanced in *CD* III/4, see Alexander Maßmann, *Bürgerrecht im Himmel und auf Erden. Karl Barths Ethik* (Leipzig: Evangelische Verlagsanstalt, 2011).

13. Nimmo, *Being in Action*, 11.

14. See Mary McClintock Fulkerson, *Places of Redemption: Theology for a Wordly Church* (Oxford: Oxford University Press, 2007); Jennifer Harvey, *Dear White Christians: For Those Still Longing for Racial Reconciliation* (Grand Rapids: Eerdmans, 2014); Brian Bantum, *Redeeming Mulatto: A Theology of Race and Christian Hybridity* (Waco: Baylor University Press, 2010); and Luke Bretherton, *Christianity and Contemporary Politics: The Conditions and Possibilities of Faithful Witness* (Malden: Wiley-Blackwell, 2010). Bantum's book offers a creative reading of Barth's Christology, and the influence of Barth can be felt throughout Bretherton's work—an indication, perhaps, that the "Barth renaissance" is beginning now to affect political theology.

15. *CD* III/1 supports this point. While one cannot separate creation and covenant—the former being the "external basis" of the covenant that Christ fulfills, the latter being the "internal basis" of the creation that Christ reconciles to God—there is a genuine distinction, and it must not be elided.

16. I borrow the distinction between "ultimate" and "proximate" contexts from David H. Kelsey, *Eccentric Existence: A Theological Anthropology* (2 vols) (Louisville: WJKP, 2009).

17. Taylor, *Theological and Political*, 222.

18. Ibid., 223.

19. Ibid., 223.

20. Ibid., 226.

21. Ibid., xvii and passim.

22. Ibid., 155.

23. Karl Barth, *Theological Existence To-day! (A Plea for Theological Freedom)*, trans. R. Birch Hoyle (Eugene: Wipf & Stock, 2011), 9.

24. A case-study in such resistance is the uproar that followed Friedrich-Wilhelm Marquardt's *Theologie und Sozialismus: Das Beispiel Karl Barths* (Munich: Chr. Kaiser, 1985).

25. I borrow here from Howard Thurman's classic, *Jesus and the Disinherited* (Boston: Beacon, 1996).

26. For more on this, see Paul Dafydd Jones, "Liberation Theology and 'Democratic Futures' (by way of Karl Barth and Friedrich Schleiermacher)," *Political Theology* 10, no. 1 (2009): 261–285.

27. Oliver O'Donovan, *The Desire of the Nations: Rediscovering the Roots of Political Theology* (Cambridge: Cambridge University Press, 1996), 286.

28. See here, exemplarily, Robin Lovin, *Reinhold Niebuhr and Christian Realism* (Cambridge: Cambridge University Press, 1995). How Barth relates to Charles Mathewes's particular construal of Christian Realism is of course an interesting issue; on this point, see Mathewes's contribution to this volume.

29. Reinhold Niebuhr's criticisms of Barth were prompted by Barth's refusal to denounce Soviet communism in suitably ferocious terms. See Gary Dorrien, *The Barthian Revolt in Modern Theology: Theology Without Weapons* (Louisville: WJKP, 2000), 134–139.

30. Reinhold Niebuhr, "We are Men and not God," *Christian Century* 65, no. 43 (1948): 1138–1140 (1140).

31. Reinhold Niebuhr, "Barth's East German Letter," *Christian Century* 76, no. 6 (1959): 167–168 (168).

32. Charles Mathewes, "The Scandalous Present and Hopeful Future of Christian Ethics," (unpublished manuscript).

33. So the final pages of Reinhold Niebuhr, *The Children of Light and the Children of Darkness: A Vindication of Democracy and A Critique of its Traditional Defense* (New York: Charles Scribner's Sons, 1960).

34. While I am not sufficiently informed about the political situations in Hong Kong, Taiwan, and other Asian contexts to make a measured judgment about what "revolt" might entail, I would encourage readers to consult a number of essays in this volume—perhaps especially those by Kin Yip Louie, Lai Pan Chiu, and Daniel Lee.

35. This being a phrase that Timothy Gorringe applies to Barth. See *Karl Barth: Against Hegemony* (Oxford: Oxford University Press, 1999).

36. Ernesto LaClau and Chantal Mouffe, *Hegemony and Socialist Strategy: Toward a Radical Democratic Politics*, 2nd edition (London: Verso, 2001), 131 (emphasis added).

37. Much more could be said about Barth's understanding of power. In this volume, Hanna Reichel creatively relates Barth's remarks about "lordless powers" to surveillance technologies. Elsewhere, Michael Jimenez has engaged the intellectual context in which Barth worked; see "Power Corrupts: Karl Barth's Use of Jacob Burckhardt's Philosophy of History," *Journal for the History of Modern Theology / Zeitschrift für Neuere Theologiegeschichte* 21, no. 1–2 (2014): 164–179.

38. Coleman, *Making a Way*, 36.

39. The Invisible Committee, *To our Friends*, trans. Robert Hurley (Cambridge: MIT Press, 2015), 195.

40. Markus Höfner, Charles Mathewes, and Kristopher Norris write about the relationship between church and world in this volume. The position I advance has especial consonance with Höfner's reading of Barth.

41. Marcella Althaus-Reid, *The Queer God* (London: Routledge, 2003), 48 and 47.

42. For more on the importance of "historical projects" for liberation theology, see Ivan Petrella, *The Future of Liberation Theology: An Argument and a Manifesto* (London: SCM, 2006).

43. Karl Barth, *Evangelical Theology*, trans. Grover Foley (Grand Rapids: Eerdmans, 1963), xii.

Part IV

DEMOCRACY AND TRADITION

CHRISTIAN ENGAGEMENT IN CIVIL SOCIETY

Religious Diversity, Democracy, and Public Theology

Conversing with Barth in a Hong Kong Context

Pan Chiu Lai

INTRODUCTION

Karl Barth (1886–1968) never visited China and he seldom talked about China, but he did mention "Chinese Walls" when commenting on Protestant theology in the nineteenth century:

> True, theology was also at work in and for the church; it was also concerned with its own proper centre, the gospel of Jesus Christ and the faith respond-ing to it; . . . However, the theologians had their eyes fixed on the world, and their thinking was necessarily conditioned by this outlook. . . . Retreat behind Chinese Walls never served theology well. It must be engaged in conversation with the contemporary world, whatever the means of the dialogue. . . . In this respect evangelical theology of the 19th century set an example never to be ignored in any vital theology.[1]

This chapter aims to investigate and explore whether, how, and to what extent, Barth's theology is relevant to recent theological debates in the Chinese-speaking world on public theology, especially debates related to the development of democracy in Hong Kong.[2]

Based on a survey of Chinese Christian discourses related to public issues, this chapter will illustrate how some Chinese theologians participating in the debates make explicit references to Barth or implicit allusions to the theo-logical position represented or championed by Barth to support their own positions. However, some of the theological discourses articulated in the debates derive from, or reflect, merely one of many possible interpretations or appropriations of Barth's theology. An alternative interpretation of Barth's theology, including his position on religion/religions,[3] as this chapter aims to show, will lead to a more comprehensive and balanced understanding of Barth's theology, as well as a different approach to public theology and the church's involvement in the development of democracy in Hong Kong.

RELIGIOUS DIVERSITY AND DEMOCRACY IN HONG KONG

Hong Kong is a religiously diversified metropolitan area. In terms of population, Christians constitute roughly 10 percent of the population of Hong Kong, but the influence of Christianity in education, social service, and so on, outperforms all other religions in Hong Kong. Among all religions in Hong Kong, Christianity has also been the most outspoken on public issues, including social, moral, cultural, and political issues. One may easily find Christians holding prayer meetings, singing hymns, and shouting slogans with Christian terminology before and/or during political demonstrations. In contrast, leaders of the other religions have tended to be rather conservative or quiet on political issues and less visible in political activities. It is not surprising to find that Hong Kong Christians seldom make reference to other religions when considering their possible responses to public issues.

In recent years, there have been several political issues which sparked off heated public debate in Hong Kong. One is the "Movement against Nationalistic Education" launched during the summer of 2012. The other is the civil disobedience movement "Occupying Central with Love and Peace," usually abbreviated to "Occupy Central" or "Occupy Central with peace" in 2013.

The "Movement against Nationalistic Education" was targeted primarily against the patriotic education embedded in the proposed "Moral, Civic and National Education" secondary school curriculum in Hong Kong. The curriculum was labeled "brain-washing" by its critics because the curriculum and the only available textbook seemed to promote not only some strongly biased "understandings" of China, for example, that the dictatorship of one political party practised in China is far better than the multiparty political system in the United States, but also some sort of emotional responses from students, especially when seeing the national flag and chanting the national anthem. The curriculum and movement provoked controversy not only among politicians, parents and teachers, but also church leaders and theologians. Against those who voiced their objections or resistance to the curriculum, Rev. Ng Chung-man, Daniel (Wu Zongwen), the senior pastor of the Evangelical Free Church of China Kong Fok Church, gave his support to the launching of national education, and he queried the rationale behind the objections articulated by some Hong Kong Christians.[4] Rev. Ng's article sparked off heated debates within Christian circles. Since the movement only lasted for several months and basically ended with the retreat of the government after a huge demonstration, its impact is incomparable to the "Occupy Central" movement.

The tentative idea of "Occupy Central" was first aired informally by Prof. Tai Yiu Ting, Benny (Dai Yaoting), a lay Christian teaching at the University of Hong Kong Faculty of Law, in a short article for a local newspaper.[5] The movement was formally launched by Prof. Tai together with Rev. Chu Yiu-ming (Zhu Yaoming), a Baptist pastor, and Prof. Chan Kin Man (Chen Jianmin), a professor of sociology of the Chinese University of Hong Kong, with a Christian background but no formal religious affiliation, and they explained the basic ideas of the movement to the mass media at a Christian church on March 27, 2013. The declared aim of the movement was to ensure that the universal suffrage to elect the chief executive of Hong Kong in 2017 should be organized according to international standards. Otherwise, they planned to organize supporters of the movement to occupy the Central District of Hong Kong. Since the district is the transportation, financial as well as political center of Hong Kong, its occupation by a large number of protesters would not only affect the economy and transportation system, but also involve certain violations of Hong Kong law. As a peaceful civil disobedience movement, the participants would pledge not to resist police arrest. With the announcement made by the Chinese government on August 31, 2013, concerning the arrangements for the 2017 election of the chief executive of Hong Kong, the commencement of movement was declared on September 28, 2013, and was further developed into the internationally known "Umbrella Movement" which ended in December 2014.

The movement provoked extensive debate among politicians, church leaders, and even Christian theologians. This was because the proposal involved serious ethical issues, including the question of whether it is ethical for Christians to take part in a civil disobedience movement. Some churches or church leaders issued statements on their positions on the issue. While the Catholic Diocese indicated that whether to take part in the movement was up to an individual's own conscience, the Anglican Church in Hong Kong expressed its reservations regarding the movement, suggesting that democracy was not a panacea to all social problems and the case was not urgent enough to warrant civil disobedience. The issue became very divisive within Christian circles in Hong Kong. The attention the movement received within Christian circles was in sharp contrast to its cold reception among some other religions in Hong Kong, including Buddhism and Daoism, which basically gave no response to the debate concerning "Occupy Central,"[6] excepting a

joint statement issued by the Colloquium of Six Religious Leaders of Hong
Kong, mentioning briefly that society should treasure the democracy and
freedom already had, and that "Extreme wild behavior will not make for the
future wellbeing of our society."[7]

The debates among church leaders and theologians involved not only
the practical issue whether to take part in the "Occupy Central," but also
basic theological and ethical issues, including the relationship of church to
state, and whether and to what extent Christians should be obedient to the
authorities. The debates eventually led to a more methodological discussion
concerning public theology.[8] Given Barth's rather well-known participation in the resistance to Nazism and his role in the drafting of the Barmen
Declaration, it should not be surprising if Barth's name was mentioned in the
debate concerning "Occupy Central."[9] Barth's name was mentioned by Rev.
Ng Chung-man at a forum with Prof. Tai Yiu-ting on "Occupy Central" held
on October 29, 2013. According to the newspaper coverage, Rev. Ng made
reference to Barth's theology to support Ng's own position that instead of
replacing an imperfect system with another imperfect system, one may better
respond positively with obedience.[10] These references to Barth indicate that
some Hong Kong Christians, one way or the other, have found Barth's theology relevant to their political context. As we will see, other than the concrete
and practical issue of "Occupy Central," Barth's theology is also involved in
the more theoretical discussion concerning public theology, albeit in a more
indirect and implicit way.

PUBLIC THEOLOGY IN THE CHINESE-
SPEAKING WORLD

In a recent issue of *Hill Road*, a bilingual theological journal published by the
Hong Kong Baptist Theological Seminary, Tang Siu-kwong, Andres (Deng
Shaoguang) and Huen Chi-wai, Freeman (Xuan Zhiwei), both professors of
the seminary, offer two critical studies of public theology.

The criticisms made by Tang and Huen on public theology are targeted primarily at Max L. Stackhouse's approach, which has been quite popular in the
Chinese-speaking world. According to Tang's understanding, Stackhouse's
approach to public theology aims to make Christian theology not only understandable but also acceptable to the public, which includes both Christians
and non-Christians. It also tends to make use of "warrants" and "criteria"
from the public domain, independent of Christian theology, to evaluate
the claims or validity of Christian theology, and to propose in what ways
Christian theology should revise its contents or articulations. This approach
risks the danger of taking the "public" as some sort of universal principle or

criterion to evaluate a particular confessional tradition of Christian "theology." For Tang, a better alternative can be found in John Webster's proposal of "theological theology," which advocates that Christian theology is only possible when based in the divine revelation of the Triune God, and the nature and purpose of theology must be determined by the content(s) of Christian confession alone. Other than its own subject matter, Christian theology needs no external justification, warrant, or criterion. Accordingly, public theology should be a secondary discipline based on or derived from dogmatic theology, which aims at offering a faithful and systematic exposition of Christian dogma.[11]

Other than the question of how, Tang also raises the question concerning who is doing the theology. According to Tang, Stackhouse's approach to public theology aims to address the public outside the church (*res public extra ecclesiam*) and become some sort of theology outside the church. However, if one follows Webster's approach, theology should be done by the church because it is the place or location for the presence of the divine Word. As the church plays a key role in the understanding of the divine economy in the public domain, how the public relates to theology is to be interpreted by the church. The only real public which theology should address is the church rather than the empire; the only possible place to conduct public theology is thus the Christian church, and not the public outside the church.[12]

These issues were also discussed in Huen's article, which criticizes public theology from a different perspective. Huen argues that the agenda set by Stackhouse, among others, wrongly assumes the false demarcation between private and public advocated by liberalism and secularism. This means that public theology fails to recognize that the church itself is also a polity as well as a group of people with their own particular way of living. In order to achieve some sort of "public-ness" defined by liberalism and secularism, this approach tends to emphasize "public" at the expense of "theology" or place "public" above "theology." Furthermore, this approach overlooks the fact that the public that Christian theology should address is the church, which makes a Christian engagement with wider society possible. As this approach focuses on seeking or articulating some sort of consensus or common ground between the church and the public outside the church, it tends to overlook the tension between one's being a citizen of a country and a disciple of Christ.[13]

The articles by Tang and Huen attracted a rather furious response from Chin Ken-pa (Zeng Qingbao), a Malaysian-born Chinese currently teaching in Taiwan, who even mocked that the criticisms of public theology launched by Tang and Huen in effect castrated "public theology" into a sort of "eunuch theology." Chin's response to Tang and Huen is mainly based on the theological mentality behind their criticisms rather than addressing directly their criticisms of Stackhouse's approach to public theology. Chin interprets the articles by Tang and Huen in light of their reservations already indicated elsewhere on the "Occupy Central" movement. Chin wonders why Tang, a scholar who had published extensively on Jürgen Moltmann and Dietrich Bonhoeffer, shifts to John Howard Yoder's theology and takes it as the basis for his queries against the "Occupy Central" movement, instead of making use of the theologies of Bonhoeffer and Moltmann to support the movement. Chin also questions why Tang queried the "Occupy Central" movement from this radically pacifist perspective, when the movement was already declared peaceful. Does this mean that any word or action against the government is inevitably violent and thus to be rejected? Will this eventually in turn justify the violence of the state against dissenting individuals? Chin also queries whether the emphasis of Tang and Huen on some sort of theological purity or pure theology and the ecclesiastical nature of theology are merely pretexts to disguise or justify their attempts to stay within the walls of the church. Chin concludes that in a pressing political situation, perhaps what should concern public theology most is not the purity of theology or theological purity.[14]

Given the particular purpose of this chapter, it will discuss neither whether the presentation and criticism of Stackhouse made by Tang and/or Huen are accurate and fair, nor whether their advocacy of an alternative approach is politically motivated, or whether the approaches to public theology advocated by other theologians can offer better alternatives. Instead, it will focus on how these debates are related to Barth's theology.

Anyone familiar with the theology of Karl Barth may discern the implicit presence of his theology in Chinese debates on public theology, even though Barth's name is rarely mentioned. In terms of the theological figures involved, John Webster, who is quoted extensively in Tang's article on public theology, is a well-known expert on Karl Barth. Webster's approach to theology, including particularly the ideas adopted by Tang, is reminiscent of some features of Barth's theology. It is well known that Yoder developed his own position largely in dialogue with Barth.[15] In terms of the theological issues involved, debates over the autonomy or purity of theology as well as its ecclesiastical nature, are fundamental to Barth's theological concerns, and his positions on these issues bear features characteristic of his theology. Although there is no particular or explicit reference to Barth's theology, it remains fair to say that Barth's theology is indirectly and implicitly involved in these debates.

CONVERSING WITH BARTH

What follows is an attempt to conduct a conversation with Barth on the political context of Hong Kong. It will focus on the controversial issues of the political "anti-nationalistic education" movements as well as "Occupy Central," and debates on public theology.

Patriotism and "Movement against Nationalistic Education"

With regard to the "Movement against Nationalistic Education," I offered a contextual and inter-disciplinary reflection on Christianity and patriotism in a chapter of my recent book, published in Chinese.[16] The chapter consisted of three main parts. In the first part, I made use of the theory of biological evolution, especially studies concerning the evolution of altruism, to explain how both the state and patriotism are products of human evolution, and patriotism as a human sentiment toward one's own country or nation is better identified as some sort of sentiment common to ordinary people rather than an absolute and universal moral obligation. The establishment of the state and the cultivation of patriotism are merely adaptation, or "survival skills," developed in the history of human evolution. The state is better understood as a product of human creativity rather than a divine creation. Furthermore, patriotism will be constrained by other human sentiments, including self-love, affection toward family members as well as universal compassion toward all human beings regardless of race and/or nationality. In the second part, I made reference to research in cultural studies and political philosophy as well as analyses of actual cases in China and Hong Kong, to highlight how it is understandable that modern nation states make use of sentiments of patriotism and patriotic education in order to achieve certain cultural hegemony to support or maintain the prevalent regime. However, given the plurality, fluidity, and ambivalence of national identity intensified by global processes of migration, more and more individual citizens tend to resist this imposed cultural hegemony and the soft-powers employed by the state, including through patriotic education. Christian theology is inevitably involved in this kind of cultural politics or resistance to the state's cultural hegemony. In the third part, I surveyed the relevant biblical materials, patristic sources as well as some examples in modern Christianity, to articulate a theological approach to patriotism appropriate to the Hong Kong context. There are five aspects to this theological approach to patriotism. First, it must be a kind of love given in freedom, rather than due to coercion, manipulation, hegemony or racial identity alone. Second, it is based on the diasporic Christian identity as a citizen of the Kingdom of God and responsible resident alien in the country in which one lives. Third, it is a critical patriotism taking serious the limitations, mistakes, and the dark side of the given country, yet accepting them with love and forgiveness. Fourth, it is integrated in an orderly and proper way with other kinds of love, including love of God, self-love, affection to family members, and so on. Fifth, patriotism should be combined with a transnational compassion toward all human beings, and transcended by an ecumenical or global vision.

The employment of secular theories aimed to disclose the secular nature of the state and the power struggle involved in the promotion of patriotism. In principle, these secular theories are separable from the theological discussion in the chapter.[17] The employment of "secular" theories is mainly as a device to counter the "grand narrative" of the secular and/ or religious advocates for patriotism, by illustrating that the theological position I argue for is not merely based on Christian tradition, but has a certain "scientific" or "objective" basis. Obviously, this seemingly "naturalistic" or "secular" discussion seems to differ radically from Barth's Christological approach to church-state relations, relating the state to the doctrine of salvation and the concept of gospel, instead of the doctrine of creation and the concept of law.[18] My chapter made no reference to Barth, but it is interesting to note that Barth's view of the state is also quite "secular" in the sense that the state is taken as a product of human creativity rather than divine creation. For Barth,

> A State is an attempt undertaken by men [*sic*] to organize the outward life of man [*sic*], with the intention of preventing individual encroachments on the rights of the whole community and at the same time encroachments of the community on the rights of individuals.[19]

Furthermore, there are also some other convergences with Barth's position, including the distinction between state and nation, the critique of nationalism as idolatry, nationhood as extension of kinship, and the "accidental order of history."[20]

I am pleased but not surprised to find that Barth advocates similar positions from a different perspective, but I am pleased and surprised to find that though Barth attempts to articulate his view from the perspective of the gospel, he does not mind if others reach a similar position through the approach of natural law.[21]

It is noteworthy that alongside Barth's advocacy for a sort of conditional obedience to the state,[22] he also indicates his reservation on, if not objection to, patriotism. He writes,

> It is quite another question whether the State has any right to try to strengthen its authority by making any kind of *inward* claim upon its subjects and its citizens; that is, whether it has any right to demand from them a particular philosophy of life (*Weltanschauung*) or at least sentiments and reactions dominated by a particular view imposed by the State from without. According to the New Testament, the only answer to this question is an unhesitating "No!"[23]

Barth further clarifies that this does not contradict the message of paying due respect to the political authority conveyed in Romans xiii:

> From Romans xiii, it is quite clear that *love* is *not* one of the duties which we owe to the state. When the State begins to claim "love" it is in the process of becoming a Church, the Church of a false God, and thus an unjust State. The just state requires, not love, but a simple, resolute, and responsible attitude on the part of its citizens. It is this attitude which the Church, based on justification, commends to its members.[24]

Barth also comments that "since the church is ecumenical (Catholic) by virtue of is very origin, it resists all abstract, local, regional and national interests in the political sphere."[25]

In line with these comments, it is quite reasonable to infer that Barth might say "*Nein*" to any patriotic education which demands a love of the state from Christians. In fact, Barth commented as follows in the first edition of his commentary on the Romans:

> Paying the oblation, but *no* incense to Caesar! Civic initiative and civic obedience, but *no* combination of throne and altar, *no* Christian patriotism, *no* democratic crusade. Strike and general strike and street fights if necessary, but no religious justification and glorification of it![26]

With mention of civil obedience, strikes and street fighting, we will turn to Barth's views on civil disobedience and violence.

Pacifism, Civil Disobedience, and "Occupy Central"

It is well known that Barth places great emphasis on an absolute and transcendent divine judgment, which may relativize indiscriminately all political ideologies and systems. However, it is important to note that, for Barth, even though all political systems are imperfect and none is absolutely good or absolutely bad, it does not mean that all of them are equally good or equally bad. On the contrary, Barth insists that some are better and some worse.[27] With regard to democracy, Barth remarks that "the gospel betrays a striking tendency to the side of what is generally called the 'democratic' state."[28] He acknowledges that democracy is not perfect, but

> Taking everything into account, it must be said that the Christian view shows a stronger trend in this direction than in any other. There certainly is an affinity between the Christian community and the civil communities of the free peoples.[29]

In contrast, regarding totalitarian states, Barth comments rather negatively,

> The statecraft that wraps itself up in darkness is the craft of a State which,
> because it is anarchic or tyrannical, is forced to hide the bad conscience of its
> citizens or officials. The Church will not on any account lend its support to that
> kind of state.[30]

There is no doubt that Barth adopts the position advocated in the New
Testament concerning paying due respect to the state. However, it is equally
important to note that for Barth, honoring or offering service to the state does
not mean to "adopt an attitude of unquestioning assent to the will and action
of the State, which is directly or indirectly aimed at the suppression of the
freedom of the Word of God"; rather, the church's honoring or rendering its
service to the State may include offering its criticism and resistance to the
state in a calm and dignified manner.[31] Barth insists that in order to provide
this service to the State, the church must have freedom in its preaching and
worship. Probably due to this consideration, Barth is particularly critical
toward the totalitarian state and tends to favor a more democratic state. He
writes,

> This right of the Church to liberty means the foundation, the maintenance, the
> restoration of everything—certainly of all human law. Wherever this right is
> recognized, and whenever a true Church makes the right use of it (and the free
> preaching of justification will see to it that things fall into their true place) there
> we shall find a legitimate human authority and an equally legitimate human
> independence; tyranny on the one hand, and anarchy on the other, Fascism and
> Bolshevism alike, will be dethroned; and the true order of human affairs—the
> justice, wisdom and peace, equity and care for human welfare which are neces-
> sary to that true order, will arise.[32]

Apart from his negative "prophecy" against tyranny, Barth endorses democracy positively. He writes,

> When I consider the deepest and most central content of the New Testament
> exhortation, I should say that we are justified, from the point of view of
> exegesis, in regarding the "democratic conception of the state" as a justifiable
> expansion of the thought of the New Testament. This does not mean that the
> separation between justification and justice, between Church and State, the fact
> that Christians are "foreigners" in the sphere of the state, has been abolished.
> On the contrary, the resolute intention of the teaching of the New Testament
> is brought out still more plainly when it is clear that Christians must not only
> endure the earthly State, but that they must *will* it, and that they cannot will it

as a "Pilate" State, but as a *just* State; when it is seen that there is no outward escape from the political sphere; when it is seen that Christians, while they remain within the Church and are wholly committed to the future "city," are equally committed to responsibility for the earthly "city," called to work and (it may be) to struggle, as well as to pray, for it; in short, when each one of them is responsible for the character of the State as a *just* state.[33]

In short, for Barth some political systems are better than others, or to be more specific, democracy is better than totalitarianism. He also encourages Christians to long for, and even take part in, political struggle for a just or better state, characterized by democracy rather than tyranny.

Although there is no concrete evidence suggesting that Barth would support the "Occupy Central" movement, he might well dispute Ng Chung-man's argument that as all political systems are imperfect, Christians should just be obedient to the political authorities and simply accept passively what has been offered. Barth may endorse active participation in a movement struggling for a better society, including a more democratic political system. In other words, Ng Chung-man quoting Barth to support his objection to the "Occupy Central" movement might reflect merely one of the possible interpretations or appropriations of Barth's theology. However, the role played by Barth in the movement against Nazism seemed to suggest that some sort of Christian participation in the resistance or even civil disobedience to a totalitarian regime is at least allowable in principle. The crucial issue is then whether Barth would endorse the strategy of civil disobedience proposed by the "Occupy Central" movement, especially if the strategy may involve breaking the law, or involve violence.

The queries raised by Tang Siu-kwong against the "Occupy Central" movement are based on the pacifist position of Yoder and focused on the ethical issue of using violence to achieve political solutions. No matter whether this kind of query is legitimate, it is interesting to note Barth's comment on the use of violence.

The Church knows God's anger and judgment, but it also knows that His anger lasts but for a moment, whereas His mercy is for eternity. The political analogy of this truth is that violent solutions of conflicts in the political community—from police measures to law court decisions, from the armed rising against a regime that is no longer worthy of or equal to its task (in the sense of a revolt undertaken not to undermine but to restore the lawful authority of the state) to the defensive war against an external threat to the lawful State—must be approved, supported and if necessary even suggested by the Christian community—for how could it possibly contract out in such situation? On the other hand, it can only regard violent solutions of any conflict as an *ultima ratio regis.* It will approve and support them only when they are for the moment the ultimate and only possibility available. It will always do its utmost to postpone such moments as far as possible. It can never stand for absolute peace, for peace at any price. But it must and will do all it can to see that no price is considered too high for the preservation or restoration of peace at home and abroad except the ultimate price which would mean the abolition of the lawful State and the practical denial of the divine ordinance. May the Church show her inventiveness in the search for other solutions before she joins in the call for violence! The perfection of the Father in heaven, who does not cease to be the heavenly Judge, demands the earthly perfection of a peace policy which really does extend to the limits of human possible.[34]

With regard to Barth's comment above, critics of "Occupy Central" might argue that according to Barth, advocates of the movement should reconsider if the measure of "Occupy Central" is really an *ultima ratio regis.* As the answer should probably be "no," the advocates of the movement would thus be advised to consider a more innovative peaceful strategy to replace "Occupy Central." However, as Chin Ken-pa might counter: why not address the violence employed by the government "from police measures to law court decisions" first? If the government were to facilitate a genuine universal suffrage, there might be no need for "Occupy Central" or discussion of it.

Theological Integrity and Public Theology

With regard to the debate discussed earlier concerning public theology, the key questions seem to be mainly methodological, including not only whether and how the doctrinal purity of Christian theology can be preserved when addressing public issues, but also whether public theology is of the church, by the church, and for the church. It is well known that Barth's theology is characterized not only by his emphasis on grounding theology on the divine revelation in Jesus Christ alone—to the exclusion of any kind of natural theology—but also his emphasis on the ecclesiastical nature of Christian theology, as underlined by the title of his magnum opus, *Church Dogmatics.* However, there exists prima facie evidence that Barth's theology is also related to political contexts or issues, and that the role of politics in Barth's theology is an important question in Barth scholarship.[35] In other words, the questions of whether and how Christian theology can preserve its purity or integrity when addressing public issues, are vital for Barth's theology. The queries made by Tang and Huen against Stackhouse's approach are reminiscent of, and very much in line with, Barth's critique of nineteenth-century Protestant theology. However, I would like to suggest that a more in-depth study of Barth's theology may indicate that Barth's understanding of theology is less restricted than that understood by Tang and Huen.

Alain Epp Weaver argues that although Barth's theology, including his view on religion/religions, is very Christocentric, it is combined with a rather universalistic understanding of salvation and the affirmation of the possibility of "secular parables of the kingdom," or witnesses of God's Word "beyond the walls of the church" (*extra muros ecclesiae*)—no matter whether these witnesses are secular or religious. These witnesses may comfort, criticize or correct the church, including the church's practice, proclamation and even dogma, and may help the church have a deeper understanding of scripture and even divine revelation. The affirmation of the possibility of these witnesses or parables offers a humble and open attitude toward these witnesses, whether Russian Communism or a donkey, beyond the boundary of the church. If one follows this approach, it is possible to develop a nonresistant public theology, which both offers a missionary witness to the non-Christian world, and receives witnesses to God's Word from non-Christian sources.[36]

The approach to public theology derived from Weaver's interpretation of Barth is quite different from the approach preferred by Tang and Huen. Relatively speaking, whereas the former tends to be more open to voices or insights from secular academic disciplines as well as other religions or ideologies without compromising the integrity of theology, the latter tend to emphasize rather one-sidedly the integrity of theology against the erosion of secular ideologies or political propaganda, advocating a more church-centered view of theology and/or divine revelation, and being skeptical or cynical about the possibility of finding consensus and forming alliances with non-Christian partners. Both approaches may claim to be consistent with Barth's theology, but the approach advocated by Weaver seems to be based on a more comprehensive and balanced interpretation of Barth's theology of religion/religions.[37] This approach underlines Barth's openness to non-Christian views on public issues. As Barth humbly and freely admits,

> In its encounter with the world it may sometimes happen that in this particular field the children of the world prove to be wiser than the children of light, so that in the question concerning its law the church has reason to learn from the world (which does not know what it knows), receiving from it the witness which it ought to give. For all its awareness of the independence of its task, it cannot exclude this possibility.[38]

This approach, as we will see, proves more fruitful for the articulation of public theology in a religious pluralistic context.

In the Chinese-speaking world there is a theological qua cultural movement called Sino-Christian theology which emerged independently from the established churches in China. Since many of the scholars associated with the movement are university professors or even public intellectuals, rather than church leaders, they are often identified as "cultural Christians" rather than "Christians" in a conventional religious sense. The Sino-Christian theology they endeavor to promote is thus widely recognized as theology outside the walls of the church.[39] This may also explain why public theology is one of the foci of attention for Sino-Christian theology. Admittedly, some of the public theologies articulated by the scholars associated with Sino-Christian theology may risk the dangers Tang and Huen caution against. However, if Christian theology must be exclusively church-based, as seems to be implied in Tang's and Huen's ecclesio-centric approach to public theology, it will entirely rule out the potential contributions of the theological discourses made by "cultural Christians" to public theology, and may also disregard contributions from lay Christian intellectuals attempting to engage discussion of public theology via their expertise in non-theological disciplines, for example, social and political sciences. Such moves would only reinforce the ghettoization or privatization of theology in China. A related but even more fundamental question is whether theological purity is the only important consideration for public theology.

David Novak mentions Barth when attempting to defend Reinhold Niebuhr from the critiques made by Hauerwas. In Novak's own words, "As a Jewish traditionalist, painfully aware of how precarious is my position in the world, I tend to feel closer to Barth than I do to Niebuhr."[40] "But when engaged in public theology, dealing with great moral issues in a secular world, I feel closer to Niebuhr."[41] For Novak, the major reason or difference is that Niebuhr's approach is "more politically savvy and more politically effective" than Barth's.[42]

> Niebuhr was so much effective in his anti-Nazism than other early (and very brave) German anti-Nazis like Barth, Bonhoeffer (Niebuhr's student), and the Confessing Church. . . . We need to remember, nonetheless, that their initial opposition to the Third Reich was theological and not ethical-political until much closer to the defeat of the Nazi regime in 1945. They were opposed to Nazism attempting to replace Christianity as the religion of the German people, but they did not see how Nazi injustice, *especially* but not exclusively directed against the Jews, was the most immediate manifestation of Nazi idolatry.[43]

Novak appreciates particularly the proactive approach based on Niebuhr's version of natural law which enable Christians, as well as Jews, to propose public policies in a secular society *ab initio*, rather than simply endorse or reject the public policy proposed by others *post factum*.[44]

Whether Novaks' comparison of Barth and Niebuhr is accurate and fair or not, it raises an important issue concerning the criteria for public theology.

In addition to theological purity or integrity, political effectiveness seems to be a legitimate criterion in evaluating various approaches to public theology. These two criteria seem to be incommensurable, and it is to be expected that theologians may have diverse views on whether and how to combine or balance these two. This criteriological question raises an even more fundamental question concerning the nature, purpose, and/or task of theology.

As I have argued elsewhere, in the Chinese-speaking world Christian theology, especially Sino-Christian theology, cannot and should not restrict itself to some sort of second-order activity aimed at seeking understanding of the Christian faith or reflecting on the proclamation and practice of the church. Any theological writing or talk (including preaching) belongs also to the first-order activity of faith and involves, knowingly or unknowingly, some sort of cultural critique, cultural negotiation, or cultural politics among various publics: the church (or religions), the academia (especially universities), and wider society. In order to achieve effective cultural critique or negotiation, theological engagement in public issues requires not only a profound understanding of Christian tradition or revelation but also a proper understanding of the dynamics of cultural change and effective strategies available.[45]

It is interesting to note that Barth upholds, probably no less than any other theologian of his time, the importance of faithful and proper understanding of divine revelation. But as I argued elsewhere,[46] he also recognizes his own theology as a "corrective theology" (*Theologie des Korrectives*).[47] According to his own account, in order to correct the bias or misguided tendencies of nineteenth-century liberal theology effectively, he deliberately risked using certain one-sided discourses to counter-balance or neutralize these.[48] In other words, in certain circumstances, Barth might prefer to make one-sided but effective theological discourses, for example, his early rejection of natural theology, than to articulate a delicately balanced, systematically organized, and comprehensively faithful account of Christian confession or divine revelation. Furthermore, if Barth's theology can be characterized as "against the stream" or even "against hegemony,"[49] for him, theology is not to be reduced to some sort of intellectual activity for the "private consumption" of the church; rather, it aims to engage itself in certain cultural critiques or negotiations within and outside church circles.

This interpretation of Barth's theology may give further freedom or flexibility to public theology in a religiously pluralistic context. In order to be politically effective, public theology in a particular context can be a fragmentary or one-sided discourse, and need not be a systematic and balanced account of all the major content of the Christian faith. For example, in the Chinese context, seeking consensus or joining forces with Confucianism may contribute to the affirmation and further enhancement of human rights in a totalitarian state. When engaging in dialogue with Confucianism on human rights, it may be advisable, for example, for Christian public theology to focus more on the Christian understanding of the human and on ethics, especially their commonalities with Confucianism, instead of a distinctive Christian doctrine of God.[50]

CONCLUDING REMARKS

The earlier discussion represents my own interpretation of Barth. What I have attempted to offer is a virtual conversation with Barth and interpretations of Barth with a view to furthering the development of public theology in the Chinese-speaking world. My interpretation of Barth might differ from some existing interpretations of Barth in the Chinese-speaking world. It might also differ from the interpretations and/or evaluations of Barth offered by Western theologians, particularly Yoder and Hauerwas,[51] who have influenced theological discourse on public theology in the Chinese-speaking world. In this sense, what is actually involved is not merely conversing with Barth, but conversing with other interpreters of Barth.

NOTES

1. Karl Barth, *Humanity of God*, trans. John Newton Thomas and Thomas Wieser (London: Collins, 1967), 16–17.

2. This research work was supported by a grant received from the Research Grants Council of Hong Kong (project No.: CUHK14405214). When making reference to Chinese publications, the family name of the author is given first according to Chinese custom, and the English translation of the title is given in square-brackets following the pinyin transliteration. Bilingual publication or journal articles with abstracts in English will be cited as English publications.

3. For the contrast between the prevalent and alternative readings of Barth's theology of religion/religions, see: Veli-Matti Kärkkäinen, "Karl Barth and the Theology of Religions," in *Karl Barth and Evangelical Theology: Convergences and Divergences*, ed. Sung Wook Chung (Grand Rapids, MI: Baker Academic, 2006), 236–257.

4. Wu Zongwen, "'Guo min jiao yu' zheng yi dai lei zhi fan si" [Reflection on the Controversy Brought Forth by "National Education"], *Guo du fu xing bao* [Kingdom Revival Times] (October 4, 2012), http://www.krt.com.hk/modules/news/article.php ?storyid=10200 (logon December 24, 2013).

5. Tai further elaborated his ideas in: Dai Yaoting, *Zhan ling Zhonghuan: he ping kang zheng xin zhan shi* [Occupy the Central: Mental War Room of Peaceful Struggle] (Hong Kong: Enrich Publishing Ltd., July 2013, August 2013).

6. On September 13, 2013, I googled the Chinese keywords "Occupy Central" with "Buddhism," and found basically no items available on the web containing these two keywords. After replacing the word "Buddhism" with "Daoism," the result was the same.

7. For an English version of the message, see: http://sundayex.catholic.org.hk/no de/1837 (logon Febuary 26, 2014).

8. Tai Yiu-ting published an article on public theology before: Benny Y. T. Tai, "Public Theology, Justice and Law: A Preliminary Note," in *Public Theology in Law and Life*, ed. Brian Edgar, Paul Babie and David Wilson (Adelaide, Australia: ATF Theology, 2012), 3–25.

9. For example, Barth's views on freedom and civil disobedience are mentioned in Zhao Chongming, *Zhan ling Zhonghuan yu jiao hui zheng zhi* [Occupy the Central and Church Politics] (Hong Kong: Logos Publishers, October 2013), esp. 161–164, 249.

10. See: *Shi dai lun tan* [Christian Times] 1367 (November 10, 2013), 7.

11. Siu-kwong Tang, "Public Theology, What Theology? Some Radical Reflections," *Hill Road* 16, no. 1 (2013): 3–30 (in Chinese with English abstract).

12. Siu-kwong Tang, "Public Theology, What Theology? Some Radical Reflections," 13, 28–30.

13. Chi-wai Huen, "Public Theology: Whose 'Public'? How 'Theological'?" *Hill Road* 16, no. 1 (2013): 31–63 (in Chinese with English abstract).

14. Zeng Qingbao, "Shi shui ba gong gong shen xue yan ge zuo gong gong shen xue" [Who Castrates Public Theology into Eunuch Theology?], *Shi dai lun tan* 1360 (September 22, 2013), 11 and 1361 (September 29, 2013), 11. Public theology (gong-gong shenxue) and eunuch theology (gonggong shenxue) sound similar in Putonghua/Mandarin, though not Cantonese. See further Chin Ken-pa, "The Ecclesiological Implications on the Political Attitude of the Chinese Authority on Christianity," in this volume.

15. See: John Howard Yoder, *Karl Barth and the Problem of War and Other Essays on Barth*, ed. Mark Thiessen Nation (Eugene, OR: Casade Books, 2003); also Kristopher Norris, "Democracy and Church: Barth and Yoder on Democratic Practice," and Markus Höfner, "Neither Self-Evident Frame nor Self-Enclosed Sect: The Christian Church in Barth's Political Ecclesiology," in this volume.

16. Lai Pinchao (Lai Pan-chiu), *Guang chang shang de han yu shen xue* [Sino-Christian Theology in Public Square] (Hong Kong: Logos & Pneuma Press, 2014), 263–309.

17. I contributed an abridged version of this chapter, leaving out the materials related to evolution, to a bilingual festschrift: Ying Fuk Tsang, Kwan Sui Man, and Wu Qing (eds.), *Festschrift in Honor of Professor Lo Lung-kwong* (Hong Kong: Chinese Christian Literature Council, 2014), 507–521.

18. Barth, *Church and State*, trans. G. Ronald Howe (London: Student Christian Movement Press, 1939), 6, 13–22.

19. Barth, *Against the Stream: Shorter Post-War Writings, 1946–1952* (London: SCM, 1954), 95.

20. See: Carys Moseley, *Nations and Nationalism in the Theology of Karl Barth* (Oxford: Oxford University Press, 2013), 1, 31, 64–65, 94–96, 189, 203–204.

21. Barth, *Against the Stream*, 43.

22. "It (i.e., the church) will give to Caesar what is Caesar's, but it can never give its unconditional sanction to any such form of mastery, to any form of the state or trend of culture." Barth, *God in Action*, English translation by E. G. Homrighausen and Karl J. Ernst, introduction by Josias Friedli (Edinburgh: T & T Clark, 1936), 34.

23. Karl Barth, *Church and State*, 76–77, emphasis original.

24. Barth, *Church and State*, 77.

25. Barth, *Against the Stream*, 40–41.

26. Barth, *Der Römerbrief (Erste Fassung)* [1919], ed. Hermann Schmidt (Zürich: Theologischer Verlag, 1985), 502f; Cf. Frank Jehle, *Ever Against the Stream: The Politics of Karl Barth*, trans. Richard and Martha Burnett (Grand Rapids: William B. Eerdmans Publishing Company, 2002), 43.

27. Barth, *Against the Stream*, 95.

28. Barth, *Against the Stream*, 44.

29. Barth, *Against the Stream*, 44.

30. Barth, *Against the Stream*, 39.

31. Barth, *Church and State*, 80–81.

32. Barth, *Church and State*, 84.

33. Barth, *Church and State*, 80–81.

34. Barth, *Against the Stream*, 41–42.

35. See George Hunsinger (ed.), *Karl Barth and Radical Politics* (Philadelphia: The Westminster Press, 1976); and also David Haddorf, "American Democracy and Trinitarian Sovereignty: Lessons from Barth," in this volume.

36. Alain Epp Weaver, "Parables of the Kingdom and Religious Plurality: With Barth and Yoder toward a Nonresistant Public Theology," *Mennonite Quarterly Review* 72, no. 3 (July 1998): 411–440. Similar interpretation of Barth can be found in Paul S. Chung, *Karl Barth: God's Word in Action* (Eugene, OR: Cascade Books, 2008), especially 449–483.

37. I advocated for similar interpretation of Barth's position on religion/religions. See: Pan-chiu Lai, "Barth's Theology of Religion and the Asian Context of Religious Pluralism," *Asia Journal of Theology* 15, no. 2 (Oct. 2001): 247–267.

38. Barth, *Church Dogmatics*, Vol. IV, Part 3, trans. G. W. Bromiley (London: T & T Clark International, 2004), 725.

39. Pan-chiu Lai and Jason Lam (eds.), *Sino-Christian Theology: A Theological Qua Cultural Movement in Contemporary China* (Frankfurt-am-Main: Peter Lang, 2010).

40. David Novak, "Defending Niebuhr from Hauerwas," *Journal of Religious Ethics* 40, no. 2 (Je 2012): 283.

41. David Novak, "Defending Niebuhr from Hauerwas," 294.

42. David Novak, "Defending Niebuhr from Hauerwas," 285.

43. David Novak, "Defending Niebuhr from Hauerwas," 293.

44. David Novak, "Defending Niebuhr from Hauerwas," 294.

45. See: Lai Pinchao, *Duo yuan, fen qi yu ren tong: shen xue yu wen hua de tan suo* [Plurality, Diversity and Identity: Explorations in Theology and Culture] (New Taipei City, Taiwan: Taiwan Christian Literature Council, 2011).

46. See: Pan-chiu Lai, "Barth's Theology of Religion and the Asian Context of Religious Pluralism," *Asia Journal of Theology* 15, no. 2 (Oct. 2001): 258–259.

47. Karl Barth, *The Word of God and the Word of Man*, trans. Douglas Horton (London: Hodder & Stoughton, 1935), 103.

48. Barth, *Church Dogmatics*, Vol. 2 Part 1, trans. T. H. L. Parker, W. B. Johnston, K. McKnight, J. L. M. Haire (Edinburgh: T.& T. Clark, 1957), 634.

49. See: Timothy Gorringe, *Karl Barth: Against Hegemony* (Oxford: Oxford University Press, 1999).

50. See: Pan-chiu Lai, "Human Rights and Christian-Confucian Dialogue," *Studies in Interreligious Dialogue* 23, no. 2 (2013): 133–149.

51. See further: George Hunsinger, "Karl Barth and the Politics of Sectarian Protestantism: A Dialogue with John Howard Yoder (1980)," in *Disruptive Grace: Studies in the Theology of Karl Barth* (Grand Rapids: William B. Eerdmans Publishing Company, 2000), 114–128; Todd V. Cioffi, "Stanley Hauerwas and Karl Barth: Matters of Christology, Church, and State," in *Karl Barth and American Evangelicalism*, ed. Bruce L. McCormack and Clifford B. Anderson (Grand Rapids, MI: William B. Eerdmans Publishing Company, 2011), 347–365.

Chapter 20

American Democracy and Trinitarian Sovereignty

Lessons from Barth and Tocqueville

David Haddorff

In dialogue with Karl Barth's trinitarian theology, this chapter explores how God's trinitarian action nurtures a political theology of authority, freedom, participation and promise, which provides a theopolitical framework for political democracy. It follows that support for democracy is based less on political arguments and more on God's gracious command to be a politically responsible witness to God's trinitarian action upon the individual and community. Central to this argument is how trinitarian theology provides a framework for political theology, and in particular, political democracy. Although drawing principally from Barth's theology, this chapter further engages the grand theorist of American democracy, Alexis de Tocqueville. The sections include: (1) God's trinitarian sovereignty: *perichoresis* and appropriation; (2) God's election and antidemocratic hegemony; (3) democratic freedom and God the creator; (4) democratic participation and God the reconciler; and (5) democratic promise and God the redeemer.

GOD'S TRINITARIAN SOVEREIGNTY: *PERICHORESIS* AND APPROPRIATION

In the concluding section of the book *Political Theology: An Introduction*, author Michael Kirwan, S. J., writes: "For eschatology and for political theology there must be a 'return to the fundamentals': the doctrine of God."[1] This statement raises the question: What is this "doctrine of God" and how does it relate to political theory and practice? One common approach is "social trinitarianism," which proposes a relational view of God, grounded in God's own internal perichoratic relationship of the three divine persons, and its application to society as a model for politics. This viewpoint rightly begins with trinitarian God, but pushes too far the analogy between human society (or persons) and the three divine persons, which risks the projection of human social relations onto God's trinitarian being. Such a view, furthermore, denies God's ineffable triune mystery and fails to adequately relate the immanent to the economic trinity, God's relations *ad intra* from God's works *ad extra*. David Kelsey recently develops a better approach in his book *Eccentric Existence*, whose trinitarian formulation, without neglecting perichoratic relations of the Father, Son, and Spirit, concentrates on God's trinitarian action as creator, reconciler, and consummator as the framework for his study of theological anthropology.[2] Like Karl Barth, Kelsey's book provides a comprehensive account of the Trinity's application to social and cultural life, including politics, and in fact, provides a useful trinitarian framework for reading Barth's own theopolitical vision in the *Church Dogmatics*. Behind this discussion of trinitarian theology is the question of God's sovereignty, which is fundamental to any theopolitical account of democracy.[3] Such an inquiry does more than simply articulate the doctrine of the Trinity as a model for politics, but asks the deeper question: *Who* is this trinitarian God and *what* is this God's political action?

To begin, we turn to Barth's first exploration of God's sovereignty, which coincides with his formal discussion of the doctrine of the Trinity in *CD* I/1, where he insists that we must always balance God's oneness in threeness and threeness in oneness.[4] Barth writes, "we cannot advance beyond these two obviously one-sided and inadequate formulations."[5] The dialectical balance between these two ways of understanding God is best expressed in the doctrines of *perichoresis* and appropriation. The doctrine of *perichoresis* explores threeness in oneness. The intra-communal relationship of the Father, Son and Spirit, says Barth, "mutually condition and permeate one another so completely that one is always in the other two and the other two in the one."[6] In contrast, the doctrine of appropriation explores oneness in threeness in God's works as revealed in Scripture, which appropriates specific works of the Triune God to a particular divine mode of being. So, for example, creation is appropriated to the Father, reconciliation to the Son, and consummation with the Spirit. Inasmuch as we equate a particular *opus ad extra* with a particular divine person, we must also say that the external works of the triune God are always undivided or indivisible. It follows that although appropriation is a convenient way to speak about God's triune action in time, it must always be kept in balance with God's being as eternal Father, Son, and Spirit, who eternally exists in perichoratic union. God freely determines to exist as Father, Son and Spirit in this eternal communion, without being dependent upon anything outside of God determining God's being and action. God is the *only* truly free being, so for humanity to be free it must stand in relation to this free God, who is the source and power of all freedom.

For a trinitarian politics of divine action, these distinctions between *perichoresis* and appropriation are fundamental, since political theology often errs when it prioritizes either one and becomes modalistic. In social trinitarianism, *perichoresis* becomes an abstraction, an idealized view of human social relations projected onto God, which is disconnected from the God of revelation and God's external works. Likewise, when appropriation is prioritized, it links God's particular modes of being with particular kinds of political theory or practice. The politics of the Father could lead to a form of centralized power, the politics of the Son could lead to anarchic pacifism or ecclesiological separateness, and the politics of the Spirit could lead to a synthesis of human and divine agency in versions of political utopianism or nationalism. In each case, God's trinitarian freedom must lose if human power is to reign supreme. Whatever God's sovereignty remains must correlate to human power or persons cannot remain free and sovereign. And yet, Barth reminds us, that God's sovereign power, his *potentia absoluta* is not an "abstract absoluteness or naked sovereignty," but a gracious gift of freedom and fellowship to humanity.[7] In the revelation of the Word of God, made visible in Jesus Christ, the trinitarian God is unveiled as the one who loves in freedom, as the eternal Father, Son and Holy Spirit, who has determined to be with and for us as creator, reconciler, and redeemer. God's sovereign self-determination is particular, not general, in that God has elected to be with us and for us, that is, to have fellowship with us even in our denial of this fellowship. "God has elected fellowship with man for himself" and at the same time, "fellowship with Himself for man."[8] God's sovereign power coexists with his determination to give the gift of freedom to humanity, enabling them to freely respond to God's gracious gift of fellowship.

If the source of political theology is the sovereignty of God's triune action, then how do we appropriate God's action into our own political actions? How does our political witness respond to God's trinitarian action? To answer this question, we briefly turn to *CD* II/2, where Barth develops his general ethics and God's command, which is always a command of grace of the triune God. God's command is not an abstract concept or ethical principle, rather it is the imperative of responsible freedom rooted in the indicative of who God is, as the gracious trinitarian commander. Since there is no generic humanity outside the humanity of Jesus Christ but only a humanity that is restored, healed, and allowed to live in free response to God's gracious command, then says Barth, the divine command, says Barth, is a "*permission—the granting of a very definite freedom,*" as it "orders us to be free."[9] This "imperative of freedom" is a calling to be included in God's purposes and share in God's work *ad extra*. Similar to his discussion of the Trinity in *CD* I/1 referred to

earlier, in *CD* III/4 Barth distinguishes between *perichoresis* and appropriation demonstrating how God's command is one and yet three in relation to
God's external works.[10] Succinctly put, there are not three commands but
one, and yet, the command comes to us in different ways of relating to the
one God. Just as theology can distinguish between God's trinitarian works,
so we can speak about the specificity of the divine command within the
three spheres of God's action. Later this understanding of God's command
will become crucial for understanding how we relate our political witness
in democracy to the actions of the triune God, but before that we turn to the
democratic musings of Tocqueville and a discussion of Barth's theology of
election, which explores further God's trinitarian sovereignty and the unity
of God's command.

GOD'S ELECTION AND
ANTIDEMOCRATIC HEGEMONY

In the introduction to *Democracy in America*, Tocqueville cautions his reader
that the book was written in light of a "religious terror exercised upon the soul
of the author."[11] The French theorist worries that once the political leveling
of popular sovereignty becomes a pervasive social and cultural force, what
happens to civilization? Although confident that God's providence is on the
side of democracy, he remains curious why God would permit the people
to rule "as God over the universe."[12] Why would God allow the people to
usurp divine sovereignty? What does this say about God and God's relationship to humanity?[13] Although God's providential will seems content to allow
democratic forces to eradicate aristocratic privilege, it risks the triumph of
popular sovereignty, which like a new religion, creates a social force that
extends through all levels of society, from the family, to the township, the
state, and the nation.[14] The power of popular sovereignty makes it more difficult to distinguish between good and evil, freedom and tyranny, participation
and complacency, and promise and material satisfaction. Hence, the idea of
popular sovereignty, which is democracy's greatest strength, also becomes
its greatest weakness, since there is no divine power to prohibit it from challenging underlying antidemocratic forms of tyranny emerging within society.
What Tocqueville finds worrisome in "America is not the extreme freedom
that prevails there but the shortage of any guarantee against tyranny."[15] The
antidemocratic threat to democracy emerges from the misuse of human freedom within democracy itself.

Likewise, Barth is obviously aware that political history reveals the
legacy of the misuse of human freedom, and that a triumph of popular sovereignty over divine sovereignty over all aspects of life can lead to disastrous

consequences. Humanity can easily fall victim to any form of "authoritarianism and collectivism," says Barth, "as for every other dishonoring, perversion and destruction of his human existence."[16] Yet unlike Tocqueville, Barth does not fear that the triumph of democracy will weaken God's sovereignty, but in fact, give greater witness to God's election and command of grace. This is because *what* this triune God does for us and with us in Jesus Christ is fundamental to *who* this God is. Furthermore, this is why God's singular command of grace through election is crucial for a theopolitical account of democracy. We spoke earlier about how both *perichoresis* and appropriation demonstrate how God's command is one and yet three in relation to God's external works. Since we discuss appropriation in later sections of the chapter, we can now address God's command as determined by *perichoresis*, that is, the one decision of the triune God, as Father, Son and Spirit in eternal relation, to elect persons into fellowship, freedom, and responsibility. Without this awareness, persons easily misuse their freedom and wreak havoc in the world through hegemonies of injustice and power, but with it they can give witness to the God that stands with us and for us in democratic society.[17]

Considering how God's election relates to political democracy, we make the first of four statements of political witness: *In our political witness to the God who elects us in Jesus Christ, we respond by affirming that both the individual and the community are called to live under God's trinitarian sovereignty as free and responsible persons.* At the basis of a free society is the free person who is elected by God to be a free person. These "individuals recognize the election of Jesus Christ as their own election."[18] Awareness of one's election affirms the election of the community, which implies that the community becomes aware that it too is reconciled to God. Barth writes that "God seeks, calls, blesses and sanctifies the many, the totality, the natural and historical groups and humanity itself, in and through the individual."[19] This awareness first takes place within the church, which in turn, gives witness to the civil community that it too is reconciled to God.[20] These lines of thought culminate in his 1946 essay, *The Christian Community and the Civil Community*, where Barth argues the Christian community is the "inner circle" and the civil community is the "outer circle" of the "visible kingdom of God." The Christian community serves as a "model and prototype" of the civil community demonstrating to the civil community, in its democratic form, how to give *witness* to Christ's rule.[21] The task of the Christian community is to remind the civil community of its true mission and task, which leads to a clear "direction and a line" of political thinking toward democracy.[22] Democracy is preferred because election heals the tension between the individual and the community by making persons *free* within the political community. This takes place through the reconciling action of the triune God to stand for and with us in the election of Jesus Christ. In Jesus Christ, as fully God and fully human, the triune God's self-determination acts in and through the covenant of grace as both the divine elector and the human elected: first, God elects to come to us in human flesh, but second, Jesus as the elected "new man," as the representative of humanity, approaches God as a free human subject. All human history, including political history, is viewed through the lens of history of Jesus Christ. Consequently, God's election affirms that the individual is "no mere delegate, but in his own right a bearer of this people's responsibility. He is no vassal, but a free citizen."[23] The democratic community becomes free and responsible through the gracious gift of the responsible "free citizen." In Jesus Christ, God's sovereignty acts with and for others as both master and servant, whose "kingdom is neither a barracks or prison, but the home of those who even, with and by him are free."[24]

Just as the correct theological account of election leads to human freedom and responsibility, a false view of election leads to hegemonic forms of antidemocratic totalitarianism. In one of the more interesting sections of his treatment of election in *CD* II/2, Barth briefly discusses two "secular imitations" of election in the political realm that emerge from false views of the election of the individual and the community. The first error is when Jesus Christ, the true elected one, is replaced with the election of the political leader as sovereign. "There is a modern concept during the last two centuries has shown itself with increasing clarity to be a kind of secular imitation of the concept of the election of Jesus Christ--the concept of the leader."[25] This "leader-concept" (*Führerprinzip*) which may begin as a regional or local reality, but it may threaten the world, as was the case during World War II, when Barth was writing *CD* II/2. The modern version of this concept Barth finds hidden in the ideology of Western individualism, where the dignity of human individuality is rejected and replaced with the freedom of this one leader, who as a pseudo-divine ruler, acts and decides on behalf of all persons who fall under the ruler's power.[26] "All freedom and all responsibility, all authority and power in the sphere, belong to him."[27] The second "secular imitation" of election, furthermore, pertains to the community, whether located in the concept of the "national people" or the "social mass." In Barth's judgment both Fascist nationalism and Communist collectivism result in a form of political totalitarianism grounded in this false idea of election. In such a system the individual exists only as a "component part" or function of the state in which the "elected community" takes precedence over the election of the individual, who "has no freedom responsibility or authority or power of his own." "In this sense the individual and his will to live," says Barth, "his conscience and understanding, his casual opinions and necessary convictions, and ultimately even his body, have all to die in order that the whole, the mass or the nation as organized in the state, may live."[28] Similar to the pseudo-election under the leader, in this collective form the person's "uniqueness and individuality" is not intrinsically valuable in itself, but only insofar as it leads to the flourishing of the elected community. Both parodies of election, therefore, are rooted in the Western individualism, but the latter concept of the elected community reveals its last stage of development in which it is "simply wearied of itself," and become "exhausted" and tired and unwilling or unable to resist the power of the "total state."[29] Similar to Tocqueville, Barth sees the totalitarian dangers of authoritarianism and collectivism rooted in the legacy of individualism incapable of disciplining itself through a participatory democracy, but unlike Tocqueville, Barth also sees these hegemonies rooted in a corrupted view of divine election, in which Jesus Christ, the elected representative, is replaced with the elected "leader," "national people," or "social mass."

When persons deny the fundamental reality of God's election, their self-awareness changes from freedom and responsibility to isolation and separateness. Individual isolation embraces secular individualism and its parodies of the election of the individual and the community. The isolated "individual," says Barth, "involves the crisis and the limit of all 'individualism,'" which has the "power to be isolated and godless," and belong "to the mass, to the *massa perditionis*." "This is the mass of men isolated over against God," continues Barth, "who has such neither are able to perform their duties and obligations toward others in the group, nor are able to maintain and vindicate their own properties when the groups."[30] Yet in election the gracious God has determined that the "godless" and "rejected," those with "no future" except to be "their own master" and have "absolute destruction," to be nothing but a "shadow reality."[31] Jesus Christ is the Lord over both the elect and the rejected, or those who claim God's sovereign lordship and those who claim their own sovereignty. In his representation of both the elect and the rejected, Jesus Christ makes it possible for both groups to move beyond opposition and standing "against on another" toward standing "alongside and for one another." "They are mutually attached to one another."[32] This means that the totalitarian victims of the parodies of election have also been reconciled to God and to those within the political community who are reconciled "free citizens." Although the negative possibility of antidemocratic hegemony of individualistic isolation exists as a "shadow reality," in the true reality of God's election the individual is transformed by the representation of Jesus Christ into a positive witness of a believing community that forms the basis for a free democratic society.

DEMOCRATIC FREEDOM AND GOD THE CREATOR

As stated earlier, Tocqueville's great insight was that the vibrancy of the American experiment in democracy thrived on personal freedom, but was also threatened by the misuse of this same freedom causing antidemocratic forces to undermine civic participation and moral character. Particularly dangerous is his unique construal of what he calls "individualism," which undermines a positive self-interest that fosters civic participation and the "welfare of the state."[33] Unlike egoism or selfishness, a positive view of self-interest leads to "law-abiding" and "self-controlled citizens." This contrasts with a destructive form of individualism, which "threatens to grow as conditions become equal."[34] Tocqueville defines individualism as that "calm feeling" which "persuades each citizen to cut himself off from his fellows in the withdrawal into the circle of his family and friends in such a way that he thus creates a small group of his own and willingly abandons society at large to its own devices."[35] Unlike egoism, individualism emerges more from wrong thinking rather than immoral character; it results more from "defects of intelligence" than "mistakes of the heart."[36] Individualism triumphs in a society where an ideology of equality triumphs over political freedom, empowering antidemocratic forces in society. Although political freedom and equality are symbiotic forces, once a society reaches a happy medium, a preoccupation with equality over freedom will lead to complacency, personal isolation, and eventually the loss of autonomy. For Tocqueville the antidote to individualism is not just democracy but *more* democracy, that is, more democratic participation and social engagement, which drives persons from their isolation into public life. A free society depends on an active free citizenry acting for the welfare of the community.

Similar to Tocqueville, we have seen how Barth uses election to critique the legacy of Western individualism. In a public gathering in the 1950s, Barth also appeals to doctrine of creation when he revises the American Declaration of Independence's Preamble in the following way: "We hold these truths to be evident, . . . that all men are created in togetherness and mutual responsibility, . . . and that they are endowed by their Creator with freedom of life within the bounds of a rightfully established common order."[37] In replacing the word "equality" and "inalienable rights" with the words "togetherness," "mutual responsibility," and "freedom of life," Barth is drawing on his anthropological understanding of the covenant as the "internal basis of creation," as persons are created to "live in freedom" within "mutual togetherness and responsibility." Barth says that a preoccupation with terms like "equality" and "individual rights" undermine the rule of constitutional law, which ought to embolden both personal and communal responsibility, which is vital for a flourishing democracy. Barth writes: "The church always stands for the constitutional State (*Rechtsstaat*), for the maximum validity and application of that twofold law (no exemption from and full protection by the law), and therefore it will always be against any degeneration of the constitutional State *(Rechtsstaat)* into tyranny or anarchy."[38] "Democracy is not in the middle between anarchy and tyranny," says Barth, "but is above both, above this dichotomy."[39] Both anarchy and tyranny are shaped by the power of *potentia* or "naked power" that "masters and bends and breaks the law," whereas democracy attempts to rise above this struggle for power through *potestas* or the "power the serves the law."[40] Barth's comments reflect his personal commitment to social democratic liberalism, but at a deeper level, his theological understanding of concepts like freedom, responsibility and community, which are developed in his doctrine of creation. For Barth these are not just political concepts but realities that exist in relation to God the creator.

The themes of freedom and responsibility are fundamentally important not only to a democracy but also to the triune God's political action in creation. With this in mind, we make our second formal statement of political witness: *In our political witness to God the creator, we respond in faith to the God who is with and for us as the Father, who creates through the Son in the power of the Holy Spirit*. This statement balances *perichoresis* and appropriation, while affirming the indivisibility of God's external works and the human response to these works. In creation the stage is set for the unveiling of God's elective grace, as the Father who loves in freedom, determines through the Son, to be a covenant God in the power of the Spirit. God's covenant of grace empowers persons, says Barth, to live in "openness of the one to the other with the view to and on behalf of the other."[41] Against individualism and equality, God's covenant-partnership, through the gift of faith empowered by the Spirit, empowers persons to truly see the other face to face, including seeing their needs and hopes, and participating in the life of the other. This "mutual openness" enables us to truly hear and speak with others, so there is a reciprocal dialogue of openness and truthfulness. This mutual seeing and conversing further leads to mutual assistance, which makes full participation in political and social justice possible. Individualism is rejected; persons are, says Barth, "neither a slave nor tyrant, but both are companions, associates, comrades, fellows and helpmates."[42]

Responsible freedom in relation to the creator respects the goodness of life itself, which calls for respect and protection of nature, nonhuman and human life, and an active life in the world as believer, worker, and citizen. As this pertains to political responsibility, says Barth, the "state cannot relieve the individual of any responsibility. On the contrary, the state is wholly a responsibility of the individual."[43] Just as it is misguided to shift "personal responsibility" to the state, it is also misguided to shift community responsibilities to the individual. Between these extremes is the dialectical movement of individual and communal responsibility for the common good of civil society. The individual as citizen, says Barth, "is asked to consider with the state what the state has to consider."[44] Responsibility with and for the state, moreover, extends to global responsibilities. The openness toward the outsider leads to an openness to communal cooperation within nations and among nations. The key principle for both forms of openness remains the same: all national histories, in all their particularity and uniqueness, point to a common humanity in covenant-partnership, made visible in its election in Jesus Christ, which remains more ontologically substantive than national differences. God's covenant history with humanity completed in Jesus Christ, says Barth, "is the centre of all history and the meaning and goal of all national history."[45] The divine command calls nations to open their doors to the outsider and the foreigner, and says Barth, "must never be barred, let alone blocked up."[46] Just as the Christian community moves from "near to far," so too, the nations ought to work toward greater cooperation with outside communities. This relationship, writes Barth, "is a kind of circle in which we have constantly to remember the necessary loyalty on the one side and openness on the other."[47]

In political witness, the individual and community are summoned to respond in *faith* to God's creative action as politically responsible citizens, who speak and act on behalf of the other, practicing openness toward the outsider. In David Kelsey's judgment, it is faith, as an "eccentric" act, embodied in practices of "doxological gratitude" that is the proper response to God the creator. It follows that human sinfulness against the creator involves misplaced faith or trust, which distorts humanity's nature, depriving its true nature, which is possible only in relationship to the triune God. Errors occur when the trust and loyalty to oneself or the natural or human environment take precedence over God's sovereignty, or vice versa, when loyalty to God leads to the neglect of God's creation or creatures. In each case, these distorted visions work at cross-purposes against human flourishing, leading to self-destructive patterns that cannot escape a "bondage to a living death."[48]

Likewise, Barth sees the sin of pride, standing against faith, as false sovereignty of the self, community, or nation above God, claiming self-justification and consequently dishonoring the triune God and God's creation.[49] Like Kelsey, Barth defines faith as "eccentric," in that, "in faith man is no longer in control of his centre."[50] In the power of the Holy Spirit, the triune God liberates humanity from the compulsion to trust false gods or powers by making possible the "acknowledgment, recognition, and confession" of faith.[51] The witness of faith defines Christian identity and provides the basis for Christian freedom, responsibility, and obedience in public life. Public confession of faith, in fact, is the opposite of misplaced trust, namely it combines commitments to God and the civil community. In declaring its faith to the world, the church's *status confessionis*, says Barth, "is decisively action, and not—or only incidentally—reaction."[52] It is never reaction because the church's confession always remains open, not closed, motivated by faith, hope, and love, not hate or resentment, and committed to the dignity of persons, communities, and the environment, and not ideology, agonistic political causes.

DEMOCRATIC PARTICIPATION
AND GOD THE RECONCILER

We have learned how Tocqueville reminds us that democracies function well when there is a high level of civic participation, which moderates anti-democratic social forces, like individualism. Without active participation, the meaning of political freedom changes from active engagement to inactive forms of action, such as voting. Once freedom is reduced to voting, the populace becomes complacent and prone toward accepting cloaked forms of despotism. By combing "centralization with the sovereignty of the people," says Tocqueville, a proactive citizenry rather blindly accepts a "single, protective, and all-powerful government but one elected by the citizens."[53] In his judgment, elected representatives are less moral than the citizenry as a whole, because they've removed themselves for local participation and become centralized bureaucrats. Thus, republican representation turns from a blessing into a curse, as elected officials draw power away from the people and toward themselves and increase "despotism in the administrative sphere," which leads to bureaucratic micromanaging of local communities. Democracy becomes a managed democracy. Following Tocqueville, Sheldon Wolin argues that this "managed democracy" exists in America today as an "inverted kind of totalitarianism," where the powerful elites use democratic structures and management devices to control society without appearing to be overtly authoritarian or oppressive. Wolin writes: "That our system actually is democratic is more of an unquestioned assumption that a matter of public discussion, and so we ignore the extent to which antidemocratic elements have been systemic, integral not aberrant."[54] Unlike classic forms of totalitarianism, which forces conflict between an all-powerful state and other associations and institutions, an inverted totalitarianism forms a symbiotic relationship in which the government and public institutions work together strengthening self-interested political and economic power arrangements.[55] Without civic participation, political representation becomes a compliant form of despotism.

The themes of participation and representation are fundamentally important not only to a democracy but also to the triune God's political action of divine reconciliation. It follows that in our third formal statement of political witness, we say the following: *In our political witness to God the reconciler, we respond in love to the God who is with and for us in the Son, sent by the Father in the power of the Spirit*. Here the reconciling work of Jesus Christ takes center stage in the events of the crucifixion and resurrection, and the justification and sanctification of the sinner. In *CD* IV/1, we see the downward movement of the Son of God, the great "high priest," who as mediator and judge justifies sinners through his atoning death on the cross. The

Lord humbly becomes the servant standing with humanity in Jesus Christ as mediator and judge, where he "renews and restores" the covenant that sinful humanity has "broken."[56] Alternatively, in *CD* IV/2, Barth explores this same event from the opposite direction of the upward movement of the Son of Man, the man of Nazareth, who acts pro nobis, as our representative, in faithful obedience toward God as the "royal man" and "exalted king," uniting humanity into "fellowship with God."[57] In both movements, the triune God accomplishes the divine work of reconciliation through actions of sending, acting, and empowering. The loving Father sends the Son, whose actions bring salvation to humanity, and are empowered and made realizable through the Holy Spirit.

Although the language of representation applies to both movements, the downward action of the Son of God in justification implies more acting on *behalf* of another, whereas the upward action of the Son of Man is acting *along with* another. God is with us and for us in these two movements. God's gracious verdict of justification repudiates, displaces, and pardons sinful humanity, whereas in sanctification the human subject is transformed and empowered to live in grateful obedience to God's command of grace. "It is one thing that God turns in free grace to sinful man," says Barth, "quite another that in the same free grace he converts man to himself."[58] Although distinguished, these divine actions of justification and sanctification remain one event of the triune God's reconciliation of the sinner. In this event the actions of Jesus Christ as representative culminates in his actions both for us and with us, in which persons are restored, liberated, and empowered to fully participate in God's reconciling action, not as co-reconciler, but as witness, in speech and action, to God's gracious purposes for church and the civil community. In short, Christ's representation empowers humanity to participate as witnesses to God's reconciliation of both the church and the civil community.

Barth's placement of the civil community (state) under reconciliation actually occurred many years earlier, in his 1928–1932 ethics lectures.[59] In later political essays, especially the 1946 essay, Barth develops this theme by making two important claims: (1) the law is the "necessary form of the gospel, whose content is grace," which places both the church and state under the authority of the gospel; and (2) the democratic state is more than just of guardian of the law and common good, but because it stands under the gospel, it becomes, in Barth's words, a "true order of human affairs—the justice, wisdom and peace, equity and care for human welfare."[60] The first time Barth discusses the state in the *Church Dogmatics* is in relation to divine justification can be found in *CD* 2/1-2, where he discusses the state in the context of God's attributes, election and divine command. In addressing God's attributes of mercy and righteousness in *CD* II/1, he claims there is a "straight line" between God's act of divine justification and a "very definite political program and task."[61] Political responsibility to the reconciler involves the two commitments of human rights and political justice, says Barth, and to reject these is to "reject God's act of divine justification."[62] In *CD* II/2 we have seen how Barth relates politics to election, so too in his discussion of God's command, he illustrates the universality and goodness of God's command with the summons to seek "the welfare of others without surrendering one's own freedom and responsibility."[63] In this way, God commands persons to "undertake and fulfill the ministry of reconciliation."[64] The true meaning and purpose of political life lies not in the actions of the state but in the actions of God's reconciliation of the church and the state. This is why, says Barth, the Christian "will always understand Caesar better than he understands himself."[65] "It is they," Barth adds, "who know what they are doing when the think and act as citizens of the state."[66] This allows the church to give witness to the state that the love of God and neighbor is possible within the practices of the civil community.

Like Barth, David Kelsey argues that just as the *love* of God and neighbor is a proper response to God's reconciliation, human sinfulness distorts love resulting in self-justifying intentions and actions, leading to self-destructive vicious cycles of entrapment. Self-justification leads to a distorted personal identity by rejecting structural reconciliation and forgiveness and instead claiming power over others or allegiance to one's political ideology. The second type of distorted personal identity desires structural reconciliation, but sees it only as a future goal of human politics rather than something already accomplished through God's actions.[67] The last type of distorted personal identity remains committed to the task of structural reconciliation in the present through political action, without acknowledging God's reconciliation. In each case, neighborly love is disconnected from love of God, and from God's action in the present and future. Similar to Kelsey, Barth argues that neighborly love is possible only when God makes persons "free for this action," namely free to be a witness to God's reconciliation.[68] Hence, the love command can never be reduced to a horizontal command to help others, but depends entirely on the vertical relationship between God and humanity, mediated by Jesus Christ. The vertical love of God makes it possible for the corrosive power of human sinfulness to be destroyed and transformed into the other-directed power of love. So, it is *agape*, says Barth, that "breaks the dominion of the sinister forces to which the man alienated from God, the neighbor and himself is subject"[69] This makes it possible for persons to live in solidarity and community under the rule of law, in the form of the gospel. In Barth's words, it empowers persons to act "correspondingly" and "freely" in obedience and responsibility so that the "the covenant of grace, becomes two-sided instead of one-sided"[70]

What is important here is not only that Barth provided a theological argument for why a social democracy is a humane form of government, but how it can become a secular witness to God's triune sovereignty. While democracy may be threatened by inverted forms of totalitarianism and management, the substance of political participation is renewed, empowered, and made visible through Son's reconciling action in the power of the Spirit. Popular sovereignty is restored and empowered through participation in Jesus Christ, as the mediator and representative, who heals the estrangement within the human community, including any form of despotism, which denies the electing God's self-determination to reconcile the political community.

DEMOCRATIC PROMISE AND GOD THE REDEEMER

Tocqueville's vision for a flourishing democracy in America was largely dependent on his positive views on the vibrancy of local politics, or politics from below, and his encounters with American evangelical Christianity. Rooted in the New England experiment, Tocqueville sees the Christianity of the New World as principally "democratic and republican."[71] There is, Tocqueville explains, "not a single religious doctrine in the United States hostile to democratic and republican institutions."[72] The churches, as associations, were responsible for society's coherent ordering of priorities, social and communal involvement, and "habits of restraint" that challenged social conformism and materialism.[73] At the same time, the churches affirm both the freedom of conscience and a transcendental moral standard, which together formed a moral social structure of governance without a state religion. It was the combination of disestablishment and religious vitality that formed the "habits of restraint" needed for a flourishing democracy. Nonetheless, Tocqueville still worried that democratic society would succumb to material pleasures and lose its promise for a democratic vision. Even though religious "habits of restraint" provide a check against excesses, Americans wrongly link their "own private fortunes and general prosperity."[74] Personal satisfaction, and what he calls, "business or industrial aristocracy," spread the false hope and promise that materialistic acquisition will bring happiness. Tocqueville's most important, and rather prophetic, statement about the despotism he fears for America, is worth quoting at length:

> I see an innumerable crowd of men, all alike in equal, turned in upon themselves in a restless search for those petty, vulgar pleasures with which they feed their souls. Each of them, living apart, is almost unaware of the destiny of all the rest. His children and personal friends are for him the whole of the human race; as for the remainder of his fellow citizens, he stands alongside them but does not

see them; he touches them without feeling them; he exists only in himself and for himself; if he still retains his family circle, at any rate he may be said to have lost his country.[75]

Tocqueville's prophetic vision of one possible future of democracy has largely come true, and yet his alternative vision of the promise of democracy also remains relevant for those persons who organize and struggle for a more democratic way of life. Although not perfect, Tocqueville reminds us that democracy is always in a state of becoming, or stated more theologically, the promise of democracy lies in its eschatological promise.

Considering this eschatological theme of promise, we look lastly at the triune action of God the redeemer and its responsive form of political witness. In so doing, we make our fourth formal statement: *In our political witness to God the redeemer, we respond in hope to the God who is with and for us in the Spirit, sent by the Father with the Son, who draws creatures to eschatological consummation.* God's eschatological consummation, like creation and reconciliation, emerges from God's being and action, as the one who eternally is giving and receiving of love, and frees humanity to further hear God's gracious eschatological promise through the Holy Spirit. "Not only was God glorious in the past," says Barth, "and not only will he be glorious and final fulfillment of his promise, but is glorious here and now in the promise of his Spirit, he himself being present and active yesterday, today and tomorrow."[76] In the promise the Spirit, Jesus Christ is not only the priestly Son of God and the kingly Son of Man, but he is also the prophetic *Christus victor*, who, writes Barth, unites Christ's "deity and humanity, of God's humiliation and man's exaltation, of the justification and sanctification of man, of faith and love."[77] In the power of the Spirit, Jesus Christ as "true witness" and "victor" unveils the eschatological knowledge of God's promised consummation of God's victory over the lordless powers of leviathan, mammon, and ideology. In the power of the Spirit, Christ's victory over the powers calls for the church to be a witness to God's Yes for the world's future, declaring that "*totus Christus* is *Christus victor*."[78] In the prophetic witness of Jesus Christ, claims Barth, "the hope of us all in the promise of the Spirit addressed to all."[79]

We saw earlier how the Spirit empowers the Christian to lead an eccentric life, one in which empowers persons to live "eccentrically" for others, living their vocation in the world. The purpose the eccentric life in response to God the redeemer, the giver of the eschatological promise, corresponds to Christ's prophetic work as it says No to the lordless powers but Yes for the individual, community, and the world. So political witness affirms not only mutual togetherness and participation but also one of "political struggle."[80] In Barth's words, the "fulfillment of political duty" means that "responsible choices of authority, responsible decisions about the validity of laws, responsible care for their maintenance, in a word, political action, which may also mean political struggle."[81] The church's struggle as witness remains free from all political ideology, which for Barth allows for it to "speak very conservatively today and very progressively or even revolutionarily tomorrow-or vice versa."[82] In the church's political witness against the powers, it also remains a positive witness to the civil community that in saying No to ideology, leviathan, mammon and other powers, the church gives witness to its future, its meaning and purpose, too belongs to God's eschatological promise of blessing and hope. This is aptly illustrated in the 1946 essay, where Barth gives twelve analogies, linking the two communities, beginning with the church as "inner witness" and moving outward to the civil community as "outer witness" to God's kingdom.[83] In the church's public witness to God's triune action of divine justification, mercy, judgment, covenant and incarnation, and the ecclesial practices of baptism, congregational equality, freedom, and service, the church demonstrates to the civil community what it means to exist as a reconciled community. These church beliefs and practices are analogously linked to forms of secular witness in the civil community, such as the constitutionally democratic insistence on impartial justice, separation of governmental powers, equality and freedom of all citizens, cultural plurality and religious diversity, and freedom of speech and of the press. In both directions the church and state serve as positive forms of political witness, who struggle for human justice and peace in the world. It follows that both communities must reject all forms of totalitarianism, anarchism, individualism, collectivism, and the unjust practices of political deception, secrecy, and coercion.

Later in *CD* IV/2, Barth demonstrates further how the church's law provides a witness to the state's law, further unveiling God's eschatological purpose for both church and state.[84] As stated earlier, all law is in the form of the gospel, which further explains why Barth thinks church law, shaped by the gospel, serves as the form of the civil law. In summary, the church law prioritizes service to the other over self-interest, gracious judgment over retribution, political trust over coercion, and the common good over individual goods. As a community of free persons, the church forms a socially and culturally diverse community while rejecting status, class, achievement, materialism, and centralized power. And, lastly, the church demonstrates to society that the law is a free gift of God that remains open-ended and dynamic. Once applied to democracy, these practices are more than just an ecclesial model for how the state ought to govern society, but it's also a vision, a promise, for a more flourishing democracy under the authority of the gospel, one that is empowered to give and receive God's eschatological blessings to the world.

Both the church and state can be a witness of *hope* to God's eschatological promise that the Spirit sent by the Father with the Son is drawing persons and communities toward eschatological flourishing. Similar to Barth, David Kelsey argues that the proper response to God's consummation is joyous hopefulness, which challenges sins of distorted or misguided hope. Misguided hope places humanity, including social roles and ideologies, as powers behind the promise for eschatological blessing, or in Kelsey's words, a "bondage to some theory about the dynamics of social and moral progress in history."[85] Ecclesial distortions can also affirm God's eschatological future blessing, but deny it in the present time, which fails to see God's redemptive power in the present time between the incarnation and the consummation. Similar to Kelsey, Barth's theology of Christian hope challenges ideologies of utopianism or dystopianism. The "eschatological difference" begins, not with optimism, pessimism, or skepticism, but God's gracious past, present, and future actions. The Holy Spirit, says Barth, is the "enlightening power of the living Lord Jesus Christ" revealing to the world that Christ is the "first and final meaning of history" and that "his future manifestation is already here and now" as a "great, effective and living hope."[86] Like faith and love, Christian hope is not an attitude or action but a hopeful and joyful response to the *divine* action of the redeemer. The promise of democracy, therefore, cannot rest in democracy itself but in the promise of its eschatological consummation. As the "inner" and "outer" circles of witness to God's triune sovereignty, the church and democratic society must struggle for justice and peace.

The substance of political promise is not possible through political struggle without the power of the Spirit's eschatological blessing; otherwise, a promethean form of defiance will rise up against God's trinitarian sovereignty and strengthen the lordless powers. The vicious cycles of distorted faith, hope, and love will lead to destructive practices that seek to overcome God's creative freedom, God's reconciling love, and God's redemptive promise with the powers of political, economic, or ideological absolutism. These possible negative outcomes do not change or alter God's triune sovereignty over the meaning and purpose of history, including democratic society. Rather they simply keep persons and communities from fully acknowledging themselves as they truly exist, namely as creatures who are loved and able to receive God's gracious eschatological blessings here and now as well as the future.

NOTES

1. S. J. Michael Kirwan, *Political Theology: An Introduction* (Minneapolis: Fortress, 2009), 197.

2. David Kelsey, *Eccentric Existence*, 2 vols. (Louisville: Westminster, 2009).

3. Fundamental to contemporary political theology is discourse about political sovereignity, and central to this discussion is engagment with the thought of Carl Schmitt. In this volume, Clifford Anderson and Devin Singh helpfully explore different aspects of sovereignty in relation to the contrasting views of Karl Barth and Carl Schmitt. See Anderson, "Constitutional Theology" and Singh, "A Tale of Two Sovereignities."

4. Karl Barth, *Church Dogmatics*, 4 vols., trans. and ed. G. W. Bromiley and T. F. Torrance (Edinburgh, 1936–77). Hereafter, all citations to the *Church Dogmatics* will be abbreviated as *CD*, followed by volume and part.

5. Barth, *CD* I/1, 368.

6. Ibid., 370.

7. *CD* II/2, 49.

8. Ibid., 162.

9. Ibid., 585, 593.

10. See *CD* III/4, 32–38.

11. Alexis de Tocqueville, *Democracy in America and Two Essays on America*, trans. Gerald E. Bevan with an Introduction and Notes by Issac Kramnik (London: Penguin Classics, 2003), 15.

12. Ibid., 71.

13. Sheldon Wolin writes that Tocqueville's anxiety was rooted in his worry that God was a "dying deity, a god who, like the absolute monarchs, had lost his potency, or by a god who changed his mind, and transferred his favor from aristocracy to the multitude. His deepest fear was that the deity might be neither and that men were condemned to live in an abandoned world, a chance arrangement devoid of any imminent meanings." Sheldon Wolin, *Tocqueville Between Two Worlds* (Princeton: Princeton University Press, 2001), 108.

14. Tocqueville reasons that God the "creator and preserver of men derives the greatest satisfaction not from the unusual propensity of the few but the widespread well-being of all. What seems to me to be a decline is, therefore, progress in his eyes; what bruises me is a pleasure to him." Tocqueville, *Democracy in America*, 820.

15. Ibid., 294.

16. *CD* II/2, 318.

17. In this volume, both Daniel Lee and Pan-chiu Lai discuss how Barth's political thought is relevant for contempoary struggles and developments within Hong Kong's democracy. See Lee's "On Becoming a Citizen" and Lai's "Relgious Diversity, Democracy, and Public Theology."

18. Ibid., 314.

19. Ibid., 313.

20. For a further discussion political democracy within the ecclesiological thought of Barth and John Howard Yoder, see Kristopher Norris' contribution to this volume: "Democracy and Church."

21. Karl Barth, *Community, State, and Church: Three Essays* (Eugene: Wipf and Stock, 2005), 186. For further discussion of Barth's political thought of church and state in relation to contemporary China, see Thomas Qu's contribution to this volume: "*Gleichnis wagen.*"

22. "Christian choices and purposes in politics tend on the whole toward the form of State, which, if is not actually realized in the so-called 'democracies,' is at any rate more or less honestly clearly intended and desired." Ibid., 182.

23. *CD* II/2, 312.

24. Ibid., 312.

25. Ibid., 311.

26. The leader "unites in himself the fullness of the election of grace, so that he is the elect, not on behalf of, but in the place of others; he is the other, besides whom there are finally no individuals, or at least no elect individuals." Ibid., 311.

27. Ibid., 311.

28. Ibid., 312.

29. Ibid., 312.

30. Ibid., 318.

31. Ibid., 457–458.

32. Ibid., 353.

33. Tocqueville, *Democracy in America*, 611.

34. Ibid., 588.

35. Ibid., 587.

36. Ibid., 588.

37. Barth, *Barth's Table Talk*, ed. John Godsey (Richmond: John Knox, 1963), 77.

38. Barth, *Community, State, and Church*, 172. For further discussion of the "rule of law" and *Rechtsstaat* in relation to Barth and Carl Schmitt, see Clifford Anderson's contribution to this volume.

39. Barth, *Barth's Table Talk*, 80–81.

40. Barth, *Community, State, and Church*, 177.

41. *CD* III/2, 250.

42. Ibid., 271.

43. *CD* III/4, 364.

44. Ibid., 465.

45. Ibid., 297.

46. Ibid., 294.

47. Ibid., 318.

48. Kelsey, *Eccentric Existence*, 423.

49. *CD* III/4, 665.

50. *CD* IV/1, 743.

51. Ibid., 758.

52. *CD* III/4, 81.

53. Tocqueville, *Democracy in America*, 806.

54. Sheldon Wolin, *Democracy Incorporated: Managed Democracy and the Specter of Inverted Totalitarianism* (Princeton: Princeton University Press, 2008), 212.

55. In his contribution to this volume, Charles Matthews, in "Whatever Happened to the Social Gospel," explores the legacy of the American Social Gospel movement and its implications for contemporary political, economic, and criminal justice. Similar to Tocqueville and Barth, Social Gospel "realism" both challenges and seeks to reform the various structures of injustice. For a discussion of Barth's "realism,"

furthermore, see Paul Dafydd Jones' contribution to this volume, "Karl Barth's *The Christian Life* and the Task of Political Theology."

56. *CD* IV/1, 251.

57. *CD* IV/2, 155.

58. Ibid., 503.

59. Karl Barth, *Ethics* (New York: Seabury, 1981).

60. Barth, *Church, Community, and State*, 79, 147–148.

61. *CD* II/1, 386.

62. Ibid., 386.

63. *CD* II/2, 719.

64. Ibid., 720.

65. Ibid., 722.

66. Ibid., 722.

67. Kelsey, *Eccentric Existence*, 875.

68. *CD* IV/2, 818.

69. Ibid., 836.

70. Ibid., 790.

71. Tocqueville, *Democracy in America*, 336.

72. Ibid., 338.

73. Ibid., 341.

74. Ibid., 627.

75. Ibid., 805.

76. *CD* IV/3, 359.

77. Ibid., 4.

78. *CD* IV/3, 216.

79. Ibid., 362–363.

80. Similar to the idea of "political struggle" in Barth's thought, Paul Dafydd Jones' essay in this volume explores the theme of "revolt" within Barth's ethics of reconcilion in *The Christian Life*.

81. Barth, *Church, State, and Community*, 144.

82. Karl Barth, *Against the Stream: Shorter Post-War Writings 1946–52* (New York, Philosophical Library, 1954), 91.

83. Barth, *Church, State, and Community*, 169–182.

84. *CD* IV/2, 729–726.

85. Kelsey, *Eccentric Existence*, 599.

86. *CD* IV/3, 681.

Chapter 21

Public Theology and Christian Social Action in Hong Kong

From the Past to the Present

Kin Yip Louie

INTRODUCTION

What is public theology? There is no unanimously accepted definition. For the purpose of this chapter, by "public theology," I mean the intellectual framework through which the church seeks to respond to pressing issues in the public square. In this sense, public theology has both a positive and a normative dimension. The positive task is to examine the public discourse and decisions of the church while also making explicit the church's implicit theological framework. The normative task is to evaluate the actions and the explicit and implicit discourses of the churches to see if they remain faithful to the gospel. Its goal is to invigorate the continuing witness of the church with critical reflection. As I shall explain in the chapter, the time has come when the Hong Kong church cannot keep silent on social justice issues and democracy. Yet, as the church seeks to engage in contemporary issues, it must avoid both the pitfall of becoming another political party and the temptation to preach with an impeccable self-righteousness. A Barthian perspective reminds us of the triumph of God's grace in the midst of pervasive sinfulness in the world and within the church. The Christian church is being sent out as the witness for the grace of God in the secular world, but the church is not yet the perfect bride of Christ.[1] This witness role also encourages the church to actively seek justice for all—without being attached to any particular grandiose theoretical framework.[2]

Public theology has become increasingly important in Hong Kong. Here are some reasons:

1. Even though Christianity is the religion of a small minority in Hong Kong (*n.b.,* surveys indicate that less than 5 percent of the Hong Kong population attends church on Sundays), its influence goes way beyond its membership numbers. These include the colonial past of Hong Kong, the rich traditions of the Christian faith, the organizational effectiveness of the churches and para-church agencies, and the educational level of many Christians. The Christian church, in the broad sense, is thus an important social institution in Hong Kong society. Due to its visibility, the attitude of the church (whether or not it actually represents the dominant social view) can have an important influence in public arena. Therefore, the public theology of the church can have a significant impact on the direction of both the church and society.

2. The influence of postmodern thinking in various forms, whether Christian or not, has penetrated and now permeates the intellectual climate of Hong Kong. One common thread in these diverse forms of post-modernism is the quest for self-identity and self-expression. Among theologians in Hong Kong, the task of self-criticism of the church has become a very fashionable enterprise. The role of the church in the political arena has become a focus of attention in examining the church's self-identity.

3. In America, public theology has become a center of controversies since the Reagan years. The Religious Right has become a permanent part of American politics, although some claim that its influence is waning. Some of the tactics and vocabulary of the culture wars in the United States have been imported into Hong Kong. However, on the whole, the culture wars in Hong Kong are quite different from those in the United States.[3] The use of American imagery raises the temperature of the debate and calls for clarification and debunking.

4. The missiology of the last fifty years has emphasized the importance of the *mission dei*. Christians are sent by God to bless the world. From mainline to charismatic churches, there is a renewed emphasis to reach out to the broader society through services and prayers. Sometimes the kinds of services provided and the content of the prayers offered by well-known church leaders are publicized on social media (such as Facebook). Sometimes this can then generate vehement denunciations from some Christians (and even non-Christians). The church leaders often find themselves unprepared to respond to such controversies. Public theology can accordingly help the church clarify its own decisions and assumptions.

5. The struggle for civil rights in recent years has sensitized Hong Kong people to social justice issues. Both within and outside of the church, there is a loud cry for the church to express her position regarding social justice and democracy.

Having given some reasons for the rising importance of public theology in Hong Kong, I will now analyze how public theology has evolved through time.

HISTORICAL DEVELOPMENTS

I do not intend to give a general history of the Protestant churches in Hong Kong, but only a quick historical survey of how the church has responded to pressing social issues over three distinct periods: 1950–1980, 1980–1997, and 1997–present.[4]

1950–1980

We begin our story after World War II. At that time, the pressing issue was poverty and the settling of immigrants. During World War II, the Hong Kong population dropped dramatically because people flocked back to the mainland to escape from the Japanese. After the war, the Communist Party came to power. People who were pessimistic about their future in a Communist regime fled to Hong Kong in large numbers. The Hong Kong population increased from under 500,000 in 1945 to over 2 million by 1950. Among these immigrants, some were Western missionaries and Chinese church leaders who were forced to leave China to avoid persecution. It is during this period that the Chinese church really took root among the local population in Hong Kong. Due to the political instability and the economic setbacks in China during the 1960s, the population influx from the mainland continued into the 1970s.[5]

Having endured much suffering on the mainland, the immigrants were looking primarily for stability and an opportunity to work and live peacefully. Most Chinese acquiesced to British rule, as the colonial government sheltered them from the political chaos in the mainland. A minority of left-leaning citizens did manage to create serious social unrest in 1967, but the memories of that uneasy time just convinced most people that British rule should not be challenged.

This means that the public theology of the church in those days was apolitical. People in society were not keen to address political issues and Christians were perhaps even less eager than others. For example, if one were to read through the Sunday church bulletins or church annual reports for the year 1967, one would seldom find references to the social unrest of that time. One would also be hard-pressed to find theological reflections on nationalism or on the right form of government. There was a small group of Chinese intellectuals who were concerned about rebuilding Confucianism to face the challenges of the twentieth century in the 1950s and 1960s and in response some Christian theologians worked on the integration of Christian faith and classical Chinese culture. But that was more a dialogue among the elites, rather than a response to popular public concerns.

Besides the general atmosphere of the society, there were also theological concerns behind such political apathy. The fundamentalist controversy of the American churches in the 1930s was transplanted to the Chinese soil through the split among American missionaries at that time. Within Chinese churches, independent revivalists such as Watchman Nee (1903–1972), John Sung (1901–1944), and Wang Ming-dao (1900–1991) championed fundamentalism. They portrayed Christian faith mostly in terms of personal sanctification. In contrast, the liberal wing of the church flourished in Christian universities and para-church organization such as the YMCA. When the Communist Party came to power, most of the prominent church leaders who came to Hong Kong belonged to the (fundamentalist) tradition of the revivalist preachers, whose primary concerns were to build up the churches and give Christians a sense of security within the church.[6]

This is not to suggest that the church ignored public issues completely. Most of those refugees from the mainland had securing a stable livelihood as their primary concern. The antebellum Hong Kong government mainly regarded the colony as a trading port, and thus was not eager to intervene in the affairs of local Chinese. In the immediate postwar era, the government was slow to change its attitude. This left ample opportunities for the churches and other voluntary organizations to fill the vacuum by providing various kinds of social services, with the provision of free food (in particular, rice, 派米) as the primary provision. With the support of Western churches and with good organization framework, the Chinese church was an important agent for relief work in meeting basic needs. At the same time, these activities gave opportunities for the church to evangelize. During that period, no tension was felt between social action and evangelism. Both were perceived to be the natural tasks of the church, and the church proceeded to do both without much critical reflection. Within society, there was also little objection concerning religious organization using social action as means of evangelism.

Gradually, as manufacturing began to flourish in Hong Kong, relief work receded into background, and Christian schools became the focus of social action. The 1960s was the golden era for the establishment of Christian primary and secondary schools, as the children of the refugees (mostly born in Hong Kong) swelled the number of school children. At first (late 1950s and early 1960s), many of these schools were small-scale and private, meaning that some of them were built on the roof of private buildings or public estates (天台學校). As the 1960s progressed, the government came increasingly to recognize that social stability required more schooling for the young. Instead of establishing a large number of schools from scratch, the government decided to utilize the expertise of religious and other charitable organizations that had already been running schools. The government subsidized these organizations (by granting land, constructing school buildings, and underwriting operational expenses every year) to establish these schools. "Subsidized schools," accordingly, became the mainstream way of students' receiving primary and secondary education in Hong Kong.

In accepting government subsidies, the churches were implicitly bargaining the scale of operation for autonomy in the content of the services provided. The Hong Kong government did not have an explicit position on the role of religion in public education. It allowed the participation of religious, organization as a matter of convenience, and there was no public debate on this issue regarding the separation of church and state in those years. However, some churches did internally debate whether their private schools should become subsidized by the government. Put positively, the government could provide financial resources beyond the reach of any church and churches could use these resources to educate and evangelize more students. Put negatively, the schools would obviously have to submit to public regulations, as well as learn to negotiate with the government. Concerning the question whether the churches should plunge into this as yet uncharted water, the majority view was that the opportunity to serve more students was simply too good to pass up. Like the government, practical advantages prevailed over philosophical considerations in the churches.[7]

In a similar way, the piecemeal relief efforts in the 1950s gradually evolved into more formal and specialized social agencies in the 1960s. Particularly after the riots in 1967, the government recognized that social services were essential to the stability of the society. In order to appropriate the financial resources of the government, the churches began to set up specialized agencies to provide social services. However, as the economy developed, providing basic needs was no longer the primary concern—professional skills were needed as well. The result, like the case in education, was the development of Christian social agencies that became more distinct from the organization of the church.

Unlike the case in education, churches engaged in serious theological debates about their role in providing social services. 1970s was the time when the postwar baby boomers became university students: this was the first generation born and raised in Hong Kong who became college-educated in large numbers. To be sure, though the percentage of young people who entered university was still small, the 1970s produced an unprecedented number of well-educated young people. That generation began to search for its mission in or contribution to society. In the United States, similar social forces produced the Woodstock generation and, in Christian circles, the New Evangelism Movement.

The Christian students of that generation also began to question their roles in society. At the same time, the Christian literature associated with the Lausanne Movement began to filter into Hong Kong. After the refugee relief works of the 1950s, many Christians felt that the church gradually slacked off from discharging her social responsibilities in the 1960s. The campus magazine *Olive* 《橄欖》 was a banner for progressive theological thinking. Two issues in particular received a lot of attention. The first was on the welfare of factory workers. Hong Kong was a world center of manufacturing (especially in clothing, toys, and watches) in the 1960s and 1970s. Beginning in the late 1960s, some young Christians became involved in a social movement that sought to improve the welfare of factory workers. A prominent Christian leader coined the phrase "the sinned against" to describe their plight, and it was one of the few locally produced theological phrases that have ever gained widespread popularity.

The second issue that received considerable attention how the church could proactively engage with popular culture. Before, when Chinese churches talked about contextualization, they usually meant classical Chinese culture such as Confucianism and Buddhism. Starting in the late 1970s, a movement sprang up to understand the urban and popular culture of Hong Kong. It was partially motivated by a concern to minister to the younger generation, and accordingly to transform popular culture. For the first time, there was a sense of responsibility among Hong Kong churches to learn and shape the secular culture around them.

We may sum up this period with a few reflections. The postwar Hong Kong was driven by the need to provide a livelihood for the tens of thousands of refugees that poured into the colony. In such a situation, practical needs trumped any theoretical concerns for the demarcation of the role of religion in the civil society. The government welcomed the efforts of religious organizations, and the churches mobilized a large portion of their limited resources to meet these needs. There was thus active participation in the public square without critical reflection of any underlying theology. As a pilgrim church living in a borrowed space, Christians of the immediate postwar generation did not feel the urge to reflect critically on their social situation.[8]

As some of the postwar generation that was born and raised in Hong Kong became the educated elite in the society, they then began to reflect on their social situation and to develop a public theology. This generation regarded Hong Kong as their home—not merely a transitory place of abode. They called the church to go beyond providing social services and to engage in social action, to transform social institutions and popular culture. They achieved some highly visible results in establishing various para-church organizations, but it is debatable how far they have changed the mentality of the mass of Christians in Hong Kong.

1980–1997

During the 1980s and 1990s, the major public issue for Hong Kong society was the returning of Hong Kong to China. After Margaret Thatcher's visit to Beijing in 1982, it soon became clear to everyone that Hong Kong would return to the sovereign rule of China in 1997. The Chinese and British government would negotiate the transition as a dialogue in diplomacy between two nations, rendering the desires of the Hong Kong people themselves irrelevant. Hong Kong people were accordingly left with this question: How should they respond to the inevitable reality? Should they rejoice? Should they repeat the story of fifty years prior and flee the Communists by emigration? And if they choose to or are forced to stay behind, what should Christians in Hong Kong do?[9]

At the time, probably many Hong Kong citizens wished for the continuation of British rule. Mainland China was still a poor nation. *Moreover, due to the many opaque political power struggles within the mainland government, Hong Kong people found it difficult to trust Beijing.* The literature about the Cultural Revolution in China that gradually got published after 1976 created further alarm among Hong Kong people about Chinese rule. After the Tiananmen Square Massacre in 1989, many were scared about the Communist regime. What message could the church bring to this anxious time?

One possible message was a silent exit. It would have been probably too embarrassing to openly advocate emigration, as such a move might be interpreted as unpatriotic or unfaithful to their sense of Chinese identity. However, many Christians and pastors did choose to emigrate to foreign countries, particularly English-speaking ones. Due to the immigration laws in the United States and the United Kingdom, religious workers such as pastors had a relatively easy time obtaining immigration visas for these countries. One prominent Bible school decided to terminate its ministry in Hong Kong and transfer the school to the United States. This exodus of pastors was noticed even outside of Christian circles. The implicit message was that personal and family concerns take precedence over the question of social mission. Leaving unresolved here the question whether such a choice was theologically justifiable, we want to stress now that these emigration decisions were often quite stressful both for the individuals concerned and for their congregations.

An alternative, more vocal voice in the church was to encourage Christians to take a positive attitude toward the future. In 1984, a group of prominent Christian leaders issued a "Confessional Statement"《信念書》[10] on the future of Hong Kong. Many of them were the same people who spoke out for social action in the 1970s. The Confessional Statement was an ad hoc statement by a group of Christians who did not represent the position of any particular denomination or Christian organization. It was nonetheless widely distributed and inspired some denominations to issue similar statements. It was probably the most influential public confessional statement by Christians on the issue of the political future of Hong Kong.

The first clause says: "We believe that God is the Creator, Redeemer and Judge, and Lord of historical development. Therefore, we believe that any change in the future of Hong Kong happen under His providence. This belief gives us the determination to strive to accomplish His will in our lives with a peaceful heart." The theological premise of the statement is the sovereignty and the providence of God. The second clause emphasizes the Bible as the standard of truth and the unacceptability of compromising the truth in any situation.[11] One can detect hints of Barthian theology in the theological framework of the statement.

Proceeding to more practical concerns, the statement urges Christians to strive to shape the future of Hong Kong along with other citizens and to "make Hong Kong into a prosperous and democratic society, respecting human rights, freedom, equality, and the rule of law." Next, it encourages Hong Kong Christians to seek to make China a free, just, and prosperous country. Alluding to Romans 13, the statement says that Christians should in general submit to secular government, but also act in a prophetic role by promoting justice in politics. Another clause admonishes the churches to accept differences in opinion, and to beware of the infiltration of secular ideologies or power into the churches. Lastly, the statement emphasizes that the church should renew herself through evangelism, discipleship, and other ministries.

Even though the statement was well-known among Christians, its practical impact (or any similar confessional statement at that time) was debatable. Its two major theological themes—the sovereignty of God and a critical acceptance of secular political power—were not controversial in Chinese churches. We may note also these themes' harmony with Barth's political theology. But any practical application of such principles can get very complicated, and the Confessional Statement offered limited guidance. For example, the sovereignty of God could mean that Christians should accept the transfer of power with confidence, for even if they faced persecution, they would be sustained by the grace of God. However, if someone had the opportunity to emigrate, how could she know whether God was calling her instead to suffer patiently under the Communist regime? When indeed individuals had no other choice but to stay in Hong Kong, it may be natural to encourage them to seek to promote the welfare of Hong Kong society and China along with other citizens. But the question remains whether citizens of Hong Kong have a prima facie moral obligation to stay.

Perhaps we should not expect any public statement to provide pastoral guidance. In any case, the Confessional Statement served to galvanize the effort to mobilize Christians to look positively toward the transfer of power. There were heated public discussions on the meaning of patriotism, and the number of public prayer meetings increased as the time drew closer to the handover. These meetings were often controversial, as an individual's participation or lack thereof in these meetings could both be interpreted politically. For instance, if a church held a public prayer meeting on the National Day of mainland China, did that symbolize healthy patriotism or an effort to appease the Communist Party? It was a time of high ideals and bitter criticism.

The majority of Christians, like the majority of Hong Kong people, could not emigrate. Most of them probably looked toward the Chinese regime with anxiety and resignation. If they asked themselves about preparing for the turnover to China, being patriotic was not their main concern. Churches prepared themselves with fervent church planting, as some feared that evangelism might be hindered and that large churches might be forced to break up. Some churches encouraged their members to remember large portions of scripture as they feared the confiscation of their religious books by the government after 1997. Their primary concern was to protect the church and to continue the Christian way of living. They were not primarily concerned about contributing to a just and free Hong Kong after the turnover.[12]

Why is there a discrepancy between the public discourse of some prominent theologians and church leaders and the actual pastoral concerns of ordinary Christians? Partially, this is a reflection of the lack of self-confidence among the churches in Hong Kong. Does what the churches say and do really matter to the future of Hong Kong? The church in mainland China debated the role of faith in the New China in the 1920s and 1930s, but their deliberations seemed to have little impact on the course of Chinese history. Though that story is not well-known among Christians, Christian suffering under the Communist regime was often paraded as an example of Christian piety. This kind of piety naturally encouraged pessimism toward Christian participation in the public square.

A related reason may be the deep-seated pragmatism in Chinese culture. Even if Christian proclamation does not make a big difference, one might nonetheless still want to be prophetic and speak truth to power. However, living under colonial rule for many years has trained the Hong Kong people to concentrate their efforts on improving ordinary life. Evangelism has thus been emphasized because such efforts are within the control of the local churches, and because church growth can be measured by the numbers of new converts. Even the provision of social services has had more measurable effects in the public arena than has their dialogue about ideological matters.

If there is a moral in this story, it may be that theologians should constantly ask themselves what sort of public theology is helpful to the church. Public theology, by definition, should respond to public issues in society. Theologians, as a critical reader of the proclamation of the church (as per a Barthian perspective on theology), should lead other Christians to engage meaningfully and profoundly with contemporary issues. But public theology also needs to speak to ordinary Christians if it wants to be effective and sustainable in the long run. Theologians need to seek to bridge their prophetic insights with the practical concerns of ordinary members. This gap will never disappear, but theologians should consider it their responsibility to attempt to bridge the gap.

Post-1997

After 1997, the worst fears of the church did not materialize. The mainland Chinese government did not drastically alter the political and social life of Hong Kong. The church suffered no curtailment of freedom, and she continued to evangelize publicly and participate in various social services. But then there were other public issues that threatened to tear the church apart.

We shall start with some non-political factors. Hong Kong was a major industrial base in the 1960s and 1970s. With the economic reforms of Deng Xiaoping and the opening up to foreign investments, China gradually became the factory of the world. Starting in the 1980s, industry in Hong Kong moved northward. As Hong Kong entered the third millennium, it transformed itself into an international financial center and major tourist city. Soon after the handover, the world economy was hit by the burst of the technology stock bubble and financial crisis of the emerging world. This external crisis, coupled with the infelicity in the execution of government policy, led to a sharp contraction of the Hong Kong economy. The grumblings of ordinary citizens gradually fermented into waves of public protest. However, with the strong growth of the economy of China after the takeover, the Hong Kong economy also resumed its growth. The GDP per capita of Hong Kong is currently the third highest in East Asia (behind Macau and Singapore, but ahead of Japan).

But underneath this prosperity is an ever-growing division between the rich and the poor. The Gini co-efficient of household income has increased from 0.43 in 1971 to 0.537 in 2011.[13] As manufacturing industries disappear, tertiary production becomes the engine of the economy. While professionals in the financial sector can earn phenomenal income, the unskilled laborers in service industries (e.g., tourism, restaurants) remain poorly paid. As predicated by economic theory (factor-price equalization), the wages of ordinary laborers in China surge, while the wages in Hong Kong remain stagnant.

Moreover, as the Hong Kong dollar is pegged to the US currency, Hong Kong suffers both significant asset inflation (primarily in the housing market) and price inflation when the Federal Reserve of United States pursues a lose monetary policy after 2008. For the younger generation, buying a home has become almost an impossible dream. All these factors have led to significant grief among the youth and the working class.

Before 1997, Hong Kong was often considered both within and without as an apolitical city. However, after 1997, political grievances have become even more explosive than economic grievances. Before the handover of Hong Kong to China, the colonial government under Chris Patton introduced a series of democratic reforms. Bracketing the question of Patton's true objective, these reforms aroused the political interest of the Hong Kong people. The promise of democratic elections in the Basic Law (a mini-constitution for Hong Kong) also aroused the people's appetite for political engagement.

When Britain negotiated with China in the 1980s, China was still considered a poor (relative to Hong Kong) and autocratic nation. In order to assuage people in Hong Kong and critics in Britain (particularly after the 1989 Tiananmen incident), China promised to give Hong Kong a democratically elected chief executive by 2017. After the handover of Hong Kong to China, the Chinese government set up an electoral committee to select the chief executive of Hong Kong. The composition and formation of the electoral committee have evolved over time. In our last election (2012), the committee had 1,200 members who were elected by members of different sectors of society. Since some sectors are very large (e.g., laborers), while other sectors have few members (e.g., financiers, Chinese medicine workers, fishermen), people in the latter have more political influence. Moreover, due to the small number of people involved and the need of many of them to do business in mainland China, it is widely perceived that Chinese government manipulates 1,200 members into voting for its favorite candidate.

While many protests and marches have occurred since the handover, perhaps the definitive one took place on July 1 march in 2003. During that time, the government established the process of drafting the national security law for Hong Kong (called Article 23). Widely interpreted as a means for the mainland government to interfere in Hong Kong affairs, most people resisted the drafting process for fear of political encroachment from the mainland. On July 1, 2003, 500,000 people (out of roughly 7 million people in Hong Kong) marched on the streets, demanding a halt to the drafting process.

There have been many marches since 2003, and the people's distrust of the Hong Kong government continues to grow. Still no one expected anything too dramatic to happen, certainly not the rise of the Umbrella Movement that began on September 9, 2014.[14] So how did that popular movement come about?[15]

The Standing Committee of the National People's Congress declared on August 31, 2014, that the candidates for the chief executive election in 2017 should be selected by a majority vote of a nominating committee with essentially the same structure as the current electoral committee. This announcement came as a great disappointment to many people. Many moderate leaders had hoped that the mainland government would give more leeway for the Hong Kong government to draw up election laws. But the Standing Committee's decision seems to be an attempt to minimize the role of the Hong Kong government. Aside from the extra step of providing universal suffrage, the mainland government has apparently decided that the selection of candidates should be continuous with the previous electoral process by a selected group of elites.

The people responded to the government's declaration with a mass demonstration on September 28, 2014, and unfortunately the police responded with teargas. All hell then broke loose. Crowds formed spontaneously on the busiest streets of Hong Kong. In three districts (Central or Admiralty, Mongkok, and Causeway Bay), people set up tents on the busy streets and slept there at night, stopping all normal traffic. The movement lasted for seventy-nine days, with the final site cleared by police on December 15. Likely no one in the beginning thought that the occupation would last as long as it did. At first, some university professors and college students played leading roles, but soon the crowd diversified to the extent that there was no longer any central leadership. Though occupation scored no immediate political success, it was an amazing testimony to the self-discipline of Hong Kong citizens that no serious violence or health issues occurred during the occupation. By the end of those seventy-nine days, many people welcomed the end of the occupation from fatigue alone, not political considerations.

Before we proceed to the challenges of the post-occupation era, let us address some theological questions. What has Jerusalem got to do with Rome? Or, does Christian faith have anything to say for the political conundrum of Hong Kong? Many Christians here give a passionate yes to the question, yet their messages contradict one another. We can capture the conflict of opinion in a nutshell: justice versus peace.

Let us begin with justice. There are a number of competing views: many people believe that the Hong Kong government serves the interest of the rich, others think that the government prioritizes the interests of mainlanders over those of the Hong Kong people, still others remain angry at our chief executive, Mr. CY Leung. The most fundamental question right now is probably whether we Hong Kong people—not the Beijing government—have the right to select our own government and determine our own fate? For many, it is a gross act of injustice to deny the right of autonomy.

To be sure, the people of Hong Kong did not have the right of self-determination under British rule. So the question becomes why this right is being demanded now. First, society has changed. The concept of "rights" is tricky, involving a value judgment. Fifty years ago, people in Hong Kong were happy if they did not need to worry about paying their next bill. As the society grew richer, people demanded more "higher order goods," such as freedom, justice, and a democratic government. In fact, these are the very things demanded by the middle class in mainland China, too. Second, the Chinese government had promised democratic elections to the Hong Kong people through the stipulations of the Basic Law of Hong Kong. Though the Bible never says "Your government shall be democratically elected," it does say "Thou shall not lie." How can Christians remain silent when the government breaks the commandments of God? Third, many here regard the Communist government as an oppressive regime. They imprison human-rights activists (such as Liu Xiaobo) and forcibly demolish church crosses. They equate loyalty to the nation with loyalty to the Chinese Communist Party. To some Christians, the CCP even qualifies as a representative of the beasts in the Book of Revelation.[16] If we do not protect our right of self-governance, other rights (including religious freedom and free speech) might be taken away from us, as well.

Let us listen to the other side: the need for peace. Bible passages such as Rom. 13:1–7 and 1 Tim. 2:1–2 tell us to submit to the government and work for peace in society. We may not like our existing government, but civil disobedience is, by definition, an act of disobedience. Two wrongs do not make a right. Second, the Umbrella Movement, as an elusive dream of democracy, seriously disrupts the rhythm of normal life, causing significant economic and other losses to many businesses and individuals. Do the demonstrators have the right to inflict these pains on other citizens? Is that what "loving our neighbors" mean? Third, the movement is creating a potentially dangerous political situation. History tells us that the Beijing government will not back down when its authority is challenged. The movement may thus actually lead to further tightening of freedoms in Hong Kong. It might also split the political scene, forcing legislative members to embrace either a militant left or a militant right. For mercy's sake, one might call for the madness to end before things get out of hand.

Taking the arguments to a higher level of theological sophistication, the justice advocates would say: we do not submit to despair. If we believe in the resurrection of dead, why can't we believe in the power of hope? Even the Chinese Communist Party cannot be more powerful than God! Moreover, should pragmatic concerns overrule our testimony to justice? Has not liberation theology taught us that God prefers the weak and the marginalized? Are you willing to stand with God against the powerful on earth?

To which the peace advocates replies: Where is your theology of humility? Jesus testified to God's justice by suffering injustice with patience and love. Organizing massive confrontations on the street is a political act, not a Christian testimony. Even if Christians feel obliged to engage in the secular political process, they should do this only when explicitly mandated by the Bible. For example, Christians should engage in the political arena for religious freedom so that they can evangelize without hindrance. For many in this peace party, same-sex marriage is another example because they contend that the Bible explicitly teaches that marriage is between one man and one woman. The Bible, on the other hand, never says "thou shall establish a democratic government on earth."

There is a third position that regards reconciliation as the major theological theme for our time. By reconciliation, we assume that the two sides have and will continue to have opposing positions. Reconciliation requires accepting the opposing party as one's brothers and sisters, refusing to vilify them, and protecting their honor. Reconciliation also involves refusing to silence one's opponents, whether by church politics (e.g., "Politics cannot be mentioned in our church") or by invectives in social media. Our political judgments and even our theological judgments are contingent and fallible. Did not Jesus tell us to keep our unity in the Spirit, that the world may know that we are his disciples?

As this brief summary of views makes clear, Christians are as divided on the matter as the society at large. It is debatable that there is a silent majority to be found among Hong Kong Christians.[17] Each party has its own theological rationale. Often, the division is drawn along generational lines. The young and the idealistic clamor for justice, while the experienced and the pragmatic advocate for peace. Most Christians probably know in their heart that justice and peace are interrelated: we cannot have real peace without justice, and justice requires us to respect the desire for peace. So the dialogue between justice and peace must continue—and it will. Returning to the focus of this volume, we now ask anew how a Barthian perspective can help us understand the past and the future of public theology in Hong Kong?

Dialogue between Barth and the Hong Kong Experience

Developing a credible public theology is a long and winding process. It requires the church to study the culture and public issues in detail—something that requires motivation to get embroiled in serious controversies while being attentive to conflicting voices. As a minority religion in Hong Kong, the church has limited resources to study matters beyond the immediate ministerial concerns. If we stretch further afield, Christianity has always been a minority religion in Chinese history. There have been periods when portions of the Chinese church engaged in heated debates in public theology,[18] but one may question the impact those debates have had either on society or on the lives of ordinary Christians. The limited impact of the Chinese church on the Chinese society at large has led to a kind of apathy toward public theology among Chinese Christians. Not surprisingly, the church in Hong Kong has historically had a very thin public theology.

That leads to our second observation: we need to learn from—without copying—Western churches with their long history of engaging in the public sphere. The German-speaking church, for better or for worse, has assumed for centuries that she has both the obligation and the authority to speak to the society and the general culture, for her history and theology deserve to be heard. Barth came from this long tradition of engagement of faith with public issues.

The various chapters in this volume have already discussed Barth's political theology in detail. I chose here to utilize Barth's insight in a more roundabout way. In one of his essays, Barth discusses the promise and ambiguity of cultural transformation.[19] In 1926, when Barth was still concerned with the influence of the liberal theology of his teachers, his lecture during a mission conference dealt with the church's proclamation of her message in the larger society. Barth wanted to differentiate between human culture and the divine Word of God, while acknowledging that we do not have access to the pure Word of God: we always hear the divine Word within our cultural context.

Barth presents his theology in a series of proposition. The first one reads: "The Church is the community instituted by God himself, the community of faith and obedience living from the Word of God, the community of the faith and obedience of sinful men."[20] This thesis emphasizes that the church is not merely a human community; its foundation and goal is the divine Word of God, not the human spirit. However, that does not mean that the church is a perfect image of the divine Word, as it is a community of sinful people. After emphasizing the divine origin of the church, Barth wants to bring in the other side of the dialectic. His fourth thesis reads: "Seen from the point of view of creation, the kingdom of nature (*regnum naturae*), culture is the promise originally given to man of what he is to become."[21] When we translate his theses into the realm of politics, it reads as follows: Seen from the point of view of creation, the kingdom of nature, politics is the promise originally given to man of what he is to become.

For Barth, the kingdom of nature is a realm where people are free to use their talents to build up the world. Human history is not directly a sacrament of God's grace, but that does not make it trivial. Our faith gives us freedom to explore different possibilities, precisely because our actions need not carry any absolute or divinized implications. Politics is about the life of the community—about making decisions for the public good. God intends for human beings to live in community and God has promised to be present in our political and cultural life, even if our political system and culture are secular.[22] Christians have the right and the mandate to engage in the political life of the society as citizens. But they will claim no special authority; they must come as servants to the community.

Similarly, his sixth thesis can be translated as follows: From the point of view of redemption or the kingdom of glory, politics is the limit set for human beings. On the other side of the human story is God who, in fulfillment of the divine promise, makes all things new. This thesis claims that the redemption of God cannot be equated with any political agenda. Indeed we should use all means, including political struggle, to pursue justice and true peace. But all such actions are, by its nature, only political actions. They do not have the same salvific function as our Lord's sacrifice. The Lord in heaven smiles upon all our political engagements, as our foolishness and selfishness in our actions are evident to Him. Yet the Lord also sees our good intentions, and sanctifies our efforts by bringing new possibilities to our political sphere. We act, not because we have all the answers, but because God is gracious in redeeming our failures.

The experience of Hong Kong churches has shown both the possibilities and the pitfalls of Christian engagement in the public sphere. In the early postwar period, the church managed to offer genuine help to the marginalized (i.e., the refugees from mainland) without a lot of strategic planning. It served the community without any theological slogans. In the eighties and nineties, a public theology based on the theme of divine sovereignty (congruent with Barthian perspective) gave the church a visible stand in society, and provided comfort and encouragement for some Christians in the colony. But the discourse in public theology left many concerns of ordinary Christians unaddressed. Nowadays, Christians are looking more than ever for guidance in theological thinking on many issues pertaining to justice and peace. But theologians on these matters are as divided as is the church![23]

A Barthian perspective teaches us to be both proactive and humble. The church should always be eager to help the needy in the society, but she should be aware of her self-righteousness. The church should also be ready to offer hope in difficult situations, without proclaiming an irrelevant (or false) variety. We theologians should have a double share of humility, as the church can often do much good without us. Our proclamation is based on our trust in God, and we have to be patient when ignored (or vilified) by others. In summary, as a minority group in Hong Kong, we are grateful for how the Lord has raised up many Christians to serve the common good. We give praise and thanks to God, but also pray: "Lord Jesus Christ, have mercy on us sinners."[24]

NOTES

1. Cf. Markus Höfner, "Neither Self-Evident Frame nor Self-Enclosed Sect: The Christian Church in Barth's Political Ecclesiology," in this volume.

2. Cf. Paul Dafydd Jones, "Karl Barth's *The Christian Life* and the Task of Political Theology," in this volume.

3. It would need another paper to compare the culture wars in Hong Kong and in the United States. In brief, some scholars and church leaders on the so-called progressive side has introduced in the last ten years the term *religious right* into the public discourse in Hong Kong, mainly to describe church leaders who fight against the LGBT or gay right movement in Hong Kong. Sometimes the same scholars will also (unfairly, in my opinion) associate the religious right in Hong Kong with a pro-Beijing political stand. The progressive party will tend to portray themselves as carrying the banner of democracy. Other issues in the culture war in the United States (e.g., abortion, gun control, nomination of court justices, the resurrection of a once (so-called) Christian nation) are not relevant for the Hong Kong setting. For more details, see Kai-man Kwan, Chi-sum Choi, *Christianity & the Debates in Contemporary Society: Morality, Politics, & the Religious Right*《基督教與現代社會的爭論：道德、政治與「宗教右派」》(Hong Kong: Tien Dao, 2012).

4. My narrative is limited to events in Hong Kong. Of course, the story in Hong Kong is very much part of the story of China. For example, many church leaders fled from mainland China to Hong Kong during the persecution of the Chinese churches in the 1950s. The rapid development of the Chinese churches in Hong Kong during the 1960s would not be possible without these leaders. For the complementary story of Christianity in China during the same period, see Kim-kwong Chan, "The Ecclesiological Implications of the Political Attitude of the Chinese Authority towards Christianity," in this volume.

5. Some historical population figures can be found in the "Report on the Task Force on Population Policy" published by the Hong Kong government, available at http://www.info.gov.hk/info/population/eng/index.htm.

6. For the history of the fundamentalist wing of the Chinese churches before World War II, see Kevin Yao, *Contending for the Truth: Fundamentalist Movement of Protestant Missionaries in China (1920–1937)*《為真爭辯－在華基督新教傳教士基要主義運動(1920–1937)》(Hong Kong: China Alliance Press, 2008).

7. For the internal debate among Baptist churches in this period on the education issue, see Vincent Lau, "Controversy over Public Funding to the Baptist Institutions in Colonial Hong Kong and the United States from the 1950s to 1970s," *Baptist History and Heritage*, Spring 2007, 85–104, available at http://www.academia.edu /7884608/Controversy_over_Public_Funding_to_the_Baptist_Institutions_in_Colon ial_Hong_Kong_and_the_United_States_from_the_1950s_to_the_1970s.

8. For further discussion on the 1970s and the yearnings of the younger generation, see Wai-luen Kwok, "The Social Participation of the Hong Kong Young Evangelicals in the Seventies,"〈七十年代香港福音派青年基督徒之社會參與〉 *CGST Journal* 32 (January 2002): 145–190. For further discussion of the social actions by the churches in Hong Kong, see Lung-Kwong Lo, *Theory and Practice of Church Community Work*《愛你的鄰舍－教會社區工作理論與實踐》(Taiwan: Campus Evangelical Fellowship, 2003).

9. Daniel Lee gives further discussions on the anxieties of Hong Kong people as they faced 1997. These issues range from the question of ethnic identity (How Chinese are Hong Kong people, really?) to economic matters (Will the Chinese government ruin the supposedly free and wonderful economy of Hong Kong?). Cf. Daniel Lee, "On Becoming Citizen: Reading Barth in the Midst of Political Change," in this volume.

10. The full name of the statement is *The Confession Statement of some Hong Kong Christians in the context of Current Social and Political Changes*, 〈香港基督徒在現今社會及政治變遷中所持的信念〉. The Chinese text is available at https://hkchurch.wordpress.com/2013/04/16/%E3%80%88%E9%A6%99%E6%B8%AF%E5%9F%BA%E7%9D%A3%E5%BE%92%E5%9C%A8%E7%8F%BE%E4%BB%8A%E7%A4%BE%E6%9C%83%E5%8F%8A%E6%94%BF%E6%B2%BB%E8%AE%8A%E9%81%B7%E4%B8%AD%E6%89%80%E6%8C%81%E7%9A%84%E4%BF%A1%E5%BF%B5/.

11. The second clause says: "Under any social or political situation, we should recognize the Bible as our ultimate stand in faith, living and ministry."

12. For an analysis of the background and the content of "Confessional Statement," see Kwok Wai-luen, "Social Participation of the Early Eighties: An Analysis of Her *Conviction*," 〈八十年代前期香港教會社會參與—《信念書》的分析〉 *CGST Journal* 30 (January 2001). For the broader context of the challenges faced by the church regarding the returning of Hong Kong to China, see Leung Ka-lun, *Minority and Minoritarianism: Discussions of Hong Kong and Chinese Churches (2)* 《少數派與少數主義: 中港教會評論集 二》 (Hong Kong: Alliance Bible Seminary, 2002).

13. *Half-yearly Economic Report 2012*, Box 5.2, http://www.hkeconomy.gov.hk/en/pdf/box-12q2-5-2.pdf.

14. It began as the Occupy Central Movement (Central is the name of Hong Kong's central business district), but soon the name "Umbrella Movement" caught on to reflect the wider concerns of the crowd. While some preferred the term "Umbrella Revolution" instead, the milder faction insisted that they were part of a people's movement, not revolution.

15. Lai Pan-chiu provides important theological reflections on the Occupy Central Movement in his chapter in this volume entitled "Religious Diversity, Democracy, and Public Theology: Conversing with Barth in a Hong Kong Context." The movement started as the Occupy Central Movement, with the goal of forcing the Hong Kong government to implement true democratic elections in 2017. Once the occupation began, the movement was renamed the "Umbrella Movement." The new nomenclature connotes a wider resistance against the perceived authoritarianism of the government. While Lai's essay describes the views of some prominent theologians and leaders, I concentrate on polarizing views among ordinary Christians.

16. Revelation 13.

17. Politicians sometimes claim that they are speaking for the silent majority. It implies that though their opponents have some very vociferous supporters, in reality their opponents represent only a small minority of citizens. Sometimes church leaders of mainline churches would adopt similar vocabulary to dismiss the radical wing in the churches.

18. See the definitive work of Wing-hung Lam, *A Half Century of Chinese Theology 1900–49* 《中華神學五十年1900–1949》 (Hong Kong: China Graduate School of Theology, 1998).

19. Karl Barth, "Church and Culture," in *Theology and Church: Shorter Writings 1920–1928*, trans. L. P. Smith (London: SCMP, 1962), 334–354. The essay comes from a lecture that Barth delivered at the Congress of the Continental Association for Home Missions at Amsterdam in June 1926.

20. Ibid., 334.

21. Ibid., 341.

22. In what sense is God present in our political life? More concretely, how can the gospel help us to reflect critically on our political agenda? Presumably our political endeavors should mirror in some ways the action of God. Alexander Massman, for example, tries to associate divine distributive righteousness of God with the human search for fairness and justice (Cf. his "Karl Barth on the Righteousness of God. The Attributes of God in Political Context," in this volume). However, as Devin Singh's paper on divine sovereignty points out, the discourse on mirroring the divine can become a form of dangerous self-justification (Cf. his "A Tale of Two Sovereignties: Karl Barth and Carl Schmitt in Dialogue," in this volume). Therefore, we have only the promise, but not the guarantee, of God's presence in our political action. See also Chloe Starr's paper on how some prominent Chinese church leaders have addressed the question of the presence (or absence) of God in the political life of China in the twentieth century.

23. As indicated in footnote 13, Lai Pun Chiu's paper gives the views of some of these theologians. One may crudely call it a debate between Anabaptist social detachment and liberation engagement. As Lai's and Daniel Lee's papers in this volume both indicate, Barth's theology may not offer a clear-cut answer for the appropriate political actions for Hong Kong Christians. But it can offer conceptual tools for analyzing the strength and pitfalls in these polarizing views.

24. Readers may know that Hong Kong went through a more violent Anti-extradition Movement in 2019, which led Beijing to push through a draconian National Security Law to silence political opposition in Hong Kong. For a discussion of Christian engagement in the Anti-extradition Movement and the theological controversies surrounding it, see Kin Yip Louie, "Theological Controversies in the Anti-Extradition Movement in Hong Kong," Unio cum Christo, vol. 6, no. 2, Oct. 2020.

Chapter 22

On Becoming a Citizen

Reading Barth in the Midst of Political Change

Daniel Lee

INTRODUCTION

Starting with a small outlying fishery village on the south coast of China, Hong Kong was "elected" to witness the rise and fall of Western colonialism. With its peculiar historical trajectory, it was deeply affected by the political ups and downs of the mainland, and yet was kept at arm's length. For both the Communist East and the capitalist West, Hong Kong was deliberately built as an outpost extending to the other. This history set the stage for all the subtleties of its politics, which are quite rare in the world and thus often obscure to foreigners. For example, its process of democratization is intriguingly long and tortuous. We have already set a record of spending more than fifteen years to democratize just half of the legislature, and its future is still quite unclear.

Hong Kong is going through an unprecedented experiment of decolonization without independence. Macroscopically speaking, it is a story of striving for a political system that can be flexible enough to fill and preserve the vulnerable buffering gap between East and West. Microscopically speaking, it is a story of transforming a subject under colonial domination into a citizen who is incited to participate in the civil community and share political responsibilities. This twofold story brings about a drastic change of political landscape, confronting the Christian Churches in Hong Kong with new cultural and political problematics. Compared with their former generation, the younger generation is much more concerned about the political system and more prepared to become directly involved in political action. So it is not unwise for Christian Churches in Hong Kong to lend a heeding ear to Oliver

O'Donovan's warning in this respect: "Rule out the political questions, you cut short the proclamation of God's saving power; you leave people enslaved where they ought to be set free from sin—their own sin and others'."[1] The question before us is no longer whether we have to deal with theo-politics or not, but how to deal with it constructively and responsibly, without compromising the church's own mission.

The difficulty of this task can hardly be overestimated. Anyone who has been caught in controversial political matters would probably agree with Karl Barth's comments:

> For, besides being Christians, we are all rather a lot of other things as well—for instance, representatives of this or that economic interest, readers of this or that newspaper, perhaps members of this or that Party.[2]

It is self-evident that the collapsing Christendom[3] within which Barth found himself is very different from our late-modern society in the Asian context. Nevertheless, his critical reflection in the midst of imminent political change still resonates in our own context. Enduring questions include: How can the Christian Church prevent itself from indulging with its own cultural and social interests, and remain free to serve God and one's neighbor? What kind of political responsibility does the Christian community share with society at large? In what manner and for what end does the Church carry out its task? Who is our political neighbor? Barth's wrestling with these questions, I believe, remains relevant to our late-modern society, and his own struggle is able to enrich our vision of political engagement. In this chapter, I first give a brief sketch of the political scenario of Hong Kong as well as its challenges to the Christian Churches in the territory. With this background in mind, I then proceed to explicate some tenets of Barth's political thought, which include (1) the very ground of freedom and hope in the midst of political turmoil, (2) the paradoxical nature of the church's political responsibility, (3) primacy of humanity in political undertaking, and (4) the dynamic notion of near and distant neighbors in political community. These aspects are particularly valuable to the Christian Church in engaging with the current situation.

POLITICAL SCENARIO OF HONG KONG AND
ITS CHALLENGES TO CHRISTIAN CHURCHES

Two "Death" Alerts

For the last few decades, Hong Kong has undergone a long period of political change. The subtlety of this change can be glimpsed by juxtaposing two "death" alerts. In 1995, two years before Britain's handover of Hong Kong to China, *Fortune Magazine* published an article with the agitating title "The Death of Hong Kong."[4] Its author prophesized with a lamenting tone that the world's most aggressively pro-business economy would soon come to an end: China's central government would high-handedly control every branch of Hong Kong government; troops of the People's Liberation Army would stroll the streets; capital controls would be imposed, coupled with the replacement of Hong Kong's independent currency with Chinese renminbi; a new court of final appeal would be established, and so on. The article asserted that communist China could not really understand and thus wholeheartedly retain the essence of Hong Kong's capitalist success and global appeal.

History proves that most of the oracles did not come true, but the cloud of "death" is still lingering in the minds of Hong Kong's inhabitants. Indeed, the theme of death has undergone a subtle twist that no one could have foreseen eighteen years ago. "This city is dying, you know?" alerted Dr. Dylan, a character in a local soap opera series in 2012. Consider the statement's wider context:

> Take a look at our world, look at the state of our city. Apart from the word "money," we can no longer tell white from black. We have all been shaped by the environment. It was as if we were all products of the same mould: to like the same food, to like the same TV program, to support the same political viewpoint, to subscribe to the same life path from birth to death. This city is dying, you know?

The words immediately became very popular in Hong Kong, arousing much public debate. Some claim that the phrase manages to touch on the deep dissatisfaction felt by many Hong Kong people, who have become skeptical of the monolithic "mammonism" of the city. If the first death alert, by and large, represents the worry of the older generation about retaining social stability and economic success, the second reveals the anxious desire of the younger generation to transcend the confines of mere economic success. The tension between these two social aspirations has been mounting beneath the ongoing political changes of the city.

A City without Politics

The root of Hong Kong's peculiar political scenario can be traced back to the colonial period. In the year of handover, Milton Friedman, the high priest of neoliberalism, strongly suggested in his article "The Real Lesson of Hong Kong" that the colonial government's earnest adherence to the laissez-faire economy amounted to the miracle of Hong Kong.[5] However, the neoliberalism in Hong Kong was actually a reduced version, in which the high degree of freedom granted to the realm of economics was not allowed to spill over into the realm of politics. It was indeed governed by "quasi-bureaucratic-authoritarian" political institutions.[6] In other words, colonial Hong Kong was carefully engineered to be a pure economic city.[7] Not until the last decade of British governance was there any politics in the modern sense of the word; and even in this case it was only administration. This political vacuum bequeathed several distinctive features to local political life: (1) with the administrative absorption of politics, there emerged a tradition of elite consensual government, which consisted of high officials, big business-people, and corporate professionals; (2) this ruling elite enjoyed substantial political advantage and had a strong belief in the superiority of an "executive-led" system; (3) the results included the passive and monolithic character of political life among the grass-roots population.[8] This was the political price we paid for economic glamour, which the *Fortune* article cherished, and which Dr. Dylan satirized.

One Country, Two Systems: An Unprecedented Experiment?

With hindsight, we could say that the author of *Fortune* article was blinded by his ignorance about the communist leaders. The latter did fully understand and really want to keep the essence of Hong Kong's capitalist success. Since the 1950s, the communist leadership had already laid down its basic policy of "long-term planning and full utilization" toward Hong Kong.[9] Early in 1972, the Chinese government managed to lift the colonial status of Hong Kong in the UN, but deliberately delayed the takeover of its governance. As a capitalist-free entrepôt, Hong Kong could function as China's window to the world. The reduced version of neoliberalism perfectly matched this orientation. The idea of "One Country, Two Systems" was basically an expansion of "long-term planning and full utilization," as well as an effort to continue the colonial legacy.

Ngok Ma, a political scientist in Hong Kong, trenchantly points out that the idea of "One Country, Two Systems" builds a firewall between the socialist system on the mainland and the capitalist system in Hong Kong, so that the operating logic of the former will not unduly interfere with the latter. Furthermore, all the elements of the political arrangement can be regarded as constituent parts of the machinery that sustains the smooth operation of Hong Kong–styled capitalism. The main objective of the idea sides with the old worry of retaining economic success. What is actually unprecedented in the arrangement is the gradual implementation of electing the chief executive and the legislature through universal suffrage. But the introduction of this institutional change lacked the resolute political ethos found in other

democratization movements in the present and the past. Instead, it was originally a political accessory subservient to the main objective. It is a political
gesture to honor the promises of "Hong Kong people running Hong Kong"
with a "High Degree of Autonomy," which were, in turn, meant to strengthen
Hong Kong citizens' confidence in continuing stability and prosperity.
Beyond its original intention, these promises, together with the process
of democratization initiated during the last decade of British governance,
unleashed a new desire to transcend the confines of mere economic success.

Struggles for Citizenship

Why do a substantial proportion of Hong Kong inhabitants want to leave the
comfort zone of reduced neoliberalism? This is another complicated story
that we cannot give a full account of here.[10] In short, neoliberalism has come
to a crisis, both locally and globally. The economic downturn, together with
a series of administrative mistakes and political misjudgment by the new government, has boosted up the popular call for policy accountability. With the
widening wealth gap, Hong Kong saw its Gini coefficient[11] reach the record
high of 0.537 in 2011, the highest in all developed regions. The grievance
toward hegemony of the financial and the real-estate development sectors has
been aggravated. With its traditional tie to big business, the fairness of the
government in policy making cannot but be called into question. The politics
of redistribution is merging with the urge for an increase in democratic participation. To counter economic difficulties, the government has accelerated
economic integration with the mainland. This unfortunately stirs up a new
and vexing problem of identity crisis. The most radical wing even advocates
fostering a distinctive identity of Hong Kong people, which is totally shielded
off from the mainland. We are now facing a whole range of conflicting
interpretations regarding the meaning of "Hong Kong people running Hong
Kong" with a "High Degree of Autonomy." Behind each interpretation stand
crucial questions: What is it meant by being a Hong Kong citizen? What
liberties and civic responsibilities exist in relation to both our fellow citizens
and the greater community on the mainland? What core values should this
citizenship spare no pains to establish, preserve, and enforce?

Church at the Crossroad

With respect to their relation to the political sphere, Christian Churches in Hong
Kong have never been so burdened by the fatal inheritance of Christendom.
Protestant community in Hong Kong is a minority in a pluralistic civil society.
According to the Government Yearbook 2011, Protestant churches have a cur-
rent registered membership of about 480,000, which is around 6.7 percent of

the whole population. With the inactive members taken out, the figure would probably decrease to less than 5 percent. However, this minority does occupy quite a considerable social space. It runs more than 639 schools and 127 nurseries, 7 hospitals and 17 clinics, more than 109 community service centers, 11 children's homes, 169 elderly services and nursing homes, 59 rehabilitation centers for mentally handicapped, disabled, and drug addicts. In addition, more than 725 para-church agencies and different Christian action groups attend to the needs of the Protestant community, as well as respond to issues that affect Hong Kong society. They support emergency relief and development projects on the mainland and in developing countries.[12] Given its humble size, the extent of the church's social participation is significant.

F. T. Ying, a church historian in Hong Kong, has studied the emergence of this impressive social involvement.[13] He points out that the postwar period was the high point during which the Protestant Church earned its social reputation. From the end of World War II to the 1960s, Hong Kong suffered from a huge influx of refugees from the mainland. The welfare and relief needs were extremely pressing, but the colonial government had no intention to launch any social-welfare planning, which had long been a perpetual concern in its home country. The challenges were finally taken up by NGOs, including various Christian organizations. They not only provided relief services such as medical care, hygiene, education and vocational training, but also transformed the concept of social welfare in Hong Kong. Because of their strenuous efforts, the colonial government in the 1970s adjusted its attitude toward social services, acknowledging the "partnership" of NGOs and becoming willing to subsidize a substantial share of welfare expenditures.

As the desire for a more robust citizenship is increasing in the civil community, the Christian Church is at a crossroads today. "Dr. Dylan" can easily be found both outside and inside the Christian community. The old pattern of social participation cannot satisfy the younger generation any longer. When it is measured against the divine requirement found in Mic. 6:8, the traditional involvement in social services seems to be one-sided, being able to reach only the demand "to love mercy" at best, but shying away from the call "to act justly." In the eyes of the younger generation, many instances of social injustice are ultimately derived from the deep-rooted structural defects of the political system. Therefore, "to act justly" in this context should necessarily include the civic responsibility to fight for a fairer system.[14] The traditional partnership with the government is sometimes being questioned as a "fatal inheritance" that desensitizes the prophetic awareness of the church. Just as the society at large is torn between conflicting interpretations of citizenship, the Christian Church is also caught in divisive debates about what political attitudes, decisions, or actions should be reckoned as the authentic Christian testimony in the midst of political change.[15]

RELEVANCE OF BARTH'S POLITICAL THOUGHT

Freedom to Serve in the midst of Political Change

"The walls of old Europe were still standing; its light, though already some-what clouded over, was still shining."[16] Here Karl Barth recalled the bygone world of his youth. In his lifetime, Barth witnessed a series of shattering changes in world politics: the breakout and end of the two World Wars, the crumbling of four imperial regimes, the emergence of the Cold War, and so on. He knew very well how ambivalent politics could be, but still considered that political involvement was integral to the life of a theologian. One of the overarching themes in his political thought is the liberating power of the gospel. If the church can approach the political problem by listening to the gospel anew, it sets itself aright with the source of genuine freedom, with which to serve God and neighbor freely without being imprisoned by its own cultural and social inheritance. In articulating this solid ground of freedom, Barth reformulated the relation of the church to the political and enlarged our imagination in engaging with it.

It is well known that Barth was dissatisfied with the Lutheran doctrine of Two Kingdoms, criticizing its making the political realm too independent of the Gospel of Jesus Christ. His Christocentric amendment was clearly seen in the second thesis of the Barmen Declaration:

> As Jesus Christ is God's assurance of the forgiveness of all our sins, so in the same way and with the same seriousness he is also God's mighty claim upon our whole life. Through him befalls us a joyful deliverance from the godless fetters of this world for a free, grateful service to his creature.[17]

Here the whole of life, including the political, is put under the reign of Jesus Christ. In his *The Christian Community in the Midst of Political Change* (1948), Barth transposes the same idea into the temporal dimension, firmly embedding any political change within the greatest change in world history:

> We may call this great change quite simply Jesus Christ in the twofold aspect of His death on the Cross and His second coming in glory. . . . Political changes, along with all other changes, take part within this intermediary time.[18]

In light of this "great change," all other changes are relativized. It does not mean that they are unimportant, but that they are not of ultimate importance. The currency of "death" language so often found in the description of politi-cal change is converted into "hope" language due to the grand narrative of God's gracious salvation. To the Christian Church, the tempting promise of political endeavor such as "no change for fifty years"[19] should not induce extreme joy with its fulfillment, nor extreme horror with its demise. In either direction, the church is distracted from the true source of its freedom. As someone who witnessed so many radical changes in world politics, Barth displayed noteworthy calm in his comments on political changes:

> Political systems change. How could it be otherwise? . . . Unfortunately, the only constant factor appears to be the element of force. In every other respect the search for new political forms and patterns seems to be never-ending.[20]

The calm does not serve as a pretext of indifference, but as a prelude to serious engagement:

> A "small" change like this cannot in any sense compete with the great change from which the Christian takes his bearings. If that is agreed, then it must be added that the "small" changes, precisely because they occur in the era and under the Lordship of Jesus Christ, are entitled to our serious interest and attention.[21]

In the midst of political change, it is quite common for the Christian Church to waver between certain old worry and certain new desire. Barth reminds the church not to fall into this twofold temptation. On the one hand, the church may indulge in the opportunity that the old political pattern has afforded it. It may mistakenly make the cause of conservative force the church's cause and God's cause. On the other hand, it may also be too hasty to jump on the bandwagon lest it miss the opportunity offered by a new pattern. It may then make the cause of revolutionary force its cause and God's cause. In both cases, Barth thinks the church would surrender its freedom on the path and become captive under ideological domination. For Barth, the only ground and safeguard of the church's freedom comes from its being put exclusively under the yoke of God's Word.[22] Only with this captivity and its corresponding freedom from ideological bondage can the church demonstrate to the civil community that citizens are also not doomed to ideological bondage, both old and new. This freedom is the very ground of all civil liberties.

The Paradoxical Nature of the Church's Political Responsibility

The immediate consequence of Barth's locating the political sphere within the orbit of God's grace in Jesus Christ is to affirm that the political sphere is neither essentially evil nor beyond the need for redemption.[23] In answering the relationship between Rom. 13 and Rev. 13, Barth emphasized,

One and the same State, Nero's Roman State, is described in the New Testament as a divine institution and as a beast from the abyss. . . . The fact that these two aspects exist: the good *ordinatio Dei* on the one hand and the *corruptio hominum* on the other, . . . certainly is a very serious problem. What we call political responsibility has to find expression between these two poles.[24]

The Christian Church has to pay attention first to the positive divine commission of the political sphere. The meaning and purpose of the political sphere is "the safeguarding of both the external, relative and provisional freedom of the individuals and the external and relative peace of their community and to that extent the safeguarding of the external, relative and provisional humanity of their life both as individuals and as a community."[25] Carrying out this commission, the political system preserves the common life from chaos, creating and preserving "a space for the fulfillment of the purpose of world history, a space for faith, repentance and knowledge."[26]

As the church acknowledges the political sphere as the gift of God, its basic attitude toward the sphere can never be indifference but gratitude. This gratitude is not expressed in the unconditional endorsement of the political system, but in making itself jointly responsible for the political sphere:

Accordingly, the various political forms and systems are human inventions which as such do not bear the distinctive mark of revelation and are not witnessed to as such—and can therefore not lay any claim to belief. By making itself jointly responsible for the civil community, the Christian community participates—on the basis of and by belief in the divine revelation—in the human search for the best form, for the most fitting system of political organization; but it is also aware of the limits of all the political forms and systems which man can discover (even with the co-operation of the Church).[27]

There is an indissoluble paradox within the church's shared responsibility for the political sphere. On the one hand, the church should know that the experiment in forging a proper political form or system can only be carried out "so far as human discernment and human ability make this possible."[28] Political systems as human inventions can never appeal to or pretend to be the distinctive mark of divine revelation. Thus, Barth insists that the church "has no exclusive theory of its own to advocate in the face of the various forms and realities of political life."[29] There is no such a thing called "*the* Christian doctrine of the just State." On the other hand, the church should not allow any secular theory to determine its participation in the human search for the proper form.[30] It can render its service to the civil community only on the basis of and by belief in divine revelation. Barth identified the command of subordinating to the civil community and its officials in Rom. 13 with this service:

> The Christian community "subordinates" itself to the civil community by mak-ing its knowledge of the Lord who is Lord of all its criterion, and distinguishing between the just and the unjust State, that is, between the better and the worse political form and reality; . . . between the State as described in Romans 13 and the State as described in Revelation 13. And it will judge all matters concerned with the establishment, preservation, and enforcement of political order in accordance with these necessary distinctions and according to the merits of the particular case and situation to which they refer. . . . It is in the making of such distinctions, judgments and choices from its own centre, and in the practical decisions which necessarily flow from that centre, that the Christian community expresses its "subordination" to the civil community and fulfils its share of political responsibility.[31]

Therefore, safeguards have been put both on the right and the left. Against the right, the Christian Church cannot indulge itself in the delusion of a new Christendom. Any form of civil religion is never an option. In political mat-ters, the church has to learn from and with others with a discerning heart, to cooperate with others in establishing, preserving, and enforcing the desired political order.[32] Yet, against the left, in its "subordinating" to the political sphere, the Christian Church cannot commit itself to such an exclusively secularized public reason as advocated by political thinkers like John Rawls. If it does so, it is not rendering a service to it, but a disservice. It does not have a political program of its own, nor can it be totally absorbed into those of oth-ers. It is always to be an uneasy companion in the political sphere, serving the latter with its disturbing presence.[33] So church politics is always dialectical. Its reflection cannot be foreclosed by certain political doctrine, being always open to new happenings and circumstance. Nevertheless, far from being arbi-trary and thus at the mercy of the dominating ideology of the time, "it will have a fixed point from which it can see and understand the events of the days and the years calmly, penetratingly and impartially."[34] From this fixed center, it will have "a constant direction, a continuous line of discoveries on both sides of the boundary which separates the political from the spiritual spheres, a correlation between explication and application."[35]

Primacy of Humanity

The inevitable consequence of the church's adherence to its constant direc-tion and continuous line is the primacy of humanity in its political concern. Barth even takes it as the criterion of the proper service which the Christian community can render in the midst of political change:

> Its first and final concern is with God and man. It is concerned with political
> systems, and their changes, . . . only inasmuch as all these things belong to man.
> The question the Church asks is what difference will these things make to the
> men on whom God has bestowed His grace in Jesus Christ?[36]

In the midst of political change, the contest between the old and the new
orders can be very severe and the cost of defeat can be very high. It is not
unusual for the involved parties to dehumanize their rivals. Unfortunately,
even theologians are often tempted to join the battle cry with the aid of theological terms or biblical statements.[37] For Barth, although the church is very
much involved in the conflicts and arguments, it is set free by God's Word
not to hate with others but to love with them. The church's real service to the
political sphere should be tested by the question of "whether it is in a position
to summon all involved in political changes to humility and modesty one with
another" and "to call them to humanity, that is to a situation in which they not
only dispute but are tolerant one with another."[38]

In his treatment of theological anthropology, Barth more fully expounds
what authentic humanity involves. In the light of Christ's becoming true man
in our midst, the basic form of true humanity is always being in encounter
with other fellow human beings. The being-in-encounter consists in (1)
mutual openness: seeing others' needs, desires and hopes; (2) mutual speech
and hearing: speaking not for one's own sake but for that of the needy other,
as well as hearing the other with all seriousness for one's own sake; (3)
mutual assistance in action.[39] With its insistence on the primacy of humanity, the church may demonstrate to the civil community its freedom from all
political propaganda, as well as what politics is actually for.

The Dynamic Notion of Near and Distant Neighbors

Almost all nation-states today have to endure the tension or even overcome
the antithesis between defending their own local interests and fulfilling their
responsibilities in the global community. For an international city like Hong
Kong, this is not something happening in the remotest end of the world, but
our daily experience. To which community should a Hong Kong citizen
attach his or her sense of belonging? Which history should be regarded as
our history? What is the right relation among the values and the corresponding responsibilities derived from our local, national and global identities?[40]
Almost all the most burning political controversies after the handover touch
on these thorny questions.

This kind of political turmoil is not unfamiliar to Barth and his reflection in
this respect is still worthy of our due attention. In the section discussing human
freedom in fellowship, Barth addresses the question of whether we should
take our relationship with our native community as in contradistinction to

other foreign communities. Is this a permanent created order and distinction? Barth fully acknowledges the fact that, as concrete human beings, we cannot but start with a life situation of certain linguistic, territorial, and historical particularity. If we are able to practice mutual openness, to engage in mutual speech and listening, and to offer mutual assistance—in short, to treat our neighbor as a true human being—it is because we have been so nurtured in our native community. Even after the bitter cup of extreme nationalism, Barth still refuses to view one's historical connection as something unredeemable:

> If he is serious in subjecting himself to the sanctification of his historical exis-
> tence, he cannot turn aside from the way of his people. He cannot leave the
> ship, even if it is in sorry straits or sinking. He cannot try to live an aesthetic or
> Christian life which is private and neutral in face of its past and present. He must
> affirm the presuppositions of its past and at his own place and time take up and
> genuinely share the problems of its future.[41]

Important as they are, our linguistic, territorial, and historical homes cannot turn out to be our prison. Barth insists that they must not be a wall but a door to our distant neighbors, because they are in connection to the history of God's saving grace in Jesus Christ:

> The history of His covenant with man, fulfilled and completed in the one Jesus
> Christ, is the centre of all history and the meaning and goal of all national his-
> tory. If His Word and command are heard and accepted by a man, this man can-
> not be concerned only with his own people. Beyond this he must be concerned
> with this greater people. He is again led out of the narrower into the wider
> sphere. Called to obedience among near neighbours, in the same obedience he
> is turned to those who are distant.[42]

For Barth, the linguistic, territorial, and historical particularities are not per-manent orders of creation. They are simply provisional and temporal disposi-tions ordained by God, and must not be artificially hypostatized. Under this arrangement, local, national, and global identities are not statically separated from one another, but dynamically on the way from one to the other. In this respect, the Christian Church reminds the political sphere of the catholicity of its vision:

> Since the Church is ecumenical (catholic) by virtue of its very origin, it resists
> all abstract local, regional, and national interests in the political sphere. It will
> always seek to serve the best interests of the particular city or place where it is
> stationed. But it will never do this without at the same time looking out beyond
> the city walls. It will be conscious of the superficiality, relativity, and temporari-
> ness of the immediate city boundaries, and on principle it will always stand for

understanding and cooperation within the wider circle. The Church will be the last to lend its support to mere parochial politics.[43]

IN PLACE OF A CONCLUSION

In recent months, a new page of paramount significance was added to the history of democratic striving in Hong Kong. The frustrated social aspirations of the younger generation burst onto the scene in the Umbrella Movement beginning on September 28, 2014. On June 18, 2015, the staunch insistence on real universal suffrage was paradoxically and tragically upheld by vetoing the political reform bill that was denounced as an offer of "fake" universal suffrage. Nothing about the process of democratization in Hong Kong can be certain, except that Hong Kong will not see its chief executive universal suffrage before 2022 and that of the legislature before 2024, if the current political procedure is to be followed. Would the old machinery live on as if it had never seen the sea of umbrellas? What long-term impact will the movement leave on the lives of our youth? How can we hope against all odds? With all the unknowns ahead of us, the Christian Church in Hong Kong may find some comfort from Barth's characteristically calm advice:

> The most important thing to be said . . . is that the Christian Church will see in such changes above all an opportunity to do penance itself. For the Christian Church a new political system necessarily means an occasion to revise the foundations of its own activities, a challenge to renewed concentration, a summons to fresh witness, all of which is appropriate since a time of political upheaval provides the incentive to seek a better knowledge of the Word of God.[44]

NOTES

1. O. O'Donovan, *The Desire of the Nations* (Cambridge: Cambridge University Press, 1996), 3.
2. *Against the Stream* (London: SCM, 1954), 127–128.
3. H. Willmer, "Karl Barth," in *The Blackwell Companion to Political Theology*, ed. P. Scott and W. T. Cavanaugh (Oxford: Blackwell, 2004), 125.
4. *Fortune Magazine*, June 26, 1995.
5. M. Friedman, "The Real Lesson of Hong Kong," *National Review*, December 31, 1997.
6. M. Sing, "Economic Development, Public Support, and the Endurance of Hong Kong's Political Institutions (1970s–1980s)," in *Hong Kong Government and Politics*, ed. M. Sing (Hong Kong: Oxford University Press, 2003), 436–465.
7. For the immigrants who had suffered from the political chaos in the mainland during the postwar period, this "apolitical" environment provided them with

the opportunity to work and live peacefully. See K. Louie, "Public Theology and Christian Social Action in Hong Kong: From the Past to the Present," in this volume; in particular, the section about the historical development.

8. N. Ma, *Hong Kong Politics: Development Process and Key Issues* (Hong Kong: Hong Kong Institute of Asia-Pacific Studies, 2010); Ambrose Y. C. King, "Administrative Absorption of Politics in Hong Kong: Emphasis on the Grass-Roots Level," in *Hong Kong Government and Politics*, ed. M. Sing (Hong Kong: Oxford University Press, 2003), 69–92; Alvin Y. So, "Hong Kong's Problematic Democratic Transition: Power Dependency or Business Hegemony?" Ibid., 466–499; Hsin-chi Kuan, "Power Dependence and Democratic Transition: the Case of Hong Kong" Ibid., 411–435.

9. Siu-kai Lau, *Hong Kong Politics after the Handover* (Hong Kong: Commercial Press, 2013), 77–109; N. Ma, *Hong Kong Politics: Development Process and Key Issues* (Hong Kong: Hong Kong Institute of Asia-Pacific Studies, 2010), 71–72.

10. For a more detailed account of the post-handover period, please refer to K. Louie, "Public Theology and Christian Social Actions in Hong Kong: From the Past to the Present," in this volume; in particular, the section about development after 1997.

11. Gini coefficient is a measure used to analyze wealth distribution in a particular country or area. The coefficient varies from 0, which indicates complete equality, with everyone having the same amount of wealth, and 1, which indicates complete inequality, with one person owning all of an area's wealth. A Gini coefficient above 0.4 is considered a precursor to social unrest.

12. *Government Yearbook 2011*, 385–386.

13. F. T. Ying, "The Political and Social Roles of Christian Churches in Hong Kong: A Retrospect," in *When Church Meets Politics: Theological Reflection on Political Praxis*, ed. S. M. Chiu (Hong Kong: Logos, 2005), 33–67.

14. Before his initiation of the Occupy Central Movement, Benny Y. T. Tai, a Christian law professor, discussed in a theological article the paramount importance of a fair system in fulfilling the demand "to act justly." When social injustices are of some systemic origin, Tai believed that "to act justly" might imply reforming of the political system. B. Tai, "Public Theology, Justice and Law: A Preliminary Look" *CGST Journal* 54 (2013): 73–94; especially, 84–88.

15. Among the major religions in Hong Kong, Christianity proves to be the most responsive on public issues. For heated debates about political issues, see also P. Lai, "Religious Diversity, Democracy, and Public Theology: Conversing with Barth in a Hong Kong Context," in this volume; in particular, section 2: Religious Diversity and Democracy in Hong Kong. Louie observes that behind the complex exchanges of the Occupy Central Movement stand the conflicting interpretations of the twin Christian virtues, namely justice and peace; K. Louie, "Public Theology and Christian Social Actions in Hong Kong: From the Past and the Present."

16. *Against the Stream* (London: SCM, 1954), 56.

17. English Translation of Barmen II from *Reformed Confessions of the Sixteenth Century*, ed. A. Cochrane (Louisville: Westminster John Knox Press, 2003), 334–335.

18. "The Christian Community in the Midst of Political Change," in *Against the Stream* (London: SCM, 1954), 82–83.

19. This is the political promise to Hong Kong people, codified in the Basic Law.

20. *Against the Stream*, 82–83.

21. Ibid., 83. Jones also observes that Barth's fiercely Christological understanding of the covenant, together with its indirect rhetorical strategy, does not render political reflection and political action marginal to dogmatic work. Quite the contrary, "human beings are now empowered to act, novelly and decisively, in the context of a covenant that is soteriologically fulfilled yet, in temporal terms, very much open." See P. D. Jones, "Karl Barth's *The Christian Life* and the Task of Political Theology," in this volume.

22. *Against the Stream*, 85–87.

23. Ibid., 84; see also G. Hunsinger, "Karl Barth and the Politics of Sectarian Protestantism," in *Disruptive Grace* (Grand Rapids: Eerdmans, 2000), 125–126.

24. *Against the Stream*, 96.

25. "Christian Community and Civil Community" (1946) in *Community, State and Church* (New York: Anchor Books, 1960), 150.

26. *Against the Stream*, 80.

27. *Community, State and Church*, 161.

28. Barmen V.

29. *Community, State and Church*, 160.

30. Jones nicely points out that the vocative "Father!" in Barth's exposition of the Lord's Prayer is resolutely iconoclastic to all political schemes, whether ecclesial or secular: "The degree to which Barth insists on the actualistic and presentist quality of the Christian's petition to God, further, serves as a nice caution that conventional wisdom, whether it be a preexisting ideological scheme or a tried-and-tested political 'game plan,' cannot presumptively set the terms for political analysis and decision-making. Insofar as the vocative, 'Father!' is sincere, it requires that Christians de-familiarize themselves with, and perhaps even obliges us to unlearn, putatively 'virtuous' or 'habitual' modes of behavior, and to attend to the possibility that God might commend unusual courses of action—or, for that matter, deft and perhaps unsavory negotiations of complex political situations." P.D. Jones, "Karl Barth's *The Christian Life* and the Task of Political Theology," in this volume.

31. *Community, State, and Church*, 162–163.

32. Over against Yoder's interpretation, Höfner sharply discerns a "deep grammar of his non-sectarian notion of the church's particularity" in Barth's political ecclesiology, in which the Christian Church cannot make the claim of being exclusively the exponent of God's kingdom over against the non-Christian society. For Barth, the church has to reckon with and be attentive to signs of Christ's prophetic work *extra muros ecclesiae*. This decisive move from the two-sided relation of the Christian Church and the non-Christian society to the three-sided relation of church, society, and the kingdom of God is of particular importance to the non-Western late-modern society like Hong Kong. It does not mean the Christian Church can then take whatever the society at large offers it, but it does mean that there should be genuine mutual learning between the Christian Church and the non-Christian society in the matter of

their joint political responsibilities. See Markus Höfner, "Neither Self-Evident Frame nor Self-Enclosed Sect: The Christian Church in Barth's Political Ecclesiology," in this volume.

33. "Christian politics are always bound to seem strange, incalculable and surprising in the eyes of the world—otherwise they would not be Christian." *Against the Stream*, 92.

34. *Against the Stream*, 90.

35. *Community, State and Church*, 180.

36. *Against the Stream*, 92–93.

37. Gerhard Sauter observed that "in the Cold War period there was a nearly totalitarian tendency among theologians toward an overjustification of responses and habits with the aid of theological terms or biblical statements. The reference to faith and lack of faith, to obedience and disobedience, was often misused in mapping the realm of decision making." "Theological Reflections on the Political Changes in Europe," in *Protestant Theology at the Crossroad* (Grand Rapids: Eerdmans, 2007), 121. Similar sentiment is emerging in Hong Kong.

38. *Against the Stream*, 93 & 145; also *Community, State and Church*, 171–172: "Since God Himself became man, man is the measure of all things, and man can and must only be used and, in certain circumstances, sacrificed, for man. Even the most wretched man—not man's egoism, but man's humanity—must be resolutely defended against the autocracy of every mere 'cause.'"

39. *CD* III.2, 222–285.

40. This problem is especially acute for the Christian Churches in the mainland under the spell of "Peace Evolution," "Patriotic Education," and "Anti-infiltration"; see Kim-kwong Chan, "The Ecclesiological Implications of the Political Attitude of the Chinese Authority towards Christianity," in this volume; in particular, the section about Post-Cold War 1991 until 2013. In Hong Kong, the tension has recently been highlighted in the "Anti-National Education Movement" in 2012, as well as the rise of parochial sentiment after the Umbrella Movement.

41. *CD* III.4, 295.

42. Ibid., 297.

43. *Community, State and Church*, 178.

44. *Against the Stream*, 84.

Chapter 23

Religion, Civil Society, and Democracy

Insights from Political Science

Jeffrey Haynes

There were few democratically elected governments, outside Western Europe and North America, until fairly recently. Instead, many countries had various kinds of authoritarian regimes—including military, one-party, no-party, and personalist dictatorships. However, during the 1980s and 1990s, the shift from unelected to elected governments was deemed so significant that Samuel Huntington gave it a name: the "third wave of democracy."[1] Today, competitive electoral politics is now taking place in around two-thirds of countries. During this near-global shift[2] from authoritarianism to various kinds of "more democratic" political arrangement, a key factor debated in the political science literature is the role of religion, including Christianity, on democratization outcomes. Often, for example, it is contended that Christianity, especially Protestant versions active in north-western Europe, is conducive to democratization and democracy. This chapter seeks to examine the role of Christianity in recent processes of democratization in order to assess their impact.

In this chapter, I assess this impact as it can be observed from the perspective of political science. It is worth noting, however, that the way religious actors "do" politics in the public sphere, including their interest in and responses to political changes, including democratization, partly depends on their theological self-understanding. This volume features several chapters which focus on this issue as argued from within religious communities, using the theology of Karl Barth as a resource. In particular, the chapters from Norris, Lai, and Anderson, explore the theological arguments of, inter alia, Barth to examine processes of democratization and democracy in various contexts and settings.[3]

The chapter starts with an overview of two recent phenomena: religious "deprivatization" and democratization. From there we turn to comparative

examination of two terms often used almost interchangeably: democratization and democracy. I follow this with a survey of three crucial actors in
democratization and democracy outcomes: the state, civil society, and political society. The chapter concludes with a brief comparative evaluation of the
role of Christianity in the democratization of two countries, one from Europe
and one from East Asia: Poland and South Korea.

RELIGIOUS DEPRIVATIZATION AND
DEMOCRATIZATION: GLOBAL PHENOMENA

There is no denying that many religious actors are now interested in political issues, including the desirability of democracy. We can see a trend that
has developed since the 1980s, during which many religions have left their
assigned place in the private sphere, becoming recognizably politically active
in various ways and with assorted outcomes. Casanova notes that in the 1980s
"what was new and became 'news' . . . was the widespread and simultaneous
refusal of religions to be restricted to the private sphere."[4] This involved a
remodeling and reassumption of public roles by religion, which theories of
secularization had long condemned to social and political marginalization.

It was once believed to be axiomatic that modernization inevitably leads to
religious privatization and secularization. As a result, there would be a fundamental, global decline in religion's social and political importance. This was
believed to be the case, regardless of religious tradition or form of political
power dominant in the context in which religion found itself. Iran's 1978–
1979 revolution posed fundamental questions in relation to this conventional
wisdom. Contemporaneously, the global Catholic Church began to play an
increasingly important role in relation to democratization in Central and
Eastern Europe, Africa, East Asia, and Latin America. These two developments not only collectively emphasized that modernization does not always
lead to secularization but also that religion can sometimes play a fundamental
role in issues of political representation and legitimacy. In sum, contrary to
once hegemonic secularization theory, there has been a widespread—some
say, global—resurgence of religion, often as a political actor in numerous
countries. This has involved various religious traditions. This emphasizes not
only that there is more than one relevant interpretation of modernization but
also that religion can and does play a role in political changes, even in parts
of the world, including Europe, that have been long regarded as inevitably
secularizing.

Globally, two phenomena are simultaneously taking place. First, there
is an *increase* in various forms of spirituality and religiosity, although this
often also implies in many cases both fragmentation and decline in societal

clout of hitherto leading religious organizations.[5] The increase in spirituality and religiosity is manifested in various ways including "new" religious and spiritual phenomena, including manifestations of "New Age" spirituality; "foreign," "exotic" Eastern religions, including Hare Krishna; "televangelism"; renewed interest in astrology, and "new" sects, such as Scientology. Note, however, that such religious entities, as Casanova points out, are "not particularly relevant for the social sciences or for the self-understanding of modernity," because they do not present "major problems of interpretation. . . . They fit within expectations and can be interpreted within the framework of established theories of secularization."[6] The point is that they are *normal* phenomena. They are examples of *private* religion. They do not individually or collectively question or challenge the extant arrangements of society, including political and social structures. Indeed, such religious phenomena are *apolitical*; and "all" they really show is that many people are interested in spiritual issues and sometimes they involve new expressions. In addition, in many European Catholic countries—for example, Ireland, Italy, Poland, and Spain—the church is fast losing moral appeal for many people, especially among the young.[7] In sum, globally the multiplicity of existing and new religious phenomena belies the idea that religion will inevitably lose its appeal for most people. In addition, innovative religious forms appear to be increasing their appeal, often at the expense of traditional religions. But from a *political* perspective these new religions are rarely of political importance.

Second, not only Christian churches—especially the Catholic Church in both transnational and national contexts—but also Islamic religious actors in many countries, as well as Jewish entities in Israel, now openly seek to articulate viewpoints on a variety of political and social issues, more readily and openly than in the past. Such religious entities typically resist state attempts to side-line them.

Three questions are central in seeking to account for religion's current political impact in many countries, including its influence on democratization outcomes. First, *why* should religious organizations seek to become actors with political goals? This occurs when religious entities feel that political and/social changes are necessary and the state is not well equipped to oversee and lead such changes, not least because the solutions it seeks are secular ones; and they do not chime well with religious interpretations. Second, how *widespread* is the phenomenon? The literature indicates that it is very extensive.[8] Third, what are the *political consequences* of religion's intervention? The short, although not very analytically helpful, answer is: they are variable.

While differing in terms of specific issues that encourage them to act politically, religious actors commonly reject the secular ideals that have long dominated theories of political development in both developed and developing countries, appearing instead as champions of alternative, confessional outlooks, programs, and policies. Seeking to keep faith with what they interpret as divine decree, they typically refuse to render to secular power holders automatic material or moral support. Instead, they are concerned with various social, moral, and ethical issues, which are, however, nearly always political to some degree. Religious actors may challenge or undermine both the legitimacy and autonomy of the state's main secular spheres, including government and more widely political society. In addition, many churches and other comparable religious entities no longer restrict themselves to the pastoral care of individual souls. Now, they raise questions about, *inter alia*, interconnections of private and public morality, claims of states and markets to be exempt from extrinsic normative considerations, and modes and concerns of government. What religious actors also have in common is a shared concern for retaining and increasing their social importance. To this end, many religious entities now seek to bypass or elude what they regard as the cumbersome constraints of temporal authority and, as a result, threaten to undermine the latter's constituted political functions. In short, refusing to be condemned to the realm of privatized belief, religion is now centrally in the public sphere, thrusting itself into issues of social, moral, and ethical—and in many places, political—contestation. However, the key point is not from which religious tradition individual religious actors come. Instead, religious actors are very often also political actors, wielding varying degrees of influence on political outcomes, while sharing a focus on a key issue: a desire to change their societies in directions where what they regard as religiously acceptable standards of behavior are central to public life, including political life. Pursuing such objectives, they use a variety of tactics and methods, operating either at the level of civil society and/or political society.

Following the end of the Cold War, both Christianity and Islam showed increasing political assertiveness, a development which seems likely to continue over the next two decades.[9] While such political assertiveness has been manifested in many countries domestically, it has also shown itself internationally and transnationally. Central to this development is the phenomenon of globalization and associated developments in communications technology. The latter permits religious entities' messages to unite or divide real or imagined communities, physically separated by international borders and thousands of kilometers. In particular, it enables diaspora populations to feel a closeness otherwise denied them and appeals to a far wider audience than previously possible. Technology is also likely to contribute to diaspora communities being increasingly affected by intra-faith discord in countries of origin, such as Pakistan and India. In addition, some governments may have to address new challenges from religious groups at home. For example, it is posited that over the next two decades, China will be home to some of the world's largest Muslim and Christian populations. The impact on China's internal politics and global attitude and focus is likely to be influenced significantly by the manner in which these two faith groups pursue their goals and seek enhanced religious freedoms. A wider point is that as religion is so fundamental to many people's identity, where tensions between different groups exist or develop, they are likely to be exacerbated by religious differences.

DEMOCRATIZATION TO DEMOCRACY: NOT A LINEAR TRAJECTORY

Questions of the relationship between religion and identity are not the concern of this chapter. Instead, we are concerned with the impact of Christianity on democratization and democracy. Democratization is a process which can occur in four not necessarily discrete stages: (1) political liberalization; (2) collapse of authoritarian regime; (3) democratic transition; and (4) democratic consolidation. *Political liberalization* is the process of reforming authoritarian rule. The *collapse of the authoritarian regime* stage refers to the stage when a dictatorship falls apart; it can be swift or slow or something in between. *Democratic transition* is a process: a material and palpable shift from authoritarian to identifiably democratic rule, identified by the election of a democratically accountable government. *Democratic consolidation* is also a process: embedding democratic institutions and developing increasingly strong perceptions among both elites and citizens that democracy is the best—indeed, *only* legitimate—way of "doing" politics.

The four stages are complementary and always in practice overlap. For example, political liberalization and transition can happen simultaneously, while aspects of democratic consolidation can appear when certain elements of transition are barely in place or remain incomplete. Or they may even be showing signs of retreating. On the other hand, it is nearly always possible to observe a concluded transition to democracy. This is when a pattern of behavior developed ad hoc during the stage in which regime change becomes institutionalized, characterized by admittance of political actors into the system—as well as the process of political decision-making—according to previously established and legitimately coded procedures. This is not to suggest that (apparent) democratic consolidation is the end of the matter: (apparent) democratic consolidation can unravel to leave a partially democratic regime which can endure for long periods of time.

Until democratic consolidation, the absence of (or uncertainty about) these accepted "rules of the democratic game" make it difficult to be sure about the eventual outcome of political transitions. This is because the transition dynamics revolve around strategic interactions and tentative arrangements between political actors with stakes in the outcome but with uncertain power resources. Key issues include: (1) defining who is legitimately entitled to play the political "game" (2) criteria determining who wins and who loses politically; and (3) limits to be placed on the issues at stake. What chiefly differentiates the four stages of democratization is the degree of uncertainty prevailing at each moment. For example, during regime transition *all* political calculations and interactions are highly uncertain. This is because political actors find it difficult to know: (1) what their precise interests are; and (2) which groups and individuals would most usefully be allies or opponents.

During democratic transitions, powerful, often inherently undemocratic, political players, such as elements within the armed forces and/or elite civilian supporters of the exiting authoritarian regime, characteristically divide into what Huntington (1991) calls "hard-line" and "soft-line" factions. "Soft-liners" are relatively willing to achieve negotiated solutions to the political problems, while "hard-liners" are unwilling to arrive at solutions reflecting compromise between polarized positions. Democratic consolidation is most likely when "soft-liners" triumph because, unlike "hard-liners," they are willing to find a compromise solution.

A consolidated democracy is in place when all political "players"—including political elites, political groups of various kinds, and the mass of ordinary people—commonly accept both formal rules and informal understandings determining political outcomes. If achieved, it signifies that groups are settling into relatively predictable positions involving politically legitimate behavior according to generally acceptable rules. More generally, a consolidated democracy is characterized by normative limits and established patterns of power distribution. Political parties emerge as privileged in this context because, despite their divisions over strategies and their uncertainties about partisan identities, the logic of electoral competition focuses public attention on them and compels them to appeal to the widest possible clientele. In addition, "strong" civil societies—that is, not overly split along class, ethnic, or religious lines—are important for democratic consolidation, primarily because a "strong"—that is, a relatively unfragmented—civil society is likely to be most effective on keeping an eye on the state and what it does with its power and making fuss if it seems to be transcending accepted limits of state power. In sum, democratic consolidation exists when all major political actors take for granted the fact that recognizably democratic processes consistently dictate governmental renewal. But this does not imply that democratic consolidation is the end state of a process: it remains a process which can be reversed.

RELIGION, DEMOCRATIZATION, AND DEMOCRACY

The third wave of democracy began in the mid-1970s with the shifts from authoritarian rule of three southern European, predominantly Christian, countries: Greece, Portugal, and Spain. From that time, democratization spread to much of the rest of the world. Yet, despite numerous relatively free and fair elections over the last four decades in many formerly authoritarian countries, ordinary people often lack the ability significantly and consistently to influence political outcomes. This is often because small groups of elites—comprising civilians, military personnel, or a combination—typically not only control national political processes but also manage more widely to dictate political conditions. Under such conditions, because power is still focused in relatively few elite hands, political systems have narrow bases from which most ordinary people are, or feel, excluded. This can be problematic because, by definition, a democracy should not be run by and for the few, but should signify a popularly elected government operating in the broad public interest. In most consolidated democracies, the political role and significance of religious actors is low. But not in all cases: in some countries (for example, Iran and Poland) religious actors, respectively Shi'i clerics and the Catholic Church, played pivotal roles in fundamental political changes.

The original system of democracy in ancient Greece was originally a form of direct governance involving citizens of a city (*polis*). Today, a minimalist definition of democracy refers to governance rooted in representative institutions whose officeholders are chosen by adult citizens via suitable electoral mechanisms. Attention to religion's role in democratization and democratic consolidation ("democracy") focuses on: (1) the historical role of religion in directly generating, opposing, and sustaining democratic states and movements; (2) the study of religious organizations as mediating institutions that strengthen civil society and thus reinforce democracy; (3) the influence of democratic political authority upon religious traditions founded on other modes of legitimate authority; (4) democratic and nondemocratic forms of governance within religious organizations; and (5) the long-term viability of religion and religious belief in modern democracies characterized by high levels of religious pluralism.

The relationship between religion, democratization, and democracy centers on three issues:

- Religious traditions have core elements which are more or less conducive to democratization and democracy;
- Religious traditions are typically multi-vocal—yet at any moment there will be powerful figures who are more or less receptive to, and encouraging of, democracy;
- Religious actors on their own rarely if ever *determine* democratization outcomes. Yet, they may in various ways, and with a range of outcomes, be significant for democratization. This may especially be the case in countries that have a long tradition of secularization.

There is a universal factor of importance to note in this context: around the world, religions have left their assigned place in the private sphere, becoming politically active in various ways and with assorted outcomes. This general re-emergence from political marginality dates from the 1980s. As already noted, this involved a remodeling and reassumption of public roles by religious actors, which theories of secularization had long condemned to social and political marginalization.

The core of secularization theory is that it was once believed inevitable that modernization would inexorably, fundamentally, and globally lead both to religious privatization and secularization. The result would everywhere be the same: elemental decline in religion's social and political importance and the rise to unchallenged prominence of various kinds of "secular"—that is, nonreligious—political actors. This was believed to be the case, regardless of religious tradition or form of dominant political power. But Iran's 1979 revolution posed fundamental questions—which continue to resonate—in relation to this conventional wisdom. Contemporaneously, the universal Catholic Church, as well as national components of the Church, began to play increasingly important roles in relation to democratization in various world regions, including: Central and Eastern Europe, sub-Saharan Africa, East Asia, and Latin America. These contemporaneous developments not only collectively emphasized that modernization does not necessarily lead to secularization but also that religion, including Christianity and Islam, may play a significant role in fundamental political changes. In sum: (1) there is more than one relevant interpretation of modernization ("multiple modernities"), with some forms of "modernization," for example, in Iran, Turkey and Poland, being heavily informed by religious values; and (2) religion may play an important role in significant political changes, even in parts of the world, such as Europe, long thought to be inevitably secularizing.

The nature of the relationship between religion, democratization, and democracy is a crucial issue in the political life of the contemporary world. Although scholars disagree about their nature and scope, there is widespread concern in many countries on three issues: the role of religious actors in (1) helping underpin or support authoritarian regimes; (2) inter-communal clashes; and (3) transnational extremist networks. In today's Europe, for example, such phenomena represent a dual challenge: first, religious communities must effectively integrate into democratic institutions while, second, policy-makers must work out and implement new policies and forms of cooperation to cope with previously unexpected threats and issues, some of which come from religious extremist actors.

Theoretically, the issue of how, or if, religious traditions and religious actors might affect the possibility of successful democratization and, once established, democracy has long been debated. During the decades immediately after World War II, many scholars agreed that political culture—which can be defined as citizens' orientation toward politics, affecting their perceptions of political legitimacy—was very important in explaining the success or failure of democratization and democracy. The political culture approach focused on how and in what ways religious traditions and actors were believed to feed into and affect a country's political culture, including citizens' preference or dislike of democracy. For example, in West Germany, Italy and Japan, cultural traditions—including Catholicism in Italy, Christian Democracy in West Germany, and a rich heritage of democracy-oriented philosophies and traditions in Japan—were said to be important, facilitating—with external assistance—the (re)making of these countries' political culture after lengthy experiences of undemocratic, totalitarian regimes.[10]

By the 1960s, Germany, Italy, and Japan were consolidated democracies. Soon after, a new theoretical orthodoxy emerged. This was linked to contemporaneous decolonization in sub-Saharan Africa, Asia, and elsewhere in the developing world. The theoretical focus in relation to both democratization and democracy shifted to institutional and economic factors: more robust, more representative institutions coupled with sustained economic growth were, it was claimed, the key reasons why countries democratized or not. At this time, the importance of cultural factors, including religion and ethnicity, were marginalized. Later, between the mid-1970s and mid-1990s, the "third wave of democracy"—which, *inter alia*, saw the shift from communist to democratic rule in many Central and Eastern European countries—helped to turn attention once again to the role of culture—including religion and ethnicity—and their role in democratic outcomes, both successful and unsuccessful. For example, in Poland at this time, the Catholic Church played a key role in undermining the country's communist regime, helping establish a post-communist, democratically accountable government.[11] The perceived pro-democracy role of the church was not however restricted to Poland, but extended to Latin America, Africa, and parts of Asia. There was also the contemporaneous rise of the Christian Right in the United States, and its considerable subsequent impact on the electoral fortunes of both the Republican and Democratic parties. Add to this the widespread growth of Islamist movements across the Muslim world, with significant ramifications for electoral outcomes in various countries, including Algeria, Egypt, Morocco, electoral successes for the Bharatiya Janata Party in India, and substantial, sustained political influence for various (Jewish) religious political parties in Israel. The overall outcome is that in recent years (where the focus has been upon, but not restricted to, the third wave of democracy), we have seen a rapid growth of religious involvement in politics, including in relation to democratization and democracy.

Various kinds of religious actors—including Christian and Islamist entities—are not necessarily pivotal to democratization processes, both successful and unsuccessful. For example, focusing on the formerly communist Central and East European region and its democratizing experience in the 1980s and 1990s, Juan Linz and Alfred Stepan argue that religion (Christianity) was *not* generally the—or even a—key explanatory factor in associated democratic outcomes (Linz and Stepan, 1996). Turning to Muslim-majority countries in the MENA and writing in the mid-1990s, Fred Halliday argues that the general failure to democratize during the third wave of democracy was not primarily due to the characteristics of Islam.[12] Instead, Halliday argued that the failure to democratize when democratization was otherwise a global trend was essentially the outcome of entrenched nonreligious social and political impediments. These included decades-long experiences of rule by "strong" individualistic leaders, associated patterns and structures of authoritarian rule, weak and often powerless institutions, and frail, fragmented civil societies, which were demonstrably incapable of pushing sustainably or collectively for democratization. Halliday also contended that while some such features might be legitimized by the state in terms of extant "Islamic doctrine" (*viz.* Wahhabism in Saudi Arabia), there was in fact nothing specifically "Islamic" about them; in other words, being Muslim did not mean you were necessarily anti-democracy or culturally and religious content with un unelected, unrepresentative, often capricious, rule by self-proclaimed "strongmen."

Samuel Huntington articulated a third view on the role of religion in democratization.[13] Different from Linz and Stepan and unlike Halliday, he averred that religions had a crucial impact, whether for "good" or "bad," on democratization outcomes during the third wave of democracy. Huntington controversially claimed that Christianity, in both Protestant and Catholic forms, was strongly connected to the remarkable spread of democracy during the third wave, a crucial component of the majority of successful democratizations during the period of the third wave (mid-1970s to late-1990s). Several other religious faiths, Huntington asserted, including Orthodox Christianity, Islam, Buddhism and Confucianism, were either not as supportive of democracy or even resolutely opposed to it. In sum, there is no consensus regarding the role of religion in recent democratization; various prominent scholars have drawn differing conclusions in this respect.

There is however agreement about when the "third wave of democracy" began: the mid-1970s, with the shifts to democracy in Greece, Portugal, and Spain. The third "wave" followed two earlier periods of comparatively swift democratization: the first and second "waves." The first wave took place during the last decades of the nineteenth and the first years of the twentieth century, when various European and North American countries democratized. The second began directly after World War II, when several countries, including Italy, Japan, and West Germany, moved decisively from authoritarian to democratic rule, strongly encouraged by, *inter alia*, the government of the United States.

Following shifts to democracy in Greece, Portugal, and Spain, authoritarian regimes in Latin America, Eastern Europe, Asia, and Africa subsequently democratized. The extent of these changes is shown by the fact that in 1972 only a quarter of countries had democratically elected governments. Twenty years later, in the early 1990s, the proportion grew to over 50 percent, and in 2015, around 75 percent of the world's 192 countries had governments characterized by their democratic election. The situation over time is summarized in table 23.1.

RELIGION, POLITICAL SOCIETY, CIVIL SOCIETY, AND THE STATE

To understand the general political importance of religious actors in the context of the third wave of democracy, it is necessary first to comprehend what they say and do in their relationship with the state. I mean something more than "mere" government when referring to the state. The state is the continuous administrative, legal, bureaucratic, and coercive system that attempts not only to manage the various state apparatuses, but in addition to "structure relations between civil and public power and to structure many crucial relationships within civil and political society."[14] As a result, almost everywhere in the world, apparently regardless of the nature of political systems and/or the level of economic development in a country, states have over time sought to reduce and control religion's political importance and involvement. That is, around the world states have sought to privatize religion, and thus considerably to reduce its political impact. Sometimes, for example, in Poland and Italy (Catholicism) and Turkey (Sunni Islam), states have attempted to erect a "civil religion" arrangement, whereby a designated religious format effectively "functions as the cult of the political community."[15] The declared purpose is to try to create and develop forms of consensual, corporate, religion, claiming to be guided by general, culturally appropriate, specific religious beliefs of intrinsic societal significance. In short, when states seek to develop "civil religions" it is an attempted strategy to try to avoid social conflicts and promote national coordination and cohesion.

Yet, religious actors' relationships with the state are by no means limited to attempts by the latter to build civil religions. In fact, in many countries, relations between religious entities and the state are not only now more visible but also increasingly problematic. Why? First, recent increases in religious challenges to the authority of the state may merely be transitory reactions in the context of the onward march of secularization. Second, even

Table 23.1   "Free," "Partly Free," and "Not Free" Countries, 1972–2015[a]

	Number of "Free" Countries	Number of "Partly Free" Countries	Number of "Not Free" Countries
1972	43	38	69
1982	54	47	64
1992	75	73	38
2002	89	56	47
2007	89	59	44
2015	89	55	51

[a] The terms "free," "partly free," and "not free," correspond respectively to the following terms: consolidated democracy, transitional democracy, and non-democracy. *Source*: http://www.freedomhouse.org/templat e.cfm?page=372 and https://freedomhouse.org/report/freedom-world/freedom-world-2015?gclid=CLG6 y__Y5sUCFSLKtAodvUsA0Q#.VWg5C2fbKUl. Last accessed July 3, 2015.

if the modern state is particularly vulnerable to legitimation crises, it does not necessarily mean that religion is again becoming *automatically* relevant to state functioning and policy-making. Third, religion-based challenges to state hegemony have roots in endeavors by the latter to assert a monitoring role *vis-à-vis* religion, in effect to control it. We can see such a development at three levels: political society, civil society, and at the level of the state itself.

In many countries, religion is being liberated from providing sometimes slavish legitimacy to secular authority. Many religious actors are now willing routinely to criticize and challenge the state in various ways in relation to a variety of issues and themes. Yet, even if heightened concern about the state's policies can be held up as evidence of the regeneration of the sociopolitical power of religion, we still need to ask further questions. The issues are themselves secular and insofar as religious agencies are active in these areas, this is a radical shift of concern from the supernatural, from devotional acts, to what are largely secular goals pursued by secular means. However, a note of caution is in order: we need to bear in mind that when religious interests act as "pressure groups"—rather than as "prayer bodies"—they are not necessarily going to be effective in what they seek to achieve. This is because the more secularized a society, the less likely it is, although by no means impossible, that religious actors will be able or willing to play a politically significant role.

Religion and Political Society

At the level of political society—that is, the arena in which the polity specifically arranges itself for political contestation to gain control over public power and the state apparatus—we can note a range of religious responses that are in part dependent upon the degree of secularization. These include (1) resistance to the disestablishment and the differentiation of the religious from the secular sphere; the goals of many so-called religious "fundamentalist" groups; (2) religious groups and confessional political parties' mobilizations and countermobilizations against other religions or secular movements and parties; and (3) religious organizations' mobilization in defense of religious, social, and political freedoms—that is, demanding the rule of law and the legal protection of human and civil rights, protecting mobilization of civil society and/or defending institutionalization of democratically elected governments. In recent times in pursuit of such goals, we can note Christian transnational mobilization in and various countries in Europe, Asia, and elsewhere.

Religion and Civil Society

Civil society is the arena where various social movements—including neighborhood associations, women's groups, religious entities, and intellectual currents—join with civic organizations, including lawyers', journalists', trade unions', and entrepreneurs' associations, to constitute themselves into an ensemble of arrangements to express themselves and seek to advance their interests. Sometimes, the concept of *civil* society is used in contrast to *political* society. Unlike the latter, civil society refers to organizations and movements—*not* political parties—formally uninvolved in both the business of government and overt political management. Note, however, that this does not necessarily prevent civil society organizations from sometimes seeking to or actually exerting political influence on various matters, including democratic outcomes and the content of national constitutions.

Regarding religion at the level of civil society, one can distinguish between hegemonic civil religions—such as Evangelical Protestantism in nineteenth-century America—and the more recent public intervention of religious entities, concerned either with single issues such as anti-abortion or with morally determined views of wider societal development, for example, in relation to homosexual rights or appropriate days for shops to open, currently a highly controversial issue in Israel. In trying to influence public policy—without themselves seeking to become political officeholders—religious actors may employ a variety of tactics, including, in no particular order: (1) lobbying the executive apparatus of the state; (2) going to court; (3) building links with political parties; (4) forming alliances with like-minded groups, both secular and from other religious traditions; (5) mobilizing followers to lobby and/ or protest; and (6) working to sensitize public opinion via mass media. The overall point is that religious actors may use a variety of methods to try to achieve their objectives.

Religion and the State

Interactions between the state and religious entities are often referred to as "church-state relations." It is necessary to point out, however, that one of the difficulties in seeking to survey the nature of contemporary church-state relations in many countries around the world is that the very concept of *church* is a somewhat parochial, Anglo-American standpoint with direct relevance only to explicitly Christian traditions. It is derived primarily from the context of British establishmentarianism—that is, maintenance of the principle of "establishment" whereby one church is legally recognized as the *only* established church. In other words, when we think of church-state relations we may assume a single relationship between two clearly distinct, unitary, and solidly but separately institutionalized entities. In this implicit model built into the conceptualization of the religion-political nexus there is but *one* state and *one* church; both entities' jurisdictional boundaries need to be carefully delineated. Both separation and pluralism must be safeguarded, because it is assumed that the leading church—like the state—will seek institutionalized dominance over rival religious organizations. For its part, the state is expected to respect individual rights even though it is assumed to be inherently disposed toward aggrandizement at the expense of citizens' personal liberty. In sum, the conventional concept of state-church relations is rooted in prevailing Christian conceptions of the power of the state of necessity being constrained by forces in society—including those of religion.

Expanding the problem of church-state relations to non-Christian contexts necessitates some preliminary conceptual clarifications—not least because the very idea of a prevailing state-church dichotomy is culture-bound. As already noted, *church* is a Christian institution, while the modern understanding of *state* is deeply rooted in the Post-Reformation European political experience. In their specific cultural setting and social significance, the tension and the debate over the church-state relationship are uniquely Western phenomena, present in the ambivalent dialectic of "render therefore unto Caesar the things which be Caesar's and unto God the things which be God's."[16] Overloaded with Western cultural history, these two concepts cannot easily be translated into non-Christian terminologies.

The differences between Christian conceptions of state and church and those of other world religions are well illustrated by reference to Islam. In the Muslim tradition, the mosque is not a church. The closest Islamic approximation to "state"—*dawla*—means, as a concept, either a ruler's dynasty or his administration. Only with the specific Durkheimian stipulation of *church* as the generic concept for *moral community*, *priest* for the *custodians of the sacred law*, and *state* for *political community* can we comfortably use these concepts in Islamic and other non-Christian contexts. On the theological level, the command-obedience nexus that constitutes the Islamic definition of authority is not demarcated by conceptual categories of religion and politics. Life as a physical reality is an expression of divine will and authority (*qudrah'*). There is no validity in separating the matters of piety from those of the polity; both are divinely ordained. Yet, although both religious and political authorities are legitimated "Islamically," they invariably constitute two independent social institutions. They do, however, regularly interact with each other. Yet, as recent and current political conflicts show in relation to, *inter alia*, Egypt and Turkey, there are on occasion sometimes serious tensions between Islamist and secular actors and the state in regard to democratization and human rights.

CHRISTIANITY AND DEMOCRATIZATION IN POLAND AND SOUTH KOREA

I complete this chapter with a brief comparative focus on Poland and South Korea, both countries that recently democratized while also seeing a major public role for Christian actors in that process. In addition, a focus on these countries enables to assess examples of politicized Christian actors from both Europe and Asia.

Poland

Around 94 percent of Poland's 37 million people are Catholics.[17] Emergence of an institutional Catholic concern with issues of social justice from the 1960s was followed, in the 1980s and 1990s, by a further period of significant international changes: the end of the Cold War, the third wave of democracy, and intensification of various aspects of globalization. During the third wave of democracy, the church was an important actor in relation to various countries, including Poland, Spain, and various African and Latin American nations. Overall, as Witte noted in the early 1990s, "twenty-four of the thirty-two new democracies born since 1973 are predominantly Roman Catholic in confession."[18]

Prior to this in Poland, the Communist state put in a policy of "cultural strangulation" toward Catholicism, designed to choke off its social importance in favor of the Communist hegemony. However, as already noted, most Poles are Catholics, and this turned out to be a significant factor in the country's shift from Communist rule in the late 1980s. Encouraged by the Pope's support, Polish Catholic activists represented both a counterculture and alternative social space to the official ideology and channels. This led, in 1980, to the creation of the Solidarity movement that articulated and expressed

Catholic social ethics as a counterstatement to those of Communism. This reflected not only a significant convergence between national and religious identity in Poland, but also, just as importantly, symbolized the failure of a Communist (secular) identity fundamentally to implant itself in the hearts and minds of most Poles, people whose cultural heritage is firmly Christian-based. In short, Poland's Christian heritage was a vital resource that helped create and then sustain opposition to communist rule.

Poland's communist government collapsed in late 1989. Flushed with success, some Polish Catholics, most of them laypeople, began to press for the "reinstatement of ecclesiastical norms in public law."[19] But they met with no sustained success—because the majority of Poles did not want it. The problem for the church was how to define its place within the post-Communist world. As Michel notes, "everything seems to indicate that it will be a challenge much more difficult than that posed by the Soviet system."[20] Why? The paradox is that while many Poles looked to the church as a nationalist focal point of anti-Communism, once democracy was won, most shifted their attention to conventional—that is, secular—political opportunity structures—especially political parties and individual political leaders—to try to achieve their sociopolitical, economic, and developmental objectives. The diminished influence of the Catholic Church was made clear when several of its aspirations—including outright opposition to abortion, divorce, and the suitability of a former Communist for the post of national president in the 1995 election—were decisively rejected by most Poles. According to Johnston, this represented both a swift and clear "distancing of Polish political culture from the Church."[21] No doubt aware of its declining influence, the church did not bother to sponsor or even overtly support a political party in the following years.

In conclusion, the important role of Catholic activists in undermining and bringing down Poland's communist government highlights that in the 1980s the church had much influence among ordinary Poles. However, the swift decline into relative political irrelevance from the 1990s—when Catholic views were unable to prevail on a range of political, social, and moral questions—suggests that many Poles were content to see the Church fulfill a significant political opposition role in the absence of secular alternatives. They were, however, less willing to afford the church a sustained political voice following the overthrow of the communist regime.

South Korea

In contrast to Poland, around 10 percent of South Koreans are Catholics, while approximately 20 percent are Protestant. Thus, around one-third of Koreans are Christians, a proportion of the population which has grown swiftly over the past forty years, during which time South Korea democratized. In South

Korea, as in Poland, interactions between state, society, and religion are strongly influenced by concerns with democracy. Notions of equity and justice, of political liberties and of human rights, form the core of such concerns. While Western Europe is understood to have developed a liberal democratic political order due to a combination of the effects of Christian belief (especially, until recently, Protestant concerns), of shared civic cultures and of longevity of sustained economic development, resulting in a relatively equitable sharing out of the fruits of economic growth, South Korea does not have this sociopolitical background. Nevertheless, it is observed that in South Korea Christianity and democracy both advance seemingly in correlation to each other. "Christian converts [a]re primarily young, urban, and middle class. . . . Christianity with its message of personal salvation and individual destiny offer[s] a surer comfort in a time of confusion and change,"[22] including the rollercoaster ride commonly known as globalization.

South Korea is of particular interest in our survey of Christianity, democracy, and democratic consolidation, as, some argue, it appears to have found the "holy grail": clear democratic advances and sustained economic growth. South Korea began displaying what Przeworski (1986: 55) calls "the signals of [democratic] opening" in the mid-1980s,[23] characterized by mass rallies and popular demands for political change. Eventually, however, an elite-dominated pacted transition from authoritarian rule ensued. Given its pacted transition, the theoretical literature would expect that the chances of limited democratization would be relatively good. Huntington suggests that democratization and eventual democratic consolidation are *only* promoted successfully if transitions involve negotiations and deals between the outgoing elite and the leading representatives of the democratic opposition.[24] Linz and Stepan (1996) argue that the constitutional compact reflected in pacted transitions, in defining the new regime's main laws, procedures and institutions, are a necessary condition to resolve existing social conflicts pacifically and favor democratization.[25] But, as both sets of authors acknowledge, there is a likely democratic price to pay. Because future stability is founded on guarantees secured by the old ruling elites, striving to protect and maintain privileges, impatient to escape judgment for any crimes committed during their rule, then stable yet limited democracies would be the result of pacted transitions.

South Korea's political transition had long roots. Pursuing, since the 1950s, a strategy of forced developmentalism, the state managed to enforce a coercive break with the traditional economy and lifestyles of its citizens. As a result, the democratic transition of the 1980s was from an authoritarian, some would say, draconian regime, highly adept at suppressing the personal liberty and political freedoms of Koreans. It is in this context that the shift to Christianity should be seen: Christianity promised both personal liberty and spiritual growth to its followers.

CONCLUSION

In this chapter I sought to engage with the issue of the relationship between Christianity, democratization, and democracy. The comparative focal points were the third wave of democracy, between the mid-1970s and the late-1990s/early 2000s and the ways in which various forms of Christianity were involved in that phenomenon. We saw that Christian actors can be pivotal in relation to democratization outcomes, as in Poland in the late 1980s and early 1990s but this is not necessarily the case. We saw in relation to South Korea that it was not so much organized expressions of Christian faith that were pivotal in the country's shift to democracy so much as the associated changes linked to conversion to Christianity which encouraged many South Koreans to demand political changes. Much of the time, however, Christian actors tend to have a rather ambivalent relationship with democratization, although on balance it can be concluded that they *tend* to be pro-democracy although this is not inevitable. This is partly because they are not necessarily recognized as legitimate actors in democratization contexts, where secular political actors are normally much more influential than religious actors.

NOTES

1. Samuel Huntington, *The Third Wave: Democratization in the Late Twentieth Century* (Norman, OK: University of Oklahoma Press, 1991).
2. I write "near-global" because the mainly Arab Middle East and North Africa, while affected considerably by the turmoil of the post-2011 "Arab Spring" events, do not show clear evidence of a regional shift to democratization, much less democracy.
3. See, in this volume, Kristopher Norris, "Democracy and Church: Barth and Yoder on Democratic Practice," Clifford B. Anderson, "Constitutional Theology: Karl Barth and Carl Schmitt on Legitimacy and the Rule of Law," and Lai Pan-chiu, "Religious Diversity, Democracy, and Public Theology: Conversing with Barth in a Hong Kong Context."
4. Jose Casanova, *Public Religions in the Modern World* (Chicago: University of Chicago Press), 6.
5. Grace Davie, *Religion in Modern Europe: A Memory Mutates* (Oxford: Oxford University Press, 2000).
6. Casanova, *Public Religions*, op. cit..
7. See Luigi Ceccarini, "The Church in Opposition. Religious Actors, Lobbying and Catholic Voters in Italy," in *Religion and Politics in Europe, the Middle East and North Africa*, ed. Jeffrey Haynes (London: Routledge, 2009), 177–201 and Anna Hennig, "Morality Politics in a Catholic Democracy: A Hard Road Towards Liberalisation of Gay Rights in Poland," in ibid., 202–226.

8. See, for example, Jeffrey Haynes (ed.), *Routledge Handbook of Religion and Politics* (London: Routledge, 2010).

9. Jeffrey Haynes (ed.), *Routledge Handbook of Religion and Politics*, 2nd ed. (London: Routledge, 2015).

10. See Juan Linz and Alfred Stepan, *Problems of Democratic Transition and Consolidation. Southern Europe, South America, and Post-Communist Europe* (Baltimore and London: Johns Hopkins University Press, 1996), Alfred Stepan, "Religion, Democracy and the 'Twin Tolerations'," *Journal of Democracy* 11, no. 4 (2000): 37–57, and Huntington, *The Third Wave*, op. cit.

11. Hennig, "Morality Politics in a Catholic Democracy," op. cit.

12. Fred Halliday, *The Middle East in International Relations. Power, Politics and Ideology* (Cambridge: Cambridge University Press, 2005).

13. Samuel Huntington, *The Clash of Civilizations and the Remaking of World Order* (New York: Free Pres, 1996).

14. Alfred Stepan, *Rethinking Military Politics: Brazil and the Southern Cone* (Princeton: Princeton University Press, 1988).

15. Casanova, *Modern Religions*, 58.

16. Luke 21:25.

17. "Statistics by Country by Catholic Population," at http://www.catholic-hierarchy.org/country/sc1.html. Last accessed July 3, 2015.

18. John Witte (ed.), *Christianity and Democracy in Global Context* (Boulder: Westview Press, 1993), 11.

19. David Martin, "Religion in Contemporary Europe," in *Religion in Contemporary Europe*, ed. John Fulton and P. Peter Gee (Lewiston, NY: Edwin Mellen), 4.

20. Patrick Michel, "Religion and Democracy in Central Eastern Europe," ibid., 34.

21. Harold Johnston, "Religious Nationalism: Six Propositions from Eastern Europe and the Former Soviet Union," in *Religion and Politics in Comparative Perspective*, ed. Bronislaw Misztal and Anson Shupe (Westport, CT; London: Praeger, 1992), 67–78.

22. Huntington, *The Third Wave*, 73–74.

23. Adam Przeworski, "Some Problems in the Study of the Transition to Democracy," in *Transitions from Authoritarian Rule: Southern Europe*, ed. Guillermo O'Donnell, Philippe Schmitter and Laurence Whitehead (Baltimore: The Johns Hopkins University Press), 55.

24. Huntington, *The Third Wave*, op. cit.

25. Linz and Stepan, *Problems of Democratic Transition and Consolidation*, op. cit.

Chapter 24

Whatever Happened to the Social Gospel?

Religion and Political Economy in the United States Today, and for the Future

Charles Mathewes

INTRODUCTION

North American theology considers Karl Barth's work dogmatic, but not particularly political, and there has been little resistance from Barthians to that assumption.[1] Few theologians deeply formed by Barth have written significant works in the arena of "political theology." (Of course, those who *have* done so—such as Jürgen Moltmann, James Cone, and Kathryn Tanner—are among the most profound and influential theologians of recent decades; but they are the exceptions that prove the rule.) And what Barthian political theology there has been, has been far more scholastic than pragmatic, content to remain in the pages of doctrinal theological tomes, and the lecture halls and seminars of exegetes, than to break into the public sphere of church or polity. On the North American scene, that is to say, Barth remains un-metabolized by the theological academy in general and political theology in particular. Figures such as Augustine, Aquinas, Calvin, Luther, Kant, Schleiermacher, Kierkegaard, Niebuhr, Rahner, and de Lubac are all explicitly and implicitly influencing discussions in theological ethics, social ethics, and political and practical theology, while Barth remains an undiscovered country. This problem is compounded by the fact that, from the other direction, Barthian theologians seem lucidly suspicious of much of what passes for political theology or even "social ethics." Barthians not infrequently insinuate that such work is theologically undisciplined, dogmatically unsound, argumentatively reactive and conceptually muddled—in short, shallow. For many Barthians, what passes for "Christian ethics" or "moral theology" is neither sufficiently Christian nor very theological.

This chapter, like others in this volume, assumes that this is a shame for political theology, and deeply inappropriate to the fundamental dynamics of Barth's theology.[2] On its best readings, Barth's theology is essentially political; not only is the only good political (and moral) theology a good dogmatic theology, but the reverse is true as well: a dogmatics that lacks purchase on the community's lived political and ethical practice is no dogmatics at all. Furthermore, an articulate and engaged Barthian political theology is especially needed now, in advanced industrial (and post-industrial) societies. Churches in these societies are, or should be, reconceiving the long-term constructive relationship between themselves and the political order as a whole— not just the state but also the larger institutional ecology of government and civil society—because both sides of the equation have changed dramatically. Paradoxically, perhaps dangerously, it is for these reasons that I propose to try to learn from the past for the future.

This essay aims, first, to describe one way of doing political theology that is broadly sympathetic to Barthian intuitions, and second, to elucidate some of the challenges that any such political theology will confront in coming decades. While the problems it identifies are common to many settings in post-industrial societies, it focuses on the particular setting of the United States because political theology is always importantly contextual; a sketch of how a dedicated effort to make one context a marginally more healthy place for Christian life (let alone human life) might cast some interesting, if indirect, light on larger issues of "political theology" that concern us all.

Such an effort is hardly unprecedented in the United States. In the past half century alone, the United States witnessed two large and well-known movements of social engagement that brought religious actors into serious transformative engagement with the public realm. First was the civil rights movement, operating most powerfully in the 1950s and early 1960s; second was the "religious right" that began in the 1970s and collapsed in the Obama era. Both of these movements, in different ways, interestingly drew inspiration from a slightly earlier, and now less well-known moment in church history, namely, the "Social Gospel" movement of the first several decades of the twentieth century. This movement served as the template for those later efforts by the churches to be involved in public life, and it deserves our direct attention. The context of our time makes its rejuvenation both urgent and very, very difficult. But what was the Social Gospel? Why is its rejuvenation needed today, and why does its rejuvenation face deep challenges? This chapter tries to answer these questions.

First, I explore what the Social Gospel was and the sorts of changes it suggested in the shape of theological engagement with politics and society. In the end, I suggest, it is impossible to avoid something like the social gospel as a mode of theological engagement in public life today, though our version of it may be undertaken on very different theological grounds. Next, I seek to identify precisely the material social challenges that should occupy future efforts to rejuvenate the social gospel. It describes the criteria that the political-theological imagination should use to identify and respond to these challenges today, criteria that bring the material challenges into view not only in secular terms (though achieving even *that* is an achievement), but also in strictly Christian terms, as challenging and undermining the disciplining and evangelizing mission of the churches. In this way, the "social gospel" can go forward as a work of the church for the church, and through being for the church, for the social order as a whole. Finally, I quickly sketch just what it is about our contemporary context that challenges the rehabilitation and restatement of the social gospel that I have urged, and makes some suggestions about how Barth's theo-political reflections can both inform and challenge the project so proposed—and how that project may challenge Barth as well.

In a way, the chapter proposes the renewed and self-conscious engagement of the churches in the reconstruction of a damaged, some would say ruined, social order. This is not meant as an *instrumentalization* of the churches for the political order, but rather as the articulation of a set of social challenges that face a particular pluralistic community in the particular theological language native to one part of that community—call them "the churches"—in order to illuminate those challenges' immediate theological salience for those churches; and the concomitant call for the churches to address those challenges in a serious and direct way, both for their own ecclesiological and evangelical reasons and for the betterment of the social order itself. Such a project will also give us the opportunity to test some of the more free-standing doctrinally generated claims about politics that originate in a more strictly systematic theological context, such as Barth's, and press questions on those claims' adequacy to the world as we find it today.

WHAT IS THE SOCIAL GOSPEL?

The "Social Gospel" is a complicated thing, of course. Many think of it, and deride it, as a too-simplistic attempt to apply a rather naïve reading of Christian love to all social problems. Such critiques are not entirely wrong, but they miss the profundity of what the Social Gospel was trying to do. Here I explain what that was.

Traditionally, the social vision of the churches was really quite straightforward: Christians should offer "supplications, prayers, intercessions, and thanksgivings . . . for kings and all who are in high positions, so that we may lead a quiet and peaceable life in all godliness and dignity" (1 Tim 2:1–2). Few thinkers swerved from this view, and in general the churches traditionally assumed that, so long as the gospel could be preached, and right worship allowed, the particular sociopolitical order was a matter of indifference.

Things changed quite dramatically in the nineteenth century, because of the profundity of social change caused by industrialization, which led to an extraordinarily tumultuous era in Christian social teachings. In fact, the "Social Gospel" was merely the Protestant American version of the larger social transformation of Christianity in the decades around 1900. Analogous developments can be seen in figures from F. D. Maurice and R. H. Tawney to Christoph Blumhardt, Karl Barth, and Jürgen Moltmann, and the tradition of Roman Catholic Social Encyclicals are quite akin to this as well. All felt the need to reconsider the shape of the Christian message and mission in response to the transforming social orders in which they were placed, and all pressed the churches toward a more vigorous and direct engagement with those social orders.

In America, Walter Rauschenbusch symbolizes this radical theological rethinking of the social teachings of the Christian churches. For him, the churches have a word to speak, a transformation to undertake in the social order itself. The proper concern of theology is the entire social order, in fact, and it will be saved by the love of God shed abroad via Christ as prompted by the church. Jesus embodied love, Paul preached love, and today, we need a modern supplement to Paul's preaching, an extension of that gospel of love and fellow-feeling in modern society's larger and less organically related structures. Rauschenbusch proclaimed that new community as a present reality, one durable enough to continue expanding until it diffused through the whole social order. In this vision, to borrow from another American theologian, the church does not have a social teaching, the church *is* a social teaching.

Rauschenbusch's proposal failed for several reasons. First of all, it failed because of history, exemplified by the apocalyptic conflagration of what we now call the *First* World War. The optimism of control and agency died, as it were, on the Somme. Other events, such as the Great Depression and the persistence of racial and national hatred, seemed also to speak against the social gospel. While the particular configuration of our social injustices could be modified, perhaps the deeper, darker energies that drive group exclusion and competition are natural to, inexpungeable from, humanity. Second, the vision was accused of purchasing social insight and social energy at the cost of a proper theological analysis of sin and grace. Most famously formulated in Reinhold Niebuhr's neo-orthodox "Christian realism," this critique was devastating. And while many later criticized Niebuhr himself— either for not being sufficiently politically radical (the critique liberationists launched in the 1960s), or for not being sufficiently theological (the critique Stanley Hauerwas launched in the 1970s), these critics usually assume the social gospel was not something they, by their criticisms of Niebuhr, had redeemed; if anything, he was seen as contaminated by problems analogous to those afflicting Rauschenbusch. No matter what one thought of Niebuhr, Rauschenbusch's Social Gospel remained politically, psychologically, and theologically inadequate. Everyone had gotten beyond it.

But "everyone" was wrong. It is a truism that we critique most vehemently that view that is most proximate to our own, and while the aforementioned criticisms have force, they are not radical rejections of the Social Gospel, but rather corrections of it.[3] Reinhold Niebuhr, Stanley Hauerwas, Emilie Townes, and Walter Rauschenbusch all share far more with each other on all these matters (and with their European counterparts Maurice, Tawney, Barth, and the encyclical-writing Popes) than they do with any theologian between their age and that of John Calvin. They agree with the Social Gospel that individualism is insufficient, that the social order is contingent and demands critical intelligence, and that the churches themselves need to provide that intelligence on their own terms, not wait upon secular thought-forms to provide it for them. Indeed almost *all* theologians today are broadly "social gospel" theologians.

This may seem an outrageous claim, but it is easily defended. After all, the details of the distinct solutions these figures offered are not nearly so interesting as the common problems they identified. When Rauschenbusch named the "Social Gospel," amid the social tumult of an industrializing America, he named a change that was very important, for the church and society, and he gave it an appropriate name, for three reasons. First, it recognized "the social" as a distinct site and topic of theological reflection. Most earlier forms of Christianity targeted only part of the issue, the Social Gospelers claimed. Christianity should not concern itself simply with the inner "spiritual" lives of individuals, and whether or not they have been saved; it must address the whole person, body and spirit, in their existence as participants in a larger social order, for the Gospel aims to create a new social order—the Kingdom of God—not just new individuals. Rauschenbusch was far from alone in this; as Karl Barth put it, in an early essay on the connections between Jesus and socialism, "perhaps nowhere else has Christianity fallen farther away from the spirit of her Lord and Master than precisely in this estimation of the relation between spirit and matter, inner and outer."[4] It is the task of the churches to speak to the whole of creation, not simply some "inner" or "spiritual" part of the human person.

Second, and entailed in the first, the Social Gospel insisted on the *contingency* of the social realm, that is, the fact that the social order is not a simple natural given of human life, that it can change, adapt, enrich, corrode. Early

Social Gospelers struggled to get their fellow Christians to see that the way things are is not the way they always have been or must be. Even in the United States—a culture putatively anchored in revolution—the tendency to naturalize contingent social orders, such as the divisions and hierarchies of leisured rich and laboring poor, of race, ethnicity, and gender, was a powerful force. Rauschenbusch's argument that the society is in crisis was a recognition that industrialization was transforming America, and the churches needed to understand and work for those changes to go the right way.

Third, the Social Gospel insisted that mere secular reason was not enough, that there would need to be an explicitly *theological* moment in the analysis of our situation and a theological component for any adequate response to it. If the first point earlier was an intra-theological debate, about the propriety of this kind of analysis as a form of theology, this last point was a debate in public discourse, about the propriety of this kind of theology as a kind of analysis, a contribution to a larger public conversation. In the burgeoning discussions of "the social" that emerged in the late nineteenth and early twentieth centuries, it would have been very easy for religious voices not to play an explicit role; it is almost entirely due to the Social Gospel that we now have a self-consciously Christian form of public witness.[5]

In short, we can say that the Social Gospel is one example of the form that Christian reflection on this-worldly life should take after the end of "Christendom," in two senses. First, it happens after the de-naturalization and de-divinization of the social order, once we have recognized that our social structures do not directly express God's will, but are rather *up to us*, so that if we find them problematic we can alter them.[6] Second, it is a form of theology developed in response to the churches' "declaration of independence," as it were, from the political authorities of the nation-state *and* from the cultural norms of the surrounding social order. The churches' independence is manifest not just in their structural disestablishment (however tacit that may be in many countries), but in the sense that those authorities must be challenged not just over the topics that they claim illegitimately as their own proper purview, but even over the topics over which those authorities have some legitimate oversight. The churches' independence is also manifest in their new self-consciousness as being distinctively *Christian*, where the possibility of a non-Christian approach is quite clearly a respectable live option, perhaps even a majority option. I take it that what Markus Höfner[7] has called Barth's "political ecclesiology" is just this sort of move; as Barth himself put it, "in this time Christian-bourgeois age has come to an end. . . . The world is reclaiming . . . its freedom (from the church). . . . But with that, the gospel's freedom over against the world has been restored to it as well."[8] Few eras of transformation are as swift and dramatic as this one; I think only of the end of the Roman Empire, with Augustine, and (perhaps) the early modern era, with Calvin. That is the magnitude of the transformation described here.

WHY DOES THE SOCIAL GOSPEL NEED TO BE RENEWED?

If we want to rehabilitate something like the Social Gospel, what shape will this rehabilitation take? What social issues in the United States are most in need of theological engagement? I think of two: the twin social crises of rising economic inequality and the continuing catastrophe of the criminal justice system. Both are massive though still under-appreciated changes to social life, changes with large implications for the overall social order's health, and for the churches' primary vocation, in ways that have not been fully recognized. The first reinforces doubt about the common good. The second reinforces doubt about the possibility of justice. Both are deeply implicated in the permanent "crisis" of racism, America's besetting, if not original, sin.

The churches should respond to these challenges by shaping their pedagogy of Christian discipleship to identify these challenges as distinct spiritual challenges, in order to enable their parishioners better to resist them in their lives, and work against them in the social order.[9] Thus the criteria used by my proposed revised social gospel are not the ones that Rauschenbusch arguably assumed and critics like Niebuhr critiqued—namely, a naïve love-monism and confidence in the durable progress of the moral community anchored in the church but extending to society. Nor is the audience immediately addressed by this social gospel the one that Niebuhr arguably assumed and critics like Hauerwas and Cone critiqued—namely, the nation and not primarily the churches. To confront these facts in this way encourages the Christian churches to be more than the "irrelevant social club[s]," that Martin Luther King called them in the early 1960s.[10] It gives Christianity a more vital and complicated role to play in the social order, and potentially enlivens the members of the Christian churches, and those outside their doors, with a more vivid picture of the Christian faith than they typically receive in churches today.

Inequality

The United States' growing inequality is a terrible challenge—both a direct challenge to the sustainability and health of our social order, and an indirect challenge to any church that aims to cultivate in its members a sacramental imagination of creation. Here I sketch the dimensions of this problem, then explain how to understand it as a challenge to proper discipleship and evangelization.

The facts of rising inequality are well known.[11] It has consequences that anyone, regardless of their religious beliefs, can acknowledge. It is culturally fragmenting: while we have become more intimately related with people who are different from us in many ways—religiously, racially, and ethnically, for example—we are growing *less* familiar with people in significantly differ- ent economic conditions than ourselves. It is socially corrupting: extremes of inequality are associated with all sorts of social dangers—greater crime, poorer education improvement across generations, less public health, and a general decline in social well-being; it seems to be a vicious cycle.[12] Finally, it is civically corrosive: Insofar as the United States is a distinctively "creedal nation," bound together by ideology more than cultural or ethnic continuity, the decay of so central a part of the national creed as social mobility is bound to have profound effects on national solidarity.

There are sufficient *secular* reasons—reasons non-Christians will readily acknowledge—to worry about these patterns, and Christian churches have full rights to those reasons, and should use them in their public speech. But beyond this litany of secular complaint, the churches should be concerned about how this situation makes more difficult their obligation to be the site in which Christians inhabit and manifest the grace of God in their lives. For these social patterns feed the worst parts of ourselves and contribute to a deep crippling of both discipleship and the churches' witness to serve their whole communities.

Consider the ways in which this setting hampers the cultivation of Christian faith in America. First of all, most Americans are simply *blind* to this rising inequality, and this blindness is itself morally culpable, and destructive of the truthful vision Christians are called to develop. Second, even as we fail to see what our world is truly like, our experience of its local manifestations encourages everyone to cultivate a zero-sum, "winner-take-all" mentality. Rising inequality damages the social compact by communicating a powerful message that we do not share a commonwealth, but instead inhabit a world of "everyone for himself," so that professing generosity, mercy, or grace, becomes a sucker's bet. Third, and as the inverse of this zero-sum mentality, we become blind to how we are always already in a position of indebtedness to others; the tone of "works righteousness" suffusing much American politi- cal speech, encourages a dangerous level of self-ignorance which corrodes our capacity for gratitude, and our concomitant ability to care for one another. Fourth and finally, all this is compounded by, and recursively works upon, other aspects of our social order, reinforcing a racism and xenophobia that are both civically acidic and morally and spiritually pernicious. It contributes to a fracturing of the people of God into different shards, shattering the Body of Christ.

In all these ways, an increasingly unequal society makes us smaller, meaner people. It encourages selfishness, narcissism, suspicion, hostility, and racial animus, and discourages generosity, sympathy, care for the neighbor, and affirmation of our common humanity and shared destiny. It subtly undermines the common good, politically, morally, psychologically, and spiritually. It concocts a toxic brew of forces that militate against the Gospel's preaching *within* the church, let alone outside of it.

This is the pathological context facing any American church that seeks to inculcate in its members a richly sacramental vision of creation, and that urges us to see ourselves and our neighbors not as heroic individualists but as mutually vulnerable and commonly dependent children of God, sharing the loving Lord's care and nurture. This context damages the churches' core evangelical practices, and hinders the churches' confession of sin, of our common weakness and need of God, and our need of one another's love and mutual support, within and without the churches. It dims Christians' vision of the world as charged with the grandeur and glory of God, which would provoke in us wondrous gratitude; it stops up our ears against the world's groaning in the labor pains of bearing a new world of redemption, which would induce in us a joyful eagerness to seek the kingdom; and it hampers us from developing a sacramental vision that would work for a new and wondrous world that is always already coming into being in our midst.

Participating in Christian community is no easy task in good times. In the United States today, it cannot be done without confronting the powers and principalities that effectively order the American social compact.[13] The churches must teach their congregants, and preach to the wider society, that ours is not a zero-sum world; we are all vulnerable and dependent, and in our politics we do share a complicated and quasi-sacramental community. For their own purposes, that is, the churches must teach a social gospel.

Criminal Justice

In turning from inequality to criminal justice, we turn from a focus on "the good" to a focus on "the right," from questions of the common good to simple justice—criminal justice most immediately, but the possibility of justice more broadly. If the challenge of the common good challenges the metaphysics, as it were, of "we the people"—of whether we *are* truly a we—this issue challenges the meta-ethics of our society—that is, whether we believe that there is justice, or ethics, at work in public life at all. As mentioned earlier, this is both a secular problem, and a set of challenges to proper discipleship and evangelization; and in the US context in particular, it manifests in a certain racialization of justice in the American polity.

The facts about American criminal justice are grim. Of course, despite the declensionist tone of some recent analyses of the criminal justice system, there never was a "golden age" of real justice in the United States. It has always been heavily punitive and terribly racially disproportionate. But the past few decades have seen an increasingly punitive turn in criminal justice, along with an ever-franker movement toward social control and a rejection of the idea of rehabilitation or reintegration after punishment. Incarcerated and paroled (but still policed) populations have skyrocketed, while civic concern for policing and punishment has given way to neoliberal economic logics of corporate prisons and low-cost, increasingly militarized policing solutions. And all this has happened in the midst of a huge *decline* in actual crime rates. From 1993 to 2012, the violent crime rate across the United States dropped by 48 percent. The last time violent crime was at the levels it is at today was 1963. Still, poll after poll shows Americans believe crime continues to rise.[14]

This situation has several interlocking features. First of all, there has been a problematic *bureaucratization* of justice. Since the 1960s there has been what William Stuntz calls a procedural "rights revolution" in American law, which has led to a *procedural* revolution in criminal justice: The system is designed not primarily to deliver justice, but to produce convicts like widgets, which is why 95 percent of all criminal cases never make it to court, but are resolved by plea deals between prosecutors and defense attorneys. Second, there has been a public *distanciation* from the justice system. Most people today are farther away from the criminal justice system, and criminality itself, than they once were. There is a large divide in who makes and enforces law, and who gets punished by it: The "justice" being delivered is enforced by police, and juries, who themselves live far away from the site of policing. Furthermore, this distancing from criminality is also true in a deeper way, for the moral anthropology of modern liberalism seduces us into a too-optimistic and simplistic vision of the human being, which has as its inverse the stigmatization and alienation of human misbehavior. Scholars from Norbert Elias through Michel Foucault to Karen Halttunen have pointed out that we increasingly fail to see any continuity between ourselves and criminals; "they" are monsters, we think, or they are sick; but either way, surely they are not in any significant continuity with us.[15] Third, the politics of crime in the United States in recent decades has become pathological. In no other context or sphere of American public life does a more immediately ethical language appear so apparently naturally than it does in speech about crime and what we continue to call, in inexcusable ignorance, the "criminal justice system." If the language of "justice" is heard in American public discourse, particularly on the lips of politicians, it is almost inevitably about punishment; and justice seems, in these moments, to be rather securely tethered to the *severity* of punishment proposed, as if the wisest Solomon were in fact the most ferocious Torquemada. No politician will risk looking "soft" by appealing for a more humane, let alone a more merciful, criminal justice system.

All this encourages citizens toward ignorance and cynicism. We protect ourselves from the knowledge of what we do to our neighbors in the name of "criminal justice" by willfully ignoring our responsibility for it; and insofar as we cannot avoid knowing it, we smother that knowledge with a self-protective cynicism which in turn corrodes whatever vestiges of hope we have for a truly decent justice system, or justice at all in this world. Hence this ignorance and cynicism undermines people's faith not just in law, but also in the idea of justice itself, encouraging us to cultivate a moral and political nihilism.

Given all this, what should the churches do? Again, as was the case with increasing economic inequality, the churches can and should make all the aforementioned points as part of their public witness. But Christians have a richer sense of their own vocation than prophetic denunciation. Churches should teach their members, and all others who have ears to hear, a more immanent, and more intimate, acquaintance with the system of public justice in the civil community. First, Christians should *confess* their responsibility for this situation, and to do this they must learn what they are responsible *for*. Christians should come to know for themselves, and help their fellow citizens see, what our criminal justice system is like. They should learn what prisons are like, and how police operate, and how the criminal justice system administers (or fails to administer) justice, and how all this relates to the ongoing reality of crime in our society. They may well be mobilized by this knowledge to agitate for prison reform, a cause that might bring together more liberal and conservative members of the churches. This kind of reformative action is not just a matter of righting a particular wrong, but also of *acknowledging responsibility*, of acknowledging our own political implication in the injustices of the justice system, and thereby of reminding ourselves of our own duties as citizens, and neighbors. It is a proper response to Jesus' call to recognize his face in the face of the victim and the weak, and even the criminal, as when Matthew quotes him as saying, "'Truly I tell you, whatever you did for one of the least of these brothers and sisters of mine, you did for me'" (Mt. 25:40).

Second, they must see—and also exhibit to the rest of society—what *criminals* are like. Criminality is human, not monstrous. They must, that is, recognize the humanity of murderers, rapists, and thieves. This will help all of us not simply to expand our own moral imaginations to include our criminal fellow humans; it will also improve our own moral self-understanding, making us see the point of the confession of sin as a practical and moral undertaking.

Third, the churches should teach their members to demand that criminal justice be just that—justice. In our courts, it should be justice that is sought, not procedural rationality. Bureaucratization and proceduralism have not been good allies of justice. Christians must demand real trials, not plea bargains.

Christians are afraid of justice; so is every human, in some way. That is understandable, but we cannot, as a society, avoid the duty of judgment. It is important that justice must ultimately be sought, not proper procedures. Christians must remind us that we cannot avoid our duties, even as citizens, to seek justice, and in doing that, they teach us an important political lesson. I turn to that next.

Conclusion: Generosity, Mercy, and the Liberal State

Through the cultivation of justice, whether criminal justice or the justice of the broader social order, a further possibility appears: the possibility of generosity or mercy, of something that goes beyond the minimum of justice. These realities are not the unique gift of the Christian churches, but reminding the polity of these possibilities is one of the churches' specific vocations in the larger social order. This applies both to economic and criminal justice, but I will take the latter as an example here.

Christians can use the frank reminder of the ultimately moral telos of our legal codes (however far off we judge that telos to be) to be a further reminder of the possibility, beyond justice, of *mercy*, both for social and evangelical power, as a message about the cosmos. We know that mercy is ontologically available for all of us, though it must be articulated in multiple diverse registers. Sheer justice and procedural politics are, thankfully, not all there is. The use of mercy is, on theological grounds, a sacramental reality: it speaks of, and participates in, realities with no native home in a worldview of sheer quid-pro-quo egalitarian justice, and it appears there both to affirm the moral energies that make us seek such justice and to graciously relativize whatever justice we manage to achieve.

This is especially important in the liberal sociopolitical orders that we all inhabit today.[16] The liberal state is all about de-theologizing, disenchanting the human sphere, or at least the explicitly political mechanisms within human society. But justice is inescapably, even if covertly, theological—that is to say, about enchantment, about a metaphysical reality. For example, the criminal justice system has an ineliminably ritualistic aspect, as regard its *visibly* meting out justice for crime through a broadly public judicial process. As Stuntz put it, "legal condemnation is a necessary but terrible thing";[17] the aroma of the apocalypse hangs about the judge as she goes about her daily work. Political and legal theorists sometimes try to capture this ritualistic dimension in a sheerly immanentist language of "legitimacy," but it seems to me that in this aspect of human political reality, more than any other, we feel the faint brush of ultimate matters. Human politics must of necessity court ultimacy, though in a liberal political era such as our own, political institutions, and the humans who enflesh them, often cannot easily be brought to acknowledge this fact, much less think through how that necessary courting ought to inform our understanding of politics and shape our inhabitation of it.[18]

This use of mercy teaches us about the limits of the polity, and politics, as well. It reminds us that full and absolute justice is not available in this dispensation, that justice is not properly speaking ours. This insight is one that Barth himself would endorse; indeed it seems of a piece with what Alexander Massmann, in his piece in this volume, calls Barth's "desecularization," and even "sacralization," of justice, and Barth's recognition that, in Christ, God has revealed God's justice to be restorative rather than retributive. But also, interestingly enough, the liberal state is itself in part built on just this insight, on the recognition that final justice is not a proper political ambition. One achievement of the liberal secular state is the centuries-long (and still continuing) distinction between the theo-ethical horizon and the secular political one; a second achievement, less frequently understood and less reliably enacted, is the recognition of our continued need to remind the secular state, and its more enthusiastic devotees, of that distinction. Law's asymptotic ambition may be to achieve a one-to-one relation between civic justice and morality, but liberal *and* Christian political thought should both insist that we should not allow that longing free rein in mobilizing and informing our legislative energies. Christians have a ground, a *theological* ground, for affirming this tension, during the world, and reminding the whole polity, Christians and non-Christians alike, of this fact; and in so doing they are simultaneously being civic *and* evangelical, in the best tradition of both Barth and the Social Gospel.

The challenges the churches face in the United States today are part of a larger challenge: to help the nation achieve something like a genuine community amid conditions of quite radical pluralism. The United States has never done this very well, but the depth of pluralism it faces now is both a crisis and an opportunity, neither of which has been fully realized. The churches in America can see the opportunities made available to them in this context, both in discipleship and in witness, as incredibly exciting. One can imagine such a project revitalizing the churches themselves, not least through a rejuvenated Social Gospel of the sort that could participate in the great social, political, and cultural tumult of a rapidly changing social order. Yet it is not without new difficulties, and I turn to them next.

WHY IS RENEWING THE SOCIAL GOSPEL SO DIFFICULT?

So the social logic, and the *theo*-social logic, of the Christian churches in modernity, after Christendom, is well-nigh inescapably marked by the presumptions first laid out in Rauschenbusch's era. Yet despite this fact, we still must recognize that putting this vision in play in America today is a major challenge. This is so especially for three reasons in particular, which I want to signify by the date 9/11, and the years 1968 and 1989.

The rise in American public consciousness of the specter of "radical Islam" since 9/11 raises challenges for anyone who wants religion in politics. (I do not mean the issue of genuine Muslims in American life, but rather the mythic figure of "radical Islam" in America today.) The ugly xenophobia and racism that are always available in American public life have conspired, in the creation of this figure, to produce potentially long-term changes to the acceptability of religious discourse, and religious actors, in American public life. Consider the basic cultural backdrop for any discussion of religion and politics in the United States today. The United States is certainly an idiosyncratic context for religion and politics, historically as well as today. But the changes represented by "9/11" do mark, I think, a rather epochal shift in American public culture, one very much still unfolding today. Consider that not long ago, the United States had as its explicit enemy the global forces of "godless communism." The godlessness of this enemy lured Americans to affirm themselves as godly—more godly, in fact, in their public culture, than they ever had been before. (Thus the motto "in God we trust" was added to the currency, and the phrase "under God" to the Pledge of Allegiance, only in the 1950s.) After 9/11, however, the central imagined enemy is no longer godless, but all too godly. Thus for the first time since H. L. Mencknen in the 1920s, we see "freethinkers" and atheists emerging as major public intellectuals precisely *as* freethinkers and atheists (thus the "New Atheists"). And it is not just fringe public intellectuals; political scientists Robert Putnam and David Campbell have identified "millennials" as the generation most skeptical of religion, most hostile to religion in politics, and not accidentally the generation most likely to associate religion with reactionary politics because of the effect of the weaponization of religion by the Right over the past few decades.[19] So, American public discourse is more ambivalent about religious actors now than it has been for a long time. This is the context in which new religious interventions must operate, and it will create fresh and complicated pressures which they will have to withstand.

The collapse of communism after 1989 is another dimension of our challenge; for this collapse effectively left global capitalism without any radical opponents, which in turn led to a pretty open field for rampant neoliberal materialism over the past couple decades. It is no surprise that this era saw the rise—heavily subsidized financially—of libertarianism as a semi-respectable political worldview (especially for young people). That is to say, both directly as a matter of economic ideology, and indirectly as a broader political ideology of selfishness, we inhabit an age in which appeals to anything like a "common good" or "justice" not immediately couched in a vocabulary of reductionistically econometric free-market reasoning, will be met with looks of incredulity and incomprehension. The collapse of any broad-based social-ist counterimagination to the triumphant economic neoliberalism regnant today—even *after* the most dramatic financial crisis since 1929, and the most devastating economic depression since the 1930s—is not simply a matter of a regrettable narrowing of the range of economic ideologies; it also means that, politically and morally, we hardly know how to articulate the depth of our problems in anything like their actual profundity.

Finally, the year "1968" represents for me the intense ideological backlash since the 1960s against the energies of the Social Gospel, and the structural challenges that any attempt to rehabilitate it will confront. Effectively those structural challenges are two: the weakening of the churches who served as "carriers" of the Social Gospel in the United States in the twentieth century, and the diffusion of their moral energies into a new institutional infrastructure of functionally secular nongovernmental organizations committed to broad-based moral reform since the 1970s.

Important here is David Hollinger's account of the kenotic travails of what he calls "Ecumenical Protestantism" in the twentieth century.[20] "Ecumenical Protestantism" is a better (because more descriptive) name for what we have often called "mainline Protestantism." It is ecumenical, both across denominations and beyond explicit Christian churches; it downplayed its doctrinal distinctiveness in order to seek alliances with other religions, and with nonreligious people and movements, in order to achieve its social aims. Its ecumenical openness was the source of its strategic energy and its stra-tegic danger. As Hollinger shows, it genuinely contributed to a substantial Christianization of the social order, welcoming greater participation of all sorts of people in the American experiment (in particular women, Jews, and African Americans); helping create a more humane environment for work-ers, the aged, the poor, and children in society; and working to keep America (after World War II) involved in the world. However, Hollinger argues, while Ecumenical Protestantism gained so much of the world, it also lost a great deal of its soul. Today, he argues, in terms of members and moral energy, the churches are husks of their former selves, while since the 1960s the energies of moral reform have become untethered from the churches. This is a real problem, though not a recently discovered one; as I noted earlier, this was also Niebuhr's critique of Rauschenbusch, and Hauerwas' critique of Niebuhr. While the past century has been helpful in thinking about the churches' vocation of social concern, it has come at some cost to that more fundamental vocation, of training its members to become fit for the weight of glory that is our eschatological destiny as citizens of the kingdom of heaven. Can the Social Gospel participate in this broader Christian pedagogy of discipleship?

If the work of thinkers like Charles Taylor and Didier Fassin is correct, we live in an age of astounding "moral revolution," rhetorically and institutionally.[21] And this "secular age" is curiously moralized in part because of the waves of Christianization that buffeted it for centuries. In the local US context, this means that there is a lively public culture of moral reform into which the churches must now operate. If the churches wish to revitalize this part of their mission, they must operate in a new institutional and moral environment where they must articulate their distinct message amid a flurry of rival voices—some sympathetic, some hostile, but all fundamentally different from them, and competing in the same space for public attention. Can the churches learn to speak in this increasingly multiply-moralized space?

CONCLUSION: THE ROLE OF THEOLOGY AND THE CHURCHES IN THIS PLURALISTIC CONVERSATION

A rejuvenated Social Gospel offers one way the churches may be engaged, in two forms. First and foremost, this approach enables the churches to offer an indirect and long-term contribution, to the overall cultural and political climate, through their practices of discipleship and evangelization: by institutionally shaping those whose practices, habits, consciences, and worldviews are formed in substantial part by the ecclesial structures that theology seeks to inform. The social and political thinkers, law professors, criminologists, and lawyers who work on these matters are in some important and necessary ways more immediate pragmatists, interested in working within the system, trying to figure out how to make it work better. Churches do not really work at such short ranges; we aim, or should aim, to have an impact decades in the future. And in the US context, we have failed, over the past forty years, to grapple with several of the largest social changes in American society.

The fact that this is a long-term project should not lead us to discount its importance. It is and must be the primary mode in which the Christian churches influence public debate: not by the immediate introduction or imposition of theological categories or frameworks on such debate, but rather by the slow and steady shaping of minds in the churches and schools and other fora where the theological voice has its primary—not its native, nor its exclusive, just its primary—home. This is historically how Christianity has primarily influenced the social imaginary: working to change the terms in which we think about our world is a deeper transformative power than pumping for one position or another within those terms.[22]

The churches also contribute more directly to public discourse by bringing into view new or hitherto obscure aspects of an issue. For example, theology has sometimes encouraged new conceptions of the person's relationship to the political community and their religious-spiritual community, as in the case of Augustine's revision of Roman patriotism in terms of Christian citizenship or Luther's reconceptualization of Christian conscience. Similarly, the churches may have practical and institutional idiosyncrasies that allow them to interact gratingly but usefully with the social order, obstructing in creative ways the smooth functioning of a system designed without full concern for justice. Perhaps Christian theology can identify certain epistemological perplexities, psychological conundrums, or sociopolitical problems that confront humans in certain contexts; perhaps theology's special idiom gives it conceptual capacities or psychological insight that allows it to do this when other approaches fail.

In these projects, a serious and sustained engagement with Barth's theo-politics may be beneficial, for both Barthian political theology and my recommended renewed Social Gospel. In Barth's work, the Social Gospel tradition will find a powerful theological interpretive lens that can simultaneously orient, energize, and regulate the churches' proclamation, both in the public square and in the churches' sanctuaries. As David Haddorf points out in his piece in this volume, Barth provides an account of God's saving action in which political activity is organic to the life of faith.[23] For Barth, the Gospel is as politically as it is "spiritually" liberatory: the freedom God delivers to humans is as much a *political* freedom as a spiritual one. For Barth humans are not essentially Lockean liberals (or worse, Hobbesians) who only secondarily and contingently coordinate their self-possessed alterities via political associations; they are social and "political" creatures all the way down. Thus Barth taught that election must be thought of as of the *community* first, and the individual only secondarily. Furthermore, the content of the gospel itself commands politics: as he famously puts it, the "command" that the redeemed hear *as* the redeemed is precisely not a determinate command to a particular action, but rather a command of permission, a "thou mayest" not a "thou must." As such, the command enables humans to freely inhabit the world that God gives us, in order properly to shape it according to the Gospel promise that in Christ God has reconciled the world to Godself—a world which very much includes the political order in which we seem increasingly to live, move, and have our being. Barth provides regulatory and self-critical resources for this endeavor as well, for this liberation is not an antinomianism; the perichoretically formed command of God orders humanity to realize fellowship between God and humans, unleashes freedom for humans from sin, and makes us capable of responsibility in the Spirit, before God—so that manifestations of this freedom will always be judged within the community that the Spirit enacts.

On the other hand, other aspects of Barth's theo-politics can be usefully challenged in this exchange, as well. A more Niebuhrian and Augustinian theologian might ask two questions in particular of Barth's work. First of all, Barth can sometimes court a perhaps too-simple and idealistic condemnation of the excesses of liberal individualism; for example, his idea that, as Haddorf puts it, "a false view of election leads to hegemonic forms of antidemocratic totalitarianism" assumes a far too-simple and idealistic vision of how thought shapes human life, and draws too tight a line between "bad" theology and all the parts of our world we might not like. Second, Barth's critique of free-standing individualism is perhaps too one-sided, and does not articulate how God might have used and continue to use the hyperbolic formulations of this individualism to teach Christians themselves the value of liberation and freedom—lessons that, Christians should forthrightly confess, found their most powerful formulations in the modern world quite often *outside* of the churches; furthermore, it fails to see how some of those hyperboles them-selves flow from earlier Christian formulations of individualism and emotiv-ism (as in forms of Pietism). Barth's critique of Western individualism, in Haddorf's account, recognizes no ironic providential reading of the history of Western thought, and sits too snugly within polemical polarizations such as the church versus "liberal individualism." In both these ways, a too-defensive response blinds itself to how Christian thought is historically implicated in evils both directly related to modernity (such as modern hyperbolic notions of freedom and individuality, against which Barth liked to inveigh), *and* to the way that Christian traditions have too often sided with reactionary and anti-liberationist forces in the history of Western civilization (which is why the Social Gospel tradition is so unusual in Christian thought), seduces us into thinking that our (self-proclaimed) theological rectitude passes easily into historical self-righteousness, and insulates us from hearing uncomfortable critiques that strike at things we judge essential.

At the same time, a more Augustinian perspective might judge this-worldly political structures as far more essentially fallen features of our political long-ings than Barth may suggest. On such Augustinian accounts, the state is an essentially and inescapably ambivalent witness to the Kingdom of God in ways Barth does not allow, and so he may not be as revolutionary as some suggest. Barth's view does not, it seems, theologically historicize the shape of "politics" itself as a human activity that may be itself misshapen after the fall. Barth may be trapped in a fallen and bourgeois imagination of politics, one more comfortable with the idea of distinct natural sphere of politics than is Augustine. For the latter, politics is never simply itself; it always longs to be the Kingdom of God, and so must be seen as part of the fallen order which God's redeeming activity will radically transfigure, so that what we call "politics" will be seen as an abortive malformation of our basic doxological orientation for the praising of God. There is no natural, pre-lapsarian form of the thing we call politics; it is a perversion of our doxologically oriented nature; it always courts idolatry. Hence Augustinians urge a more fugitive relationship between the churches and the political forms in which they find themselves, whether they are an *imperium* (as in Augustine's time) or a state (as in the modern world). For them Barth does not fundamentally confront the (at best) dialectical nature of politics' witness to God. (Interestingly, this may be why a certain kind of "Barthian Thomism" has emerged in recent years in the Anglophone world—Barth may be more sympathetic to a Thomist construal than an Augustinian eschatological account.[24]) But however this tension gets engaged and managed, it is clear that a collaboration between Barth's political-theological intuitions and the particular conditions eliciting a renewed Social Gospel in the United States may well bear much fruit.

A renewed Social Gospel will thus speak of matters traditionally of concern, but seek out how to root those concerns more thoroughly in the church's vocational context of spiritual pedagogy. As the core of this pedagogy, the churches should teach parishioners to *see the social world aright*, to give them a good "sociological imagination," and then to show them how to act, how to respond appropriately to the situation properly perceived. They will thus care about the social order both in itself—for its current situation may be so scandalous as to make our efforts at proper worship of God hypocritical and thus offensive to the Lord—and also as a foreshadowing of the kingdom: a potential icon, if you will, of the coming Kingdom. So preached, the Social Gospel can continue to have diagnostic bite, prescriptive promise, and pedagogical and disciplining power, in our churches today, as well as being a word badly needed in our societies as a whole.

NOTES

1. Many thanks to Markus Höfner, Paul Jones, Evan Sandsmark, Heike Springhart, Kris Norris, and the whole group of scholars who gathered at Bochum to discuss our papers. For its faults I have only myself to thank.

2. I note especially connections between this chapter and that of Paul Jones on this point.

3. Gary Dorrien, *Soul in Society: The Making and Renewal of Social Christianity* (Minneapolis: Augsburg Fortress Press, 1995).

4. On p. 104 in "Jesus and the Movement for Social Justice," pp. 98–113 in *Karl Barth: Theologian of Freedom*, ed. Clifford Green (Minneapolis: Augsburg Fortress, 1991). For more, see also George Hunsinger, ed., *Karl Barth and Radical Politics* (Philadelphia: Westminster Press, 1976).

5. This kind of theological and ethical reflection emerged in complicated dialectical conversation with the emergence of the academic discipline of sociology, not as part of a professionalization moment in philosophy.

6. This partly explains the connection between Social Gospel and the language of "crisis" which it first popularized.

7. Cf. Markus Höfner, "Neither Self-Evident Frame nor Self-Enclosed Sect: The Christian Church in Barth's Political Ecclesiology," in this volume.

8. *Das Evangelium in der Gegenwart*, pp. 33–34, found on p. 168 of Eberhard Busch, *The Great Passion: An Introduction to Karl Barth's Theology* (Grand Rapids, MI: William B. Eerdmans, 2004).

9. This understanding of mission is like Barth's account of the church's "gathering," "upbuilding," and "sending" by the Spirit in *Church Dogmatics*. See *Church Dogmatics* IV/1 §62, IV/2 §67, and IV/3.2 §72 (Edinburgh: T&T Clark, 1961, 1962).

10. Martin Luther King, Jr., *Why We Can't Wait* (New York: Signet Classic, 2000), p. 80.

11. See Martin Gilens, *Affluence and Influence: Economic Inequality and Political Power in America* (Princeton: Princeton University Press, 2014), Robert Frank, *Falling Behind: How Rising Inequality Harms the Middle Class* (Berkeley: University of California Press, 2013), and Joseph Stiglitz, *The Price of Inequality: How Today's Divided Society Endangers Our Future* (New York: W.W. Norton, 2012). For more on all this see my "A Social Gospel for the Twenty-First Century," pp. 14–35 in *Virginia Theological Seminary Journal* (Summer 2015).

12. Richard Wilkinson and Kate Pickett, *The Spirit Level: Why Equality is Better for Everyone* (New York: Penguin, 2010).

13. The term "powers and principalities" admits of several different construals; I follow Paul Dafydd Jones' analysis of Barth's theological account of the "Powers" (in §78), especially how the revolt *against* the Lordless powers is always also a positive gracious working *for* the Kingdom.

14. See http://www.prisonpolicy.org/graphs/incarceration1925-2008.html. See also Ernest Drucker, *A Plague of Prisons: The Epidemiology of Mass Incarceration in America* (New York: New Press, 2011), Vesla M. Weaver and Amy E. Lerman, "Political Consequences of the Carceral State," pp. 817–833 in *American Political Science Review* 104, no. 4 (November 2010), Michelle Alexander, *The New Jim Crow: Mass Incarceration in the Age of Colorblindness* (New York: The New Press, 2010), and William Stuntz, *The Collapse of American Criminal Justice* (Cambridge MA: Harvard University Press, 2011).

15. See Karen Halttunen, *Murder Most Foul: The Killer and the American Gothic Imagination* (Cambridge, MA: Harvard University Press, 2000).

16. My understanding of liberalism may be surprisingly un-demonizing to some readers, including some Barthians. For more on what I take liberalism to be, see my "Augustinian Christian Republican Citizenship," pp. 218–249 in Michael Jon Kessler, *Political Theology for a Plural Age* (New York: Oxford University Press, 2013).

17. William Stuntz, *The Collapse of American Criminal Justice*, p. 311.

18. See Bonnie Honig, *Emergency Politics: Paradox, Law, Democracy* (Princeton: Princeton University Press, 2009).

19. Robert Putnam and David Campbell, *American Grace: How Religion Divides and Unites Us* (New York: Simon and Schuster, 2010); see also Douglas Laycock,

"Religious Liberty and the Culture Wars," pp. 839–880 in *University of Illinois Law Review* 2014, no. 3 (2014).

20. David Hollinger, *After Cloven Tongues of Fire: Protestant Liberalism in Modern American History* (Princeton: Princeton University Press, 2013).

21. See Charles Taylor, *A Secular Age* (Cambridge, MA: Harvard University Press, 2007), Didier Fassin, *Humanitarian Reason: A Moral History of the Present* (Berkeley: University of California Press, 2012).

22. For historical studies of several of these episodes, see Kate Cooper, *The Fall of the Roman Household* (Cambridge University Press, 2011), and Peter Brown, *Through the Eye of a Needle: Wealth, the Fall of Rome, and the Making of Christianity in the West, 350–550 AD* (Princeton: Princeton University Press, 2012).

23. See David Haddorf, "American Democracy and Trinitarian Sovereignty: Lessons from Barth and Tocqueville," in this volume.

24. Those who have spoken of the idea of a "Barthian Thomism" include Nigel Biggar and Eric Gregory, but they have fellow travelers among a number of scholars, from Eugene Rogers through Jennifer Herdt.

Chapter 25

Civil Societies and Biblical Value Systems in the West

Michael Welker

The towering theologians in the 1930s and 1940s in Germany were, at least from our perspective today, Karl Barth (1886–1968) and Dietrich Bonhoeffer (1906–1945). For both great theologians the strong concentration on God's revelation in Jesus Christ is formative.[1] A strong Christological orientation of faith is directed against aggressive nationalism, political ideology, and the glorification of racist hegemony and war, against tyrannical suppression and persecution of countless fellow human beings. The Barmen Declaration and its strong political emanations stand for this exemplary move in "theo-politics"—if one wants to use this term for political resistance in the name of the living God and the resurrected Christ. Are there any theo-political challenges at the beginning of the twenty-first century that require moving beyond these central theological positions and the figures of thought and orientation connected with them?

The twentieth century brought a growing ecumenical consciousness to the Christian churches, a differentiated sensitivity to liberation theologies and the striving for social justice and protection of human dignity, and finally strong ecological concerns, locally and globally. It generated a continuously intensified search for a pneumatological grounding of Christian theology[2] and sensitivity to global developmental processes and global interdependencies. The last decades brought nothing less than a revolutionary development in the digital exploration of the world and in highly accelerated and intensified global communication. All these developments have strong repercussions on moral moods and also on many forms of human faith and piety.

We do not only face, like Barth and Bonhoeffer, dominant and dangerous ideological powers, centralized political forces with enormous impacts of brutality, endangerment, and suppression. We do not only have to ask with both of them for more convincing spiritual orientations than a subjectivist faith or a theism of "absolute dependence" could offer. We are also aware that dualized and dualizing forms of theological and political orientations seem to be too weak to grasp and represent our contemporary political, religious, and moral situation.

Today, we see ourselves surrounded by a very dense network of constant media signals from all over the world, witnessing countless contexts of violence and terror, suffering and distress; the constant self-alarming of the global community surrounds us in many voices. For many people, this situation brings into question any belief in and talk of faith in a mighty and merciful God. Bonhoeffer's message in his famous letters from prison was: "only the suffering God can help!" Following the philosopher Martin Heidegger, Jürgen Moltmann spoke of the "crucified God." But how can the suffering and crucified God help in a world full of violence and unequal distribution of suffering and pain among human beings?

It belongs to the great challenges at the beginning of the twenty-first century to recognize the saving and ennobling power of God at work in the Holy Spirit and in the inconspicuous reign of Christ. At the same time, we have to see that the powers of the cosmos and of nature are not salvific. The creation, called "good" in the first chapter of the Bible, is indeed TOB, life-furthering, but it is not paradise, and it is not divine. Earthly life is not salvific—it lives at the expense of other life and at the same time it is frail and finite. The mathematician and philosopher Alfred North Whitehead was right in stating: "life is robbery."[3] Nature shows an abundance of order and beauty, but it is also full of powers of self-endangerment and self-destruction. And human beings can use the freedom and capacities given to them to intensify and accelerate these powers of self-destruction and self-endangerment in irresponsible and deeply frightening ways. The biblical traditions call this abuse sin.

If we do not want to encourage illusionary or cynical attitudes toward this real constitution of nature and world, we have to strive for an honest creation theology and faith, and we have to focus on the powers of God, which does not transport us into a dream world, but wants to orient, sustain, save, and ennoble us in a world of frailty, finitude, endangerment, and self-endangerment under the power of sin.

At the same time, we should focus on real societal, social, cultural, and political conditions in our environments if we do not want to deal with illusions of "theo-politics" and all sorts of moral wishful thinking. In the following, we will therefore start with a concentration on forms of societal organization in the Western world, called "civil society." A sketch follows of some basic features of civil society in Germany and its connection to religious and ecclesial impulses in social and societal life. We will finally ask for formative symbolisms and normative configurations in biblical and Christian faith traditions, which have and still shape civil societal motivations, calling for action.

WHAT IS CIVIL SOCIETY?

It is not easy to define the contours and texture of so-called civil societies. Since they are also often called the "third sector," it might be tempting to approach them with the so-called three-sector theory. The economic three-sector hypothesis has been developed by the British and Australian economist Colin Clark and the French economist Jean Fourastié.[4] It says that in societies with low per capita income the primary sector deals with the extraction of raw materials and has 70 percent of the workforce. The secondary sector with 20 percent of the workforce deals with manufacturing, and the tertiary sector with 10 percent of the workforce deals with services. Countries in a more advanced phase of development with a median national income shift to a ratio of 40 percent primary, 40 percent secondary, and 20 percent tertiary sector. In countries with a high national income, the sector of services dominates the output of the economy. With only 10 percent of the workforce in the primary sector, 20 percent manufacturing, and 70 percent of services, we see a reversal of the ratios.

It is very likely that the transformation of a society into one dominated by the services workforce is favorable for the emergence and development of a civil society. Therefore, the three-sector theory should not be ignored in reflections on the emergence of civil societies. The term "third sector," however, indicates here the differentiation of this sector of public life from the state and from the market. In addition, it is differentiated from the family, which is particularly important to take into account when the family is very large, rich and influential, functioning as a social network.

A civil society operates in a multitude of associations in which people come together and cooperate voluntarily, as a rule unpaid and without interests in economic profit and achievement of public careers (thus the difference from the market and politics). Although some civil societal associations follow local or regional interests, the active respect or rather the promotion of central societal values and the "common good" should be visible. An association under the motto "Get rid of foreigners!" cannot claim to be a civil societal association; neither can a group of friends that builds swimming pools for each other. I would even argue that bowling, stamp-collecting, and canary bird-breeding clubs should not be called civil societal associations. The mere differentiation from state and market and the "advancement of shared interests"[5] are not enough.

On the other hand, the civil society should not only be associated with the so-called "new social movements" that have gained enormous national and international visibility since the 1970s and are very often connected with political protest: the associations and movements for human rights, for equality, the rights of women, minority rights, against racism, the environmental movements and groups, again local and global, and the movements for the protection of animals gain a clear visibility and clear contrast over against injustice and careless politics and ecologically brutal economic interests. But the concerns of the civil societies go beyond those conventionally considered to revolve around human rights, social justice, and development of a concept of improving people's lives.

It is therefore quite clear that organized activities concerning nonprofit sports, nonprofit activities to improve fellow citizens' health and education, and nonprofit work for schools and kindergartens fall in the realm of civil society activities. Nonprofit work for the conservation of the arts and architectural treasures, for the development and presentation of musical skills, unpaid work in public libraries and museums—all this belongs to the spectrum of civil societal engagements. A whole cluster of values emerges as guiding all these activities: a mutual respect and the banning of coercive force against fellow human beings, affirmation of the state of law, respect for human rights and for the rights of freedom, public openness to the activities and rules of democratic participation, this search for justice and truth and the engagement for an open society that accepts a plurality of interests and tolerance for different styles of life, worldviews, and traditions of faith.

CIVIL SOCIETY AND RELIGION IN GERMANY AT THE BEGINNING OF THE THIRD MILLENNIUM AS A CONCRETE MODEL AND EXAMPLE

To a great extent German civil society is organized in associations and unions called "*Vereine*." About 600,000 registered *Vereine* exist in Germany today, six times more than fifty years ago. In addition, the country has 16,000 foundations, many of them with capital below 500,000 EUR. About one-third of the population is seen to be active in all sorts of engagement in civil society. With these figures Germany holds a middle rank compared to other European countries.

Ranked in terms of the quantity of participating members, the key areas seem to be:

• sports and social activities
• health and healthcare

- church and religion
- culture, music, and education
- engagement for the elderly
- engagement for children and youth
- political, environmental, and social interest groups
- local civic engagements, fire departments and emergency services, and so on

In terms of political and media influences as well as international interconnectedness, the ranking, of course, looks very different. A few searches on the internet can provide a strong impression of the many German civil societal associations, globally connected, active in human-rights issues, anti-discrimination and equality concerns, working for ecological issues and the protection of specific environments. The German union for the protection of animals, to give just one example, has 750 local unions with 500 homes for animals and has more than 800,000 members.

The third largest area of civil societal engagement in Germany comprises churches and religious communities. This is partly due to the presence of six welfare associations (*Wohlfahrtsverbände*), five of which are very large, one Protestant and one Roman Catholic; only the Association of the Jews is a small one. The Roman Catholic *Caritas* has 560,000 employees and an equal number of volunteer workers, and it covers an enormous number of social societal activities. Of a similar size is the Protestant *Diakonie* with 450,000 employees and 700,000 voluntary and unpaid coworkers involved. The large secular welfare associations are also most impressive as civil societal powers. They have half a million employees altogether and many, many volunteers: The German Red Cross, Arbeiterwohlfahrt and Paritätischer Wohlfahrtsverband, with many big associations such as the German AIDS Society, German Cancer Society, German Lifesaving Society, German Youth Hostel Organization, German Homes for Children, SOS Children's Villages, Pro Familia, and so on. As can be seen, there are loose boundaries between civil societal organizations and the organizations of the large welfare associations with employed and paid members, partly supported by state funds and tax privileges.

The strong connection of ecclesial and diaconal organizations is not only quantitatively most impressive, but is also an important breeding ground for civil societal value systems and forms of organization. Even about twenty years ago, the Princeton sociologist Robert Wuthnow stated "that the role of religion has been a central aspect of the civil-society debate, if for no other reason than the fact that churches, synagogues, and other places of worship have played a vital role in efforts to rebuild and maintain voluntary bases of self-government."[6] "In Russia, for example, new converts to the Orthodox

Church have been struggling to rebuild civil society on a parish basis from
the bottom up, and, if the efforts are proving successful, then the statistics
are at least heartening because 30 percent of Russians age 18 to 25 have
become Christians since 1988 and the number of churches in Moscow alone
has quadrupled in this period."[7] Today we hear of an impressive 60 percent
belonging to the Russian Orthodox Church in a formerly oppressively secularized country. But have they built up a civil society? If so, what are the
forms and textures and the political and societal concerns? If not, what distinguishes the development in Russia from emergent civil societies in other
countries?

Wuthnow acknowledges that many religious leaders, in many countries,
"Protestants and Catholic alike, are hopeful that Christianity can be a spiritual and ethical force in the formation of a new civilization that will be more
democratic and economically vibrant."[8] But he also rightly asks whether
genuinely Christian and biblical values promoted the evolution of civil societies as opposed to secular democratic ideals, which we associate more with
philosophers of the Enlightenment. "To insist that Christianity always has a
healthy influence on civil society because it is true or good or humanitarian,
therefore, is to ride roughshod over the difficult terrain of social reality, and
the contemporary debate is no exception."[9]

It is therefore important to identify clear modes of interdependence
between religious value orientation and institutionalized practiced social
action, which is undoubtedly for the individual and common good. The connection of a genuinely Christian and biblical orientation and diaconal work
can provide such an orientation. With respect to institutionalized diaconal
work, it is the connection of justice and mercy as early as in the biblical law
traditions that has been formative for the Occidental ethos.

LAW AND SPIRIT: BIBLICAL VALUE
SYSTEMS AND CIVIL SOCIETY

The connection of justice and mercy already in the biblical law traditions
has become one of the most important impulses in shaping civil societies.
The power of mercy in biblical law is tremendous.[10] I have proposed defining mercy as "the free, creative self-withdrawal in favor of the other or in
favor of others." Many people try to assert that mercy is a natural tendency
in life. This, however, is highly questionable, at least without strong further
qualifications. Natural life lives at the cost and expense of other life. Even if
we are vegetarians we have to destroy an enormous amount of life to sustain
ourselves. Mercy, however, is not just self-limitation in the midst of this
natural tendency of life to sustain itself at the expense of others. Mercy is a

creative, supporting, and freeing activity in favor of the frail, the weak, the poor, and the person in need.

The activity of mercy is essential for family life. No baby, no child could be raised without massive free and creative self-withdrawal in its favor. The solidarity between the generations is expressed in mercy for the sick, the frail, the old and the dying. In family life and close friendships, mercy is often blessed by love and turns into a *joyful* free and creative self-withdrawal in favor of others. The experience of receiving and giving mercy and love and the acknowledgment that we all are in need of mercy at least in specific phases of our life lead to a subtle self-experience. The biblical traditions very often cultivate such a self-experience with dualities. One of the most famous dualities is the double identity of the slave in Egypt and the free person living in the blessed land. The "motive clause" of the Old Testament traditions argues for the practice of mercy with the poor and the stranger "because you know how it feels to be a stranger and because you are grateful to God who has freed you from slavery in Egypt with mighty hand and outstretched arm" (cf. Ex 22:20; 23:9; Lev. 19:34; Deut. 10:19; 23:8; 26:5). Basic human experiences rooted in family life are thus moved into the broad social realm and gain moral, political, even legal and religious importance. The mercy laws in favor of the widows and orphans, the poor and the weak, not only in one's own family, but in one's whole social environment, gain an enormous normative shaping power. The normativity of the law reaches beyond the capacity of conflict solution into the capacity of social transformation. This is particularly clear in the so-called slave laws, which require the freeing of slaves, at least of Hebrew slaves, after six years of slavery (Ex 21:2ff.). The legal routinizing of almsgiving and tithing in favor of the poor and needy points in the same direction. Mercy becomes an instrument for social stabilization and transformation.

The mercy laws not only learn from family ethos but also recursively strengthen this ethos and the radiating power of family life and love. They even strengthen the legal culture and religious symbolisms and practices. With respect to the juridical law, laws of mercy strengthen and challenge its competence. On the one hand, no case can fall outside the purview of the law; no person, however weak, poor and miserable, can fall beyond the reach of the law. On the other hand, the systematic orientation of the law toward compassion demands the continual refinement of the legal culture and its progression toward humanization and universalization.

The mercy code of the law enables us to deal with the strange paradox that plagues all moral and legal evolution. Many human societies have the desire to improve the juridical law and develop their moral matrices. However, how can this be done without destroying the binding force of law and morals, their capacity to provide "security of expectations"? The mercy code of the law allows for transformation without relativization. It allows for the balancing of normative stability and creative innovation.

Mercy laws finally connect the moral and legal attempts to strive for justice and to care for the weak with religious orientation. In the religious perspective on the just and merciful God, the biblical traditions open broad historical horizons. They extend memories and expectations over vast historical time spans. The just and righteous God will deal with human beings in time spans that reach far beyond the imagination of human courts or of individual and communal moral memory.

Again we see a recursive strengthening of the religious imagination and communication. The "fatherly" mercy, the care for justice and love, provides an understanding of the powers of the divine that can deal with the very sobering insight that natural life has to live at the expense of other life, that robbery and death are essential parts of natural existence. Enormous counterforces are discovered and unleashed that shape a diaconal, mutually supportive, and humane culture. Sensitivities for distortions on the one hand (the whole area of sin, trespasses, temptations, and evil) and for moral refinement (the whole area of love, forgiveness, and ennoblement in many forms) are cultivated, can become taught and practiced.

The teaching and practice of justice, mercy, and love can become self-referential; the teaching of teaching, the teaching of healing, the teaching of good legal and religious practices can become essential for the whole society and its culture. The cultivation of memories and expectations becomes part of the value system. Communities seeking truth and justice and salvation are established in institutionalized and in fluid forms.

Another biblical symbol and value system of growing importance for the development of civil societies can be seen in the Spirit narratives and traditions. These narratives and traditions support a contemporary interest in the so-called "plurality and diversity" of social life and organizations. The figure of the "pouring of the spirit" on male and female, old and young, masters and slaves (Joel 2) and on people from different traditions, cultures, and languages (Acts 2), the power of the Spirit to endow people with very different gifts and to establish communities with different "members" for mutual strengthening and support, can offer helpful orientation against monistic, monohierarchical, dualistic political and religious forms of thought and organization.

The biblical insight that these more complicated forms of social organization can be crucial in dealing with normative distortions, with limits of moral, legal, political and religious regulations and steering, can provide an orienting power in shaping pluralistic civil societies without plunging into social chaos and relativism. We do not yet have a long history and routines of praxis in dealing with these more demanding symbolisms and forms of thought. For the benefit of sound civil societies it will be important to rise to the theological, academic, and educational challenges connected with the biblical insights into the power of the Spirit. This Spirit is not just a mental and intellectual phenomenon, but also a normative and freeing energy that constitutes complex interactive social associations that treasure the values of justice and mercy. When Germany, after the horrors of Nazi dictatorship and two World Wars, tried to regain trust and recognition among the peoples, it established itself as a *"Rechtsstaat"* and *"Sozialstaat,"* a state of law and a welfare state. This was a good choice, deeply rooted in the biblical law traditions and their basic normative dynamics.

NOTES

1. Dietrich Bonhoeffer, *Widerstand und Ergebung: Briefe und Aufzeichnungen aus der Haft, Dietrich Bonhoeffer Werke 8* (Gütersloh: Kaiser, 1998); Karl Barth, *Kirchliche Dogmatik*, III / 1–3 (Zurich: TVZ); cf. Michael Welker, *Theologische Profile. Schleiermacher—Barth—Bonhoeffer—Moltmann* (Frankfurt: Hansisches Verlagshaus, 2009).

2. For the German context, see: Jürgen Moltmann, *Der Geist des Lebens: Eine ganzheitliche Pneumatologie* (Gütersloh: Kaiser, 1991, new edition 2010); Michael Welker, *Gottes Geist: Theologie des Heiligen Geistes* (Neukirchen-Vluyn: Neukirchener Verlag, 1993, 6th ed. 2015), for Pentecostal pneumatology: Frank D. Macchia, *Baptized in the Spirit: A Global Pentecostal Theology* (Grand Rapids: Zondervan, 2006); Young-hoon Lee, *The Holy Spirit Movement in Korea: Its Historical and Theological Development* (Oxford: Regnum Books International, 2009); Michael Welker (ed.), *The Work of the Spirit: Pneumatology and Pentecostalism* (Grand Rapids: Eerdmans, 2006).

3. Alfred North Whitehead, *Process and Reality: An Essay in Cosmology, Gifford Lectures 1927–28*, corrected ed. (New York: Free Press, 1978), 105.

4. Jean Fourastié, *Die große Hoffnung des 20. Jahrhunderts* (Cologne: Bund Verlag, 1954).

5. Cf. the programmatic statements of CIVICUS, The World Alliance for Citizen Participation (civicus.org).

6. Robert Wuthnow, *Christianity and Civil Society: The Contemporary Debate* (Valley Forge: Trinity Press International, 1996), 4.

7. Cf. Nathaniel Davis, *A Long Walk to Church: A Contemporary History of Russian Orthodoxy*, 2nd ed. (Boulder: Westview Press, 2003).

8. Wuthnow, *Christianity*, 4.

9. Wuthnow, *Christianity*, 6.

10. Cf. Michael Welker, "The Power of Mercy in Biblical Law," *Journal of Law and Religion* 29, no. 2 (2014): 225–235 (in the following, I refer to some ideas of this text).

Index

About the Editor

Markus Höfner is senior research associate at the Institute for Hermeneutics and Philosophy of Religion, Zürich University, Switzerland. His publications include *Sinn, Symbol, Religion. Theorie des Zeichen und Phänomenologie der Religion bei Ernst Cassirer und Martin Heidegger* [Meaning, Symbol, Religion: Theory of Signs and Phenomenology of Religion in Ernst Cassirer and Martin Heidegger] (2009); *Ewiges Leben. Ende oder Umbau einer Erlösungsreligion?* [Eternal Life: End or Modification of a Religion of Redemption?] (ed. with Günter Thomas, 2018); and *Gottes Gegenwarten* [God's Presences] (ed. with Benedikt Friedrich, 2020).

About the Contributors

Clifford B. Anderson is associate university librarian for research and digital strategy and professor of religious studies at Vanderbilt University, Nashville, Tennessee. His publications include *The Crisis of Theological Science: A Contextual Study of the Development of Karl Barth's Concept of Theology as Science from 1901 to 1923* (dissertation, 2005), *Karl Barth and American Evangelicalism* (ed. with Bruce L. McCormack, 2011), and *Karl Barth and the Making of Evangelical Theology: A Fifty-Year Perspective* (ed. with Bruce L. McCormack, 2015).

Kim-Kwong Chan is a retired ordained minister of the Christian Nationals' Evangelism Commission. His publications include *Protestantism in Contemporary China* (with Alan Hunter, 1993), *Religious Freedom in China: Policy, Administration, and Regulation—A Research Handbook* (with Eric Carlson, 2005), and *Understanding World Christianity: China* (2019).

Chin Kenpa is professor in the Department of Philosophy at Fu Jen Catholic University, Taiwan. His publications include *God, Relation, and Discourse: Critical Theology and the Critique of Theology* (2007, in Chinese), *What Is Sino-Theology?* (2015, in Chinese), *Horizons of the Blind: Deconstruct(ive) ing Theology* (2017, in Chinese), and *Publicity and Revolution: The Radical Theology in China 1910–1950* (2020, in Chinese).

David Haddorff is associate professor of theology and ethics at St. John's University, New York. His published books include *Dependence and Freedom: The Moral Thought of Horace Bushnell* (1994); an extensive monograph: "Karl Barth's Theological Politics" in the reprint of Karl Barth's *Community, State, and Church: Three Essays* (2004*)*; and, most recently, the book *Christian Ethics as Witness: Barth's Ethics for a World at Risk* (2010), where he examines Barth's theological ethics in relation to current ethical issues in politics, economics, and the environment.

Angela Dienhart Hancock is associate professor of homiletics and worship at Pittsburgh Theological Seminary, Pittsburgh, Pennsylvania. Her publications include *Karl Barth's Emergency Homiletic, 1932–1933: A Summons to Prophetic Witness at the Dawn of the Third Reich* (2013) and chapters on Barth and preaching in *The Oxford Handbook of Karl Barth* (ed. Paul Dafydd Jones and Paul Nimmo, 2019) and *What Is Jesus Doing? Divine Agency in the Life of the Church and the Ministry of the Pastor* (ed. Edwin van Driel, 2020). She is an ordained minister of the Presbyterian Church in the United States.

Jeffrey Haynes is emeritus professor of politics at London Metropolitan University and former director of the Centre for the Study of Religion, Conflict, and Cooperation, London. His recent books include *From Huntington to Trump: Thirty Years of the Clash of Civilizations* (2019), *The United Nations Alliance of Civilisations and the Pursuit of Global Justice: Overcoming Western versus Muslim Conflict and the Creation of a Just World Order* (2018), and *World Politics: International Relations and Globalisation in the 21st Century* (with Peter Hough et al., 2017).

Oliver Hidalgo is senior research associate in the Department of Political Science at the University of Münster and adjunct professor of political science at Regensburg University, Germany. His publications include *Die Antinomien der Demokratie* [The Antinomies of Democracy] (2014), *Staat und Religion: Zentrale Positionen zu einer Schlüsselfrage des Politischen Denkens* [State and Religion: Main Positions Concerning a Key Issue of Political Thought] (ed. with Christian Polke, 2017), and *Politische Theologie. Beiträge zum untrennbaren Zusammenhang zwischen Religion und Politik* [Political Theology: Contributions to the Inseparable Relationship between Religion and Politics] (2018).

Paul Dafydd Jones is associate professor of religious studies in the Department of Religious Studies, University of Virginia, Charlottesville. His publications include *The Humanity of Christ: Christology in Karl Barth's Church Dogmatics* (2008, 2011); *The Oxford Handbook of Karl Barth* (ed. with Paul D. Nimmo, 2019); and numerous articles, chapters, and reviews. With Paul T. Nimmo, he is the co-editor of the T&T Clark series Explorations in Reformed Theology. With Charles T. Mathewes, he co-directs the project on "Religion and Its Publics" at the University of Virginia.

Grace Y. Kao is professor of ethics and director of the Center for Sexuality, Gender, and Religion (CSGR) at Claremont School of Theology, Claremont, California. Her publications include *Grounding Human Rights in a Pluralist World* (2011), *Asian American Christian Ethics: Voices, Methods, Issues* (ed. with Ilsup Ahn, 2015), and *Encountering the Sacred: Feminist Reflections on Women's Lives* (ed. with Rebecca Todd Peters, 2018). Learn more about her work at drgracekao.com.

Volker Küster is professor of comparative religion and missiology and chairs the Center for Intercultural Theology at the Protestant Theological Faculty, Johannes Gutenberg-University, Mainz, Germany. His publications include *The Many Faces of Jesus Christ: Intercultural Christology* (2001), *A Protestant Theology of Passion: Korean Minjung Theology Revisited* (2010), *Einführung in die interkulturelle Theologie* [Introducing Intercultural Theology] (2011), and *God/Terror: Ethics and Aesthetics in Contexts of Conflict and Reconciliation* (2021).

Pan Chiu Lai is a professor in the Department of Cultural and Religious Studies at the Chinese University of Hong Kong. His publications include *Sino-Christian Theology: A Theological Qua Cultural Movement in Contemporary China* (ed. with Jason Lam, 2010); "Religious Diversity and Public Space in China: A Reconsideration of the Christian Doctrine of Salvation" in *Interactive Pluralism in Asia: Religious Life and Public Space* (ed. by Simone Sinn and Tong Wing Sze, 2016); and "Karl Barth and Universal Salvation: A Mahayana Buddhist Perspective" in *Karl Barth and Comparative Theology* (edited by Christian T. Collins Winn and Martha Moore-Keish, 2019).

Daniel Lee is the Eleanor and Wayne Chiu Associate Professor for Theological Studies and director of the Center for Faith and Public Values at the China Graduate School of Theology, Hong Kong. His publications include *The Holy Spirit as Bond in Calvin's Thought: Its Functions in Connection with the Extra Calvinisticum* (2011) and *Total Grace and Filial Gratitude* (2016).

Kin Yip Louie is the Heavenly Blessings Professor for Theological Studies at the China Graduate School of Theology, Hong Kong. His publications include *The Beauty of the Triune God: The Theological Aesthetics of Jonathan Edwards* (2013), *The Search for Christendom: History of the Medieval Church* (in Chinese, 2017), and *A Call to Political Engagement* (in Chinese, ed. with Joyce Sun, 2017).

Alexander Massmann is an affiliated lecturer at the Faculty of Divinity at the University of Cambridge, United Kingdom. His publications include *Citizenship in Heaven and on Earth: Karl Barth's Ethics* (2015), *Deathless Hopes: Reinventions of Afterlife and Eschatological Belief* (ed. with Christopher B. Hays, 2018), and *Modifying Our Genes: Theology, Science, and Playing God* (with Keith Fox, 2021).

Charles Mathewes is the Carolyn M. Barbour Professor of Religious Studies in the Department of Religious Studies at the University of Virginia, Charlottesville. His publications include *A Theology of Public Life* (2007), *Understanding Religious Ethics* (2010), and *The Republic of Grace: Augustinian Thoughts in Dark Times* (2010).

Kristopher Norris has served as a professor of public theology and ethics at Wesley Theological Seminary, Washington DC, and Virginia Theological Seminary, Alexandria. His publications include *Kingdom Politics: In Search of a New Political Imagination for Today's Church* (2015) and *Witnessing Whiteness: Confronting White Supremacy in the American Church* (2020).

Gert Pickel is professor of sociology of religion in the theological faculty at Leipzig University, Germany. His publications include *Church and Religion in Contemporary Europe: Results from Empirical and Comparative Research* (ed. with Olaf Müller, 2009), *Transformations of Religiosity: Religion and Religiosity in Central and Eastern Europe 1989–2010* (ed. with Kornelia Sammet, 2012), and *Religionspolitik in der Bundesrepublik Deutschland: Fallstudien und Vergleiche* [Politics of Religion in the Federal Republic of Germany: Case Studies and Comparisons] (ed. with Antonius Liedhegener, 2016).

Thomas Xutong Qu (瞿旭彤) is associate professor in the Department of Philosophy, School of Humanities, Tsinghua University, People's Republic of China. His publications include *Barth und Goethe. Die Goethe-Rezeption Karl Barths 1909–1921* [Barth and Goethe: The Reception of Goethe by Karl Barth 1909–1921] (2014) and "Kritischer müsste Kants Kritik sein: Eine nachkantische Interpretation von Barths Beziehung zu Kant" ["Kant's Critic Should Be More Critical: A Post-Kantian Interpretation of Barth's Relationship with Kant"] in *Gottes Gegenwart–God's Presences: Festschrift für Günter Thomas zum 60. Geburtstag* (edited by Markus Höfner and Benedikt Friedrich, 2020).

Hanna Reichel is associate professor of reformed theology at Princeton Theological Seminary, Princeton, New Jersey. Her publications include *Theologie als Bekenntnis: Karl Barths kontextuelle Lektüre des Heidelberger Katechismus* [Confessing Theology: Karl Barth's Contextual Reading of the Heidelberg Catechism] (2015), *Menschenbilder und Gottesbilder: Geschlecht in theologischer Reflexion* [Images of God and Hu/Man: Theological Reflections on Gender Studies] (2019) (ed. with Dirk Evers and Laura-Christin Krannich), and *"Zu schauen die schönen Gottesdienste des Herrn"* ["To Gaze on the Beauty of the Lord and to Seek Him in His Temple"] (2013) (ed. with Tobias Habicht and Stefan Karcher).

Devin Singh is associate professor of religion in the Department of Religion at Dartmouth College, Hanover, New Hampshire. His publications include *Divine Currency: The Theological Power of Money in the West* (2018) and *Reimagining Leadership on the Commons* (ed. with Randal Joy Thompson and Kathleen A. Curran, 2021).

Chloë Starr is professor of Asian Christianity and theology at Yale University Divinity School, New Haven, Connecticut. Her publications include *Red-Light Novels of the Late Qing* (2007), *Reading Christian Scriptures in China* (2008), and *Chinese Theology: Text and Context* (2016).

Günter Thomas is professor of systematic theology in the Protestant Theological Faculty at Bochum University, Bochum, Germany, and research associate in the Faculty of Public Theology at the University of Stellenbosch, South Africa. His publications include *Neue Schöpfung: Theologische Untersuchungen zum "Leben der kommenden Welt"* [New Creation: Theological Analyzes Concerning the Hope of the "Life of the World to Come"] (2009), *Dogmatics after Barth: Facing Challenges in Church, Society, and the Academy* (ed. with Rinse H. Reeling Brouwer and Bruce McCormack, 2012), *Exploring Vulnerability* (ed. with H. Springhart 2017), *Responsibility and the Enhancement of Life* (ed. with H. Springhart, 2017), and *Gottes Lebendigkeit: Beiträge zur Sytematischen Theologie* [God's Vitality: Contributions to Systematic Theology] (2019). He is chairman of the Annual Karl-Barth Conference in Switzerland.

Michael Welker is a senior professor of systematic theology, director of the Research Center International and Interdisciplinary Theology at the University of Heidelberg, Germany, and an honorary professor at Seoul Theological University. He is a member of the Heidelberg and the Finnish Academies of Arts and Sciences. Barth Prize 2016; Gifford Lectures 2019. His publications include *Gottes Geist* ([7]2019) [= God the Spirit, [2]2013], *Gottes Offenbarung: Christologie* ([4]2019) [= God the Revealed:

Christology, 2013], and *Images of the Divine and Cultural Orientations: Jewish, Christian, and Islamic Voices* (ed. with William Schweiker, 2015).

Martin Wendte is senior research associate in the Protestant Theological Faculty at Tübingen University, Tübingen, Germany, and pastor of the Protestant Church in Ludwigsburg, Germany. His publications include *Gottmenschliche Einheit bei Hegel: Eine logische und theologische Untersuchung* [Divine-Human Unity per Hegel: A Logical and Theological Analysis] (2007), *Die Gabe und das "Gestell". Luthers Metaphysik des Abendmahls und die technische Spätmoderne* [The Gift and the "Gestell": Luther's Metaphysics of the Lord's Supper and Late-modern Technicity] (2013), and *Rationalität im Gespräch: Philosophische und Theologische Perspektiven* [Rationality in Conversation: Philosophical and Theological Perspectives] (ed. with Markus Mühling et al., 2016).